THE IPC SOLUTION

STUDENT RESOURCES

- Interactive eBook
- Graded Quizzes
- New Practice Quiz Generator
- New Trackable Activities
- Flashcards
- Interpersonal Simulations
- Interactive Video Activities
- Ethical Case Studies
- Chapter Summaries
- Glossary
- Web Links
- Review Cards

Students sign in at **www.cengagebrain.com**

INSTRUCTOR RESOURCES

- All Student Resources
- Engagement Tracker
- LMS Integration
- Instructor's Manual
- PowerPoint® Slides
- Prep Cards
- Discussion Questions

Instructors log in at **www.cengage.com/login**

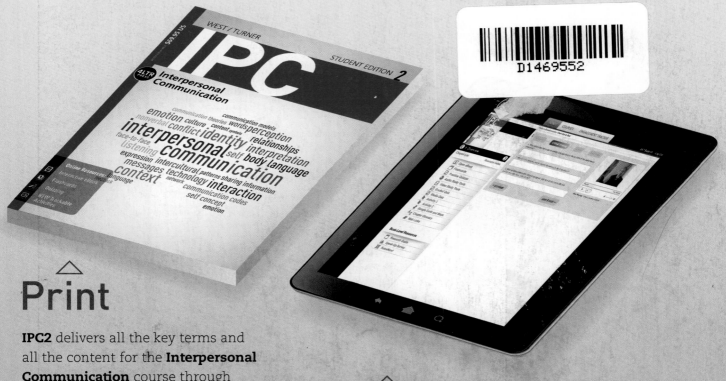

D1469552

Print

IPC2 delivers all the key terms and all the content for the **Interpersonal Communication** course through a visually-engaging and easy to reference print experience.

CourseMate

CourseMate provides access to the full **IPC2** narrative, alongside a rich assortment of quizzing, flashcards, and interactive resources for convenient reading and studying.

IPC2

Richard West

Lynn H. Turner

Vice President, General Manager, 4LTR Press and the Student Experience: Neil Marquardt

Product Director, 4LTR Press: Steven E. Joos

Product Manager: Riccardo Nuzzo

Content Developer: Patricia Hempel

Product Assistant: Mandira Jacob

Marketing Director: Stacey Purviance

Content Project Manager: Corinna Dibble

Manufacturing Planner: Doug Bertke

Production Service: MPS Limited

Sr. Art Director: Stacy Shirley

Cover/Internal Designer: KeDesign, Mason, OH

Cover Image: Thinkstock

Intellectual Property

    Analyst: Ann Hoffman

    Project Manager: Farah Fard

For product information and technology assistance, contact us at
Cengage Learning Customer & Sales Support, 1-800-354-9706

For permission to use material from this text or product,
submit all requests online at **www.cengage.com/permissions**
Further permissions questions can be emailed to
permissionrequest@cengage.com

Library of Congress Control Number: 2014950548

ISBN: 978-1-285-85551-6

Student Edition with CourseMate:

ISBN: 978-1-285-07708-6

Cengage Learning
20 Channel Center Street
Boston, MA 02210
USA

Cengage Learning is a leading provider of customized learning solutions with office locations around the globe, including Singapore, the United Kingdom, Australia, Mexico, Brazil, and Japan. Locate your local office at: **www.cengage.com/global**

Cengage Learning products are represented in Canada by Nelson Education, Ltd.

To learn more about Cengage Learning Solutions, visit **www.cengage.com**

Purchase any of our products at your local college store or at our preferred online store **www.cengagebrain.com**

Printed in the United States of America
Print Number: 02   Print Year: 2015

1 Introduction to Interpersonal Communication   2

2 Communication, Culture, and Identity   26

3 Communication, Perception, and the Self   46

4 Communicating Verbally   68

5 Communicating Nonverbally   88

6 Listening and Responding Effectively   110

7 Communicating and Emotion   130

8 Sharing Personal Information   152

9 Communicating Conflict   174

10 Communicating in Close Relationships   196

11 Communicating in Context:
Families, Friends, and Romantic Partners   218

References   239

Index   251

© vikpit / Shutterstock 160089440

CONTENTS

1 Introduction to Interpersonal Communication 2

1-1 The Evolution of Interpersonal Communication 4

1-2 Defining Interpersonal Communication 6

1-3 Models of Communication 7

    1-3a Mechanistic Thinking and the Linear Model 7

    1-3b Feedback and the Interactional Model 9

    1-3c Shared Meaning and the Transactional Model 10

    1-3d The Interpersonal Communication Continuum 12

1-4 The Value of Interpersonal Communication 14

1-5 Principles of Interpersonal Communication 15

    1-5a Interpersonal Communication Is Unavoidable 16

    1-5b Interpersonal Communication Is Irreversible 16

    1-5c Interpersonal Communication Is Symbolic 16

    1-5d Interpersonal Communication Is Rule Governed 17

    1-5e Interpersonal Communication Is Learned 17

    1-5f Interpersonal Communication Has Both Content and Relationship Levels 18

    1-5g Interpersonal Communication Involves Ethical Choices 18

1-6 Myths About Interpersonal Communication 19

    1-6a Interpersonal Communication Solves All Problems 19

    1-6b Interpersonal Communication Is Always a Good Thing 19

    1-6c Interpersonal Communication Is Common Sense 20

    1-6d Interpersonal Communication Is Synonymous with Interpersonal Relationships 20

    1-6e Interpersonal Communication Is Always Face-to-Face 20

1-7 Interpersonal Communication Ethics 20

    1-7a Five Ethical Systems of Communication 21

    1-7b Understanding Ethics and Our Own Values 24

1-8 The Communication Core: Competency and Civility 25

2 Communication, Culture, and Identity 26

2-1 Defining Culture 28

    2-1a Culture Is Learned 29

    2-1b Culture Creates Community 30

    2-1c Culture Is Multileveled 31

2-2 Diversity in the United States: A Nation of Newcomers 32

2-3 Why Study Intercultural Communication? 33

    2-3a Technological Imperative 33

    2-3b Demographic Imperative 34

    2-3c Economic Imperative 34

    2-3d Peace Imperative 35

    2-3e Self-Awareness Imperative 35

    2-3f Ethical Imperative 35

2-4 Dimensions of Culture 36

    2-4a Uncertainty Avoidance 36

    2-4b Distribution of Power 36

    2-4c Masculinity-Femininity 37

    2-4d Individualism-Collectivism 37

2-5 Challenges of Intercultural Communication 39

    2-5a Ethnocentrism 39

    2-5b Stereotyping 40

    2-5c Anxiety and Uncertainty 40

    2-5d Misinterpretation of Nonverbal and Verbal Behaviors 41

    2-5e The Assumption of Similarity or Difference 41

2-6 Skill Set for Intercultural Understanding 42

    2-6a Know Your Biases and Stereotypes 42

    2-6b Tolerate the Unknown 43

    2-6c Practice Cultural Respect 44

    2-6d Educate Yourself 44

    2-6e Be Prepared for Consequences 45

    2-6f Relate to the Individual, Not the Culture 45

3 Communication, Perception, and the Self 46

3-1 Understanding Perception: A "See/Saw" Experience 47

    3-1a Attending and Selecting 48

    3-1b Organizing 49

    3-1c Interpreting 50

    3-1d Retrieving 51

3-2 Influences on Perception 52

    3-2a Culture 52

    3-2b Sex and Gender 52

3-2c   *Physical Factors* 54
3-2d   *Technology* 54
3-2e   *Our Sense of Self* 54

3-3   Understanding the Self: The "I's" Have It 55
3-3a   *Self Concept* 55
3-3b   *Self Awareness* 56
3-3c   *Self Esteem* 56
3-3d   *Self Fulfilling Prophecy* 57

3-4   Identity Management: Let's Face It 58
3-4a   *Identity Management and Facework* 59

3-5   Online Identity Management 61
3-5a   *Screen Names* 61
3-5b   *Personal Home Pages* 61

3-6   Skill Set: Improving Perception Checking and Self-Concept 64
3-6a   *Understand Your Personal Worldview* 65
3-6b   *Realize the Incompleteness of Perception* 65
3-6c   *Seek Explanation and Clarification* 65
3-6d   *Distinguish Facts from Inferences* 65
3-6e   *Be Patient and Tolerant* 65
3-6f   *Have the Desire and Will to Change* 65
3-6g   *Decide What You Would Like to Change* 66
3-6h   *Set Reasonable Personal Goals* 66
3-6i   *Review and Revise* 66
3-6j   *Surround Yourself with "Relational Uppers"* 66

4 Communicating Verbally 68

4-1   Understanding Verbal Symbols 70
4-1a   *Words Are Symbolic* 70
4-1b   *Words Evolve Over Time* 71
4-1c   *Words Are Powerful* 72
4-1d   *Meanings for Verbal Symbols May Be Denotative or Connotative* 72
4-1e   *Words Vary in Level of Abstraction* 73

4-2   Factors Affecting Verbal Symbols 75
4-2a   *Culture and Ethnicity* 75
4-2b   *Sex and Gender* 79
4-2c   *Generation* 80
4-2d   *Context* 80

4-3   The Destructive and Constructive Sides of Verbal Symbols 81
4-3a   *The Destructive Side of Verbal Symbols* 81
4-3b   *The Constructive Side of Verbal Codes* 85

4-4   Skill Set for Improving Verbal Communication 86
4-4a   *Owning and Using I-Messages* 86
4-4b   *Understanding the Ladder of Abstraction* 86
4-4c   *Indexing* 87
4-4d   *Probing the Middle Ground* 87

5 Communicating Nonverbally 88

5-1   Principles of Nonverbal Communication 90
5-1a   *Nonverbal Communication Is Often Ambiguous* 91
5-1b   *Nonverbal Communication Regulates Conversation* 91
5-1c   *Nonverbal Communication Is More Believable Than Verbal Communication* 92
5-1d   *Nonverbal Communication May Conflict with Verbal Communication* 92

5-2   Nonverbal Communication Codes 92
5-2a   *Visual-Auditory Codes* 93
5-2b   *Contact Codes* 97
5-2c   *Place and Time Codes* 101

5-3   Cultural Variations in Nonverbal Communication 103
5-3a   *Body Movement* 103
5-3b   *Facial Expressions* 103
5-3c   *Personal Space* 104
5-3d   *Touch* 104

5-4   Technology and Nonverbal Communication 105

5-5   Skill Set for Increasing Nonverbal Communication Effectiveness 106
5-5a   *Recall the Nonverbal-Verbal Relationship* 106
5-5b   *Be Tentative When Interpreting Nonverbal Behavior* 107
5-5c   *Monitor Your Nonverbal Behavior* 107
5-5d   *Ask Others for Their Impressions* 107
5-5e   *Avoid Nonverbal Distractions* 108
5-5f   *Place Nonverbal Communication in Context* 108

6 Listening and Responding Effectively 110

6-1   Lend Me Your Ear: Differences Between Hearing and Listening 111

6-2   The Components of the Listening Process 113
6-2a   *Receiving* 113
6-2b   *Responding* 114
6-2c   *Recalling* 114
6-2d   *Rating* 115

6-3   The Value and Importance of Listening 115

6-4   The Barriers: Why We Don't Listen 116
6-4a   *Noise* 117
6-4b   *Message Overload* 118
6-4c   *Message Complexity* 118
6-4d   *Lack of Training* 118

6-4e Preoccupation 119
6-4f Listening Gap 119

6-5 Poor Listening Habits 119
6-5a Selective Listening 119
6-5b Talkaholism 120
6-5c Pseudolistening 120
6-5d Gap Filling 120
6-5e Defensive Listening 121
6-5f Ambushing 121

6-6 Personal Styles of Listening 121
6-6a People-Centered Listening Style 122
6-6b Action-Centered Listening Style 122
6-6c Content-Centered Listening Style 122
6-6d Time-Centered Listening Style 122

6-7 Culture and the Listening Process 123

6-8 Skill Set for Effective Listening 124
6-8a Evaluate Your Current Skills 124
6-8b Prepare to Listen 124
6-8c Provide Empathic Responses 125
6-8d Use Nonjudgmental Feedback 126
6-8e Practice Active Listening 127

7 Communicating and Emotion 130

7-1 Defining Emotion: More Than Just a Feeling 131
7-1a Two Category Systems for Emotion 132
7-1b Emotion, Reason, and the Body 133

7-2 Explaining Emotion: Biology and Social Interaction 134
7-2a The Biological Theory of Emotion 134
7-2b The Social Interaction Theory of Emotion 135

7-3 Emotion and Communication 136
7-3a Metaphors for Emotion 137
7-3b Cues for Emotional Communication 138

7-4 Influences on Emotional Communication 139
7-4a Meta-Emotion 139
7-4b Culture 139
7-4c Gender and Sex 141
7-4d Context 142

7-5 Recognizing Destructive and Constructive Aspects of Emotional Communication 144

7-6 Skill Set for Emotional Communication 147
7-6a Know Your Feelings 147
7-6b Analyze the Situation 148
7-6c Own Your Feelings 149
7-6d Reframe When Needed 149
7-6e Empathize 150

8 Sharing Personal Information 152

8-1 Definition of Self-Disclosure: Opening Up 153
8-1a Intentionality and Choice 153
8-1b Private Information and Risk 154
8-1c Trust 155
8-1d Self-Disclosure as a Subjective Process 156

8-2 Factors Affecting Disclosure 157
8-2a Individual Differences 157
8-2b Relational Issues 157
8-2c Culture and Ethnicity 158
8-2d Gender and Sex 159
8-2e Channels 159

8-3 Principles of Self-Disclosure 160
8-3a We Disclose a Great Deal in Few Interactions 160
8-3b Self-Disclosures Occur Between Two People in a Close Relationship 162
8-3c Self-Disclosures Are Reciprocal 162
8-3d Self-Disclosures Occur over Time 163

8-4 Explaining Self-Disclosure 163
8-4a Communication Privacy Management Theory 163
8-4b Social Penetration 164
8-4c The Johari Window 165

8-5 Reasons for Revealing and Concealing Personal Information 167
8-5a Reasons for Revealing Personal Information 167
8-5b Reasons Not to Self-Disclose 169

8-6 Skill Set for Effective Disclosing 171
8-6a Use I-Statements 171
8-6b Be Honest 171
8-6c Be Consistent and Focused with Your Verbal and Nonverbal Communication 171
8-6d Choose the Appropriate Context 171
8-6e Be Sure Your Disclosure Is Relevant 171
8-6f Estimate the Risks and Benefits 172
8-6g Predict How Your Listener Will Respond 172
8-6h Be Sure the Amount and Type of Disclosure Are Appropriate 172
8-6i Estimate the Effect of the Disclosure on Your Relationship 173

9 Communicating Conflict 174

9-1 Defining Conflict 175
9-1a Interaction 176
9-1b Interdependence 177
9-1c Perception 178

9-1d Incompatible Goals 178

9-1e Types of Conflict 178

9-1f Myths About Conflict and Communication 181

9-1g Factors Influencing Interpersonal Conflict 182

9-2 Communication Patterns in Conflict 184

9-2a Symmetrical Escalation 184

9-2b Symmetrical Withdrawal 184

9-2c Pursuit-Withdrawal/ Withdrawal-Pursuit 184

9-2d Symmetrical Negotiation 184

9-3 The Destructive and Constructive Sides of Interpersonal Conflict 185

9-3a Destructive Aspects of Interpersonal Conflict 185

9-3b Constructive Aspects of Interpersonal Conflict 186

9-4 Explaining Conflict 187

9-4a The Four-Part Model 187

9-4b The Explanatory Process Model 188

9-5 The Relationship of Conflict to Power 190

9-5a Using Power 190

9-5b Sex Differences 192

9-5c Empowerment 192

9-6 Skill Set for Effective Conflict Management 192

9-6a Lighten Up and Reframe 193

9-6b Presume Goodwill and Express Goodwill 193

9-6c Ask Questions 193

9-6d Listen 194

9-6e Practice Cultural Sensitivity 194

10 Communicating in Close Relationships 196

10-1 Understanding Close Relationships 198

10-2 Thinking and Talking About Close Relationships 199

10-2a Relationships as Cultural Performances 199

10-2b Relationships as Cognitive Constructs 200

10-2c Relationships as Linguistic Constructions 200

10-3 Influences on Close Relationships 201

10-3a Attraction 201

10-3b Culture 202

10-3c Gender and Sex 202

10-3d Electronic Media 203

10-4 Developing Interpersonal Relationships Through Stages 204

10-4a Initiating 205

10-4b Experimenting 205

10-4c Intensifying 206

10-4d Integrating 206

10-4e Bonding 206

10-4f Differentiating 207

10-4g Circumscribing 207

10-4h Stagnating 207

10-4i Avoiding 207

10-4j Terminating 208

10-5 Explaining Communication in Close Relationships 208

10-5a Systems Theory 208

10-5b Dialectics Theory 210

10-5c Social Exchange Theory 213

10-6 Skill Set for Communicating in Close Relationships 214

10-6a Communication Skills for Beginning Relationships 214

10-6b Communication Skills for Maintaining Relationships 215

10-6c Communication Skills for Repairing Relationships 216

11 Communicating in Context: Families, Friends, and Romantic Partners 218

11-1 Family Relationships 219

11-2 Close Friendships 225

11-2a Model of Childhood Friendship 228

11-2b Adult Friendships 229

11-3 Romantic Relationships 231

11-3a Saying "I Love You" 233

11-4 Skill Set: Strategies to Improve Your Interpersonal Communication with Family Members, Close Friends, and Romantic Partners 235

11-4a Take Time to C.A.R.E. 235

11-4b Recognize Your History Together 236

11-4c Find Ways to Keep the Relationship "Alive" 236

11-4d Ensure Equity When Possible 236

References 239

Index 251

1 | Introduction to Interpersonal Communication

LEARNING OUTCOMES

- **1-1** Identify the evolution of interpersonal communication in the communication field
- **1-2** Define and describe the interpersonal communication process
- **1-3** Explain three prevailing models of human communication
- **1-4** Understand the value of interpersonal communication
- **1-5** Identify the principles of interpersonal communication
- **1-6** Describe the myths related to interpersonal communication
- **1-7** Compare and contrast five ethical systems of communication
- **1-8** Explain the communication "core" of competency and civility

After you finish this chapter, go to **PAGE 25** for **STUDY TOOLS.**

THEORY/MODEL PREVIEW

Semiotics Theory

Each day, we engage one of the most ancient of all behaviors: interpersonal communication.

We head off to work and greet people on the bus, in the office, in the carpool, or on the street. We talk to our roommates and discuss last night's party over breakfast. Or, we wake up and soon find ourselves in the middle of a heated exchange with a family member about dirty dishes. Although each of these situations differs, they all underscore the pervasiveness of interpersonal communication in our lives.

Still, not everyone is comfortable talking to others. In fact, some people are quite nervous about communicating.

The extent to which people exhibit anxiety about speaking to others is called **communication apprehension**. Communication apprehension is a legitimate and real experience that researchers believe usually negatively affects our communication with others (Richmond, Wrench, & McCroskey 2012). People with communication apprehension can go to great lengths to avoid communication situations because communicating can make them feel shy, embarrassed, and tense. At times, some individuals find themselves fearful or anxious around people from different cultural groups. This **intercultural communication apprehension** (Liu, 2008; Neuliep, 2012) not only impairs quality face-to-face conversations, but also can affect whether or not we wish to communicate with someone *at all*. We return to culture and communication in Chapter 3.

communication apprehension A fear or anxiety pertaining to the communication process.

intercultural communication apprehension A fear or anxiety pertaining to communication with people from different cultural backgrounds.

Even if we don't experience or suffer from communication apprehension, we often have difficulty getting our message across to others. We may feel unprepared to argue with a supervisor for a raise, to let our apartment manager know that the hot water is not hot enough, or to tell our partner "I love you." At times throughout the day, we may struggle with what to say, how to say something, or when to say something. We also may struggle with listening to certain messages because of their content or the manner in which they are presented. In addition, communication may seem difficult when others don't respond as we'd wish or when others don't even seem to pay attention to us.

This book is about improving your ability to interact with other people. Improving your skills in interpersonal communication will assist you in becoming more effective in your relationships with a variety of people, including those with whom you are close (e.g., family members, friends, coworkers) and those with whom you interact less frequently (e.g., health care providers, contractors, babysitters).

Throughout this course, you will see how research and theory associated with interpersonal communication inform everyday encounters. You will also be introduced to a number of useful communication skills that you can immediately apply to your life. We believe that the theoretical and practical applications of interpersonal communication are intertwined to the extent that we cannot ignore the mutual influence of one upon the other—after all, theories inform practice, and practice grows out of theory. At the same time, we agree with Robert Craig (2003), a communication professor and researcher, who maintains that the communication discipline can influence and enhance people's lives only by being practical. So, we take a practical approach with this book in the hope that you will be able to use what you learn to make effective communication choices in your own interpersonal relationships.

Our first task is to map out a general understanding of interpersonal communication. We begin this journey by providing a brief history of how interpersonal communication came about in the field of communication.

1-1 THE EVOLUTION OF INTERPERSONAL COMMUNICATION

Let's overview the communication discipline to give you a sense of its evolution. For a more expansive view of the communication field, we encourage you to look at additional sources that provide a more comprehensive presentation (Craig, 2003; Friedrich & Boileau, 1999; Simonson, Peck, Craig, & Jackson, 2013). You can find the full citations for these sources in the References section at the end of this book.

What we call communication studies today has its origins in ancient Greece and Rome, during the formation of what we now know as Western civilization. Being skilled at communication was expected of all Greek and Roman citizens (i.e., landowning and native-born). For example, citizens were asked to judge murder and adultery trials, travel as state emissaries, and defend their property against would-be land collectors. This sort of public communication was viewed primarily as a way to persuade other people, and writers such as Aristotle developed ways to improve a speaker's persuasive powers. His book, the *Rhetoric*, described a way of making speeches that encouraged speakers to incorporate logic, evidence, and emotions and to consider how the audience perceived the speaker's credibility and intelligence.

Aristotelian thinking dominated early approaches to communication for centuries. But as time went on, interest grew in providing speakers with practical ways to improve their communication skills in situations other than public persuasion. Being pragmatic was essential in order to reach the broadest possible audience. Today, in what we can call the modern era, communication scholars have begun to move beyond the focus on skills to form a more theoretical and philosophical approach to communication. They began trying to answer the question "How do I come to know, to believe, and to act?" in relation to communication. Yet, another question is also important: "How do we translate all of this theory into practice?"

Contemporary communication courses—like the one you're enrolled in now—were first taught in English departments in the early 1900s. These courses, staying true to early Greek and Roman thinking, emphasized public speaking and were taught by English teachers who had some training in public communication. The English department was considered the appropriate place for communication courses because it was believed that written and spoken communication were synonymous. However, scholars who specialized in the study of public speaking (we call them communication scholars today) were unhappy with this arrangement. They maintained that there were clear differences between the two forms of communication.

In 1913, this debate grew so intense that when the National Council of Teachers of English held its annual convention in Chicago, a group of public speaking teachers proposed that they form their own association, the National Association of Academic Teachers of Public Speaking. This was the beginning of the modern-day National Communication Association, an organization comprised of more than 8,000 communication teachers, researchers, and practitioners who study over 50 different areas of communication. One of the largest fields of the communication discipline is interpersonal communication, which explores communication within many different relationships, including those between parents and children, teachers and students, supervisors and employees, friends, and spouses, to name just a few.

Even though we engage in interpersonal communication daily, it is often difficult to disentangle from everything else we do. To arrive at the definition of interpersonal communication, it helps first to distinguish it from other types of communication. Scholars have identified the following kinds of situations in which human communication exists: intrapersonal, interpersonal, small group, organizational, mass, and public. You may notice that the communication department at your school is organized around some or all of these communication types. Many schools use these categories as an effective way to organize their curriculum and course offerings.

Note that these communication types build on each other because they represent increasing numbers of people included in the process. In addition, keep in mind that although these communication types differ from one another in some significant ways, they aren't mutually exclusive. For example, you may engage in both intrapersonal and interpersonal communication in

a single encounter, or interpersonal communication may take place in an organizational context. With these caveats in mind, let's take a closer look at the six types of communication:

▶ **Intrapersonal communication:** communication that is internal to communicators; communication with ourselves. We may find ourselves daydreaming or engaging in internal dialogues even in the presence of another person. These are intrapersonal processes. Intrapersonal communication includes imagining, perceiving, or solving problems in your head. For instance, intrapersonal communication takes place when you debate with yourself, mentally listing the pros and cons of a decision before taking action.

▶ **Interpersonal communication:** the process of strategic message transaction between people (usually two) who work toward creating and sustaining shared meaning. We will discuss this definition in more detail later in this chapter.

▶ **Small group communication:** communication between and among members of a task group who meet for a common purpose or goal. Small group communication occurs in classrooms, the workplace, and in more social environments (e.g., sports teams or book clubs).

▶ **Organizational communication:** communication with and among large, extended environments with a defined hierarchy. This context also includes communication among members within those environments. Organizational communication may involve other communication types, such as interpersonal communication (e.g., supervisor/subordinate relationships), small group communication (e.g., a task group preparing a report), and intrapersonal communication (e.g., daydreaming at work).

▶ **Mass communication:** communication to a large audience via some mediated channel, such as television, radio, the Internet, or newspapers. At times, people seek out others using personal ads either on the Internet or in newspapers or magazines. This is an example of the intersection of mass communication and interpersonal communication.

▶ **Public communication:** communication in which one person gives a speech to a large audience in person. Public communication is also often called public speaking. Public speakers have predetermined goals in mind, such as informing, persuading, or entertaining.

Each of these communication types is affected by two pervasive influences: culture and technology. In the 21st century especially, acknowledging these two influences is crucial to our understanding of interpersonal communication and human relationships. First, it's nearly impossible to ignore the role that culture plays as we communicate with others. Over the past several

© iStock.com/Rich Legg

decades, scores of immigrants have arrived in the United States, bringing with them various customs, values, and practices. As a result, we now live in a country where intercultural contact is both necessary and commonplace, making effective communication with others even more critical than it would be ordinarily. The ever-increasing presence of intercultural relationships—such as those between exchange students and their host families, and U.S. parents and their children adopted from other countries—has prompted researchers to study the effects of these blended populations on communication effectiveness (e.g., Galvin, 2006). We will delve deeper into the topic of culture, community, and communication in Chapter 3.

A second influence upon the various communication types is technology. As you know from your own online experiences, it is now possible to communicate with another person without ever having face-to-face contact. Years ago, interpersonal communication was limited to sending letters or talking with someone personally. But today, relationships are routinely initiated, cultivated, and even terminated via electronic technology and people derive various perceptions of others through their online interactions (Hanna & Walther, 2013). This phenomenon has stimulated research on technology, relationships, and interpersonal communication (see, e.g., Walther & Jang, 2012; Walther, Van Der Heide, Ramirez, Burgoon, & Pena, 2014). Technology not only has made interpersonal communication easier and faster, but has shaped the very nature of our communication and our relationships. Our conversations have become abbreviated, such as when we look at our caller ID and answer the phone with "And when did you get home from vacation?" instead of "Hello?" We develop close relationships with others via online dating services (e.g., Match.com), and our social networking sites (e.g., Facebook and Twitter) allow us to have tens of millions of "friends and followers." Throughout this book, we will integrate technology's effect on the different topics related to interpersonal communication, providing you a chance to understand its influence in your relationships with others.

1-2 DEFINING INTERPERSONAL COMMUNICATION

We define **interpersonal communication** as the strategic process of message transaction between people to create and sustain shared meaning. Three critical components are embedded in this definition: process, message exchange, and shared meaning. Let's look at each in turn.

When we state that interpersonal communication is strategic, we mean to suggest that you are deliberative in your interpersonal efforts. That is, we don't wish to have intimate communication with everyone with whom we interact; we are selective. In fact, it would be both exhausting and inappropriate to do so. Therefore, we retain an internal interpersonal barometer, exchanging personal messages with those whom we feel we need or want to communicate.

Stating that interpersonal communication is a **process** means that it is an ongoing, unending, vibrant activity that is always changing. When we enter into an interpersonal communication exchange, we are entering into an event with no definable beginning or ending, and one that is irreversible. For example, consider the moments when you first meet and begin communicating with classmates during a small group activity in class. Chances are that for the first few minutes everyone in the group feels a little awkward and uncertain. Yet, after you all introduce yourselves to one another, it's highly likely that you all feel more comfortable. This shift from feeling uncertain to feeling comfortable is the ongoing interpersonal communication process in action.

The notion of process also suggests that it is not only individuals who change but also the cultures in which they live. For instance, today's U.S. society is very different than it was in the 1950s. The climate of the United States in the 1950s can be characterized as a time of postwar euphoria, tempered by an (irrational) concern about communism. The feminist movement of the 1970s had yet to occur, and for many white middle-class families, gender roles were restricted and traditional. Women's roles were more rigidly defined as nurturers and primary caretakers for children, whereas men's roles were relegated to emotionless financial providers. These roles influenced decision making in many families (Turner & West, 2015). Nowadays roles are less rigid. Thousands of dads stay at home to care for children, and millions of moms work outside the home. And more than ever, couples make all kinds of decisions together about the family. Consider a couple communicating in the 1950s about an issue such as contraception and another couple discussing the same issue today. In what ways do you think the dialogues would be similar or different?

The second element of our definition of interpersonal communication highlights **message exchange**. In this regard, we mean the transaction of verbal and nonverbal *messages*, or information being sent simultaneously between people. Messages, both verbal and nonverbal, are the vehicles we use to interact with others. But messages are not enough to establish interpersonal communication. For example, consider an English-speaking communicator stating the message "I need to find the post office. Can you direct me there?" to a Spanish-speaking communicator. Although the message was stated clearly in English, no shared meaning results if the Spanish speaker is not bilingual.

Meaning is central to our definition of interpersonal communication because meaning is what people extract from a message. As you will learn in Chapter 4, words alone have no meaning; people attribute meaning to words. We (co)create the meaning of a message even as the message unfolds. Perhaps our history with someone helps us interpret the message. Perhaps a message is unclear to us and we ask questions for clarity. Or maybe the message has personal meaning to us and no one else understands the personal expressions used. Meaning directly affects our relational life. As Steve Duck and Julia Wood (1995) state: "We suspect that 'good' and 'bad' relational experiences are sometimes a matter of personal definition and personal meaning, but always intertwined, sometimes seamlessly, in the broader human enterprise of making sense of experience" (p. 3). In other words, achieving meaning is achieving sense making in your relationships.

When we say that people work toward creating and sustaining meaning, we are suggesting that there must be some shared meaning for interpersonal communication to take place. Because meaning is affected by culture in more ways than language differences, we have to be careful not to assume that our meaning will automatically be clear to others

interpersonal communication The process of message transaction between two people to create and sustain shared meaning.

process When used to describe interpersonal communication, an ongoing, unending, vibrant activity that always changes.

message exchange The transaction of verbal and nonverbal messages being sent simultaneously between two people.

meaning What communicators create together through the use of verbal and nonverbal messages.

and result in shared meaning (Martin & Nakayama, 2012). For example, Martin and Nakayama note that in the United States, many people tend to dislike Monday, the first day of the work week, and enjoy Friday, which is the end of the workweek. However, many Muslims around the world dislike Saturday, which is the first day of the week for Muslims after Friday, the holy day. Therefore, cultural expressions such as TGIF (thank God it's Friday) may not communicate the same meaning to all people, even when accurately translated.

To underscore the importance of culture, we discuss various cultural groups throughout every chapter of this text. And, we recognize that although there are many differences among various cultures, some similarities exist. In each chapter, we strive to present conclusions about cultural communities that reflect consistencies in research and honor the integrity of the various populations.

1-3 MODELS OF COMMUNICATION

To further comprehend the interpersonal communication process and to provide more information about the evolution of the communication field, we draw upon what theorists call models of communication. **Communication models** are visual, simplified representations of complex relationships in the communication process. They help you see how the communication field has evolved over the years and provide a foundation you can return to throughout the book. The three prevailing models we discuss will give you insight into how we frame our definition of interpersonal communication. Let's start with the oldest model so you can see the development of the interpersonal communication process.

1-3a Mechanistic Thinking and the Linear Model

More than 60 years ago, Claude E. Shannon, a Bell Telephone scientist, and Warren Weaver, a Sloan Cancer Research Foundation consultant, set out to understand radio and telephone technology by looking at how

FIGURE 1.1   LINEAR MODEL OF COMMUNICATION

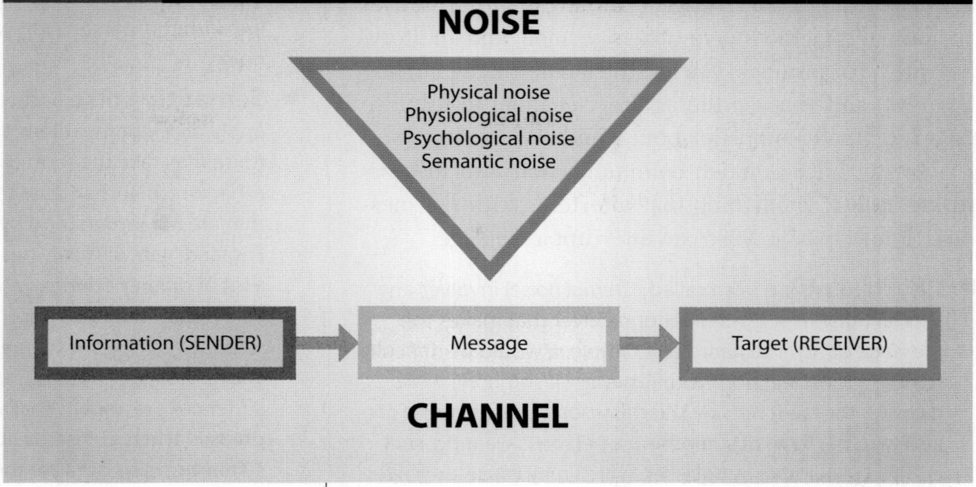

NOISE

Physical noise
Physiological noise
Psychological noise
Semantic noise

Information (SENDER) → Message → Target (RECEIVER)

CHANNEL

© Cengage Learning®

information passed through various channels (Shannon & Weaver, 1949). They viewed information transmission as a linear process, and their research resulted in the creation of the **linear model of communication**.

The linear approach frames communication as a one-way process that transmits a message to a destination. Think about when you were a child. You may have played "the telephone game," which included punching a tiny hole in the bottoms of two plastic cups, and inserting kite string or thread through each hole. Using the cups to "talk into" and to "listen with" illustrates the one-way communication we're discussing with the linear model. You talk and someone hears you. That is the essence of the linear model.

Several components comprise the linear model of communication (see Figure 1.1). The **sender** is the source of the **message**, which may be spoken, written, or unspoken. (If American Sign Language is your primary form of interpersonal communication, your messages will necessarily be both linguistic and nonverbal.) The sender passes the message to the **receiver**, the intended target of the message. The receiver, in turn, assigns meaning to the message. All of this communication

communication models Visual, simplified representations of complex relationships in the communication process.

linear model of communication A characterization of communication as a one-way process that transmits a message from a sender to a receiver.

sender The source of a message.

message Spoken, written, or unspoken information sent from a sender to a receiver.

receiver The intended target of a message.

takes place in a **channel**, which is a pathway to communication. Typically, channels represent our senses (visual/sight, tactile/touch, olfactory/smell, and auditory/hearing). For instance, you use the tactile channel to hug a parent, and you use the auditory channel to listen to your roommate complain about a midterm exam.

In the linear model, communication also involves **noise**, which is anything that interferes with the message. Four types of noise can interrupt a message:

▶ **Physical noise** (also called *external noise*) involves any stimuli outside of the sender or receiver that makes the message difficult to hear. For example, it would be difficult to hear a message from your professor if someone were mowing the lawn outside the classroom. Physical noise can also take the form of something a person is wearing, such as "loud jewelry" or sunglasses, which may cause a receiver to focus on the object rather than the message.

▶ **Physiological noise** refers to biological influences on message reception. Examples of this type of noise are articulation problems, hearing or visual impairments, and the physical well-being of a speaker (i.e., whether he or she is able to deliver a message).

▶ **Psychological noise** (or *internal noise*) refers to a communicator's biases, prejudices, and feelings toward a person or a message. For example, you may have heard another person use language that is offensive and

derogatory while speaking about a certain cultural group. If you were bothered by this language while communicating with this person, you were experiencing psychological noise.

▶ **Semantic noise** occurs when senders and receivers apply different meanings to the same message. Semantic noise may take the form of jargon, technical language, and other words and phrases that are familiar to the sender but that are not understood by the receiver. If you live in New England, you will likely hear people say "wicked" to mean a lot of different things (e.g., a large amount, odd, etc.). If you're from the South, you will likely hear people say "fixin' to go," which means the person is getting ready to leave. If you're "stoked," this term, from the 1960s Southern California surfer culture, means that you are excited. These sorts of phrases and their use could be considered conversational semantic noise because the words and phrases may not be known.

The linear view has been studied with **context**, or surrounding, in mind. Context is multidimensional and can be physical, cultural, psychological, or historical. The **physical context** is the tangible environment in which communication occurs. Examples of physical contexts are the hotel van on the way to the airport, the dinner table, the apartment, and the church hall. Environmental conditions such as temperature, lighting, and space are also part of the physical context. For example, consider trying to listen to your best friend talk about her financial problems in a crowded coffee shop. The environment does not seem conducive to receiving her message clearly and accurately.

The **cultural context** refers to the rules, roles, norms, and patterns of communication that are unique to particular cultures. Culture always influences the communication taking place between and among people, requiring us to look at the backgrounds of communicators. Newcomers, for instance, may have difficulties assimilating into U.S. culture, often illustrated by the use of language within the family. Language serves as a primary factor affecting the quality of interpersonal communication within the family (Scollo & Carbaugh, 2013). So, for example, if grandparents and grandchildren have difficulty communicating with each other because the grandparents speak primarily Spanish and the grandchildren speak primarily English, it's likely that meaning will be jeopardized.

The **social-emotional context** indicates the nature of the relationship that affects a communication encounter. For example, are the communicators in a particular interaction friendly or unfriendly, supportive or unsupportive? Or do they fall somewhere in between? These factors help explain why, for instance, you might feel completely anxious in one employment interview but very comfortable in another. At times you and an

channel A pathway through which a message is sent.

noise Anything that interferes with accurate transmission or reception of a message. *See also* physical noise, physiological noise, psychological noise, and semantic noise.

physical noise Any stimuli outside of a sender or a receiver that interfere with the transmission or reception of a message. Also called *external noise*.

physiological noise Biological influences on a sender or a receiver that interfere with the transmission or reception of a message.

psychological noise Biases, prejudices, and feelings that interfere with the accurate transmission or reception of a message. Also called *internal noise*.

semantic noise Occurs when senders and receivers apply different meanings to the same message; may take the form of jargon, technical language, and other words and phrases that are familiar to the sender but that are not understood by the receiver.

context The environment in which a message is sent.

physical context The tangible environment in which communication occurs.

cultural context The cultural environment in which communication occurs; refers to the rules, roles, norms, and patterns of communication that are unique to a particular culture.

social-emotional context The relational and emotional environment in which communication occurs.

© imtmphoto/Shutterstock.com

interviewer may hit it off, while at other times you may feel intimidated or awkward. The social-emotional context helps explain the nature of the interaction taking place.

In the **historical context**, messages are understood in relationship to previously sent messages. Thus, when Jessie tells Tina that he missed her while they were separated over spring break, Tina hears that as a turning point in their relationship. Jessie has never said that before; in fact, he has often mentioned that he rarely misses anyone when he is apart from him or her. Therefore, his comment is influenced by their history together. If Jessie regularly told Tina he missed her, she would interpret the message differently.

We will return to the notion of context often in this book. For now, keep in mind that context has a significant influence on our relationships with others. Furthermore, context involves people and their conversations and relationships. If we don't consider context in our interactions with others, we have no way to judge our interpersonal effectiveness.

Although the linear model was highly regarded when it was first conceptualized, it has been criticized because it presumes that communication has a definable beginning and ending (Anderson & Ross, 2002). In fact, Shannon and Weaver (1999) later emphasized this aspect of their model by claiming that people receive information in organized and discrete ways. Yet, we know that communication can be messy. We have all interrupted someone or had someone interrupt us. The linear model also presumes that listeners are passive and that communication occurs only when speaking. But we know that listeners often affect speakers and are not simply passive receivers of a speaker's message. With these criticisms in mind, researchers developed another way to represent the human communication process: the interactional model.

1-3b Feedback and the Interactional Model

To emphasize the two-way nature of communication between people, Wilbur Schramm (1954) conceptualized the **interactional model of communication**. Schramm's model shows that communication goes in two directions: from sender to receiver and from receiver to sender. This circular, or interactional, process suggests that communication is ongoing rather than linear. In the interactional model, an individual in a conversation can be both sender and receiver, but not both simultaneously (see Figure 1.2).

The interactional approach is characterized primarily by **feedback**, which can be defined as responses to people, their messages, or both. Feedback may be verbal (meaning found in words) or nonverbal (meaning found in smiles, crossed arms, etc.). Feedback may also be internal or external. **Internal feedback** occurs when you assess your own communication (e.g., by thinking "I never should have said that"). **External feedback** is the feedback you receive from other people (e.g., "Why did you say that? That was dumb!").

A person can provide external feedback that results in important internal feedback for him- or herself. For example, let's say that Alexandra gives Dan the following advice about dealing with the death of his partner: "You feel sad as long as you need to. Don't worry about what other people think. I'm sick of people telling others how they should feel about something. These are *your* feelings." While giving Dan this external feedback, Alexandra may realize that her advice can also be applied to her own recent breakup. Although she may intend to send Dan a comforting message, she may also provide herself internal feedback as she deals with her relational circumstances.

Like the linear model, the interactional model has been criticized primarily for its view of senders and receivers—that is, one person sends a message to another person. Neither model takes into consideration what happens when nonverbal messages are sent at the same time as verbal messages. For example, when a father disciplines

historical context A type of context in which messages are understood in relationship to previously sent messages.

interactional model of communication A characterization of communication as a two-way process in which a message is sent from sender to receiver and from receiver to sender.

feedback A verbal or nonverbal response to a message. *See also* internal feedback and external feedback.

internal feedback The feedback we give ourselves when we assess our own communication.

external feedback The feedback we receive from other people.

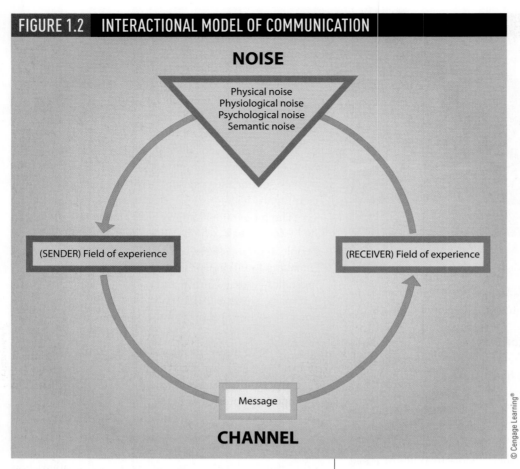

FIGURE 1.2 INTERACTIONAL MODEL OF COMMUNICATION

NOISE

Physical noise
Physiological noise
Psychological noise
Semantic noise

(SENDER) Field of experience

(RECEIVER) Field of experience

Message

CHANNEL

© Cengage Learning®

his child and finds the child either looking the other way or staring directly into his eyes, the father may "read" the meaning of the child's nonverbal communication as inattentive or disobedient. What happens if the child doesn't say anything during the reprimand? The father may still make some meaning out of the child's silence ("Don't just stand there with that blank stare!"). The interactional view acknowledges that human communication involves both speaking and listening, but it asserts that speaking and listening are separate events and thus does not address the effect of nonverbal communication as the message is sent. This criticism led to the development of a third model of communication: the transactional model.

1-3c Shared Meaning and the Transactional Model

Whereas the linear model of communication assumes that communication is an action that moves from sender

transactional model of communication A characterization of communication as the reciprocal sending and receiving of messages. In a transactional encounter, the sender and receiver do not simply send meaning from one to the other and then back again; rather, they build shared meaning through simultaneous sending and receiving.

to receiver, and the interactional model suggests that the presence of feedback makes communication an interaction between people, the **transactional model of communication** (Barnlund, 1970; Watzlawick, Beavin, & Jackson, 1967) underscores the fact that giving and receiving messages is simultaneous and mutual. In fact, the word *transactional* indicates that the communication process is cooperative. In other words, communicators (senders and receivers) are both responsible for the effect and effectiveness of communication. In a transactional encounter, people do not simply send meaning from one to the other and then back again; rather, they build shared meaning. Perhaps Dr. Martin Luther King Jr.'s words best underscore the transactional model: "It really boils down to this: that all life is interrelated. We are all caught in an inescapable network of mutuality, tied into a single garment of destiny."

A unique feature of the transactional model is its recognition that messages build upon each other, underscoring an exchange of sorts. Furthermore, both verbal and nonverbal behaviors are necessarily part of the transactional process. For example, consider Alan's conversation with his coworker Hurit. During a break, Hurit asks Alan about his family in Los Angeles. He begins to tell her that his three siblings all live in Los Angeles and that he has no idea when they will be able to "escape the prison" there. When he mentions "prison," Hurit looks confused. Seeing Hurit's puzzled facial expression, Alan clarifies that he hated Los Angeles because it was so hot, people lived too close to each other, and he felt that he was being watched all the time. In sum, he felt like he was in a prison. This example shows how much both Alan and Hurit are actively involved in this communication interaction. Hurit's nonverbal response to Alan prompted him to clarify his original message. As this exchange

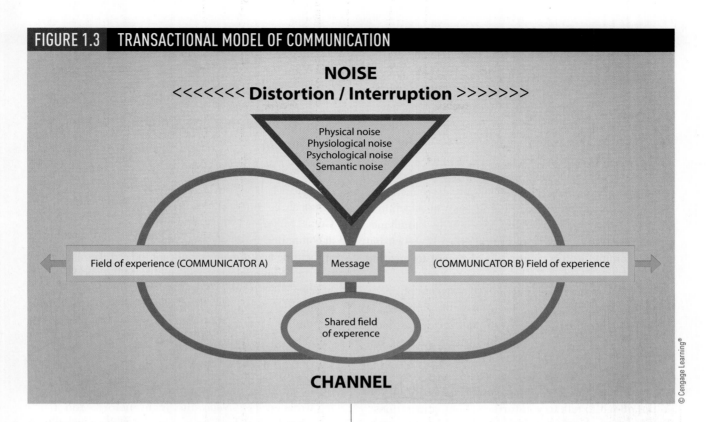

FIGURE 1.3 TRANSACTIONAL MODEL OF COMMUNICATION

NOISE
<<<<<<< **Distortion / Interruption** >>>>>>>

Physical noise
Physiological noise
Psychological noise
Semantic noise

Field of experience (COMMUNICATOR A) — Message — (COMMUNICATOR B) Field of experience

Shared field
of experience

CHANNEL

© Cengage Learning®

shows, the nonverbal message works in conjunction with the verbal message, and the transactional process requires ongoing negotiation of meaning.

Note that the transactional model in Figure 1.3 is characterized by a common field of experience between communicator A and communicator B. The **field of experience** refers to a person's culture, past experiences, personal history, and heredity, and how these elements influence the communication process.

People's fields of experience overlap at times, meaning that people share things in common. Where two people's fields of experience overlap, they can communicate more effectively than if overlap was not present. And as they communicate, they create more overlap in their experiences. This process explains why initial encounters often consist of questions and answers between communicators, such as "Where are you from?" "What's your major?" "Do you ski?" The answers to these questions help establish the overlap in the communicators' experiences: "Oh, I was in Chicago over the holidays last year"; "Really, that's my major, too"; "Yeah, I don't ski, either."

Fields of experience may change over time. For instance, in class, Alicia and Marcy have little in common and have little overlap in their fields of experience. They just met this term, have never taken a course together before, and Alicia is 18 years older than Marcy. It would appear, then, that their fields of experience

would be limited to being women enrolled in the same course together. However, consider the difference if we discover that both Alicia and Marcy are single parents, have difficulty finding quality child care, and have received academic scholarships. The overlap in their fields of experience would be significantly greater. In addition, as the two continue in the class together, they will develop new common experiences, which, in turn, will increase the overlap in their fields of experience. This increased overlap may affect their interactions with each other in the future.

Interpersonal communication scholars have embraced the transactional process in their research, believing that human communication "is always tied to what came before and always anticipates what may come later" (Wood, 1998, p. 6). Wood believes that many misunderstandings occur in relationships because people are either unaware of or don't attend to the transactional communication process. Consider her words:

> The dynamic quality of communication keeps it open to revision. If someone misunderstands our words or nonverbal behavior, we can say or do something to

field of experience The influence of a person's culture, past experiences, personal history, and heredity on the communication process.

clarify our meaning. If we don't understand another person's communication, we can look puzzled to show our confusion or ask questions to discover what the other person meant. (p. 6)

In summary, early communication models showed that communication is linear and that senders and receivers have separate roles and functions. The interactional approach expanded that thinking and suggested less linearity and more involvement of feedback between communicators. The transactional model refined our understanding by noting the importance of a communicator's background, by demonstrating the simultaneous sending and receiving of messages, and by focusing on the communicators' mutual involvement in creating meaning.

Before we move on to the next discussion, consider that our notion of communication models is continually evolving. New technologies, for instance, necessarily influence the communication process between communicators, as noted earlier in the chapter. Consider, for example, emailing a close relative asking to borrow money. Next, your relative decides to call you on the phone to talk to you further about your request. You then both decide to talk face-to-face about the situation/request. How does this infusion of technology affect the meaning? Is meaning jeopardized or enhanced because of multiple channels? The transactional model may soon become outdated as technology shapes how we view, and enact, the communication process. Communication scholars may reconsider the transactional model to take into account email, emoticons, and geographically dispersed people. In sum, we recognize that the communication behaviors and roles described

Fields of experience shape the efficacy of our communication. How might these communicators' fields of experience overlap? How might they diverge? How is this conversation shaping their respective fields of experience?

© iStock.com/SilviaJansen

by the models are not absolute and can vary depending on the situation.

With this foundation, let's now discuss the nature of interpersonal communication.

1-3d The Interpersonal Communication Continuum

With these models in place, we need to address one additional area that will help you understand the interpersonal communication process. Four decades ago, Gerald Miller and Mark Steinberg (1975) proposed looking at communication along a continuum. It was a unique view at the time and remains significant today. Like many interpersonal communication researchers, Miller and Steinberg believed that not all human communication is interpersonal. Our interactions with others can be placed on a continuum from impersonal to interpersonal (see Figure 1.4).

Think about the various interactions you have that could be considered impersonal or closer to the impersonal end of the continuum. You sit next to a person in the waiting room of your dentist and ask whether he watched *Fox News* the night before. You tell a man hawking tickets to a sold-out Celtics game that you're not interested. You tell the woman sitting next to you at a wedding that you're a friend of the groom. Typically, these linear episodes remain on the impersonal end of the continuum because the conversations remain superficial. You do not acknowledge the people in these examples as unique individuals who are important in your life.

Now, consider the many times you talk to people on a much deeper level. You share confidences with a close friend with whom you have tea. You laugh with your grandfather about a treasured family story. You commiserate with a classmate who is disappointed about a grade. In these cases, your communication is not superficial. You share yourself and respond to the other person as a unique individual.

These two ends of the continuum—impersonal and interpersonal—are the extremes. But, most of our communication encounters with others aren't so binary. Rather, most fall in between or along various points on the continuum. Your talks with a professor, coworker, or car mechanic may not be particularly emotionally fulfilling but probably have a personal dimension to them. Your professor sometimes delicately asks what personal problems might have caused a failing grade on an exam. A coworker may share family stories. And a car mechanic may ask if you have enough money for a new transmission. Each of these interactions entails some degree of closeness but not a lot of emotional depth.

FIGURE 1.4 THE CONTINUUM OF INTERPERSONAL COMMUNICATION

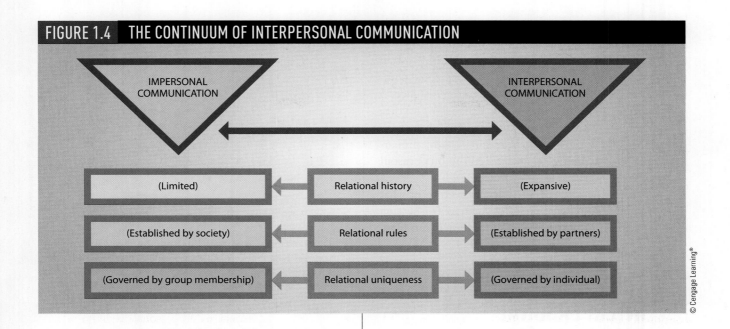

© Cengage Learning®

What will determine the extent to which an encounter is impersonal, interpersonal, or in between? Three issues are particularly important: relational history, relational rules, and relational uniqueness.

First, **relational history** pertains to the prior relationship experiences that two people share. For example, Rolanda and Maria have worked as servers in a restaurant for several years. Their relational history is apparent when you consider the amount of time they have spent together. This history may include working the same hours, sharing with each other their personal feelings about their boss, or having social times with each other's friends. Their relational history, then, spans both their professional and personal lives. This rich history enables their conversations to be interpersonal rather than impersonal.

Relational rules indicate what the people in a relationship expect and allow when they talk to each other. Relational rules, often unstated, differ from social rules in that the two relational partners negotiate them themselves as opposed to having them set by an outside source. It is true that others may influence the interpersonal rules (e.g., a supervisor's rules may have an impact on workplace relationships). Nonetheless, most relational rules are constructed by the relational partners and at times, the two may have to consider external influences on those rules. Rules help relational partners negotiate how information is managed and stored (Petronio, 2002, 2013). For example, one relational rule that Rolanda and Maria may share is the belief that all restaurant gossip should remain private. Another one of their relational rules may

communicate the need to be professional while on the job and to avoid tasteless jokes about one another or other coworkers.

A final influence on the relationship continuum is **relational uniqueness**, which pertains to how communicators frame their relationship and compare it to others. In other words, how is their relationship unique from others? In the relationship between Rolanda and Maria, they know and treat each other as unique individuals, not as generic coworkers. Thus, Rolanda asks Maria for help in making a financial decision because she knows that Maria has a good head for business. And Maria refrains from teasing Rolanda when she drops a tray because she knows Rolanda is sensitive about being clumsy. Their relational history and rules help develop their sense of relational uniqueness.

Again, much of our communication isn't purely impersonal or interpersonal; rather, it falls somewhere between the two ends of the continuum. Moreover, the relationship you have with someone doesn't always indicate whether your communication is personal or not. At times, personal communication occurs in our

relational history The prior relationship experiences that two people share.

relational rules Negotiable rules that indicate what two relational partners expect and allow when they talk to each other.

relational uniqueness The ways in which the particular relationship of two relational partners stands apart from other relationships they experience.

impersonal relationships. For example, you may consider telling your dry cleaner about your divorce or confiding to a fellow passenger that you are deathly afraid of flying. At other times, we may have impersonal communication in our close relationships. For instance, a couple with five children may be too exhausted to worry about being sensitive, loving, and compassionate with each other. Feeding the kids, bathing them, preparing their lunches, and getting them to the bus present enough challenges.

Now that you are getting a clearer picture of what interpersonal communication is, let's turn to a discussion of the value of interpersonal communication in our lives.

1-4 THE VALUE OF INTERPERSONAL COMMUNICATION

Most of you are seeking a college degree in order to secure an excellent job. Along the way, do not ignore the importance of interpersonal communication. In job interviews, interpersonal communication skills are essential. Understanding how to employ these skills effectively relates directly to getting a job (DuBrin, 2014). The National Association of Colleges and Employers reports that interpersonal skills are among the top skills employers look for in new hires across professions. And, among the top reasons why employees fail to advance in the workplace, almost one-third of CFOs report poor interpersonal communication skills. Clearly, without some knowledge and skill in interpersonal communication, you may have a difficult time finding a job in today's marketplace. There are other reasons, in addition to job success, that we need to learn about interpersonal communication. Most of us desire long-term, satisfying relationships, and effective interpersonal communication can help us establish such relationships. Learning about interpersonal communication can improve our lives physically, emotionally, and psychologically and can improve our relationships with others. A number of recent conclusions by both the academic and medical communities, including the American Cancer Society and the National Institutes of Health (e.g., American Cancer Society, 2013; Fong & Longnecker, 2010; Kosky & Schlisselberg, 2011) show the value of communication and relationships:

▶ Communication skills make a major impact on the well-being of cancer patient.

© Monkey Business Images/Shutterstock.com

▶ Older people with the ability to communicate in extended interpersonal networks improve their physical and emotional well-being.

▶ Effective doctor-patient communication is central to the delivery of effective health care.

▶ The American Cancer Society encourages cancer patients to establish interpersonal relationships with their physicians. These relationships involve taking the time to ask questions, making concerns known, sharing information, and making choices.

▶ Patient perceptions of quality end-of-life care are directly related to the communication between doctor and patient.

An additional benefit of studying interpersonal communication—and one that many of you are likely seeking—is that it can improve relationships with your family and friends. Communicating in close relationships can be tough. Yet, think about the advantages, for instance, of (1) improving your listening skills with a roommate, (2) using more sensitive language with a sibling, (3) employing nondefensive reactions in your conflicts with parents, and (4) accepting responsibility for your feelings in your conversations. These are a few areas that we explore in this book. We dedicate Chapter 11 to family, friends, and romantic relationships, knowing that these types remain among the most challenging and exciting in our lives.

Another value associated with learning about interpersonal communication pertains to the classroom. Research has shown that using your communication skills in the classroom may improve your academic performance. For instance, students who are considered to have high degrees of interaction involvement in class are more likely to increase their learning, motivation, and satisfaction with the course (Myers & Claus, 2012). Learning to listen, to participate, and to be involved in class, then, has lasting positive effects on your learning and grades.

A final way that learning about interpersonal communication can improve your life is that it can help you gain information about yourself. Psychologist Abraham Maslow (1954/1970) calls this the process of

The "People-Centered" Professions

Whether we want to call them jobs that require "social skills" or "people skills," they are in high demand. Each of these professional pursuits requires both knowledge and skill in interpersonal communication. Jenna Goudreau (2012) asserts that if you feel your expertise extends to persuading, supporting, and/or teaching others as well as relishing opportunities to work with others, then you're in luck. Analyzing the results from a jobs outlook resource. Goudreau finds that "social [interpersonal] skills rank No. 1 among job skills in highest demand." Citing a study that extrapolated data from the U.S. Department of Labor's Occupational Information Network (O*NET), she presents some compelling information regarding professions that required skills in "persuasion, negotiation, social perceptiveness, instructing others, coordinating efforts and service orientation." In other words, O*NET gathers information from those occupations that necessitate interpersonal communication skills. A number of career options were identified, each providing a relatively high salary and "high earnings growth potential." Managers round out the top jobs involving quality interpersonal communication skills.

© iStock.com/Imageegaml

Marketing, construction, administrative services, and social/community services managers were among the highest paid and highest in demand. Yet, they require a high degree of interpersonal adeptness because these positions "deal directly with people on a daily basis." Furthermore, those interested in sales and health care will also find jobs increasing in demand as the "economy moves toward services and technology." Still, Goudreau concludes that technical skills quickly become outdated but the interpersonal communication skills "have a long shelf life."

---

self-actualization. When we are self-actualized, we become the best person we can be. We are tapping our full potential in terms of our creativity, our spontaneity, and our talents. When we self-actualize, we try to cultivate our strengths and reduce our shortcomings. At times, others help us to self-actualize. For instance, in the movie *As Good As It Gets*, Jack Nicholson's character, Melvin, suffers from an obsessive-compulsive disorder. His love interest, Carol, portrayed by Helen Hunt, has her own family problems but tries to help Melvin overcome some of his idiosyncrasies. In a poignant exchange that occurs during their first date, Carol becomes distressed and tells Melvin that she will leave the restaurant unless he gives her a compliment. Carol pleads, "Pay me a compliment, Melvin. I need one quick." Melvin responds by saying, "You make me want to be a better man." Although Melvin clearly frames the compliment from his vantage point, he still, nonetheless, manages to help Carol see her value through his eyes.

Overall, then, we can reap a number of benefits from practicing effective interpersonal skills. Aside from the fact that it allows us to function every day, becoming

adept at interpersonal communication helps us in the workplace, improves our health, and aids us in our relationships with family and friends. We have now set the stage for examining some principles and misconceptions about interpersonal communication.

1-5 PRINCIPLES OF INTERPERSONAL COMMUNICATION

To better understand interpersonal communication, let's explore some major principles that shape it. Interpersonal communication is unavoidable, irreversible, symbolic, rule governed, and learned, and has both content and relationship levels.

> **self-actualization** The process of gaining information about ourselves in an effort to tap our full potential, our spontaneity, and our talents, and to cultivate our strengths and eliminate our shortcomings.

1-5a Interpersonal Communication Is Unavoidable

Researchers have stated that "you cannot *not* communicate" (Watzlawick, Beavin, & Jackson, 1967). Read that phrase again. This means that as hard as we try, we cannot prevent someone else from making meaning out of our behavior—it is inevitable and unavoidable. No matter what poker face we try to establish, we are still sending a message to others. Even our silence and avoidance of eye contact are communicative. It is this quality that makes interpersonal communication transactional. For instance, imagine that Kate and her partner, Chloe, are talking about the balance in their checking account. In this scenario, the two engage in a rather heated discussion because Kate has discovered that $300 cannot be accounted for in the balance. As Kate speaks, Chloe simply sits and listens to her. Yet Kate can't help but notice that Chloe is unable to look her in the eye. Kate begins to think that Chloe's shifting eyes and constant throat clearing must signify something deceptive. Although Chloe hasn't spoken a word, she is communicating. Her nonverbal communication is being perceived as highly communicative. We return to the impact that nonverbal communication has on creating meaning in Chapter 5.

1-5b Interpersonal Communication Is Irreversible

There are times when we wish that we hadn't said something. Wouldn't it be great if we could take back a comment and pretend that it hadn't been spoken? Think about the times you told a parent, a partner, a roommate, or your child something that you later felt was a terrible thing to say. Or what about the times you told a good friend that you couldn't stand his nose piercing ("What exactly were you thinking? You look like a freak!") or her new car ("You paid how much for that? Have you ever heard of the phrase 'ripped off?!'"). Although we might later wish to eat our words, the principle of **irreversibility** means that what we say to others cannot be reversed.

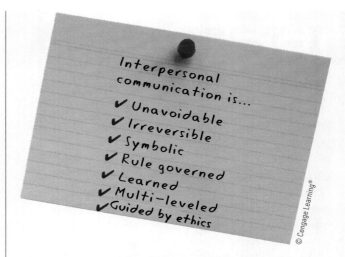

irreversibility The fact that our communication with others cannot be "unsaid" or reversed.

semiotics theory A theory that examines the study of symbols in relation to their form and content.

symbols Arbitrary labels or representations (such as words) for feelings, concepts, objects, or events.

In fact, the principle of irreversibility affects even mediated interpersonal communication such as email. Think about sending an email that was written in haste. It may have been filled with personal attacks against someone because you were upset and venting. Now imagine that email getting into the hands of the person you were slamming. An apology may help, but saying you're sorry does nothing to erase the original message. The irreversibility of your message becomes apparent.

1-5c Interpersonal Communication Is Symbolic

The study of the use of symbols and their form and content is part of **semiotics theory**. One important reason interpersonal communication occurs is because symbols are mutually agreed upon by the participants in the process. **Symbols** are arbitrary labels or representations for feelings, concepts, objects, or events. Words are symbols. For instance, the word *table* can represent a place to sit. Similarly, the word *hate* represents the idea of hate, which means strong negative feelings for someone or something.

The word *fear* suggests that symbols may be somewhat abstract, and with this abstraction comes the potential for miscommunication. For instance, consider how hard it would be for someone who has never attended college to understand the following:

I have no idea what the *prereqs* are. I know that the *midterm* is pretty much *objective*. And the *prof* doesn't like to follow the *syllabus* too much. I wish that stuff was in the *undergrad* catalog. I'm sure I'd rather do an *independent study* than take that class.

In the semiotic tradition, "communication is easiest when we share a common language, that words can mean different things to different people so miscommunication

Semiotics Theory

The theory of semiotics has focused primarily on the role that symbols play. For many semiotic researchers, the stories we share with others have symbolic value. As you reflect upon a few of your "academic stories," consider which ones you would interpret as "symbolic." That is, think about those stories that have value and have the potential to provide meaning to others. Whether it's about your first exam, an ex-roommate, social event, or other experience, share a narrative that provides some insight into your college life.

is a constant danger" (Craig, 2007, p. 78). Ultimately, people are the interpreters of what constitutes meaning in language.

Because the verbal symbols used in this message are not understood by everyone, the message would be lost to someone who had never encountered words such as those italicized. This example underscores the importance of developing a transactional viewpoint because communication requires mutual understanding. In Chapter 4, we look in more detail at the importance of language in interpersonal relationships.

1-5d Interpersonal Communication Is Rule Governed

Consider the following examples of communication rules:

▶ As long as you live under my roof, you'll do what I say.

▶ Always tell the truth.

▶ Don't talk back.

▶ Always say "thank you" when someone gives you a present.

▶ Don't interrupt while someone is talking.

You probably heard at least one of these while growing up. We noted earlier that rules are important ingredients in our relationships. They help guide and structure our interpersonal communication. **Rules** essentially say that individuals in a relationship agree that there are appropriate ways to interact in their relationship. Like the rules in our childhood, most of the rules in our relationships today tell us what we can or can't do. Susan Shimanoff (1980) has defined a rule as "a followable prescription that indicates what behavior is obligated, preferred, or prohibited in certain contexts" (p. 57). In other words, Shimanoff, like many other communication researchers, thinks that we can choose whether or not we wish to follow a rule. Ultimately, we must decide whether the rule must be adhered to or can be ignored in our interpersonal exchanges.

To understand this principle, consider the Chandler family—a family of three who finds itself homeless. The Chandlers live day to day in homeless shelters in a large city in the South. The family members agree on a communication rule explicitly stating that they will not discuss their economic situation in public. This rule requires all family members to refrain from talking about what led to their homelessness. Each member of the family is obligated to keep this information private, an intrafamily secret of sorts. Whether or not people outside the Chandler family agree on the usefulness of such a rule is not important. Yet, one test of the rule's effectiveness is whether family members can refrain from discussing their circumstances with others. If the rule is not followed, what will the consequences be? Rules, therefore, imply choice, and participants in a relationship may choose to ignore a particular rule.

1-5e Interpersonal Communication Is Learned

People obviously believe that interpersonal communication is a learned process. Otherwise, why would we be writing this book, and why would you be taking this course? Yet, as we mentioned at the beginning of this chapter, we often take for granted our ability to communicate interpersonally. Still, we all need to refine and cultivate our skills to communicate with a wide assortment of people. You must be able to make informed communication choices in changing times.

You're in this course to learn more about interpersonal communication. Yet, you've also been acquiring this information throughout your life. We learn how to communicate with one another from television, the Internet, our peer group, and our partners. Early in our lives, most of us learn from our family. Consider this

rule A prescribed guide that indicates what behavior is obligated, preferred, or prohibited in certain contexts.

dialogue between Amanda Reid and her 7-year-old son, Luke:

> **Luke:** Mom, what's Holly's dad's name?
>
> **Amanda:** Mr. Letteri.
>
> **Luke:** No, Mom—what's his *real* name?
>
> **Amanda:** Honey, I told you. Mr. Letteri.
>
> **Luke:** Doesn't he have a name like I do?
>
> **Amanda:** Little kids call him Mr. Letteri. Grown-ups call him Kenny.
>
> **Luke:** Why can't I call him Kenny?
>
> **Amanda:** Because you're not a grown-up and because he is older than you, you should call him Mr. Letteri.

Clearly, Amanda is teaching her child a communication rule that she believes leads to interpersonal effectiveness. She tells her son that he should use titles for adults. Implied in this teaching is that kids do not have the same conversational privileges as adults. Interestingly, this learned interpersonal skill evolves with age. For example, at age 24, what do you think Luke will call Kenny Letteri? This awkwardness about names is frequently felt by newlyweds as they become members of their spouse's family. Does a husband call his wife's mother "Mom," or does he call her by her first name? Of course, his mother-in-law may ask to be called "Mom," and yet her son-in-law may be uncomfortable with accommodating her request, especially if his own mother is still alive.

1-5f Interpersonal Communication Has Both Content and Relationship Levels

Each message that you communicate to another contains information on two levels—content and relationship. The **content level** refers to the information contained in the message. The words you speak to another person and how you say those words constitute the content of the message. Content, then, includes both verbal

content level The verbal and nonverbal information contained in a message that indicates the topic of the message.

relationship level The information contained in a message that indicates how the sender wants the receiver to interpret the message.

ethics The perceived rightness or wrongness of an action or behavior.

and nonverbal components. A message also contains a **relationship level**, which can be defined as how you want the receiver of a message to interpret your message. The relational dimension of a message gives us some idea how the speaker and the listener feel about each other. Content and relationship levels work simultaneously in a message, and it is difficult to think about sending a message that doesn't, in some way, comment on the relationship between the sender and receiver (Knapp & Vangelisti, 2005). In other words, we can't really separate the two. We always express an idea or thought (content), but that thought is always presented within a relational framework. Consider the following example:

> Father Felix is a Catholic priest who is the pastor of a large parish in the Rocky Mountains. Corrine Murphy is the parish administrative assistant. Both have been at the parish for more than 10 years and have been good friends throughout that time. One of the most stressful times in the church is during the Christmas season. The pastor is busy visiting homebound parishioners, while Corrine is busy overseeing the annual holiday pageant. With this stress comes a lot of shouting between the two. On one occasion, several parishioners hear Father Felix yell, "Corrine, you forgot to tell me about the Lopez family! When do they need me to visit? Where is your mind these days?" Corrine shoots back, "I've got it under control. Just quit your nagging!" The parishioners listening to the two were a bit taken aback by the way they yelled at each other.

In this example, the parishioners who heard the conversation were simply attuned to the content dimension and failed to understand that the 10-year relationship between Father Felix and Corrine was unique to the two of them. Such direct interpersonal exchanges during stressful times were not out of the ordinary. Father Felix and Corrine frequently raised their voices to each other, and neither gave it a second thought. In a case like this, the content should be understood with the relationship in mind.

1-5g Interpersonal Communication Involves Ethical Choices

Although we will address this topic in more detail a bit later in the chapter, we wish to point out that **ethics** remains instrumental in your interpersonal communication. Ethics is the perceived rightness or wrongness of an action or behavior. Researchers have identified ethics as a type of moral decision making, determined in large part by society (Spinello, 2014). In our conversations

© Pressmaster/Shutterstock.com

1-6a Interpersonal Communication Solves All Problems

We cannot stress enough that simply being skilled in interpersonal communication does not mean that you are prepared to work out all of your relational challenges and problems. Surely, as we noted earlier, communication will not work sometimes. You may communicate clearly about a problem, but not necessarily be able to solve it. Also, keep in mind that communication involves both speaking and listening. In advising appointments, for instance, many students have revealed to us that they try to "talk out a problem" with their roommates. Although this may seem to be a great strategy, we hope that this talking is accompanied with listening. We are confident that you will leave this course with an understanding of how to communicate thoughtfully and skillfully with others in a variety of relationships. We also hope you realize that simply because you are talking does not mean that you will solve all of your relationship problems.

1-6b Interpersonal Communication Is Always a Good Thing

National best-selling self-help books and famous self-improvement gurus have made huge amounts of money promoting the idea that communication is the magic potion for all of life's ailments. Most often, communication is a good thing in our relationships with others. We wouldn't be writing this book if we didn't think that! Yet, there are times when communication results in less-than-satisfying relationship experiences. A relatively new area of research in interpersonal communication is called "the dark side" of communication (Cupach & Spitzberg, 2014). We refer to such difficult communication as "destructive" communication.

Destructive interpersonal communication generally refers to negative communication exchanges between people. People can communicate in ways that are manipulative, deceitful, exploitive, homophobic, racist, and emotionally abusive (Cupach & Spitzberg, 1994). In other words, we need to be aware that communication can be downright nasty at times and that interpersonal communication is not always satisfying and rewarding. Although most people approach interpersonal communication thoughtfully and with an open mind, others are less sincere. To contrast destructive communication, we also discuss constructive (or, the bright side) interpersonal communication, which focuses on the altruistic, supportive, and affirming reasons that people communicate with others. Look for discussions of destructive and constructive interpersonal communication throughout the chapters of this book.

with those whom we have a close relationship, nearly every encounter is guided by ethics. What you say, how you say, the expectations you have of others' communication abilities, the conversational topic, among others, can all function prominently in our interpersonal communication with our friends, families, coworkers, and others. If we apply a technological lens, the ethical effects do not diminish. For instance, if you're on a listserv, what consequences exist for the communicator who chooses to use inflammatory language to insult you? Do you jump into the thread or do you choose to move on? Ethical choices confront all of us in a number of important and different ways.

In this chapter so far, we have explored the definition of interpersonal communication in some detail and have described several principles associated with interpersonal communication. Now that you know what interpersonal communication is, let's focus on some of the misconceptions about interpersonal communication.

1-6   MYTHS ABOUT INTERPERSONAL COMMUNICATION

Dr. Phil's advice. The Internet. Old tales that never were proven true. Whatever the source, for one reason or another, people operate under several misconceptions about interpersonal communication. These myths impede our understanding and enactment of effective interpersonal communication.

1-6c Interpersonal Communication Is Common Sense

Consider the following question: If interpersonal communication is just a matter of common sense, why do we have so many problems communicating with others? We need to abandon the notion that communication is simply common sense.

It is true that we should be sure to use whatever common sense we have in our personal interactions, but this strategy will get us only so far. In some cases, a skilled interpersonal communicator may effectively rely on his or her common sense, but there are many situations where our common sense simply fails to "kick in" (think, for example, of those heated arguments, the euphoria we feel when we first start dating someone, and other highly emotional moments). In these and other cases, we need to make use of an extensive repertoire of skills to make informed choices in our relationships. One problem with believing that interpersonal communication is merely common sense relates to the diversity of our population. As we discuss in Chapter 3, cultural variation continues to characterize U.S. society. Making the assumption that all people intuitively know how to communicate with everyone ignores the significant cultural differences in communication norms. Even males and females tend to look at the same event differently (Ivy, 2012). To rid ourselves of the myth of common sense, we simply can take culture and gender into consideration.

1-6d Interpersonal Communication Is Synonymous with Interpersonal Relationships

We don't automatically have an interpersonal relationship with someone merely because we are exchanging interpersonal communication with him or her. Interpersonal communication *can lead to* interpersonal relationships, but an accumulation of interpersonal messages does not *automatically* result in an interpersonal

relationship. Sharing a pleasant conversation about your family with a stranger riding on the bus with you doesn't mean you have a relationship with that person.

Relationships do not just appear. William Wilmot (1995) remarked that relationships "emerge from recurring episodic enactments" (p. 25). That is, for you and another person to develop an interpersonal relationship, a pattern of intimate exchanges must take place over time. Relationships usually will not happen unless two people demonstrate a sense of caring and respect, and have significant periods of time to work on their relational issues.

1-6e Interpersonal Communication Is Always Face-to-Face

Throughout this chapter, much of our discussion has centered on face-to-face encounters between people. Indeed, this is the primary way that people meet and cultivate their interpersonal skills with each other. It is also the focus of most of the research in interpersonal communication. Yet, as each of us knows by now, massive numbers of people utilize the Internet in their communication with others and people are finding life partners online. This mediated interpersonal communication requires us to expand our discussion of interpersonal communication beyond personal encounters. In the spirit of inclusiveness, we incorporate technological relations into our interpretation of interpersonal communication. Discussing the intersection of technology and interpersonal communication is necessary to capture the complexity of our various relationships.

Thus far, this chapter has given you a fundamental framework for examining interpersonal communication. We close by examining a feature of the interpersonal communication process that is not easily taught and is often difficult to comprehend: ethics.

1-7 INTERPERSONAL COMMUNICATION ETHICS

Communication ethicist Richard Johannesen and his colleagues (2007) concluded that "ethical issues may arise in human behavior whenever that behavior could have significant impact on other persons, when the behavior involves conscious choice of means and ends, and when the behavior can be judged by standards of right and wrong" (p. 1). In other words, ethics is the cornerstone of interpersonal communication.

Earlier, we noted that interpersonal communication involves ethical choices. And, a primary goal of ethics

Interpersonal communication is NOT...
- ✗ Always a problem solver
- ✗ Always a good thing
- ✗ Common sense
- ✗ Synonymous with interpersonal relationships
- ✗ Always face-to-face

is to "establish appropriate constraints on ourselves" (Englehardt, 2001, p. 1). Ethical decisions involve value judgments, and not everyone will agree with those values. For instance, do you tell racist jokes in front of others and think that they are harmless ways to make people laugh? What sort of value judgment is part of the decision to tell or not to tell a joke? In interpersonal communication, acting ethically is critical. As Raymond Pfeiffer and Ralph Forsberg (2005) concluded, "To act ethically is, at the very least, to strive to act in ways that do not hurt other people, that respect their dignity, individuality, and unique moral value, and that treat others as equally important to oneself " (p. 7). If we're not prepared to act in this way, one can conclude that we do not consider ethics important. Overall, being ethical means having respect for others, shouldering responsibility, acting thoughtfully with others, and being honest. The following section fleshes out these ethical behaviors more thoroughly.

TABLE 1.1   ETHICS ON THE JOB: VIEWS OF THE MOST ETHICAL OCCUPATIONS

Please tell me how you would rate the honesty and ethical standards of people in these different fields—very high, high, average, low, or very low?
Nov. 26-29, 2012

Occupation	%Very high/High
Nurses	85
Pharmacists	75
Medical doctors	70
Engineers	70
Dentists	62
Police officers	58
College teachers	53
Clergy	52
Psychiatrists	41
Chiropractors	38
Bankers	28
Journalists	24
Business executives	21
State governors	20
Lawyers	19
Insurance salespeople	15
Senators	14
HMO managers	12
Stockbrokers	11
Advertising practitioners	11
Members of Congress	10
Car salespeople	8

Ethics is necessarily part of not only our personal relationships but our work relationships as well. To get a sense of the interplay between ethics and various jobs, consider Table 1.1, which shows what the U.S. public views as being the most and least ethical occupations. See if you agree with how the country views ethical occupations and if your career choice is found among those listed. What do you think the rankings look like today?

1-7a Five Ethical Systems of Communication

We make value judgments in interpersonal communication in many ways. Researchers have discussed a number of different ethical systems of communication relevant to our interpersonal encounters (e.g., Andersen, 1996; Englehardt, 2001; Jensen, 1997). We will discuss five of them here. In addition, because the field of communication has agreed on a code of ethical behavior, we have provided you ethical values as they relate to communicating with others (see Table 1.2). As we briefly overview each system, keep in mind that these systems attempt to let us know what it means to act morally.

CATEGORICAL IMPERATIVE

The first ethical system, the categorical imperative, is based on the work of philosopher Immanuel Kant (Kant, 1785;

To illustrate the relationship between communication ethics and corporate social responsibility, *Forbes* magazine published the insights of Don Knauss, chairman and CEO of Clorox, a company with a 100-year tradition of customer service, on the role of ethics in business-customer relationships. Knauss clearly embraces ethical business practices as he concludes: "We know that in order to build and maintain trust with our customers we have to first develop a company-wide reputation for integrity." To accomplish this, Knauss claims that all employees must take part in an online training course on ethics as well as enroll in "refresher" courses that cover different ethical practices. Furthermore, Clorox employees, vendors, and subsidiaries must also abide by a company code of conduct that covers a variety of subjects—from human rights to labor and safety. These internal ethical policies and practices, however, are accompanied with external support. For instance, Knauss writes that "any activity we engage in with customers will be fair and defensible, no exceptions." In addition, to ensure a corporate culture of trust, if a customer is not ethical in its treatment of employees or in dealing with Clorox, Knauss believes in "cutting off a large customer." He concludes, "Whatever a management team can do to engender that trust with customers, with suppliers or with whichever constituency it's dealing with—consistent with a set of values and principles that it just will not violate—is only to its long-term benefit." Knauss

Company codes of social responsibility are becoming increasingly common in the U.S.

contends that when a company models ethical behavior, business relationship improve, allowing for, of course, an improvement in the "bottom line."

Thompson, 2013). Kant's **categorical imperative** refers to individuals following moral absolutes. This ethical system suggests that we should act as though we are an example to others. According to this system, the key question when making a moral decision is: What would happen if everyone did this? Thus, you should not do something that you wouldn't feel is fine for everyone to do all the time. Kant also believed that the consequences of actions are not important; what matters is the ethical principle behind those actions.

> **categorical imperative** An ethical system, based on the work of philosopher Immanuel Kant, advancing the notion that individuals follow moral absolutes. The underlying tenet in this ethical system suggests that we should act as an example to others.

> **utilitarianism** An ethical system, developed by John Stuart Mill, suggesting that what is ethical will bring the greatest good for the greatest number of people. In this system, consequences of moral actions, especially maximizing satisfaction and happiness, are important.

For example, let's say that Mark confides to Karla, a coworker, that he is in the early stages of leukemia. Although the company has health benefits and although the type of leukemia is treatable, Karla decides to tell no one else because Mark fears some repercussions to revealing his health status. Elizabeth, the supervisor, asks Karla if she knows what's happening with Mark because he misses work and is always tired. The categorical imperative dictates that Karla tell her boss the truth, despite the fact that telling the truth may affect Mark's job, his future with the company, and his relationship with Karla. The categorical imperative requires us to tell the truth because Kant believed that enforcing the principle of truth telling is more important than worrying about the short-term consequences of telling the truth.

UTILITARIANISM

The second ethical system, **utilitarianism**, was developed in 1861 by John Stuart Mill (Mill, 1863; Su,

2013). According to this system, what is ethical is what will bring the greatest good for the greatest number of people. Unlike Kant, Mill believed the consequences of moral actions are important. Maximizing satisfaction and happiness is essential. For example, suppose you're at a friend's house and her younger sister is crying incessantly. You notice your friend grabbing her sister, shaking her, and yelling for her to be quiet. Afterward, you observe red marks on the child's arms. Do you report your friend to the authorities? Do you remain quiet? Do you talk to your friend?

Making a decision based on utilitarianism or what is best for the greater good means that you will speak out or take some action. Although it would be easier on you and your friend if you remained silent, doing so would not serve the greater good. According to utilitarianism, you should either talk to your friend or report your friend's actions to an appropriate individual.

THE GOLDEN MEAN

The **golden mean**, a third ethical system, proposes that we should aim for harmony and balance in our lives (Gensler, 2013). This principle, articulated more than 2,500 years ago by Aristotle, suggests that a person's moral virtue stands between two vices, with the middle, or the mean, being the foundation for a rational society. The application of the golden mean to communication is rooted in the ability to find a "middle ground" so that communicators are less inclined to honor the extremes of a discussion. Aristotle felt that thoughts or behaviors—when taken to excess—-are neither productive nor especially valuable.

Let's say that Cora, Jackie, and Lester are three employees who work for a small social media company. During a break one afternoon, someone asks what kind of childhood each had. Cora goes into specific detail, talking about her abusive father: "He really let me have it, and it all started when I was 5," she begins before launching into a long description. In contrast, Jackie only says "My childhood was okay." Lester tells the group that his was a pretty rough childhood: "It was tough financially. We didn't have a lot of money. But we really all got along well." In this example, Cora was on one extreme, revealing too much information. Jackie was at the other extreme, revealing very little, if anything. Lester's decision to reveal a reasonable amount of information about his childhood was an ethical one; he practiced the golden mean by providing a sufficient amount of information but not too much. In other words, he presented a rational and balanced perspective. In this case, note that revealing too much and revealing too little may make another awkward or uncomfortable. Finding the "balance"

in self-disclosure is especially difficult—a topic we discuss in greater detail in Chapter 8.

ETHIC OF CARE

An **ethic of care**, the fourth ethical system, means being concerned with connection. Carol Gilligan first conceptualized an ethic of care by looking at women's ways of moral decision making. She felt that because men have been the dominant voices in society, women's commitment toward connection has gone unnoticed. Gilligan (1982) initially felt that an ethic of care was a result of how women were raised. Although her ethical principles pertain primarily to women, Gilligan's research applies to men as well. Some men adopt the ethic, and some women do not adopt the ethic. In contrast to the categorical imperative, for instance, the ethic of care is concerned with consequences of decisions.

Suppose that Ben and Anthony are having a conversation about whether it's right to go behind a person's back and disclose that he or she is gay. Ben makes an argument that it's a shame that people won't own up to being gay; they are who they are. If someone hides his or her sexuality, Ben believes that it's fine to "out" that person. Anthony, expressing an ethic of care, tells his friend that no one should reveal another person's sexual identity. That information should remain private unless an individual wishes to reveal it. Anthony explains that outing someone would have serious negative repercussions for the relationships of the person being outed and thus shouldn't be done. In this example, Anthony exemplifies a symbolic connection to those who don't want to discuss their sexual identity with others.

SIGNIFICANT CHOICE

The fifth ethical system, **significant choice**, is an ethical orientation conceptualized by Thomas Nilsen (1966). Nilsen argued that communication is ethical to the extent that it maximizes people's ability to exercise free choice. Information should be given to others in a noncoercive way so that they can make free

golden mean An ethical system, articulated by Aristotle, proposing that a person's moral virtue stands between two vices, with the middle, or the mean, being the foundation for a rational society.

ethic of care An ethical system, based on the concepts of Carol Gilligan, that is concerned with the connections among people and the moral consequences of decisions.

significant choice An ethical system, conceptualized by Thomas Nilsen, underscoring the belief that communication is ethical to the extent that it maximizes our ability to exercise free choice. In this system, information should be given to others in a noncoercive way so that people can make free and informed decisions.

Exposing a friend's secrets may violate the ethic of care.

experiences be completely revealed to a partner? How do you treat an ex-friend or ex-partner in future encounters? Is it ever okay to lie to protect your friend? These kinds of questions challenge millions of interpersonal relationships.

Raymond Pfeiffer and Ralph Forsberg (2005) conclude that when we are confronted with ethical decisions, "we should not ignore our society's cultural, religious, literary, and moral traditions. Our values have emerged from and are deeply enmeshed in these traditions. They often teach important lessons concerning the difficult decisions we face in life" (p. 8).

The five ethical systems, summarized in Table 1.2, can give you strategies for making ethical decisions. However, making sense of the world and of our interpersonal relationships requires us to understand our own values. And, these values are apparent not only in our face-to-face conversations, but in our online conversations as well. Ethical behavior is essential when we communicate with people whom we don't see or with whom we have no shared physical space. We return to this topic throughout the book as we discuss the various themes and skills related to interpersonal communication.

We need to understand that because ethical choices can have lasting physical, emotional, financial, and psychological consequences, a sense of ethics should guide us on a daily basis. Being aware of and sensitive to your decisions and their consequences will help you make the right choices in these changing times.

and informed decisions. For example, if you place a personal ad on an Internet dating site and fail to disclose that you are married, you are not ethical in your communication with others. However, if you give information regarding your relationship status and other details, you are practicing the ethical system of significant choice.

1-7b Understanding Ethics and Our Own Values

Ethics permeates interpersonal communication. We make ongoing ethical decisions in all our interpersonal encounters and these ethical choices are especially important in our very close relationships. Questions of ethics are all around us: Should someone's past sexual

TABLE 1.2	ETHICAL SYSTEMS OF INTERPERSONAL COMMUNICATION	
Ethical System	**Responsibility**	**Action**
Categorical imperative	To adhere to a moral absolute	Tell the truth
Utilitarianism	To ensure the greatest good for the greatest number of people	Produce favorable consequences
Golden mean	To achieve rationality and balance	Create harmony and balance for the community and the individual
Ethic of care	To establish connection	Establish caring relationships
Significant choice	To enable free choice	Maximize individual choice

Adapted from Englehardt, 2001.

1-8 THE COMMUNICATION CORE: COMPETENCY AND CIVILITY

One central theme guides the writing of this book: the communication core. Throughout the text, you will explore many topics associated with interpersonal communication. As you try to digest the material, keep in mind that there are critical, or core, behaviors that we believe will assist you in becoming more adept and effective in your interpersonal communication. Let's explain this a bit further.

We believe that you have an abundance of choices available to you in your communication with others, and we hope that you will always choose to become a more effective communicator. Yet, we know that our communication with others is sometimes filled with anxiety, confusion, unpleasantness, excitement, and angst. Having a toolbox of ways to adapt and respond appropriately to all sorts of communication situations will help you achieve the meanings you intend to convey.

To be effective in your communication with others requires two critical ingredients: competency and civility. **Communication competency**, or the ability to communicate with knowledge, skills, and thoughtfulness, should be foremost when trying to meet a communication challenge. When we are competent, our communication is both appropriate and effective. We use communication appropriately when we accommodate the cultural expectations for communicating, including using appropriate rules, understanding the different roles we play, and being "other-centered" when possible. Acquiring meaning is essential and this occurs when each communicator has achieved his or her goals in a conversation or a relationship. As you read the following chapters, you will be introduced to a lot of information about interpersonal communication. Developing a large repertoire of useful skills and applying them appropriately is a hallmark of a competent communicator.

A second ingredient of being an effective communicator is civility. **Civil communication** is the acceptance of another person as an equal partner in achieving meaning during communication. Civility requires sensitivity to the experiences of the other communicator. When we are civil communicators, we avoid sending hateful emails to others, accept that not all communication encounters will go our way, acknowledge multiple viewpoints, and avoid harming others. And, although most people would state that being civil is critical in society, "we do not yet know enough about what makes people more civil to one another" (Poole & Walther, 2002, p. 11). Therefore,

learning about interpersonal communication will assist you in being part of a *civil*ization.

These days, civil communication seems to be lacking. We have witnessed profanity in Congress, name-calling on talk radio, family members openly attacking each other on television talk shows, and people belittling individuals who lack "appropriate" language skills. On a more personal level, you may have been the recipient of incivility by classmates and even close friends. As interpersonal communicators, we should remain intolerant of such uncivil interactions. Throughout this book, as we introduce various skill sets necessary to achieve effective communication and quality relationships, we offer ways to enhance civil communication.

Now more than ever and because of the integration of technology in our lives, we live in changing times. Communication skills that were once effective may have to be revisited. Adapting to the cultures and individuals around us is paramount in a country where race, ethnicity, gender, age, sexual identity, economic status, religion, and belief systems pervade contemporary conversations. As you learned earlier in this chapter, interacting with others is often challenging because of the various fields of experience of communicators. These backgrounds clearly influence the sending, receiving, and interpretation of a message.

communication competency The ability to communicate with knowledge, skills, and thoughtfulness.

civil communication The acceptance of another person as an equal partner in achieving meaning during communication.

STUDY TOOLS

DON'T FORGET TO CHECK OUT WWW. CENGAGEBRAIN.COM!

CHAPTER 1 FEATURES THE FOLLOWING RESOURCES:

☐ Ethics & Choice: Lenora

☐ Communication Assessment Test: Personal Report of Communication Apprehension

☐ Interactive Activities

2 | Communication, Culture, and Identity

LEARNING OUTCOMES

2-1 Recognize and understand the interpretation and complexity of culture

2-2 Understand the importance of cultural diversity in the United States and beyond

2-3 Identify reasons for the importance of intercultural communication

2-4 Describe the dimensions of cultural variability

2-5 Explain the obstacles to achieving intercultural effectiveness

2-6 Employ strategies to improve intercultural communication

After you finish
this chapter, go to
PAGE 45 for
STUDY TOOLS.

THEORY/MODEL PREVIEW

Context Orientation Theory; Cultural Variability Theory

Most people communicate with the mistaken belief that others will understand them.

For instance, some people use personal expressions or inside jokes when in reality, these words, phrases, and stories are not universally understood. And, especially in the United States, most people don't think twice about using the English language to make their point, despite the fact that many people who live in the United States speak different languages and are members of various cultural groups where English is not a primary language.

In addition, most English speakers employ their own nonverbal codes without thinking about how nonverbal communication differs across cultures. For example, looking someone directly in the eyes during a conversation is a valued norm in the United States but is viewed as disrespectful or a sign of aggression in many parts of the world. In addition, many people in the United States value emotional expressiveness, yet research shows that some cultural groups, especially those in Eastern cultures, do not freely express their feelings (Davis, Greenberger, Charles, Chen, Zhao, & Dong, 2012). Today more than ever, much of the meaning in our interactions with others depends on the cultural backgrounds of the communicators.

Our discussion in this book, thus far, has focused on the interpersonal communication process. This chapter focuses on one important and decisive influence upon that process: culture. Culture pervades virtually every component of interpersonal communication, and cultural diversity is a fact of life. By thinking about and understanding culture, we can learn a lot about the ways that we and others communicate in a multicultural society.

The emphasis of this chapter is on intercultural communication. For our purposes, **intercultural communication** refers to communication between and among individuals and groups whose cultural backgrounds differ. Some researchers distinguish between communication across national cultures (e.g., people from Japan and from the United States) and communication between groups within one national culture (e.g., African Americans and Asian Americans). In this text, we refer to all such encounters as intercultural encounters. In many U.S. communities, these intercultural encounters were once very rare because most communities were comprised primarily of Caucasians who were fully assimilated into the dominant culture. But, clearly times are changing as nonwhite babies born now comprise the majority of births and U.S. Census estimates indicate that the "White majority" will dissipate by 2043 (Tavernise, 2012).

We live in a society that is more culturally diverse than ever. We describe this cultural complexity in this chapter and look at the significant issues associated with culture and interpersonal communication. The words of Larry Samovar, Richard Porter, and Edwin McDaniel (2013) underscore our rationale for this chapter: "What members of a particular culture value and how they perceive the universe are usually far more important than whether they eat with chopsticks, their hands, or metal utensils" (p. 26). Knowledge of others' cultural values and practices enhances intercultural communication.

For intercultural communication to occur, individuals don't have to be from different countries. In a diverse society such as the United States, we can experience intercultural communication within one state, one town, or even one neighborhood. You may live in an urban center where it's likely that people from various cultural backgrounds live together. As authors, we find ourselves in

intercultural communication Communication between and among individuals and groups from different cultural backgrounds.

China remains the largest yet one of the most misunderstood countries in the world. More and more people are traveling to China; in fact, many U.S. businesses continue their economic engagement with this country of nearly 1.5 billion people. Gary Stoller (2013) writes that China's business market and booming tourism has prompted many newcomers to travel to places like Hong Kong with little, or no, understanding of the cultural expectations. Stoller asserts that cultural etiquette is necessary in order to win business and sustain credibility. Many rules and appropriate cultural expectations exist. For instance, punctuality is key in China, and being late is a sign of disrespect. Should a business card be given to you and you don't understand Mandarin, you are expected to look at the card—even if you don't know the language. Failing to do so is also a sign of disrespect. Interruptions should not occur. Within two days of meeting a Chinese business executive, an email should be sent "recapping all the positive points made at the meeting and

reconfirming what was understood and agreed on to move forward." Stoller warns readers that many other Chinese customs should be considered and adhered to, particularly as they pertain to eating and drinking. He cites an international sales director who states, "The key for China is to always be patient and polite."

---

this exciting cultural stew. In the South End of Boston, for instance, it is common to see people with Caribbean, Cambodian, and Latino backgrounds all living on the same street. In Milwaukee, one would be able to find both Polish and Mexican communities on the south side of the city.

Trying to understand people who may think, talk, look, and act differently from us can be challenging at times. Just think about the words people use to describe those who may be culturally different from them: *odd, weird, strange, unusual,* and *unpredictable.* These associations have existed for centuries. Consider the words of fifth-century Greek playwright Aeschylus: "Everyone is quick to blame the alien." Today the "alien" takes many shapes and forms, with many of us embracing the diversity and heterogeneity in the population and many others rejecting it.

Intercultural communication theorists (e.g., Asante, Miike, & Yin, 2014) argue that humans cannot exist without culture. Our individuality is constructed around culture. As we will learn in Chapter 3, our identities are shaped by our conversations and relationships with others. Our cultural background enters into

this mix by shaping our identity, our communication practices, and our responses to others. We tend to use other people as guideposts for what we consider to be "normal." And, in doing so, we can focus on how others from diverse cultures differ from us. For instance, when Jean from the United States meets Cheng from China in her philosophy class, she might notice how he smiles more frequently than his U.S. counterparts. Jean might also observe that Cheng is much more deferential to the professor than are she and her U.S. friends since he always asks permission to speak. Yet this comparison is incomplete. Intercultural scholars and practitioners believe that although this classroom difference exists, a host of cultural similarities exist between Cheng and his U.S. student peers. We note this point because this chapter explores both what factors culturally bind us as well as what elements divide us.

2-1 DEFINING CULTURE

Culture is a very difficult concept to define, partly because it is complex, multidimensional, and abstract. Some researchers (e.g., Kroeber & Kluckhohn, 1993) have discovered over 300 different definitions for the word! For our purposes, we believe that **culture** is the

culture The shared, personal, and learned life experiences of a group of individuals who have a common set of values, norms, and traditions.

Cultural Awareness and Human Resource Management

A robust and productive working environment requires a "culturally and linguistically diverse workforce." So says an intellectual center that focuses on aging and cultural diversity. Human resource (HR) professionals are key to achieving such a work climate. The center posits that HR professionals should strive to ensure that cultural diversity is paramount in both the employment and training of employees. Because of the job duties required of HR personnel, cultural awareness comes in various shapes and forms: recruitment ("Consider the demographics of your local community when recruiting new staff"), staff education and development ("Include a cultural diversity component in all staff orientation"), and organizational supports ("Address cultural diversity in all organizational policies and practices"). The center further calls for a number of other key considerations for HR professionals: working on securing bilingual staff, encouraging staff to learn a second language, providing facilities for a variety of religious and

spiritual observances, reviewing assessment programs and practices for cultural bias, advertising job vacancies in "ethnic media," among other recommendations. The center, while focused on aging in particular, shows that an understanding of intercultural communication is essential for those who wish to pursue a career in human resource management.

---

shared, personal, and learned life experiences of a group of individuals who have a common set of values, norms, and traditions. These standards, patterns of communication, and cultural customs are important to consider in our communication with others. They affect our interpersonal relationships within a culture, and the three are nearly impossible to detach from our understanding of intercultural communication.

As we define the term *culture*, keep in mind that we are embracing a "global" interpretation. That is, we acknowledge culture to include these commonly held components:

▶ Age (e.g., adolescents, senior citizens)

▶ Race/ethnicity (e.g., African American, Cherokee)

▶ Sexual identity (e.g., bisexuals, transgendered individuals)

▶ Spiritual identity (e.g., Catholic, Muslim)

▶ Geographic region (e.g., New Englanders, Midwesterners)

▶ Family background (e.g., single parent, cohabiting couples)

▶ Ability (e.g., visual impairments, physical challenges)

Our examples reflect this expansive view of culture. We now look at three underlying principles associated with our definition of culture: culture is learned, culture creates community, and culture is multileveled.

2-1a Culture Is Learned

We aren't born with knowledge of the practices and behaviors of our culture. People learn about a culture through the communication of symbols for meaning and we do this learning both consciously and unconsciously. We can learn about culture directly, such as when someone actually teaches us ("Here is how we celebrate Hannakah"), and indirectly, such as when we observe cultural practices from afar, particularly on the Internet or on television. In the United States, our family, friends, and the media are the primary teachers of our culture. Yet, we caution against accepting everything that we read or see. For instance, if you read a blog about a cultural community, keep in mind that one person does not necessarily "speak" for that community. We will address a related skill set that aims to improve your intercultural competency.

Let's look at an example of a learned ritual that varies depending on culture. Bradford Hall (2005) observes some differences in dating in New Zealand and the United States. In New Zealand, it is uncommon for someone to exclusively date another unless he or she has gone out with that person in a group of friends first. Even television shows in New Zealand suggest that romantic relationships begin in groups. Furthermore, exclusive dating in New Zealand occurs only after the couple makes long-term relationship plans. As Hall observes (and as most of you already know), in the United States, exclusive dating does not have to be preceded by group interactions, and many people in exclusive dating relationships in the United States haven't made long-term plans.

When you have acquired the knowledge, skills, attitudes, and values that allow you to become fully functioning in your culture, you are said to be enculturated. **Enculturation** occurs when a person learns to identify with a particular culture and a culture's thinking, way of relating, and worldview. Enculturation allows for successful participation in a particular society and makes a person more accepted by that society. Learning about a

society usually takes place within a family or close relationships. Ilsa becomes enculturated, for instance, when as a little girl she learns the rules about not using profanity, dressing "like a girl," and going to church each Sunday. Although she is young, she is slowly being enculturated into the United States, and this process will continue—both directly and indirectly—throughout her lifetime.

Whereas enculturation occurs when you are immersed in your own culture, **acculturation** exists when you learn, adapt to, and adopt the appropriate behaviors and rules of a host culture. Acculturated individuals have effectively absorbed themselves into another society. However, you don't have to sacrifice your personal set of principles simply because you've found yourself in another culture. For example, some immigrants to the United States may attend school in a large city such as Phoenix or Miami. These individuals may adapt to the city by using its services, understanding the laws of the city, or participating in social gatherings on campus. But, they may return to many of their cultural practices while in their homes, such as participating in spiritual healings or eating a family meal with multiple family generations present. To sum up, enculturation is first-culture learning, and acculturation is second-culture learning.

2-1b Culture Creates Community

Central to our definition of culture is the assumption that it helps to create a sense of community. We view **community** as the common understandings among people who are committed to coexisting. In the United States, communities are filled with a number of cultures within cultures, sometimes referred to as **co-cultures** (Orbe, 1998; Orbe & Roberts, 2012). For example, a Cuban American community, a Lebanese American community, and a community of people with disabilities are all co-cultures within one larger culture (the United States). Each community has unique communication behaviors and practices, but each also subscribes to behaviors and practices embraced by the larger U.S. culture. Membership in a co-culture provides individuals with opportunity and **social identity**—the part of one's self that is based upon membership in a particular group. Still, such membership may be problematic. For instance, some research (Buzzanell, 1999; Fernandez & Greenberg, 2013) continues to show that

enculturation The process that occurs when a person—either consciously or unconsciously—learns to identify with a particular culture and a culture's thinking, way of relating, and worldview.

acculturation The process that occurs when a person learns, adapts to, and adopts the appropriate behaviors and rules of a host culture.

community The common understandings among people who are committed to coexisting.

co-culture A culture within a culture.

social identity The part of one's self that is based on membership in a particular group.

The Chinese American co-culture has a long and vibrant history. In this photo, a dragon costume delights the crowd during a parade celebrating the Chinese New Year. With which co-cultures do you associate?

if you are a member of an unrepresented or marginalized co-culture, you are disadvantaged in job interviews because "interview protocols" are determined by dominant groups.

Many times, the two cultures mesh effortlessly; however, sometimes a **culture clash**, or a conflict over cultural expectations, occurs. For instance, consider what the reaction might be of a new immigrant from Mexico who is learning English as he tries to assimilate into a small group with three students who have lived in the United States their entire lives. Imagine the challenge of understanding slang ("dog and pony show," "jerry-rigged," etc.). Or, consider the reaction of a recently immigrated Islamic woman, who is accustomed to wearing a hijab (a headscarf or veil that covers the head and chest and is worn primarily by Muslim females). In France and other countries, there are now federal laws prohibiting the wearing of the hijab in public. Many Western people do not embrace such modesty in dress and therefore may ridicule or express fear of the head covering. Each of the preceding scenarios is opportunistic for culture clashes.

Finally, although a much less profound example than those above, a culture clash occurred several years back when the MTV show *Jersey Shore* filmed in Florence, Italy. The citizens of Florence were overwhelmingly outraged about characters such as Nicole "Snooki" Polizzi and Mike "The Situation" Sorrentino claiming to be Italian. The native Italians were not amused, and "No Grazie, Jersey Shore" signs began appearing all over the city.

Still, cultural conflicts are not necessarily bad; in fact, having the opportunity to view a situation from a different cultural point of view can be productive. Rebecca Evans (2013), a writer for *Construction News,* indicates that across the globe, culture clashes have resulted in increased productivity. She writes that when a new hospital was being built in Sweden, the contractor (who worked in both the United Kingdom and Sweden) integrated various managerial styles and viewed it less as a difficulty and more as a step in a positive direction. Michael Jonas (2007) observes that "culture clashes can produce a dynamic give-and-take, generating a solution that may have eluded a group of people with more similar backgrounds and approaches" (p. D2).

2-1c Culture Is Multileveled

On the national level of culture, we assume that people of the same national background share many things that bind them in a common culture: language, traditions, etc. Thus, we expect Germans to differ from the Hmong based on differing national cultures. However, as discussed in the previous section, cultures can be formed on other levels, such as generation, sexual identity, gender, race, and region, among others. For example, in many parts of the country, regionalisms exist. People who live in the middle of the United States (in states such as Kansas, Illinois, Iowa, Nebraska, Indiana, and Wisconsin) are often referred to as "Midwesterners." People who live in Vermont, New Hampshire, Maine, Massachusetts, Rhode Island, and Connecticut are called "New Englanders." Both Midwesterners and New Englanders have their own unique way of looking at things, but the two regions also share a reputation in common—namely, pragmatic thinking and an independent spirit.

A second example of the multileveled nature of a co-culture is a culture that develops around a certain age cohort. People who grew up in different time frames grew up in different cultural eras, as the labels we attach to various generations suggest—for example, Depression Babies of the 1930s or Flower Children of the 1960s. The

culture clash A conflict over cultural expectations and experiences.

J. Emilio Flores/Stringer/Getty Images News/Getty Images

culture of the Great Depression in the 1930s reflected the efforts of people trying to survive during troubling financial times. Thus, values of frugality and family unity dominated. In contrast, the 1960s was a prosperous era in which individualism and protest against the government flourished. As people age, they often find it difficult to abandon many of the values they learned during childhood. Now, consider the Millennials (born between the early 1980s and early 2000s) and the various values they represent and uphold. This group weathered the economic troubles during the 2010s, but many lost their jobs and had to rely on governmental support. Are their struggles to "survive" similar to the Depression Babies of the past?

Our discussion about culture thus far has focused on a general framework for understanding culture. We continue our cultural journey by addressing U.S. diversity and its value.

2-2 DIVERSITY IN THE UNITED STATES: A NATION OF NEWCOMERS

Intercultural contact is pervasive in the United States. This diversity affects family structure, corporations, religious institutions, schools, and the media. With more than 300 million citizens, our nation is a heterogeneous mix of various cultures. See Figure 2.1 for a look at how ancestral groups, and their root cultures, are distributed across the United States. The increase in diversity over the past several years is not without consequence. Rubin Martinez (2000) observes that our diversity can be challenging: "All across the country, people of different races, ethnicities, and nationalities, are being thrown

together and torn apart . . . it is a terrifying experience, this coming together, one for which we have of yet only the most awkward vocabulary" (pp. 11–12).

Native or indigenous peoples were the first to inhabit and reside in the United States. Since that time, scores of immigrants have ventured to this nation. Julio Guerrero (2013) notes that Latinos, most of whom are from Mexico, are the fastest-growing cultural group in the United States, growing considerably over the past decade in particular. The United States traditionally supports cultural newcomers. However, a backlash of sorts is increasing. For example, an "English only" movement has gained momentum across the country. Politicians and activists, feeling that the arrival of new cultural groups in the United States risks dividing the country along language and cultural lines, continue to try to make English the official language of the country. In 1996, the U.S. House of Representatives passed the English Language Empowerment Act, which would have made English the official language of the United States. It never became law, but the efforts continue and illustrate the extent to which others are willing to codify a nationalistic posturing (see www.us-english.org for a review of different themes, strategies, and events related to an "English-only" movement).

Over the past few decades, immigration has caused increased anxiety in the United States, prompting intercultural misunderstandings and relational challenges. The Migration Policy Institute (www.migrationpolicy.org), for instance, notes that since the terrorist attacks in 2001, there have been significant immigration developments, including increased deportation, fence building along the Mexico–United States border, denying driver's licenses to those given deportation relief, and a host of other activities and laws designed to "control the immigration problem." By some estimates, there are

FIGURE 2.1 DIVERSITY IN THE UNITED STATES

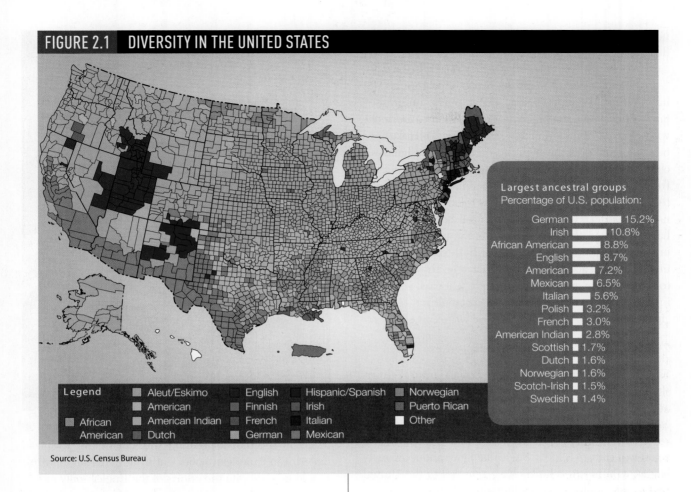

Largest ancestral groups
Percentage of U.S. population:

German	15.2%
Irish	10.8%
African American	8.8%
English	8.7%
American	7.2%
Mexican	6.5%
Italian	5.6%
Polish	3.2%
French	3.0%
American Indian	2.8%
Scottish	1.7%
Dutch	1.6%
Norwegian	1.6%
Scotch-Irish	1.5%
Swedish	1.4%

Legend
- African American
- Aleut/Eskimo
- American
- American Indian
- Dutch
- English
- Finnish
- French
- German
- Hispanic/Spanish
- Irish
- Italian
- Mexican
- Norwegian
- Puerto Rican
- Other

Source: U.S. Census Bureau

some 11 million undocumented living and working immigrants in the United States (Capps, Bachmeier, Fix, & Van Hook, 2013), so this topic will continue to resonate within families and across society for years to come.

Many decades ago, anthropologist Edward T. Hall (1959) noted that "culture is communication and communication is culture" (p. 169). In other words, we learn how, where, why, when, and to whom we communicate through cultural teachings. Conversely, when we communicate, we reproduce and reinforce our cultural practices. Hall's words still apply today. The United States is more diverse than ever, and almost everyone has been exposed to this growing diversity in some way. The nation's growing diversity has been hotly debated, with some cultural critics believing that the increase in diversity is "destroying society" (Haug, 2013), while others believe that understanding diversity allows for the "growth of an individual" (Hathaway, 2013). Regardless of the divergent opinions on this matter, cultural variability continues to be a critical part of our country's evolution.

With such diversity, learning how to communicate effectively with members of different cultures is a hallmark of a thoughtful and effective communicator. Let's explore this issue further by examining the importance of intercultural communication.

 ## 2-3 WHY STUDY INTERCULTURAL COMMUNICATION?

Intercultural communication scholars Judith Martin and Thomas Nakayama (2013) note several reasons to study intercultural communication. We identify six "imperatives," or critical reasons, based on Martin and Nakayama's work, and provide their application to interpersonal relationships. At the heart of this discussion is our belief that intercultural communication will continue to be important well beyond the class you are currently taking.

2-3a Technological Imperative

The extent to which technology has changed the United States cannot be overstated. Computers ushered in so much more than ways to communicate online. Personal computers prompted the Information Age which, even now, continues to move in unpredictable ways. Few will dispute the fact that the Internet remains the most significant influence on culture and interpersonal relationships.

Technological changes increase opportunities for intercultural communication and at times, unforeseen encounters. For example, consider Yolanda's experience with *eBay*, an online auction site. When Yolanda finds out that she holds the high bid on an antique handkerchief she wants to buy, she discovers that the seller is from a small town in Italy. Yolanda emails the seller and tells him that her grandmother has relatives in a town in northern Italy. He emails back to tell her that he, too, has relatives in that same town. As the two continue to email each other, they realize that both sets of relatives in Italy know each other! Later that year, they all Skype together—an event they decide to repeat each year. The implications of technology on our intercultural relationships continue to change even as we write this chapter.

2-3b Demographic Imperative

Earlier in this chapter, we noted that cultural diversity continues to shape and reshape the United States, and we provided information about the demographic changes in the United States. Yet many co-cultures within the country reject the notion that "blending" into a national culture is ideal. Since dialogues about diversity began, writers and scholars have referred to the United States as a "melting pot," a metaphor that evokes a unified national character formed as a result of immigration. In the past, immigrants frequently changed their names, clothes, language, and customs to "fit in."

In contrast, more contemporary metaphors for diversity in the United States include a symphony, mosaic, kaleidoscope, or salad, suggesting that diversity provides for unique textures and prisms. In these metaphors, different cultures retain their unique characteristics even while becoming a part of the U.S. culture. Think about a salad with all sorts of ingredients, including lettuce, tomatoes, croutons, cranberries, carrots, among others. Each has its own "taste," yet each contributes to the larger "taste" of the salad. Metaphors also suggest that the larger culture can accommodate and appreciate the contributions of co-cultures and co-cultural values. For example, in the United States, it's not uncommon for our food, dress, religion, and street signs to identify individual cultural groups. Intercultural signs abound. We eat at Korean restaurants, witness Saudi men wearing a thawb (an ankle-length

Photodisc/Getty Images

white shirt), and read greeting cards celebrating Kwanzaa (an African American holiday affirming African culture). In addition, despite the efforts of the English-only movement we mentioned earlier, signs and labels in some parts of the country are written in two languages—for example, Spanish and English in the Southwest, and French and English in northern New England.

As a country, the United States will always be populated with individuals whose backgrounds are multicultural. Popular figures such as Tiger Woods, Alicia Keys, Vince Vaughn, Keanu Reeves, Nicki Minaj, and Dwayne "The Rock" Johnson all have a rich multicultural ancestry. Such unique cultural configuration will continue since the U.S. Census shows that the number of mixed race households grew more than 30 percent from 2000 to 2010 (U.S. Census Bureau, 2012). We need to keep in mind the demographic shifts now occurring at unprecedented rates.

2-3c Economic Imperative

Today, only a handful of places on Earth are completely out of touch with the rest of the world. This phenomenon is referred to as the **global village**, which means that all societies— regardless of size—are connected in some way (McLuhan, 1964). No country is economically isolated any longer. For instance, with the exception of Canada and the United Kingdom, in 2013, eight of the top

global village The concept that all societies, regardless of size, are connected in some way. The term also can be used to describe how communication technology ties the world into one political, economic, social, and cultural system.

10 U.S. economic exports go to countries where English is not the dominant language (IndexMundi, 2012). Therefore, the United States depends on other countries for its economic sustainability. Today, because of the availability of cheap labor, U.S. firms continue to send work and workers overseas, a practice called **outsourcing**. People in business and industry, education, media, and politics communicate with others of different cultures, if for no other reason than that it is cost-efficient to do so. All of these exchanges of human resources represent one piece of the process known as globalization.

Workers from other countries who come to the United States often receive no training in intercultural similarities and differences (Palmer, 2002). The result can be problematic: "[International workers] can't be expected to learn our [United States] customs through osmosis" (p. 13A). We would add that citizens of the United States can't be expected to learn about others through osmosis, either.

2-3d Peace Imperative

The Lakota Indians have a saying: "With all beings and all things we shall be as relatives." Yet, as Martin and Nakayama (2013) ask, is it really possible for cultures to work together and get along on one planet? Our current state of world affairs makes it difficult to answer this question. On one hand, the Berlin Wall has been torn down; on the other hand, other types of walls have been put up. For instance, centuries of violence in the Middle East and Africa, coupled with tensions between China and Taiwan, make this a challenging time for cultural understanding. We're not suggesting that if cultures understood each other, cultural warfare would end. Rather, we believe that learning about other cultures aids in understanding conflicting points of view, perhaps resulting in a more peaceful world. Looking at an issue from another's perspective, as we will learn in Chapter 3, is critical to interpersonal relationships and communication.

2-3e Self-Awareness Imperative

As we will discuss in Chapter 3, each of us has a **worldview**, which is a unique way of seeing the world through our own lens of understanding. Worldviews can help you understand your "place and space" (e.g., privilege, level of comfort talking with others, etc.) in society. Although these perspectives are often instinctive, they are directly derived from our cultural identity. When we have a clear understanding of who we are and what forces brought us to our current state, we can begin to understand others' worldviews. For example, remember what it was like when you first discovered your sexual identity. Some of you may have experienced a physical attraction to a member of the opposite sex, while others may have been attracted to a person of the same sex. A same-sex attraction likely affects you differently if you adhere to a religion that considers same-sex attraction immoral than if you come from a spiritual background that accepts GLBT (gay men, lesbians, bisexuals, and transgendered) individuals. Becoming personally aware of your own worldview and the worldviews of others will inevitably help you manage the cultural variation in your relationships and allow you to reflect on your own cultural assumptions.

2-3f Ethical Imperative

Recall from Chapter 1 that ethics pertains to what is perceived as right and wrong. Culturally speaking, ethics can vary tremendously (Buber, 1970). That is, different fields of cultural experience dictate different opinions of what constitutes ethical behavior. For example, let's consider behavior associated with the family that may be viewed differently in the United States versus in China. Historically, in China, boys were valued more than girls; and until 2013, parents were required by Chinese policy to have only one child (Mashru, 2012). As a result, when a mother gives birth to a girl in China, the child may have been abandoned or given up for adoption to allow the parents to try again to have a boy. As noted, however, Chinese officials have "loosened" this policy because of an "elderly boom," whereby seniors cannot work and need support from younger generations. That responsibility generally falls to the female and thus, the policy has been revisited. Still, a multiple-child household is only possible if one of the parents is a single child (Yang, 2013).

You may agree or disagree with this practice based upon your ethical perspective(s). Regardless of our personal opinions, each of us has an ethical obligation to ensure that cultural behaviors are depicted in the context of cultural values. We also have an ethical obligation to ensure that we fully understand cultural practices before deciding whether to impose our own cultural will on others.

We summarize the six imperatives in Table 2.1. Each imperative is accompanied by examples of how that imperative applies to the study of intercultural communication.

---

outsourcing A practice in which a nation sends work and workers to a different country because doing so is cost-efficient.

worldview A unique way of seeing the world through one's own lens of understanding, directly derived from our cultural identity.

TABLE 2.1 REASONS FOR STUDYING INTERCULTURAL COMMUNICATION

Imperative Type	Example
Technological imperative	*Email* is facilitating communication between and among cultures. The Internet facilitates cross-cultural understanding of societies around the world.
Demographic imperative	The *influx of immigrants* from Mexico, Russia, and Vietnam has changed the workforce in the United States.
Economic imperative	The *global market* has prompted overseas expansion of U.S. companies. Business transactions and negotiation practices require intercultural understanding.
Peace imperative	*Resolution of world conflicts*, such as those in the Middle East, requires cultural understanding.
Self-awareness imperative	*Self-reflection* of cultural biases aids in cultural sensitivity. Understanding personal *worldviews* promotes cultural awareness.
Ethical imperative	*Cultural values* are frequently difficult to understand and accept. We have an ethical obligation to appreciate the cultural variations in dating, marriage, and intimacy.

© Cengage Learning®

2-4 DIMENSIONS OF CULTURE

Dutch management scholar Geert Hofstede (1980, 1984, 1991, 2001, 2003) examined work attitudes across 40 cultures. His work showed that four dimensions of cultural values were held by more than 100,000 corporate managers and employees in multinational corporations: uncertainty avoidance, distribution of power, masculinity-femininity, and individualism-collectivism. These four areas comprise **cultural variability theory**, and we address each below.

2-4a Uncertainty Avoidance

It seems as though regardless of geographic location, people have a desire to reduce their uncertainty (Berger, 1988; Craig, 2013). The notion of **uncertainty avoidance** can be tricky to understand. Overall, the concept refers to how tolerant (or intolerant) you are of uncertainty. Those cultures that resist change and have high levels of anxiety associated with change are said to have a high degree of uncertainty avoidance. Because cultures with a *high* degree of uncertainty

cultural variability theory A theory that describes the four value dimensions (uncertainty avoidance, distribution of power, masculinity-femininity, individualism-collectivism) that offer information regarding the value differences in a particular culture.

uncertainty avoidance A cultural mind-set that indicates how tolerant (or intolerant) a culture is of uncertainty and change.

power distance How a culture perceives and distributes power.

avoidance desire predictability, they need specific laws to guide behavior and personal conduct. The cultures of Greece, Chile, Portugal, Japan, and France are among those that tolerate little uncertainty. Risky decisions are discouraged in these cultures because they increase uncertainty.

Those cultures that are unthreatened by change have a *low* degree of uncertainty avoidance. The cultures of the United States, Sweden, Britain, Denmark, and Ireland tend to accept uncertainty. They are comfortable taking risks and are less aggressive and less emotional than cultures with a high degree of uncertainty avoidance.

Intercultural communication problems can surface when a person raised in a culture that tolerates ambiguity encounters another who has little tolerance. For instance, if a student from a culture with high uncertainty avoidance is invited to a party in the United States, he or she will probably ask many questions about how to dress, what to bring, exactly what time to arrive, and so forth. These questions might perplex a U.S. host, who would typically have a high tolerance for uncertainty, including a laid-back attitude toward the party—"Just get here whenever." Recall that cultures with high uncertainty avoidance prefer to have rules and clear protocol more than cultures with low uncertainty avoidance.

2-4b Distribution of Power

How a culture deals with power is called **power distance**. Citizens of nations that are *high* in power distance (e.g., the Philippines, Mexico, India, Singapore, and Brazil) tend to show respect to people with higher status. They revere authoritarianism, and the difference between the powerful and the powerless is clear. Differences in age, sex, and income are exaggerated in these cultures, and people accept these differences.

India is an example of a culture that is high in power distance, exemplified by the caste system of the Hindu people. The caste system is a social classification that organizes people into four castes or categories: *brahmins* (priests), *kashtryas* (administrators/rulers), *vaisyas* (businesspeople or farmers), and *sudras* (laborers) (Kumar, 2013). Each caste has various duties and rights. This caste hierarchy inhibits communication among caste groups. In fact, only one group (the priests, who historically have been afforded full respect) has the prerogative to communicate with all other social groups.

The cultures that are *low* in power distance include the United States, Austria, Israel, Denmark, and Ireland. People in these cultures believe that power should be equally distributed regardless of a person's age, sex, or status. Cultures with low degrees of power distance minimize differences among the classes and accept challenges to power in interpersonal relationships. Although included on the list of cultures low in power distance, the United States is becoming higher in power distance because of the growing disparity between rich and poor (Jandt, 2013).

Intercultural encounters between people from high and low power distance cultures can be challenging. For instance, a supervisor from a high power distance culture may have difficulty communicating with employees who come from lower power distance cultures. Although the supervisor may be expecting complete respect and follow-through on directives, the employees may be questioning the legitimacy of such directives.

2-4c Masculinity-Femininity

Hofstede (2001) identifies *masculinity-femininity* as the extent to which cultures represent masculine and feminine traits in their society. For our purposes, masculinity

is not the same as "male," and femininity is not the same as "female," although the use of these terms still reinforces stereotypical notions of how men and women should behave. **Masculine cultures** focus on achievement, competitiveness, strength, and material success—that is, characteristics stereotypically associated with masculine people. Money is important in masculine cultures. Masculine cultures are also those in which the division of labor is based on sex. **Feminine cultures** emphasize sexual equality, nurturance, quality of life, supportiveness, and affection—that is, characteristics stereotypically associated with feminine people. Compassion for the less fortunate also characterizes feminine cultures.

Hofstede's research showed that countries such as Mexico, Italy, Venezuela, Japan, and Austria are masculine-centered cultures, where the division of labor is based on sex. Countries such as Thailand, Norway, the Netherlands, Denmark, and Finland are feminine-centered cultures, where a promotion of sexual equality exists. The United States falls closer to masculinity.

What happens when a person from a culture that honors such masculine traits as power and competition intersects with a person from a culture that honors such feminine traits as interdependence and quality of life? For example, suppose that a woman is asked to lead a group of men. In Scandinavian countries, such as Denmark and Finland, such a task would not be problematic. Many political leaders in these countries are feminine (and female), and gender roles are more flexible. Yet, in a masculine culture, a female leader might be viewed with skepticism, and her leadership might be challenged.

2-4d Individualism-Collectivism

When a culture values **individualism**, it prefers competition over cooperation, the individual over the group, and the private over the public. Individualistic cultures have an "I" communication orientation, emphasizing self-concept, autonomy, and personal achievement. Individualistic cultures—including the United States, Canada,

Ben Bloom/Stone/Getty Images

masculine culture A culture that emphasizes characteristics stereotypically associated with masculine people, such as achievement, competitiveness, strength, and material success.

feminine culture A culture that emphasizes characteristics stereotypically associated with feminine people, such as sexual equality, nurturance, quality of life, supportiveness, affection, and a compassion for the less fortunate.

individualism A cultural mind-set that emphasizes self-concept and personal achievement and that prefers competition over cooperation, the individual over the group, and the private over the public.

Cultural Variability Theory

One intriguing and complex component of cultural variability theory is the masculine/feminine dimension. Essentially, this portion of the theory advances that generally, males are masculine and females are feminine. Still, we all know that feminine males and masculine females are also part of many global societies. Comment on the potential problems and opportunities of using terms like *masculine* and *feminine* to describe men and women around the globe.

Britain, Australia, and Italy—tend to reject authoritarianism (think, for instance, how many rallies have occurred in the United States denouncing U.S. presidents and their policies) and typically support the belief that people should "pull themselves up by their own bootstraps."

collectivism A cultural mind-set that emphasizes the group and its norms, values, and beliefs over the self.

context orientation theory The theory that meaning is derived from either the setting of the message or the words of a message and that cultures can vary in the extent to which message meaning is made explicit or implicit.

Collectivism suggests that the self is secondary to the group and its norms, values, and beliefs. Group orientation takes priority over self-orientation. Collectivistic cultures tend to value duty, tradition, and hierarchy. A "we" communication orientation prevails. Collectivistic cultures such as Colombia, Peru, Pakistan, Chile, and Singapore lean toward working together in groups to achieve goals. Families are particularly important, and people have higher expectations of loyalty to family, including taking care of extended family members.

Interestingly, the collectivistic and individualistic intersect at times. For instance, in the Puerto Rican community, a collectivistic sense of family coexists with the individualistic need for community members to become personally successful. Hector Carrasquillo (1997) observed that "a Puerto Rican is only fully a person insofar as he or she is a member of a family" (p. 159). Still, Carrasquillo points out that younger Puerto Ricans have adopted more independence and have accepted and adapted to the individualistic ways of the U.S. culture. We see, therefore, that even within one culture, the individualism-collectivism dimension is not static.

Look at the summary of Hofstede's four dimensions of culture provided in Table 2.2. As we did in the previous sections, we provide representative cultures as identified by Hofstede. Keep in mind that because his results are based on averages, you will most likely be able to think of individuals you know who are exceptions to the categorization of nations.

One additional cultural dimension merits consideration: context. Recall from Chapter 1 that context is the surrounding in which communication takes place. Intercultural communication theorists find that people of different cultures use context to varying degrees to determine the meaning of a message. Scholars have referred to this as **context orientation theory** (Hall & Hall, 1990). Context orientation theory answers the

TABLE 2.2	HOFSTEDE'S CULTURAL DIMENSIONS

Dimension	Description
Uncertainty avoidance	Cultures high in uncertainty avoidance desire predictability (e.g., Greece, Japan). Cultures low in uncertainty avoidance are unthreatened by change (e.g., United States, Great Britain).
Distribution of power	Cultures high in power distance show respect for status (e.g., Mexico, India). Cultures low in power distance believe that power should be equally distributed (e.g., United States, Israel).
Masculinity-femininity	Masculine cultures value competitiveness, material success, and assertiveness (e.g., Italy, Austria). Feminine cultures value quality of life, affection, and caring for the less fortunate (e.g., Sweden, Denmark).
Individualism-collectivism	Individualistic cultures value individual accomplishments (e.g., Australia, United States). Collectivistic cultures value group collaboration (e.g., Chile, Columbia).

© Cengage Learning®

following question: Is meaning derived from cues outside of the message or from the words in the message?

The cultures of the world differ in the extent to which they rely on context. Researchers have divided context into two areas: high context and low context (Victor, 1992). In **high-context cultures**, the meaning of a message is primarily drawn from the surroundings. People in such cultures do not need to say much when communicating because there is a high degree of similarity among members of such cultures. That is, people typically read nonverbal cues with a high degree of accuracy because they share the same structure of meaning. Native American, Indian, Japanese, Chinese, and Korean cultures are all high-context cultures. On a more fundamental level, high-context communities are less formal, and the relational harmony is valued and maintained as decisions are made.

In **low-context cultures**, communicators find meaning primarily in the words in messages, not the surroundings. In such cultures, meanings are communicated explicitly; very little of the conversation is left open to interpretation. As a result, nonverbal communication is not easily comprehended. Self-expression, then, becomes a relational value. Examples of low-context cultures include Germany, Switzerland, United States, Canada, and France.

Think about how cultural differences in context might affect interaction during conflict episodes, job interviews, or dating. If one person relies mainly on the spoken word and the other communicates largely through nonverbal messages, what might be the result? Or, if one person's communication is direct and expressive, what are the consequences and implications if the other communicator employs silence and indirect forms of communication?

So far in this chapter we have discussed why you need to understand intercultural communication. We're confident that you are beginning to appreciate the cultural diversity in your lives and that you are prepared to work on improving your intercultural communication skills. A critical step toward understanding your culture and the cultures of others is to understand the problems inherent in intercultural communication, a subject we outline below.

2-5 CHALLENGES OF INTERCULTURAL COMMUNICATION

Although intercultural communication is important and pervasive, becoming an effective intercultural communicator is easier said than done. In this section, we explain five obstacles to intercultural understanding: ethnocentrism, stereotyping, anxiety and uncertainty, misinterpretation of nonverbal and verbal behaviors, and the assumption of similarity or difference.

2-5a Ethnocentrism

Ethnocentrism is the process of judging another culture using the standards of your own culture. Ethnocentrism is derived from two Greek words, *ethnos*, or "nation," and *kentron*, or "center." When combined, the meaning becomes clear: nation at the center. Ethnocentrism is a belief in the superiority of your own culture. The term's application to populations and communities has its roots tracing back to the 1800s (Bizumic, 2014). Myron Lustig and Jolene Koester (1999b) claim that cultures "train their members to use the categories of their own cultural experiences when judging the experiences of people from other cultures" (p. 146). Normally, ethnocentric tendencies exaggerate differences and usually prevent intercultural understanding.

At first glance, being ethnocentric may appear harmless. Few people even realize the extent to which they prioritize their culture over another. For instance, you will note that throughout this book, we work to avoid the use of the single term, *American*. Like many researchers and practitioners, we believe that *American* can refer to people in North America, Central America, and South America. To suggest that the word pertains only to those in the United States is ethnocentric (and inaccurate).

We tend to notice when people from other cultures prioritize their cultural customs. For example, although many people in the United States value open communication, not all cultures do. Many Asian cultures (e.g., China and Japan) revere silence. The Chinese philosopher Confucius said, "Silence is a friend who will never betray." Now, consider what happens in conversations when the Western and Eastern worlds meet. Let's say that Ed, a young business executive from the United States, travels to China to talk to Yao, another executive, regarding a business deal. Ed is taken aback when, after he makes the offer, Yao remains silent for a

---

high-context culture A culture in which there is a high degree of similarity among members and in which the meaning of a message is drawn primarily from its context, such as one's surroundings, rather than from words.

low-context culture A culture in which there is a high degree of difference among members and in which the meaning of a message must be explicitly related, usually in words.

ethnocentrism The process of judging another culture using the standards of one's own culture.

few minutes. Ed repeats the specifics of the offer, and Yao acknowledges his understanding. This standstill in their discussion leads Ed to believe that Yao is going to reject the offer. However, if Ed had studied Chinese culture sufficiently before his trip, he would know that to the Chinese, silence generally means agreement. One speaks only if he or she has something of value to add. Ed's cultural ignorance may cost the company both money and respect. And the inability to look beyond his own Western view of silence represents ethnocentrism.

2-5b Stereotyping

Consider the following statements:

▶ Old people are crabby and complain a lot.

▶ Italians love to use their hands while speaking.

▶ Teenagers have no interest in politics.

▶ Boys don't cry.

These statements are **stereotypes**—the "pictures in our heads" (Lippman, 1922, p. 3), or the fixed mental images of a particular group and communicating with an individual as if he or she is a member of that group. We have all stereotyped at one point or another in our lives. Stereotypes are everywhere in U.S. society, including politics ("All politicians are crooked"), medicine ("Doctors know best"), entertainment ("Hollywood celebrities use Botox"), journalism ("The media are so liberal"), and sports ("They're just dumb jocks"). Such statements generalize the perceived characteristics of some members of a group to the group as a whole.

© Minerva Studio/Shutterstock.com

stereotypes Fixed mental images of a particular group; communicating with an individual as if he or she is a member of that group.

in-group A group to which a person feels he or she belongs.

out-group A group to which a person feels he or she does not belong.

You may not have thought about this before, but stereotypes can be good or bad. Think about the positive stereotypes of firefighters, police officers, emergency personnel, and other rescue workers after the terrorist attacks on the United States on September 11, 2001. Words like *heroic, compassionate, daring,* and *fearless* have all been attributed to these groups of individuals, regardless of the cultural identification of the members of these groups. However, right after the attacks, many Arabs living in the United States were accused of being terrorists simply because of their Middle Eastern identity, and people used hurtful and hateful speech while interacting with Arab Americans. The point is that we must be willing to look beyond the generalizations about a particular group and communicate with people as individuals (we talk further about stereotyping in Chapter 3).

2-5c Anxiety and Uncertainty

You may feel anxiety and uncertainty when you are introduced to people who speak, look, and act differently from you. Most societies have few guidelines to help people through some of the early awkward intercultural moments. People commonly question what words or phrases to use while discussing various cultural groups. Most of us want to be culturally aware and use language that doesn't offend, yet we frequently don't know what words might be offensive to members of cultures other than our own. For example, you might wonder whether you should refer to someone as American Indian or Native American or another as African American or black. These cultural references can be problematic, even in the communities that are affected by the terminology.

Our family and friends remain influential on our perceptions. In particular, their observations and reactions to cultural differences are often passed on to us. And they can prompt us to either feel that we are members of what social scientists call an in-group or an out-group. **In-groups** are groups to which a person feels he or she belongs, and **out-groups** are those groups to which a person feels he or she does not belong.

Perceptions of belonging are directly proportional to the level of connection an individual feels toward a group. Let's say that Lianna and Nate, a devoutly Christian married couple, meet Nate's best friend, Rose. Although Rose is Jewish, she feels that she has in-group affiliation with the couple and communicates with them comfortably. Now suppose that Lianna and Nate meet Rose's mom, Sandra, an atheist who believes that the couple spends too much time talking about "being saved." Sandra will likely view Lianna and Nate as an out-group member because she does not feel a sense of belonging with the husband and wife. Being a member of either an in-group or an out-group can influence our degree of comfort in intercultural communication.

2-5d Misinterpretation of Nonverbal and Verbal Behaviors

Speakers expect to receive nonverbal cues that are familiar. However, nonverbal behaviors differ dramatically across and within cultures. An Asian proverb states that "those who know, do not speak; those who speak, do not know." If Paola is a person who believes that communication must be constant to be effective, she may struggle with interpersonal exchanges with the Western Apache or the Asian Indian who value silence. However, as is true of other facets of culture, nonverbal communication varies within cultures as well as between cultures. For instance, although Italians might gesture more than people from the United States in general, not all Italians use expansive gestures. We could certainly find someone from Italy who gestures less than someone we pick from the United States. We return to the topic of culture and nonverbal communication in Chapter 5.

In addition to nonverbal differences, verbal communication differences exist between and among cultures and co-cultures. For example, generational diversity can exist with word usage. Words such as *smooching* and *necking* once referred to an act most people today refer to as *kissing*. Yet, today's generations are using the phrase "make out" to cover a wide array of emotional and physical activities (we cover the use of language extensively in Chapter 4). We must understand nonverbal and verbal differences between (co)-cultures if we are to achieve meaning in our intercultural relationships.

2-5e The Assumption of Similarity or Difference

This assumption suggests that intercultural communication is possible because it simply requires homing in on people's inherent similarities. At the other end of the continuum is the belief that people from different cultures are vastly different from one another, and therefore communication between them is difficult if not impossible. Assuming similarity fails to appreciate difference, and assuming difference fails to appreciate cultural commonalities.

In the United States, we need to be careful when we place a premium on what some may call the "American way." We are ethnocentric if we believe that other cultures should do things the way that we do things here or if we hold cultures in higher esteem if they imitate or practice cultural customs. In many cases, people who are unfamiliar with U.S. traditions often question these

OKAY   NOT OKAY   BETTER CHECK FIRST

practices. For instance, in a 2013 survey on Reddit, a social news and entertainment website, a question was posed to those outside the United States: "What aspect of [U.S.] culture strikes you as the strangest?" The responses were far-ranging and included the following:

▶ "Being able to buy anything you want at Wal-Mart—you [can] buy 24 rolls of toilet paper and a 12 gauge shotgun in the same store."

▶ "Having a weird version of Puritanism—It's pretty infuriating to live somewhere where something as natural and beautiful as the human body is viewed as taboo and 'corrupts' our youth, but a guy getting his head cut off or getting beaten to death is perfectly okay for kids to watch."

▶ "Cheerleaders—dressing up young girls in short skirts and getting them to dance around and cheer on young men strikes me as odd."

▶ "Being obsessed with being the best country in the world." (Wile & Weisenthal, 2013)

Clearly, some of these posts have more significant cultural resonance than others (e.g., the obsession with being the best). Still, each reflects the fact that simply because something is practiced or revered in the United States does not mean that it is similarly practiced or revered in other cultures. Assuming similarity across cultures, then, is problematic.

We have given you a number of issues to consider in this chapter so far. First, we defined culture and co-culture and discussed the dimensions of culture. We then proceeded to outline several reasons for studying intercultural communication. Next, we addressed some of the most common challenges to intercultural communication. We now offer you some suggestions for improving your intercultural effectiveness in relationships.

2-6 SKILL SET FOR INTERCULTURAL UNDERSTANDING

In this section, we present several ways to improve your communication with people from different cultures. Because most cultures and co-cultures have unique ways of communicating, our suggestions are necessarily broad. As we have emphasized in this chapter, communicating with friends, classmates, coworkers, and others from different cultural backgrounds is both exciting and challenging. In the end, knowing your intercultural sensitivity (Chen & Starosta, 2000) is a good first step.

© alexmillos/Shutterstock.com

2-6a Know Your Biases and Stereotypes

Despite our best efforts, we enter conversations with biases and stereotypes. How do we know we have biases and stereotypes? Listening carefully to others' responses to our ideas, words, and phrases is an excellent first step. Have you ever told a story about a cultural group that resulted in a friend saying, "I can't believe you just said that!" That friend may be pointing out that you should rethink some culturally offensive language or risk facing challenges from others during conversations.

We need to avoid imposing our predispositions and prejudices on others. Perceptions of different cultural groups are frequently outdated or otherwise inaccurate and require a constant personal assessment. Facing your biases and even your fears or anxieties is an essential first step toward intercultural effectiveness.

Recall that ethnocentrism is seeing the world through your own culture's lens. We may like to think that our particular culture is best, but as you have seen through our many examples, no culture can nor should claim preeminence. We first need to admit that to an extent, we all are biased and ethnocentric. Next, we need to honestly assess how we react to other cultures. As we mentioned

Intercultural Sensitivity Scale

Below is a series of statements concerning intercultural communication. There are no right or wrong answers. Please work quickly and record your first impression by indicating the degree to which you agree or disagree with the statement.

> 5 = strongly agree; 4 = agree; 3 = uncertain;
> 2 = disagree; 1 = strongly disagree

Please put the number corresponding to your answer in the blank before the statement.

_____ 1. I enjoy interacting with people from different cultures.

_____ 2. I think people from other cultures are narrow-minded.

_____ 3. I am pretty sure of myself in interacting with people from different cultures.

_____ 4. I find it very hard to talk in front of people from different cultures.

_____ 5. I always know what to say when interacting with people from different cultures.

_____ 6. I can be as sociable as I want to be when interacting with people from different cultures.

_____ 7. I don't like to be with people from different cultures.

_____ 8. I respect the values of people from different cultures.

_____ 9. I get upset easily when interacting with people from different cultures.

_____ 10. I feel confident when interacting with people from different cultures.

_____ 11. I tend to wait before forming an impression of culturally distinct counterparts.

_____ 12. I often get discouraged when I am with people from different cultures.

_____ 13. I am open-minded to people from different cultures.

_____ 14. I am very observant when interacting with people from different cultures.

_____ 15. I often feel useless when interacting with people from different cultures.

_____ 16. I respect the ways people from different cultures behave.

_____ 17. I try to obtain as much information as I can when interacting with people from different cultures.

_____ 18. I would not accept the opinions of people from different cultures.

_____ 19. I am sensitive to my culturally distinct counterpart's subtle meanings during our interaction.

_____ 20. I think my culture is better than other cultures.

_____ 21. I often give positive responses to my culturally different counterpart during our interaction.

_____ 22. I avoid those situations where I will have to deal with culturally distinct persons.

_____ 23. I often show my culturally distinct counterpart my understanding through verbal or nonverbal cues.

_____ 24. I have a feeling of enjoyment toward differences between my culturally distinct counterpart and me.

Interaction Engagement items are 1, 11, 13, 21, 22, 23, and 24. Respect for Cultural Differences items are 2, 7, 8, 16, 18, and 20. Interaction Confidence items are 3, 4, 5, 6, and 10. Interaction Enjoyment items are 9, 12, and 15, and Interaction Attentiveness items are 14, 17, and 19.

---

previously, you can listen to others for their reactions. Looking inward is also helpful; ask yourself the following questions:

▶ What have I done to prepare myself for intercultural conversations?

▶ Do I use language that is biased or potentially offensive to people from different cultures?

▶ What is my reaction to people who use offensive words or phrases while describing cultural groups—am I silent? If so, do I consider my silence problematic?

▶ How have my perceptions and biases been shaped? By the media? By school? By talking to others?

These are among the questions you should consider as you begin to know yourself, your perceptions, and how you may act on those perceptions. We all need to understand our outdated and misguided views of others that have falsely shaped our impressions of other cultures. Recognizing that your family, friends, coworkers, school, and the media influence your prejudices is critical. Getting rid of the unwanted or misguided biases is essential if we are to begin to forge intercultural relationships with others.

2-6b Tolerate the Unknown

Earlier in the chapter, we noted that some cultures tolerate uncertainty more easily than others. Although we noted that the United States is one such culture, tolerating things of which you are unaware does not always come naturally. We may wish to *think* we are tolerant, but the truth is that differences can bother us at times.

You may be unfamiliar with various cultural practices of coworkers, craftspeople you hire for home repair, and others whose backgrounds and fields of experience differ from yours. For instance, consider the Romanian who is accustomed to greeting people by kissing the sides of both cheeks. Think about the colleague who greets you in another language other than your own. Or, perhaps as an able-bodied person you are unable to identify with someone

problems, raise children, and manage interpersonal relationships. **Cultural imperialism** is a process whereby individuals, companies, and/or the media impose their way of thinking and behaving upon another culture. With cultural imperialism, a belittling of another culture occurs. We can avoid this practice by using cultural respect. This requires us to show that we accept another culture's way of thinking and relating, even though we may disagree with or disapprove of it. Different societies have different moral codes, and judging a culture using only one moral yardstick can be considered both arrogant and self-serving.

When you practice cultural respect, you empathize with another culture. **Cultural empathy** refers to the learned ability to accurately understand the experiences of people from diverse cultures and to convey that understanding responsively (Ting-Toomey & Chung, 2005). When you are empathic, you are on your way to appreciating the life experiences of another person or social group. In other words, try to reach beyond the words to the feelings that the communicator is trying to show. You become other-oriented and engage in the sort of civil communication we referred to in Chapter 1.

Developing cultural respect involves trying to look at a culture from the inside. What is it like to be a member of another culture? Avoid reading verbal and nonverbal communication solely from your own cultural point of view (Chapter 5 has more to say about nonverbal communication and culture). Refrain from becoming easily frustrated or insulted if another person is not using your language or is having a hard time communicating.

2-6d Educate Yourself

Aside from taking this course in interpersonal communication, you can take advantage of numerous opportunities to educate yourself about other cultures. First, read. That's right: Read all that is available to you about other cultures. Browse magazines and books that are dedicated to culture, intercultural communication, and intercultural relationships. And, canvas the web. Many websites allow you to travel virtually across cultures. Some links provide you information about cultures all over the world and in particular, some discuss business practices and protocols of dozens of global communities (see, e.g., www.educationworld.com and www.worldbiz.com). If you're interested in, say, religion or spirituality or the various tribal nations, many online resources are valuable (e.g., www.adherents.com, www.Nativeculturallinks.com). These are just a few of the active websites that students have chosen as important intercultural opportunities. This information will provide you a backdrop for future reference and will allow you to discover more about your own culture as well.

who relies on a wheelchair for mobility. Some cultural behaviors are simply different from yours and it may take time to understand the differences. Be patient with yourself and with others. If you encounter a cultural unknown, think about asking questions For some of us, being tolerant is not a challenge at all; others of us need to work at it. Regardless of competency level, being unaware or uncomfortable in an intercultural encounter will likely prevent you from experiencing a satisfying intercultural relationship.

2-6c Practice Cultural Respect

Various traditions, customs, and practices allow cultures and co-cultures to function effectively. Skilled intercultural communicators respect those cultural conventions. No one culture knows "the right way" to solve work

cultural imperialism The process whereby individuals, companies, and/or the media impose their way of thinking and behaving upon another culture.

cultural empathy The learned ability to accurately understand the experiences of people from diverse cultures and to convey that understanding responsively.

Second, educating yourself requires that you learn about cultures through others. Participate in community lectures and discussions about cultural groups. Talk to people who represent another race, religion, nationality, or other cultural group. Be interested in their experiences, but avoid patronizing them. Don't accept everything written about culture and communication as truth. Be rigorous and critical in your reading and tentative in your acceptance. Be willing to seek out information that is based on both research and personal experience.

2-6e Be Prepared for Consequences

Although we may make a serious effort to be thoughtful and considerate, having a conversation with an individual from a different (co)-culture can be challenging. So many issues operate simultaneously in a conversation—verbal and nonverbal differences, nervousness, cultural customs, rules, symbols, and norms. We may try to attend to all of these aspects of our conversation, but things still may go awry. There is no way to completely control all the things that can go astray in our cultural dialogues and cultural stumbling may happen. What we can work toward, however, is preempting potential problems.

© iQoncept/Shutterstock.com

2-6f Relate to the Individual, Not the Culture

Although we know that we have drawn on some generalizations to make some of the points in this chapter, we remain concerned about painting broad cultural strokes to define individuals. Identifying with the person and not the cultural group is paramount in intercultural communication.

Accepting individual cultural uniqueness is important. First, as we learned earlier, there are variations within cultures and co-cultures. For instance, not all Christians have the same beliefs about abortion rights, nor do all elderly people sit around playing Words with Friends. Second, people's communication behaviors and skills can vary tremendously within cultures. Some people use a lot of personal space in conversations, whereas others use little. Some people are direct and forthright in their dialogues, but others are more reserved and timid. Some individuals may be reluctant to share personal tragedies; however, others may have no qualms with such disclosure. Constantly reminding yourself that not all members of a certain cultural group think alike, act alike, and talk alike allows you to focus on the person instead of the group to which he or she belongs.

STUDY TOOLS

DON'T FORGET TO CHECK OUT COURSEMATE AT WWW.CENGAGEBRAIN.COM!

CHAPTER 2 FEATURES THE FOLLOWING RESOURCES:

☐ Ethics & Choice: Roommates

☐ Communication Assessment Test: Intercultural Sensitivity Scale

☐ Interactive Activities

3 | Communication, Perception, and the Self

LEARNING OUTCOMES

3-1 Identify the components in the perception process

3-2 Explain the influences on the perception process

3-3 Discuss the dimensions of self-concept

3-4 Identify the relationship between identity management and facework

3-5 Delineate two online identity markers

3-6 Select skills for perception checking

After you finish this chapter, go to **PAGE 67** for **STUDY TOOLS.**

THEORY/MODEL PREVIEW

Symbolic Interactionism Theory; Interaction Management Theory; Implicit Personality Theory; Attribution Theory; Social Information Processing Theory

©iStock.com/Media

Look around you right now—at your apartment, office, or dorm room. Are people milling around? Is music playing?

Is the television on? Is your computer turned on and logged on to a particular website? Is your cell phone ringing? What are you wearing? Do you hear noises outside? Are you sick or healthy?

Now think about how you felt the last time you had a heated argument with another person. What did you find particularly aggravating about the argument? How did you feel about yourself as you engaged in the conflict? What reactions did you receive from the person you were arguing with during the exchange? Did anyone "win" the argument? If so, how did that happen? How do you think you will handle the next conflict with this person?

You answered these 14 questions based on two important topics in interpersonal communication: perception and the self. As you stopped to consider what was around you, you perceived your immediate surroundings. Some things you may have noticed before we prompted you to do so. However, you may not have thought about other things until we mentioned them. In both cases, you were engaged in the perception process.

As you thought about the last argument you had, we hope you inevitably looked at another critical part of interpersonal communication: the self. We asked you to think about your personal reactions to the conflict and how the conflict affected you. Even in a split second, you may have thought about the effect of the conflict on your relationship with the other person. You also may have reflected on how your identity influenced the type of conflict and the way the conflict developed. These considerations are part of your "self."

We discuss the perception process and an understanding of the self together in this chapter for a few

reasons. First, we perceive the world around us with a personal lens (Taheri, 2013). That lens is necessarily part of our perceptions. Second, we can't talk about perception unless we talk about how those perceptions influence and affect all aspects of our self. Finally, we believe that perceiving requires an understanding of the self. In other words, we can't begin to unravel why we recognize some things and ignore others without simultaneously figuring out how our individual identity functions (sometimes unconsciously) within those realizations. Perception and individual identity are inextricably linked; that is, you can't talk about one without referencing the other (Belin, Capanella, & Ethofer, 2013).

Our focus in this chapter is on face-to-face communication between people. Furthermore, because of the increasing intersection between identity and online communication, we will also delve into this dynamic interplay. To get a common foundation of understanding, we begin by explaining the perception process in face-to-face communication.

3-1 UNDERSTANDING PERCEPTION: A "SEE/SAW" EXPERIENCE

In most of our interpersonal encounters, we form an impression of the other person. These impressions, or perceptions, are critical to achieving meaning. The process of looking at people, things, activities, and events can involve many factors. For instance, in a face-to-face meeting with a teacher to challenge a low grade on a paper, you would probably notice not only your instructor's facial reactions and body position, but also your own. You might also be attentive to the general feeling you get as you enter the instructor's office. And you would probably prepare for the encounter by asking other students what their experiences with the instructor had been with respect to grade challenges.

Perceiving an interpersonal encounter, then, involves much more than hearing the words of another

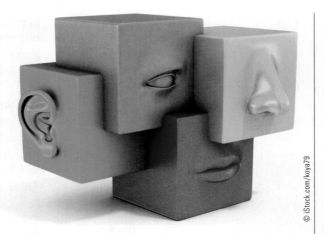

person. Perception is an active and challenging process that involves all five senses: touch, sight, taste, smell, and hearing. Through perception, we gain important information about the interpersonal communication skills of others and of ourselves. For our purposes, then, we define **perception** as a process of using our senses to respond to stimuli. The perception process generally occurs in four stages: attending and selecting, organizing, interpreting, and retrieving. Because perception is so instrumental to all of our interpersonal communication, we describe each stage (see Table 3.1).

perception The process of using our senses to understand and respond to stimuli. The perception process occurs in four stages: attending and selecting, organizing, interpreting, and retrieving.

attending and selecting stage The first stage of the perception process, requiring us to use our visual, auditory, tactile, and olfactory senses to respond to stimuli in our interpersonal environment.

mindful Having the ability to engage our senses so that we are observant and aware of our surroundings.

selective perception Directing our attention to certain stimuli while ignoring other stimuli.

3-1a Attending and Selecting

The **attending and selecting stage** requires us to use our visual, auditory, tactile, and olfactory senses to respond to stimuli in our interpersonal environment. When we are attentive and selective, we are mindful. Ellen Langer (1989) believes that mindful communicators pay close attention to detail. Being **mindful** means being observant and aware of your surroundings. In the case of interpersonal communication, this includes engaging senses such as sight and touch.

We are constantly bombarded with stimuli that make it almost impossible to focus on every detail of an encounter. As a result, we use **selective perception**. When we selectively perceive, we decide to attend to things that fulfill our own needs, capture our own interests, or meet our own expectations. We pay attention to some things while ignoring others.

In our relationships with others, we use selective perception all the time. For example, let's say that Luke has decided to end his relationship with Melissa. He explains that he thinks it is in her best interest as well as his for them to break up. However, he says that he has learned a lot while in the relationship. Luke continues talking, telling Melissa several of the things he feels he learned from being with her, and explains that he is grateful to have spent time with her.

As Melissa selectively perceives this unexpected conversation, she probably attends to the reason that Luke is breaking up with her. Regardless of everything else Luke says, Melissa listens for a particular piece of information. As a result, she filters and ignores other information, such as what Luke learned while being in the relationship. As would most people in such a situation, Melissa wants to know what motivated Luke's decision to break up. In addition to selectively perceiving his words,

TABLE 3.1 STAGES OF THE INTERPERSONAL PERCEPTION PROCESS

Stage	Description	Example
1. Attending and selecting	It involves sorting out stimuli. We choose to attend to some stimuli and to ignore others.	At the campus library, Kendrick notices his friend talking to a woman he had wanted to meet and date.
2. Organizing	It involves categorizing stimuli to make sense of them.	Kendrick creates the belief that his friend and the woman are close.
3. Interpreting	It involves assigning meaning to stimuli.	Kendrick decides not to ask his classmate out for a date because she is already dating his friend.
4. Retrieving	It involves recalling information we have stored in our memories.	Kendrick remembers that the two were together at a concert on campus a few weeks earlier.

© Cengage Learning®

© iStock.com/koya79

Melissa may also selectively attend to some of Luke's nonverbal signals, such as whether or not he has averted his eye contact or whether his vocal tone varies while delivering the news.

In this example, Melissa could consider a number of different stimuli—Luke's behaviors, the time of day, the noises in the room, and so on. But, she remains focused on fulfilling her need to hear why the relationship no longer works for Luke.

3-1b Organizing

After we are done selecting and attending to stimuli in our environment, we need to organize them in such a way that we can make sense of them. The **organizing stage** in the perception process requires us to place what are often a number of confusing pieces of information into an understandable, accessible, and orderly fashion. We frequently categorize when we organize. For example, patients organize information they receive from physicians to reduce their uncertainty about their illness. Because doctors tend to use language that is highly abstract and usually technical, patients must organize the doctors' confusing information into specific and understandable bits of information. In a diagnosis of Alzheimer's disease, for example, a patient (and his/her family) may receive an inordinate amount of information, ranging from costs to medications to treatments to the emotional toll on family members. As with all families in these situations, the volume of information will have to be recognized, prioritized, and ultimately organized. For instance, Barbara Germino and her research team (2013) found that patients who organize and manage their illness (breast cancer) reduce their uncertainty and end up with a clearer understanding of their disease.

When we organize, we usually use a **relational schema** (Batanova & Loukas, 2014), which is a mental framework or memory structure that people rely on to understand experience and to guide their future behavior. Each of us requires a recognized way of understanding something or someone. Therefore, we employ schema to help sort out the perception process. Each time we communicate, we use a relational schema to facilitate that communication. For example, you may classify your boss according to *leadership style* (autocratic, diplomatic, yielding, etc.), *work ethic* (hard working, lazy, etc.), or *personality characteristic* (rude, compassionate, insincere, etc.). These schemata help you recognize aspects of your boss's communication effectiveness without having to do a lot of thinking. Workers frequently use these types of classifications to help them organize the numerous messages given by a supervisor. For example, if the only types of messages that Jenny gets from her boss are insensitive and rude, she will inevitably categorize all of her boss's comments in that manner, regardless of whether the messages are framed that way.

When organizing, we look for consistencies rather than inconsistencies. Most of us would have a difficult time trying to communicate with each person in an individual manner as we meet in the subway, in the elevator, on the street, and in the grocery store. We, therefore, seek out familiar patterns of classifications: children, men, women, and so forth. Our decision of which classification to use is a selective process because when we choose to include one category, we necessarily ignore, eliminate, or devalue another.

Organizing is essential because it expedites the perception process. However, as convenient as it may be, the impulse to lump people into recognizable categories can be problematic. Using broad generalizations to describe groups of people is considered stereotyping. Recall from Chapter 2 that **stereotyping** includes having fixed mental images of a particular group and subsequently communicating with an individual as if he or she is a member of that group. In many cases, stereotypes get in the way of effective perception. When we stereotype others, we use schema without being concerned with individual differences, and such categorization is problematic when we begin to adopt a fixed impression of a group of people.

Consider the following dialogue between JJ and Ryan, two students who happen to be on the school football team, as they talk about their first day of class. In this scene, JJ obviously uses a unique schema to communicate about nontraditional-aged learners in his class. He stereotypes this group of people as having free time, not wanting to help other students, and being uninvolved in campus activities. Ryan attempts to dispel JJ's perceptions by focusing on the value of nontraditional students in class and reminding JJ that he wouldn't want to be treated like a stereotype.

organizing stage The second stage of the perception process, in which we place what are often a number of confusing pieces of information into an understandable, accessible, and orderly arrangement.

relational schema A mental framework or memory structure that we rely on to understand experience and to guide our future behavior in relationships.

stereotyping Categorizing individuals according to a fixed impression, whether positive or negative, of an entire group to which they belong.

JJ:	What's with all the old people in this class?
Ryan:	What do you mean, "old?"
JJ:	I mean, they don't have to take all these classes. They're in like one or two classes? It's crazy—they only have to worry about one thing.
Ryan:	What are you talking about? I had a few of what you call "old" students in my group in methods class, and to be honest, they really made a difference. One helped me get through the stats part of the class.
JJ:	And they ruined the curve, right?
Ryan:	Ah…no. I think the professor was more willing to listen to them when it came to curving the midterm. What is with you? Do you like it when everyone assumes you're a dumb jock just because you play football? I don't think so!

We encounter problems when we act upon our stereotypes in the perception process. When we perceive people to possess a particular characteristic because they belong to a particular group, we risk communication problems. Perceiving men as lacking emotion, immigrants as recipients of public assistance, or car dealers as slick and dishonest makes honest and ethical communication difficult. People who stereotype in this way oversimplify the complex process of perception. It's a delicate balance—we need some shortcuts so that all the stimuli bombarding us doesn't overwhelm us, but not so many shortcuts that we treat people unfairly.

3-1c Interpreting

Consider the following two sets of words and phrases:

A. *beer, lake, taxes, student ID, rifle, cell phone*

B. *Canada, cheddar cheese, Mercedes-Benz, wheelchair, the Pope*

interpreting stage The third stage of the perception process, in which we assign meaning to what we perceive.

As you looked at both sets of words and phrases, chances are you tried to find some commonality or difference among them. And, despite the fact that the lists were simply random words we chose with no intention, you may have begun to find some ways in which the words are related. This process is at the core of interpretation.

After attention/selection and organization are complete, we are then ready to interpret. At the **interpreting stage**, we assign meaning to what we perceive. Interpreting is required in every interpersonal encounter. And, despite our best efforts, we often fail to bring everything we know about something to the interpretation stage, resulting in a bias or a misinterpretation. We need to understand the source's objective(s) in communicating with us, something that requires us to be transactional.

As we established when we discussed the transactional nature of communication in Chapter 1, we need to achieve meaning for interpersonal communication to occur. What should you think of the friend who tells you to "get lost" after an argument? Do you take him literally? Or, what about the neighbor who decides to build a fence and then proceeds to tell you that she loves being your neighbor? How do you assign meaning to the comment made by your sibling who says, "So, do you want a closer relationship with me or not?"

The process of interpreting something is not simple; it is influenced by relational history, personal expectations, and knowledge of the self and other. First, your relational history, a concept we addressed in Chapter 1, affects your perception. Consider how you would perceive a statement by a close friend with whom you have had a relationship for more than 11 years versus a coworker with whom you have had a professional relationship for about a year. Because of your previous relationship experiences, perhaps your friend can get away with being sarcastic or pushy. However, your past experiences with the coworker are limited, and you may not be so open to sarcasm or pushiness.

Second, your personal expectations of an individual or situation can also affect how you interpret behavior. Let's say that you work in an office in which the department supervisor, Jonathan, is grouchy and intimidating. Consequently, whenever department meetings are held, workers avoid expressing their views openly, fearing verbal backlash. At one of these meetings, how would you talk about ways to improve efficiency in the office, fearing that Jonathan would react harshly?

Powerful symbol of serenity. . .or just a pile of rocks? It all depends on interpretation.

© iStock.com/Barcin

In addition to relational history and personal expectations, your knowledge of yourself and others can greatly affect your interpretation of behavior. For instance, are you aware of your personal insecurities and uncertainties? Do they influence how you receive off-the-cuff or insensitive comments? What do you know about your own communication with others? Do you recognize your strengths and shortcomings in an interpersonal encounter? Finally, what do you know about the other person? What shared fields of experience can be identified in your encounter? What assumptions about human behavior do you and others bring into a communication exchange? Such questions can help you assess how much knowledge you have about yourself and about the other communicator.

3-1d Retrieving

So far, we have attended to and selected stimuli, organized them, and interpreted them to achieve meaning in the encounter. The **retrieving stage** of perception asks us to recall information stored in our memories. At first glance, retrieving appears to be pretty straightforward. Yet, as you think about it further, you'll see that the retrieval process involves selection as well. At times, we use **selective retention**, a behavior that recalls information that agrees with

our perceptions and selectively forgets information that does not. Here is an example that highlights the retrieval process and some potential conflict associated with it.

Crystal sits with her friends as they talk about Professor Wendall. She doesn't really like what she hears. They talk about how boring the professor is and that his tests are too hard. They also make fun of his southern drawl as they imitate his teaching. Crystal remembers that she had Professor Wendall for a class more than 2 years ago, but she doesn't recall him being such a bad professor. In fact, she remembers the biology course she took from him as challenging and interesting. It doesn't make sense that her friends don't like Professor Wendall.

So, why do Crystal's friends and Crystal perceive Professor Wendall differently? Crystal has retrieved information about her professor differently. He may have ridiculed students, but Crystal doesn't recall that. She remembers his accent, but she does not remember it causing any problems. She also recollects Wendall's exams to be fair. Thus, Crystal's retrieval process has influenced her perception of Professor Wendall in the classroom.

The selective perception process such as that of Crystal's begins as infants. In fact, Tobias Grossman (2013) found that babies begin processing and weeding out emotions as young as one year. He noted that while newborns look at faces and listen to voices, it is the retrieval of the familiar mother's voice that they prefer. Grossman believes that this affirming retrieval can be traced back to prenatal experience insofar as the infant is continually exposed to the familiarity (and comfort) of the voice of its mother.

retrieving stage The fourth and final stage of the perception process, in which we recall information stored in our memories.

selective retention Recalling information that agrees with our perceptions and selectively forgetting information that does not.

So far, we have examined the perception process and its components. As we know, interpersonal communication can be difficult at times. Understanding how perception functions in those encounters helps clarify potential problems. We now turn our attention to several influences on our perception process. As you will learn, a number of factors affect the accuracy of our perceptions.

3-2 INFLUENCES ON PERCEPTION

When we perceive activities, events, or other people, our perceptions are a result of many variables. In other words, we don't all perceive our environment in the same way because individual perceptions are shaped by individual differences. We now discuss five factors that shape our perceptions: culture, sex and gender, physical factors, technology, and our sense of self.

3-2a Culture

Culture is an important teacher of perception (Martin & Nakayama, 2013) and provides the meaning we give to our perceptions (Chen & Starosta, 2006). In Chapter 2, you learned how culture pervades our lives and affects communication. With regard to perception, culture dictates how something should be organized and interpreted. For instance, Bantu refugees from Somalia perceive time differently after they arrive in the United States. In Somalia, clocks and watches are rare. In the United States, we learn to be punctual and watch the clock or our watch regularly. In addition, William Hamilton (2004) notes:

> Bantu parents learn that hitting their children is discouraged, though that was how they were disciplined in Africa. . . . They learn that Fourth of July fireworks are exploded to entertain not kill, and that being hit by a water balloon, as Bantu children were in one incident at school, is a game and not a hateful fight. (p. A14)

As another example, in the United States, most people expect others to maintain direct eye contact during conversation. This conversational expectation is influenced by a European American cultural value. However, traditional Japanese culture does not dictate direct eye contact during conversation (Bizumic, 2014), so we may feel that a classmate from Japan is not listening to us during conversation when he or she doesn't maintain eye contact. As

© iconspro/Shutterstock.com

a final illustration, the teachings of Islam and Christianity guide many Lebanese American families in virtually every decision of life, including birth, death, education, courtship, marriage, divorce, and contraception (Hashem, 2004). This adherence to religious principles may be difficult for someone without any religious connection to understand. Recall that each time you communicate with another person, you're drawing upon relational schema, a topic we discussed earlier. It may be difficult for two people with differing cultural backgrounds to sustain meaning if they are using two different schemata. You can see, then, that cultural heritage affects how people perceive the world. In turn, that same cultural heritage affects how people communicate with and receive communication from others. Cultural variation is sometimes the reason we can't understand why someone does something or the reason why others question our behavior. Although it's natural to believe that others look at things the same way you do, remember that cultures can vary tremendously in their practices, and these differences affect perception.

3-2b Sex and Gender

Sex refers to the biological makeup of an individual (male or female). **Gender** refers to the learned behaviors a culture associates with being a male or female. For example, we have a masculine or feminine gender. If we possess both masculine and feminine traits in equally large amounts, we are called *androgynous*. Possessing relatively low amounts of masculinity and femininity is

sex The biological makeup of an individual (male or female).

gender The learned behaviors a culture associates with being a male or female, known as masculinity or femininity.

FIGURE 3.1   GENDER ROLES IN COMMUNICATION

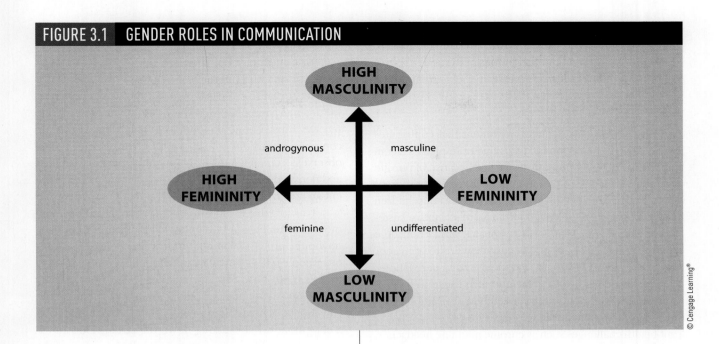

© Cengage Learning®

termed *undifferentiated* (see Figure 3.1). It is possible to be a masculine female or a feminine male.

Researchers have investigated the relationship between perception and sex. Looking at perceptions of body type, researchers found that boys and girls in kindergarten and second grade differed in preferences for body types. Girls preferred a thinner figure than boys, and girls perceived thinness as both attractive and feminine. Boys preferred more athletic builds by kindergarten and were indirectly communicating "preferences for being smart, moderately strong, and somewhat prone to fighting" (Miller, Plant, & Hanke, 1993, p. 56). Other researchers have noted that when asked to compare themselves with others, college-aged women—more than men—were inclined to compare themselves with professional models when evaluating their sexual attractiveness and weight (Franzoi & Klaber, 2007). In fact, a website exists, mybodygallery.com, that allows women (but not men) to compare their bodies to other women!

Perceptual differences such as those above are a result of the way men and women have been raised. **Gender role socialization** is the process by which women and men learn the gender roles appropriate to their sex (e.g., being masculine if you are biologically a male). This socialization usually affects the way the sexes perceive the world. Messages about masculinity and femininity are communicated to children early in life, and these messages stick with us into adulthood. Sandra Bem (1993) notes that when we understand and organize our world around masculinity and femininity, we are using a **gender schema**. Specifically, she believes that through a schema, we process and categorize beliefs,

ideas, and events as either masculine or feminine. If new information doesn't fit our gender schema, Bem maintains that we simply discard it.

Think about your perceptions of the following situations:

▶ A 5-year-old boy playing house with a 6-year-old neighbor girl

▶ A retired elderly male dancing with another male at a New Year's Eve party

▶ A newborn girl wearing a pink dress with flowers

▶ An adolescent female helping her father change the oil in his car

Do any of these situations contradict how you normally view male and female behavior? Does the age of the person make a difference? If so, why? What contributes to these perceptions? Parents? Media? Teachers? Peers? Games? In all likelihood, each of these—in some way—has helped shape your current perceptions.

Men and women frequently look at things differently, depending on what gender schema they bring to a circumstance (Ivy, 2012). As people sort out the various stimuli in their environment, gender cannot be ignored or devalued. Certainly, men and women can reject gender

gender role socialization The process by which women and men learn the gender roles appropriate to their sex. This process affects the way the sexes perceive the world.

gender schema A mental framework we use to process and categorize beliefs, ideas, and events as either masculine or feminine in order to understand and organize our world.

prescriptions and help society expand its perceptual expectations. However, most people continue to look at their worlds with rigid interpretations of the sexes, resulting in perceptions that may be distorted or inaccurate.

3-2c Physical Factors

Our physical makeup is another element that contributes to variations in perceptions. *Age* is one example. We seem to perceive things differently as we age because of our life experiences. Being single and in debt at age 19 is different than being in debt as a single parent of three young children at age 45. No one is relying on a single teenager for sustenance, whereas a parent needs to consider his or her three children at home. The aging process allows us to frame our life experiences. Our *health*, too, helps shape perceptions. We broadly define health to include such things as fatigue, stress, biorhythms, and physical ability. For example, consider the perceptual challenges of those who have significant health challenges such as chronic migraine headaches. Perceptions of work and home relationships will likely be influenced if an individual is in constant pain. Additionally, some people simply do not have the physical *ability* to see another person's behaviors or to listen attentively to his or her words. Others need some accommodation to be able to attend to stimuli in their surroundings. Our senses vary, often according to our physical limitations. Imagine the difficulty a physically challenged individual experiences trying to navigate nonaccessible curbs compared with someone who does not require motorized accommodation such as a wheelchair. If you don't use a wheelchair, you won't perceive the curbs as potential obstacles.

3-2d Technology

Now more than ever, technology affects our perceptions. The Internet in particular—which has little oversight and relatively little accountability—requires us to be critical in our perceptions. We need to remember that websites have been created by a variety of people with different backgrounds (e.g., psychiatrists, talk show hosts, gun manufacturers, etc.). Keep in mind that the trustworthiness of websites varies.

Technology makes possible the cultivation of online relationships. If, for instance, you visit a dating website and find a match, you need to remember that you are relying on text written onscreen and a downloaded picture. The picture may be inauthentic or out-of-date, or you might be the victim of someone who gives false information. Further, you are unable to read the facial expressions, listen to the

self-concept A relatively stable set of perceptions we hold of ourselves.

vocal characteristics, look at the clothing, watch the body movement, and observe the eye contact of the other person, all critical parts of the perception process outlined above. In sum, the Internet can leave us relationally shortchanged because we can't perceive the whole picture—we are receiving only what the other person wants us to receive. Likewise, we communicate only what we wish to communicate to the other person. As Sue Barnes (2003) observes, "screen names, signature lines, personal profiles, and personal Web pages can be carefully designed to present an image of self" (p. 133).

The Internet is not the only technological development that affects our perceptions. For example, consider how our perceptions are altered when we observe various people with smartphones, handheld game consoles, or Bluetooth headsets. For instance, what do you think when you see a teenager talking on a cell phone? Now, consider your reaction to an older man in a suit talking on a cell phone while walking down the street. Do you experience any difference in perception? Now, change the context. A teenager is sitting with her mother at the bus stop, and the older man is driving in his Mercedes-Benz. Does the context make a difference in your perceptions?

We can't escape the influence that technology has on our perceptions. This influence occurs in both overt and covert ways. We may be conscious of how our perceptions change, or be unaware of technology's influence. Nowadays, the reaction we have to electronic technology ranges from indifference to awe. At times, we expect everyone we meet to own some technology; other times, we are impressed by the latest technology, privately vowing to own it once we have enough money! As you continue to understand your own perceptual behaviors, keep in mind that technology plays a significant role in how those perceptions are developed and sustained (we return to the topic of technology a bit later in the chapter).

3-2e Our Sense of Self

A final factor that shapes our perceptions is self-concept, which we discuss further in this chapter. For now, it's important to point out that our perceptions of ourselves are influential in the perception process. We define **self-concept** as a relatively stable set of perceptions a person holds of himself or herself. Our self-concept is rather consistent from one situation to another. For instance, our core beliefs and values about our intellectual curiosity or charitable ways stay fairly constant. Self-concept is flexible, though; for example, our beliefs about our ability to climb a mountain may differ at age 30 and age 65.

Self-concept affects our perceptions of others' feelings about us. Generally, statements from people we trust and respect carry more weight than statements from those

Few terms resonate more with technophiles than *selfie*. *Selfie*—the 2013 *Oxford Dictionary* word of the year (and a topic we return to in Chapter 4), is a self-portrait people take with their smartphones. The selfie, according to Dan Zak (2013), has afforded people to perceive the world and themselves in personal ways. Zak calls a selfie a "self-portraiture" that allows people to present themselves in strategic ways. Zak states that every day, "Facebook spits out a photo of a friend who has turned a smartphone camera on him or herself. There is a practiced tilt of the head, to avoid additional chins. There is the palm tree or infinity pool in the background to record momentary privilege. There is the artfully arranged cleavaged or the casually flexed triceps, to establish oneself as fit, desirable, deserving of exhibition in the carousel museum of social media." What Zak is inferring here is that selfies allow for a presentation of the self that transcends authenticity. A psychologist quoted by Zak notes that self-portraitures are "good for self-empowerment." We rely on selfies because, as Zak notes, "selfies say: I'm

© iStock.com/pixdeluxe

not alone because I can share my aloneness." Zak cites a literature professor who quotes poet Ralph Waldo Emerson: "the mark of wisdom is seeing the miraculous in the commonplace and showing ourselves to each other because we find something of worth in ourselves." Indeed, selfies are technological self-presentations online and these snapshots provide a lens into an individual's sense of self.

we don't. Consider, then, the way you would perceive the same words depending on whether they came from a close friend or from a classmate. Suppose, for instance, that you perceive yourself to be an excellent listener. If a classmate tells you that she thinks you don't listen well, you might not be as willing to consider changing your behavior as you would if a close friend made the same observation.

Thus far, we have given you a sense of what perception is, noted why it's important in interpersonal communication, and identified some significant influences on the perception process. Throughout our discussion, you have seen that it's virtually impossible to separate our sense of self from our perceptions. Now, we dig further into the self and explain the importance of the self in interpersonal communication. We start by explaining the self and its dimensions.

3-3 UNDERSTANDING THE SELF: THE "I'S" HAVE IT

How do you see yourself? This is the key question guiding our discussion of the self. Answering this question is not easy. Certainly, we realize that you can't answer this question in a word or two. Previously, we noted that self-concept is both fixed and flexible. It makes sense, then, that you would inevitably begin your answer to this question with "Well, it depends."

This chapter will help you formulate and clarify a response to this question. If you think "it depends," you're partially correct. However, there are ways to articulate a more complete response. We hope that you will think about this question as you read this section. We are guided by the following principle as we introduce this information: To have a relationship with someone else, you must first have a relationship with yourself. In other words, communication begins and ends with you. Let's explore self-concept and what it entails.

3-3a Self-Concept

Earlier, we defined self-concept as a relatively fixed set of perceptions we hold of ourselves. The self-concept is everything we believe about ourselves. This collection of perceptions is more stable than fleeting, but that does not mean that our self-concept is permanent. One reason self-concept changes is because it emerges from our various interpersonal encounters with others. George Herbert Mead (1934), more than 80 years ago, posited that communication with others shapes personal identity. This theory is called the **symbolic interactionism theory**.

To begin our discussion, consider two versions of the following story regarding Terrence Washington. As a self-employed painter, Terrence relies on small projects to make a living. His recent surgery to correct tendonitis has caused him to be laid up at home, unable to continue to paint homes. His inability to take on jobs has not only caused him some financial problems, but has also affected his psychological well-being. Terrence feels useless and can't seem to shake a sense of self-doubt.

Now consider Terrence's situation again. This time, though, Terrence's friends visit him, assuring him that this circumstance is only temporary. One friend suggests that Terrence help her figure out a color scheme for her living room. Another friend gets Terrence a temporary job advising customers in a local paint store. Although he is unable to paint homes, Terrence finds himself as busy as ever. His self-doubt begins to dissipate, and his feelings about himself take on a positive cast.

The two examples result in different self-concepts for Terrence. In the first example, we see a man who is beginning to doubt his own abilities, and whose self-concept will likely proceed into a negative spiral: He wants to get better, but to get better he needs to feel good about himself. Because he doesn't feel good about himself, he won't get better. The second scenario underscores the importance of others in our self-concept.

symbolic interactionism theory The theory that our understanding of ourselves and of the world is shaped by our interactions with those around us.

self-awareness Our understanding of who we are.

self-esteem An evaluation of who we perceive ourselves to be.

self-worth How we feel about our talents, abilities, knowledge, expertise, and appearance.

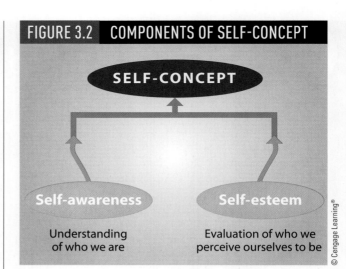

FIGURE 3.2   COMPONENTS OF SELF-CONCEPT

SELF-CONCEPT

Self-awareness — Understanding of who we are

Self-esteem — Evaluation of who we perceive ourselves to be

© Cengage Learning®

Terrence's friends positively affect his career prospects, and, in turn, his self-concept.

Terrence's self-concept is influenced by both an awareness of himself and an assessment of his potential. These influences—self-awareness and self-esteem—are the two primary components of self-concept (Figure 3.2).

3-3b Self-Awareness

Self-awareness is our understanding of who we are. According to symbolic interaction theorists, we begin our lives as blank slates—that is, we are born with no consciousness of who we are. We rely on our parents, guardians, or family members to help us recognize ourselves. When we hear our parents cooing to us, for instance, we realize that we exist. The adults around us soon start speaking to us in baby talk. This talk may not sound all that important, but it initiates the process of self-awareness that continues throughout our lifetimes.

In Terrence Washington's case, his self-awareness as an adult stems from the belief that he is a painter who has successfully made a living painting other people's homes. Understanding self-awareness serves as the first step toward understanding our self-esteem.

3-3c Self-Esteem

Self-esteem is a bit more complicated than self-awareness. Our **self-esteem** is an evaluation of who we perceive ourselves to be. In a sense, our self-esteem is related to our **self-worth**, or how we feel about our talents, abilities, knowledge, expertise, and appearance. Our self-esteem comprises the images we hold—that is, our social roles (e.g., father, receptionist, electrician, etc.), the words we use to describe these social roles (e.g., doting grandparent, courteous police officer, skilled nurse, etc.), and how others see us in those roles (e.g., competent, negligible, thorough, etc.). Ann Frymier and Marjorie Nadler (2013) also point out that the self-esteem of the source affects how you receive a message. This is especially important in situations where you are required to offer feedback. In an interview situation, for example, if your interviewer is awkward or uncomfortable and fumbling through the interview, then you, as the potential employee, may have a difficult time achieving meaning. Clearly, the interviewer's communication skills do not elicit an opportunity for clarity.

We develop our self-esteem as a result of overcoming setbacks, achieving our goals, and helping others in their pursuits (Sternberg & Whitney, 2002). Even when we fail, our feelings of self-worth may not be jeopardized if we think we have beaten obstacles along the way. Think, for instance, about the difficulties of divorce. For many married couples, divorce is an acrimonious process pitting one spouse against the other. Yet, some ex-spouses survive these breakups as friends. Elizabeth Graham (1997, 2003) found that ex-spouses do not remain angry forever after a divorce; indeed, some become very good friends. What appears to be an insurmountable relational episode, then, can actually result in some couples being able to talk to one another on intimate terms. Some couples, overcoming obstacles, report being able to retain some of the original feelings of affirmation they once held for each other. Clearly, the self-esteem of such couples is positively affected by the ability to manage the divorce effectively.

Other people do not always enhance our feelings of self-worth. Regardless of how many family or friends surround us during difficult times, it might be the case that nothing helps us feel better about ourselves. At times, others may unwittingly contribute to our negative self-perceptions. For example, if you try to encourage someone after the loss of a relational partner by showering him with platitudes or cliché phrases (e.g., "I'm sure you'll make it" or "Hey, not all relationships were meant to be"), you may unknowingly cause your friend to feel worse.

Like our self-concept, self-esteem may fluctuate. One day we consider ourselves to be excellent, and the next day we are down on ourselves. This variation in self-esteem is often due to our interactions with others in our lives and the feedback we've received. We usually listen more carefully to those we admire or whose previous advice was worthwhile. We generally reject the opinions of those we don't know. Most of us are able to understand that one situation shouldn't necessarily affect our feelings of self-worth.

Finally, some writers have talked about the relationship between self-esteem and "selfies" (those self-portraits people take of themselves with their smartphones) (see IPC Around Us). Regardless if you believe it's a technological exercise in narcissism or a "feel-good creative way" to promote yourself, Jessica Yadegaran (mercurynews.com, 2013) concludes that personal snapshotting has taken off. She cites numerous individuals, including image and psychology experts, who contend that these pictures promote one's well-being and help in feelings of self-worth. The positive comments apparently lift the spirits of those who are otherwise down. The selfies result in positive comments for many, providing further support for one's value. Yet, Yadegaran also notes that selfies can damage one's self-esteem in that they can cause individuals to lose contact with their "authentic selves." Without this authenticity, our relationship building becomes more challenging. We will address more about relationships and technology in Chapters 10 and 11.

3-3d Self-Fulfilling Prophecy

The self is also formed, in part, by the predictions you make about yourself. When predictions about a future interaction lead you to behave in ways that make certain that the interaction occurs as you imagined, you have created a

Self-esteem is bolstered by personal accomplishments, the cultivation of expertise, and the performance of valuable social roles. How might military service affect self-esteem?

FIGURE 3.3 **STAGES OF SELF-FULFILLING PROPHECIES**

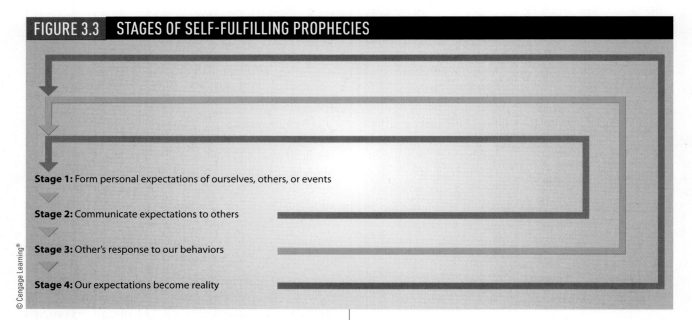

Stage 1: Form personal expectations of ourselves, others, or events

Stage 2: Communicate expectations to others

Stage 3: Other's response to our behaviors

Stage 4: Our expectations become reality

© Cengage Learning®

self-fulfilling prophecy. Our self-concepts frequently lead to self-fulfilling prophecies. These prophecies may either be *self-imposed*, which occurs when your own expectations influence your behavior, or *other-imposed*, which occurs when the expectations of another person influence your behavior. Self-fulfilling prophecies can take place within a number of interpersonal situations, from the family to the workplace. Consider the following:

▶ Mario is nervous about talking to someone he respects and admires, thinking that he probably is going to blunder when he speaks with that person. When he meets the person, he trips over his words.

▶ Ana approaches a job interview thinking that her job expertise and communication skills will get her the job, and she prepares thoroughly for the interview. The job is offered to her.

Although each of these prophecies is different, self-fulfilling prophecies usually follow a pattern. First, we form expectations of ourselves, others, or particular events. Next, we communicate that expectation to others. Third, others respond to our behaviors. Fourth, our expectations become reality, and our expectations confirm and reinforce our original thinking about ourselves. However, each stage returns to the first stage, because the original perception prompted the prophecy itself (Figure 3.3).

self-fulfilling prophecy A prediction or expectation about our future behavior that is likely to come true because we believe it and thus act in ways that make it come true.

identity management theory The theory that explains the manner in which you handle your "self" in various circumstances; includes competency, identity, and face.

Here is an example of how self-fulfilling prophecies function in a person's life. As a young child, Rachael felt that she was ugly and awkward. As a result, she wasn't particularly social and avoided talking to people face-to-face, especially in social settings (*Step 1:* Form expectation of event). While attending a wedding reception, Rodney, one of the guests at her table, asked Rachael to dance. She told him that she was not a good dancer, was not interested in making a fool of herself on the dance floor, and did not want to dance with Rodney (*Step 2:* Communicate expectation to other). When Rodney returned to his seat, he thought to himself: "Wow, she is shy! And talk about not wanting to hang out with people" (*Step 3:* Others respond to behavior). At the same time, Rachael thought that Rodney did not want to talk to her because she was not as pretty or outgoing as the other women at the reception (*Step 4:* Confirmation of original perception).

As you can tell, the self doesn't simply develop without being influenced in some way. After you gain an understanding of yourself, you can begin to address how you present yourself to others. Researchers refer to this as identity management, which is the topic we explore in the next section.

3-4 IDENTITY MANAGEMENT: LET'S FACE IT

At the heart of our discussion of the self is identity management theory (Cupach & Imahori, 1993, 2005). **Identity management theory** refers to the communication practices we employ to influence how others will perceive us. In a general sense, one's identity is viewed as "what is attached to an individual due to his or her membership in a particular category," such as sex, age, occupation, and so on (Heisterkamp & Alberts, 2000). This theory suggests that people behave according to their goals and that a person's competency and identity all work together in our interactions with others (Imahori, 2006). When we manage our identities, we decide on a particular communication behavior to influence how others perceive us. Another important reason to communicate our identities is to be active citizens. As Nikolas Coupland and Jon Nussbaum (1993) state, "To be our social selves, to be individuals functioning within social and political communities, we need to *voice* our identities and so participate in the reproduction of these communities" (p. 1).

One of the first people to discuss identity management was sociologist Erving Goffman (1959). Goffman believed that identity is best explained by comparing it to theatrical performances. He believed that "when an individual appears before others, he [or she] will have many motives for trying to control the impression they receive of the situation" (p. 15). Goffman goes on to say that we play characters in a performance and are concerned about "coherence among setting, appearance, and manner" (p. 25). In other words, we are actors who "perform" for the audiences around us. And, subsequently, "the performer requests that the audience takes his or her performance seriously" (Dillard, Browning, Sitkin, & Sutcliffe, 2000, p. 405).

This image of a theatrical production may seem a bit odd to you. After all, who wants to admit to "acting" in an interpersonal encounter? We're not like the monarchy who "hold court" with the public or the Pope, who is often associated with "having an audience." Still, Goffman believes that we all take on particular social roles and manage these roles to achieve meaning in our relationships with others.

Identity management does not happen without some risk and consequence. For instance, suppose Victor, a 25-year-old graduate student, decides to move back in with his parents for financial reasons, one of a group of people that Katherine Newman (2013) calls "boomerang kids" who are part of an "accordion family." The rules that were once part of the household (e.g., "No profanity" or "Clean up your room") may now seem out of date to Victor. As he figures out how to act at home and, in turn, formulate his "new identity," he may reject the household rules because he feels that he is too old to have to abide by them. Yet, what happens if his mom or dad requires adherence to the rules? Aren't they also managing their identity as Victor manages his? How

Victor handles these different identities will affect the quality of the interpersonal communication he has with his parents.

Because identity management requires some risk, we may find ourselves in situations that compromise our sense of self. We become preoccupied with protecting the image we decide to present to others. In doing so, we are engaged in facework, a topic we now explore in more detail.

3-4a Identity Management and Facework

In interpersonal interactions, people shape their identities to display a particular sense of self, one essential theme of this chapter. When we get into conversations with others, we offer our identity and hope that others will accept it. This is critical to our self-concept overall and to our self-esteem in particular. The image of the self—the public identity—that we present to others in our interpersonal encounters is called face. Generally, face is somewhat automatic (Cupach & Metts, 1994). The metaphor of face pervades U.S. society. We talk about "saving face," "in your face," and, especially in this book, "face-to-face" communication all the time. **Face** is how you want to be perceived by others, how you want others to treat you, and how you end up treating others. The essence of face is politeness and one cannot ignore that this politeness necessarily includes dignity and respect for others (Kádár & Haugh, 2013).

We take it for granted that there is a give and take in maintaining face. In other words, following the transactional nature of communication that we identified in Chapter 1, both communicators in an interaction are responsible for **facework**, the set of coordinated behaviors that help us either reinforce or threaten our competence. Facework is usually a two-person event in an interpersonal relationship. As Cupach and Metts (1994) conclude, "Face is not merely what one individual dictates. Rather, partners negotiate (usually subtly) who each other 'is' with respect to one another" (p. 96).

We present two types of face in our conversations with others: positive face and negative face. **Positive face** pertains to our desire to be liked by

---

face The image of the self we choose to present to others in our interpersonal encounters.

facework The set of coordinated behaviors that help us either reinforce or threaten our competence.

positive face Our desire to be liked by significant people in our lives and have them confirm our beliefs, respect our abilities, and value what we value.

When we receive messages that do not support either our positive or negative face, our identities become threatened.

significant people in our lives. It is the favorable image that people present to others, hoping that others validate that image. We have positive face when others confirm our beliefs, respect our abilities, and value what we value. That's not to say that individuals have to agree with everything we have to say or with everything we believe—that would be impossible! Most of us simply want to relate to people who make efforts to understand, appreciate, and respect our perceptions and competencies.

When one "loses" face (e.g., a threat to positive face), the consequences can be very real. A study by Gina Masullo Chen (2013), for example, found that those using social media sites similar to Facebook used retaliatory aggression such as "destroying" the face of those who experience rejection and criticism. In particular, if a participant was rejected from joining particular groups ("We don't want you in our group") or criticized once in a particular group ("No offense, but when we saw your profile, we laughed"), that person was more likely to send "virtual ticking bombs" to those group members. In addition, those where positive face was assaulted were less likely to send "virtual smiley faces." The results, according to Chen, show that aggressive techniques undertaken in this way were efforts in restoring positive face.

negative face Our desire that others refrain from imposing their will on us, respect our individuality and our uniqueness, and avoid interfering with our actions or beliefs.

self-monitoring Actively thinking about and controlling our public behaviors and actions.

Negative face refers to our desire for others to refrain from imposing their will on us. Negative face is maintained when people respect our individuality and avoid interfering with our actions or beliefs. Again, this is not to say that people will simply become dutiful and obedient in our conversations without challenging us. Rather, we're suggesting that people periodically need to feel autonomous and want others to be flexible enough to respect this need in interpersonal encounters.

When we receive messages that do not support either our positive or negative face, our identities become threatened. Face threats can jeopardize meaning in an interpersonal encounter. As Joseph Forgas (2002) concluded, "to fail in a performance leads to loss of face, which upsets the pattern of social intercourse" (p. 29). If our positive face is threatened—such as when another person challenges our skills—we have to figure out how to deal with the threat to our identity. For instance, let's say that Pat is a hairstylist and that Nola, a client of 19 years, threatens Pat's positive face by asking Pat, "Where *did* you find this color? In your attic?" Because Pat takes pride in her abilities, this insult may be difficult to overcome. Pat will have to figure out a way to preserve her positive face with Nola. Indeed, this process happens frequently in our lives, and we have to learn how to handle these face threats. In the United States, we are normally not conditioned to help others "save" their face (Pan, 2000), although people in other cultures (e.g., Asian cultures) are attuned to maintaining everyone's face in an interaction.

As we discuss the topic of identity management, recognize that managing our identities is important because so much of our interpersonal meaning is based on our competency, identity, and face. Working on your identity management requires (1) timing (saying "I hate meaningless jobs" in a job interview), (2) focusing on the present (staying attuned to the content of the message rather than the impression you're making), and (3) practicing self-monitoring. People vary in their abilities to pay attention to their own actions and the actions of others (Snyder, 1979). The term **self-monitoring** refers to the extent to which people actively think about and control their public behaviors and actions. Self-monitoring is important in identity management because people who are aware of their behaviors and the effects of their behaviors in a conversation are viewed as more competent communicators. Be careful, however. Practicing self-monitoring too much will result in being preoccupied with details that may be unimportant. On the other hand, being ignorant of your strengths and shortcomings in a conversation is just as problematic. Finding a reasonable middle ground in self-monitoring is critical in identity management.

© Tyler Olson/Shutterstock.com

3-5 ONLINE IDENTITY MANAGEMENT

On the Internet, individuals typically communicate who they are through identity markers. An **identity marker** is an electronic extension of who someone is. In other words, an identity marker is an expansion of the self. Two primary identity markers exist on the Internet: screen names and personal home pages.

3-5a Screen Names

As in face-to-face relationships, online relationships inevitably require introductions. Yet, unlike in interpersonal relationships, we can introduce ourselves online by using names that are odd, silly, fun, editorial, or outright offensive. These screen names are nicknames and often serve to communicate the uniqueness of the sender of a message. Many screen names function as a way for communicators to protect their identities from others until more familiarity and comfort develops.

People use a wide variety of screen names. Some are shaped by fiction (e.g., MadMadHatter or hobbitfeets), others by popular culture (e.g., IDOLfan) and still others by a desire to reinforce personal values (e.g., veganvixen420 or xNODISHONORx). Haya Bechar-Israeli (1996) observes that many people place a great deal of importance on their screen names and nicknames and that they invest a great deal of thought in their creation. According to Bechar-Israeli, "References to collective cultural, ethnic, and religious themes in nicknames might indicate that the individual belongs to a certain social group" (p. 12). Her research shows that rather than frequently changing their names, people tend to keep their names for a period of time, which underscores the fact that they commit themselves to a screen identity.

At first glance, screen names may seem unimportant in building an electronic discussion and relationship. However, unlike your name (which was probably given to you at birth), screen names are created by the individual and reflect some degree of creativity, a value that others may consider important when encountering people online. And despite the relative stability of screen names, people can change their names much more easily

in virtual life than in real life. If you encounter someone who is verbally offensive online, you can leave a chat room, establish a different name, and reenter the chat room under an entirely different alias. Even wigs and cosmetic surgery can't achieve such a transformation so quickly! Finally, most of our given names at birth (e.g., Nate, Luisa, Maggie) communicate little to others. On the other hand, screen names give others insight into people's interests or values. A screen name such as STALKU, for example, can tell others a lot.

3-5b Personal Home Pages

If an individual wants to communicate a great deal of personal information, a personal home page may be the first step. Personal home pages present a number of features that depict who the person is, such as a resume or portfolio; information on personal hobbies and genealogy; photographs of the person and his or her family members, friends, pets, and home; and links to groups with advocacy causes or contacts.

Communicating one's identity via a personal home page is often enlightening to others. Personal websites can contain information that may be deliberate or accidental. First, as is the case with personal interactions, people may strategically present themselves in a certain way on their personal web pages. Digital photos, slick graphics, funky fonts, interesting links, and creative screen names may communicate a sense of organization, creativity, insight,

identity marker An electronic extension of who someone is (e.g., screen name).

and invitation. These sorts of intentional markers may be consciously presented on web pages so that others have a comprehensive understanding of who the person is and can find out a bit about his or her attitudes, beliefs, and values. The message is clear: "I'm a person you want to meet. I've got it together online. You can imagine how together I will have it when you meet me." However, some personal home page designers would do well to remember a corollary of Murphy's law: If nothing can go wrong, it will anyway! Someone may have the best intentions of communicating clarity and authenticity, but they go awry. Consider the following greeting on a personal home page: "Welcome to my home page. I hoop you get a kick out of reading the different stories about me." Or, what about the web page that had inadvertently been linked to a pornographic website? And then there are those websites that are filled with odd photos ("That's me kissing the neighbor's cat") or those with too much disclosure ("Feel free to use the 'Past Romances' dropdown"). It's likely that with these sorts of things, many will choose to skip over a home page rather than engage it. As in face-to-face encounters, although we may mean well, the words (and pictures and links) sometimes come out wrong.

Throughout this chapter, we have emphasized the link between our perceptions, our sense of self, and our communication with others. The following four conclusions regarding perception, the self, and interpersonal communication illustrate how the three are closely related.

One conclusion regarding the intersection of perception, self, and interpersonal communication suggests that each person operates with a personal set of perceptions. **Implicit personality theory** suggests that we fill in the blanks when identifying characteristics of people, using a few characteristics to draw inferences about others. We believe that certain traits go together and communicate with people on this basis. For example, consider how you fill in the following sentences (choose from the words in parentheses):

> ▶ Dr. Hess is warm, sensitive, and (intelligent, dumb).

> ▶ Dr. Aldine is rude, distant, and (compassionate, unreliable).

Choosing "intelligent" in the first sentence and "unreliable" in the second sentence illustrates the **halo effect**, which states that you will match like qualities with each other. A **positive halo** occurs when you place positive qualities (warm, sensitive, and intelligent) together. A **negative halo** exists when you place negative qualities (unintelligent, rude, and temperamental) together. Once we form an impression (positive or negative) of another, we may begin to interact with the other person in a way that supports the impression.

Implicit personality theory enables us to effectively manage a lot of information about another person. However, be careful of overusing implicit personality behaviors when communicating with others. Don't perceive characteristics in a person that don't exist. Responding to people according to such predispositions can lead to problems in interpersonal communication.

A second conclusion on the symbiotic nature of perception, self, and interpersonal communication relates to perceptual problems. In general, perceptual errors can cause problems in our communication with others. For example, **attribution theory** (Heider, 1958) examines how we create explanations or attach meaning to someone's behavior. Fritz Heider once said that we are all "naive psychologists" in that we try to uncover reasons for people's actions, yet we may have no real understanding of the person or the circumstances surrounding the actions.

Our attributions are often influenced by our feelings for another person. For instance, have you ever arranged to meet someone for coffee and that person showed up late? What were your thoughts while waiting? If the person was someone you liked, you may have attributed the lateness to something out of his or her control, such as car trouble, congested traffic, disobedient children, and so forth. If the person was someone you didn't know well or didn't like, you may have attributed the delay to something within the person's control. Perhaps you viewed the person's behavior as intentional. Yet, the person might have been late because of unforeseen circumstances. We may be "naive," then, to the number of different influences on behavior. In Chapter 7, we look further into how feelings and emotions affect our relationships with others.

In addition to the preceding two conclusions, we also believe that the self undergoes a continual process of modification. Our sense of who we are changes as our relationships change. In other words, our identity—like communication—is a process, not a constant. This

implicit personality theory The theory that we rely on a set of a few characteristics to draw inferences about others and use these inferences as the basis of our communication with them.

halo effect The result of matching like qualities with each other to create an overall perception of someone or something.

positive halo The result of placing positive qualities (e.g., warm, sensitive, and intelligent) together.

negative halo The result of grouping negative qualities (e.g., unintelligent, rude, and temperamental) together.

attribution theory A theory that explains how we create explanations or attach meaning to another person's behavior or our own.

Attribution Theory

Attribution theorists are primarily concerned with trying to understand and make sense of what prompted various events or what caused an individual's actions or conduct. In essence, attribution theory helps describe the cognitive processes that we use when we try to explain another's behavior. Think about a relationship you have with your roommate, best friend, or work colleague. Now, consider an event that occurred with this person and which remains unresolved (e.g., dating a person 20 years older, quitting a job over the phone, etc.). Discuss how attribution principles can be applied to these events.

conclusion implies that we, and our relationships, are changing. Consequently, our interpersonal communication should reflect these changes. Think about the way you were as a sophomore in high school, and look at who you are now. Your perceptions of your own strengths and shortcomings have inevitably changed over the years. Imagine what it would be like if you didn't change or if others didn't change.

Finally, our fourth conclusion is clear: The self responds to a variety of stimuli. To understand this conclusion, consider the fact that we respond to people (e.g., father or grandparent), surroundings (e.g., noise level or lighting), and technology (e.g., an Internet site or a television program). Each has the capacity to affect the self.

Before we close this chapter, we wish to identify the interplay among the perception process, the self, and our online conversations and relationships. Communication theorists have advanced the notion that our online relationships are important and that it's possible, and even likely, that we can have quality online relationships (Walther, 1992, 2008, 2012). Walther contends that we can establish and maintain relationships online (we adapt to the medium); and although nonverbal cues are at a minimum, our perceptions and presentations of our various selves provide for a mutually satisfying relationship. We will look at Walther's thinking throughout this book, but for now let's briefly examine

the roles that perception and self-presentation play in our online relationships. One central component of Walther's thinking related to the current discussion is **impression management**, which is the unconscious or strategic effort to influence another's perceptions. He believes that communicators will try to "fill in the blanks" with respect to incomplete perceptions (think about implicit personality processes). Subsequently, we may make attributions of another's behavior (think about attribution processes). Online, we use a "perceptual personality" framework ("You sound just like my uncle Martin; he's my favorite relative") and this framing influences the direction of the relationship.

The online relationship between two communicators does not require both to be at their computers, laptops, or smartphones at the same time. This "asynchronous communication" provides for further perception checking. That is, when we send a text or message online, before pressing "Send," we have time to reflect on the message, edit it, and review it. The difference in elapsed time affords for both online interactants to cultivate a certain type of relationship. Suppose, for instance, that Michael and Ben have been communicating back and forth since meeting on a dating website. Although they haven't met, they have sent texts and emails with personal disclosures and words that suggest a future together. In sum, the couple has, in their eyes, established an intimate relationship, and their perception of such a relationship is illustrated by the content sequencing of messages.

Perceptions, however, remain insufficient in online relationship development. The self also manifests itself in a number of curious, yet important ways. Social networking sites (SNS) such as Facebook are filled with people who wish to provide a number of different self-presentations (West & Turner, 2014). Many SNS allow users to use a number of different behaviors to establish and maintain a particular online identity/self-image (e.g., displaying relational status such as divorced or single, using pictures, etc.). This identity is based on how senders and receivers present themselves to others. Some, for instance, may desire to show that they are animal lovers and participate in chat rooms dedicated to pets or display pictures of their pets. Others may wish to show that they are open about their past and discuss alcoholic episodes. Still others may wish to demonstrate their intellectual

impression management A component of Walther's social information processing theory; the unconscious or strategic effort to influence another's perceptions.

Salesperson

In his blog, Kyle Porter, the CEO of SalesLoft, succinctly notes, "No longer is 'just winging it' sufficient for the sales professional" (Porter, 2013). Porter illuminates a number of different skills necessary to become a competent salesperson, many of which underscore the importance and the interplay of perception and the self. Furthermore, he notes that "sales professionals must combat their limited time and reduced influence by honing in on the fundamentals." What are those fundamentals? He identifies several. A person's "attitude" is essential in that "the ability to bounce back from rejection" is critical in order to keep moving forward. The customer's "preferred choice of digital medium" is also pivotal. Being digitally savvy and perceiving which social media is preferred by a customer assists a salesperson tremendously. A third fundamental is the ability to handle a customer's objections. Perceiving which objections are critical and manageable and which are secondary or impossible to address "separates the weak from the strongest of professionals." Porter's recommendations align with identity management, whereby a salesperson knows how to handle him- or herself in various circumstances. Sometimes, a sale is quick; other times, it can linger. Porter is underscoring the need for sales professionals to take into consideration time, timing, people, and personal competency as these experts ascertain their next strategic move.

curiosity by quoting philosophers or providing links to published works. Clearly, there is a strategic effort to present one's self online and individuals are tacitly aware of these efforts.

Finally, three selves exist in online environments: the **actual self** (attributes of an individual), the **ideal self** (attributes an individual ideally possesses), and the **ought self** (attributes the individual should possess) (Gibbs, Ellison, & Heino, 2006). These various selves are frequently employed strategically, and they are often managed online in real time (while someone is communicating with the other). Furthermore, we gather and accrue the impressions we receive from online presentations, providing a more comprehensive understanding of our online partners.

---

actual self Attributes of an individual.

ideal self Attributes an individual ideally possesses.

ought self Attributes an individual should possess.

By now, you should have a clear idea about the importance of perception and the self in communicating with others. How can you work toward checking your perceptions so that you don't make erroneous assumptions about others or their behavior? What can you do to improve your self-concept? How do our perceptions and self-concepts function in our interpersonal communication? Let's look at a number of skills to consider as you respond to these questions.

3-6 SKILL SET: IMPROVING PERCEPTION CHECKING AND SELF-CONCEPT

When we check our perceptions, we attempt to rid ourselves of our predisposed biases and images of people. Checking our perceptions also helps build meaning in our relationships. Let's examine the skill set related to perception checking.

3-6a Understand Your Personal Worldview

Each of us enters a communication situation with a unique **worldview**, a personal frame for viewing life and life's events. Your worldview is your conception and perception of the environment around you—both near and far. Your worldview differs from that of your classmate. You may believe that humans are basically good creatures, while your classmate may have a more cynical view of humanity, citing war, famine, and greed. We all enter interpersonal encounters with various worldviews, and we need to recognize the influence that these views have on our communication.

3-6b Realize the Incompleteness of Perception

There is no possible way for us to perceive our environment completely. By its nature, perception is an incomplete process. When we attend to certain aspects of our surroundings, as you learned earlier, we necessarily fail to attend to something else. If you are working on a group project and think a group member is lazy, you should check your perception further. Perhaps there is some other issue, such as working a late-night job or caring for a sick relative, that is contributing to the group member's behavior. And don't forget that people, objects, and situations change, thereby making it important to update your perceptions periodically.

3-6c Seek Explanation and Clarification

We need to double-check with others to make sure that we are accurately perceiving a person, situation, or event. Seeking explanation and clarification requires us to foster a dialogue with others. Trying to understand whether your perceptions are accurate communicates to others that you are eager to gain an accurate understanding, which will help you achieve meaning in interpersonal exchanges.

Consider the following encounter between Wes and Lee. The two have been happily dating for a month, but their 15-year age difference has prompted Wes to reconsider his future with Lee. Wes calls Lee at 10 p.m. to let her know that they had better stop dating. Lee is puzzled by the call because the last time the two were together, three nights earlier, Wes talked about how much he enjoyed being with her. Lee wonders how things could have changed so quickly. Immediately, Lee feels defensive and thinks that Wes is breaking up with her because he is critical of her manner of communicating. She knows she criticizes a lot, and her previous boyfriends didn't like that. She doesn't realize that their age difference is really what is troubling Wes.

Most likely, Lee could have avoided her feelings of confusion, frustration, and anger if she had sought out clarification and explanation of Wes's perceptions. If she had, they could have arrived at a more amicable end to their relationship or perhaps even reconciled.

3-6d Distinguish Facts from Inferences

One way to explain and to clarify is to distinguish facts from inferences. **Facts** are statements based on observations; **inferences** are personal interpretations of facts. Looking at the tense lips and angry look on a woman at the baggage claim at an airport may prompt you to draw the conclusion that she is unhappy that the airline lost her luggage. But this is your inference, not a fact.

During the perception process, we need to be careful not to confuse facts and inferences. Remember implicit personality theory, which we explained earlier? Take extra care and avoid filling in the blanks or extending a perception beyond the facts. At the very least, recognize when you are using an inference.

3-6e Be Patient and Tolerant

We cannot overemphasize the importance of being patient and tolerant in your perceptions. Because we live in an "instant society," we expect things to happen quickly. However, you can't expect to develop quality communication skills overnight; they take time and practice to learn. The effort is worth it, because without patience and tolerance, you won't be able to check the accuracy of your perceptions.

When you improve your sense of self, you are on your way toward increasing your self-awareness and enhancing your self-esteem. In turn, your relationships improve. In this section, we explore five skills necessary to improve your self-concept.

3-6f Have the Desire and Will to Change

As we mentioned earlier in the chapter, our self-concept changes as we grow. Therefore, we should be willing

worldview A unique personal frame for viewing life and life's events.

fact A piece of information that is verifiable by direct observation.

inference A conclusion derived from a fact, but it does not reflect direct observation or experience.

to change our self-concepts throughout our lifetimes. If you want to be more sensitive to others, make that commitment. If you'd like to be more assertive, take the initiative to change. Having the desire or will to change your self-concept is not always easy. We grow comfortable with ourselves even when we recognize ways we'd like to change. We need to realize that a changing self-concept can help us grow just as much as it can help our relationships grow.

3-6g Decide What You Would Like to Change

After you establish a will to change, describe what it is specifically about yourself that needs to change. In addition, describe why you feel a change may be needed. Are others telling you to change? If so, why are they suggesting that? Are their concerns legitimate, or are you uncritically accepting their judgments?

3-6h Set Reasonable Personal Goals

Always strive to have reasonable goals and avoid setting goals that are impossible to meet. Otherwise, you may feel a sense of failure. A reasonable goal for a college student might be to do all the assigned reading in each class for a semester. Studying hard, reading and rereading the classroom readings and textbook, participating in class when appropriate, and being a good listener seem like reasonable and attainable goals. Setting a goal of getting a perfect grade point average, writing error-free

Brad Wrobleski/Masterfile

Our self-concept often changes as we grow older. Sometimes we want to change the way we see ourselves but we're not sure we can. By taking a calculated risk, you may find that the way you see yourself—and, in turn, the way you see others—can change dramatically.

papers, and understanding the course content without asking questions seems unreasonable. And don't expect to be someone you are not. Avoid societal expectations of perfection. Look beyond the superficial expectations that we find in the media.

3-6i Review and Revise

At times, you may make changes to your self-concept that are not entirely beneficial. Think about the implication of these changes and consider revising them if necessary. For instance, you may have tried to be more accommodating to your family members, but the result was that your integrity was trampled. Perhaps you made some changes at work, trying to engage people who annoy you daily, and now you're having trouble getting your work finished on time because these people stop to talk throughout the day. Perhaps some of your past behaviors now need to be refreshed.

Consider Hillary, who, at age 18, described herself as a "really boring person." To bolster her self-esteem and to assert her independence, Hillary decided to get a tattoo, much to the surprise and shock of her parents. As an 18-year-old, she felt that she was an adult and didn't have to abide by her parents' rules. Now, as a 30-year-old, Hillary is rethinking her image-boosting behavior. She thinks that the tattoo, located on her right forearm, communicates an image that is contrary to the one she wants to convey as a middle school teacher. Now, it seems, demonstrating independence is not as important to her self-concept as it used to be.

Occasions in which you revise past changes may force you to think about whether changes to your self-concept were justified in the first place or whether they are appropriate for you now. For Hillary, her reflections on whether or not the tattoo was important at age 18 no doubt occupy her mind from time to time. At age 30, she probably regrets being so impulsive in her behavior without thinking about the consequences.

3-6j Surround Yourself with "Relational Uppers"

Think, for a moment, about the amount of stress in your life right now. You may be working full-time, raising children, taking a full course load, coping with a health issue, feeling overwhelmed by bills, or having a hard time with a particular course. Now think about hanging around people who do nothing but tell you that you need to change. Or consider interpersonal relationships with people who constantly tell you that you are deficient in one way or another. We believe that you need to avoid these types of people in favor of **relational uppers**, those people who support and trust you as you improve your self-concept. Take care to surround yourself with relational uppers, because these individuals will be instrumental for you to achieve your potential.

relational uppers People who support and trust us as we improve our self-concept.

STUDY TOOLS

DON'T FORGET TO CHECK OUT COURSEMATE AT WWW.CENGAGEBRAIN.COM!

CHAPTER 3 FEATURES THE FOLLOWING RESOURCES:

☐ Ethics & Choice: Karena and Nick

☐ Communication Assessment Test: Self-Monitoring Scale

☐ Interactive Activities

4 | Communicating Verbally

LEARNING OUTCOMES

4-1 Describe the attributes of verbal symbols and explain their relationship to language and meaning

4-2 Identify how factors such as culture, gender, generation, and context affect verbal symbols

4-3 Explain the ways in which verbal symbols may be used destructively and constructively

4-4 Demonstrate skill and sensitivity in using verbal communication

After you finish this chapter, go to **PAGE 87** for **STUDY TOOLS.**

THEORY/MODEL PREVIEW

Triangle of Meaning, Framing Theory; Symbolic Interaction, Linguistic Determinism/Relativity, Two-Culture Theory; Muted Group Theory

Humans depend on verbal symbols for interpersonal communication for two major reasons. First of all, verbal language *connects us to others.*

Language is instrumental in both initiating social relationships (e.g., see research on flirting—Weber, Goodboy, & Cayanus, 2010) and maintaining them (e.g., see research on sibling relationships—Myers, Byrnes, Frisby, & Mansson, 2011). It isn't an overstatement to say that interpersonal relationships are constructed and reconstructed in conversation (Duck, 2007; Duck & McMahan, 2011). When we think about our friendships or our work and family relationships, we recall things we have said to one another. These conversations may have made us laugh, cry, or left us feeling happy, frustrated, or some mix of emotions. However we have felt, talk has created the fabric of our relational lives. When Tommy tells Pat he loves her or when Alissa talks to her mother about a problem she's having with her roommate on campus, they are using words to establish and reestablish that a relationship exists between them.

Furthermore, verbal language *differentiates members of an in-group from those of an out-group.* Some researchers (Dunbar, 1998) argue that this was a large part of the reason humans developed verbal language systems. In an example of this important aspect of language, a reader wrote to the *New York Times* blog about gay/straight etiquette, "Civil Behavior," asking why it's okay for gay men to refer to other gay men as "girl" or "Mary" but not okay for a straight man to do so. In his response, Steven Petrow (2013) wrote the following:

Words like "Mary," "girl" and even that commonly used B-word are sometimes used as terms of endearment

© Instudio 68/Shutterstock.com

among gay men, notably those of our generation. Even so, it *does* matter whether you're gay or not—a straight man who calls a gay one "Mary" is on thin ice. [emphasis added]

Petrow quoted some responses to his post on Facebook about this topic, one of which observed that people who belong to a group can "re-appropriate" a slur term, invest it with a more positive meaning, and use the term without penalty, but that people outside the group cannot do the same. Petrow notes that the Food Network star Paula Deen's admission of her use of the N-word in the past caused her problems (including the loss of her job at the Food Network) for just this reason: she was not a member of the group, and thus couldn't "re-appropriate" the word and use it without negative repercussions.

One way that people accomplish both connection to and differentiation from others is through code switching. **Code switching** involves the ability to speak in a way that connects us to a certain group and then to switch and connect to a different group with a different type of language. NPR correspondent Gene Demby (2013) talks about how people move relatively easily from speaking to their boss in proper English with jargon appropriate to their workplace, to speaking in slang to their friends after work. Demby's blog contains a humorous example of code switching by the comedy duo Key and Peele (npr.org).

Despite their importance to us, the verbal and nonverbal systems we use to interact with others are imprecise and can sometimes have dramatic (even if unintended) effects. Misunderstandings, misinterpretations, and inaccuracies often result from our necessary dependence on these symbol systems. In this chapter, we will discuss verbal symbols and describe their unique attributes. Although we have separated our presentation of verbal and nonverbal message systems into two chapters, it's important to remember that they are inextricably intertwined,

> **code switching** Shifting back and forth between languages, sometimes in the same conversation or in different situations.

Young adults are masters of language that assigns in-group and out-of group status.

and it's very often the interplay between them that makes meaning. When Jorge tells his sister, Amelia, that he hates her with a laugh and a friendly push on her shoulder, Amelia knows to interpret the words differently than she would if Jorge scowled and turned his back on her.

4-1 UNDERSTANDING VERBAL SYMBOLS

To begin our discussion, we need to distinguish among the related terms *language*, *verbal symbols*, and *grammar*. **Language** is the overall system consisting of both verbal symbols and grammar enabling us to engage in meaning making with others. **Verbal symbols** are the words or the vocabulary that make up a language. **Grammar** refers to a set of rules dictating how words can be combined to make a meaningful message.

Verbal symbols are important to a language system, but they must be accompanied by grammatical rules telling us how to use them. If a man walked up to you and said, "Look on sky balloon is hanging," you would assume

language A system comprised of vocabulary and rules of grammar that allows us to engage in verbal communication.

verbal symbols Words or vocabulary that make up a language.

grammar The rules that dictate the structure of language.

encoding The process of putting thoughts and feelings into verbal symbols, nonverbal messages, or both.

decoding The process of developing thought based on hearing verbal symbols, observing nonverbal messages, or both.

he was not a native English speaker or that something was wrong with him. The words in the sentence are all recognizable as part of the English vocabulary, but their arrangement does not follow any rules for a sentence in English. The processes of **encoding**, or putting our thoughts into meaningful language, and **decoding**, or developing a thought based on hearing language, require that those involved in the conversation possess a shared vocabulary and understanding of the rules of grammar.

Discussion of the rules of grammar is beyond the scope of this book. However, we do want to turn our attention to verbal symbols, which form the building blocks of interpersonal communication. Verbal symbols have five specific attributes: they are symbolic, their meanings evolve, they are powerful, their meanings are denotative and connotative, and they vary in levels of abstraction. These five attributes help us understand how verbal symbols are used in interpersonal communication.

4-1a Words Are Symbolic

Symbols are arbitrary, mutually agreed-on labels or representations for feelings, concepts, objects, or events. Because words are arbitrary symbols, there is not a direct relationship between the word and the thing. For instance, the letters *c-a-t* form an agreed-on symbol for the actual furry animal English speakers call a cat. The Spanish word *gato* and the German word *katze* are equally arbitrary symbols used to represent the same animal. Figure 4.1 illustrates this concept by graphically

FIGURE 4.1   THE TRIANGLE OF MEANING

thing

thought
(furry feline house pet)

word
(cat)

representing the thought, the thing, and the word that stands for the thing on the three points of the triangle of meaning, a theory also referred to as the semantic triangle (Ogden & Richards, 1923). This illustration shows that the word is *not* the thing but merely a symbol we have agreed to use to stand for it. By agreeing on symbols, we can engage in communication with one another about things.

Usually, a group of speakers (or a culture) records their agreement about the meaning of words in a dictionary. However, a dictionary is not static because language and the verbal symbols that constitute it keep changing over time.

4-1b Words Evolve Over Time

As time passes, some words become out of date and aren't used any longer. For example, the words *petticoat*, *girdle*, *dowry*, and *typewriter* are becoming obsolete and disappearing from our vocabulary. Some expressions that were popular in earlier times simply aren't used now, illustrating that language is susceptible to fads and fashion. If you are younger than 80 years old, you probably have never used the phrase *the bee's knees*, 1920s slang that meant something was wonderful or "hot." In the 1950s and 1960s, it was common for people to say "toodle-loo" instead of "good-bye"; and when couples wanted to go find a romantic spot, they'd tell others that they were "going to the submarine races" although there was no evidence of any water nearby! Some researchers talk of words and phrases as having "careers," in the course of which their meaning may undergo dramatic changes (Bowdle & Gentner, 2005).

Sometimes words experience a revival after they had been popular during an earlier era. For example, the word *groovy* was popular in the 1960s, fell out of favor for a while, and then became trendy again in the late 1990s with the release of the Austin Powers movies. *Groovy's* revival didn't last long among the larger population, but smaller segments of society still use the word frequently.

Often our vocabulary changes as a result of social changes. For example, contemporary speakers generally favor the words *African American* and *Latino/a* over the words *Negro* and *Hispanic*. These sorts of language changes might be ridiculed as political correctness and thought of as an overconcern for how things are said. But confusing political correctness with important language reform is a mistake. Changing language to give people respect and to be accurate is a goal that shouldn't be trivialized. Furthermore, using language that is appropriate to a culture's evolution strengthens a person's credibility.

For instance, the words *colored*, *Negro*, *Afro-American*, *African American*, and *person of color* reflect changes in the position of black people in the United States. The words are not synonyms but actually have different meanings, according to some researchers (McGlone, Beck, & Pfiester, 2006). *African American* communicates an emphasis on ethnicity rather than race, and *person of color* is more positive than *nonwhite*.

Similarly, as we mentioned in Chapter 2, the words used to describe people with disabilities have evolved. For example, when Dale tells his parents about his friend Abby, who uses a wheelchair because she has muscular dystrophy, he calls her a *person with a disability*. He doesn't use the word *handicapped* or *crippled* because language reform has helped him see people in wheelchairs as people first, not as their disabilities. He knows Abby as a great friend with a biting sense of humor who happens to use a wheelchair to get around.

Additionally, we've observed an evolution in verbal symbols around issues of gender identity. The website for GLAAD (Gay & Lesbian Alliance Against Defamation; www.glaad.org) includes guidance for journalists in using the most currently acceptable terminology for writing about transgender people. For instance, the site offers the following advice about terms that are problematic and terms that are preferred by members of the transgender community:

Problematic: "sex change," "pre-operative," "post-operative"

Preferred: "transition"

Referring to a sex change operation, or using terms such as pre- or post-operative, inaccurately suggests that one must have surgery in order to transition. Avoid overemphasizing surgery when discussing transgender people or the process of transition. (GLAAD, 2013)

Verbal symbols continue to evolve, and their meanings change. For instance, the words *calling card* used to mean an engraved card that you left at the home of someone whom you had just visited. Today, we still use the term *calling card*, but now it refers to prepaid cards for making phone calls. Similarly, the word *gay* used to refer to being happy and lighthearted, as in "we'll have a gay old time." Today, *gay* is a sexual identity. Incidentally, the term *gay* was chosen intentionally by people in gay communities because of the positive associations it carried from its former meaning.

In addition, people coin new terms or create new meanings for existing words—such *defriend*, *epic*, *fiscal cliff*, and *flash mob*, to name a few—that give labels to recent innovations and capture current experiences. As Paul McFedries (2004) observes, "When there's a new invention, service, trend or idea, we need a new way to describe these things. The emerging vocabulary becomes a mirror to the culture" (p. 12). This is the case because vocabularies tend to reflect the current times. The third edition of the *Oxford English Dictionary* (OED) (2013) contains many new words (e.g., *buzzworthy*) as well as revisions to older words (e.g., the use of *it* to mean "fashionable"), reflecting the impact of popular culture on vocabulary and usage.

Each year the researchers and editors of the OED choose a "word of the year" that best reflects the mood of the times. In 2013, the word chosen was *selfie*, the self-portraits people snap with their smartphones. *Selfie* won the word of 2013 title over several competitors including "'twerk,' the sexually provocative dance move . . . 'showrooming,' the practice of visiting a shop to look at a product before buying it online at a lower price; . . . 'Bitcoin,' the digital currency that gained widespread media attention . . . [and] 'binge-watch,' a verb that describes watching many episodes of a TV show in rapid succession" (Hui, 2013). *Selfie* has been added to the online version of the OED and is being considered for addition to the more conservative print version.

4-1c Words Are Powerful

Certain words have the power to affect people dramatically. As we've said previously, words are arbitrary symbols, so their power is not intrinsic; it derives from our having agreed to give them power. And, as we've mentioned, these agreements change over time. For example, in the 17th century, the word *blackguard* was a potent insult, but that's no longer the case today. Other words, however (such as *ass*) have taken on power they didn't have in the 17th century (Duck, 2007).

People have made many words powerful. For instance, in March 2010, activists gathered in Massachusetts to protest the derogatory use of the word *retard* in everyday speech. According to protestors, elimination of the term from common parlance would promote tolerance for and inclusion of those with intellectual disabilities. Said Craig Smith, founder of the equal rights group Massachusetts Advocates Standing Strong (MASS), "When that word's used, it's a sign of ignorance. That's the bottom line. We can change people's way of thinking" (*Boston Herald*, 2010). This case points to the power that some gave the term *retard*.

The power of words in the English language is further illustrated by a study examining how the phrase "think positive" affected breast cancer patients (Kitzinger, 2000). The study found that in general, that phrase sent a message that if you don't get better after being diagnosed with breast cancer, it's because you're not being positive enough. This phrase, then, had a great deal of power, often making patients feel inadequate or responsible for their own illness.

In another example of how much power people give words, both conservative and liberal groups have requested that certain (different) words be banned from student textbooks (Ravitch, 2003). Words such as *devil*, *dogma*, and *cult*, and words that make comparisons, such as *economically disadvantaged*, have all been considered dangerous, and various groups have asked to ban them. The fact that people label a word as taboo indicates that they think it is highly charged and powerful.

After a word becomes taboo, it often becomes even more powerful. For instance, Robin's daughter Kate was 10 years old before she knew that all families didn't ban the word *fat*. Robin had struggled with her weight all her life and was very sensitive about her body. As a result, the family never used the word *fat*, and it became a very powerful word in their house. While visiting a friend, Kate was surprised when she heard the family joking around about gaining weight and calling each other fat. Even though her friend's family found it acceptable to use the word *fat*, Kate still couldn't bring herself to use the forbidden word.

4-1d Meanings for Verbal Symbols May Be Denotative or Connotative

Denotative meaning refers to the literal, conventional meaning that most people in a culture have agreed is the meaning of a symbol. Denotation is the type of meaning

denotative meaning The literal, conventional meaning that most people in a culture have agreed upon.

found in a dictionary definition. For instance, Merriam-Webster Online (2013) defines the word *gun* as follows:

GUN:

1. a: *a piece of ordnance usually with high muzzle velocity and comparatively flat trajectory*

  b: *a portable firearm (as a rifle or handgun)*

  c: *a device that throws a projectile*

2. a: *a discharge of a gun especially as a salute or signal*

  b: *a signal marking a beginning or ending*

3. a: *Hunter*

  b: *Gunman*

4. *something suggesting a gun in shape or function*

5. *throttle*

These definitions form the denotative meaning of the word *gun*. Denotative meanings can be confusing; because the dictionary provides more than one meaning for *gun*, a listener hearing someone use the word, *gun*, must decide if the speaker is using definition 1a, 1b, 1c, 2a, 2b, and so forth.

The connotative meaning of a term can be even more confusing because the meaning varies from person to person. **Connotative meanings** derive from people's personal and subjective experience with a verbal symbol. For example, someone who had a close friend or relative shot to death would have a different emotional or connotative meaning for *gun* than would a hunter or a police officer. Although all of these people would be aware of the denotative meanings of *gun*, their definition of the word would be colored by their personal connotative meanings.

4-1e Words Vary in Level of Abstraction

Words fit on a continuum from concrete to abstract. If a word is **concrete**, you are able to detect its **referent** (the thing the word represents) with one of your senses. Stated another way, concrete words are those that you can see, smell, taste, touch, or hear. The more a word restricts the number of possible referents, the more concrete the word is. For instance, if Sara has 15 relatives but only 3 brothers, then *brother* is a more specific, concrete term than *relative*, and *Scott* (the name of one of Sara's brothers) is more specific than either of the two other terms. The word *relative* is the term with the fewest restrictions, so it is the most abstract. We can envision a ladder of abstraction (see Figure 4.2) that begins with the most concrete symbol for a referent and moves to the most abstract.

FIGURE 4.2 THE LADDER OF ABSTRACTION

Abstract

sounds

music

punk music

punk music popular in the 1980s

music The Clash recorded

"Rock the Casbah"

Concrete

Some referents are naturally somewhat **abstract**. Ideas such as *love* and *justice* do not have terms that correspond to the lower rungs of the ladder of abstraction. Language skills allow us to talk about the concepts involved in abstract terms. For example, when we speak about *justice*, we use other abstract terms, such as *fairness*, to get our message across. To make our ideas more concrete so others can better understand our meaning, we often use figures of speech such as metaphors and similes. Metaphors equate two terms—for example, "*Love* is a *roller-coaster ride*." Similes make comparisons using the word *like* or *as*—for example, "*Justice* is like *redistributing portions of a pie*."

Although they do not provide perfect descriptions, figures of speech can be beautiful, allowing language to soar to poetic heights and enabling us to see something in a new way. Yet, it is also true that some metaphors are used so often that they become "frozen" or "conventional" and we don't even recognize that they are metaphoric ("my mood is down") (Sopory, 2006).

Sometimes the comparisons provided by metaphors and similes don't help us understand meaning

connotative meaning The meaning of a verbal symbol that is derived from our personal and subjective experience with that symbol.

concrete Able to be seen, smelled, tasted, touched, or heard.

referent The thing a verbal symbol represents.

abstract Not able to be seen, smelled, tasted, touched or heard.

better but, rather, mislead us (Geary, 2011), allowing us to believe that two things are alike when, in fact, they are not. For instance, Campbell (2013) points out that the commonly used comparison between the plethora of images that people are subjected to in modern society and a flood is misleading. Campbell argues that the natural image of a flood (over which people have little to no control) obscures the fact that people *can* exert conscious control over what images to view. As another example, political speech commonly attempts to guide listeners to conclusions that are favorable to the speaker, and it may use metaphoric language to do so. Siner (2013) observed that President Obama introduced the possibility of problems with the Affordable Care Act website (HealthCare.gov) in 2013 by using the word "glitch." Siner quotes an October 1, 2013, speech by Obama where he said, "Now, like every new law, every new product rollout, there are going to be some glitches in the sign-up process along the way that we will fix. I've been saying this from the start." As Siner points out, glitches usually connote small, easily fixable problems, and people are used to experiencing them while working with computers. However, she also observes that the more extreme problems with HealthCare.gov, and the attendant political fall-out surrounding it, may actually end up changing the meaning of *glitch* rather than the other way around.

One theory about how figures of speech affect us is **framing theory** (Lakoff, 2003; Lecheler & DeVreese, 2012). Framing theory argues that when we compare two unlike things in a figure of speech, we are unconsciously influenced by the comparison. In a way, the figure of speech creates a frame through which we view the terms. For example, comparing differences between men and women to war (i.e., the "battle of the sexes") focuses our thinking on oppositions and a basic animosity between the sexes. We don't consciously reflect on this—the metaphor just leads us to make this association. Imagine how our thinking might differ if we instead used the lens of diversity to frame our discussions of gender rather than the lens of battle (DeFrancisco & Palczewski, 2014).

When referents are not right in front of us, we can visualize them through the **process of abstraction** (the ability to move up and down the ladder of abstraction from specific to general and vice versa). For instance, let's say that Jay wants to tell his friends about his fabulous new red Ford Mustang GT. As he uses descriptors to talk about his car in its absence, his friends are able to imagine it pretty clearly. Later, Jay sees a friend, Lois, who just totaled her car. Jay decides to tell Lois about his new car, but he uses words that are less concrete, leaving out the brand name and color so that Lois won't feel too bad about losing her car when Jay has such a great one.

Because words vary in their level of abstraction, meaning is often ambiguous. This ambiguity may be unintentional or strategic. For instance, if Jane lacks the verbal skills of clarity and the ability to fit her vocabulary to her audience, her communication may seem vague, even though she doesn't intend it to be. However, sometimes it may serve a purpose to be ambiguous. Researchers have described this phenomenon in two ways: strategic ambiguity and equivocation.

Strategic ambiguity refers to how people talk when they do not want others to completely understand their intentions (Carmon, 2014; Eisenberg, 1984). In organizations, people (especially at the management level) may leave out cues on purpose to encourage multiple interpretations by others. It's possible that ambiguity helps people deal with tensions in an organization. To promote harmony, leaders of organizations may have to be ambiguous enough to allow for many interpretations while simultaneously encouraging agreement

framing theory A theory arguing that when we compare two unlike things in a figure of speech, we are unconsciously influenced by the comparison—it acts like a frame to filter our thinking.

process of abstraction The ability to move up and down the ladder of abstraction from specific to general and vice versa.

strategic ambiguity Leaving out cues in a message on purpose to encourage multiple interpretations by others.

© iStock.com/HelpingHandPhotos

(Eisenberg, 1984). This strategy can also be used by a person in a conflict. Saying something like "That's an interesting idea" is ambiguous enough that it might end the argument.

Equivocation is a type of ambiguity that involves choosing your words carefully to give a listener a false impression without actually lying. If your grandmother sends you a birthday gift that you don't like, but you value your relationship with your grandmother and don't want to hurt her feelings, you might equivocate in your thanks. You might say, "Thank you so much for the sweater, Grandma. It was so thoughtful of you to think about keeping me warm in the cold winters!" You have not said the sweater was attractive, nor have you said you liked it, so you haven't lied overtly. However, if you are a good equivocator, you have given your grandmother the impression that you are really pleased with a sweater that you, in fact, dislike. Keep in mind that such a tactic could have long-term consequences. In this case, you could receive similar unwanted sweaters for several birthdays to come.

Equivocating involves saying things that are true but misleading. It should be no surprise that the language of advertising makes use of equivocation. When an ad says that a car's seats "have the look and feel of fine leather," that means that they are *not* made of fine leather, but the use of the words *fine leather* leads an unsuspecting listener to think that they are. In addition, the word *virtually* is a good equivocal word. The phrase *virtually spotless* means that the described item has some spots on it, but the phrase leads you to believe otherwise.

Sometimes *euphemisms* are a kind of equivocal speech. **Euphemisms** are milder or less direct words substituted for other words that are more blunt or negative. They are used to reduce the discomfort related to an unpleasant or sensitive subject. For example, we say we're going to the *restroom* even though we're not planning to rest, we refer to a person's *passing* rather than their death, or we talk about *adult entertainment* rather than pornography.

 ## 4-2 FACTORS AFFECTING VERBAL SYMBOLS

We understand and use words differently depending on a variety of factors. In this section, we discuss the relationships between verbal symbols and culture and ethnicity, gender, generation, and context. Although we discuss these factors in isolation, they can form many

Idioms have understood meanings within a culture but exact translations don't always make sense.

combinations. For example, an elderly African American man living in the United States talking to his granddaughter at home uses verbal symbols quite differently than a young Asian woman living in South Korea speaking to a group of business associates at their company's annual meeting.

4-2a Culture and Ethnicity

On the most basic level, culture affects verbal symbols (and vice versa) because most cultures develop their own language. Thus, people of Kenya tend to speak Swahili, and those living in Poland usually speak Polish. This section addresses some of the many other ways that culture and ethnicity relate to language.

Let's first look at idioms. An **idiom** is a word or a phrase that has an understood meaning within a culture, but that meaning doesn't come from exact translation. People who are learning a language have to learn the meaning of each idiom as a complete unit; they cannot simply translate each of the words and put their meanings together. For example, in English we say "it

equivocation A type of ambiguity that involves choosing our words carefully to give a listener a false impression without actually lying.

euphemism A milder or less direct word substituted for another word that is more blunt or negative.

idiom A word or a phrase that has an understood meaning within a culture but whose meaning is not derived by exact translation.

was a breeze" when we mean that something was easy. If someone tried to translate "it was a breeze" without knowing it functions as an idiom, they would mistake the statement's meaning. However, a listener also has to pay attention to context. If "it was a breeze" is the response to the question "What messed up all the papers I had laid out under the window?" English speakers know not to access the statement's idiomatic meaning but rather to rely on the meaning of each word.

In another example, Madeline works for the International Student Center at Western State University, and she hears some of the international students complaining that U.S. students are unfriendly. When Madeline asks why they feel this way, they tell the following story: A group of American and international students were seated together in the Student Union. When they parted company, the U.S. students said, "See you later," but made no attempt to do so later on. The international students believed that the U.S. students failed to keep their promise for future interactions. Madeline explained to the international students that "see you later" is an example of a particular type of idiom called *phatic communication*. **Phatic communication** consists of words and phrases that are used for interpersonal contact only and are not meant to be translated directly word for word. This type of communication can be thought of as content-free because listeners are not supposed to think about the literal meaning of the statement; rather, they are expected to respond to the polite contact the speaker is making. When you see someone and say, "Hi, how are you doing?" you probably don't really want to know the details about how the other person is doing—you're just making contact. "How's it going?" or "How're you doing?" should elicit a response such as "Okay—how about you?" If you said, "How's it going?" as you walked by your acquaintance Katy, and she grabbed your arm and started to tell you about her recent breakup or the big fight she had with her brother, you would likely be surprised and might think that Katy was odd.

Next we'll discuss some verbal behaviors thought to characterize two specific ethnic groups: African Americans and Mexican Americans. There are many other groups we could examine, but these two are the most studied in terms of the effects of ethnicity on language. Although the findings do not apply to every member of these two groups, African Americans and Mexican

Americans are often considered distinct language groups. Both groups tend to spend a great deal of time with their own members in social and neighborhood settings, and most people in both groups identify with race as a way of establishing personal identity (Johnson, 2000).

AFRICAN AMERICAN SPEECH

Some research suggests that African American speech is more assertive than European American speech (Craig & Grogger, 2012; Ribeau, Baldwin, & Hecht, 2000). According to this research, in a conversation between Renée, an African American, and Lee, a European American, Lee might say, "Is everything okay between us?" and Renée might respond "You know what's wrong—just say it." African Americans and European Americans may truly differ in how assertive their speech is, or this finding may be complicated by perceptions. One study found that African American women think European American women are highly conflict avoidant. European American women reported their belief that African American women are assertive and confrontational. However, neither group of women characterized themselves as highly avoidant or confrontational (Shuter & Turner, 1997).

Black speech is also seen as vibrant and enduring (Alim, 2012; Smitherman, 2000). Black speech has had a long evolution, and many of its words and phrases have found their way into the vocabulary of white speakers. For example, when white speakers say "Back in the day" or "She thinks she's all that" or use words like *hip*, *phat*, or *testify*, they owe a debt to African American speakers. In addition to being rooted in tradition, black speech is often humorous, witty, and wise (Powers, 2013).

The Linguistic Society of America issued a resolution making this same assertion. They passed this resolution in support of the Oakland, California, school board's decision to recognize Black English (variously known as African American Vernacular English [AAVE] or Ebonics). The Linguistic Society stated:

> The systematic and expressive nature of the grammar and pronunciation patterns of the African American vernacular has been established by numerous scientific studies over the past thirty years. Characterizations of Ebonics as "slang," "mutant," "lazy," "defective," "ungrammatical," or "broken English" are incorrect and demeaning. (Linguistics Society of America, 1997)

CHICANO ENGLISH

Chicano English, spoken by Mexican Americans, is also frequently studied by researchers. Mexican Americans form only a part of the Latino/a culture. This culture includes Cubans, Puerto Ricans, Chileans, Peruvians, Columbians, and many more. It is difficult to generalize

phatic communication Communication consisting of words and phrases that are used for interpersonal contact only and are not meant to be translated verbatim.

TABLE 4.1   THE LANGUAGE OF A PARTICULAR SPEECH COMMUNITY: PRISON VOCABULARY

Birds on the line	A warning that someone is listening to the conversation
Bling bling	A warning that officers are coming
Bonaroo	A prisoner's best clothes
Buck Rogers time	A parole date so far in the future that the prisoner can't imagine being released
Cat nap	A short sentence
Escape dust	Fog
T-Jones	A prisoner's mother

© Cengage Learning®

about all Latino/as, but national, ancestral, and language ties seem to be important to Latinos/as, and "the Spanish language also functions to create and cement cultural unity" (Johnson, 2000, p. 167).

Mexican Americans, like other Latino/as, exhibit great variety in terms of their bilingualism (Vallejo, 2012). Some Mexican Americans speak English or Spanish exclusively, others speak Spanish in private and English in public, whereas still others engage in code switching, shifting back and forth between languages, sometimes in the same conversation. When Luís says to José, "Yo no le creí, you know" ("I didn't believe him, you know") (Silva-Corvalán, 1994), he demonstrates code switching by saying the statement in Spanish and ending with the slang English phrase "you know," as an English speaker would.

On a broader level, remember that culture pertains to more than just national origin. Cultures or co-cultures can form around people who share certain things in common, such as religious beliefs or professional experiences. People become **speech communities** when they share norms about how to speak; what words to use; and when, where, and why to speak (Labov, 1972). In this way, a speech community resembles a national or ethnic culture. One example of a unique speech community is people who are incarcerated. Prison vocabulary is rich and quite different from the English spoken by those outside prison walls. In fact, a San Diego consulting firm that prepares convicts to serve their sentences has compiled a dictionary to acculturate future prisoners to prison culture (Rough Guide, 2007). See Table 4.1 for examples of prison vocabulary.

Symbolic interaction theory (SI) explains how words relate to culture (Blumer, 1969; Mead, 1934). SI says that cultures are held together by their common use of symbols and that things do not exist in an objective form; they exist based on cultural agreement about them. In short, "all the 'things' that make up our world, including ourselves, are products of symbolic actions,

constituted and created through the communication process" (Trenholm, 1986, p. 37). Symbolic interactionism, then, points us to an understanding of how culture or society is tied to words.

Another framework that links culture and verbal symbols is the **Sapir-Whorf hypothesis**, a theory put forth simultaneously by anthropologists Benjamin Whorf and Edward Sapir (Hoijer, 1994; Worf, 1956). In its most extreme version, the Sapir-Whorf hypothesis argues that words determine our ability to perceive and think. In this form, the theory is known as **linguistic determinism**.

Both Whorf and Sapir believed that culture affects our thinking through the vehicle of language. Researchers have suggested that without a word for something in the environment, a person has difficulty perceiving that thing or thinking that it is important. For example, the radio show, Radiolab (2012), discussed the relationship between a culture's language and people's ability to perceive (or pay attention to) colors. They referred to Jules Davidoff's research testing the Himba, an indigenous people living in Northern Nambia. The Himba have no separate word in their language for blue, and when Davidoff presented research participants with four

speech community A group of people who share norms about how to speak; what words to use; and when, where, and why to speak.

symbolic interaction theory The theory that our understanding of ourselves and of the world is shaped by our interactions with those around us.

Sapir-Whorf hypothesis A theory that points to connections among culture, language, and thought. In its strong form, this theory is known as linguistic determinism, and in its weak form, it is known as linguistic relativity.

linguistic determinism A theory arguing that our language determines our ability to perceive and think about things. If we don't have a word for something in our language, this theory predicts that we won't think about it or notice it.

cards, three colored green and one colored blue, the participants were not able to tell what made the cards different. It took them a long time, and some help to "see" that one of the cards was a different color from the others (Guy, 2012).

The principle that language determines what you perceive and think about is apparent in the comments of Elizabeth Seay (2004), who studied Native American languages in Oklahoma:

> Learning new languages can bring unnoticed ideas into focus. The Comanches have a word for the bump on the back of the neck which is thought to be a place where the body is centered. The Muscogee-Creeks single out the particular kind of love that children and their parents and grandparents feel for each other, using a word that also means "to be stingy." (p. 17)

These examples, along with many others (such as the fact that the Chinese have no word for *privacy*) support the idea that language determines how we think and that speakers of different languages perceive the world in different ways. However, not all researchers agree with linguistic determinism. Even Benjamin Whorf wondered if linguistic determinism might be overstating the case. He devised another theory, **linguistic relativity** (Whorf, 1956), which states that language influences our thinking but doesn't determine it.

Even though compelling examples illustrate both linguistic determinism and linguistic relativity, empirical evidence hasn't completely supported the theories' assertions. One of the most famous examples illustrating the Sapir-Whorf hypothesis (the example of the number of words the Inuit have for snow) has been called into question. The Inuit example states that they have many words for *snow* because it is so crucial to their everyday lives. In addition, supposedly the Inuit actually see snow differently from others whose lives are not as dependent on snow. Whereas English speakers simply see monolithic white "stuff," due to having only one word, *snow*, the Inuit see all the varieties their language allows. Whorf didn't specify how many Inuit words for *snow* exist; some say about two dozen, but the numbers vary. The *New York Times* once mentioned that there were 100, although this example has been shown to be inaccurate (Pullum, 1991). Although the Inuit do use many different terms for snow, other languages allow their speakers to perceive the same variety through phrases and modifiers (*fluffy*, *slushy*, *good packing*, and so forth).

The Arabic language doesn't have a single word for *compromise*, which some have said is the reason that Arabs seem to be unable to reach a compromise. Yet, the Arabic language does provide several ways to articulate the concept of compromise, the most common being an expression that translates in English to "we reached a middle ground" (Nunberg, 2003). This example illustrates **codability**, which refers to the ease with which a language can express a thought. When a language has a convenient word for a concept, that concept is said to have high codability. Thus, the existence of the word *compromise* gives that idea high codability in English. When a concept requires more than a single word for its expression, it possesses lower codability. It is accurate, then, to say that the idea of compromise has lower codability in Arabic than in English. However, having a phrase rather than a single word to express an idea does not mean that the idea is nonexistent in a given culture, only that it is less easily put into the language code (Nunberg, 2003). Thus, we can see that even linguistic relativity has to be modified somewhat because of humans' capacity to create words and add descriptors to existing words. Still, the basic premise of the Sapir-Whorf hypothesis, that the words people use have an impact on how they perceive and process the world, has resonance for us. For instance, some evidence suggests that bilingual speakers thought differently when they spoke in different languages (Barner, Inagaki, & Li, 2009).

linguistic relativity A theory stating that language influences our thinking but doesn't determine it. Thus, if we don't have a word for something in our language, this theory predicts that it will be difficult, but not impossible, to think about it or notice it.

codability The ease with which a language can express a thought.

THEORY SPOTLIGHT:

Linguistic Determinism/Relativity

Which version of the theory do you think has the most value to you in explaining verbal symbol use in IPC: linguistic determinism or linguistic relativity? Explain your answer by giving an example. Can you think of a concept that you've experienced for which we do not have a specific term in the English language? If you can, how do you express that experience and what does that tell you about the theory?

Cultures dictate attitudes toward verbal symbols as well as certain language practices. For example, in the United States, speech functions primarily as a vehicle for expressing one's ideas clearly and forcefully. The Chinese have the attitude that actions are more powerful than words, exemplified in proverbs such as "Talk does not cook rice." Other language traditions include the following:

▶ In the Lakota tradition, it is sacrilegious to say the name of a dead person in public.

▶ Jewish people believe that children should not be named for any living person.

▶ The Japanese avoid saying words in wedding toasts that refer to home or going back home.

▶ In traditional Native American communities, silence is an important way to communicate respect.

▶ In England, death is supposed to be ignored and not spoken about, even to express condolences.

4-2b Sex and Gender

The impact of sex and gender on language and verbal symbols has been studied extensively. However, despite decades of research examining and comparing men and women's communication behaviors, we still don't have definitive information. Early research held that women and men spoke very differently. Women were seen as using a different vocabulary from men that included, among other things, more words for colors (e.g., *mauve*), more polite words and phrases (e.g., "Would you please open the door?" rather than "Open the door"), and more modifiers (e.g., *very* and *so*) (Lakoff, 1975).

Some researchers have theorized that children play in sex-segregated groups (Pelligrini, 2010) and that the different ways of interacting within the groups result in different speech behaviors (Maltz & Borker, 1982). In studies by Maltz and Borker, little girls tended to play in small groups to which it was difficult to gain entry; however, after a girl was accepted in the group, it was

easy for her to speak up and be heard. Furthermore, the preferred play activities for girls were creative interactions like house and school, which involve the players in setting the rules. In contrast, little boys played in large groups to which it was easy to gain access but difficult to be heard. These boys played baseball, war, and soccer, which have set rules. Thus, whereas girls learned negotiation and cooperation, boys learned assertive communication behaviors and that little talk is necessary for play.

This belief that sex operates in the same way as culture in establishing different rules, norms, and language patterns for men and women came to be known as the **two-culture theory** (Maltz & Borker, 1982). This theory was grounded in the notion that "differences in men's and women's language use reflects [sic] different experiences, different worlds" (Mulac, Bradac, & Gibbons, 2001, p. 121). Much of Deborah Tannen's (e.g., 2001) writing comparing women's and men's language use stems from the two-culture theory. For instance, she argues that women prefer "rapport" talk, or talking for pleasure, while men prefer "report" talk, or talk that accomplishes a task.

Although some research in the last two decades has supported the idea that men and women speak differently in the ways described above (e.g., Coates & Cameron, 1989; Mulac et al., 2001; Treichler & Kramarae, 1983; Wood, 1998), other studies (e.g., Canary & Hause, 1993; Goldsmith & Fulfs, 1999; Turner, Dindia, & Pearson, 1995) question whether women and men actually differ much in their speech. For example, in an analysis of more than 1,200 research studies, researchers found that the differences in communication behavior attributable to sex totaled only around 1 percent (Canary & Hause, 1993).

Do women and men really communicate differently? That question is difficult to answer. However, keep in mind that sex makes a big difference in U.S. society. People in the United States consistently remark on sex even when sex distinctions aren't important to the situation. For example, a grade school teacher commands, "Quiet, boys and girls!" rather than "Quiet, students!" or "Quiet, children!" Similarly, a performer's usual greeting to the audience is "Good evening, ladies and gentlemen." Given this interest in dividing people based on sex, the fact that some sense of language community based on sex arises in the United States is not surprising. Perhaps more tellingly, men and women's language use is perceived differently even when it's essentially the same (DeFrancisco & Palczewski, 2014; Kirtley & Weaver, 1999). Despite the weaknesses of the two-culture approach, sex continues to be a factor that affects

© Olesya Feketa/Shutterstock.com

two-culture theory A theory asserting that sex operates in the same way as culture in establishing different rules, norms, and language patterns for men and women.

© Blend Images/Shutterstock.com

expectations for how people use verbal symbols, which in turn impacts how people are heard and understood.

4-2c Generation

As we discussed earlier in this chapter, one of the functions of language is differentiating in-group members from those on the outside. One of the tasks of each generation is to distinguish itself from the generation that came before it. Generational differences form age cohorts that, to some extent, share experiences and beliefs. The members of any age cohort—for example, Gen Y, the Baby Boomers, Millennials, or the Greatest Generation—share a popular culture, which leads to a common language. Slang such as *cheaters* (eyeglasses), *gams* (a woman's legs), *none of your beeswax* (none of your business), and *hitting on all sixes* (giving 100 percent effort) peppered the talk of youth in the 1920s and 1930s but is rarely, if ever, heard today.

Technological changes may affect language across generations as well. Lytle (2011) reports that students use language forms from social media (such as LOL, laugh out loud; IDK, I don't know; SMH, shaking my head; and BTW, by the way) in their high school assignments. Lytle notes that teachers are uncomfortable with the situation, but their discomfort varies by age. Many of the older teachers simply do not understand what their students are submitting. The younger teachers understand the "text speak" but they are concerned about what they see as a dramatic decline in students' writing abilities. Lytle states that when college admission officers receive applications that are written like texts, they tend to toss them immediately.

Email addresses may also indicate age differences. Many young people opt for creative email names like Venus-chick, Juliaiscoolia, and so forth. However, what seems cool to a 16-year-old can seem embarrassing a few years later, especially as colleges use emailed applications. One young woman, whose email name is "artzyfartzygirl," said that she plans to change the name when she sends emails for college applications so admission committees don't get the wrong idea about her (Sweeney, 2004). A study reported by Jeanna Bryner (2007) on MSNBC.com showed that young people recognize that some email names are unprofessional. Two hundred college students rated actual email names on various criteria, including professionalism. Names deemed unprofessional included gigglez217, bacardigirl, bighotdaddy, and drunkensquirl.

On the other hand, Baby Boomers who are becoming grandparents wish for younger-sounding names for their grandchildren to call them (Matchen, 2009). The consensus of the grandparents was that "Grandma" or "Grandpa" sounds too old. They want names such as Nanno, Gigi, Granmissy, Bubbles, Mimi, and Pops. Baby Boomers becoming grandparents believe they have a different type of relationship with their grandchildren than their grandparents had with them and these less conventional names reflect that connected, hip relationship. Furthermore, Baby Boomers generally don't think of themselves as old, so they invent new names to avoid the connotations of the "blue-haired old granny stereotype" that come with the name "Grandma." Matchen also points out that changing demographics mean that more children have living great-grandparents, and perhaps Baby Boomers wish to have different names to distinguish themselves from the older generation.

4-2d Context

Contextual cues subsume all the other elements we have discussed because the culture, ethnicity, gender, and generation of the people who are interacting factor into the context. Generally, in communication research, the context involves the setting or situation in which the encounter takes place. Thus, as we discussed in Chapter 1, *context* means all of the elements surrounding the people who are interacting. Here, we briefly address situation, time, relationship, and nonverbal contextual cues. You can understand the impact of situation if you think

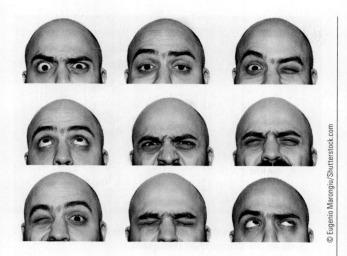

of the same statement, "You have good legs," being said in each of the following situations:

▶ By construction workers to a woman walking by a construction site

▶ By a coach to an athlete running on a track

▶ By a doctor to a child in the doctor's office

Although the words remain the same, each of these situations would create a different sense of the meaning of the statement.

As we discussed previously in this chapter, the meanings of words can change over time. In the 1940s and 1950s, females over the age of 18 referred to themselves as *girls* without a negative connotation. In the 1970s, some feminists rejected the word *girl* as demeaning when applied to adult females. In the 1990s and more recently, some feminists have reclaimed that word and use the term *girrl power* with positive connotations. However, many women in their 40s and 50s still reject the term *girl* and do not use it or like to hear it, retaining negative connotations for it.

Relationships between speakers also contribute to the contextual cues that affect meaning. People who are close to you can say things that would be considered impolite if said by mere acquaintances. Teasing, joking, use of swear words, and various forms of humor known as "loving abuse" depend on a strong prior relationship between the speakers. If the relationship isn't positive, these types of interactions would probably be judged as insulting rather than friendly. Of course, even among good friends or family members, people can go too far, and a comment that was intended to be humorous can be interpreted as insulting.

Rhunette Diggs and Kathleen Clark (2002) discuss how racial considerations can complicate a comment meant to be a joke between friends. Diggs and Clark write an account of their own interracial friendship, begun in graduate school and sustained over several years after graduation. At a birthday party for Diggs, Clark, who was the only white person present, made a joke about Diggs being obedient. Although Clark meant it as a humorous jibe between friends, Diggs framed the comment as problematic, in large part because of the interracial context. Diggs saw the comment as giving her outsider status, being labeled by a white person.

As we discuss in Chapter 5, people depend on nonverbal cues to interpret verbal codes. If someone comments that you look nice, you probably check their tone and facial expressions to confirm that their verbal comment is sincere. If the speaker sounds sarcastic in tone, you will undoubtedly believe that you don't look good in their eyes. The nonverbal part of the context is powerful and persuasive in helping people make sense of verbal codes.

In sum, when we communicate, we are doing much more than exchanging words. The verbal symbols we use are powerful, ever-evolving abstractions that have both denotative and connotative meanings. They are affected by culture, gender, generation, and context. You have seen that the meaning of a statement often goes beyond the simple definitions of each word. We will now address how verbal symbols operate destructively and constructively in interpersonal communication.

4-3 THE DESTRUCTIVE AND CONSTRUCTIVE SIDES OF VERBAL SYMBOLS

Verbal symbols are not inherently positive or negative. Rather, the value of verbal symbols is determined by how people use them. Verbal symbols in the English language may be easily used for negative ends; they may be exclusionary and derisive, enable verbal abuse, provide inaccurate impressions, mislead listeners, and promote stereotypes. However, they may also be used to support, to include others, and to connect in positive ways with others.

4-3a The Destructive Side of Verbal Symbols

Here we discuss four processes: static evaluation, polarization, reification, and muting that illustrate ways words can be inaccurate, misleading, and unhelpful. We then discuss sexist, racist, and homophobic language, all of which reveal the very negative side of verbal symbols.

STATIC EVALUATION
Verbal symbols reflect **static evaluation** when they conceal change. When we speak and respond to people

> **static evaluation** The tendency to speak and respond to someone today the same way we did in the past, not recognizing that people and relationships change over time.

today the same way we did 10 years ago, we engage in static evaluation. To a degree, we need to think that people and things are stable. If we recognized that everything is in a constant state of flux, it would be difficult to talk or think because we would be paralyzed by the notion of how little control we have. However, if we ignore change, we cause other problems. And words contribute to these problems because labels aren't always updated to indicate the changes that take place over time.

For instance, *Mom* is what you call your female parent regardless of whether you are 4, 18, or 40 years old. However, your relationship with your mother, as well as you and your mother herself, all change greatly over time. The word *Mom* doesn't help us to see these changes, and, in fact, it tends to obscure them. When parents say to their children, "No matter how old you get, you will always be my little baby," they are naming the very problem that exists with static evaluation.

POLARIZATION

Polarization occurs when people utilize the either/or aspect of the English language and use words that cast topics in extremes. When we refer to people as smart *or* dumb, nice *or* mean, right *or* wrong, we are polarizing. Polarization is troubling because most people, things, and events fall somewhere between the extremes named by polar opposites. Most people are good some of the time and bad some of the time. Labeling them as one or the other fails to recognize their totality. For example, when Kayla tells her friend Marsha about her professor, Dr. Lee, she focuses on how much she dislikes Lee. Kayla says, "He is such a sarcastic jerk! I cannot stand his class. All he ever does is make fun of students. He doesn't even realize how many stupid things he says!" Although Kayla is entitled to her opinion of Dr. Lee as a poor teacher, her use of such words as *jerk* and *stupid* is polarizing.

Polarization is also problematic because of static evaluation. If we settle on an extreme label for someone at one time and then encounter the same person later, we will probably not take into account the possibility that the person may have changed over time. For example, let's say that Christie briefly dated Rick in high school when they

Symbols such as flags are potent, but they are not the same as the things they represent.

© ArtisticPhoto/Shutterstock.com

were both juniors, but she broke it off because she thought he was too immature. Two years later, they meet at a party in college. Christie remembers Rick from high school and immediately thinks of the polarizing term *immature*. Keeping this word in her mind will hinder Christie's ability to see Rick's changes and interact with him appropriately. Polarization also causes communication problems because of reification, which we address next.

REIFICATION

Reification is the tendency to respond to words, or labels for things, rather than the things themselves. Thus, if we call someone by an extreme label, reification suggests that is how we will respond to them, regardless of what they might do. Reification is often referred to as confusing the symbol and the thing. When people have a strong reaction to a symbol such as a national flag or a school mascot, they are fusing the symbol (flag or mascot) with the thing itself (their country or their school). Although symbols are potent, they are not the same as the things they represent. People who cut up the U.S. flag or burn it may be as patriotic as those who fly the flag in front of their home each day.

MUTING

Verbal symbols fail users by letting some experiences and ideas go unnamed, creating what theorists call **lexical gaps**. Lexical gaps indicate that language does not serve all its users equally. The **muted group theory** (Kramarae, 1981) explains what happens to people whose experiences are not well represented by the verbal symbols in their language. The theory states that if some groups of people have a lot of unnamed experiences (or lexical gaps), they'll have trouble articulating their thoughts and feelings, will seem awkward, and may be regarded as too silent or too talkative. They may also feel that something must be wrong with them because their language doesn't give them an adequate vocabulary for their unique

polarization The tendency to use "either/or" language and speak of the world in extremes.

reification The tendency to respond to words, or labels for things, as though they were the things themselves.

lexical gaps Experiences that are not named.

muted group theory Theory that explains what happens to people whose experiences are not well represented in verbal symbols and who have trouble articulating their thoughts and feelings verbally because their language doesn't give them an adequate vocabulary.

Britt Peterson (2013) writes in the *Boston Globe* about the influence that baseball has had on the English language spoken in the United States. Peterson observes that "baseball lingo is more than a way to talk about what happens on the field. The sport has had an outsize influence on everyday English." Peterson argues that baseball has had an impact on how we talk about race and gender, as well as how we use metaphors, and give people nicknames, among other linguistic practices. For example, Peterson notes that during the government shutdown in 2013, legislators and the media used language drawing from "America's preferred metaphor for nearly everything under the sun: baseball." Peterson quotes Senator Charles Schumer as exhorting House Speaker John Boehner to "Just step up to the plate and do it," and comments that the Huffington Post accused the White House and Senate Democrats of "refusing to play ball" when the House sent back amended spending bills.

© iStock.com/Diane39

experiences. For example, Mary wants to talk about how her boyfriend uses flattery to manipulate her into doing more of the housework than he does. She is troubled when he says things like, "Oh, you're so much better at cooking, cleaning, and so forth, than I am—can't you just do it?" Yet, when Mary tries to describe this experience, she has to tell a long story because she can't find a single word that pinpoints exactly what he's doing (Kramarae, 1981).

Additionally, the theory suggests that groups are muted when language draws more on others' experiences than their own. Some researchers say that expressions from sports ("hit it out of the park") and war ("he attacked all his opponents' ideas") show that English is shaped more by the experiences of men than women (DeFrancisco & Palczewski, 2014; Johnson, 2000).

Other researchers suggest that African Americans (Orbe, 1998) and fathers (Chopra, 2001) are also muted by the English language. For instance, African Americans can be muted when language labels their experiences and behaviors in pejorative ways. When black speakers are said to be "aggressive" or "confrontational," they are being judged by white standards. Furthermore, when Black English is marginalized and considered substandard, black speakers are muted. When parenting is assumed to be mainly a woman's experience and the words *parent* and *mother* are used interchangeably, fathers are muted.

Language is flexible, and people can come up with new words that fill lexical gaps. As we've discussed, people invent words all the time. However, gaining acceptance of new words isn't always easy. For example, feminists point to the trouble they have had getting people to use *Ms.* instead of *Miss* and *Mrs.*

SEXIST LANGUAGE

Sexist language refers to language that is demeaning to one sex. Most of the research has examined how language can be detrimental to women. Some researchers assert that the fact that English uses the generic *he* is an example of sexism in language. The **generic *he*** refers to the rule in English grammar, dating from 1553, that requires the masculine pronoun *he* to function generically when the subject of the sentence is of unknown gender, or includes both men and women. For instance, in the following sentence, *his* would be the correct word to fill in the blanks using the generic *he* rule: "A person should do ___ homework to succeed in ___ classes." Researchers have argued that this rule excludes women because *he* isn't truly generic; rather, it conjures up images of male people (Gastil, 1990; Ivy, Bullis-Moore, Norvell, Backlund, & Javidi, 1995; Martyna, 1978).

sexist language Language that is demeaning to one sex.

generic *he* The use of the masculine pronoun *he* to function generically when the subject of the sentence is of unknown gender or includes both men and women.

TABLE 4.2 ELIMINATING SEXISM IN LANGUAGE

Sexist Language	Nonsexist Alternative
The scholar opened his book.	The scholar opened a book.
The pioneers headed West with their women and children.	The pioneer families headed West.
You're needed to man the table.	You're needed to staff the table.
Beth was salesman of the month.	Beth was the top seller this month.
Playing computer games cost the company a lot of man-hours.	Playing computer games cost the company a lot of productive time.
Manhole cover	Sewer access cover
Freshman	First-year student
Postman	Letter carrier
A person needs his sleep.	People need their sleep.
Mankind	Humankind, humanity

© Cengage Learning®

Another example of language that some people think is sexist is **man-linked words**. These words—such as *chairman*, *salesman*, *repairman*, *mailman*, and *mankind*—include *man* but are supposed to operate generically to include women as well. Man-linked expressions such as *manning the phones* and *manned space flight* are also problematic. In addition, the practice of referring to a group of women and men as *guys*, as in "Hey, you guys, let's go to the movies," reinforces sexism in language. Relatively easy alternatives to these exclusionary verbal symbols are becoming more commonplace (Earp, 2012), and we may be on our way to seeing much less of this type of sexism in language (see Table 4.2).

Other examples of sexism in language include the practice of women taking their husband's surname after marriage, the wealth of negative terms for women, and the lack of parallel terms for the sexes. When a woman marries, she attains the honorific *Mrs*. Yet, *Mrs*. has no

man-linked words Words that include the word *man* but are supposed to operate generically to include women as well, such as *mankind*.

male counterpart; men remain *Mr*. regardless of marital status. In addition, referring to a married woman by her formal married name (e.g., Mrs. John Jones) obscures her identity under that of her husband.

Some researchers have pointed to the fact that there are more derogatory terms for women than there are for men. See how many negative terms you can think of that label women (i.e., *slut*, *bitch*, etc.) and then do the same for men. Your first list is probably longer. Researchers have also noted that parallel terms for men and women are not, in actuality, parallel (Pearson, West, & Turner, 1995). As Table 4.3 illustrates, many of the feminine words exist only to mark the person as a female. Language offers opportunities to "gender-tag human referents more or less automatically, that is, without stopping to consider how such usages reinforce the importance of gender-categorization" (Stringer & Hopper, 1998, p. 218). This is known as *semantic derogation*, or the use of one term (for males) with a positive connotation and its supposed parallel term (for females) with a negative connotation (e.g., *master* and *mistress*).

RACIST LANGUAGE

The feminist movement has sensitized us to sexism in language, but we have to remain alert to language that systematically offends one group, including racist language (language that demeans those of a particular ethnicity). In the 21st century, most people avoid overt racial slurs, but language can be racist in other, more subtle ways. The practice of associating negativity with black ("blackmail," "the bad guys wear black hats," "you're the black sheep of the family") perpetuates racial stereotypes on a subtle level. When Miranda, a white woman, met Lyle,

TABLE 4.3 "PARALLEL" TERMS FOR WOMEN AND MEN

Female	Male	Female	Male
mistress, stewardess	*master, steward*	*majorette, waitress*	*major, waiter*
governess, actress	*governor, actor*	*comedienne, hostess*	*comedian, host*
spinster, slut	*bachelor, stud*	*songstress, sculptress*	*singer, sculptor*

© Cengage Learning®

a black man, she hadn't known too many black people before. She tried to speak in a way that wouldn't offend him. It didn't even occur to her that Lyle would find her use of the terms *dark side* and *blackball* troubling. Some researchers argue that racism comes from being taught language that reflects a thought system that values one race over another. For example, when whites are taught from a Eurocentric perspective and don't learn anything about African or Asian history or accomplishments, racism flourishes (Asante, 1998).

HOMOPHOBIC LANGUAGE

When the actor Alec Baldwin used a word perceived as a slur to gay men in an altercation with a photographer in 2013, MSNBC suspended his new talk show *Up Late*, and Baldwin received a great deal of negative press. Baldwin apologized and acknowledged the power of language to wound others, saying, "I did not intend to hurt or offend anyone with my choice of words, but clearly I have—and for that I am deeply sorry. Words are important. I understand that, and will choose mine with great care going forward" (quoted in Carter, 2013).

While Baldwin's case was high profile, it certainly wasn't an isolated incident of homophobic language use. A 2003 national study of 9th- to 12th-grade students across the United States (reported in Snorton, 2004) found that 66 percent of students report using homophobic language, such as "that's so gay" to describe something that is wrong, bad, or stupid, and 81 percent report hearing homophobic language in their schools frequently or often. The survey found that four out of five lesbian, gay, bisexual, and transgender students reported hearing homophobic remarks often in their school. Furthermore, over 80 percent of the time, faculty or staff did not intervene when such language was used. In 2013, the television show *Big Brother* was criticized repeatedly for the homophobic language used by some of the contestants (Boyle, 2013), as well as racist and sexist words some of them used.

4-3b The Constructive Side of Verbal Codes

Although verbal symbols can cause the problems we just discussed, verbal communication (coupled with nonverbal communication) is our only means to connect with others. Through language, we can express confirmation, or the acknowledgment, validation, and support of another person (Schrodt, Ledbetter, & Ohrt, 2007). Through the use of **confirmation**, we can build supportive relationships with others. Confirming messages help another person understand that you are

paying attention to him or her and that you recognize that person as an equal. You don't have to agree with someone to confirm him or her—you simply have to express that you are hearing that person and paying attention. For example, when Maddy listens intently to her sister, Charlene, complain about their mother, she confirms that she cares enough about Charlene to pay attention. Even though Maddy doesn't agree with Charlene (Maddy has a positive relationship with their mother), Charlene feels confirmed. There's some evidence that when parents confirm their children, it improves the children's mental health outcomes (Schrodt et al., 2007). In contrast, **disconfirmation** occurs when someone feels ignored and disregarded. Disconfirmation makes people feel that you don't see them—that they are unimportant. See Table 4.4 for examples of confirming and disconfirming responses to others.

We can also use language to develop inclusion rather than exclusion. Using the language of inclusion means that you are thoughtful and attentive to when others seem to be offended and that you ask what in your language might have given offense. Although we might accidentally exclude someone from time to time, through careful

TABLE 4.4	DISCONFIRMING AND CONFIRMING COMMUNICATION
Disconfirming	**Confirming**
Ignoring	Attending
Silence	Appropriate talk
"You don't matter to me."	"You matter to me."
"You're on your own."	"We're in this together."
"You shouldn't feel that way."	"I hear how you feel."

© Cengage Learning®

confirmation A response that acknowledges and supports another.

disconfirmation A response that fails to acknowledge and support another, leaving the person feeling ignored and disregarded.

language use we can build supportive relationships. In addition, as we discuss in Chapter 6, we can use empathic language to connect with others. When we try to understand another's feelings, we show we care enough about that person to spend time and energy listening, and we can establish genuine relationships.

Verbal codes also help us solve problems. When we use open-ended questions (e.g., "What do you think is wrong?" or "How would you like me to respond to you?"), we can work toward problem solving in our interpersonal relationships. Verbal symbols help us explain our position while conveying that we're also interested in the other person's position.

4-4 SKILL SET FOR IMPROVING VERBAL COMMUNICATION

To improve your verbal communication skills, we suggest cultivating an attitude of respect for others. To do so, you need to engage in **perspective taking**, which means acknowledging the viewpoints of those with whom you interact. For example, if you talk frequently with a friend who is a different ethnicity than you, perspective taking requires you to understand that ethnicity matters, and that your friend will have somewhat different experiences from yours as a result.

Marsha Houston (2004), a communication studies scholar who is African American, writes that she doesn't like it when white women friends try to empathize with

perspective taking Acknowledging the viewpoints of those with whom we interact.

her by saying that they know exactly how she feels about racism because they have experienced sexism (or some other "ism"). Houston says that it erases her experience to state that your experience is just like it. Listening to others before assuming that you already know exactly what their experience is will help you in perspective taking.

In addition to developing respect for others and working on perspective taking, you can practice four skills to help you be more effective in using verbal symbols: owning and using I-messages, understanding the ladder of abstraction, indexing, and probing the middle ground.

4-4a Owning and Using I-Messages

Each of us must take responsibility for our own behaviors and feelings in communication with others. *Owning* refers to our ability to take responsibility for our own thoughts and feelings, and is often accomplished through I-messages. *I-messages* acknowledge our own position, whereas *you-messages* direct responsibility onto others, often in a blaming fashion. For example, if you are bored during a lecture, you could communicate this to the professor with a you-message ("Your lecture is boring") or an I-message ("I'm having trouble getting involved in this material"). I-messages help prevent defensiveness in the listener because they focus on the speaker's feelings and actions. See Table 4.5 for more examples of how to change you-messages to I-messages.

4-4b Understanding the Ladder of Abstraction

Earlier in the chapter, we mentioned that you engage in the process of abstraction by using words at different levels on the ladder of abstraction. For example: *vehicle, car, black 2014 Chevy Cruze*. The first term allows the listener to imagine a wide range of vehicles, the second term narrows the field somewhat, and the third restricts the referent much more. The more abstract you are, the more you allow a listener to interpret what you mean. The more concrete you are, the more you direct the listener to your precise meaning.

Being skillful in this area requires you to diagnose when a situation needs specificity and when general information might suffice. A simple guideline suggests that the better you know someone, the less concrete you have to be. For example, when two people have a developed relationship, they may understand each other without providing a concrete description. So, when Tom tells Martha that he wants to spend some time relaxing, she knows

TABLE 4.5	YOU-MESSAGES AND I-MESSAGES
You-Messages	**I-Messages**
You are insensitive.	I need you to pay attention to me.
You make me mad.	I get angry when you ignore me.
You don't understand anything.	I don't feel understood when you interrupt me.
You never listen to me.	I want you to put down the paper when I talk to you.
You are so rude.	I was hurt when you said you thought my hair looked bad.
You're a liar.	I need to be able to trust you, and I feel betrayed because you didn't tell me the truth about the car accident.

© Cengage Learning®

Verbal Clarity in the Restaurant Business

The restaurant business is a fast-paced, customer-oriented business. There is no time for confusion about what wait staff or management need to say. It is critical for restaurant employees to overcome challenges to effective verbal communication. Jackie Lohrey (2014) observes that poor communication practices can lead to errors in ordering, and will result in dissatisfied customers who may never return to your restaurant. Wait staff are encouraged to understand cooking jargon, and be able to translate it for customers in terms they will easily grasp. Clarity and being concrete are valued skills for restaurant employees. Managers should set

© iStock.com/Brian McEntire

guidelines for clear, effective verbal communication to ensure that the restaurant workers operate as a team, and the restaurant runs smoothly.

from her 5 years of experience with him that he means he wants to go into his workshop and would appreciate not being disturbed. Tom doesn't need to tell Martha concretely what the abstract term *relaxing* means to him at this point in their relationship. However, when Tom is at work and tells a new coworker that they need to get a project finished as soon as possible, he probably should specify that *as soon as possible*, in this case, means by the end of the week. Otherwise, the coworker could spend eight hours working to finish the project, only to discover that Tom didn't need the project finished that soon.

4-4c Indexing

A way to avoid static evaluation, one of the problems we mentioned earlier, involves dating your statements to indicate that you are aware something may have changed (Korzybski, 1958). **Indexing** requires that you acknowledge the time frame of your judgments of others and yourself. For example, if Alex notes that Rucha is self-centered, he would index that by saying, "Yesterday, when she wouldn't stop talking about herself, Rucha acted so self-centered." Indexing reminds us that the way people act at one given time may not be the way they are for all time.

4-4d Probing the Middle Ground

Probing the middle ground is a skill that helps you avoid polarization in your verbal communication. When you are tempted to label something with an extreme judgment, try to explore the shades of gray that might be more descriptive of the behavior. For instance, if you

think someone is against you, try to discover the places where you agree so you can see that the person disagrees with you on some things but not on all things. If you are tempted to label someone as irresponsible, try to discover the areas where the person has acted responsibly so you can see that he or she is not completely at one extreme on the responsibility scale. Thinking about the middle ground will help restrain you from polarizing or using extreme labels that can easily become inflammatory.

indexing Avoiding generalizations by acknowledging the time frame in which we judge others and ourselves.

STUDY TOOLS

DON'T FORGET TO CHECK OUT COURSEMATE AT WWW.CENGAGEBRAIN.COM!

CHAPTER 4 FEATURES THE FOLLOWING RESOURCES:

☐ Ethics & Choice: Trivializing Culture

☐ Communication Assessment Test: Vocabulary Test

☐ Interactive Activities

5 | Communicating Nonverbally

After you finish this chapter, go to **PAGE 109** for **STUDY TOOLS.**

LEARNING OUTCOMES

5-1 Identify the primary principles of nonverbal communication

5-2 Explain and exemplify the types of nonverbal communication

5-3 Articulate the relationship between nonverbal communication and culture

5-4 Identify the relationship between nonverbal communication and technology

5-5 Apply a variety of strategies to improve skills in nonverbal communication

THEORY/MODEL PREVIEW

Interaction Adaption Theory; Expectancy Violations Theory; Social Information Processing Theory

We all communicate without saying a word, and we all "speak" without talking.

Nonverbal communication has been called the "unspoken dialogue" (Burgoon, Buller, & Woodall, 1996), and scholars have noted its importance in conversations. Some researchers report that around 65 percent of overall message meaning is conveyed nonverbally (Moore, Hickson, & Stacks, 2009) (see Figure 5.1), while others report up to 97 percent of emotional meaning in a face-to-face conversation is conveyed nonverbally (Mehrabian & Ferris, 1967). From a historical perspective, employing nonverbal communication to understand others is a practice that has been with us since ancient China and India. David Matsumoto, Mark Frank, and Hui Sung Wang (2012) reveal that over thousands of years, the Chinese have relied on the nose, eyes, and chin, for instance, to judge another's character. In India, it has been customary, since 1000 B.C., to detect a liar by looking at whether the person is dragging a big toe on the ground and/or avoiding eye contact.

When we attend to nonverbal behaviors, we draw conclusions about others, and others simultaneously draw conclusions about us. This process is part of the transactional nature of communication we discussed in Chapter 1. The influence of nonverbal behavior on our perceptions, conversations, and relationships cannot be overstated. Although we are unaware of our use of nonverbal communication, it is always present in our interactions with others and remains a critical part of how we achieve interpersonal meaning.

This chapter explores nonverbal communication and its value in our lives. We focus our discussion on

FIGURE 5.1 COMMUNICATION OF INTERPERSONAL MEANING

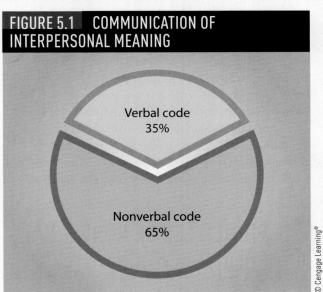

Verbal code
35%

Nonverbal code
65%

© Cengage Learning®

how nonverbal behavior functions, both directly and indirectly, in our daily activities. Before we move on in our discussion about nonverbal communication,

let's spend a few moments interpreting it. **Nonverbal communication** encompasses all behaviors—other than spoken words—that communicate messages and have shared meaning between people. To this end, we can define nonverbal communication as a process of sending and receiving nonlinguistic cues. This interpretation has three associated parameters. First, electronic communication is not included in our definition. Second, when we note that there is "shared meaning," we are saying that a national culture agrees on how to construe a behavior. For example, in many co-cultures in the United States, when a parent sees a child do something unsafe, the parent might wag his or her index finger. The child must know the meaning behind this nonverbal shaming technique to respond to the parent's reprimand. Third, as we mentioned in Chapter 4, verbal and nonverbal

nonverbal communication All behaviors—other than spoken words—that communicate messages and that have shared meaning between people.

" Say what's on your mind, Harris—the language of dance has always eluded me. "

communication usually work together to create meaning, although there are clear distinctions between the two (Table 5.1).

Nonverbal communication is central to our relational lives. Howard Giles and Beth Le Poire (2006) illustrate that the way people communicate nonverbally influences (1) how relationships are established,

interaction adaptation theory A theory that suggests individuals simultaneously adapt their communication behavior to the communication behavior of others.

TABLE 5.1   DIFFERENCES BETWEEN VERBAL AND NONVERBAL COMMUNICATION

Verbal Communication	Nonverbal Communication
Single channel (words)	Multichanneled
Intermittent	Continuous
Significantly shaped by culture	Significantly shaped by biology
Can be clear or ambiguous	Inherently ambiguous
Normally content centered	Normally relational
Mostly strategic and voluntary	Frequently involuntary
Subject to verification	Instinctively credible

Adapted from Andersen, P. (2008). Nonverbal communication: Forms and functions. Long Grove, IL: Waveland.

maintained, and dissolved; (2) the diagnosis of health-related problems such as autism; (3) the number of sexual partners a person has; (4) how babies show emotional distress; (5) marital satisfaction and stability; and (6) perceptions of beauty. These reasons are just a snapshot of why the area of nonverbal communication is valued and essential to discuss in a book on interpersonal communication.

Nonverbal communication competence requires us to be able to encode and decode nonverbal messages (Burgoon & Hoobler, 2002). We also have to use nonverbal communication ourselves to get across our meaning. Being able to adapt to people around you is a hallmark of a competent nonverbal communicator. **Interaction adaptation theory** suggests that individuals simultaneously adapt their communication behavior to the communication behavior of others (Burgoon, Stern, & Dillman, 2007; Hubbard, 2009; Kennedy-Lightsey & Dillow, 2011). The better we are able to adapt, the better we are able to understand the meaning of a message. Suppose, for example, that Rosa and her roommate, Nadine, are in a noisy place talking about the problems related to how clean their dorm room is. Nadine is practicing interaction adaptation if, when Rosa leans forward to talk about the topic, Nadine simultaneously leans forward to listen to the story. This "postural echo" suggests that Nadine is not only mirroring Rosa's behavior but also trying to understand Rosa's meaning.

With our definition of nonverbal communication established, we're now ready to explore some of the principles of nonverbal communication before moving on to discuss nonverbal communication codes and culture.

5-1 PRINCIPLES OF NONVERBAL COMMUNICATION

Although it is often overlooked or downplayed, nonverbal communication is a vital aspect of interpersonal communication. Consider the times when we don't say a word but manage to "say" so much. Imagine hugging a close friend at her father's funeral. Or, think about holding hands with your partner during a romantic movie. In these situations, nonverbal communication is likely more powerful than any words you could say.

As we relate the following information, we are mindful of the many challenges and difficulties related to communicating nonverbally. Several learning, psychological, and physical disabilities, for instance, frequently prevent meaning from being achieved. An individual with Asperger syndrome, in particular, may experience challenges in meaning making since this autistic disorder usually results in people having a hard time communicating without words. In addition, we acknowledge that many people who have various physical challenges, including vision impairment, for example, may find the nonverbal communication process disquieting.

We also need to recall the uniqueness of the intersection of nonverbal communication and technology. In Chapter 4 and throughout this book, we discuss the role that both verbal and nonverbal cues play in online relationships. As we review the following material with you, although most of the research in nonverbal communication has failed to address the nonverbal communication–technology association, we will include this critical topic when appropriate. With this in mind, we now explore four principles of this type of communication.

5-1a Nonverbal Communication Is Often Ambiguous

One reason nonverbal communication is so challenging in our relationships is that our nonverbal messages often mean different things to different people, which can lead to misunderstandings. Compared to verbal messages, nonverbal messages are usually more ambiguous. For example, suppose that Lena prolongs her eye contact with Jason and, in turn, Jason refocuses on Lena. While Lena may be showing some attraction to Jason, he may be returning the eye contact because he believes that something is wrong. Clearly, the same nonverbal behavior (eye contact) can elicit two different meanings.

Mark Knapp, Judith Hall, and Terrence Horgan (2014) capture the challenge of nonverbal communication by noting that it is more difficult to understand because it is intangible and more abstract. A major reason for this ambiguity is that many factors influence the meaning of nonverbal behaviors, including shared fields of experience, current surroundings, and culture. Consider the following conversation between a father and son as they talk about the son staying out past his curfew:

Father: I told you to be home by 11! It's past midnight now. And get that smirk off your face!

Son: You might have told me 11, but you didn't say anything when I asked if I could stay out 'til 12. You didn't say for sure either way. Remember when I asked while you were changing the oil on the truck? You didn't even look at me. I couldn't hear you mumbling under the car. And, how am I . . .

Father: You heard what you wanted to hear. I told you . . .

Son: I swear, Dad. I thought my curfew was midnight. And I've stayed out 'til midnight before.

This scenario between father and son suggests a few things about the ambiguous nature of nonverbal communication. First, the father seems to be annoyed by his son's smirk. Is he truly smirking, or is the father misinterpreting his son's facial expression because he is angry? Second, the son took his dad's verbal message about the 11 p.m. deadline less seriously because his father neglected to make eye contact when delivering it. In addition, the son thought that his dad hesitated when he asked about a later curfew, and also claimed that he couldn't clearly hear his father's response from under the car, further eroding the power of the father's verbal communication. In this example, ambiguity results from the interaction of the verbal and nonverbal behaviors of both the father and son.

5-1b Nonverbal Communication Regulates Conversation

People use nonverbal communication to manage the ebb and flow of conversations. Nonverbal regulators allow speakers to enter, exit, or maintain the conversation. Who talks when and to whom, referred to as **turn taking**, is based primarily on nonverbal communication. For instance, if we want a chance to speak, we usually lean forward, toward the speaker. When we don't want to be interrupted in a conversation, we may avoid eye contact and keep our vocal pattern consistent so that others don't have an opportunity to begin talking until we are finished. When we are ready to yield the conversation to another,

turn taking In a conversation, nonverbal regulators that indicate who talks when and to whom.

Grammy-winning French techno group Daft Punk emphasizes visual components in their highly popular music. They do not speak or show their faces.

we typically stop talking, look at the other person, and perhaps make a motion with our hands to indicate that it is now okay for the other person to respond.

In our technological relationships, consider how regulation functions. During texting, for example, regulating can take a few forms. We may use ellipses points ("I wanted to say one more thing here. . . .") to show we want to continue a sequence; or to demonstrate support of another person, we may use an emoticon ("I'm so sorry. Must be pretty hard for you 😢 ").

5-1c Nonverbal Communication Is More Believable Than Verbal Communication

As noted earlier, although nonverbal communication is often ambiguous, people generally believe nonverbal messages over verbal messages. You've no doubt heard the expression "Actions speak louder than words." This statement suggests that someone's nonverbal behavior can influence a conversational partner more than what is said. A job candidate being interviewed may verbally state her commitment to being professional, yet if she wears jeans and arrives late to the interview, these nonverbal cues will likely cause the interviewer to regard her statement with skepticism.

Consider how Esther reacts to the nonverbal communication of the customers at a local coffee shop where she is a barista. She continues to make judgments on the likelihood of customers giving tips based upon their pleasant conversational tone and their well-dressed appearance. However, as we learned in Chapter 3,

> **mixed message** The incompatibility that occurs when our nonverbal messages are not congruent with our verbal messages.

perceptions may be inaccurate or incomplete. One of the biggest tippers for Esther may be an old curmudgeon with a dirty jacket!

5-1d Nonverbal Communication May Conflict with Verbal Communication

Although nonverbal and verbal communication frequently operate interdependently, sometimes our nonverbal messages are not congruent with our verbal messages. We term this incompatibility a **mixed message**. When a friend asks you "What's wrong?" after observing you with tears in your eyes, and you reply, "Nothing," the contradiction between your nonverbal and verbal behavior is evident. When a physician purses her lips or frowns as she reveals to her patient that the prognosis "looks good," she gives a mixed message. Or, consider a wife, who after being asked by her husband if she loves him, shouts, "Of course I love you!" Most of us would agree that angrily shouting to express our affection sends a mixed message.

When confronted with a mixed message, people have to choose whether to believe the nonverbal or the verbal cues. Because children are generally not sophisticated enough to understand the many meanings that accompany nonverbal communication, they rely on the words of a message more than the nonverbal behaviors (Knapp et al., 2014). In contrast, adults who encounter mixed messages pay the most attention to nonverbal messages and neglect much of what is being stated. The multiple messages that originate from the eyes, voice, body movement, facial expressions, and touch usually overpower the verbal message. Adults are more adept at interpreting levels and complexities of communication, including the varying nonverbal messages.

5-2 NONVERBAL COMMUNICATION CODES

Extensive study of nonverbal communication indicates that we employ several different forms of nonverbal codes in our conversations with others. Later in the chapter, we will look at a number of these codes and

TABLE 5.2 CATEGORIES OF NONVERBAL COMMUNICATION

Code	Nonverbal Category
Visual-auditory	Kinesics (*body movement*)
	Physical appearance (*body size, body artifacts, attractiveness*)
	Facial communication (*eye contact, smiling*)
	Paralanguage (*pitch, rate, volume, speed, silence*)
Contact	Haptics (*touch*)
	Space (*personal space, territoriality*)
Place and time	The environment (*color, lighting, room design*)
	Chronemics (*time*)

© Cengage Learning®

discuss their cultural implications. In this section, we examine a classifying system articulated by Burgoon et al. (1996), which is set out in Table 5.2. This system includes visual-auditory codes, contact codes, and place and time codes.

5-2a Visual-Auditory Codes

As their name reflects, visual-auditory codes include categories of nonverbal communication that you can see and hear. These categories are kinesics (body movement), physical appearance (such as attractiveness), facial communication (such as eye contact), and paralanguage (such as pitch level and whining).

KINESICS (BODY MOVEMENT)

Body communication is also called **kinesics**, a Greek word meaning "movement." Kinesics refers to the study of how people communicate through bodily motions. Kinesic behavior is wide-ranging; it can include anything from staying put at a party after being asked to leave to gesturing during a speech.

The primary components of kinesics are gestures and body posture/orientation. Gestures have been analyzed for almost 2,500 years. For example, writings by the Greek philosopher Aristotle explain that gestures are important when delivering a public speech. Michael Corballis (2011) notes that gestures preceded verbal communication by tens of thousands of years. What can we learn from gestures? First, gestures can be both

intention and unintentional. Second, we need to consider the context of gestures to understand them. Think about the gestures that the following individuals would use: parking lot attendant, nurse, radio disc jockey, landscaper, and auctioneer. What gestures would they have in common? What gestures are unique to these occupations? In the classroom setting, gestures such as raising a hand, writing on a whiteboard, pointing, and waving at a student to come sit in a particular seat are common. Janet Bavelas (1994) describes several gesture types. As you review each, keep in mind that cultural variations exist:

▶ **Delivery gestures** signal shared understanding between communicators. Clifton, for example, nods his head to let his friend, Kaitlin, know that he understands what she is talking about.

▶ **Citing gestures** acknowledge another's feedback. For instance, in a conversation with her employee, Cindy uses a citing gesture when she disagrees with what her employee is saying—she raises her hand, palm flat to the receiver, her index finger extended upward.

▶ **Seeking gestures** request agreement or clarification from the speaker. For instance, we may extend both our arms out, keep our palms flat, and shrug. This gesture is used when someone is communicating "I don't know what you mean."

▶ **Turn gestures** indicate that another person can speak or are used to request the conversation floor. We referenced this behavior earlier in the chapter when we discussed the regulating function of nonverbal messages. Turn gestures include pointing at another to indicate it is his or her turn, or extending your hand outward and rotating your wrist in a clockwise motion to show that the other person should continue speaking.

In addition to gestures, our body posture and orientation reveal important information. Posture has been associated with emotions and the English

kinesics The study of a person's body movement and its effect on the communication process.

delivery gestures Gestures that signal shared understanding between communicators in a conversation.

citing gestures Gestures that acknowledge another's feedback in a conversation.

seeking gestures Gestures that request agreement or clarification from a sender during a conversation.

turn gestures Gestures that indicate another person can speak or that are used to request to speak in a conversation.

language contains several expressions depicting this relationship (e.g., "Don't be so uptight," "I won't take this lying down," etc.). Posture is generally a result of how tense or relaxed we are. For example, your body posture would likely differ depending on whether you were reading this chapter while you were alone in your room or in the waiting room of a hospital. **Body orientation** refers to how we turn our legs, shoulders, and head toward (or away) from a communicator. Lillian Glass (2013) found that body orientation affects conversations and the extent to which people believe what we say. Moreover, she noted that people will frequently change their body position based on their credibility. For example, typically, when people communicate with someone of higher status, they tend to stand directly facing him or her. Conversely, those with higher status tend to use a leaning posture when speaking to subordinates.

PHYSICAL APPEARANCE

In interpersonal exchanges, physical appearance plays a role in our evaluations of others ("How could he have done that?! He's such a good-looking guy"). Physical appearance encompasses all of the **physical characteristics** of an individual, including body size, skin color, hair color and style, facial hair, and facial features (e.g., blemishes, skin texture, etc.).

How does physical appearance influence our interpersonal communication? Although we are unable to discuss every aspect of physical appearance, a few thoughts merit attention. Certainly, skin color has affected the communication process. Even today—decades after civil rights legislation—some people won't communicate with people who are of a particular race or ethnicity. Body size, too, can influence our interpersonal relationships. Do you find yourself making judgments about people who appear overweight or too thin? What is your first assessment of a person who is more than 6 feet tall? What is your initial impression of a bodybuilder? Do you evaluate women who shave their body hair differently from women who choose not to shave?

In our technological world, our and another's physical appearance can be quite influential in perceptions of our relationships. Catalina Toma and Jeffrey Hancock (2010) found that online, we generally view physical attractiveness through the photographs that individuals place in their profiles. However, they caution that these photos are pretty subjective and "highly malleable" (p. 338), meaning that we can manipulate them by selecting the most flattering pictures that make us look younger and more attractive. Therefore, the authenticity of physical appearance must be taken in conjunction with the possibility of a photograph that is less than authentic.

Body artifacts refer to our possessions and how we decorate ourselves and our surroundings. Clothing, for example, can convey social status or group identification. Furthermore, some writers (*Forbes*, 2012) indicate that clothing can communicate quite a bit, including spending

© iStock.com/sandr2002

---

body orientation The extent to which we turn our legs, shoulders, and head toward or away from a communicator.

physical characteristics Aspects of physical appearance, such as body size, skin color, hair color and style, facial hair, and facial features.

body artifacts Items we wear that are part of our physical appearance and that have the potential to communicate, such as clothing, religious symbols, military medals, body piercings, and tattoos.

© Gregory James Van Raalte/Shutterstock.com

habits, emotional states, social position, economic level, and the sorts of morals and values we support.

Other examples of the influence of clothing are all around us. In the corporate world, tailored clothing bolsters one's status among many peers. During Kwanzaa, a holiday celebration in African American communities, participants frequently wear traditional African clothing, which serves as a nonverbal connection among African Americans. People who wear religious symbols, such as a crucifix or the Star of David, may be exhibiting religious commitments. Military clothing is usually accompanied by medals or stripes to depict rank, which suggests military accomplishment. Many of you may have body piercings or tattoos, and these can communicate many different messages. Yet, although some of you may adorn yourself with these nonverbal body symbols to show your nonconformity, some job interviewers may view them as expressions of too much independence and future unwillingness to be a team player at work.

Physical appearance also includes the level of attractiveness of the interpersonal communicators. Research exists on interpersonal attractiveness. Knapp et al. (2014) have compiled a number of conclusions based on their review of the research findings. Two seem particularly pertinent to our discussion. First, generally speaking, people seek out others who are similar to themselves in attractiveness, just as they seek out others who are similar to themselves in other characteristics. If you are a nonsmoker, are you likely to be compatible with a smoker? If you are vegetarian, will you be attracted to a carnivore? Although people are not so narrow and simplistic insofar as they use only one behavior to determine attractiveness, it is true that we are interested in being around those people who are similar to us.

Second, Knapp and his team (2014) note that physically attractive people are often judged to be more intelligent and friendly than those not deemed attractive. This conclusion resonates in a number of different environments, including the classroom. For example, researchers note that people pay closer attention to those who they view are viewed as physically attractive (Williams, 2011). However, in the business setting, "more attractive women in executive roles are often the victims of prejudice, taken less seriously and often resented, thus feeling the pressure to come up with glasses and hairstyles that project a more severe aura" (Jones, 2004, p. 3B). It's clear, then, that although many try to avoid its influence, physical attractiveness affects perceptions and impressions of credibility.

FACIAL COMMUNICATION

More than any other part of the body, the face gives others insight into how someone is feeling. Our facial expressions cover the gamut of emotional meaning, from eagerness to exhaustion. We often have difficulty shielding authentic feelings from others because we usually don't have much control over our facial communication. This fact further explains the point we made earlier in this chapter, that people tend to believe our nonverbal codes over our verbal codes—it's tough to hide our feelings. While looking at an infant or toddler, try suppressing a smile. When talking to a parent who has lost a child in a war, repressing a sad look on your face is probably impossible. It's simply too challenging to control a region of our body that is so intimately connected to our emotions.

The part of the face with the most potential for communication is the eye. For most of us, our eyes remain instrumental in both aesthetic and practical ways. For instance, some research indicates that as we view artwork through our eyes, we establish a viewing "strategy" (e.g., linking pieces of art together) as we process the visual stimuli (Sharma & Chakravarthy, 2013). Eye behavior is complex. We can look directly into someone's eyes to communicate a number of different things, including interest, power, or anger. We roll our eyes to signal disbelief or disapproval. We avoid eye contact when we are uninterested, nervous, or shy. Our eyes also facilitate our interactions. We look at others while they speak to get a sense of their facial and body communication.

© ollyy/Shutterstock.com

Simultaneously, others often look at us while we speak. We also make judgments about others simply by looking at their eyes, deciding if they are truthful, uninterested, tired, involved, or credible. Although our conclusions may be erroneous, most people rely on eye contact in their conversations.

Finally, smiling is one of the most recognizable nonverbal behaviors worldwide. When we go to the Department of Motor Vehicles, most of us are not all that excited to smile for the camera. Still, smiling usually has a positive effect on an encounter. As Sarah Stevenson (Psychology Today, 2012) puts it, "Each time you smile you throw a little feel-good party in your brain."

Smiling also may entice others to act as good Samaritans. In an experiment testing the effects of smiling on helping behavior, Nicolas Gueguen and Marie-Agnes De Gail (2003) report that smiling at others encourages them to assist in tasks. Studying 800 passersby, the research team had eight research assistants ask others for help. One group of assistants smiled at some of the people exiting a grocery store. A few seconds later, passersby had an opportunity to help an assistant who dropped a computer diskette on the ground. Results showed that the previous smile of a stranger enhanced later helping behavior. That is, those who were smiled at earlier were more likely to help the stranger with the computer disk.

Smiling has various conversational effects. Smiling at another usually results in a more pleasant encounter. However, smiling at ill-conceived times may prompt others to react unfavorably. In conflict, for instance, smiling is often perceived as an inappropriate and poorly timed behavior. Smiling during a heated exchange can aggravate an already difficult situation, unless the smile is used to ease tensions. Smiling has multiple meanings (e.g., a smirk and a sneer communicate two different things), so context is definitely important when we interpret another's smile.

PARALANGUAGE (VOICE)

To introduce the concept of paralanguage, let's examine the story of Charles. A few weeks ago, Charles lost his mother, a woman whom he considered his best friend.

When people around the office ask him how he's doing, he always responds, "She lived a good, long life." However, his good friend, Melissa, can hear a "voice" that is different from the one Charles normally uses. For example, sometimes when Charles says that he feels fine and that no one should be concerned about him, Melissa hears a different message. She "feels" his pain during his silence. She "listens to his pain" when Charles laughs awkwardly. Melissa is clearly drawing conclusions about the paralinguistic cues from Charles.

This story underscores a vocal characteristic called **paralanguage**, or vocalics, which is the study of a person's voice. Paralanguage refers not to *what* a person says but to *how* a person says it. Paralanguage covers a vast array of nonverbal behaviors such as pitch, rate, volume, inflection, tempo, and pronunciation, which we call **vocal qualities**. We also consider **vocal distractors** (the "ums" and "ers" of conversation) and the use of silence as vocal qualities. Paralanguage also encompasses such nonverbal behaviors as crying, laughing, groaning, muttering, whispering, and whining; we call these **vocal characterizers**. Don't underestimate the usefulness of studying these paralinguistic behaviors. They give us our uniqueness as communicators, help us differentiate among people, and influence people's perceptions of us and our perceptions of them.

Our vocal qualities include the rate (speed), volume (loudness/softness), inflection (vocal emphasis), pitch (highness/lowness), intensity (volume), tempo (rhythm), and pronunciation associated with voices. Vocal qualities lead listeners to form impressions about a speaker's socioeconomic status, personality type, persuasiveness, and work ethic (Griffin, 2014). One way to tap into these vocal nuances is to practice saying the same sentence with various rates, volume, inflection, sighs, and tempo. For example, try saying the following statement to show *praise*, then *blame*, and then *exasperation*:

You really did it this time.

The next time you want to borrow a friend's car, tell your father a secret, ask your professor a question, or engage in a debate with your roommate about religion or politics, you will probably utilize a number of different vocal qualities.

The "ums" in our conversations may seem unimportant, but these vocal distractors compose an increasingly researched area of vocal qualities because they can predict whether a conversation will continue and the fluency of that conversation. How do you react when you hear a speaker use these disfluencies? You may find them appropriate for many social situations, but what happens in more professional settings, such as formal presentations

---

paralanguage The study of a person's voice. Also called *vocalics*. Nonverbal behaviors that include pitch, rate, volume, inflection, tempo, and pronunciation as well as the use of vocal distractors and silence.

vocal qualities Nonverbal behaviors such as pitch, rate, volume, inflection, tempo, and pronunciation.

vocal distractors The "ums" and "ers" used in conversation.

vocal characterizers Nonverbal behaviors such as crying, laughing, groaning, muttering, whispering, and whining.

at work, job interviews, or oral reports for a class? When vocal distractors are used excessively, people view them as bad habits that can jeopardize credibility.

SILENCE

We include silence in our discussion of the vocal qualities of paralanguage because a person's use of his or her voice includes the decision not to use it. Strange as it may sound, in our relationships, we should all exercise our right to remain silent. However, how many of us do? Society seems to have a love affair with talking. Self-help books (such as *Communication Miracles for Couples*) exclaim that communication is the way to relational bliss and long-lasting happiness. Therapists tell their patients to open up and communicate. And what adolescent doesn't hear from a parent: "Talk to me!" We live in a culture that places a premium on the spoken word.

Yet, at times, as we touched on in Chapters 2, honoring silence may be the most powerful way to communicate to another person. Silence communicates and informs the communication process in a number of ways. First, silence indicates that we need some time for reflection. Silence gives us a chance to think about the circumstances or events surrounding an interpersonal relationship. For instance, if you have been battling with your sibling, taking some time to withdraw from the conversation can help you refocus on the original issue and how you want to go about resolving it.

Silence can also be part of the destructive side of communication we talked about in Chapter 1. At times, silence serves as an interpersonal weapon. In online relational life, think about the numbers of times you have either not received a response from someone to a question or concern. Or, consider the times where you decided to avoid communication and simply not respond to another.

In face-to-face relationships, silence can be consequential. Suppose that Andrew and Jess, who have been married for 6 months, are having a fight about whether or not they can afford to have a child. Because Andrew is not comfortable talking about this topic so early in their marriage, he remains silent on the issue. In contrast, Jess wants to talk about it because she feels that having children is an important part of being married. Each time Jess tries to bring up the subject, Andrew simply says he doesn't want to talk about it and leaves the room.

You may have been the target of this "silent treatment" or may have decided yourself that giving this sort of punishment in a relationship was necessary. Silence can be a frustrating nonverbal behavior to respond to, as Jess probably knows all too well. What does a person say or do when another person is not saying or doing anything? A sort of communication spiral ensues: someone wants to jump-start the conversation to get the issues clarified and resolved; but after the issues are clarified, the fighting continues, resulting in one or both people shutting down. Unfortunately, using silence to hurt or undermine another person is commonplace. Understanding when silence is effective and when it sabotages the interpersonal communication process takes time and experience.

Vocal characterizers such as laughing, moaning, or whining also communicate a great deal about how to interpret verbal messages. For example, if Illeana tells José, "I'm so over you," but does so with laughter, José probably can infer that the comment should not be taken seriously. Or, suppose Ron is a member of a task group at work. Each time the group meets, his coworker Linda complains about the time it takes to get the group together, the assignment, and the time constraints. Linda's whining about the task will likely affect Ron's conversations with her.

5-2b Contact Codes

Contact codes include touch (haptics) and space (such as personal space). These two areas are among the most discussed and important areas in interpersonal communication. The two areas are also linked in many ways. For instance, quickly think about the last time when you noticed someone touched you or you touched another person. Now, quickly think about how various space differences functioned in those interactions. The interrelationship between these two nonverbal codes merits their consideration together.

TOUCH (HAPTICS)

Touch communication, or **haptics**, is the most primitive form of human communication. Research has concluded

© mmarcol/Shutterstock.com

haptics The study of how we communicate through touch.

that touch has lasting value. Ben Benjamin and Ruth Werner (2004) support this claim:

> Human touch can completely change the way the body functions. From your heart rate to your blood pressure to the efficiency of your digestive system, welcomed touch can make your body work better. Humans need touch. We crave it, we hunger for it, and we get sick and can even die from the lack of it. (pp. 30, 31)

Touch behavior is the ultimate in privileged access to people. That is, when you touch another person, you have decided—whether intentionally or unintentionally—to invade another's personal space. When forced into circumstances where everyone is close—for example, standing in a crowded elevator, sitting next to someone on the train or bus, or standing in a line—we normally offer an apology or an excuse if we accidentally touch someone. Interestingly, at public celebrations like Mardi Gras and New Year's Eve parties, touching another person doesn't seem as intrusive. In fact, some people enjoy it!

Touch behavior is an ambiguous form of communication, because touching has various meanings depending on the context. Touching another person takes different forms and signals multiple messages. Shaking hands upon meeting someone, making love, slapping an old friend on the back, physically abusing a partner, rubbing a partner's neck, and tickling a small child are all examples of touch behavior. Desmond Morris (2002) reports that there are 457 types of body contact, from the rare (e.g., kissing a hand) to the more common (stylist cutting hair). Touch has several functions (Jones & Yarbrough, 1985):

▶ Touch is used for positive affect, which includes healing, appreciation, and affection. The nurse who touches the senior in the convalescent home is expressing tactile support to her patient.

▶ Touch has a playful function; it serves to lighten an interaction. This type of touch is apparent when two kids wrestle each other or when baseball players slap each other on the butt after a home run.

▶ Touch is used to control or direct behavior in an encounter. Touching another person while saying "move aside" is an example of touching to control.

▶ Ritualistic touch refers to the touches we use on an everyday basis, such as a handshake to say hello or good-bye.

proxemics The study of how people use, manipulate, and identify their personal space.

personal space The distance we put between ourselves and others.

intimate distance The distance that extends about 18 inches around each of us that is normally reserved for people with whom we are close, such as close friends, romantic partners, and family members.

▶ The task function pertains to touch that serves a professional or functional purpose. For instance, hairstylists and dentists are allowed to touch you to accomplish their tasks.

▶ A hybrid touch is a touch that greets a person and simultaneously demonstrates affection for that person. For instance, kissing a family member hello is an example of a hybrid touch.

▶ Touch that is accidental is done without apparent intent. This type of touching includes touching in close spaces, such as intimate restaurants, in elevators, at crowded restaurants, or at a religious service.

SPACE AND DISTANCE

An episode of *Seinfeld* may come to mind as we mention the phrase "close talkers." Spatial communication is important in conversation. **Proxemics**, the study of how communication is influenced by space and distance, is historically related to how people use, manipulate, and identify their space. **Personal space** is the distance we put between ourselves and others. We carry informal personal space from one encounter to another; think of this personal space as a sort of invisible bubble that encircles us wherever we go. Our personal space provides some insight into ourselves and how we feel about other people. For instance, some research shows that happily married couples stand closer to one another (11.4 inches) than those who are maritally distressed (14.8 inches) (Crane, Dollahite, Griffin, & Taylor, 1987).

Anthropologist Edward T. Hall (1959) was the first to devise categories of personal space. His system suggests that in most co-cultures in the United States, people communicate with others at a specific distance, depending on the nature of the conversation. Starting with the closest contact and the least amount of personal space, and moving to the greatest distance between communicators, the four categories of personal space are intimate distance, personal distance, social distance, and public distance (Figure 5.2). Examine Hall's categories and think about your own interpersonal encounters.

Intimate distance covers the distance that extends from you to around 18 inches. This spatial

Raul Reyes (RGJ.com, 2013) pointedly asks the question "When is a handshake more than a handshake?" Discussing the handshake between President Obama and Cuban president Raul Castro at the funeral of former South African president Nelson Mandela, Reyes notes that the nonverbal behavior elicited a "torrent of criticism." The handshake unleashed a great deal of concern from politicians, in particular. U.S. senators were quoted as saying that the handshake provided Castro "propaganda to continue to prop up his dictatorial, brutal regime," and President Obama "should have asked him [Castro] about those basic freedoms Mandela was associated with that are denied in Cuba." Reyes expresses exasperation at the outbreak of criticism, noting that the president would have avoided a lot of handshakes if he had taken these senators' advice, given that the Chinese vice president was present and China has a record of human rights abuses. Reyes captures the moment of the gathering by stating that the event "was not about political grievances. It was about coming together *despite* political grievances." Former president

Mandela was a close friend of the Cuban president, and "it would have been needlessly rude for Obama to snub Castro." Reyes concludes that the president does not "deserve criticism for shaking Castro's hand" and that "his gesture was appropriate, polite, and entirely befitting of a statesmen." The handshake—a nonverbal symbol usually associated with a greeting or salutation—now carries much more significance than many anticipated.

FIGURE 5.2   EDWARD T. HALL'S FOUR TYPES OF PERSONAL DISTANCE

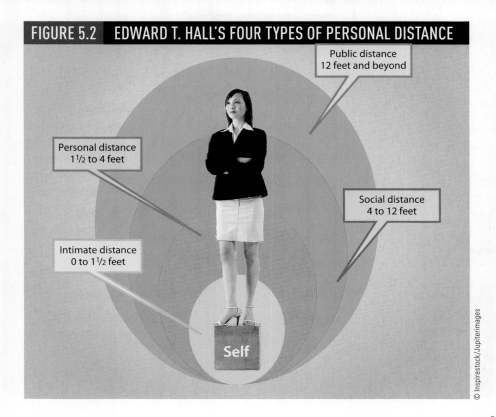

Public distance
12 feet and beyond

Personal distance
1½ to 4 feet

Social distance
4 to 12 feet

Intimate distance
0 to 1½ feet

Self

zone is normally reserved for those people with whom you are close—for example, close friends, romantic partners, and family members. Of course, in some situations, you have little choice but to allow others within an intimate distance (e.g., attending a movie or theater production, sitting on a train, watching a rock concert, etc.). If you let someone be a part of your intimate distance zone, you are implying that this person is meaningful to you. In fact, zero personal space—in other words, touch—suggests a very close relationship with someone because you are willing to give him or her part of your private space.

Personal distance, ranging from 18 inches to 4 feet, is the space most people use during conversations. This distance allows you to feel some protection from others who might wish to touch you. The range in this distance type allows those at the closest range to pick up your physical nuances (such as dry skin, acne, body smells, etc.). However, we are still able to conduct business with those at the far range—which Hall (1959) calls "arm's length"—but any signs of nonverbal closeness are erased. Examples of relationships accustomed to personal distance are casual friends or business colleagues.

Social distance, which is 4 to 12 feet, is the spatial zone usually reserved for professional or formal interpersonal encounters. Some office environments are arranged specifically for social distance. Tables are aligned in a particular way, and cubicles are set up specifically to encourage social distance (rather than intimate distance or personal distance). As a result, many business transactions take place within social distance. Water cooler chats or conversations in a break room at work also characterize the social zone. Whereas in the intimate and personal spatial zones we can use a lower vocal volume, social distance typically requires increased volume.

At the **public distance**, communication occurs at a distance of 12 or more feet. This spatial zone allows listeners to scan the entire person while he or she is speaking. The classroom environment exemplifies public distance. Most classrooms are arranged with a teacher in the front and rows of desks or tables facing the teacher. Of course, this setup can vary, but many classrooms are arranged with students more than 12 feet from their professor. Public distance is also used in large settings, such as when we listen to speakers, watch musicals, or attend television show tapings.

A theoretical model can help us understand the differences in distance between people. The **expectancy violations theory** (Burgoon, 1978, 2009; West & Turner, 2014) states that we expect people to maintain a certain distance in their conversations with us. If a person violates our expectations (if, for instance, a work colleague stands in our intimate space while talking with us), our response to the violation will be based on how much we like that person. That is, if we like a person, we're probably going to allow a distance violation. We may even reciprocate that conversational distance. If we dislike the person, we will likely be irritated by the violation and perhaps move away from the person. According to this theory, the degree to which we like someone can be based on factors that include our assessment of his or her credibility and physical attractiveness. Personal space violations, therefore, have consequences on our interactions.

Before moving on, let's address one final point about space. Whereas personal space is that invisible bubble we carry from one interaction to another, **territoriality** is our sense of ownership of space that remains fixed. Humans mark their territories in various ways, usually with items or objects that are called **territorial markers**. For example, perhaps you go to a coffee shop each morning and stake out your table with a newspaper. Or, maybe you live near a house that has a fence that separates its yard from the neighbor's. Although one doesn't always own a particular

---

personal distance Ranging from 18 inches to 4 feet, the space most people use during conversations.

social distance Ranging from 4 to 12 feet, the spatial zone usually reserved for professional or formal interpersonal encounters.

public distance 12 feet or more, this space is closely associated with a speaker and audience.

expectancy violations theory A theory stating that we expect other people to maintain a certain distance from us in their conversations with us.

territoriality The sense of ownership of space that remains fixed.

territorial markers Items or objects that humans use to mark their territories, such as a newspaper set on a table in a coffee shop.

THEORY SPOTLIGHT:

Expectancy Violations Theory

A key component related to expectancy violations theory is the notion of response. That is, people will have various responses to personal space violations. Now, imagine sitting in your school's cafeteria and although a number of tables are free, a person sits right next to you at your table. The two of you are now alone at the eight-seat table. What criteria would you use to determine whether this behavior was a violation? And, what criteria would you use to determine how you would handle the violation?

territory, we nonetheless presume "ownership" by the sheer frequency with which we occupy a space or by the markers we use to communicate that the territory is "ours." In a sense, we believe that we have proprietary rights over some particular location. If, for example, you take the train each morning to work and sit in the same seat, you have claimed your territory. If someone were to occupy your seat one day, the only thing you could do about it besides merely experience displeasure would be to ask the person to leave.

5-2c Place and Time Codes

We do not often think of place and time codes when we think of nonverbal communication, but they affect us deeply. The categories of nonverbal communication included in place and time codes are environment (such as color and smell) and chronemics (time).

THE ENVIRONMENT

Where you sit, sleep, dance, climb, jog, write, sing, play, sew, or worship are all parts of your **physical environment**. How we utilize the parts of the environment, how we manage them, and their influence upon us are all part of nonverbal communication. Or, as Burgoon and her research team (1996) concluded, "Humans have always altered the environment for their purposes, interpreted meaning from it, and relied on environmental cues for guides to behavior" (pp. 109–110). Our physical environment entails a number of features, including the smell (e.g., restaurant), clutter (e.g., attic, garage, basement, closet), and sounds (e.g., music, chatter) of our surroundings. But what do we do to the environment, and what does it "do" to us? Let's explore three prominent environmental factors that affect communication between people: color, lighting, and room design.

Tourist areas such as Las Vegas make prominent use of neon lights and signs at night to attract crowds with the promise of excitement and abandon.

© Kobby Dagan/Shutterstock.com

Color is one of the most subtle environmental influences. Most researchers conclude that color affects our moods and perceptions. In other words, color has symbolic meaning in the environment and in our society (Sadka, 2004). Consider the colors in our everyday lives and their meanings. Red, for instance, embodies an interesting contradiction: It both facilitates togetherness and incites anger. Couples share their (red) hearts of candy on Valentine's Day; later, this same couple may "see red" when they get into a fight. The color blue also has several meanings. Many people associate blue with calmness (think about lakes and oceans), whereas others feel "blue" when they are sad or depressed. Yellow (joy) and purple (wisdom) are less paradoxical.

Our perceptions of color, which can be based on cultural interpretations, can affect our perception of the physical environment. Do you feel that a certain color is most conducive to learning? Now, notice the color of your communication classroom. Do you prefer bold and bright colors, or are you more of an earth-tone person? One reason that so many educational and work environments remain neutral in coloring is because these benign colors generally have a calming effect and function to enhance learning and productivity (Meghani, 2009).

In addition to color, the *lighting* of the environment can influence and modify behavior. Tracy Bedrosian and her research team (2013) discovered that color of environmental lighting may induce depression and alter our neural structures. The effect of lighting on worker productivity has been investigated for many decades (Roethlisberger & Dickson, 1939). Lighting levels also seem to affect behavior within interpersonal interactions. Next time you're in a department store, look at how the lighting level varies in the different departments. Some departments, such as cosmetics, have soft lighting because it makes the customer look good and thus more inclined to buy the store's beauty products. Or, think about how lighting in dimly lit restaurants affects our behavior; it may prompt us to feel relaxed, causing us to prolong our evening (and increase our dinner tab). Brightly lit restaurants, such as McDonald's or Wendy's, may increase people's rate of eating (thus, the term *fast food*), allowing these places to move people in and out in an efficient way.

Room design, including room size, also affects communication. For example, many retirement villages are now being designed to allow for both independence and interaction. Individual living units similar to small

physical environment The setting in which our behavior takes place.

condominiums are built to promote privacy, but the units converge to form a meeting room where activities, events, and group functions take place.

TIME (CHRONEMICS)

Chronemics, the study of a person's perception and use of time, helps us to understand how people perceive and structure time in their dialogues and relationships with others. Time is an abstract concept that we describe using figures of speech (which we discussed in Chapter 4)—for example, "time is on your side," "time well spent," "time to kill," "time on your hands," "don't waste time," "on time," and "quality time." Dawna Ballard and David Seibold (2000) observed the reciprocal relationship between time and communication. They believe that communication creates a person's understanding of time, and yet our sense of time restricts our communication.

Edward T. Hall (1959) noted three time systems. *Technical time* is the scientific measurement of time. This system is associated with the precision of keeping time. *Formal time* is the time that society formally teaches. For example, in the United States, the clock and the calendar are our units of formal time. We know that when it's 1 a.m., it's usually time to sleep, and at 1 p.m. we find ourselves at work or school. Furthermore, in the United States, our arrangement of time is fixed and rather methodical. We learn to tell time based on the hour, and children are usually taught how to tell time by using the "big hand" and the "little hand" as references. *Informal time* is time that includes three concepts: duration, punctuality, and activity.

▶ *Duration* pertains to how long we allocate for a particular event. In our schedules, we may earmark 40 minutes for grocery shopping or an hour for a religious service. Some of our estimates are less precise. For instance, what does it mean when we respond "Be there right away"? Does that mean we will be there in 10 minutes, an hour, or as long as it takes? And, despite its vague and odd-sounding nature, the statement "I want it done yesterday" is clear to many.

▶ *Punctuality* is the promptness associated with keeping time. We're said to be punctual when we arrive for an appointment at the designated time. Despite the value placed on punctuality in the United States, friends may arrive late to lunch, professors late to class, physicians late to appointments, and politicians late to rallies. (In fact, with the tendency of some people to always be tardy, we may question why we even make appointments in the first place.)

© Denizo71/Shutterstock.com

▶ *Activity* is related to chronemics. People in Western cultures are encouraged to "use their time wisely"—in other words, they should make sure their time is used to accomplish something, whether it's a task or a social function. Simultaneously, they should avoid being so time occupied that others view them as focused and obsessive. Our use and management of time are associated with status and power. For example, the old adage "time is money," which equates an intangible (time) with a tangible (money), suggests that we place a value on our use of time. And as a country with individualistic values (see Chapter 2), the United States is a society that supports the belief that time is intimately linked to status and power.

Suppose, for instance, that Joan arrives at an interview 5 minutes late. Joan probably won't get the job,

chronemics The study of a person's perception and use of time.

because punctuality is an important value to communicate to a future boss. However, let's say that the interviewer, Mr. Johansen, is 5 minutes late for the interview. Of course, he would not lose his job. Similarly, John's optometrist could be late for his appointment with no consequence, but if John is late for his own appointment, he might have to pay a "no show" fee.

Let's look at a few more examples. Some professors are regularly late for class, but these same professors have policies about student punctuality. And many of you have waited in long lines for a school loan, concert tickets, or a driver's license. If you truly had power, you wouldn't have to spend time waiting in line; you'd have someone wait in line for you! Time is clearly related to status and power differences between individuals (Moore et al., 2009).

We have spent a great deal of time identifying the primary types of nonverbal communication so you can better understand their comprehensive nature. We continue this chapter by considering how culture affects nonverbal messages. As we learned in Chapter 2, culture influences virtually every aspect of interpersonal communication. Understanding various cultural influences on nonverbal behavior helps you realize that not everyone shares your beliefs, values, and meanings. Particularly in the area of nonverbal communication—which, as we noted earlier in the chapter, is often ambiguous and open to interpretation—remembering cultural variations helps us become more competent communicators.

5-3 CULTURAL VARIATIONS IN NONVERBAL COMMUNICATION

We could write an entire text about the influence of culture on nonverbal behavior. In fact, several books examine this topic in detail (e.g., Martin & Nakayama, 2013; Samovar, Porter, McDaniel, & Roy, 2013). Nonverbal behaviors convey different meanings among (co-)cultures. We learn how to interpret nonverbal behaviors as children. Yet, as we note in elsewhere in this book, the U.S. population is so culturally diverse that we can't always rely on these interpretations; the meaning of nonverbal communication between and among cultures can vary. Unless you are sensitive to this variation, you may have a tough time communicating with someone with a different cultural background from you. To provide you with a sense of how culture affects nonverbal behavior, we give you a glimpse into this area. Let's explore a few conclusions related to

body movement, facial expressions, personal space, and touch.

5-3a Body Movement

Kinesic behavior is one area where nonverbal communication and culture intersect. For example, research has shown that greetings vary from one culture to another. For instance, most Westerners are accustomed to shaking hands upon meeting. In other cultures, however, the handshake is not common. In Japan, as many of you know, individuals bow when they meet to express mutual respect. What you may not know is that the person with the lower status initiates bowing and is expected to bow deeper than the individual with higher status. The person with elevated status decides when the bowing ends.

Gesturing has also been studied across cultures. For instance, Mexicans, Greeks, and people from many South American countries are dramatic and animated while speaking. Mexicans tend to use lots of hand gestures in their conversations, and Samovar et al. (2013) note that Italians "talk with their hands" in expressive gestures. However, people in a number of Asian cultures consider such overt body movements rude, and Germans generally consider bold hand gestures too flashy. As illustrated in Chapter 2, the A-OK sign used in the United States carries different meanings around the world, such as sexual connotation in some European communities.

Another cultural difference in nonverbal communication is the way the concept of "two" is communicated. For example, in the United States, people use the forefinger and the middle finger, whereas Filipinos hold up the ring finger and the little finger and the French use the thumb and forefinger. Such cultural combinations require each of us to be aware that "one size doesn't fit all" as we discuss kinesic behavior.

5-3b Facial Expressions

Since the eye is the foundation of the face, it's logical that this area has been studied extensively. The extent to which a person looks at another during a conversation is culturally based. Members of most co-cultures in the United States are socialized to look at a listener while speaking (Nakayama & Martin, 2013). It's common for two people from the United States to look at each other's eyes while communicating. In this country, frequent eye aversion may communicate a lack of trust. However, in other cultures, such as Japan and Jamaica, direct eye contact is perceived as communicating disrespect.

With respect to those who have no eyesight, culture still functions prominently. For example, Francie Latour (2014) interviewed a researcher (Osagie Obasogie) who had interviewed over 100 people who were blind since birth. In her interview, Obasogie states that "we kind of live in this world where people think that everything is postracial. . . . And I'm really trying to challenge that notion" (p. K2). His research shows that blind people are also introduced to racial challenges. He found that some of his participants were instructed by their parents to "smell" race. In another situation, a landlord saw a black person walk into a white (blind) woman's house to which the landlord rang her doorbell and asked, "Is everything OK? I saw a black person walk into your house." Obasogie concludes that what he's amazed with is that racial boundaries are "patrolled" for blind individuals by parents, dating partners, and others. Clearly, even those with no vision are confronted with difficulties related to race.

While we tend to focus on cultural differences, research has also uncovered similarities across cultures. Collectively, research conducted as far back as the early 1970s (Ekman, 1972, 1973; Ekman & Friesen, 1971) has shown that facial expressions are universal. In television crime shows, you may have seen microexpressions uncovered in crime labs. Indeed, this sort of investigation is at the heart of what Ekman undertook nearly five decades ago. That is, six expressions have been shown to be judged consistently across cultures: anger, disgust, fear, happiness, sadness, and surprise. Today, there may be some variation because of the co-cultural backgrounds of communicators, but essentially this universality remains.

5-3c Personal Space

Spatial distances have been the focus of research in intercultural communication. And, personal space is essential to understand since in the United States, as previously discussed, we tend to clearly demarcate our territory. Edward Hall and Mildred Reed Hall (1990) discuss the territoriality of Germans and the French:

> Germans . . . barricade themselves behind heavy doors and soundproof walls to try to seal themselves from others in order to concentrate on their work. The French have a close personal distance and are not as territorial. They are tied to people and thrive on constant interaction. (p. 180)

In addition, interpretations of personal space vary from culture to culture. People in many South American countries, such as Brazil, require little

© iStock.com/tbradford

personal space in an interaction. Arabs, Hungarians, and Africans similarly reduce conversational distance (Lewis, 1999). Generally speaking, people from individualistic cultures (e.g., the United States, Germany, and Canada) require more space than do those from collectivistic cultures (e.g., Costa Rica, Venezuela, and Ecuador). The personal space requirements of people from collectivistic cultures can be partially explained by the fact that people from those cultures tend to work, sleep, and have fun in close proximity to one another (Martin & Nakayama, 2013).

5-3d Touch

Researchers have also investigated touch behavior within a cultural context. For example, Tiffany Field (1999) found that adolescents from the United States touched each other less than adolescents from France. Field observed friends at McDonald's restaurants in Miami and Paris and found that the U.S. teenagers did less hugging, kissing, and caressing than their French counterparts. However, the U.S. adolescents engaged in more self-touching, such as primping, than the French adolescents.

Some cultures accept more same-sex touching than others. For example, men frequently hold hands in Indonesia, and men frequently walk down the street with their arms around each other in Malaysia (interestingly, this touch may be construed as physically intimate, yet both countries remain among the least accepting of gay relationships). Such overt touching, however, may be frowned upon in Japan or in Scandinavia.

In the United States, touching is usually avoided. To get a sense of the extent to which you avoid touch,

TABLE 5.3 CULTURE AND NONVERBAL COMMUNICATION

Nonverbal Type	Nonverbal Behavior	Cultural Difference
Kinesics	Greeting another	**United States*:** Varies; generally, shaking hands **Japan:** Bowing
Facial expression	Eye contact during conversation	**United States*:** Varies; generally, conversation direct **Cambodia:** Indirect
Proxemics	Personal space during conversation	**United States*:** Varies; generally, large **Costa Rica:** Small
Haptics	Same-sex touching during conversation	**United States:** Gaining acceptance; tends to vary from women to men **Malaysia:** Same-sex hand-holding is common

© Cengage Learning®

*Due to the co-cultural differences in the United States, broad cultural generalizations about the behavior are difficult.

complete the Touch Avoidance Inventory at www .cengagebrain.com.

As you can see from the variety of cultural differences in nonverbal behavior discussed in this section and summarized in Table 5.3, nonverbal behaviors should always be understood within a cultural context. We cannot assume that others automatically understand our nonverbal displays, because their meanings can differ significantly within and across cultures. Further, the U.S. population continues to grow more diverse. Being sensitive to cultural communication differences and seeking clarification will help you in your interpersonal relationships.

5-4 TECHNOLOGY AND NONVERBAL COMMUNICATION

The interplay between the digital environment and nonverbal communication remains an important area. It's clear that every generation has, in some way, been introduced to technology. Whether it's the printing press, telegraph, telephone, computer, fax, voice mail, email, or texting, the evolution of technology has occurred for centuries. Yet, those generations who have relied extensively on their cell phones and the Internet have been particularly challenged with being adept at nonverbal communication effectiveness. Mark Bauerlein (2009) writes that because of the ease of checking email, Facebook, and stock quotes, digital natives might "improve their adroitness at the keyboard, but when it comes to their capacity to 'read' the behavior of others, they're all thumbs" (p. W 11). Regardless of whether or not you agree with this sentiment, one essential rings true: technology has forever altered nonverbal communication. Consider the various nonverbal codes we identified earlier. Now think about how various technologies can, and have affected these codes. Our "nonverbal literacy" has unquestionably been affected by the introduction of various mediated communications. When we are walking with our cell phones, many of us "forget" to look up, sometimes stumbling into another, ultimately impinging on another's personal space. When you are at dinner with a companion, you may receive a text and read it, only to look up and see your date frustrated as you averted your eye contact. Constantly looking at your tablet PC while talking to a family member may suggest that you value the technology over the conversation.

We already know that the communication process is transactional, a point we introduced in Chapter 1. This co-creation then requires the attainment of interpersonal meaning. Is meaning achieved, however, when one person is talking and another is responding to texts? If one is looking away and ignoring the other's words, concurrently sending an instant message, is there meaning? What sort of meaning is acquired as two

Proxemic behavior can communicate a great deal about the relationship between people.

friends simultaneously tweet each other? These and a host of other considerations must be acknowledged as we try to unpack the challenge of sending and receiving nonverbal communication with mediated technologies.

Mehgan Green (2012) candidly addresses this interplay in her research. See if you can empathize with her insights:

> To start writing I had to first turn off the TV (a mediated form of communication whose effects I know interfere with my ability to get work done). Then I had to exit my iTunes, put my phone in the other room (on silent so I couldn't hear the messages I was missing), exit my Skype account, log out of my email, exit my favorite blog, get off all the news websites and finally the hardest part . . . log out of Facebook (p. 1).

Greene's words may seem humorous, but her point should not be overshadowed. She laments the fact that "there is a lack of concentration on the loss of nonverbal literacy" (p. 1).

One theoretical framework underscoring this discussion is **social information processing (SIP) theory** (Walther, 2011; West & Turner, 2014), a model we briefly addressed in Chapter 3. Focusing on online relationships, Walther contends that our online relationships

social information processing (SIP) theory a theory that contends that people have the ability to establish online relationships and that these relationships are equal to or greater than the intimacy achieved in face-to-face relationships.

with others have the same potential for intimacy that our face-to-face relationships have. That is, we are able to manage our impressions and self-images online without ever speaking to another person. Walther (2011) claims that we accrue impressions of others and do this primarily through words; we don't need to talk to another person. Walther (2008) argues that "our language and writing are held to be highly interchangeable with nonverbal cues" (p. 393). SIP asserts that self-presentations online, including emoticons (a topic we discuss further in Chapter 7) and pictures are communicative. Furthermore, chronemic cues also function prominently online. That is, the timing of our messages to others—the pace of our response to an email, the ongoing accrual of messages over time, or the decision to respond or not—is critical in online relationships. Walther and other SIP scholars, then, are asking us to suspend our traditional interpretation of nonverbal communication and paradoxically, view the words we use as nonverbal cues.

5-5 SKILL SET FOR INCREASING NONVERBAL COMMUNICATION EFFECTIVENESS

As stated previously, nonverbal behavior is difficult to pin down with precision. We may think we understand what a person's hand gesture or eye behavior means, but there are often multiple ways to interpret a particular nonverbal behavior. Therefore, we must be cautious when we interpret messages. We now turn our attention to identifying six skills for improving nonverbal communication effectiveness. As you practice these skills, keep in mind that you may have to alter your verbal communication (a topic we examined in Chapter 4) since nonverbal communication is closely aligned with what we say.

5-5a Recall the Nonverbal-Verbal Relationship

Throughout this chapter, we have reminded you that nonverbal communication is often best understood with verbal communication. That is, we need to pay attention to what is said in addition to the nonverbal behavior. Most of us blend nonverbal and verbal messages. We raise our voice to underscore something we've said. We frown when we tell a sad story. We motion with our hands when we tell others to get going.

iStock.com/Grafissimo

interpretation of this nonverbal communication by asking the professor if he has time to talk to her. Also consider the cultural background of communicators. We identified how nonverbal communication varies between and among co-cultures; this is an important foundation to draw upon as you interpret the meaning of a nonverbal message.

5-5c Monitor Your Nonverbal Behavior

Being a self-monitor is crucial in conversations (Gangestad & Snyder, 2000). Becoming aware of how you say something, your proximity to the other person, the extent to which you use touch, or your use of silence are just as important as the words you use. This self-monitoring is not easy. For example, let's say that Tracy is in a heated exchange with her roommate, Sue, who refused to pay the cable bill. When Tracy tries to make her point, it's not easy for her to think about how she is saying something or whether or not she is screaming or standing too close. Like most people, she simply wants to make her point. However, Tracy's nonverbal communication can carry significance, particularly if Sue is focusing on it and Tracy is ignoring it. You need to look for meaning in both your behavior and the behavior of others.

5-5d Ask Others for Their Impressions

When applying for a job, we ask others for their interview strategies. When going out on a date, we ask friends how we look or smell. When choosing a class, we may ask our friends about their experiences with a particular professor. Yet, when we try to improve our communication with others, we generally neglect to ask others about our nonverbal effectiveness. Whom should we consult to ensure accuracy and clarity in our nonverbal communication?

The easy answer is that we should ask someone with whom we are close. Our close relationships can provide us valuable information, such as that our silent reactions to others' disclosures make them uncomfortable or that

And, when young toddlers are angry, we see them jump up and down on the floor while they scream, "No!" These examples illustrate the integration of nonverbal and verbal messages. We need to remain aware of this relationship to achieve meaning in our conversations. In addition, we need to be aware that our nonverbal and verbal message should match. Imagine Luke, for instance, telling an interviewer, "My biggest strength as an employee is that I'm a great listener," only to follow up that statement by glancing down at a recent text coming in on his cell phone while the interviewer discusses the company's mission.

5-5b Be Tentative When Interpreting Nonverbal Behavior

In this chapter, we have reiterated the ambiguous nature of nonverbal communication, including cultural differences in nonverbal expressions. Because of individual differences, we can never be sure what a specific nonverbal behavior means. For example, when Ashley walks into Professor Fairfield's office, she may be confident in thinking that he is busy. After all, there are books everywhere, the phone is ringing, and the professor is seated behind a desk with many papers on it. However, these environmental artifacts and conditions may not be accurately communicating the professor's availability. Ashley needs to clarify and confirm her

Body Language and Personal Space in the Nursing Profession

The ebbs and flows of the nursing profession are often based upon the relationship that a nurse has with his or her patient. Helping patients heal is a primary goal of what it means to be an effective nurse and the conversations that nurses have with patients are instrumental. These conversations necessarily take into consideration the importance of kinesic and proxemic behavior. Kim Holland (nursetogether.com, 2013) expresses the value of being aware of body language and personal space as she provides specific recommendations related to nursing communication. She contends that patients can "see the mood" through the actions of a nurse. To this end, Holland provides several recommendations related to the interplay between nonverbal communication and nursing. First, being aware of one's eye contact, while seemingly easy, is not always practiced. Nurses need to stay adept at establishing and engaging their eye contact with patients since "patients see our hearts through our eyes." A second concern relates to an area of the body not always considered: the shoulders. Holland believes that nurses often carry their stress in their shoulders and tight stressful shoulders affect

© iStock.com/monkeybusinessimages

posture and comfort, thereby influencing productivity. Third, Holland notes that a nurse's hands can be quite calming to patients as can a simple pat on the back that can inspire patient confidence. Finally, a nurse's use of personal space is also crucial. When a discussion happens, is it occurring next to the patient's bed or standing at the door? In highly consequential conversations (e.g., medicine dosage, medical diagnosis, etc.), Holland believes that nurses should move closer to a patient. In doing so, nurses "show respect and open communication" and they can "better observe facial expressions." In sum, being an effective nurse requires an understanding of the power of nonverbal communication.

our constant eye rolling during a conflict is irritating. Our close relational partners are more inclined to inform us whether our verbal and nonverbal communication are consistent. Those who are close to us are more likely to be up-front with us about any communication deficiencies.

5-5e Avoid Nonverbal Distractions

The old saying "Get out of your own way!" has meaning when we communicate nonverbally. At times, our nonverbal communication can serve as noise in an interpersonal exchange. Consider, for example, playing with your hair, shifting your eyes, using vocal distractors, or texting while talking to someone. Are you having a personal conversation with someone in a noisy bar? The person is likely to focus more on your nonverbal displays than on what you are saying. In turn,

it's likely that meaning would be obscured or little meaning would be exchanged in the interaction.

5-5f Place Nonverbal Communication in Context

Earlier in this chapter, we discussed the fact that we live in a society that embraces simplistic notions associated with nonverbal communication. For instance, in the 1970s and 1980s, John Molloy (1978) made millions of dollars from his book *Dress for Success.* This simplistic source told business professionals how to dress to look "professional" and to be taken seriously in the workplace. Scores of companies embraced the basic suggestions of the book and used its conclusions to mandate changes to corporate attire.

However, when discussing human behavior, we need to avoid such superficial ideas about our nonverbal communication. We should pay attention to nonverbal cues, but we should place them in appropriate context. Be careful of assigning too much meaning to a wink, a handshake, a pair of dangling earrings, or a voice that sounds uptight. These may carry no significant meaning in a conversation. To acquire meaning, you must consider the entire communication process, not just one element of it.

STUDY TOOLS

DON'T FORGET TO CHECK OUT WWW.CENGAGEBRAIN.COM!

CHAPTER 5 FEATURES THE FOLLOWING RESOURCES:

☐ Ethics & Choice: Kyle

☐ Communication Assessment Test: Touch Avoidance Inventory

☐ Interactive Activities

6 | Listening and Responding Effectively

LEARNING OUTCOMES

6-1 Recognize the difference between hearing and listening

6-2 Describe the components of the listening process

6-3 Explain the value and importance of listening

6-4 Recognize obstacles to listening

6-5 Name the common poor listening habits

6-6 Identify four styles of listening

6-7 Explain how culture affects listening

6-8 Utilize a variety of techniques to enhance your listening effectiveness

After you finish this chapter, go to **PAGE 129** for **STUDY TOOLS.**

THEORY/MODEL PREVIEW

Working Memory Theory

© S_L/Shutterstock.com

Listening is one of the most utilized skills in our interpersonal communication, but the skill that is attended to the least.

Interestingly, most people believe that they are good listeners, but in fact, research shows that people are not at all efficient in their listening. Listening has been identified as a "forgotten skill," a "lost art," and "the most critical business skill of all" (Ferrari, 2012). Clearly, listening is a conversational imperative, and without quality listening, our interpersonal communication would suffer.

Despite its value, so many of us experience listening deficiencies. For instance, in the course of an average day, most of us don't listen with complete attention to the barrage of messages from the media, our friends, family, and coworkers. Some of these messages are not altogether useful for us ("And let me tell you about my niece's new boyfriend"); others we've heard over and over again ("When I was a teenager . . ."); others don't make sense to us ("When I cook, I usually think of Gayle's wedding dress"); and still other messages we tune out ("Wait, I know about that bank's mission statement").

Let's be clear: Failing to listen can have serious consequences. Consider Abby, a 21-year-old college junior who decided to go to campus counseling services because she was feeling depressed. Or, think about Dana, a 31-year-old single father who brought his toddler into the doctor's office because of an ongoing cough. Now think about Manuel, a 55-year-old construction site supervisor who meets the building inspector to talk about cutting costs on a project that has already run over budget. Each

of these scenarios requires a listener-receiver (a counselor, a physician, and a building inspector), and without effective listening, the costs can be devastating.

This chapter discusses the importance of listening, explores reasons why we don't always listen, and suggests ways we can overcome our bad listening habits. Unlike other chapters, it's more difficult to unpack the impact of listening on our online relationships. First, no communication research exists that helps us understand this dynamic. Second, the listening process and its relationship to the online world is rather tough to disentangle. Therefore, most of what you will read relates to the face-to-face experiences we have with others.

Listening is a communication behavior that we may think we all understand, but we need to explain it further to have a common foundation. We begin our discussion by first differentiating listening from hearing. Although the two terms are often used interchangeably, hearing and listening are different processes and mean different things.

LEND ME YOUR EAR: DIFFERENCES BETWEEN HEARING AND LISTENING

Let's begin by interrogating a commonly held, but erroneous myth: listening and hearing are the same thing. They are not. Hearing occurs when a sound wave hits an eardrum. The resulting vibrations, or stimuli, are sent to the brain. For our purposes, we define **hearing** as the physical process of letting in auditory stimuli without trying to understand that stimuli. We can pay attention to several stimuli and simultaneously store stimuli for future reference. When we try to organize the stimuli,

hearing The physical process of letting in audible stimuli without focusing on the stimuli.

we have to retrieve previous experiences and information to match it to the current stimuli. Again, all of this "processing and storage" is done at the same time, and all of it is conducted at the point in the communication process that we call hearing.

To help understand the complex intersection between stimuli and our cognitive processes, **working memory theory** (Baddeley, 2012) was conceptualized. Working memory theory explains why we direct our attention to relevant information and suppress irrelevant information while allowing our thinking processes to coordinate multiple tasks. Working memory temporarily holds information over a short period of time and allows you to "delegate" the things you experience to the parts of the brain that can take action.

We introduced you to the issue of stimuli in Chapter 3. With respect to its relationship to working memory theory, consider the following. When Kirsten sits at The Beanpot Cafe drinking coffee and reading the morning paper online, she hears all types of noises, including people ordering coffee, couples laughing, and even the folk music coming from the ceiling speakers. However, she is not paying attention to these background noises. Instead, she is hearing the stimuli without thinking about them. Kirsten must be able to tune out these stimuli

working memory theory A theory stating that we can pay attention to several stimuli and simultaneously store stimuli for future reference.

THEORY SPOTLIGHT:

Working Memory Theory

An individual's working memory allows for completing tasks and blocking out distractions so you can stay focused. College life is replete with an abundance of irrelevant and ancillary distractions, making it more difficult for you to hone in on the learning process. Think about a number of these interruptions and academic noises and identify a few. Next, how is your memory able to organize these various extraneous stimuli and provide relevance to those people and events that assist you to focus? In other words, how can you participate in activities and sustain your attention on matters related to your education?

because otherwise she wouldn't be able to concentrate on reading the paper.

Like Kirsten, we find ourselves hearing a lot of stimuli throughout our day, whether it's the hum of an air conditioner, dishes breaking in a restaurant, or the sounds of fire trucks passing on the street. Most of us are able to continue our conversations without attending to these noises.

Being a good listener is much more than letting in audible stimuli. Listening is a communication activity that requires us to be thoughtful. The choices we make when we listen affect our interpersonal encounters. As we alluded to earlier, people often take listening for granted as a communication skill in interpersonal relationships. As Harvey Mackay (2011) concluded, "Listening is the hardest of the 'easy' tasks; if you want to be heard, you must know how to listen." Unlike hearing, listening is a learned communication skill. People often have a difficult time describing what being an effective listener is, but they seem to know when another person is not listening. And, listening is often viewed as a passive process. As Andrew Wolvin (2010) concludes, "The word 'just' is all too often frequently used to describe listening in the admonition 'Just listen' (p. 2). This reduces listening to a simple behavior that requires little engagement."

THE COMPONENTS OF THE LISTENING PROCESS

With this framework, we define **listening** as the dynamic, transactional process of receiving, responding to, recalling, and rating stimuli and/or messages from another. When we listen, we are making sense of the message of another communicator. Let's briefly break down this definition.

Listening is dynamic because it is an active and ongoing way of demonstrating that you are involved in an interpersonal encounter. Furthermore, listening is transactional because both the sender and the receiver are active agents in the process, as we discussed in Chapter 1. In other words, listening is a two-way street that requires both "motorists to navigate." We can't just show that we listen; we need others to show us *they know* we are listening.

The remaining four concepts of the definition require a more detailed discussion. We already know that hearing is a starting point in the listening process. Stimuli have to be present, but much more is required. The **four "Rs" of listening**—receiving, responding, recalling, and rating—make up the listening process (see Figure 6.1). Each of the following sections reviews a component of the listening process and the specific skill it requires. Also, because we wish to encourage you to practice your listening continuously, we include a few remarks for improving that skill. We will have broader skill recommendations later in the chapter.

6-2a Receiving

When we receive a message, we hear and attend to it. **Receiving** involves the verbal and nonverbal acknowledgment of communication. We are selective in our reception and usually screen out those messages that are least relevant to us. We also have a problem receiving all of the messages since our attention spans are rather short, lasting from around 2 to 20 seconds (Wolvin & Coakley, 1996). And, then there is a loss of listening abilities. Do you find yourself putting in your ear buds or head set on to listen to your music? This can lead to hearing loss and consequently, can lead to problems in receiving a message.

When we are receiving a message, we are trying to be mindful—a concept we discussed in Chapter 3. Mindfulness, you may recall, means we are paying close attention to the stimuli around us. **Mindful listening** requires us to be engaged with another person—the words, the behaviors, and the environment. Mindful listening has been employed in professional contexts, including treatment of adults with autism or Down syndrome (King,

FIGURE 6.1   THE LISTENING PROCESS

Stage 1	Receiving	→	Acknowledge the message
Stage 2	Responding	→	Provide feedback
Stage 3	Recalling	→	Remember the essence of the message
Stage 4	Rating	→	Evaluate the message

© Cengage Learning®

Baxter, Rosenbaum, Zwaigenbaum, & Bates, 2009) and those with multiple sclerosis (Hendrick, 2010).

The following two suggestions should improve your ability to receive messages effectively. First, eliminate unnecessary noises and physical barriers to listening. If possible, try to create surroundings that allow you to receive a message fully and accurately. Avoid answering your cell phone, watching ESPN, or texting your roommate if someone is talking to you. Second, try not to interrupt the reception of a message. Although you may be tempted to cut off a speaker when he or she communicates a message about which you have a strong

Texting, working on the computer, or watching TV while talking to someone will make you unlikely to receive their message fully or accurately.

listening The dynamic, transactional process of receiving, responding, recalling, and rating to stimuli, messages, or both.

four "Rs" of listening The four components of the listening process: receiving, responding, recalling, and rating.

receiving The verbal and nonverbal acknowledgment of a message.

mindful listening Listening that requires us to be engaged with another person—the words, the behaviors, and the environment.

opinion, yield the conversational floor so you can receive the entire message and not simply a part of it.

6-2b Responding

Responding means giving feedback to another communicator in an interpersonal exchange. Responding suggests the transactional nature of the interpersonal communication process. That is, although we are not speaking to another person, we are communicating by listening. This suggests that responding is critical to achieve interpersonal meaning.

Responding, which lets a speaker know that the message was received, happens during and after a conversation. So, when Kenny uses both head nods and words (e.g., "I get it," "Yep, you make sense," etc.) during his conversation with his girlfriend, Keri, he's providing both nonverbal and verbal feedback. And, if, after the two have stopped talking, Kenny hugs and holds her, he is still responding to his girlfriend's message.

You can enhance the way you respond in several ways. Adopting the other's point of view is important. This skill (which we talk about later in this chapter) is particularly significant when communicating with people with cultural backgrounds different from your own. Also, take ownership of your words and ideas. Don't confuse what you say with what the other person says. Finally, don't assume that your thoughts are universally accepted; not everyone will agree with your position on a topic.

6-2c Recalling

Recalling involves understanding a message, storing it for future encounters, and remembering it later. We have sloppy recall if we understand a message when it is first communicated but forget it later. When we do recall a conversation, we don't recall it word for word; rather, we remember a personal version (or essence) of what occurred (Bostrom, 1990). Recall is immediate, short-term, or long-term (Bostrom & Waldhart, 1988).

Michele Tine (2013) reminds us that people's recall abilities vary. For instance, in a study of rural (and urban) poverty, Tine found that low-income rural children recalled tasks differently than their high-income rural counterparts. She believes that these recall differences may be attributed to poor economic and environmental

---

responding Providing observable feedback to a sender's message.

recalling Understanding a message, storing it for future encounters, and remembering it later.

chunking Placing pieces of information into manageable and retrievable sets.

---

conditions, an area that has often been overlooked in listening research.

Let's consider another situation: Suppose another person criticizes you for recalling a conversation incorrectly. You might simply tell the other person that he or she is wrong. This is what happens in the following conversation between Matt and Dale. The two have been good friends for years. Matt is a homeowner who needed some painting done, and Dale verbally agreed to do it. Now that Dale has given Matt the bill, the two remember differently their conversation about how the bill was to be paid:

Dale:	Matt, you said you'd pay the bill in two installments. We didn't write it down, but I remember your words: "I can pay half the bill immediately and then the other half 2 weeks later." Now you're trying to tell me you didn't say that?
Matt:	That's totally not it at all. I told you that I'd pay the bill in two installments *only* after I was happy that the work was finished. Look, I know this isn't what you want to hear, but the hallway wall is scratched and needs to be repainted. I see gouges on the hardwood floors by the living room, and look at the paint drips on the molding in the dining room.
Dale:	I told you that I'd come in later to do those small repairs, and you said you'd pay me.
Matt:	Sorry, bud, I don't remember it that way.

© Cengage Learning®

Matt and Dale clearly have different recollections of their conversation. Their situation is even more challenging because both money and friendship are involved.

A number of strategies can help you improve your ability to later recall a message. First, repeating information helps clarify terms and provide you an immediate confirmation of whether the intended message was received accurately. Second, using *mnemonic* (pronounced "ni-MON-ik") devices as memory-aiding guides will likely help you recall things more easily. Abbreviations such as MADD (for Mothers Against Drunk Driving) and PETA (People for the Ethical Treatment of Animals) use acronyms as mnemonic devices. Finally, chunking can assist you in recalling. **Chunking** means placing pieces of information into manageable

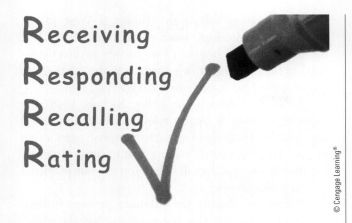

Receiving

Responding

Recalling

Rating

and retrievable sets. For example, if Matt and Dale discussed several issues and subissues—such as a payment schedule, materials, furniture protection, paint color, timetables, worker load, and so on—chunking those issues into fewer, more manageable topics (e.g., finances, paint, and labor) may have helped reduce their conflict.

6-2d Rating

Rating means evaluating or assessing a message. When we listen critically, we rate messages on three levels: (1) we decide whether or not we agree with the message, (2) we place the message in context, and (3) we evaluate whether the message has value to us.

You don't always agree with messages you receive from others. However, when you disagree with another person, you should try to do so from the other's viewpoint. Rating a message from another's field of experience allows us to distinguish among facts, inferences, and opinions (Brownell, 2012), and these three are critical in evaluating a message. Although we briefly explored facts and inferences in Chapter 2, let's refresh you on the subject. Facts are verifiable and can be made only after direct observation. Inferences fill in a conversation's "missing pieces" and require listeners to go beyond what was observed. **Opinions** can undergo changes over time and are based on a communicator's beliefs or values.

When we evaluate a message, we need to understand the differences among facts, inferences, and opinions. Let's say, for example, that Claire knows the following:

▶ Her best friend, Oliver, hasn't spoken to her in 3 weeks.

▶ Oliver is calling other people.

▶ Claire has called Oliver several times and has left messages on voice mail.

These are the facts. If Claire states that Oliver is angry at her, or that he doesn't care about her well-being, she is not acting on facts. Rather, she is using inferences and expressing opinions. And, her views may not be accurate at all.

Here are two suggestions that will help you improve your ability to rate messages. First, if possible, detect speaker bias. At times, messages are difficult to listen to. One reason for this may be the speaker's bias; information in a message may be distorted because a speaker may be prejudiced in some way ("Anyone with that accent sounds pretty dumb to me"). Second, listeners should be prepared to change their position. After you have rated a message, you may want to modify your opinions or beliefs on a subject because of new information or because you were quick to evaluate. Learn to become more flexible in your thinking.

6-3 THE VALUE AND IMPORTANCE OF LISTENING

It's probably hard to find people who will admit the following: "I'm a really bad listener." Although we like to think we are good listeners, we all need help in this area. Listening is an ongoing interpersonal activity that requires lifelong training. Active listening, a behavior we discuss in more detail later in the chapter, is particularly crucial. Because we listen for a variety of important reasons (see Figure 6.2), listening needs to be a high priority in our lives. Let's offer a few more reasons why studying this topic has lasting value.

Listening is essential to our relationships with others, whether they are coworkers, family members, friends, or other important people in our lives. Several conclusions merit some consideration. Listening is used

FIGURE 6.2 WHY WE LISTEN

Listening for **information**

Listening for **advice**

Listening for **enjoyment**

Listening to **help others**

Listening for **cultural understanding**

© Cengage Learning®

rating Evaluating or assessing a message.

opinion A view, judgment, or appraisal based on our beliefs or values.

at least three times as much as speaking and at least four times as much as reading and writing (Grognet & Van Duzer, 2002).

Employers rank listening as the most important skill on the job (Carnevale & Smith, 2013). Listening expert Michael Purdy suggests that hourly employees spend 30 percent of their time listening; managers, 60 percent; and executives, 75 percent or more (Purdy, 2004). Liz Simpson (2003), a writer for the *Harvard Management Communication Letter*, offers the following advice to those in the workplace: "To see things from another's point of view and to build trust with her [him], you have to listen closely to what she [he] says" (p. 4).

Researchers and writers have called listening a 21st-century skill (Stuart, 2010) because it's now more important than ever. Sheila Bentley (2000) remarked that "new technology and changes in current business practices have changed whom we listen to, what we are listening for, when we listen to them, and how we listen to them" (p. 130). Listening errors can debilitate worker productivity (Lumley & Wilkinson, 2014); and because of what Howard Gardner and Katie Davis (2013) call the "App Generation," young people today have focused more on their smartphones and have failed to practice effective listening with others.

Good listening skills are valuable in other types of interpersonal relationships as well. For example, successful medical students must develop effective listening skills because, on average, a medical practitioner may conduct over 250,000 interviews during a 40-year career (Meldrum, 2011). Additional research reported by Donaghue (2007) shows that doctor-patient communication, of which listening is identified as paramount, is especially pivotal in health care. Many hospitals, responding to national surveys on patient satisfaction, are now requiring assessments of a physician's listening skills for fear of malpractice suits. Answers to questions such as "During this hospital stay, how often did doctors listen carefully to you?" will now be collated and provided to patients to use to make health care choices.

Other contexts require skill in listening. In the educational context, researchers have found that effective listening is associated with more positive teacher-parent relationships (Castro, Cohen, Tohar, & Kluger, 2013) and more positive student learning (Bond, 2012). On the home front, many family conflicts can be resolved

American Sign Language (ASL) A visual rather than auditory form of communication that is composed of precise hand shapes and movements.

by listening more effectively (Turner & West, 2013). And, in our friendships, some research has shown that the intimacy level between two friends is directly related to the listening skills brought into the relationship (Worthington & Fitch-Hauser, 2011).

Although it dates to the 1940s (Nichols, 1948), the topic of listening is clearly relevant today. You would have trouble thinking of any interpersonal relationship in your life that doesn't require you to listen. Improving your listening skills will help improve your relational standing with others.

Before we discuss the listening process further, we should point out that not everyone has the physical ability to hear or listen. Although our discussion in this chapter focuses on those who are able to hear physiologically, we are aware that many individuals rely on another communication system to create and share symbols: **American Sign Language** (ASL). ASL is among the fastest-growing languages in the United States (Modern Language Association, 2010). A visual rather than auditory form of communication, ASL is composed of precise hand shapes and movements. According to the "About ASL" page of a website dedicated to American Sign Language (www.aslinfo.com), approximately half a million people communicate in this manner in the United States and Canada alone. In fact, ASL is seen as an instinctive communication method for visual learners who aren't hearing impaired. The hard-of-hearing and deaf communities have embraced ASL, and it is used to create and sustain communication within the community.

With this important recognition, we now turn our attention to the challenges people have with listening. You already know that listening is important in our personal and professional lives. Yet, for a number of reasons, people don't listen well. We now present several obstacles to listening.

 ## 6-4 THE BARRIERS: WHY WE DON'T LISTEN

People don't want to acknowledge that they are often poor listeners. As we present the following context and personal barriers to listening, try to recall times when you have faced these problems during interpersonal encounters. We hope that making you aware of these issues will enable you to avoid them or deal with them effectively. Table 6.1 presents examples of these obstacles in action.

TABLE 6.1 BARRIERS TO LISTENING

Barrier Type	In Action
Noise (physical, semantic, physiological, psychological)	Marcy tries to listen to Nick's comments, but his racist words cause her to stop listening.
Message overload	As a receptionist for a church, Carmen's daily tasks include reading about 20 emails, listening to approximately 10 voice mails, opening nearly 50 pieces of mail, and answering about 40 phone calls. When the minister approaches her with advice on how to organize the church picnic, Carmen's message overload interferes with receiving the minister's words accurately.
Message complexity	Dr. Jackson tells her patient, Mark, that his "systemic diagnosis has prevented any follow-up"; Mark tunes out because he doesn't understand what she means.
Lack of training	Jamie is asked to supervise a task force at work. He has never taken a course on communication, and he does not have any formal training in listening. He struggles with wanting to listen to the group and wishes he better understood how to listen.
Preoccupation	As Sara talks with Kevin, a coworker, she tries to listen to him talk about his job, but she is thinking about what time she will need to leave work to get to her little brother's graduation that evening. Sara also continues to search the Web to find her last-minute graduation gift.
Listening gap	As Loretta tells her grandkids how she and her husband met, the 6- and 7-year-olds grow impatient and tell their grandma to hurry up.

© Cengage Learning®

6-4a Noise

As we mentioned in Chapter 1, the physical environment and all of its distractions can prevent quality listening. Noise, you will remember, is anything that interferes with the message. Suppose, for instance, that a deaf student is trying to understand challenging subject matter in a classroom. Attempting to communicate the professor's words, the signer begins to sign words that are incorrect because she doesn't understand the content. Or, the signs are slurred or incoherent because the signing is too fast. These distractions would certainly influence the reception of the message by the deaf student.

Distractions can include physical, semantic, physiological, and psychological noise that prevent a listener from receiving the sender's message. Let's clarify each type of noise a bit further. **Physical noise** is any external distraction that prevents meaning between communicators. We may have difficulty listening to our boss at work because a printer is running. Maybe a friend is not able to listen to you at a bar because the music is too loud. Perhaps the noisy dishwasher at home interferes with a parent-child conversation. We run into physical distractions on a daily basis.

Semantic noise results from a sender using language that is not readily understood by a receiver. Semantic noise may take the form of antiquated words

© iStock.com/Olmarmar

physical noise External disturbances that interrupt the meaning between a sender and receiver.

semantic noise Disruption that results from a sender using language that is not readily understood by a receiver.

or phrases, or language that is confusing or filled with jargon. If you are listening to your grandfather talk about reverse home mortgages, you may "check out" of the conversation because his language may be too technical or irrelevant to you.

The third type of noise, **physiological noise**, is any physical, chemical, or biological disturbance that interferes with communication. For example, it's difficult to listen when you have a migraine headache.

Finally, **psychological noise** occurs when the sender and/or receiver have biases and prejudices that distort the message meaning. Think of this as mental interference in message meaning. We may enter a conversation with preconceptions or stereotypes that affect our understanding of what the other person is going to say, and our assumptions may get in the way of effective listening. For example, you may be a volunteer at Planned Parenthood and therefore, it may be difficult for you to be open-minded when a colleague talks to you about the right to protest at medical facilities that provide reproductive services.

6-4b Message Overload

Senders frequently receive more messages than they can process, which is called **message overload.** With the advent of more and more (social) media and advanced media technology, multitasking is now commonplace

© iStock.com/German

---

physiological noise Interference in message reception because of physical, biological, or chemical functions of the body.

psychological noise The biases or prejudices of a sender or receiver that interrupts the meaning of a message.

message overload The result when senders receive more messages than they can process.

---

both at work and home. The average worker in the United States handles about 200 messages in 1 day (BBC News, 1999); and the McKinsey Global Institute reported 28 percent of our work week is spent reading, sorting, sending, and deleting email (Chui et al., 2012). We used to visit a coworker's desk just a few feet away, but now we email her. Before, we'd visit a neighbor to borrow something; now we call him instead. We tweet out our opinions on sports and steroids. We can't get pictures up fast enough on Facebook. We now find ourselves talking on the phone while downloading a document, sending an email while chatting with a roommate, and text messaging while driving (*please* don't do this!). With all of this technological maneuvering, who wouldn't be tired of listening at some point during the day?

6-4c Message Complexity

Messages we receive that are filled with details, unfamiliar language, and challenging arguments are often difficult to understand. For example, at the "closing" of a property sale, many homebuyers are overwhelmed by the number of documents they have to sign; the complex federal, state, and local laws they are told about; and the stress of signing financial papers that will put them in debt for 30 years or more. This is a great deal to manage and listen to, and it's likely that the unfamiliar and cumbersome language will negatively affect their listening skills. This can be a serious problem, because important information is communicated at the "closing." Many people in technical professions are changing their behaviors. For example, experts in science, technology, engineering, and math (STEM) are spending considerable time and resources making their messages less complex and more amenable to laypeople's understanding (National Governors Association, 2008).

6-4d Lack of Training

Both the academic and corporate environments include opportunities to learn about listening, but more could be done. Because listening is a learned activity, we are seeing more and more schools—including Capital Community College, the University of Northern Iowa, Nassau Community College (New York), Penn State University, and the University of Maryland—offer courses on the topic. Still, most students' preparation in listening is limited to a chapter such as the one you are reading now. And, consider the tens of millions of people who have never enrolled in an interpersonal communication class! Finally, more and more employers are realizing that increased productivity, positive employee morale, and a healthy organizational climate can be attributed to listening (Hall, 2013).

6-4e Preoccupation

Even the most effective listeners become preoccupied at times. When we are preoccupied, we are thinking about our own life experiences and everyday troubles. Those who are preoccupied may be prone to what Anita Vangelisti, Mark Knapp, and John Daly (1990) call **conversational narcissism**, or engaging in an extreme amount of self-focusing to the exclusion of another person. Those who are narcissistic are caught up in their own thoughts and are inclined to interrupt others (Honeycutt, Pence, & Gearhart, 2013). Most of us have been narcissistic at one time or another; think of the many times you've had a conversation with someone while you were thinking about your rent, your upcoming test, or your vacation plans. Or, think about trying to hijack a conversation to make it personally relevant ("Oh, you think your surgery was bad! Let me tell you what I went through!"). Although such personal thoughts may be important, they can obstruct our listening. Narcissism, however, has some rather profound implications in our perception process. In one study, for instance, auditors from an accounting firm found that client narcissistic communication positively influenced auditor perceptions of a client's assessment to be fraudulent (Johnson, Kuhn, Apostolou, & Hassell, 2013).

Preoccupation can also result from focusing on the technology in front of us. How many times have you been on the phone and typing at your computer at the same time? How often have you been told to "listen up" by a friend, only to simultaneously text-message another friend. This preoccupation with technology while others are communicating with us can undercut effective and engaged listening.

6-4f Listening Gap

We generally think faster than we speak. In fact, research shows that we speak an average rate of 150 to 200 words per minute, yet we can understand up to 800 words per minute (Wolvin & Coakley, 1996). That is, we can think about three or four times faster than we can talk. The **listening gap** is the time difference between your mental ability to interpret words and the speed at which they arrive to your brain. When we have a large listening gap, we may daydream, doodle on paper, or allow our minds to wander. This drifting off may cause us to miss the essence of a message from a sender. It takes a lot of effort to listen to someone. Closing the listening gap can be challenging for even the most attentive listeners.

6-5 POOR LISTENING HABITS

Poor listening is something that usually occurs over our lifespan. For one reason or another, we have picked up behaviors that do little to develop and maintain quality interpersonal relationships. Although some of these occur more frequently than others in conversations, each is serious enough to affect the reception and meaning of a message. Table 6.2 offers some tips to help you overcome the poor listening habits we discuss next.

6-5a Selective Listening

You engage in **selective listening**, or **spot listening**, if you attend to some parts of a message and ignore others. Typically, you selectively listen to those parts of the message that interest you. For an example of how spot listening can be problematic, consider what happens when jurors listen to a witness' testimony.

TABLE 6.2 — HOW TO OVERCOME POOR LISTENING HABITS

Poor Listening Habit	Strategy for Overcoming Habit
Selective listening	Embrace entire message.
Talkaholism	Become other-oriented.
Pseudolistening	Center attention on speaker.
Gap filling	Fill gap by mentally summarizing message.
Defensive listening	Keep self-concept in check.
Ambushing	Play fair in conversations.

© Cengage Learning®

conversational narcissism Engaging in an extreme amount of self-focusing during a conversation to the exclusion of another person.

listening gap The time difference between our mental ability to interpret words and the speed at which they arrive at our brain.

selective listening Responding to some parts of a message and rejecting others.

One juror may listen to only the information pertaining to *where* a witness was during a crime to assess the witness's credibility. Another juror may selectively listen to *why* a witness was near the crime scene. Their spot listening prevents them from receiving all relevant information about the crime. Controlling for such selective listening first requires us to glean the entire message. Attending to only those message parts that interest you or tuning out because you believe that you know the rest of a message may prompt others to question your listening skills.

6-5b Talkaholism

Some people become consumed with their own communication (McCroskey & Richmond, 1995). These individuals are **talkaholics**, defined as compulsive talkers who hog the conversational stage and monopolize encounters. When talkaholics take hold of a conversation, they interrupt, directing the conversational flow. And, of course if you're talking all the time, you don't take the time to listen. For instance, consider Uncle Jimmy, the talkaholic in the Norella family. The nearly 15 members of the Norella clan who gather each Thanksgiving dread engaging Uncle Jimmy in conversation because all he does is talk. And talk. Some family members privately wonder whether Jimmy understands that many of his more than a dozen relatives would like to speak. But without fail, he comes to dinner with story after story to tell, all the while interrupting those who'd like to share their stories, too.

Not all families have an Uncle Jimmy, but you may know someone who is a talkaholic—that is, someone who won't let you get a word in edgewise. If you are a talkaholic and have the urge to interrupt others, take a deep breath and refrain from talking until your conversational partner has finished speaking. If you find yourself talking in a stream of consciousness without much concern for the other person, you are susceptible to becoming a talkaholic. Remember that other people like to talk, too.

talkaholic A compulsive talker who hogs the conversational stage and monopolizes encounters.

pseudolisten To pretend to listen by nodding our heads, looking at the speaker, smiling at the appropriate times, or practicing other kinds of attention feigning.

gap fillers Listeners who think that they can correctly guess the rest of the story a speaker is telling and don't need the speaker to continue.

6-5c Pseudolistening

We are all pretty good at faking attention. Many of us have been indirectly trained to **pseudolisten**, or to pretend to listen by nodding our heads, by looking at the speaker, by smiling at the appropriate times, or by practicing other kinds of attention feigning. The classroom is a classic location for faking attention. Professors have become adept at spotting students who pseudolisten; many of their nonverbal behaviors give away pseudolistening. Or, consider a less strategic fake listening experience; imagine that you just received word that you failed an exam and you're out to dinner with your roommate and her parents. You may pseudolisten because of what is on your mind. You can correct this poor listening habit by making every effort to center your attention on the speaker.

6-5d Gap Filling

Listeners who think that they can correctly guess the rest of the story a speaker is telling and who don't need the speaker to continue are called gap fillers. **Gap fillers** often assume that they know how a narrative or interpersonal encounter will unfold. They also frequently interrupt; when this happens, the

listener alters the message, and its meaning may be lost. Although an issue may be familiar to listeners, they should give speakers the chance to finish their thoughts.

6-5e Defensive Listening

Defensive listening occurs when people view innocent comments as personal attacks or hostile criticisms. Consider Jeannie's experiences. As the owner of a small jewelry shop in the mall, she is accustomed to giving directions to her small staff. Recently, one of her employees commented: "Look, Jeannie, I think you could get more young girls in here if you brought in some rainbow beads. The young ones love them." Jeannie's response was immediate: "Well . . . here's what I recommend: Why don't you find a lot of money, get your own store, and then you can have all of the rainbow beads you want! I've been in this business for almost 10 years, and I think I know what to buy! Why is it that everybody thinks they know how to run a business?"

Jeannie's response fits the definition of defensive listening. Those who are defensive listeners often perceive threats in messages and may be defensive because of personal issues. In this example, Jeannie may not have any animosity toward her employee; she simply may have misinterpreted the comment. To ensure that you are not a defensive listener, keep your self-concept in check. Don't be afraid to ask yourself the following question: "Am I too quick to defend my thoughts?"

6-5f Ambushing

People who listen carefully to a message and then use the information later to attack the individual are **ambushing**. Ambushers want to retrieve information to discredit or manipulate another person. Gathering information and using it to undercut an opponent is now considered routine in politics. Divorce attorneys frequently uncover information to discredit their clients' spouses. Ambushing in this manner should be avoided; words should never be viewed as ammunition for a verbal battle.

Listening to others can be tough and yet by now, we're sure you agree that if we aren't practicing quality listening, we are less likely to have quality relationships. We now focus on the styles of listening that you and others are likely to manifest in your conversations with others.

6-6 PERSONAL STYLES OF LISTENING

Typically, we adopt a style of listening in our interpersonal interactions. A **listening style** is a predominant and preferred approach to the messages we hear. We adopt a listening style to understand the sender's message. In general, listening requires us to think about the relationships we have with others and the tasks that are assigned to us. Providing a template for these listening styles, Charles Johnston, James Weaver, Kittie Watson, and Larry Barker (2000) have identified four: **p**eople-centered, **a**ction-centered, **c**ontent-centered, and **t**ime-centered. We call this establishing a "P-A-C-T" between communicators (see Figure 6.3).

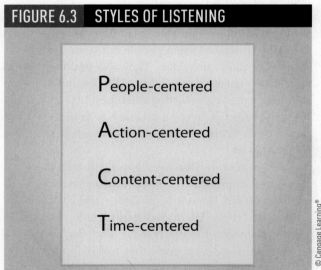

FIGURE 6.3   STYLES OF LISTENING

People-centered

Action-centered

Content-centered

Time-centered

© Cengage Learning®

defensive listening Viewing innocent comments as personal attacks or hostile criticisms.

ambushing Listening carefully to a message and then using the information later to attack the sender.

listening style A predominant and preferred approach to listening to the messages we hear.

6-6a People-Centered Listening Style

The style associated with being concerned with other people's feelings or emotions is called the **people-centered listening style**. People-oriented listeners try to compromise and find common areas of interest. Research shows that people-centered listeners are less apprehensive in groups, meetings, and interpersonal situations than other types of listeners (Sargent, Weaver, & Kiewitz, 1997; Watson & Barker, 1995). People-centered listeners quickly notice others' moods and provide clear verbal and nonverbal feedback, feedback that can make a tremendous difference in a person's life. For instance, in one study (Campbell, Carrick, & Elliott, 2013), those who practiced person-centered listening with terminally ill patients included them in diagnostic decision making and in their overall care.

6-6b Action-Centered Listening Style

The **action-centered listening style** pertains to listeners who want messages to be highly organized, concise, and error free. These people help speakers focus on what is important in the message. Action-centered listeners want speakers to get to the point and are often frustrated when people tell stories in a disorganized or random fashion. They also **second-guess** speakers—that is, they question the assumptions underlying a message (Kirtley & Honeycutt, 1996). If a second-guesser believes a message is false, he or she develops an alternative explanation which is viewed as more realistic.

Action-centered listeners also clearly tell others that they want unambiguous feedback. For instance, as an action-centered listener, a professor may tell her students that if they wish to challenge a grade, they should simply delineate specific reasons why they deserve a grade change and what grade they feel is appropriate.

6-6c Content-Centered Listening Style

Individuals who engage in the **content-centered listening style** focus on the facts and details of a message. They consider all sides of an issue and welcome complex and challenging information from a sender. However, they may intimidate others by asking pointed questions or by discounting information from those the listener deems to be nonexperts. Content-centered listeners are likely to play devil's advocate in conversations. Therefore, attorneys and others in the legal profession are likely to favor this style of listening in their jobs.

6-6d Time-Centered Listening Style

When listeners adopt a **time-centered listening style**, they let others know that messages should be presented with a consideration of time constraints. That is, time-oriented listeners discourage wordy explanations from speakers and set time guidelines for conversations, such as prefacing a conversation with "I have only 5 minutes to talk." Some time-centered listeners constantly check the time or abruptly end encounters with others.

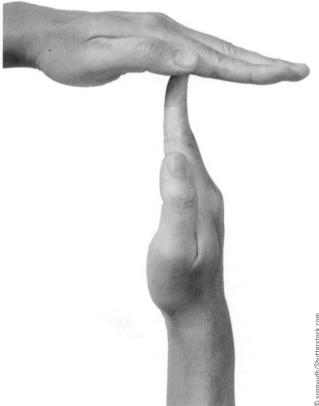

© songvudh/Shutterstock.com

---

people-centered listening style A listening style associated with concern for other people's feelings or emotions.

action-centered listening style A listening style associated with listeners who want messages to be highly organized, concise, and error free.

second-guess To question the assumptions underlying a message.

content-centered listening style A listening style associated with listeners who focus on the facts and details of a message.

time-centered listening style A listening style associated with listeners who want messages to be presented succinctly.

One of your authors has a friend who lives on an island. Her time-centered listening is an inside joke to her friends because she keeps looking at her watch so that she doesn't miss the island ferry to her home. Whether being invited to dinner or to a movie, she is intent on letting others know that she can't go too far from the ferry terminal.

Which of the four listening styles is the best? It's not a trick question because it all depends on the situation and the purpose of the interpersonal encounter. In fact, William Mickelson and S. A. Welch (2013) comment that "listening is a complex, intricate process such that within a single conversation, all types of listening may be present" (p. 158).

You may need to change and adapt your listening style to meet the other person's needs. For example, you might need to be a time-centered listener for the coworker who needs information quickly, but you might need to be person centered while speaking to your best friend about his divorce. However, remember that just because you have adjusted your style of listening does not mean that the other person has adjusted his or her style. You will both have to be aware of each other's style. Know your preferred style of listening, but be flexible in your style depending on the communication situation.

Our listening style is often based on our cultural background. So, let's now turn our attention to the role of culture in listening. When speakers and listeners come from various cultural backgrounds, message meaning can be affected.

value direct communication, or speaking one's mind. Some collectivistic cultures, such as China, respect others' words, desire harmony, and believe in conversational politeness. In fact, listening (*tinghua*) is one of the key principles in Chinese communication. While listening to others, communicators need to remember that differences in feedback (direct or indirect) exist. Let's explore a few examples of the interface of culture and listening.

Richard Lewis (1999) suggests that listening variations across cultures affect the ability to be an effective salesperson. For example, Lewis points out that for the French, listening for information is the main concern. For citizens of several Arab countries, however, listening is done for know-how or for gain. And Lewis indicates that people in some cultures, such as Germany, do not ask for clarification; asking a presenter to repeat him- or herself is seen as a sign of impoliteness and disrespect. As a practical application of this information, consider how a salesperson's recognition of these cultural differences might positively affect his or her company's bottom line.

Donal Carbaugh (1999) offers additional information on ways that culture and listening work together. Looking at listening as a personal opportunity to interrelate with the environment, Carbaugh cites an example of the Blackfeet Indians:

> Blackfeet listening is a highly reflective and revelatory mode of communication that can open one to the mysteries of unity between the physical and spiritual, to the relationships between natural and human forms, and to the intimate links between places and persons. (p. 265)

6-7 CULTURE AND THE LISTENING PROCESS

As we learned in Chapter 2, we are all members of a culture and various cocultures. We understand that cultural differences influence our communication with others. Because all our interactions are culturally based, culture affects the listening process (Worthington & Fitch-Hauser, 2012). Much of the research in this area pertains to race, ethnicity, and ancestry.

Recall from Chapter 2 our discussion of individualistic and collectivistic cultures. We noted that the United States is an individualistic country, meaning that it focuses on an "I" orientation rather than a "we" orientation. Individualistic cultures

Former Blackfeet Tribal Chief Earl Old Person leads an informal listening conference with several tribal representatives. The Blackfeet Tribe is renowned for being a culture that promotes the cultivation of listening skills.

Catherine Karnow/Encyclopedia/Corbis

In fact, Native American communities have come together to form an "Intertribal Monitoring Association on Indian Trust Funds" (www.itmatrustfunds.org) with the sole purpose of having "listening conferences." Representatives from various tribal nations gather to listen to how the federal government is adhering to Trust Fund Standards, to provide tribal forums, and to keep up-to-date on policies and regulations on federal initiatives, among others. These listening conferences have been taking place for over 15 years.

In a study that examined both Iranian and U.S. students, Ali Zohoori (2013) looked at the perceptions of listening competency. Zohoori notes that while Iran continues to transition into the digital age, the primary forms of listening that occur are related to appreciative or aesthetic listening (e.g., listening to poetry or music, etc.). Zohoori looked at both high school and college students. The results showed that while both cultures were generally similar in their perceptions of listening competency, the U.S. students perceived themselves to be better listeners than their Iranian counterparts. Zohoori points out that this may be the case because self-praise is not a cultural value in Iran and modesty remains important. Furthermore, several similarities were observed between both cultures in their perceptions of recalling, responding, and rating listening behaviors.

The common thread in these examples is the notion that while cultures vary in their value systems, listening remains a critical part of the various cultural communities. Staying culturally aware of these variations as you consider the message of another person is important.

What strategies can you use to become a better listener with individuals from various (co-)cultures? First, don't expect everyone else to adapt to your way of communicating (recall our discussion of ethnocentrism in Chapter 2). Second, accept new ways of receiving messages and practice patience with senders who may not have a similar cultural background. Third, wait as long as possible before merging another's words into your words—don't define the world on your terms. Finally, seek clarification when possible. Asking questions in intercultural conversations reduces our processing load, and we are better equipped to translate difficult concepts as they emerge.

In the rest of the chapter, we review effective listening skills you should practice. We know that improving your listening habits is a challenging and lifelong process. So, you shouldn't expect changes to your listening behaviors to happen overnight.

6-8 SKILL SET FOR EFFECTIVE LISTENING

This section outlines five primary skills for improving listening. Whether we communicate with a partner, boss, close friend, family member, coworker, or another, we all must choose whether we will develop good or bad listening habits. And yes, this is a *choice* for you. Let's explore the following guidelines for effective listening.

6-8a Evaluate Your Current Skills

The first step toward becoming a better listener is assessing and understanding your personal listening strengths and weaknesses. To begin, think about the poor listening habits you have seen others practice. Do you use any of them while communicating? Which listening behaviors do you exhibit consistently, and which do you use sporadically? Also, which of your biases, prejudices, beliefs, and opinions may interfere with receipt of a message?

In addition, we have stressors and personal problems that may affect our listening skills. For example, if you were told that your company was laying off workers, how would this affect your communication with people on a daily basis? Could you be an effective listener even though you would find yourself preoccupied with the financial and emotional toll you would experience if you were downsized? In such a situation, it would be nearly impossible to dismiss your feelings, so you should just try to accept them and be aware that they will probably affect your communication with others.

6-8b Prepare to Listen

After you assess your listening abilities, the next step is to prepare yourself to listen. Such preparation requires both physical and mental activities. If you are hearing impaired, you may have to ask for some assistance to ensure that the message is delivered to you accurately. You may have to locate yourself closer to the source of the message (of course, depending on who the speaker is, your physical proximity will vary). If you have problems concentrating on a message, try to reduce or remove as many distractions as possible, such as your laptop or TV. Have you ever had a friend or parent say, "Will you please stop texting and listen to me?" Before being confronted with this question,

A teen's empathy skills continue to be important to cultivate. Sue Shellenbarger (2013) observes that in adolescence, "critical social skills that are needed to feel concern for other people and understand how they think are undergoing major changes." She continues by noting that empathy skills continue rising steadily in girls at age 13. Boys, however, do not begin until age 15 to shows gains in what she calls "perspective taking." Shellenbarger provides research that shows that between ages 13 and 16, adolescent males show a decline in their ability to recognize and respond to others' feelings. She adds, "Fortunately, the boys' sensitivity recovers in the late teens." The research demonstrates that those kids who cultivate empathy skills "form healthy relationships and argue less with their parents." Furthermore, empathic skills are learned skills that children can experience themselves—by being affirmed by adults who respond favorably to their feelings. Some research also concludes that teen boys may suppress empathic feelings so they can participate in jokes and teasing that often characterize teenage boy groups.

Finally, Shellenbarger argues that fathers play an important role in families. Those teens with supportive dads state that they feel better after talking over anxieties with their father, allowing for an enhanced ability to be empathic. After the Boston Marathon bombing in 2013, for instance, one parent stated that he and his sons talked about how a runner who lost her legs must feel when walking into a restaurant where everyone was wearing

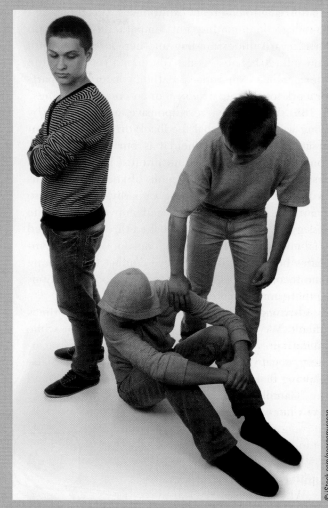

© iStock.com/georgemuresan

shorts. Clearly, teaching empathy is a "vital social skill." (online.wsj.com; 10/15/13)

---

set your phone aside and prepare for the conversation you're about to have.

To prepare yourself mentally, do your homework beforehand if you are going to need information to listen effectively. For example, if you want to ask your boss for a raise, you would want to have ready a mental list of the reasons why you deserve a raise and possible responses to reasons why you do not. If you are a student, reading the material before class will make the lecture or discussion much more meaningful because you will have the background knowledge to be able to offer your thoughts

on issues as they arise. In your personal relationships, you should be prepared to consider other points of view as well as your own.

6-8c Provide Empathic Responses

When we use empathy, we tell other people that we value their thoughts. **Empathy** is the process

> **empathy** The process of identifying with or attempting to experience the thoughts, beliefs, and actions of another.

of identifying with or attempting to experience the thoughts, beliefs, and actions of another. Empathy tells people that although we can't feel their exact feelings or precisely identify with a current situation, we are trying to co-create experiences with them. You are said to be empathic (not "empathetic") when you work toward understanding another person. As Judi Brownell (2012) observed, "You do not *reproduce* the other person's experiences. Rather, you and your partner work together to *produce*, or co-create, meanings" (p. 185). We show we're responsive and empathic by giving well-timed verbal feedback throughout a conversation, not simply when it is our turn to speak. Doing so suggests a genuine interest in the sender's message and has the side benefit of keeping us attentive to the message. To show empathy, we must also demonstrate that we're engaged nonverbally in the message. This can be accomplished through sustained facial involvement (avoiding a blank look that communicates boredom), frequent eye contact (maintaining some focus on the speaker's face), and body positioning that communicates interest.

Learning to listen with empathy is sometimes difficult. We have to show support for another while making sure that we are not unnecessarily exacerbating negative feelings. For instance, examine the following dialogue between two friends, Camilla and Tony. Camilla is angry that her boss did not positively review her work plan:

Camilla: He's self-righteous—that's all there is to it. He didn't even say that my idea made sense. I think he's just jealous because he didn't come up with it first.

Tony: Yeah, I bet you're right. He really didn't show you any respect. And because he's the boss, I'm sure he wanted to take the credit.

© Cengage Learning®

Although Tony meant to show empathy, he may have unintentionally perpetuated the idea that Camilla's boss was a "bad" man. Because Tony seems to be supporting her thoughts, Camilla will have a difficult time

nonjudgmental feedback Feedback that describes another's behavior and then explains how that behavior made us feel.

changing her perception of her boss. This negative view won't help Camilla in future conversations with her boss. Now, consider an alternative response from Tony that doesn't reinforce Camilla's negative perception:

Camilla: He's self-righteous—that's all there is to it. He didn't even say that my idea made sense. I think he's just jealous because he didn't come up with it first.

Tony: Wow, you're obviously frustrated with him . . . you sound like you want to quit. I know that it's rough for you right now, but hang in there.

© Cengage Learning®

In this example, Tony not only demonstrated some empathic listening skills, but helped Camilla redirect her thinking about her boss. When Tony changed the direction of the conversation in this way, Camilla could consider less resentful impressions of the situation. Helping others alleviate their anxiety is a necessary emotional support skill for many interactions (Burleson, 2003).

6-8d Use Nonjudgmental Feedback

Many of us provide feedback with little concern for how the receiver will interpret it. Particularly with those whom we have close relationships such as family members, we may not think twice about providing feedback—regardless of its content. When we give **nonjudgmental feedback**, we describe another's behavior and then explain how that behavior made us feel. As we will discuss in Chapter 7, centering a message on your own emotions without engaging in accusatory finger wagging can help reduce interpersonal conflict.

Consider the difference between the following statements:

▶ "You are so rude to come in late. You made me a nervous wreck! You're pretty inconsiderate to make me feel this way!"

▶ "When you come home so late, I really worry. I thought something had gone wrong."

In heated moments especially, taking ownership of your feelings and perceptions, as in the second

IPCAREERS

Mental Health Counselor

It has been referred to as a "grunt job" and "an endless experience of sadness." Yet, those who pursue a career as a mental health professional also identify it as "richly rewarding." Sarah Maurer (innerbody.com, 2013), a writer who advocates on behalf of mental health counselors, notes that the profession—while not for everyone—is filled with dedicated, thoughtful, and other-centered listeners. In fact, Maurer offers that whether it's through diagnosis, support, or education, a mental health expert must adapt to and adopt various communication styles, most prominently "the ability to listen attentively." By guiding clients in "talk therapy" that are practiced in safe settings through role play, counselors are ethically compelled to toss aside poor listening habits, including pseudo-listening, talkaholism, and selective listening. In addition, Maurer underscores the fact that the four major components of listening

© iStock.com/Christopher Futcher

(receiving, responding, recalling, rating) are essential in this career option. Specifically, she points out that "mental health counselors have the unique opportunity to help people develop the emotional resilience to navigate life's challenges with calm, confidence and optimism." Certainly, each of the four "Rs" function prominently in such a journey.

statement, is difficult. Owning your feelings rather than blaming others for your own feelings results in more effective interpersonal communication.

6-8e Practice Active Listening

We define **active listening** as a transactional process in which a listener communicates reinforcing messages to a speaker. When we actively listen, we show support for another person and his or her message. In our interpersonal relationships, active listeners *want to* listen rather than feel *obligated to* listen. Particularly in close relationships with others, demonstrating that you are actively involved in the conversation will help both

your credibility as a communicator and your relationship standing with others. Additional elements of active listening are paraphrasing, dialogue enhancers, questions, and silence. We briefly discuss each of these in the following subsections.

PARAPHRASING

Active listening requires **paraphrasing**, or restating the essence of another's message in our own words. Paraphrasing is a perception check in an interpersonal encounter; it allows us to clarify our interpretation of a message. When paraphrasing, try to be concise and simple in your response.

paraphrasing Restating the essence of a sender's message in our own words.

For instance, you can use language such as "In other words, what you're saying is . . ." or "I think what I heard is that you . . ." or "Let me see if I get this right." Such phrases show others that you care about understanding the intended meaning of a message.

DIALOGUE ENHANCERS

Active listening requires us to show the speaker that even though we may disagree with his or her thoughts, we accept and are open to them. As we noted earlier, speakers need support in their conversations. **Dialogue enhancers** take the form of supporting expressions such as "I see" or "I'm listening." Dialogue enhancers should not interrupt a message. They should be used as indications that you are involved in the message. In other words, these statements enhance the discussion taking place.

QUESTIONS

Asking well-timed and appropriate questions in an interpersonal interaction can be a hallmark of an engaged active listener. Asking questions is not a sign of ignorance or stupidity, unless your questions are trying to trap the speaker or are meant to deceive or manipulate the sender. What question asking demonstrates is a willingness to make sure that you receive the intended meaning of the speaker's message. If you ask questions, you may receive information that is contrary to your instincts or assumptions, thereby avoiding gap filling, a problem we identified earlier. Don't be afraid to respectfully ask questions in your relationships with others. Your input will likely be met with gratitude as the other communicator realizes your desire to seek information.

SILENCE

Author Robert Fulghum (1989) comments in *All I Really Need to Know I Learned in Kindergarten* that silence is a big part of a satisfying life (we already addressed this importance in Chapter 5). As we noted elsewhere, keeping quiet is usually not viewed as a virtue in many Western societies. In fact, in the self-help book sections in U.S. bookstores, you will likely find no books on the importance of keeping quiet because the culture rewards talkativeness.

Silence is a complicated concept in conversations and in the listening process. Indeed, at times, we should honor **silent listening**, which requires us to stay attentive and respond nonverbally when another person is struggling with what to say. Despite the challenge, particularly with a subject area of which we know a great deal, we need to allow the entire message to be revealed before jumping in. We also need to be silent because sometimes words are not needed. For example, after a conflict has been resolved and two people are looking at each other and holding each other's hands, they don't need to speak to communicate. In this context, silence may be more effective than words in making the people in the relationship feel closer.

However, as noted in our discussion of nonverbal communication (Chapter 5), silence is not always positive. It can also be used to manipulate or coerce another person in an interpersonal exchange. This is an example of the debilitative side of communication

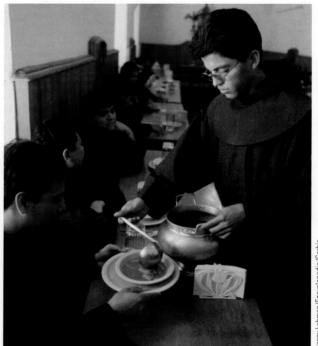

Danny Lehman/Encyclopedia/Corbis

The value of silence is not lost on monks who take a vow of silence as part of their spiritual practice. In such a tradition, practicing silence is not meant as a way to reject others but as a means to clear away noise so the monks are better able to listen.

dialogue enhancers   Supporting statements, such as "I see" or "I'm listening," that indicate we are involved in a message.

silent listening   Listening that requires individuals to listen attentively and nonverbally to another person.

that we discussed in Chapter 1. For instance, giving someone "the silent treatment"—that is, refusing to talk to someone—may provoke unnecessary tension. Also, imposing your own code of silence in an encounter may damage a relationship. For example, if you choose to remain silent in an interpersonal conflict, you will most likely exacerbate the problem and cause your conversational partner to be even more conflicted.

7 | Communicating and Emotion

LEARNING OUTCOMES

7-1 Understand the definition of emotion in all its complexities

7-2 Describe the differences between biological and social explanations for emotion

7-3 Explain the relationship between emotion and interpersonal communication

7-4 Clarify the influences on emotional communication

7-5 Recognize the destructive and constructive aspects associated with emotional communication

7-6 Employ skills for emotional communication to increase satisfaction in interpersonal interactions

THEORY/MODEL PREVIEW

Biological Theory; Social Interaction Theory

After you finish this chapter, go to **PAGE 151** for **STUDY TOOLS.**

Everyone experiences the powerful impact of emotion: the joy of falling in love, the grief of losing a loved one, the pride in an accomplishment, the embarrassment of a public mistake, or the anger that boils up when we think that someone is standing in the way of a cherished goal.

Emotional experiences shape our lives and our relationships, and are often what we remember most about interpersonal encounters. For example, Jay barely remembers any of his high school teachers now that he's 32. But his ninth-grade English teacher, Ms. Laurent, is someone he'll never forget. He often thinks of how she helped him feel proud of his work and optimistic about his future. Emotion often influences how we judge interpersonal interactions. For instance, when Angie thinks back to her friendship with Rosa, she's glad it's over because of all the arguments between them, which left Angie feeling angry and depressed most of the time. Angie had to conclude that she and Ros had an unhealthy relationship.

In this chapter, we investigate emotion and its power ful relationship to the interpersonal communication process We all know intuitively how important emotion is, but ofte we don't have enough information about emotion—it isn a subject discussed much in school, for instance. But if w don't pay attention to emotion, we can't be competent com municators. As with so many aspects of interpersonal com munication, we need to gain adequate knowledge before w can develop our skills, and so we'll begin by defining emotior

DEFINING EMOTION: MORE THAN JUST A FEELING

Defining the term **emotion** is complicated. Some researchers (e.g., Fehr & Russell, 1984; Ortony, Clore, & Foss, 1987) argue that emotion involves only one person's feelings (e.g., anger, fear, anxiety, happiness). Other researchers (Planalp & Fitness, 1999) include in their definition those emotions we feel in relationship with others, such as envy and love. Still other scholars (Buzzanell & Turner, 2012; Tracy, 2005) differentiate between *real* feelings and *manufactured* feelings that are produced because some outside norm dictates that they are appropriate. For instance, if you are a server in a restaurant, your job requires you to smile and act happy around your customers even if you've had a horrible day, and don't feel like smiling at all. Manufacturing a feeling that you're not actually experiencing is called *emotion labor*.

In this book, we define emotion as the critical internal structure that orients us to, and engages us with, what matters in our lives: our feelings about ourselves and others. Thus, the term *emotion* encompasses both the internal feelings of one person (e.g., when Joe feels anxious before he meets Ana's parents) as well as feelings that can be experienced only in a relationship (e.g., when Joyce feels competitive when she hears how well Barb did on the chemistry exam). Emotion labor falls outside the definition we're using here.

The definition of emotion also rests on the notion of process. Although we have names for discrete emotions such as fear, sadness, depression, ecstasy, and so forth, emotion is often experienced as a blend of several

> **emotion** The critical internal structure that orients us to, and engages us with, what matters in our lives: our feelings about ourselves and others. Emotion encompasses both the internal feelings of one person (e.g., anxiety or happiness) as well as feelings that can be experienced only in a relationship (e.g., jealousy or competitiveness).

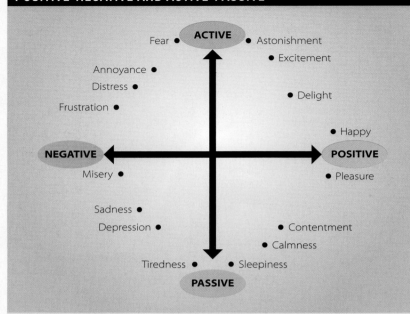

FIGURE 7.1 CATEGORY SYSTEM FOR EMOTIONS: POSITIVE-NEGATIVE AND ACTIVE-PASSIVE

Based on Guerrero, L. K., Andersen, P. A., & Trost, M. R. (1998). *Handbook of communication and emotion.* San Diego, CA: Academic Press, p. 14.

7-1a Two Category Systems for Emotion

To capture the complexity of emotion, some researchers have created category systems classifying common emotions in the United States. These systems focus on attributes of emotion, such as **valence** (whether it reflects a positive or negative feeling), **activity** (whether it implies action or passivity), and **intensity** (how strongly felt it is).

One system (Russell, 1978, 1980, 1983) categorizes emotion along two dimensions at once: valence and activity. This system allows us to see how specific emotions cluster together depending on whether they are active-negative, active-positive, passive-negative, or passive-positive (see Figure 7.1). For example, when Luis feels an emotion such as excitement, we can see on Figure 7.1 that it is positive and implies some action. When he feels an emotion such as contentment, the figure shows that it's less positive and less active than excitement.

Another system for classifying individual emotion is based on its intensity. Robert Plutchik's (1984) emotion cone provides a graduated image of emotional range

emotions (Ross, Shayya, Champlain, Monnot, & Prodan, 2013). Strategic embarrassment is an example of an emotional blend. Although embarrassment is an unpleasant emotional state, people sometimes plan embarrassing situations for others, and planning an embarrassing moment for someone else is often socially acceptable (Bradford & Petronio, 1998). For example, it is a common practice among adolescents to use strategic embarrassment in the following way: Tom knows that his friend, Jesús, is interested in Amy. He also knows that Jesús is shy and won't introduce himself to her. As Amy and Jesús pass in the school hallway, Tom purposely pushes Jesús into Amy. Jesús is embarrassed, but he recognizes that Tom actually has helped him connect with Amy, producing a blend of emotion (Bradford, 1993).

To explicate our definition of emotion more completely, we'll now discuss two category systems for emotion and explore the relationships among emotion, reason, and physicality, or the body.

valence An attribute of emotion that refers to whether the emotion reflects a positive or negative feeling.

activity An attribute of emotion that refers to whether the emotion implies action or passivity.

intensity An attribute of emotion that refers to how strongly an emotion is felt.

Emotion and interpersonal communication often go hand in hand. Not only does emotion influence how, when, and why we communicate with others, but our displays of emotion communicate messages themselves. These Habitat for Humanity volunteers don't have to say a word; their smiles communicate the pride and pleasure they take in helping others and making a difference in their community.

FIGURE 7.2 EMOTION CONE

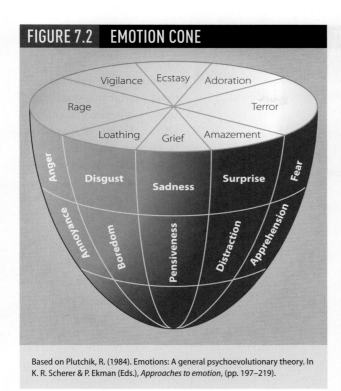

Based on Plutchik, R. (1984). Emotions: A general psychoevolutionary theory. In K. R. Scherer & P. Ekman (Eds.), *Approaches to emotion*, (pp. 197–219).

FIGURE 7.3 COMMON DUALISMS IN WESTERN THOUGHT

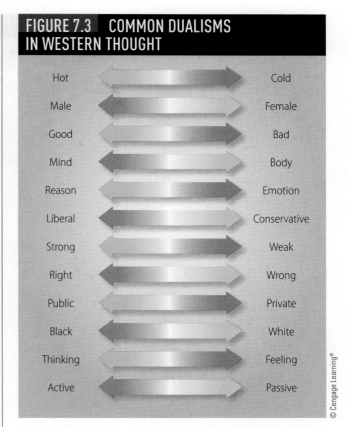

© Cengage Learning®

(see Figure 7.2). The lowest level of each vertical slice represents the mildest version of the emotion, and each successive level represents a more intense state. This system points to the impact of labeling an emotion with a particularly intense name. For example, if Jenna says she is bored in French class, that statement carries a much different meaning, and is far less intense, than if she says she loathes French.

7-1b Emotion, Reason, and the Body

From the preceding discussion, you can see that emotion is a complicated concept. One of the complexities of emotion is that it's often framed within the either/or framework that characterizes Western thought. This either/or thinking, also known as *dualism*, originated in the 18th century with philosophers Immanuel Kant and René Descartes. It is a way of thinking that constructs polar opposite categories to encompass the totality of a thing, prompting us to think about it in an either/or fashion. **Dualism** creates the problem of polarization that we discussed in Chapter 4. For example, dualism encourages us to think about all of temperature as either hot or cold, all of gender as either feminine or masculine, and all of a person as either good or bad. Figure 7.3 lists common dualisms that pervade our language and thinking.

When we phrase things as either/or choices, we can't see a third (or fourth) possibility. Many in the United States believe that the government shutdown in 2013, as well as the Congress and President Obama's general lack of productivity during this time, was due in large part to either/or thinking (Novack, 2013). When members of Congress believe that they and their political opponents do not share any goals, and they frame issues in terms of good or evil, it is difficult to negotiate and get things done for the country. William Ury (2010) refers to thinking outside dualism as conceptualizing "the third side," and he suggests that negotiating for the third side is the only way to resolve conflict among people.

Dualism encourages us to consider a person to be split into two parts—mind and body—that operate completely independently (TenHouten, 2012). The historic division between mind and body is further split when the mind is seen, in another dualism, as either reason or emotion. And dualism is illustrated whenever someone says to another in a conflict, "Stop being hysterical about this! You have to be reasonable." Yet, reason is dependent on emotion. Hunches and gut reactions show emotion in service of reason. Emotion helps us to decide between competing alternatives when all else is equal. How do you choose between a brown scarf and a black scarf when both look equally good with your coat? How do you choose whether to go visit your friend Mark or stay home and watch TV, when either alternative sounds fun? We would be paralyzed by indecision if we didn't have emotional responses to help us make decisions.

> **dualism** A way of thinking that constructs polar opposite categories to encompass the totality of a thing. Dualism prompts us to think about things in an either/or fashion.

TABLE 7.1   EMOTIONS, PHYSICAL REACTIONS, AND COGNITIONS

Emotions	Physical Reactions	Cognitions
Joy	Warm temperature Fast heartbeat	"I am so happy, and this feels different."
Anger	Fast heartbeat Tense muscles	"I feel anger, and I want to do something."
Sadness	Lump in throat Tense muscles	"I am feeling sadness wash over me."
Shame	Hot flushes Fast heartbeat	"I am ashamed. What can I do?"

© Cengage Learning®

The process of perception illustrates the relationships among reason, body, and emotion. When we perceive something, we first attend to stimuli. So, let's say that stimuli are coming toward you and you feel threatened in some way, believing that your safety is at risk. That is, you feel the emotion of fear. This insight involves reason. You must first notice that something dangerous is happening (e.g., someone approaches you looking threatening). In this step, you compare your knowledge of a nondangerous event to what is actually happening, and you see the discrepancy (e.g., you say to yourself, "I could have no one bothering me, but that's not happening now"). You also have to determine the importance of this behavior and evaluate the context (e.g., you and this person are friends playing football, or you are walking down a dark alley and the person is a stranger). All these judgments are part of the cognitive element of emotion. Emotion also has a physiological component. For example, if someone approaches you with a scowl on his or her face, you are likely to experience physiological reactions such as accelerated heart rate, breathing changes, a lump in your throat, and tense muscles. Table 7.1 presents a listing of common emotions with their accompanying cognitive and physical elements.

Despite our knowledge of these connections, dualistic thinking persists in many arenas. For instance, thinking about emotion as separate from reason and the body is often reflected in medical school curricula, although there are some recent efforts to change this (O'Callaghan, 2013). Many courses in medical school teach students to treat physical symptoms, but relatively few address the thoughts and feelings of patients and their families. However, on some level we understand that emotion, the body, and reason are inextricably linked. Our language helps us see the connections. Think about words we use to describe emotion: *heartache, heartsick, heartened, heartless, heartfelt, lighthearted*. All these words indicate our instinctive knowledge of the connections between emotion and the body (the heart).

Experiencing emotion seems to affect people's physical functioning in ways that are not simply physical manifestations of the emotion. Pressman, Gallagher, and Lopez (2013) found that physical health was impacted in positive ways from experiencing positive emotions, and in negative ways from negative emotions. Furthermore, these researchers produced evidence that this effect was shared by people all around the world, regardless of other factors such as poverty and stage of development. Pressman and her colleagues conclude that there is no escaping the strong connection between physical and emotional health. They state that "emotion matters for health around the globe" (p. 544). In sum, we see that emotion is internal but impacts all our feelings about ourselves and others. Further, emotion is often experienced in blends, and may combine both positive and negative feelings. Emotion also can be understood in terms of its activity and intensity. Finally, we argue that, despite a Western tendency to see things as either/or, emotion is best explicated in the context of reason (or cognitions) and physicality (or the body).

 ## 7-2 EXPLAINING EMOTION: BIOLOGY AND SOCIAL INTERACTION

Many theories help us understand emotion. We'll now review two theories that explain how emotions originate: the biological and social (Hochschild, 1983).

7-2a The Biological Theory of Emotion

Proponents of the biological theory agree with Charles Darwin and others that emotion is mainly biological, related to instinct and energy. Because advocates of this view believe that emotions are similar across many types of people, they propose that people from a variety of cultures should experience feelings in the same manner.

This theory assumes that emotion exists separately from thought and that we need thought only to bring a preexisting emotion to our conscious awareness. For example, let's say that Maura is arguing with her friend, Rolanda, about how to plan a campus event. While they

Charles Darwin believed that the majority of emotional gestures cross all cultures.

talk, Maura is thinking about advancing her ideas in the argument and is not paying any attention to the emotion she is experiencing. However, as she walks away from Rolanda, she notices that she's slightly irritated because Rolanda disagrees with her about the best way to advertise the event. Although Maura had been experiencing emotion during the argument, she needed introspection, or thought, to bring it to her attention.

Darwin placed importance on observable emotional expressions, not the meaning associated with them. Darwin argued that these "gestures" of emotion were remnants of prehistoric behaviors that served important functions. For instance, when we bare our teeth in rage, our behavior is a remnant of the action of biting. When we hug someone in an expression of affection, our action is a remnant of the act of copulation. And when our mouths form an expression of disgust, our action is a remnant of the need to regurgitate a poisonous substance or spoiled food. Thus, in the biological theory, "emotion . . . is our experience of the body ready for an imaginary action" (Hochschild, 1983, p. 220). Furthermore, Darwin argued that people enact these gestures as a result of experiencing emotion. However, he also asserted that the opposite is true—that is, when people enact a certain gesture, they experience the related emotion. Darwin also believed that these emotive gestures (with a few exceptions, such as weeping and kissing) are universal, meaning that they cross all cultures.

7-2b The Social Interaction Theory of Emotion

The social interaction theory (Gerth & Mills, 1964) acknowledges that biology affects emotion and emotional communication. However, proponents of this theory are also interested in how people interact with social situations before, during, and after the experience of emotion. In this way, the theory adds social factors, like interactions with others, to the biological basis for explaining emotion (Hareli & Hess, 2012).

Let's say that Catherine finds out on Tuesday that her best friend, Lita, is having a party on Friday. Lita hasn't invited Catherine. The social theory is interested in the following questions: What elements in Catherine's cultural milieu contribute to how she perceives being left off the guest list? That is, do any contextual elements affect her experience of emotion? For example, if Catherine's birthday is coming up, she might think Lita is giving her a surprise party. The biological theory of emotion considers these questions unimportant, but they are central to the social theory.

Like the biological theory, the social theory talks about gesture. However, the social theory focuses on how the reactions of others to our gestures help us define what we are feeling. Let's say that Catherine tells another friend, Alex, about not being invited to the party, and she starts to cry because she feels hurt. Alex interprets Catherine's tears as a manifestation of anger, saying to Catherine, "You must be really mad!" Catherine hears this and agrees, "Yes, I can't believe that jerk didn't invite me after all the times she's been to my parties!" Catherine's sense of her own emotional experience may have been confused before she talked to Alex, but his interpretation swayed her and influenced how she labeled

THEORY SPOTLIGHT:

Social Interaction Theory/ Biological Theory

What kinds of questions would you ask using the social interaction theory of emotion if you wanted to understand how you felt after breaking up with a significant other? How would these questions differ from those you'd ask using the biological theory?

TABLE 7.2 THE BIOLOGICAL AND SOCIAL THEORIES OF EMOTION

	The Biological Theory	The Social Theory
Definition of emotion	Biological processes	Feeling states resulting from social interaction
Relationship of emotions to cognitions	Separate	Interrelated
Assumption of universality	Yes	No
Concern with subjective meaning	No	Yes

© Cengage Learning®

her emotion. See Table 7.2 for a comparison of the biological and social theories.

Now that we have defined emotion and discussed some theories that help us understand it, we are ready to address our primary concern in this chapter: how emotion relates to interpersonal communication.

7-3

EMOTION AND COMMUNICATION

Emotion clearly affects interpersonal communication. It influences how we talk to others, how others hear what we say, and how our communication affects our relational outcomes (Theiss & Solomon, 2007). For example, people who feel betrayed by a relational partner have many communication choices to express their feelings. Research shows that if they use explicit strategies to forgive their partner, their relationships improve (Waldron & Kelley, 2008). Emotion permeates communication from birth to death. One study showed that the emotion embodied in the final conversation with a loved one before death makes a big difference in the survivor's ability to cope with the loss (Keeley, 2007). Furthermore, some research (Kennedy-Lightsey, Martin, Thompson, Himes, & Clingerman, 2012) demonstrates that self-disclosures, risk taking, and emotion were all related when people thought about telling personal information to their friends.

Interpersonal communication can be influenced by the feelings of those around us through **emotional contagion**, or the process of transferring emotion from one person to another (Du, Fan, & Feng, 2011). Emotional contagion occurs when one person's feelings "infect" those around them. You have probably experienced emotional contagion yourself. Think of a time when you were with a friend who communicated in a nervous manner. Didn't you find yourself becoming nervous, too, just watching her fidget? Or you may have become depressed yourself after spending time with a friend who expressed that he was down in the dumps. Conversely, if you are around someone who expresses positive feelings, you usually find your own mood brightening and your communication becoming more upbeat. Goleman (2006) calls this *emotional afterglow.*

In examining the relationship between interpersonal communication and emotion, we need to clarify several terms. **Emotional experience** refers to feeling emotion and thus is intrapersonal in nature (Jorie felt nervous before her interview). **Communicating emotionally** suggests that the emotion itself is a part of the way the message is delivered (Roberto yells at his wife, Tessa, telling her that she is making them late for their dinner reservations). **Emotional effects** relate to how

emotional contagion The process of transferring emotions from one person to another.

emotional experience The feeling of emotion.

communicating emotionally Communicating such that the emotion is not the content of the message but rather a property of it.

emotional effects The ways in which an emotional experience impacts communication behavior.

© iStock.com/Franck-Boston

emotional experience impacts communication behavior (when Sophie ran into her friend, Laura, at the mall and accidentally called her Deanna, the name of another friend, Sophie was so embarrassed and flustered that she was unable to conduct the rest of the conversation with Laura without stammering and stuttering). **Emotional communication** means actually talking about the experience of emotion to someone else (Alex told Patrick how he was feeling about the possibility of adopting a child as a single dad). Clarifying these terms allows us to see the myriad ways that emotion and interpersonal communication intersect. In this chapter we devote most of our attention to the latter term, *emotional communication*, or talking about our feelings to someone. When we engage in emotional communication, we need a vocabulary to express the emotions we are experiencing. So, the first part of this section focuses on the language used in the United States to portray emotion—that is, the metaphors we employ to articulate our feelings. The second part of this section discusses how we use verbal and nonverbal cues in emotional communication.

7-3a Metaphors for Emotion

As we discussed in Chapter 4, people often employ figurative language, especially metaphors, to talk about abstract ideas such as emotion. Research (e.g., Locock, Mazanderani, & Powell, 2012) suggests that metaphors help people communicate complicated emotions that are difficult to express in literal language. We also use metaphoric language to distinguish among various emotions as well as to clarify "the subtle variations in a speaker's emotional state (e.g., *get hot under the collar* refers to "[a] less intense state of anger than does *blow your stack*" [Leggitt & Gibbs, 2000, p. 3]). Table 7.3 lists some common metaphors for emotion.

Our figurative language often implies that emotion has a presence independent of the person experiencing it—as in the phrase "she succumbed to depression." Emotions are frequently framed as opponents ("he struggled with his feelings") or as wild animals ("she felt unbridled passion") (Kovecses, 2000). We speak of guilt as something that "haunts" us, fear as something that "grips" us, and anger as something that "overtakes" us (Hochschild, 1983).

TABLE 7.3	COMMON METAPHORS FOR EMOTIONS
Anger	
A hot fluid in a container	She is boiling with anger.
A fire	He is doing a slow burn.
Insanity	George was insane with rage.
A burden	Tamara carries her anger around with her.
A natural force	It was a stormy relationship.
A physical annoyance	He's a pain in the neck.
Fear	
A hidden enemy	Fear crept up on him.
A tormentor	My mother was tortured by fears.
A natural force	Mia was engulfed by fear.
An illness	Jeff was sick with fright.
Happiness	
Up	We had to cheer him up.
Being in heaven	That was heaven on earth.
Light	Miguel brightened up at the news.
Warm	Your thoughtfulness warmed my spirits.
An animal that lives well	Tess looks like the cat that ate the canary.
A pleasurable physical sensation	I was tickled pink.
Sadness	
Down	He brought me down with what he said.
Dark	Phil is in a dark mood.
A natural force	Waves of depression swept over Todd.
An illness	Lora was heartsick.
A physical force	The realization was a terrible blow.

Adapted from Kovecses, Z. (2000). *Metaphor and emotion: Language, culture, and body in human feeling.* Cambridge: Cambridge University Press

Although these phrases are evocative of the feelings that various emotions engender, they leave the impression that people are not responsible for their emotion—that is, that people are acted upon by emotional forces beyond their control. This way of talking about emotion fits in with our earlier discussion of the division between emotion and reason. Such language depicts emotion as something that

emotional communication Talking about our feelings to another person.

can make us lose our minds completely as we are over-whelmed by forces beyond our rational control.

7-3b Cues for Emotional Communication

As we discussed in Chapters 4 and 5, the tools we have for communicating are verbal and nonverbal cues. In this section, we'll briefly discuss nonverbal and verbal cues that we use for emotional communication. We'll also discuss how people use combinations of these cues.

NONVERBAL CUES

Facial expressions are obviously one of the most important means for communicating emotion. When people view photos of facial expressions for a variety of emotions, they are generally accurate in their ability to discern one emotion from another (Gosselin, Kirouac, & Dore, 1995). Perhaps the most researched facial expression is the smile. Smiles usually indicate warmth and friendliness, but, as we mentioned in Chapter 5, smiles can be interpreted to mean something other than positive emotion. For example, Donna's boss, Melanie, often uses a smile as a mocking gesture. Therefore, when Melanie approaches Donna's office with a smile on her face, Donna feels nervous, and braces herself for some type of unpleasant interaction. Further, nonverbal cues can mean multiple things at the same time. So, a smile you receive from the host when you arrive at a holiday party may be an expression of genuine happiness in seeing you as well as a part of a well-learned greeting ritual (Hareli & Hess, 2012).

Although it is not as well researched as the face, the voice is probably equally important in conveying emotion. How loudly people talk, how high-pitched their tone is, how fast they talk, how many pauses they take, and so forth give clues to emotion. In addition, the tone of a person's voice can provide clues to whether the emotion they are expressing is positive or negative. For example,

© Ioannis Pantzi/Shutterstock.com

when Jack calls his coworker, Theo, one morning before work, Theo can tell right away by the way Jack says "hello" that something is wrong. Before Jack explains his problem verbally, Theo is cued by the tone in Jack's voice.

Emotion is "embodied." This means that "people scratch their heads, clench their fists, shake, gesture wildly, hug themselves, pace the floor, lean forward, fidget in their seats, walk heavily, jump up and down, slump, or freeze in their tracks" (Planalp, 1999, pp. 46–47) when they're communicating emotion. However, there isn't a great deal of research on gestures and body movement. Some research has indicated that depressed people gesture less than those who are not depressed (Segrin, 1998).

One study (Miller, 2007) investigated how caregivers can communicate compassion nonverbally through place and time codes. Caregivers stated that they tried to show compassion to patients by being on time to see them, and by structuring the environment so that the temperature is comfortable and so forth. One obstetrician in this study said that an environmental concern was organizing appointments so that pregnant women weren't coming to the office at the same time as women struggling with fertility issues.

VERBAL CUES

Although we are discussing how people talk about emotion, it is the case that people often fail to state a specific emotion directly (Shimanoff, 1985, 1987). Instead, they use indirect cues. For example, Max guesses that Russ is angry with him when Russ calls Max an idiot and tells him that he wants to be alone. Russ doesn't tell Max any direct information about his emotion, but calling him a name and saying that he wants to be by himself are indirect verbal indicators of Russ's emotional state. In this way, people fail to actually use *emotional communication* (talking to another about feelings) but rather *communicate emotionally* (demonstrate emotions in the way they communicate).

This leaves listeners in the rather tricky position of inferring others' emotional states (Leggitt & Gibbs, 2000). For instance, let's say that Isabella invites Ruth over for dinner, and Ruth shows up an hour late. When Isabella greets Ruth by saying sarcastically, "Nice of you to show up on time," Ruth gets the idea that Isabella is angry. Ruth would also probably get the same message about Isabella's emotional state if she asked Ruth rhetorically, "Do you ever look at your watch?" In neither case did Isabella say she was angry directly, but her comments were indirect indicators of anger. Later in this chapter, we discuss using I-messages to verbalize emotions, which can prevent the confusion that might result from indirect communication.

© iStock.com/boophotography

COMBINATIONS OF CUES

Verbal and nonverbal cues can be discussed separately, but in practice people usually communicate emotion through a mixture of cues. People often use verbal and vocal cues while gesturing and displaying facial expressions. For example, when Dwight surprises Pat with a vacation to Acapulco, Pat tells him that she's happy in a high-pitched voice while grinning and giving him a hug. Sometimes, however, cues are conflicting or incongruent. When Sandy tells her son, Jake, that she is angry that he hasn't put away all his toys, but she laughs indulgently, her nonverbal and verbal communication conflict with each other. Especially in cases of conflicting cues, people rely on other information to try to discern meaning. We discuss some of these other influences in the following section.

7-4 INFLUENCES ON EMOTIONAL COMMUNICATION

In this section, we explain a few areas that will help you understand that emotional communication is not a fixed behavior in our conversations with others. Emotional communication is influenced by several factors, including meta-emotion, culture, gender and sex, and context.

7-4a Meta-Emotion

How people communicate about emotion is influenced by a related topic: meta-emotion. **Meta-emotion** means emotion about emotion (Jäger & Bartsch, 2006). People who study emotion tend to focus on specific emotions, without paying much attention to how people feel about expressing certain emotions. For example, in the case of anger, "some people are ashamed or upset about becoming angry, others feel good about their capacity to express anger, and still others think of anger as natural, neither good nor bad" (Gottman, Katz, & Hooven, 1997, p. 7).

Differences in the effects of communicating emotion may result in part because of meta-emotion. Let's compare the emotions of two couples who have been dating for a year: Andrea and José, and Marla and Leo. Andrea's expression of love for José is accompanied by the meta-emotion pride. She is proud of her ability to engage in a committed relationship. José feels the same way. On the other hand, when Marla expresses love to Leo, she experiences the meta-emotion shame for becoming so vulnerable in a relationship. Communication transactions between Andrea and José will likely differ significantly from those between Marla and Leo because one couple is proud of their commitment whereas one part of the other couple (i.e., Marla) feels shame.

7-4b Culture

Remember from our discussion of the biological theory of emotion that Darwin asserted that emotions are primarily universal—that is, people of all cultures respond to the same emotions in the same way. Few people agree with that assertion today. Although some emotional states and expressions—such as joy, anger, and fear—might be universal, the current focus of research is on differences in emotional communication across cultures (Jack, Caldara, & Schyns, 2012). As we've discussed throughout this text, culture is an important influence on most communication behaviors. The brief review in this section gives you an overview of how different cultures think about emotion and how emotion is communicated in various cultures.

CULTURES AND THINKING ABOUT EMOTION

Cultures differ in how much they think and talk about emotion (Planalp & Fitness, 1999). One study (Kayyal & Russell, 2013) demonstrates, for example, that while

meta-emotion Emotion felt about experiencing another emotion.

the English and Arabic languages both have the ability to translate words for emotions (such as happiness, sadness, fear, anger, embarrassment, etc.), these translations do not provide equivalent definitions for their native speakers, and English and Arabic speakers identified different facial expressions for the same emotion word. The meanings of these emotions tended to vary by culture although the translation made it seem as though the two languages were talking about the same emotion. The only emotion out of 12 that were tested that was equivalent across the two languages was *happiness* (English) or *farah* (Arabic).

Planalp and Fitness (1999) state that 95 percent of Chinese parents report that their children understand the meaning of *shame* or *xiu* by age 3, whereas only 10 percent of U.S. parents say their children do. Because of this difference, it seems that shame plays a more important role in Chinese culture than it does in U.S. culture. Yet, one study (Seiter & Bruschke, 2007) found that Chinese respondents suffered less from shame after engaging in deception than did U.S. respondents. One explanation for this difference might be that deception is more acceptable in China than it is in the United States. Another explanation might be that U.S. and Chinese respondents defined shame differently. There is some evidence (Hurtado-de-Mendoza, Molina, & Fernández-Dols, 2013) that collectivist cultures (like China) conceptualize shame as more publicly shared and less threatening than do individualistic cultures (like the United States). It is important to consider not just the emotion but also what triggers the emotion and how the emotion is framed within the culture.

Some other research (Planalp & Fitness, 1999) notes that the Chinese think less about love than do people in the United States. Furthermore, when the Chinese do think of love, they have a cluster of words to describe "sad-love," or love that does not succeed; such words are absent in U.S. culture. Other research (Lazarus, 1991) points to a similar dynamic in Japanese culture. In Japanese stories, when a conflict exists between a couple and the families of the couple, it is resolved in favor of the families, even when that means the couple has to give each other up. In Japan, stories that end with the lovers separating because of family objections are celebrated as showing the right way to resolve this problem. In contrast, in the United States and other Western European cultures, many of the stories in books, magazines, and movies end with the couple staying together against the wishes of their families. In these cultures, listeners cheer the lovers on, enjoying the triumph of romantic love.

HOW EMOTION IS COMMUNICATED ACROSS CULTURES

People of different cultures express emotion differently (Aune & Aune, 1996). For instance, people from warmer climates have been found to be more emotionally expressive than those from colder climates. In addition, people from collectivistic cultures (such as Korea, China, and

individualistic expression   *collectivist expression*

Japan), are discouraged from expressing negative feelings for fear of their effect on the overall harmony of the community. Thus, people from these cultures are less inclined to express negative feelings. This does not mean that people from collectivistic cultures do not have negative feelings; it simply means that emotional restraint in communication is a shared cultural value (Martin & Nakayama, 2014). People from individualistic cultures like the United States have no such cultural value—in fact, emotional openness is valued—so they are more expressive of negative emotions.

7-4c Gender and Sex

Gender and sex differences in communication (as well as other behaviors) are widely researched (Hastie & Cosh, 2013). In the United States, many activities are divided according to sex, so people are interested in the ways in which men and women are presumed to differ. For example, although gender roles are in flux in the United States, parenting is still seen as primarily the responsibility of women, whereas men are expected to work to pay the bills. The two sexes are expected to do different things and have different strengths in the workplace and at home (Buzzanell & Turner, 2012). In this section, we review research that examines emotion and gender stereotypes and then explore research on the expression of emotion and gender.

EMOTION AND GENDER STEREOTYPES

Of course, the stereotypical view holds that women are more emotional, more emotionally expressive, and more attuned to the emotions of others than are men. Agneta Fischer (2000) wonders why women are thought to be the emotional sex while men are perceived to be unemotional. She asserts:

> As far back as I can remember I have encountered emotional men; indeed, I have met more emotional men than emotional women. My father could not control his nerves while watching our national sports heroes on television (which made watching hardly bearable); my uncle immediately got damp eyes on hearing the first note of the Dutch national anthem; a friend would lock himself in his room for days when angry; a teacher at school once got so furious that he dragged a pupil out of the class room and hung him up by his clothes on a coat-hook; one of the male managers at our institute was only able to prevent having a nervous breakdown by rigidly trying to exercise total control over his environment; and a male colleague's constant embarrassment in public situations forced him to avoid such settings altogether. (p. ix)

Fischer's point is not that men are *more* emotional than women. Rather, she observes that all these examples of men expressing emotion go unnoticed because they do not support the stereotype we have of men as unemotional.

Stephanie Shields (2000) makes a similar point when she argues that emotional expression (or lack of it) defines the essence of femininity and masculinity. She notes that people even use gender stereotypes to make judgments about their own emotions. Shields reports on an earlier study that she and her colleagues conducted (Robinson, Johnson, & Shields, 1998, as cited in Shields, 2000), in which participants played a competitive word game. In the study, participants were asked about their emotional experience both immediately after playing and then a week later. The researchers found that the reports about the emotions matched gender stereotypes more closely the longer after the event the reports were recorded. The researchers concluded that when the participants forgot exactly how they felt, they used stereotypes (i.e., men are stereotyped as more stoic and women as more emotional) to provide an answer.

Another study (Shields & Crowley, 1996) also showed the power of gender stereotypes on emotion. This study asked college students to read an emotion-provoking scenario and then to answer open-ended questions about the scenario. The scenario was identical for all participants except that in some cases the protagonist was male and in others female. The scenario stated one of the following:

> "Karen was emotional when she found out that her car had been stolen."

> "Brian was emotional when he found out that his car had been stolen."

The researchers found that the respondents judged the word *emotional* in the scenario differently depending on whether they read the Karen version or the Brian version. If participants thought the protagonist was Karen, they attributed the cause of her emotion more to her personality than to her situation, and they imagined her reaction was extreme and hysterical. Respondents who thought Brian's car was stolen downplayed the word *emotional* in the story and described his emotion as what any person might feel who had worked hard making money to buy a car. The researchers concluded that the respondents used gender stereotypes to answer the questions.

EMOTIONAL EXPRESSION AND SEX AND GENDER

Researchers are interested in the differences between men and women in nonverbal expressions of emotion, such as smiling. Three differences are well documented

© Valery Sidelnykov/Shutterstock.com

and may be caused by men and women conforming to stereotyped gender roles (Hall, Carter, & Horgan, 2000). First, women smile more than men in social situations. Second, men and women also differ in nonverbal expressiveness, or facial animation and the liveliness of gestures. Again, women tend to demonstrate their emotional states by using more nonverbal cues than men do (Hall et al., 2000; Jones & Wirtz, 2007). Finally, women are also more accurate than men in figuring out what others' emotional states are based on nonverbal cues.

Scholars have also investigated sex differences in the verbal expression of emotional support to others. In general, men are less likely to give emotional support to a person in distress, and when they do provide it, they are less focused on emotion and less person-centered than women (Burleson, Holmstrom, & Gilstrap, 2005). The results of one study (Burleson et al.) suggest that men provide poorer emotional support than women because they see good emotional support as not fitting a masculine gender identity.

As people age, these gender stereotypes seem to exert less influence on their behaviors. Men tend to become more emotionally expressive, and women become more instrumental or task oriented. A study of 20 married couples over the age of 60 who had been married for an average of 42 years shows this change. The researchers interviewing the couples found the men to be expressive about their emotions (saying things like they fell in love with their wives at first sight and reporting how nervous they'd been to meet her parents), whereas wives were more matter-of-fact in their accounts (Dickson & Walker, 2001).

7-4d Context

The contexts in which we express emotion are infinite: we express emotion at work, with friends, in our families,

feeling rules The cultural norms used to create and react to emotional expressions.

at school, over the phone, in person, and so on. We discuss two specific contexts here: historical period and social media.

HISTORICAL PERIOD

The book *American Cool* (Stearns, 1994) traces the changes in emotional communication in the United States from the Victorian period (beginning approximately in the 1830s) to the 1960s. The main thesis is that the Victorians were much more emotionally expressive than U.S. citizens of the 1960s. A North American in the 1960s favored "cool" over the emotional excesses of the Victorians. This is because culture is governed by **feeling rules**, or "the recommended norms by which people are supposed to shape their emotional expressions and react to the expressions of others" (p. 2), and the feeling rules of U.S. culture changed considerably from the Victorian period to the 1960s.

In the 1890s, men in the United States were instructed to express their anger. However, 70 years later, child-rearing experts warned parents not to encourage boys to express anger, arguing that an angry man is possessed by the devil. In the area of romantic love, Victorian men were also encouraged to be expressive, in contrast to the 1960s vision of male love as primarily

© Victorian Traditions/Shutterstock.com

sexual and silent. A love letter written by a man of the Victorian era illustrates the flowery emotional expression that was the norm:

> I don't love you and marry you to promote my happiness. To love you, to marry you is a mighty END in itself. . . . I marry you because my own inmost being mingles with your being and is already married to it, both joined in one by God's own voice. (Stearns, 1994, p. 3)

Obviously, a man in Victorian times would be influenced by the feeling rules of his time and would express himself much differently than a man of the 1960s, who would be equally influenced by a very different set of feeling rules. Today, we have different feeling rules as well, although the influence of "cool" is still strong in contemporary U.S. society.

ELECTRONIC MEDIA

As we discussed in Chapter 1, the channel for a communication transaction influences the communication. Because more and more of our communication time is spent in electronic communication or on social media, online emotional communication is a worthwhile subject of study. Email and other social media that are print only have been seen as somewhat impoverished forms of communication because they lack a nonverbal dimension (Bazarova, Taft, Choi, & Cosley, 2013). The emoticon is one way that users of social media express nonverbal communication online. **Emoticons** are icons that can be typed on the keyboard to express emotions. They are used to compensate for the lack of nonverbal cues online, and are sometimes called quasi-nonverbal communication (Lo, 2008). Additionally, graphical emoticons (*emojis* in Japanese) have been used to express emotion in texts and blogs among other online communications (Aoki & Uchida, 2011). Aoki and Uchida point out that *emojis* can be used to differentiate similar emotions within a text. They note that the verbal statement "The dish I ordered wasn't good" accompanied by two different *emojis* will convey two different emotional meanings.

Emotional communication is obviously vital to online interactions; a preliminary online search yielded more than 8 million sites in at least eight languages that deal with emoticons and *emojis*. Most Western emoticons look like a face (eyes, nose, and mouth) when rotated 90 degrees clockwise. Emoticons originating in East Asia are usually interpreted without rotation and can incorporate nonstandard characters. Table 7.4 presents examples of commonly used emoticons and their translations.

Some research (Rourke, Anderson, Garrison, & Archer, 2001) argues that when people are experienced

"I forgot to put a smiley face on my sarcastic email to you."

© Cartoonresource/Shutterstock.com

users of social media, it is just as rich a communication process as any other, including face-to-face. Furthermore, communication online doesn't necessarily inhibit

TABLE 7.4 EMOTICONS

Common Western Emoticons	
:) :-) :] =) :D xD	Happiness, sarcasm, laughing, or a joke
:(:-(:[>:(:'(	Unhappiness, sadness, or disapproval
:| :-| :-\ :-/	Indifference, confusion, or skepticism
:-P ;-) ;-P :3	Cute, playful, or joking

Common Eastern Emoticons	
(^_^) (^-^) (^o^)	Happiness, sarcasm, laughing, or a joke
(>_<) (;_;) (._.) ಠ_ಠ	Unhappiness, sadness, or disapproval
(´_ゝ`) (¬_¬) O_o	Indifference, confusion, or skepticism
(~_^) (^_~) ◕‿◕ (˙ω˙)	Cute, playful, or joking

emoticon An icon that can be typed on a keyboard to express emotions; used to compensate for the lack of nonverbal cues in computer-mediated communication.

emotional expression; one study (Rourke et al., 2001) found that 27 percent of the total message content online consisted of emotional communication. Yet a *New York Times* online article (Williams, 2007), while stating that emoticons are widely used and important to help avoid misunderstandings, also notes that some people are offended when they see the "smileys" or "frownys" appear in a message. One real estate agent quoted in the article commented that it didn't make her feel any better to see a : (on an email saying she'd lost a deal worth hundreds of thousands of dollars. In fact, she found it highly annoying!

7-5 RECOGNIZING DESTRUCTIVE AND CONSTRUCTIVE ASPECTS OF EMOTIONAL COMMUNICATION

As we discussed earlier in this chapter, some classification systems of specific emotions use positive and negative (i.e., valence) as a primary dimension for categorizing those emotions. We're all familiar with negative emotions: embarrassment, guilt, hurt, jealousy, anger, depression, and loneliness, to name a few. Jealousy (Elphinston, Feeney, Noller, Connor, & Fitzgerald, 2013) and hurtful messages (e.g., Bippus & Young, 2012; Young & Bippus, 2001) have received attention from researchers interested in how this type of emotional communication operates in relationships. One study (Young & Bippus) found that if hurtful messages were phrased humorously, they were perceived as less intentionally hurtful and caused fewer wounded feelings.

Some negative emotions are the polar opposites of positive emotions. For example, empathy, a positive emotion, is the opposite of the negative emotion *schadenfreude,* a German word that, loosely translated, means to take pleasure in another's misfortune. (The term is derived from the German words for "damage" and "joy.") In 2012, some reporters (e.g., Denn, 2012) used schadenfreude *to* describe how many people felt when they saw Paula Deen's reputation tarnished when she revealed she had Type 2 diabetes and had been suffering from it for several years while she'd been touting recipes for foods high in fat and sugar. Some people think that the public's fascination with the problems of celebrities like Lindsay Lohan and Charlie Sheen stems from schadenfreude. But schadenfreude is not a feeling only limited to our responses to public

figures. Some research indicates people also feel it toward their friends, perhaps as a response to competition for a romantic partner (Colyn & Gordon, 2013). Colyn and Gordon found that people responded with schadenfreude when a friend suffered a (hypothetical) misfortune that lowered their physical appeal.

The fact that schadenfreude blends two emotions should come as no surprise. Emotion is often experienced in blends, and destructive and constructive, love and hate, are often entangled with one another. In fact, negative emotions might not always be destructive. Expressions of anger can be functional in certain contexts, including the following example (Tavris, 2001):

A 42-year-old businessman, Jay S., described how his eyes were opened when he overheard his usually even-tempered boss on the phone one afternoon: "I've never heard him so angry. He was enraged. His face was red and the veins were bulging on his neck. I tried to get his attention to calm him down, but he waved me away impatiently. As soon as the call was over, he turned to me and smiled. "There," he said. "That ought to do it." If I were the

Christie Aschwanden (2013) comments in the *New York Times* online that many people took a "wicked delight" in seeing Tiger Woods' empire come crashing down in 2009. She speculates that this is because Woods had seemed to have the perfect life prior to being exposed as a womanizer who cheated on his wife repeatedly with a variety of women, including paid escorts. Aschwanden observes that our joy in seeing Woods's fall is aptly described as *schadenfreude,* the German-derived word for delight in another's misfortune. Aschwanden quotes Dr. Richard Smith who has written a book about schadenfreude and states that this emotion, while perverse, serves an important function. Smith argues that humans seem to be hard-wired for social comparisons, and these comparisons may cause another emotion: envy. Aschwanden cites Smith as saying that schadenfreude can soothe our feelings of envy. As Aschwanden concludes, "When envy invokes pain, schadenfreude provides a potent antidote." Furthermore, schadenfreude is a passive emotion, meaning that we do nothing and still we're able to see the powerful fall. This, according to Aschwanden, is part of the emotion's great appeal: "It's the lack of participation on the part of the witness that gives schadenfreude its gleefulness and makes its acknowledgment

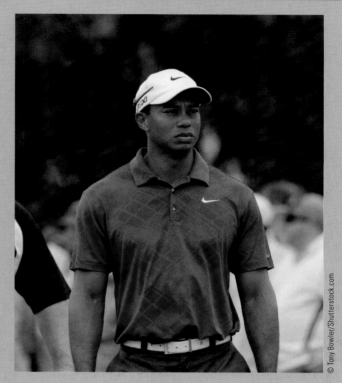

© Tony Bowler/Shutterstock.com

permissible—your secret target has fallen and you had nothing to do with it."

---

guy he'd been shouting at, let me tell you, it would have done it, too. (p. 251)

The boss's yelling and showing anger accomplished a goal. There are no simple guidelines specifying when talking is better than yelling because the context, the receiver, the sender, and the social goal all make a difference. It may even be that the categorization of an emotion or even a mode of emotional communication as either destructive or constructive is problematic because it all depends on whether the context called for the emotion, the sender and the receiver expected the emotion, and the social goals of the situation were accomplished through the emotional communication (Tavris, 2001). As Tavris states, "the calm, nonaggressive reporting of your anger (those 'I-messages' that so many psychologists recommend) is the kindest, most civilized and usually most effective way to express anger, but even this mature method depends on its context" (p. 250). Sometimes losing your cool is an effective way to get your partner's attention.

Some research (e.g., Côté, Decelles, McCarthy, Van Kleef, & Hideg, 2011) suggests that possessing emotional intelligence may actually lead people to be more negative and manipulative in their behaviors with others. Côté and her colleagues found that university employees who possessed the highest emotional skills often used them to embarrass peers and to engineer situations for their own gain or advancement. Grant (2014) notes that in our enthusiasm for the benefits of emotional intelligence, we have tended to ignore its negative aspects like manipulation of others.

Communication that offers comfort, social support, warmth, affection, forgiveness, or desire falls on the positive end of the emotional spectrum. However, like the destructive side, the constructive side of emotional communication does not present a simplistic picture. Some of the research on social support provides a glimpse at the mixture of constructive and destructive that is expressed simultaneously. David Spiegel and Rachel Kimerling (2001) introduce an example from a support group for family members of breast cancer patients by saying, "The expression of positive feelings often brackets the expression of painful sadness" (p. 101). Following is the vignette they report:

> A 20-year-old daughter was tearfully coming to terms with the sudden downhill pre-terminal course of her mother's breast cancer: "I see this black hole opening up in my life. I don't think I will want to live without my Mom. She would stay up at 2 A.M. and talk me through my misery for two hours. She won't be there, but I don't want to make her feel guilty for dying." Her father, also at the family group meeting, held her hand and tried to comfort her, but he clearly was overwhelmed by his own sadness and his lifelong fear of strong emotion and dependency on him by others. The husband of another woman whose breast cancer was progressing rapidly started to comfort her but found his voice choked with emotion: "I am sure you will get through this—there's so much love in your family." "Why are you crying?" the father asked. "I don't know," he replied, and everyone, tearful daughter included, found themselves laughing. (p. 101)

The mix of sadness and laughter in that example shows the complex tapestry of emotional communication. Another instance that shows a mixture of emotion was reported in the *Annals of Behavioral Medicine* (Ullrich & Lutgendorf, 2002). When college students were asked to write their feelings about a traumatic event as well as their efforts to understand and make sense of it, they became more aware of the benefits of the trauma, such as improved relationships, greater personal strength, spiritual growth, and a greater appreciation of life. The authors concluded that the process of communicating their thoughts and emotion made a negative event seem more positive, or at least to contain some positive aspects.

Another example of the complexity involved in classifying emotional communication as constructive or destructive can be seen in the emotional communication of forgiveness. Forgiveness, which is based in numerous religious teachings, represents positive emotional communication because it allows for peace and reconciliation. Some research suggests that forgiving provides important benefits for the forgiver as well as the forgiven (e.g., Strelan, McKee, Calic, Cook, & Shaw, 2013).

Nelson Mandela, the first black president of South Africa and the statesman widely credited with leading the emancipation of the country, freeing blacks from oppressive white rule, died in 2013. The many accounts of his life, written in the immediate aftermath of his death, focused on his amazing ability to forgive.

© Leszek Glasner/Shutterstock.com

Mandela had been imprisoned by the government for 27 years, had experienced and witnessed enormous brutality, yet he argued for reconciliation and enacted forgiveness in his life and leadership. Keller (2013), writing in the *New York Times* about Mandela's ability to exhibit forgiveness, says that when Mr. Mandela was asked in 2007 how he could keep from hating his oppressors, he answered as follows: "Hating clouds the mind. It gets in the way of strategy. Leaders cannot afford to hate."

Dean Murphy (2002) writes about the power and problematic nature of forgiveness. He cites Roger W. Wilkins, a civil rights activist and history professor at George Mason University, who also notes that people need to forgive for their own sense of self-preservation. Wilkins observes, "After a while you figure it out for yourself: you can't be consumed by this stuff because then your oppressors have won. . . . If you are consumed by rage, even at a terrible wrong, you have been reduced."

However, Wilkins recognizes the limits of forgiveness when he reflects on the bombing of the 16th Street Baptist Church in Birmingham, Alabama, in 1963, which killed four young black girls. In 2002, Bobby Frank Cherry was convicted of the bombing deaths and sentenced to life imprisonment. He has not asked for forgiveness and continues to deny his guilt. This makes things complicated because forgiveness requires participation from both sides. In this case, Wilkins suggests that people can purge hatred from their hearts without actually forgiving.

Deakin (2013) relates another difficult case: In 2011, Lauren Dunne Astley was murdered by her former boyfriend just a few weeks after she graduated from high school. Her parents have responded to the tragedy with grace, and have reached out to the parents of Lauren's killer in forgiveness. They have devoted themselves to working toward an end to dating violence and to changing the cultural stereotypes that push some men

FIGURE 7.4 THE INTERDEPENDENCE OF THE CONSTRUCTIVE AND DESTRUCTIVE SIDES OF EMOTIONAL COMMUNICATION

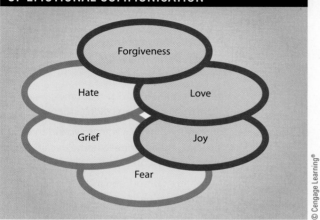

Forgiveness

Hate

Love

Grief

Joy

Fear

© Cengage Learning®

to violence. Her parents have said that they find forgiveness liberating.

Forgiveness highlights the positive and negative sides of emotion in tandem. To experience the liberation of forgiveness, Lauren's parents had to suffer the torment of grief. Lauren's father, Malcolm Astley, says forgiveness is helpful to him, calling grief "the hard form of caring" (Deakin, 2013, p, 8). Figure 7.4 illustrates the interdependence of the constructive and destructive sides of emotional communication.

7-6 SKILL SET FOR EMOTIONAL COMMUNICATION

Competence in expressing emotion and in listening and responding to the emotional communication of others is critical to your success as an interpersonal communicator (Hesse & Rauscher, 2013). Some have called this competence *emotional intelligence*. This concept has received a great deal of attention since the 1995 publication of Daniel Goleman's best-selling book by that title. Goleman notes that communicative skills are central to emotional intelligence (E-IQ) and that E-IQ is required to be successful in contemporary society. To help you develop emotional communication competence, we provide

several skills for you to consider: knowing your feelings, analyzing the situation, owning, reframing, and empathizing.

7-6a Know Your Feelings

Competence in emotional communication begins with your ability to identify the emotion or mix of emotion you are experiencing at a particular time. This skill requires you to do several things:

1. **Recognize the emotion you're feeling.**
2. **Establish that you are stating an emotion.**
3. **Create a statement that identifies why you are experiencing the emotion. (You may or may not choose to share this statement with anyone else; it is sufficient that you make the statement to yourself.)**

RECOGNIZING YOUR EMOTION

This step requires you to stop for a moment and ask yourself what your emotional state is at the present. In other words, you are to take a time out from the ongoing process and take your emotional temperature. It is important not to skip this step, because it involves making a link between yourself and outer reality. To name your feelings signals how you perceive them and alerts you to what your expectations are. For instance, when you recognize that you are irritable, that tells you that you have less patience than usual, and you may expect others to make allowances for you. The opposite process occurs as well. When you give a feeling a name, you respond to that label, which triggers perceptions and expectations.

This step is difficult for several reasons. First, in the heat of an emotional encounter, you may not be prepared to stop and take a time out. Second, we are often so detached from our feelings that it is difficult to name them. And third, some people are simply less aware than others of their emotional states. If you are "low affective oriented" (Booth-Butterfield & Booth-Butterfield, 1998), you will be relatively unaware of your own emotional experiences.

You need to practice this skill and work on methods to overcome these obstacles. For example, in a highly charged emotional interaction, you can repeat a phrase such as "It's time to take a time-out," or

© Polina Lobanova/Shutterstock.com

you can make a prior agreement with a relational partner that you will check every half hour to see if a time out is needed. You might want to list emotions in a journal so that you can consult the list to remind yourself of the variety of emotion you might be experiencing. You can also monitor your physical changes to check for signals of emotion. As we noted in Table 7.1, emotion is often accompanied by physiological conditions such as a hot flush, a lump in the throat, and so on. And you can monitor your thoughts to see how they might relate to feelings.

ESTABLISHING THAT YOU ARE STATING AN EMOTION

This step in the process provides a check to see that you are really in touch with emotion language. It isn't enough to simply say "I feel"; you must be sure that what follows really is an emotion. For instance, if you say, "I feel like seeing a ball game," you are stating something you want to do, not an emotion you are experiencing. A phrase highlighting emotion would be "I feel restless because I have been working on this project all weekend and I'd like to get out and see a game."

© iStock.com/YazolinoGirl

CREATING A STATEMENT THAT IDENTIFIES WHY YOU ARE FEELING THE EMOTION

This step involves thinking about the antecedent conditions that are contextualizing your feelings. Ask yourself, "Why do I feel this way?" and "What led to this feeling?" Try to put the reasons into words. For example, statements such as the following form reasons for emotion:

▶ "I am angry because I studied hard and got the same grade on the exam that I got when I didn't study."

▶ "I am feeling lonely. All my friends went to spend the weekend upstate and left me alone at home because I couldn't take time off from work."

▶ "I am feeling really happy, proud, and a little anxious. I finally got the job I wanted, and I worked especially hard to make a good impression at the interview. All the prep work I did paid off. But now I have to actually make good on everything I said I could do!"

▶ "I'm feeling guilty. I told my boyfriend I couldn't see him tonight because I had to study, but I really just felt like having a night to myself."

Going through this exercise should help you clarify why you are experiencing a particular emotion or emotional mix. It also should point you in a direction to change something if you wish to. For instance, if you wish to reduce your guilt, tell your boyfriend that you need some time to yourself occasionally without having to give him a reason.

7-6b Analyze the Situation

After identifying your emotion, analyze the situation by asking yourself these questions:

1. **Do you wish to share your emotion with others?** Some emotional experiences are not ready for communication—that is, you may not completely understand the emotion yet or you may feel that you would quickly slide into conflict if you communicated the emotion. Or, you might decide that you are comfortable with the emotion and that you don't ever need to share it. For example, if you are looking through your high school yearbook and feel nostalgia for the time you spent there, you might enjoy your memories and not feel the need to talk about it with anyone. If you wake up early one morning and experience a beautiful sunrise, you may feel joy without needing to tell anyone about it.

2. **Is the time appropriate for sharing?** If you decide you want to communicate an emotion to someone else, an analysis of the situation helps you decide if the time is right. If your partner is under a great deal of stress at work, you may want to wait until the situation improves before talking about your unhappiness at how little time you spend together. If you just found out you are pregnant with a wanted baby

and your best friend has recently suffered a miscarriage, you also might decide to wait to share your joy.

3. ***How should you approach the communication?*** Analyzing the situation helps you think about how to share your emotion. If you are angry with your boss, you need to consider if and/or how to express your anger. Obviously, anger at a boss and anger at a partner provide entirely different situational constraints. Because the workplace climate is not conducive to emotional communication, you may decide not to tell your boss how you feel even though you would like to do so.

4. ***Is there anything you can do to change the situation if needed?*** Your analysis allows you to think about how and whether to change the situation. In the case of a workplace issue, you might consider instituting new norms at work, accepting the way things are, or looking for a new job.

7-6c Own Your Feelings

As we discussed in Chapter 4, **owning** is the skill of verbally taking responsibility for your feelings, and is often accomplished by sending **I-messages**, which show that speakers understand that their feelings belong to them and aren't caused by someone else. For skillful emotional communication, I-messages take the following form:

"I feel ____ when you ____, and I would like ____."

For example, let's say that Vanessa is unhappy that her boyfriend, Charles, spends more time with his buddies than with her. Vanessa's I-message would be something like the following:

"I feel unhappy when you spend four nights a week with your friends, and I would like you to spend one of those nights with me."

I-messages differ from you-messages, in which I place the responsibility for my feelings on you. If Vanessa had sent a you-message to Charles, she might have said:

"You are so inconsiderate. All you do is hang out with your friends. I can't believe I am staying with you!"

You can see that Charles's reaction might be more positive to the I-message than to the you-message. Using I-messages does not guarantee that you will get what you ask for. Charles could still tell Vanessa that he wants to spend four nights with his friends. But I-messages help to ensure that Charles hears what Vanessa wants and that he doesn't get sidetracked into a defensive spiral where he argues with her characterization of him as inconsiderate. The I-message focuses on Vanessa's emotion, which is what she wants to talk about with Charles.

7-6d Reframe When Needed

Reframing refers to the ability to change the frame surrounding a situation to put it in a more productive light. When Jane Brody (2002) wrote about methods for reducing hostile tendencies, she alluded to the skill of reframing. Brody quotes Dr. Norman Rosenthal, a psychiatrist in the Washington, DC, area who specializes in depression and anger. Rosenthal comments that a friend often grew angry when waiting in his car at long red lights. The friend's wife reframed for him by reminding him that "the red light doesn't care, so he might as well save his fury" (p. D7). Rosenthal suggests that it is easier for people to reframe their thinking about something than it is to change the world. He goes on to say that after you discover what makes you mad, you can reframe those irritants by changing the messages you give yourself. If you think of other people as rude, that frame may cause hostility. If you change the frame to respecting yourself for being polite, you will probably feel less anger and hostility.

© iStock.com/Exkalibur

owning Verbally taking responsibility for our own thoughts and feelings.

I-message A message phrased to show we understand that our feelings belong to us and aren't caused by someone else.

reframe To change something that has a negative connotation to something with a more positive connotation (e.g., a problem can become a concern, or a challenge can become an opportunity).

I-Messages and the Teaching Profession

As Kelly Cherwin (higheredjobs.com, 2011) asserts, effective teaching may depend just as much on a teacher's emotional intelligence as it does on the teacher's intellectual prowess. One reason that this is the case, according to Cherwin, is because "not every student learns through the same methods, is motivated in the same manner, or acts in the same way in a classroom (live or online). So, it seems apparent that recognizing differences in teaching and learning styles, as well as being able to connect with your students, is important to produce a beneficial outcome." One skill that Cherwin advocates is the use of I-messages. She acknowledges that when teaching, it is inevitable that a teacher will become frustrated or upset. Teachers need to learn to manage these emotions and not demonstrate visible anger toward their students. They also need to take responsibility for their emotions and not blame their students. Cherwin argues that one way to do this is to focus on "I" rather than "you" when making statements about

© bikeriderlondon/Shutterstock.com

the emotional situation. She states, "For example, instead of saying, 'You are not working hard enough to understand this concept,' say, 'I am confused about what is making this concept difficult to understand. Let's try together to understand what is not making sense.'" Cherwin concludes that if teachers can master the art of managing their emotions and using I-messages, they will avoid putting their students on the defensive, which should help students open their minds and increase their learning.

7-6e Empathize

As we discussed in Chapter 6, empathy is the ability to put yourself in another's place so you are able to understand his or her point of view. Empathy is dependent, to a degree, on trust. And this is a concern because there is some evidence that trust is eroding in U.S. culture (Cass, 2013). Some research (e.g., Piff, 2012) suggests that the erosion in trust may be caused by widening economic disparities in the United States. Kristof (2013) observes that wealthy people, more so than the less well-off, seem to respond to others without empathy, suggesting that problems people experience generally are their own fault. He also notes that the poorest 20 percent of the population donate a larger percentage

of their income to charity than do the richest 20 percent. Stern (2013) states that it's possible that wealthy people's relative isolation from the poor contributes to their lack of empathy. Stern quotes Patrick Rooney, the associate dean of Indiana University School of Philanthropy, who told him that "greater exposure to and identification with the challenges of meeting basic needs may create 'higher empathy' among lower-income donors." Thus, we can see that empathy has far-reaching implications for our society.

In interpersonal communication, empathy is often accomplished through the skill of **active listening**, which calls for you to suspend your own responses for a while so you can concentrate on the other person. In active listening, you usually allow the other person a full hearing (no interruptions), and when it's your turn, you say something like "You sound really troubled by your relationship with your dad. Tell me more about how you're feeling." Sometimes people find active

active listening Suspending our own responses while listening so we can concentrate on what another person is saying.

listening difficult to do and comment that repeating back what you've heard sounds corny. But, however you express it, empathy is a valuable skill, and people experiencing strong emotion usually feel the benefits of empathy. When Tommy comes storming into his fraternity house, throwing his books on the table, and swearing about his problems with his girlfriend, Chloe, he would probably appreciate it if someone listened to him with empathy.

Often our response to hearing someone's emotional outburst is to attempt to solve his or her problem ("Here's what you should say to her the next time you see her"), question the person ("How long has she been acting like this?"), tell a story about a similar problem that you have had ("Hey, I know just how you feel, my ex-girlfriend did the same thing! That's why I dumped her"), or evaluate the person's problem ("You know, all couples fight—it's not that big a deal"). Although some of those responses might prove useful later, empathizing is the best approach for early in the conversation because it keeps the focus on the person who is expressing the emotion and allows him or her to set the pace and the content of the conversation. In this way, that person can explore how he or she really feels while you lend a listening ear.

Although these skills take practice, knowing your feelings, recognizing your emotion, being able to identify reasons for your emotion, phrasing an emotion statement, analyzing the situation, owning, reframing, and empathizing all contribute to your interpersonal communication competence in emotional encounters.

STUDY TOOLS

DON'T FORGET TO CHECK OUT COURSEMATE AT CENGAGEBRAIN.COM!

CHAPTER 7 FEATURES THE FOLLOWING RESOURCES:

- ☐ Ethics & Choice: Marco
- ☐ Communication Assessment Test: Emotional Intelligence (EIQ)
- ☐ Interactive Activities

8 | Sharing Personal Information

LEARNING OUTCOMES

8-1 Understand the complexity of self-disclosure

8-2 Identify the effects of individual differences, relational issues, culture, gender and sex, and channel on self-disclosing

8-3 Describe the principles of self-disclosure

8-4 Present explanations for self-disclosing behavior

8-5 Explain the reasons for engaging and not engaging in self-disclosures

8-6 Use a variety of techniques to enhance effectiveness in self-disclosing

After you finish this chapter, go to **PAGE 173** for **STUDY TOOLS.**

THEORY/MODEL PREVIEW

Communication Privacy Management Theory; Social Penetration Theory; Johari Window

© iStock.com/Courtney Keating

Self-disclosure is one of the most researched behaviors in the communication discipline.

Most interpersonal communication scholars believe self-disclosure is a critically important communication skill because it helps relationships develop and contributes to strengthening our self-concept. Ample evidence shows that greater disclosure is related to greater emotional involvement in a relationship (Such, Espinosa, García-Fornes, & Sierra, 2012) and that "disclosure is central to how people define what constitutes intimacy" (Lippert & Prager, 2001, p. 294). Furthermore, relational partners tend to like themselves and each other more after they have self-disclosed to one another (Sprecher, Treger, & Wondra, 2013).

Researchers believe that self-disclosure and relationship development go hand-in-hand—and you probably think so, too. Most people can think of a time when a relationship became closer after one or both partners shared something personal. Because self-disclosure is integral to our interpersonal relationships, we need to examine this communication skill more closely. What does it really mean to self-disclose? Is it always a helpful behavior? What are the risks? What exactly are the boundaries between intimate information and information we're willing to make public? How can we become skillful self-disclosers? In this chapter, we'll discuss this exciting, complex interpersonal communication behavior.

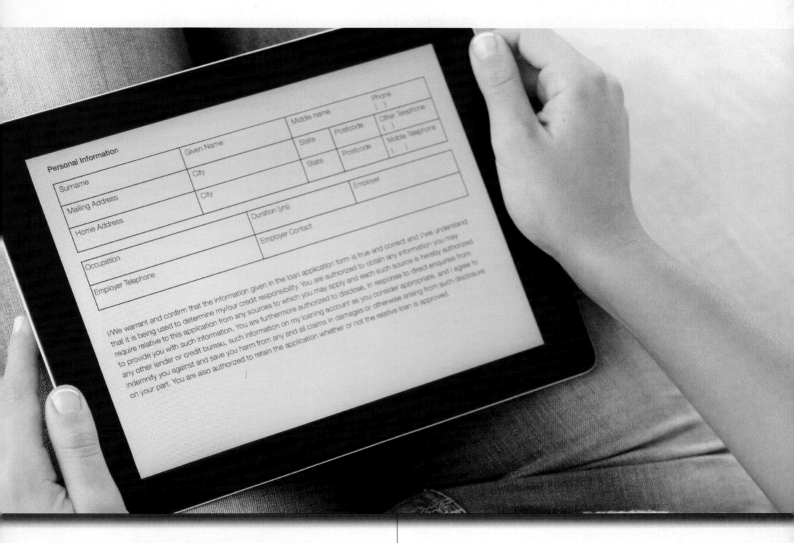

8-1 DEFINITION OF SELF-DISCLOSURE: OPENING UP

Self-disclosure is personal information, shared intentionally, that another person would have trouble finding out without being told. Statements such as "I think I really like Dan," "I feel the most myself when I'm at family gatherings," "I'm disappointed in my progress in my career," or "I am concerned about our relationship—I'm having trouble trusting you like I used to" all may be self-disclosures.

Implicit in our definition is the fact that self-disclosures are verbal behaviors. We do reveal information about ourselves nonverbally—for example, by dressing in certain clothes, wearing a wedding ring, or making facial expressions—but these types of revelations don't fit our definition of self-disclosure because they don't have the same intentionality as information we reveal verbally

to a specific person. Nonverbal behaviors are more generally sent—for example, everyone we come in contact with sees what we wear. Our definition highlights several important features of self-disclosing, all discussed in this section: intentionality and choice, personal information and risk, and trust. In addition, our definition points to the fact that decisions about choice, risk, and trust are subjective. That means what feels like risky information to Janis seems like no big deal to Olivia.

8-1a Intentionality and Choice

When you engage in self-disclosure, you choose to tell another person something about yourself. When Mike tells Elizabeth that he fears he isn't smart enough to make it in medical school, his disclosure is a conscious,

self-disclosure Evaluative and descriptive information about the self, shared intentionally, that another would have trouble finding out without being told.

voluntary decision to confide a vulnerability to a friend. Mike isn't coerced into telling Elizabeth his concerns; rather, he freely discloses them. Although disclosures sometimes slip out unintentionally (e.g., when someone is drunk, overly tired, or otherwise impaired), these "slips" don't meet our definition for real self-disclosure.

We choose *whether* or not to tell something, and we also choose *how* to tell it. For instance, Mike tells Elizabeth about his fear of failing in medical school, but he withholds the information that he did poorly on the MCAT (the standardized exam for potential medical students). Mike is in control of how much he tells and, therefore, how vulnerable he allows himself to be in his relationship with Elizabeth.

As we choose whether and how much to self-disclose in our interpersonal relationships, we negotiate the boundaries between privacy and openness. Sandra Petronio (2000) observes that being both known by others and yet unknown "is essential to our communicative world" (p. xiii). Selectively self-disclosing helps us create the balance among what is private to ourselves, what is shared with intimates, what is disclosed to close friends, and what is known to many others.

8-1b Private Information and Risk

Self-disclosure involves information that another would not be easily able to discover without being told; it must be private information rather than public. **Public information** consists of facts that we make a part of our public image—the parts of ourselves that

we present to others. Usually, people strive to present socially approved characteristics in public information. Some researchers use the metaphor of the theater to describe life, and they refer to public information as what is seen "on stage."

Private information reflects the self-concept. Private information consists of the assessments—both good and bad—that we make about ourselves. It also includes our personal values and our interests, fears, and concerns. In the "life as theater" metaphor, private information is what is kept "backstage." When we're backstage, we can forget about some of the social niceties that are important for public information. The following dialogues illustrate the concepts of public and private information. The first conversation is between Gwen and her boss at Clarke Meat Packing Plant, Ms. Greene; the second is between Gwen and her best friend, Robin, who doesn't work at the plant.

Gwen:	Ms. Greene, I need to take a personal day on Friday.
Ms. Greene:	That's a problem, Gwen. Our new plant policy is that we don't allow personal days if they'll result in having to pay other workers overtime. As I look at the work flowchart, I see that there are only two workers scheduled for that shift. So, I'm afraid I'll have to deny your request.
Gwen:	I'm kind of surprised to hear that. When did that policy go into effect?
Ms. Greene:	It's been our policy for the past 6 months now . . . didn't your union rep inform you?
Gwen:	Ah . . . no, um, I don't think he did, but I may have missed the meeting—I can check with the rep. In the meantime, what should I do about Friday?
Ms. Greene:	I suggest you come to work, Gwen. But if you don't like the conditions here, you can always look for another job.
Gwen:	I like working here, Ms. Greene. I don't want another job.

In this dialogue, Gwen displays public information. She tries to show her supervisor that she is a cooperative, dedicated worker who enjoys working at the plant and who takes responsibility for her own problems (e.g., she

public information Personal facts, usually socially approved characteristics, that we make part of our public image.

private information Assessments, both good and bad, that we make about ourselves, including our personal values and our interests, fears, and concerns.

volunteers to talk to the union rep). In the next dialogue, Gwen is free to exhibit private information with her best friend.

Gwen: Oh, Robin, I'm so mad! Greene won't let me take a personal day on Friday. The entire plant is being run on the fickle whims of the bosses these days!

Robin: Whoa, slow down, Gwen. What happened?

Gwen: I asked that jerk for a personal day on Friday, and she said no because she'd have to pay someone else overtime. I hate my job. She even came out and told me if I didn't like it I could take a walk. I wish I could—I should start looking for a new job, but I hate the job hunt. Maybe I'm too lazy to make a change because it seems like so much work. But, it would serve them right if I did leave, and I didn't give any notice. I can't stand that place!

When displaying private information, Gwen is unconcerned about presenting herself as competent and responsible. Instead, she vents her emotions and reveals some of her less than positive self-assessments: she feels she might be lazy and she doesn't like change or job seeking. In short, she self-discloses.

Some researchers (e.g., Mathews, Derlega, & Morrow, 2006) have noted that past research on self-disclosure has left it to the researcher to define private information. But they wanted to know what people thought was personal, so they asked study participants to describe what constituted highly personal information. They received answers ranging from self-concept to death and illness (see Table 8.1 for a summary of their findings). However, changes in communication practices as a result of social media have left many people wondering if the concept of privacy itself is changing or if it is possible to keep any information private now (Richards, 2013). Certainly social media sites like Facebook may be changing what we consider to be private as opposed to public, and they may even be changing the nature of self-disclosure (Fox, Warber, & Makstaller, 2013). But, even in the era of Facebook, you can see where risk comes into play when we self-disclose. Self-disclosure involves sharing who we really are with another and letting ourselves be truly known by them. The scary part is that we may be rejected by the other person after we have exposed ourselves in this fashion. Risk may also be inherent in the situation or the topic of self-disclosures. Some

TABLE 8.1 HIGHLY PERSONAL TOPICS FOR SELF-DISCLOSURE

Topic	Example
Self-concept	I may not have the drive to succeed in life.
Romantic relationships	When my boyfriend and I broke up, he wouldn't talk to me at all for a month. He ignored my emails and calls.
Sex	I'm a virgin, and I feel that makes me special.
Psychological problems	I am an alcoholic.
Abuse	My father put his hands around my throat and pinned me to a wall.
Death/Illness	My middle brother passed away right before my eyes.
Family relationships	My father left when I was seven and never looked back.
Moral issues	I hit a car on purpose.
Unplanned pregnancy	I recently became pregnant, and I'm not married.
Friendships	I hate my best friend's girlfriend.
Miscellaneous	I had to declare bankruptcy at the age of 24.

Adapted from Mathews et al., 2006, "What is highly personal information and how is it related to self-disclosure decision-making? The perspective of college students." *Communication Research Reports*, 23, 88–89.

research (Theiss & Solomon, 2007) takes on this notion by examining sexual self-disclosures. The researchers don't mean telling another person about sex in general but rather speaking to a partner before engaging in sex, and talking about personal preferences with regard to sexual behavior. They note that people rarely talk specifically about sex, and when they do it is often indirect communication rather than a clear self-disclosure. They comment that it's important to take the risk to disclose at this time to avoid unwanted or unsafe sexual encounters.

8-1c Trust

The concept of trust explains why we decide to take the plunge and reveal ourselves through self-disclosure. When we are in a relationship with a trusted other, we feel comfortable self-disclosing because we believe that our confidante can keep a secret, will continue to care for us, and won't get upset when we relate what we are

thinking. Our perception of trust is a key factor in our decision to self-disclose, and most self-disclosures take place in the context of a trusting relationship.

8-1d Self-Disclosure as a Subjective Process

As you've probably noticed, whether information is considered self-disclosure depends on subjective assessments made by the discloser. The degree of risk involved is a personal judgment; what one person considers risky might be information that someone else would find easy to tell. Taking this fact into consideration, let's make a distinction between *history* and *story.*

History consists of information that sounds personal to a listener but is relatively easy for a speaker to tell. Disclosures that are classified as history may be told easily because of the teller's temperament, changing times, or simply because the events happened a long time ago and have been told and retold. For instance, Nell was the driver in a serious car accident when she was 19, and a good friend of hers was badly injured. The

story of the accident and its aftermath is a dramatic one, but it doesn't feel risky to tell it because she has told it so many times that it has become routine, and her friend eventually completely recovered. In another example, Melanie, who married Jeff in 1975, used to feel nervous about telling people that her husband had been married once before. She really didn't know anyone who'd been divorced, and she felt it was kind of shameful to be married to a divorced person. By 2015, when she and Jeff had been married for 40 years and the divorce rate in the United States was quite high, Melanie stopped being concerned about that disclosure.

In contrast, **story**, or true self-disclosure, exists when the teller *feels* the risk he or she is taking in telling the information. A disclosure should be considered story (or authentic) even if it doesn't seem personal to the average listener. For instance, when Donna told her friend, Oscar, that she had never known a Mexican American person before, Oscar thought that she was simply making a factual observation. However, to Donna, that admission felt very risky. She was afraid that Oscar would think less of her and judge her as provincial because she was unfamiliar with people other than white European Americans such as herself. Donna was engaging in story even though Oscar heard it as history.

Another way to think about history and story relates to the topic of a disclosure. Some topics seem inherently more or less personal than others. For example, you could share a great deal of information about a topic such as sports without seeming to become very personal ("I love the Cincinnati Bengals," "I think the Saints are the most improved team in the NFL," "I believe that professional athletes make too much money"). However, topics such as sex or money seem intrinsically more personal. Thus, disclosures are typed based on **topical intimacy**. However, a person can reveal an actual disclosure (i.e., story) about what seems to be a low-intimacy topic. For instance, Jill might feel she's taking a risk to tell her feminist friends that she's a devoted Green Bay Packer fan. The reverse is also true; a person can reveal very little really personal

history Information that may sound personal to another person but is relatively easy for us to tell.

story Information we feel we are taking a risk telling another.

topical intimacy The level of intimacy inherent in a topic.

information about a high-intimacy topic. For example, when Mike says he wants to take a course in the sociology of sex, he may not think he's risking much. The distinction between real self-disclosure and simple disclosures all depends on the risk the teller feels while talking to a listener.

At this point in our discussion, you may be thinking of self-disclosure as an event in which one person tells another something of consequence. In fact, this is the way many researchers have approached self-disclosure. However, some people think that disclosures aren't discrete, finite events; rather, they are processes that occur on a continuum. Some research (e.g., Dindia, 1998; Thoth, Tucker, Leahy, & Stewart, 2013) indicates that self-disclosing is an ongoing process. Dindia, for instance, investigated how gay men told others about their sexual identity, and she found that her respondents described coming out as a process. She quotes one of her participants as saying, "I . . . am in the process of coming out. . . . When you say, 'hey, I'm gay.' That's the beginning. Yeah, [first you come] out to yourself and then [you] slowly [come] out to other people as well" (p. 87). Self-disclosures are unfinished business because there is always something more or someone else to tell.

information secret from her friend, Trish. Some people are comfortable telling personal disclosures to every one of their close friends but one; others may only wish to confide in one close friend.

8-2b Relational Issues

Self-disclosures wax and wane over the life of a relationship. Telling each other every secret may be important early in the relationship, but in long-term friendships, marriages, or partnerships, self-disclosures account for a much smaller amount of communication time. "Getting to know you" is an important part of developing a new relationship, but as relationships endure and stabilize, the participants need to disclose less because they already know a great deal about one another (Knapp, Vangelisti, & Caughlin, 2014).

Researchers suggest that some general patterns of self-disclosure may be related to the life of a relationship (see Figure 8.1). The first pattern pictured represents the general scenario we've described: People meet, get to know each other, begin to tell each other more and more personal information, and then decrease their disclosures as the relationship endures. This pattern shows a gradual increase in self-disclosing that parallels the growth of the relationship until the relationship stabilizes; at that point, self-disclosures decrease. Some evidence (Bosch, 2012) suggests that, along with other changes, self-disclosures diminish in long-term marriages without a corresponding diminishment of satisfaction.

The second pattern pictured in Figure 8.1 represents two people who know each other as casual friends for a long time before escalating the relationship with self-disclosures and increasing intimacy. The long-term relationship is characterized by low self-disclosures and then a spike up before a leveling off of openness. Let's look at an example. Steven, an emergency room nurse at a local hospital, has worked for several years on the same shift as Amanda, an ER physician at the hospital. They

8-2 FACTORS AFFECTING DISCLOSURE

Although our definition of self-disclosure is fairly straightforward, the discussions of history and story, as well as considerations of self-disclosure as a process, show that self-disclosing is not a simple concept or skill. A complete understanding of self-disclosure requires consideration of many factors, including individual differences, relational issues, cultural values, gender and sex, as well as channel. We explore each below.

8-2a Individual Differences

People have different needs for openness. Whereas David has no problem telling his friends all about his personal feelings, Selena saves disclosures of that nature for her family and most intimate friends. Think about your own tendencies to share information with others in your life. Do you believe that some things are better left unsaid, or do you think that friends and family should know everything about you?

Even people who have a high need to disclose don't wish to tell everyone everything. Although Deanna might tell her partner, Eric, about the fact that she was sexually abused by her stepfather, she may want to keep that

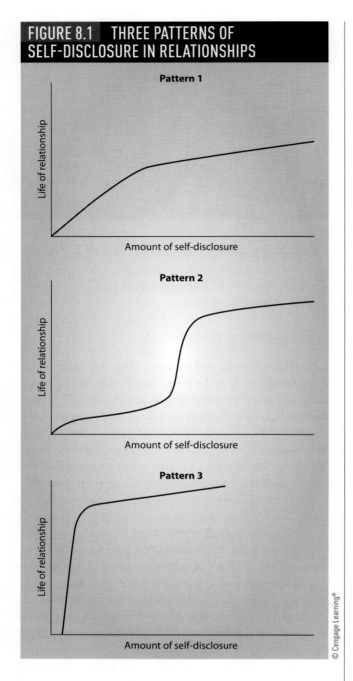

FIGURE 8.1 THREE PATTERNS OF SELF-DISCLOSURE IN RELATIONSHIPS

Pattern 1

Life of relationship

Amount of self-disclosure

Pattern 2

Life of relationship

Amount of self-disclosure

Pattern 3

Life of relationship

Amount of self-disclosure

© Cengage Learning®

The third pattern, sometimes referred to as "clicking," shows a high incidence of self-disclosing almost immediately in the relationship. Researchers refer to these relationships as ones that just "click" from the start rather than needing a gradual build. For example, Ben and Marcus met 20 years ago as 12-year-olds at football camp. They immediately found each other easy to talk to and enjoyed being together. Now, two decades later, they still enjoy an open and deep friendship.

Researchers explain the clicking process by suggesting that people carry around relationship scripts in their heads, and when they find someone who fits the main elements of that script, they begin acting as though all the elements are there. In other words, let's say that some of the things Ben expects in a friend are to have the same interests he has, resemble him physically, be open and attractive, and have a good sense of humor. When he finds all those characteristics in Marcus, he quickly begins acting as though they have a developed friendship. If Marcus has a similar response, we should see the clicking pattern. Again, in this third pattern, there is a leveling off of self-disclosures over time.

In all three patterns in Figure 8.1, self-disclosures eventually level off—and, in many cases, they eventually decrease dramatically if relationships last a long time. However, when new issues arise, even longtime friends or couples who have been together many years will self-disclose. Self-disclosures may also increase if people feel that their relationship has fallen into a rut and they wish to bring back some of its earlier excitement and intensity. Furthermore, if self-disclosures decrease suddenly and radically between people, the decrease may signal that a relationship is in trouble (Carmel, 2012).

Finally, although we may disclose the same information to several people, the way we frame our disclosure may vary based on our relationship with the person involved. For example, Jim tells both his mother and his good friend, Rose, that he has received a cancer diagnosis. When Jim tells his mother, he concentrates on how hopeful his doctor is, and how early the cancer was detected. When Jim tells Rose, he focuses on his own fears and feelings of vulnerability.

8-2c Culture and Ethnicity

Like all the behaviors we discuss in this text, self-disclosing is moderated by cultural prescriptions and values. For example, some evidence suggests that Asian Indians' sense of appropriate self-disclosure differs from those of North Americans and Western Europeans. Asian Indians might be considered overly private by North American or Western standards (Hastings, 2000). Parents and children in Pakistan self-disclose to each other less often than parents and children who are native to the United

have spoken to each other a lot about working conditions and emergency health care. Although Steven and Amanda don't know each other well, they like each other and respect each other's medical skills and steadiness in an emergency. One night, Steven's father suffers a stroke and is brought into the emergency room. When his dad dies a few hours after being admitted, Steven finds comfort in sharing his feelings with Amanda. This tragedy leads to increased disclosures between them. One year later, they refer to each other as best friends. This pattern shows that, as with the first pattern, Amanda and Steven's disclosures will eventually decrease over time.

States. Most Japanese also self-disclose less than North Americans, primarily because privacy is a Japanese cultural value. Most Asians believe that successful persons do not talk about or exhibit feelings and emotions, whereas most North Americans and Western Europeans believe that a willingness to disclose feelings is critical to relationship development.

The amount of self-disclosure deemed appropriate by a culture relates to whether it is a high-context or low-context culture. As we have discussed previously in this text, high-context cultures (such as China and Japan) derive meaning mainly from activity and overall context, not verbal explanation; the reverse is true in low-context cultures (such as the United States). Thus, explicit verbal disclosures are unnecessary in high-context cultures. For example, some research confirms that the Chinese value actions rather than talk in developing relationships (Martin & Nakayama, 2013). In addition, differences in how self-disclosure is valued depends on whether a culture is collectivist or individualistic. One study showed that husbands' marital satisfaction and self-disclosing behaviors were dependent on whether they came from a collectivist or individualistic culture (Quek & Fitzpatrick, 2013). Another study (Schwartz, Galliher, & Rodríguez, 2011) suggests that acculturation might have an impact on self-disclosing behaviors. The researchers surveyed Latino/as living in the United States and found that more acculturated Latino/as disclosed more to white American friends than did less acculturated Latino/as.

Some researchers (e.g., Martin & Nakayama, 2013; Parks, 1982) have observed that scholars, students, and teachers focus on the communication behavior of self-disclosure because of a Western bias that favors openness over privacy and disclosure over withholding information. These researchers criticize the cultural biases that cause Westerners to value disclosure more highly than privacy and secrecy, and suggest that cultures that value privacy should not be seen as deficient, or evaluated in comparison to a Western standard.

8-2d Gender and Sex

Many people believe that gender or sex is a major factor in self-disclosing behaviors. However, the research remains inconclusive on this topic. Some studies suggest that in general, women in the United States seem to self-disclose more than men, and they value self-disclosures more (Ivy, 2012; Wood, 2013). This belief was confirmed in research (Sheldon, 2013) showing that when female friends talked, they usually related emotional disclosures both online and face-to-face. Waldman (2013) describes research showing that adult, white, heterosexual men have fewer friends than any other group. Moreover, the friendships these men do have are more superficial than those formed by

The common stereotype holds that women disclose a great deal about themselves and men disclose very little. However, research shows that the differences between men's and women's self-disclosures are not that dramatic.

women, lacking in self-disclosure and trust. Yet an analysis of 205 studies examining sex differences in self-disclosure (Dindia & Allen, 1992) found that the differences between women and men were rather small. In fact, other researchers (Mathews, Derlega, & Morrow, 2006) found no sex differences in self-disclosing behaviors.

Biological sex might not be as important to differences in self-disclosure as other issues such as gender role or the composition of the couple. In terms of gender role, men who are **androgynous** (meaning they embody both masculine and feminine traits) believe that self-disclosure characterizes close relationships. Androgynous men desire friends who want to share themselves through talk, and they want to do the same. With reference to sex composition, male-male pairs seem to disclose the least and female-female pairs the most (Burleson et al., 2005).

Because the way in which gender or sex influences self-disclosing behavior is complex and uncertain, you might be tempted to fall back on stereotypes depicting disclosing women and silent men. However, most of the research doesn't support such a conclusion. The overall differences between women and men as self-disclosers, and communicators in general, are relatively small, and they are more likely to be the result of other factors, such as power, culture, and so forth, rather than simply an outcome of biological sex (DeFrancisco & Palczewski, 2014).

8-2e Channels

Hollenbaugh and Everett (2013) observe that more and more of our relationships are being formed and maintained online, and this phenomenon raises questions for our conclusions about interpersonal communication. We

---

androgynous Having both masculine and feminine traits.

have to test whether or not our beliefs about communication behaviors, such as self-disclosure, which were formed based on face-to-face relationships, still hold true online. Davis (2012), for example, noted that adolescents in Bermuda experience self-disclosure and friendship in unique ways online. Other researchers (e.g., Nguyen, Bin, & Campbell, 2012), however, argue that many expectations about online self-disclosure are contested when the empirical literature is examined. Nguyen and her colleagues surveyed the literature comparing online and offline communication and found that online channels did not necessarily increase the amount of personal disclosure by users. Other factors such as the relationship between communicators, the specific online venue, and the context of the interaction had a moderating effect on the amount of disclosure.

Hollenbaugh and Everett (2013) examined self-disclosure specifically on blogs. They were particularly interested in the notion that anonymous disclosing online would help disclosers overcome their concern about jeopardizing a relationship with someone they know. The researchers found, contrary to expectations, that anonymity did not increase self-disclosures in all cases. When bloggers shared a photo of themselves, they actually self-disclosed more than when there was no visual to identify them. But, when they shared their real names, some bloggers did tend to disclose less.

Another study examined anonymity in the context of disclosing sexual assault online (Moors & Webber, 2012). The researchers found that disclosers did seem to like the anonymous online forum as a place where they could talk about this sensitive and traumatic topic. Several of them indicated that they saw the online venue as one place they could disclose when they had nowhere else to turn. Yet, a small but troubling number of unsupportive and negative responses to people's disclosures by other posters caused the researchers to sound a note of caution. They suggest more monitoring of websites to prevent this.

Callaghan, Graff, and Davies (2013) warn that when reading studies about online self-disclosure, we should interpret their results based on whether they were performed in a laboratory or in a naturalistic setting. They found that respondents tended to self-disclose more in a lab with a researcher present than in a natural online channel that they chose themselves.

In sum, this brief review of studies investigating online disclosures suggests that the channel may make a difference in how people approach self-disclosure. However, we need to look at more factors than simply whether disclosures take place online or offline in order to make good conclusions and build theory explaining this communication behavior.

PRINCIPLES OF SELF-DISCLOSURE

From our discussion so far, you should have a picture of the self-disclosure process and how it's affected by factors we've mentioned, such as relational issues, culture, gender and sex, as well as channel. To focus this picture further, we now examine four principles, or norms, of self-disclosure: we disclose a lot in a few encounters, self-disclosures generally occur in the context of a close relationship between two people, self-disclosing is reciprocal, and self-disclosures occur gradually over time. Of course, these are general principles, and sometimes you may find yourself disclosing, or listening to another's disclosure, in ways that don't totally adhere to one or more of these principles. However, these norms do hold true for the most part in terms of describing self-disclosing behaviors.

8-3a We Disclose a Great Deal in Few Interactions

This principle suggests that if we examine our total communication behavior, self-disclosures are somewhat rare. Some researchers (e.g., Rosenfeld, 2000) estimate that only approximately 2 percent of our communication can be called self-disclosure. We generally spend a lot more time in small talk than in the relatively dramatic behavior of self-disclosure.

For instance, think about a typical day any one of us might have. We'll illustrate this day with the activities of Joe. Maybe Joe gets up at 7 a.m. and mumbles a morning greeting to his roommates as he hurries to get showered and dressed. He grabs a fast-food breakfast at

KJ Dell'Antonia (*The New York Times*, 2013) blogs in "Motherlode" about how she had no intention of self-disclosing to her children one morning when she was driving the three of them to school. But, somehow, it just happened. She mentioned to them that one time she had suffered a severe case of food poisoning and had to go to the hospital. That led to the children questioning her about the experience, and she ended up telling them that it was the time she had a stillborn daughter who would have been her second child. Dell'Antonia realized that she had never really talked to any of her children about this loss, and she felt that she might have waded into deep waters with the conversation. Thinking something like "in for a penny, in for a pound," she told the children about her feelings at the loss of the baby, and they talked about how their family would have been different if the baby had lived. Dell'Antonia honestly admitted that her youngest child might not have been born in that case. As they speculated about these issues, Dell'Antonia reflected on the results of her self-disclosures, saying, "If you had asked me at 7:30 this morning whether my children were ready to contemplate those kinds of contradictions in some way beyond the abstract, I'm not sure what I'd have said. But by 7:40, we were all the way in." She left the conversation hoping that her honesty and

openness would be good for her children, but not really knowing for sure.

a drive-through and then goes to his part-time job. At work, he has to give guidance to and take instructions from a variety of people. He might spend a little bit of time complaining to his coworkers that he's tired and has a great deal to do. Joe makes some phone calls and places orders, types up a report, and files some paperwork. For lunch, he meets a friend, and the two of them chat about a movie they both saw last week. They engage in some trivial gossip about another friend who might be getting divorced. Joe leaves lunch to hurry over to campus to take two classes. He doesn't speak much in class because he's busy taking notes during the lectures. After the classes, Joe heads over to the coffee shop to study. He orders a latte and sits at a table to read the week's assignment. Joe leaves the coffee shop and stops at the store on the way home to pick up the ingredients for a quick dinner. He runs into a friend at the grocery store and exchanges a few words before hurrying home. When he gets home, he turns on television and watches a reality show while he's putting dinner together. Over dinner the TV remains on; then Joe cleans up the dishes and sends a few texts. Joe falls into bed around midnight.

In that scenario of a typical day, Joe probably didn't self-disclose at all, even though he did talk to many people. The kinds of interactions in the day described were routine, phatic, or instrumental and did not involve

sharing much personal information. However, on another day, he might call a friend and spend an hour talking about a problem that has been bothering him. This generalized example about self-disclosure indicates that we disclose a large amount in a few interactions. Most of our interactions are short, routine, and relatively impersonal. Only a few of our interactions are truly self-disclosive. Yet, because of the emotional impact that self-disclosure has on us and on our relationships, we (and researchers) pay it more attention than some of our other communication behaviors, which actually take up more of our time.

8-3b Self-Disclosures Occur Between Two People in a Close Relationship

Although it is possible for us to tell personal information to small groups of people (or even to large groups, such as on Facebook pages), generally researchers have believed that self-disclosure occurs when only two people are present. Further, how much and how frequently we self-disclose depend in great part on the nature of our relationship with another person. People disclose the most in relationships that are close (e.g., in marital, cohabiting, or family relationships and close friendships). In a study examining why people tell family secrets to others, the researchers (Vangelisti, Caughlin, & Timmerman, 2001) found that people had to think their relationships were secure to feel comfortable enough to self-disclose.

However, a principle is only true *most* of the time, and there are some exceptions to this generalization. The main exception is called "the bus rider phenomenon" or "strangers on a train" (Thibaut & Kelley, 1959). This notion refers to self-disclosures made to strangers rather than to close friends or relatives. The phenomenon derives its name from the fact that such self-disclosures may often occur on public transportation such as buses, planes, or trains where two people are confined together for a period of time with not much to do but talk to each other. In such cases, the relationship between the people is temporary and transient rather than close and ongoing. We're sure that many of you have heard a stranger's life story while traveling across the country on public transportation, or perhaps you, yourself, have shared personal information with strangers in this context.

dyadic effect The tendency for us to return another's self-disclosure with one that matches it in level of intimacy.

reciprocity The tendency to respond in kind to another's self-disclosure.

8-3c Self-Disclosures Are Reciprocal

The essence of this principle is the tendency to respond in kind. Most research suggests that the self-disclosures of one member of a pair will be reciprocated with self-disclosures by the other. The **dyadic effect** describes the tendency for us to return another's self-disclosure with one that matches it in level of intimacy. For example, if Leila tells her friend, Victoria, that she was raped when she was 18 by a guy she was dating, Victoria's reciprocal disclosure would have to be about something equally serious and intimate. The dyadic effect suggests that Victoria would be unlikely to respond by simply telling Leila that at one time she dated a basketball player.

Reciprocity is sometimes explained by noting that it keeps people in the relationship on an equal footing. If two people have reciprocated disclosures, then they have equalized the rewards and the risks of disclosing. In addition, researchers (e.g., Grice 1975) observe that disclosure reciprocity may be governed by global conversational norms such as the requirement that a response has to be relevant to the comment that preceded it. Thus, when Leila tells Victoria her story about date rape, Victoria responds with a story about how she narrowly escaped date rape herself. In doing so, Victoria matches Leila's intimacy level and keeps the conversation on the same topic.

However, conversations involving self-disclosures do not always contain immediate responses of reciprocal self-disclosures like the one we just described between Leila and Victoria. Victoria doesn't have to reciprocate immediately; she may simply listen with empathy while Leila tells her story. Instead of telling about her own experience after hearing about Leila's, Victoria might express empathy and encourage Leila to tell her more about what

happened, how she feels about it now, and so forth. Research suggests that expressing concern for the speaker is actually a better response (because it makes a more favorable impression on the discloser) than responding with a matching self-disclosure (Berg & Archer, 1980).

Does this mean that the norm of reciprocity is wrong? Not exactly. People in close relationships don't have to engage in immediate reciprocity, but they should reciprocate within the conversation at some point, or in a later conversation in the near future. In other words, Leila would be unhappy about the conversation (and maybe her relationship with Victoria) if Victoria never revealed anything personal about herself. But Victoria's self-disclosures don't have to come immediately after Leila's to satisfy the norm of reciprocity.

When people are just getting to know one another, the need for immediate reciprocity is strong (Sprecher, Treger, Wondra, Hilaire, & Wallpe, 2013) and tends to result in positive outcomes for a relationship. As relationships develop and mature, this need is relaxed, and reciprocal disclosures may no longer need to occur even within the same conversation. In these cases, the participants simply trust that disclosures will equalize over the course of their relationship. Sarah might simply listen to her sister, Miranda, as she discloses that she is thinking about divorcing her husband, without disclosing anything to Miranda at all. But Sarah has disclosed a lot to Miranda in the past and will continue to do so in the future.

8-3d Self-Disclosures Occur over Time

Disclosures generally happen incrementally over time. We usually tell a low-level self-disclosure to a relationship partner first and then increase the intimacy level of our disclosures as time goes by and our relationship with that person continues and deepens. In our previous example of Leila and Victoria, this principle suggests that Leila would make her disclosure about date rape after she had already disclosed other, lower-level personal information about herself (e.g., that she had flunked calculus and she was thinking of leaving the university to go into a training program to become a real estate agent). This principle illustrates how relationship development and self-disclosure are intertwined. Learning more about one another changes a relationship, and the nature of the self-disclosures changes as the relationship matures or deteriorates.

This principle also refers to the fact that time affects the meaning of disclosure. For example, when Bethany tells her boyfriend early in their relationship that she's afraid to assert herself around authority figures, he might respond with empathy and support. He might even think it's appealing that Bethany needs him to help her be assertive. But, if Bethany and her boyfriend stay together, the same disclosure 20 years later could be heard as an indication that Bethany refuses to grow up and take any responsibility for herself. In this case, the disclosure would probably not be met with empathy and support.

8-4 EXPLAINING SELF-DISCLOSURE

People have suggested many ways to explain the process of self-disclosure so that we can understand it more clearly. We discuss two theories in this section: Communication privacy management and social penetration. We also introduce a model of the self, the Johari Window, and illustrate how it can help us understand self-disclosure.

8-4a Communication Privacy Management Theory

Sandra Petronio (2002, 2010) developed **communication privacy management theory (CPM)** to explain how and why people decided to reveal or conceal private information to others. Before discussing the theory itself, we need to talk about the polar oppositions of openness and privacy.

In early research on self-disclosure, theorists asserted that self-disclosures created our sense of self and contained the essence of being human. Sidney Jourard (1971) is probably the researcher who has most influenced our positive response to self-disclosure. He suggested that we must engage in self-disclosure to be psychologically and physically healthy. His position came to be known as the "ideology of intimacy" (Bochner, 1982; Parks, 1982) because he believed that disclosing to create intimacy with another was the most important thing a person could do.

More recently, people have rejected this idea in favor of emphasizing the benefits of privacy and even deception (Horan & Booth-Butterfield, 2013). Some researchers now contend that concealing information can have positive effects on relationships. For example, Leda Cooks (2000) writes about discovering that the man who had raised her was not her birth father. Her mother told her this secret when Cooks was 30, revealing that no other members of the family, not even the man Cooks considered her father, knew the truth. Cooks was dumbfounded,

communication privacy management theory (CPM) A theory focusing on how people manage information that they consider to be private.

Communication Privacy Management

Is the concept of owning private information still viable in the age of the Internet? Is it still possible for people to be in complete control of the boundaries around their private information? Do we really get to choose who co-owns information with us or do the principles of this theory have to change to accommodate the easy access to our private information that people have today?

but she eventually decided to keep the secret, believing that in doing so she would preserve her relationship with her custodial father and, more importantly, with her brother, to whom family meant everything.

CPM takes this position and notes that there are good reasons for sharing and equally good reasons for

© kezza/Shutterstock.com

social penetration theory A theory of self-disclosure and relational development that illustrates how sharing increasingly more personal information intensifies a relationship's intimacy level.

withholding private information. One of the key principles of CPM involves the rules that people create to govern when and how information is shared with others. These rules are developed based on some of the influences on self-disclosing that we discussed earlier in the chapter: gender, culture, individual motivations, reciprocity, and risk, for instance.

Furthermore, CPM argues that boundaries are created around private information. The person who might tell something about themselves is considered to "own" the information; if that person tells another, the boundary around the information expands and the two people now "co-own" the private information. Sometimes boundary turbulence arises because the rules about sharing private information are unclear. If Craig tells his daughter Ella that his wife, Kay, Ella's stepmother, is worried about losing her job, boundary turbulence may ensue if Kay hadn't wanted to reveal that information to Ella. Craig can claim that he didn't know that, but Kay will still maintain that her expectations for privacy were violated. The theory predicts that some resolution has to occur at this point. Perhaps Kay will redraw her boundaries and include Ella as a co-owner of the information. Or perhaps Kay will redraw her boundaries to exclude Craig from future private disclosures.

8-4b Social Penetration

Social penetration theory (Altman & Taylor, 1973; West & Turner, 2014) says that people, like onions, have many layers. A person's layers correspond to all the information about them, ranging from the most obvious to the most personal. For example, when two strangers meet, some information—such as their clothing style, approximate height and weight, and hair color—is easily observable. This information makes up the outer layer of the person. Other information—such as gender (masculinity, femininity, androgyny), how a person feels about his or her height and weight, and whether his or her hair color is natural or dyed—is less accessible, and conversation is necessary to "peel" these layers of the onion away. Through interaction, people may choose to reveal these deeper layers of themselves to one another and, in so doing, perhaps intensify their relationship.

Social penetration theory pictures all the topics of information about a person—such as their interests, likes, dislikes, fears, religious beliefs, and so forth—along the perimeter of an onion that has been sliced in half (see Figure 8.2). We can have a relationship with a casual friend in which the only topics we discuss are at the surface layer of the onion. For example, Alissa may know that her friend, Zach, is interested in mixed martial arts, likes cat videos on YouTube, listens to electronic music,

FIGURE 8.2 THE SOCIAL PENETRATION MODEL

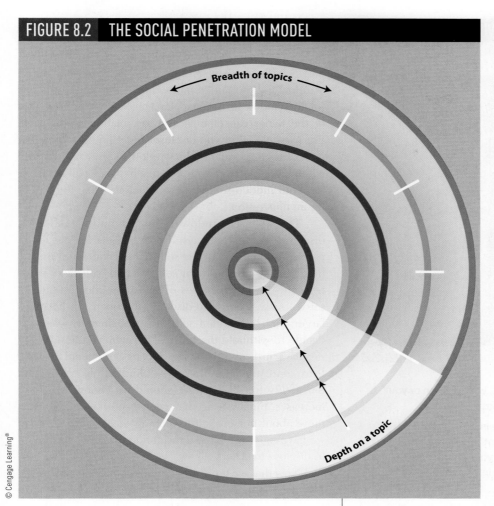

Breadth of topics

Depth on a topic

© Cengage Learning®

is afraid of snakes, loves to travel, has four brothers, and is a member of the Catholic Church. Zach knows that Alissa loves to dance, is a business major, has a sister and two brothers, wants a pet pig, went to Spain a year ago, had an internship last semester, and can't carry a tune.

In this example, Alissa and Zach's relationship has a fair degree of **breadth** (i.e., they both know information about the other across several different topics) but not much depth. **Depth** occurs when they tell each other how they feel about the topics—for example, that Zach's experiencing a crisis in his Catholic faith or that Alissa is much closer to her youngest brother than anyone else in her family, and she feels estranged from her parents. Some relationships have a great deal of breadth without depth, and vice versa. Other relationships have a great deal of both—for example, an extremely close friend or partner would probably know a lot about us in a variety of areas. Yet other relationships involve not much of either, as when a distant relative knows only a few things about us not in much depth. The degree to which you self-disclose controls the social penetration described by the model. Using Figure 8.2 as an example, you could

draw a separate diagram for each of your friends and relatives to determine how much depth and breadth you have in each relationship.

8-4c The Johari Window

The Johari Window is a model used to illustrate the self-disclosure process. Although "Johari" sounds like a term that comes from a mystical language, it is simply a combination of the first names of its creators, Joseph Luft and Harry Ingham (Luft, 1970). Luft and Ingham were interested in the self, and the model they created can help us understand more than just self-disclosure (e.g., it can be used as a tool for self-awareness). For our purposes here, we examine how the window can be applied to the self-disclosure process.

The **Johari Window** provides a pictorial representation of how "known" you are to yourself and others. As Figure 8.3 illustrates, the model is a square with four panels. The entire, large square represents your self as a whole. It contains everything that there is to know about you. The square is divided by two axes: one representing what you know about yourself and one representing what you have revealed about yourself to others. The axes split the window into four panes: the open self, the hidden self, the blind self, and the unknown self.

▶ The **open self** includes all the information about you that you know and have shared with others through disclosures. Whenever you tell someone a piece of

breadth A dimension of self-disclosure indicating the number of topics discussed within a relationship.

depth A dimension of self-disclosure indicating how much detail we provide about a specific topic.

Johari Window A model used to understand the process of self-disclosure consisting of a square with four panels that provides a pictorial representation of how "known" we are to ourselves and others.

open self In the Johari Window, the pane that includes all the information about us that we know and have shared with others through disclosures.

FIGURE 8.3 THE JOHARI WINDOW

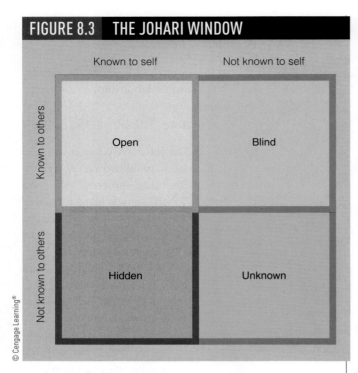

In Figure 8.3, all the quadrants are the same size, but the Johari Window is a person-specific model, meaning that we need to draw a different window for each person with whom we interact. For instance, your Johari Window for you and your mother will differ from your Johari Window for you and your professor. Also, the sizes of the panes can change as your relationships evolve. For example, after you disclose something personal to a professor, in redrawing the window of your relationship with that professor, your open-self panel will increase and your hidden-self panel will decrease. See Figure 8.4 for an illustration.

The Johari Window helps us understand self-disclosure in many ways. First, self-disclosures emanate from the parts of the self that are known to us: the hidden self and the open self. Second, self-disclosures regulate the relative sizes of the open and the hidden selves. As we choose to disclose, the open self becomes larger, and the hidden self becomes smaller; when we decide to withhold disclosures, we achieve the opposite result. Third, as others provide us with feedback, we learn more about ourselves, the blind self decreases, and our ability to self-disclose (should we choose to do so) increases. Finally, as we have new experiences and learn more about ourselves, the unknown self decreases, and we have more available information that we may choose to disclose to others.

Now that we understand more about self-disclosure, we will examine why people choose to self-disclose to

information about yourself (e.g., your opinion or your concerns), the open self increases.

▶ The **hidden self** contains the information that you are aware of but have chosen not to disclose. When you decide that it is too soon to tell your friend that you used a lot of drugs in high school, that information remains in the hidden self.

▶ The **blind self** encompasses information that others know about you, although you are unaware of this information. For example, if you have a tendency to twist the rings on your fingers or chew gum loudly when you are nervous, others watching you know this, but you aren't conscious of your habit.

▶ The **unknown self** consists of the information about you that neither you nor others are aware of. Neither you nor any of your friends or family might know that you have a capacity for heroism. If you're never tested, that information might remain forever in the unknown self. Luft and Ingham believed that there is always something about each person that remains a mystery. So, there are always things about you to learn and discover.

hidden self In the Johari Window, the pane that includes the information about ourselves that we are aware of but have chosen not to disclose.

blind self In the Johari Window, the pane that includes information others know about us that we are unaware of.

unknown self In the Johari Window, the pane that includes the information about ourselves that neither we nor others are aware of.

FIGURE 8.4 THE JOHARI WINDOW AFTER SELF-DISCLOSURE

Known to self | Not known to self

Known to others

Open

Blind

Not known to others

Hidden

Unknown

© Cengage Learning®

their relational partners, or why they decide to withhold private information from these same partners.

8-5 REASONS FOR REVEALING AND CONCEALING PERSONAL INFORMATION

People have many reasons for both disclosing and keeping personal information private, as CPM has suggested. Because our definition focuses on information that is shared intentionally, not things that are blurted out by accident, it is important to examine how people think about the disclosure process. First, we will consider reasons why people choose to share personal information with another. Then, we'll examine reasons for concealing the same information.

8-5a Reasons for Revealing Personal Information

Several specific motivations encourage people to take a risk and reveal themselves to another. Some of the reasons represent factors specific to an individual, whereas others relate to the relationship between people. Table 8.2 presents these motivations, and this section briefly discusses each of them.

TO EXPERIENCE CATHARSIS AND IMPROVE PSYCHOLOGICAL HEALTH AND CONTROL

One reason psychologists are so interested in the concept of self-disclosure is probably because individuals are believed to experience **catharsis**, or a therapeutic release of tensions and negative emotion, through disclosing (Omarzu, 2000). Although, as we've mentioned, the position has moderated somewhat, in general, engaging in self-disclosure is seen as a method for helping individuals achieve psychological health (Smyth, Pennebaker, & Arigo, 2012). The adage "A trouble shared is a trouble halved" expresses the common wisdom that self-disclosing about troubles provides some relief from those troubles. In one study that tested that assumption (Hamid, 2000), 243 Chinese workers in Hong Kong filled out questionnaires about occupational stress and disclosing to a best friend. The researcher found that disclosing to a best friend did reduce the workers' perception of occupational stress.

Sometimes the desire for catharsis or a sense of control over an unpredictable situation can lead to inappropriate self-disclosures. Tamara Afifi and her colleagues (2007) investigated this type of disclosing behavior by examining parents who disclose information about their divorce to their children. The researchers found that parents who felt out of control and stressed tended to engage in more inappropriate disclosures. When parents felt that their partners had not treated them well in the divorce and they weren't getting what they wanted, they tended to confide in their children even though they knew it wasn't healthy for them.

TO IMPROVE PHYSICAL HEALTH

Some evidence supports the belief that self-disclosure provides physical as well as psychological benefits for disclosers. In a 1959 article in the *Journal of Mental Hygiene*, Sidney Jourard stated that self-disclosure promotes physical health and that failure to disclose may cause ill health. This was a controversial position in 1959, and few others followed up on Jourard's thesis. Yet, it is a viable argument today because a great deal of evidence supports the relationship between self-disclosing and physical health (Smyth et al., 2012).

TABLE 8.2	REASONS TO SELF-DISCLOSE
Individual Reasons	**Relational Reasons**
To achieve catharsis (therapeutic release of tensions) and to maintain psychological health and control	To initiate a relationship
	To maintain or enhance a relationship
To maintain physical health	To satisfy expectations for a close relationship
To attain self-awareness	To achieve relational escalation (can be manipulative)

© Cengage Learning®

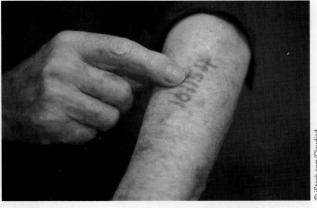

catharsis A therapeutic release of tensions and negative emotion as a result of self-disclosing.

© iStock.com/Claudiad

For example, a study of Holocaust survivors found that people who disclosed the most about their experiences showed better physical health than those who concealed more (Pennebaker, Barger, & Tiebout, 1989). Likewise, researchers (Osborn, Berg, Hughes, Pham, & Wiebe, 2013) found that adolescents with Type 1 diabetes had better results in managing their disease when they were not secretive and self-disclosed to their parents. Other researchers conducted a 9-year study of gay men with HIV-positive status (Cole, Kemeny, Taylor, Visscher, & Fahey, 1996). They found that men who concealed their sexual identity and their health issues had more deterioration in their immune systems, a quicker onset of AIDS, and lived a shorter time with AIDS than did men who self-disclosed. In addition, a large body of research supports the contention that disclosing has a positive impact on blood pressure levels and resistance to cardiovascular disease (e.g., see Tardy, 2000).

TO ACHIEVE SELF-AWARENESS

Self-disclosures provide us with the means to become more self-aware. We're able to clarify our self-concepts through the feedback we receive from others when we disclose, and by the process of hearing ourselves disclose. For example, when Kara discloses to her sister, Martha, that she feels stupid for not learning how to swim until she was an adult, Martha responds by praising Kara for having the courage to tackle a new skill later in life. Martha tells Kara that she is really proud of her and feels that she is setting a good example for their children that it's never too late to learn. Kara is pleased to hear her sister's comments. As she reflects on them, she realizes that persisting with swimming lessons was worthwhile, even though it was more difficult to learn at age 35 than it would have been at age 5. After talking to Martha and thinking about their conversation, Kara feels really good about herself.

When George discloses to his friend Julia that he is thinking about quitting his job and starting his own business, he surprises himself. Although he had been feeling

© marekuliasz/Shutterstock.com

discontented with work, until he heard himself tell Julia that he wants to start his own business, he hadn't really been sure of this. When he puts that thought into words for Julia, he begins to clarify his feelings for himself. This process is pictured in the Johari Window, which we described earlier; as we listen to ourselves disclose and receive feedback, we increase the side of the window that is known to us.

TO INITIATE A RELATIONSHIP

As we discussed previously, disclosers are prompted to tell private information as a way of developing a new relationship with someone who seems interesting. One study (Vittengl & Holt, 2000) supports the idea that self-disclosures help develop new relationships: "Self-disclosure within get-acquainted conversations is accompanied by liking or feelings of social attraction to conversational partners and by an increase in positive emotions" (p. 63). Here it is important to remember that "social attraction" includes friends, partners, coworkers, and so forth, not simply romantic and/or sexual attraction.

To illustrate these findings, let's examine the case of Anita and Zoe. Anita is a working single mother attending the local community college part time and holding down a part-time job as an administrative assistant at a law firm. Because she's so busy, she hasn't made many friends at school or work. One day when she is rushing to finish a project at the firm, she bumps into Zoe. Anita had met Zoe, who is also a single mother, during her orientation. Zoe works full-time at the law firm and mentors new employees.

When they met, Anita had thought that it would be nice to get to know Zoe, but she just hadn't had the time. When they bump into each other, Anita is worrying about her son, Brad, who has been getting into fights at school. Zoe says "hi" in a friendly way and asks if Anita would like to have coffee later. Although Anita really doesn't have the time, she says yes and is surprised when, over coffee, she finds herself telling Zoe some of her concerns about Brad. Zoe listens with empathy and then responds that her son had some behavior problems when he was Brad's age, too, and that she, like Anita, had worried that her work schedule might have been partly to blame. Zoe mentions that she and her son had benefited from some counseling sessions with the school psychologist. When Zoe and Anita part, they both think that they have begun a friendship.

TO MAINTAIN EXISTING RELATIONSHIPS

Existing relationships also benefit from self-disclosures. In an interesting study examining why people tell others about their dreams, researchers found that 100 percent of their participants attributed their disclosures to some

© Photosani/Shutterstock.com

everything about me. I love him and trust him and pretty much share everything with him" (p. 141).

TO ESCALATE A RELATIONSHIP

As we've discussed, self-disclosing provides a way to get to know someone and to allow that person to know you. This process escalates a relationship, often moving it to a more intimate level. Casual acquaintances may become close friends after they spend some time telling each other personal information about themselves. For example, when Javier tells his friend, Elena, that he used to suffer from bulimia and that he still worries every day that he might slip back into his old binge-and-purge habits, Elena feels honored that Javier trusts her with this information. His self-disclosure makes her feel closer to him and advances their relationship to a deeper level.

However, as we discuss throughout the text, communication can be used for destructive purposes as well as positive goals. Indeed, self-disclosures can be used to manipulate a relational partner. For example, a person can offer an inauthentic self-disclosure (or history) to manipulate a relational partner, through the norm of reciprocity, into revealing something truly personal. In this manner, the relationship may escalate faster than it would have otherwise, which might be the devious objective of the first discloser. Or, one person may say "I love you" early in a relationship, without necessarily meaning it, simply to advance the intimacy of the relationship.

8-5b Reasons Not to Self-Disclose

Although opening up to another person provides benefits, there are also compelling reasons to keep our secrets to ourselves. As communication privacy management theory suggests, both desires are extremely important. We want to be open with our partners, but at the same time, we want to maintain our secrets. Although ethical questions arise when we keep something that is critically important from someone else, most of the time, maintaining privacy is ethical. We need to remember that it's our choice as to whether we disclose. People choose not to disclose for the following reasons, which we discuss below: avoiding hurt and rejection, avoiding conflict, maintaining individuality, and avoiding stress.

TO AVOID HURT AND REJECTION

Perhaps the most common reason for keeping a secret is because we believe that the person we reveal it to may use the information to hurt us or may reject us when they know our inner selves. For example, Mick doesn't tell his friend, Marci, that he served time in a juvenile detention center for multiple DWIs (tickets for driving

type of relational goal (Ijams & Miller, 2000). People said that they told a relational partner about a dream to enhance closeness, warmth, and trust. The authors quote one of their respondents, who explained why revealing dreams was important:

> My brother and I have a good sibling relationship. We tell each other everything that goes on in our dreams. Each time we reveal something, the bond between us strengthens. It seems melodramatic, but there is a strong bond between us. (p. 141)

TO SATISFY EXPECTATIONS OF WHAT CONSTITUTES A GOOD RELATIONSHIP

As we mentioned earlier, the ideology of intimacy dictates that we should be completely open and self-disclosive with people in intimate relationships. If we fail to do so or if we consciously keep secrets from intimate others, we often believe that our relationships are flawed or not as good as we want them to be. Self-disclosing allows us to see our relationships in a positive light.

As an example, in the study about dreams referred to previously (Ijams & Miller, 2000), some study participants said that they told a partner about their dream because the partner was already close to them, and the participants' expectation was that in a close relationship people tell each other everything, including their dreams. As one of their respondents stated: "He knows while intoxicated) because he fears that she will be angry, respect him less, or bring it up in a taunting way in an argument. All of these negative outcomes are reasons for keeping a secret private.

Furthermore, if we share a really critical piece of information about ourselves, even with a sympathetic friend, we have given this friend some potential power over us, and we can't be absolutely sure that our friend would never use this power against us or in a way that we would not like. When Audra confides in Allen that she thinks she's a lesbian, she figures he's a trustworthy confidante because he is a longtime friend who is gay himself. However, she doesn't realize that Allen feels strongly that one's sexual identity is nothing to hide. Allen tells several mutual friends about Audra's disclosure. Although Audra doesn't believe that being a lesbian is shameful, she wasn't ready to tell their friends yet; she was still getting used to the idea herself. She was extremely hurt by what she saw as Allen's betrayal.

TO AVOID CONFLICT AND PROTECT A RELATIONSHIP

Some secrecy may actually be helpful in a relationship. If people believe that sharing personal information would cause stress in their relationship, and they don't think the information is necessary for their partner to know, they may choose to conceal the information. For example, Lois thinks she doesn't need to tell her friend, Raymond, that she voted Republican in the last election. Lois knows Raymond is a staunch Democrat, and she believes the disclosure would cause a conflict that could harm their relationship. A study of Chinese business people (Hamid, 2000) found that disclosing to one's mother was negative for the relationship because it increased feelings of stress in both parties.

© Lightspring/Shutterstock.com

In another example, Marsha does not like her brother's wife. When Marsha chooses not to tell this to her brother, Hal, she figures that her silence keeps the relationship between them more peaceful. Because Marsha knows that Hal is happy with his wife, it seems irrelevant to reveal that she isn't. This secret does not affect their relationship much, because they live in different cities separated by thousands of miles, and Marsha and Hal keep in touch mainly by email and phone.

Finally, because you don't know exactly how your relational partner will respond, disclosing may feel like an unwise risk to your relationship. Some research indicates that if you disclose to someone who responds in a negative fashion, you are likely to feel badly about the interaction, the other person, and about your relationship with the other person (Afifi & Guerreo, 2000; Roloff & Ifert, 2000). Some people may believe disclosing isn't worth that risk.

TO KEEP YOUR IMAGE INTACT AND MAINTAIN INDIVIDUALITY

Some people withhold self-disclosures because they're concerned that if they begin disclosing, they will lose control and be unable to stop. Furthermore, these people fear that disclosures will bring with them unrestrained emotionality, perhaps causing them to cry uncontrollably. In a related vein, some people worry that self-disclosing will cause them to lose their sense of mystery and individuality. For instance, Caitlin may fear that if Nolan knows all about her, she won't seem interesting to him any longer. And Gary's fear is that if he tells his friend, Lyle, all about himself, he'll disappear into the relationship and stop being a unique individual.

If someone has established a particular role in a relationship, he or she may fear changing that role and image by self-disclosing something that puts that image into question. Lucy and Rebecca have been friends for 5 years. In their relationship, Rebecca often turns to Lucy, who has been married for 15 years, for advice when she has problems with a boyfriend. When Lucy and her husband fight, she doesn't feel comfortable confiding in Rebecca because it seems to negate her identity as a happily married person who gives support but doesn't need to ask for it.

TO AVOID STRESS

Although it is possible that telling someone something personal can relieve the stress of keeping a secret, some evidence indicates that self-disclosures sometimes

LIFEJACKET UNDER YOUR SEAT

© Luba V Nel/Shutterstock.com

actually increase stress. For instance, Valerian Derlega and his colleagues (1993) give the following example:

> Bill, 20, and Mark, 21, are juniors at a state university. They are flying together to Florida for spring break. Bill is uncomfortable about flying, and he tells Mark about being nervous. Mark, in turn, describes an unpleasant experience when, on another flight, his plane had mechanical problems. As the plane takes off, neither of them is feeling very good. Somehow, talking about their fears made them feel worse rather than better. (p. 103)

Similarly, Anita Vangelisti and her colleagues (2001) observe that continuing to think and talk about stressful issues can result in more stress. They note that stress is reduced only when the disclosures begin to reflect a positive outlook.

SKILL SET FOR EFFECTIVE DISCLOSING

Although we may have good reasons for keeping silent at times, we need to refine our self-disclosing skills for those times when we wish to open up. In this section, we outline important techniques for building our self-disclosing skills.

8-6a Use I-Statements

Owning, or the use of I-statements, which we've discussed in previous chapters, is the most basic verbal skill for self-disclosing. Saying "I think," "I feel," "I need," or "I believe" indicates that you accept that what you're saying is your own perception, based on your own experiences and affected by your value system. When you self-disclose using owning, you take responsibility for your feelings and experiences. In addition, your listener realizes that you are speaking for yourself and not trying to make a generalization. Compare these two disclosures: (1) Edward tells Mike, "I don't know if I will really be happy going to college in New York. It's so far away from my family—I

© iStock.com/Mikosch

know I'll be homesick." (2) Edward says to Mike, "It's important to stay near home for college. It's not good to put too much distance between family members." When Edward uses the latter phrasing, he doesn't own his feelings; instead, he presents them as a general rule that all people should consider when deciding where to go to college. The first statement Edward makes is an owned self-disclosure, focusing on his own, unique feelings.

8-6b Be Honest

Honesty in self-disclosure refers to being both clear and accurate. If you are too ambiguous and unclear, your self-disclosures may not be "heard" as real disclosure. Yet, if you and your partner know each other very well, you may be able to offer disclosures more indirectly. For instance, if you know that your partner is struggling with several deadlines at work, you will be able to hear a disclosure in your partner's sarcastic comment: "I had a great day at work today. What a pleasure palace that job is!" Generally speaking, however, you need to be clear and accurate in your disclosures. If you are dishonest or inaccurate while disclosing, you are defeating the purpose of self-disclosure.

8-6c Be Consistent and Focused with Your Verbal and Nonverbal Communication

Consistency means that your nonverbal communication should reinforce, not contradict, your verbal communication. For example, if Shannon tells Josie that she's really upset about her grades this semester but smiles while saying it, Josie may be confused about whether Shannon is upset or not. Focusing means that your nonverbal communication adds meaning to the issue at hand and doesn't distract from your message. For instance, if Maya continually taps her pencil against a table while telling her mother that she wants to quit school, her mother may be distracted by the gesture and have trouble concentrating on Maya's disclosure.

8-6d Choose the Appropriate Context

This refers to an assessment of the appropriateness of the disclosure to the situation itself. If Ron is at a company picnic, for instance, he may decide that it isn't the time or place to tell his boss that he is unhappy at work and wants more responsibility. He may wait to disclose his feelings until an appropriate occasion, such as a yearly review or a private meeting.

8-6e Be Sure Your Disclosure Is Relevant

Relevancy means that you are able to weave your disclosure naturally into the conversation. When Jeff and Noel

Self-Disclosure Decisions in Journalism

It has often been thought that journalists were supposed to be completely neutral and objective, and stand at a distance from the stories they covered. Certainly, they were not supposed to be the story, themselves. However, recently several news anchors have disclosed their sexual identities, and there is some suggestion that a knowledge of self-disclosing principles was very helpful as they navigated this disclosure decision (Emmrich, 2014). For instance, Anderson Cooper stated that initially he felt that as a journalist he should adhere to the standard of neutrality and not discuss his personal life, but he finally concluded that "in a perfect world, I don't think it's anyone else's business, but I do think there is value in standing up and being counted. I'm not an activist, but I am a human being and I don't give that up by being a journalist." Several news anchors have chosen to come out in a rather casual way, perhaps in an effort to avoid becoming a story themselves. Robin Roberts, of *Good Morning America* on ABC, made a passing reference to her longtime partner, Amber, on a Facebook post. While at CNN, Thomas Roberts attended the annual meeting of the National Lesbian and Gay Journalists Association and made a low-key announcement. Sam Champion,

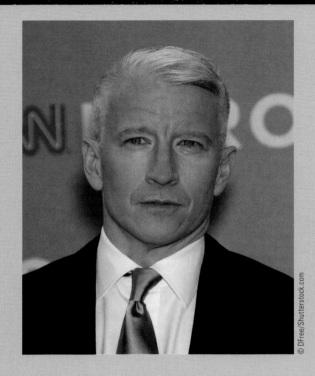

© DFree/Shutterstock.com

of ABC, noted during a broadcast, that he was "so lucky to have this person in my life," indicating his partner, Rubem Robierb, who was shown on camera standing in the wings. In all these cases, the anchors evaluated the risks and benefits, and sought to find appropriate contexts for their self-disclosures.

go out bowling together for the first time, for instance, they begin talking about their involvement in sports in the past. The situation and the topic seem to invite Jeff to tell Noel that he is insecure about his athletic abilities. If Jeff and Noel were at a restaurant talking about a movie they had both recently seen, that topic wouldn't have been so inviting for Jeff's disclosure.

8-6f Estimate the Risks and Benefits

To be competent in self-disclosure, you need to be able to estimate and balance its risks and benefits. As mentioned previously, there are compelling reasons to reveal and to withhold disclosures, many of which pertain to issues of self-identity. To be effective at self-disclosing, you need to practice judging when the benefits outweigh the risks, and vice versa.

8-6g Predict How Your Listener Will Respond

Your ability to decode messages of warmth, concern, and empathy on the part of the other person will help you make judgments about when to tell and when to be silent. Mark knows that his partner, Sean, is a sympathetic listener. Therefore, although Mark feels some fear about revealing his past experiences with homelessness, he feels that Sean is ready to hear about them.

8-6h Be Sure the Amount and Type of Disclosure Are Appropriate

Although, as we've said before, there are a few exceptions to this rule, the amount and type of disclosure should match the perceived intimacy level of the relationship. On a first date, it's probably unwise to tell all

"Yes, I wear a dress and hack people to death, but I'm still right for this job."

your insecurities and past indiscretions. Early in your relational life, you and your partner should share talk time. You don't want to dominate the conversation with long self-revelations. You should attempt to pace your disclosures so that they roughly match the developing intimacy of your relationship.

8-6i Estimate the Effect of the Disclosure on Your Relationship

Think about how the disclosure might affect the relationship. For example, Jake asks himself if telling Rochelle about his growing interest in her will actually cause the end of their friendship. Ellie considers whether telling Marc about her trouble with commitment in the past will hurt or intensify their relationship. Of course, you can never know for sure what the specific effects a disclosure will have, but making well-founded assessments of effects is an important skill to develop.

STUDY TOOLS

DON'T FORGET TO CHECK OUT COURSEMATE AT WWW.CENGAGEBRAIN.COM!

CHAPTER 8 FEATURES THE FOLLOWING RESOURCES:

- ☐ Ethics & Choice: Theo
- ☐ Communication Assessment Test: Exploring Your Approach to Self-Disclosure
- ☐ Interactive Activities

9 | Communicating Conflict

LEARNING OUTCOMES

9-1 Understand the complexities of conflict

9-2 Detail communication patterns in conflict

9-3 Identify the destructive and constructive sides of conflict

9-4 Describe two theories of interpersonal conflict

9-5 Identify the relationship between power and conflict

9-6 Employ skills for communicating during conflict that afford increased satisfaction in interpersonal interactions

After you finish this chapter, go to **PAGE 194** for **STUDY TOOLS.**

THEORY/MODEL PREVIEW

The 4-Part Conflict Model; The Explanatory Process Model

Most people think engaging in conflict is an unpleasant and even nasty experience (Sonnentag, Unger, & Nägel, 2013; Turner & Shuter, 2004).

Yet it's impossible to interact with others without sometimes experiencing conflict; conflict is an unavoidable part of life. Conflicts are common in interpersonal communication because we're all unique individuals, and differences between people are what prompt conflict. Not all differences cause conflict, however. Sometimes, people recognize differences between them that do not matter enough to cause conflict. For example, let's say that Lauryn really likes Lady Gaga, and her cousin, Tess, can't stand Lady Gaga. If Lauryn and Tess don't live together, don't go to concerts together, and don't talk about music when they see each other, this difference will probably not precipitate conflict between them.

How much conflict arises from people's differences also depends on what stage they're in in their relationship.

When people first meet, they usually focus on their similarities, thus reducing opportunities for conflict. Part of the fun of getting to know someone is discovering all the things you have in common. However, later in the relationship, you may notice and discuss differences. Think back to the first time you met someone you later became good friends with or dated. Your early encounters with this person probably had fewer conflicts than your later interactions (Knapp, Vangelisti, & Caughlin, 2014).

Another factor influencing conflict between people has to do with the type of relationship they share. In some relationships, people notice differences relatively quickly because the nature of the relationship implies differing interests, concerns, and bases of power. For example, in a relationship between a worker, Carlos, and his boss,

Manuel, their job titles indicate that despite the fact that they work for the same company, they'll have divergent perspectives. Manuel's job as boss dictates that he's responsible for maximizing productivity and minimizing expense. This goal may run counter to Carlos' needs and desires as an employee. Furthermore, the power relationship between the two is not equal. Manuel has the power to punish or reward Carlos in ways that aren't reciprocal. These inherent differences make workplace friendships or romances tricky (although not impossible) to negotiate. Parent-child and teacher-student are other types of relationships in which intrinsic differences between the roles played offer ripe arenas for difference and, thus, conflict. Some people suggest that relationships between people of different cultures or even relationships between men and women maximize differences, and provide opportunities for more conflicts than do relationships between more similar people.

In short, unless you only talk to people who are exactly like you, or you never develop a relationship beyond its initial stages, or you are able to avoid any

discussions about areas of difference with another, conflict in interpersonal communication is inevitable. What is not preordained, however, is how you and your partner deal with the normal conflicts of daily life. You do have some control in this crucial arena, and can implement skills that will influence how the conflict proceeds and affects your relationship. Before we learn about how to manage conflict, we'll first define the term, examining its complexities including: types of conflict people engage in; common myths that people hold about interpersonal conflict; and factors that exert an influence on the experience of conflict.

9-1 DEFINING CONFLICT

We've all experienced conflict, but often it comes as a surprise. We're left scratching our heads, wondering what happened. Knowing what conflict is all about won't stop you from experiencing discord, but it can be the first step

The holidays often become a fertile breeding ground for family conflict, according to Olga Khazan (theatlantic .com, 2013). Khazan explains that families fight for many reasons when they get together to celebrate. Two that she discusses at length are what she calls "small differences" and "minor annoyances." First, she points to Freud's theory called "the narcissism of the small difference." As Khazan states, it's the small differences between people who are otherwise quite similar that can cause great aggravation and lead to conflict. She offers that this may be the case because we focus more on the differences between us and family members than we do on our similarities. So, if you and your sister look a lot alike but she votes Democratic and you vote Republican, Khazan predicts a political conflict over the turkey dinner.

Khazan points to another reason for family conflicts that she calls minor annoyances or "social allergens." Social allergens refer to those little annoying habits that people have that tend to drive you wild when you're exposed to them over time. When your uncle has the habit of clearing his throat excessively or your brother always uses the phrase "to be sure" before giving his opinion about something, annoyance may build up as

© iStock.com/steele2123

you listen. These cumulative annoyances are especially difficult when families are under the same roof and increasingly interdependent on one another.

Khazan suggests some methods for dealing with these two conflict starters, including reframing them so you can regard them as positives rather than annoyances. She notes, for instance, that rather than asking yourself how it's possible that you can be related to such idiots, you should instead marvel that such diversity could come from the same genetic pool.

in helping you manage it better. **Interpersonal conflict** is commonly defined as "the interaction of interdependent people who perceive incompatible goals and interference from each other in achieving those goals" (Folger, Poole, & Stutman, 2013, p. 5). Several key parts of this definition include interaction, interdependence, perception, and incompatible goals. We will discuss each one of these fundamental terms individually, to help us understand the meaning of conflict.

9-1a Interaction

Here, **interaction** means that conflicts are created and sustained through verbal and nonverbal communication (Canary, Cupach, & Serpe, 2001; Roloff, 1987). Some

© Edtw/Shutterstock.com

interpersonal conflict The interaction of interdependent people who perceive incompatible goals and interference from each other in achieving those goals.

interaction A condition necessary for conflict, given that conflicts are created and sustained through verbal and nonverbal communication.

conflicts involve yelling, crying, swearing, and screaming. Other conflicts consist of icy silences, cold shoulders, frowns, and withdrawal. However, regardless of the behaviors, remember that the definition specifies that conflict is interaction *between* people. In other words, if Cate is talking to James the same way she always does, even though internally she's angry with him, they aren't engaging in conflict by this definition. They enter into conflict only when she says or does something that shows how she feels, and James responds with disagreement.

Because this text is focused on explaining interpersonal communication, we emphasize the expression of conflict through verbal and nonverbal cues. However, this focus doesn't mean that we are not interested in the thoughts people have during conflicts. Our emphasis is on how our thoughts influence what we say; for students of communication, interaction is in the foreground, and cognition is in the background, but the two work together, each affecting the other (Bodie, Honeycutt, & Vickery, 2013).

One study (Sillars, Roberts, Leonard, & Dun, 2000) examined the relationship between thoughts and communication behaviors in marital conflict. The researchers asked 118 married couples to discuss a current issue that caused conflict for them, and then to watch videotapes of their own discussion. This method allowed the researchers to probe how the couples thought about their conflict communication. The researchers noted that *thought* and *talk* go together: "To appreciate the subtlety and complexity of communication in conflict, it is helpful to consider what people are thinking as they interact" (pp. 480–481).

The study found that in severe conflicts especially, husbands and wives tended to construct individual accounts that didn't agree with each other. Thus, as wives watched the tapes and recalled what they were thinking, they generated a very different picture from what their husbands thought about the same tape. The researchers comment that selective perception is a central dynamic in conflict interactions; people's differing thought patterns impacted the ways they conducted the conflict.

9-1b Interdependence

Interdependence means that the people involved in the conflict are in some type of a relationship together that requires them to rely on one another. Parties must feel some degree of interdependence to experience conflict. If you are completely independent of another person, then generally a conflict won't arise. The person simply isn't important enough to you to bother engaging in conflict with them.

Let's say that Lola meets Justin at a party. Justin doesn't interest Lola much, and Lola finds herself disagreeing with his loudly stated views. Justin is talking about a recent case on campus where a woman has accused a basketball player of date rape. Justin proclaims that the accuser was probably asking for it, because the campus paper had reported that she was drunk at the time of the alleged attack. Lola listens for a while, getting a little agitated as she hears so much that she thinks is absolutely wrong. She decides to talk to someone else and politely excuses herself. On the other hand, if Lola and Justin are good friends, they may find that their different opinions on this case will lead to conflict. It wouldn't be as easy for Lola to just walk away from a good friend with whom she disagrees.

Interdependence brings up one of the striking ironies of conflict. Although people's need for others is a basic, fundamental human desire, people rank conflicts with others one of the most critical stressors they experience. As one researcher (Kowalski, 2001) observes, "it is ironic that the same relationships that people seek so eagerly are the source of many, perhaps most, of their greatest frustrations and unhappiness" (p. 297). Our connection to others provides us both pleasure and pain, both the joy of feeling understood and the conflict surrounding differentiation. When Jeff thinks of his happiest moments, he usually thinks of the times he has spent with his best friend, Ray. However, Jeff's unhappiest time is also associated with Ray. Ray had thought that Jeff was flirting with Ray's girlfriend, and he'd been furious, not speaking to Jeff for a week, even when they were at basketball practice and classes together. Jeff had felt

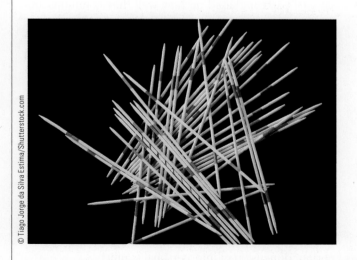

interdependence A condition necessary for conflict, given that people involved in conflict rely on each other, need each other, and are in a relationship with each other.

a lot of pain and anxiety because he thought that their friendship was over. Finally, Ray realized that Jeff wasn't really guilty, and they were able to resume their friendship. Jeff found it surprising that being around the same friend could sometimes be so much fun and other times feel like torture.

9-1c Perception

Perception, as we discussed in Chapter 3, refers to the psychological process involved in sensing meaning. The definition we provided for conflict states that conflict exists when interdependent people *think* that they have incompatible goals. For example, Carmen wants to go on a family vacation to Florida. She misunderstands a statement that her husband, Dave, makes and jumps to the conclusion that he disagrees with her preferred vacation destination. Even though Carmen and Dave really agree on where to take their vacation, if Carmen believes they disagree, they will probably experience conflict. This type of conflict persists until the parties come to understand that their goals really are similar.

Of course, the opposite situation may occur as well: Ana and Bonnie believe that they both hold the same opinion about their boss, Dawn, so they do not engage in any conflict on the topic. In fact, however, Ana holds a much more positive opinion of Dawn than Bonnie does, but because they don't talk about Dawn much, they do not realize they disagree.

Some researchers emphasize the importance of perception to the conflict process when they apply a competence model to interpersonal conflict. Competency suggests that people judge themselves and their conversational partners based on how well they communicate and how successful they are in reaching their conversational goals (Spitzberg & Cupach, 1984, 1989; Wright et al., 2013). When applying this model to conflict, one study (Canary et al., 2001) found that people's perceptions of competency during the conflict directly affected the relationship. The researchers found results resembling this example: if Josie and Kerry have an argument about cleaning their apartment, and each perceives that they both behaved competently during their conflict, they will be more satisfied and happier with one another (and their relationship) than they would be if they'd had the exact same conflict but *thought* they'd behaved less competently. Therefore, researchers argue that perception of communication competence is an extremely important dimension of interpersonal conflict.

image conflict A conflict with another about one's sense of self.

9-1d Incompatible Goals

The definition of conflict specifies that friction results when people's goals differ (as in "I want to study, but Jon wants me to go to a party with him") at the same time that they think others stand in the way of the achievement of personal goals (as in "I want to get promoted at work, but my supervisor wants me to stay in her department"). This feature of the definition implies that conflict is goal oriented. For instance, imagine two sisters, Karla and Meredith, who spend a lot of time together. One Sunday, Karla wants to go to the beach, and her sister wants to stay home and have a barbeque. Because Karla's goal isn't compatible with what Meredith wants, they will engage in conflict if they are dependent on one another to accomplish their goals. If Karla needs Meredith to drive her to the beach and Meredith needs Karla to start the barbeque, or even if they simply just want to be together for the day, they are interdependent and have incompatible goals, which will likely cause conflict between them, according to our definition.

9-1e Types of Conflict

Now that we have a basic, working definition of conflict, we can further our understanding by learning about various conflict types. We'll discuss six types: image, content, value, relational, meta-, and serial conflicts. Understanding these different types helps us gain a better sense of conflict communication.

IMAGE CONFLICTS

Image conflicts concern self-presentation. For example, if Ellie considers herself to be a competent adult, she may engage in conflict with her mother when her mother offers suggestions about how to manage her career. Ellie may feel that her mother isn't respecting her as an adult and, as such, is challenging Ellie's

© tommaso lizzul/Shutterstock.com

image of herself. Sometimes image conflicts result from a problem of misperception; Ellie believes her mother still thinks of her as a child, but that isn't really the case. This type of conflict is especially difficult when two different images are, in fact, in play. If Ellie's mother does still view Ellie as a child, they actually do have two competing images. A similar problem can exist when a parent pushes a child to grow up faster than the child feels comfortable doing. In that case, the parent views the child as an adult, whereas the child may still see herself or himself as a child. Sometimes, image conflicts may masquerade as another type of conflict, but at the core of an image conflict is a disagreement about self-definition.

CONTENT CONFLICTS

Content conflicts are often called "substantive" because they revolve around the substance of a specific issue. Interdependent people fight about myriad topics. Maeve calls her Internet provider to complain about the service, and the service provider tells her there is no evidence to support her complaint. Nanette likes a tree on her property line, but her neighbor thinks its roots are responsible for cracking his driveway. Matt hates to bowl, and his best friend, Drew, loves bowling. Ginna wants to spend some of their savings on a vacation, and her husband, Sean, thinks that would be a waste of money. Penny thinks that the data for her work group's presentation should be rechecked, and the other members of the group think they've been checked sufficiently. Lou believes that even though he works part time, he should be respected as a member of the company and allowed a say in company policies; however, the full-time workers don't want the part-timers involved in those matters. Although all of these examples involve topics of disagreement, some of these content conflicts have undertones of the other types of conflicts within them. As we discuss the subsequent types, we'll point out this overlap.

Some researchers suggest subdividing content conflicts (Johnson, Becker, Wigley, Haigh, & Craig, 2007). These researchers think that content conflicts can either focus on **public issues**, meaning issues outside the relationship, or involve **private issues** that relate more closely to the relationship, and in this way resemble the relational conflict type we'll discuss later. For instance, when Stan and Frank disagree about whether Barack Obama was a good president, they are debating a public issue. When Stan complains that Frank has no time to hang out with him anymore because he is always spending time with his new girlfriend, they are tackling a private issue. Not surprisingly, research finds that people enjoy arguments about public issues more than conflicts about private issues.

VALUE CONFLICTS

Value conflicts are conflicts focused specifically on questions of right and wrong. The neighbors who are arguing about the tree on their property line may be having a values conflict if they are discussing it in terms of ecosystems and environmental protection. When people disagree about gun control, gay rights, U.S. immigration laws, or capital punishment, they are usually engaging in value conflicts because opinions on these topics largely depend on value judgments made by the participants. For example, arguments about gun control often hinge on the value placed on human life compared to the value placed on freedom of choice.

RELATIONAL CONFLICTS

Relational conflicts focus on issues concerning the relationship between two people. When Rachel and Taylor argue about how much Taylor respects Rachel's opinions, they are having a relational conflict. Couples who argue about how much they should tell their in-laws about their financial situation compared to how much they should keep private, are engaging in relational conflict. Our previous example of Ginna and Sean's fight about whether to spend savings on a vacation could be classified as a relational conflict if it centers on how they make decisions in their relationship. The disagreement would be a values conflict if it underscores a difference in how the two value money.

---

content conflict A conflict that revolves around an issue. Also called *substantive conflict.*

public issue An issue outside a relationship that can cause a content conflict.

private issue An issue related to a relationship that can cause a content conflict.

value conflict A conflict in which the content is specifically about a question of right and wrong.

relational conflict A conflict that focuses on issues concerning the relationship between two people.

meta-conflict A conflict about the way a conflict is conducted.

META-CONFLICTS

Meta-conflicts are conflicts about the way you conduct conflict. Any time people engage in conflict about any topic, they may also be concerned about *how* they're conducting the conflict communication. If Jennifer and Dominic argue repeatedly, they may also reflect on their conflict process, and this reflection may lead to meta-conflicts. When Jennifer tells Dominic that she hates it when he interrupts her, and Dominic replies that he wouldn't do that if she'd get to the point, they are engaging in meta-conflict. Meta-conflicts can happen at any time, but they are especially likely in long-term relationships.

To read short dialogues that illustrate these five types of conflict, see Table 9.1. In addition, Figure 9.1 presents a dialogue and a picture that show how these conflict types overlap. Even though the types cannot be completely separated, being able to identify what kind of conflict you're having is useful in helping you decide how to manage it.

SERIAL CONFLICTS

Serial conflict is a sixth conflict type, but it differs from the other five types because it doesn't refer to the subject or the underlying focus of the conflict.

FIGURE 9.1 OVERLAP IN TYPES OF CONFLICTS

Conflict Dialogue

Andre: It's a real shame that all these states are legalizing medical marijuana. People will abuse the system and get prescriptions even if there's nothing wrong with them. Drugs are illegal for a reason!

Michael: I really thought I knew you, Andre, but that just blew me away. Alcohol and tobacco are legal, and they're much more harmful than marijuana. With proper regulation, marijuana can be a beneficial treatment for a number of illnesses.

Values
How should substances be controlled?

Content
Should medical marijuana be legal?

Image
Did we really know each other well?

Relational
Can we still be friends though we disagree?

© Cengage Learning®

serial conflict Conflict that recurs over time in people's everyday lives, without a resolution.

TABLE 9.1 TYPES OF CONFLICT

Image Conflict	
Marilyn:	Mom, why do you still treat me like a child? I'm 22 years old!
Mom:	Marilyn, you are always going to be my little girl.
Marilyn:	That's ridiculous, Mom. You have to let me grow up.
Content Conflict	
Fred:	Jeff, I don't think that New York has the largest state population. I'm pretty sure I read that it was California.
Jeff:	No, it's New York.
Fred:	Well, we can look it up.
Value Conflict	
Amy:	Travis, I can't believe we're so close to getting married, and I am just finding out that you don't want to have kids! To me, that's what marriage is all about.
Travis:	Are you kidding? I never believed that marriage is all about having kids. What about love, companionship, and fun? Aren't those the things that marriage is all about?
Relational Conflict	
Angela:	Marlee, I know this sounds funny, but I feel kind of left out when you and I are together with Justine. We used to be best friends, and now it seems like you don't even want to be around me if you have the chance to hang out with her.
Marlee:	That's not exactly true, Angela.
Angela:	It sure feels that way to me.
Marlee:	I know I've been spending a lot of time with Justine, but that's just because we have the same major and are in a lot of classes together.
Meta-conflict	
Laura:	I'm tired of hearing you take that tone with me!
Adrianne:	What are you talking about?
Laura:	You just did it now—you sound so patronizing whenever we disagree about anything. It sounds like you think you're so superior.
Adrianne:	That is totally not true. I don't think that at all.
Laura:	Well, it sounds like you do.

© Cengage Learning®

Instead, it refers to a timeframe for the conflict. Up to this point, we've been talking about conflicts as discrete episodes, with specific starting points ("I'm so sick of you using up all the hot water every morning") and specific ending points ("Okay, okay, I'll take a quicker shower"). Serial conflicts are those that recur over time in people's everyday lives, without a resolution ("Last week you said you'd take a quicker shower, but you aren't doing that. It's the same thing over and over." "Well, you're always on my back! We've argued about the hot water for months. Leave me alone about the stupid shower, already."). Researchers (Bevan et al., 2007; Malis & Roloff, 2006) find that these serial conflicts tell us a lot about relational communication. In relationships with a long history (such as dating, marriage, or families), partners are likely to have unsettled issues that come up repeatedly whether they want them to or not. Some research (e.g., Carr, Schrodt, & Ledbetter, 2012) has attempted to discover what factors sustain these serial arguments in some relationships. Factors such as whether the participants believe the conflict to be resolvable, as well as their perceptions of the intensity of the conflict affect how likely it is to recur (those conflicts perceived as irresolvable and very intense seem to be the ones that turn into serial arguments).

9-1f Myths About Conflict and Communication

Another way to understand what conflict is consists of examining what it is not. Thus, we turn our attention to false beliefs, or myths, about the nature of interpersonal conflict. As we've stated previously, conflict is a normal part of life, but many people find it unpleasant. Perhaps as a result, people talk a great deal about conflict, and this tends to generate myths about it. We'll discuss the following very common (but mistaken) beliefs: conflict is just miscommunication, all conflict can be resolved through good communication, and it is always best to talk through conflicts.

MYTH #1: CONFLICT IS JUST MISCOMMUNICATION
Many people believe that all conflict results from miscommunication or unclear communication. However, it's possible to communicate perfectly clearly to others, and still disagree. For instance, if Tim wants to go to Harvard and his parents tell him they do not want him to go to school so far away from home, Tim and his parents may continue to argue about this topic even though they've all clearly communicated their positions. The problem in this case is not that they haven't been clear; rather, they disagree about whose goal is more important and, possibly, who has the power in their relationship to make such a decision.

MYTH #2: ALL CONFLICT CAN BE RESOLVED THROUGH GOOD COMMUNICATION
The corollary to the myth of miscommunication is the notion that all conflicts can be resolved through good communication. This myth tells us that if we master a certain set of skills for managing conflict, we can resolve all of our conflicts. Although we offer a set of skills later in this chapter, we recognize that some conflicts persist, and partners may have to agree to disagree on some things. For example, no amount of good communication practices will convince Harry to vote for a Libertarian candidate even though his son, Michael, tries to persuade him that the Libertarian candidate in the current election advocates better policies than does the Republican candidate. Harry simply states that he has voted Republican his whole life and is proud to continue doing so.

MYTH #3: IT IS ALWAYS BEST TO TALK THROUGH CONFLICTS
Underlying the first two myths is the idea that it's always best to talk about conflicts. People often believe that they need to communicate more to reach a mutually satisfying solution to their conflicts. Indeed, people derive many benefits from talking through issues that bother them (e.g., Merrill & Afifi, 2012) However, this myth obscures the benefits that accrue from avoiding certain topics rather than talking about them in great detail (Guerrero & Afifi, 1995; Petronio, 2013; Wang, Fink, & Cai, 2012). Sometimes continuing to talk about a point of disagreement just exaggerates and prolongs the problem. Some arguments are not that important, and if you ignore them, they really will go away. For instance, when Mel broke the rain gauge in their backyard, Tina was angry. However, because she realized that it was just a $20 item and that getting into a big discussion about it wouldn't be productive for their relationship, she didn't

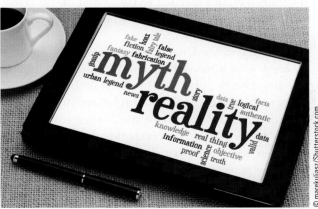

say anything. Within a day or two, Tina had completely forgotten the incident and was no longer angry.

Although we acknowledge that many people subscribe to these myths about conflict, it's important to realize they are not accurate. Not all conflicts are based on misunderstandings, are resolvable, or are best dealt with by talking. Remember that communication is an important part of managing interpersonal conflict, but conflict management isn't just about communicating well.

9-1g Factors Influencing Interpersonal Conflict

In this section, we broaden our understanding of conflict by briefly discussing two factors that affect conflict interaction: gender and sex, and culture. Although we review them separately, these variables most often act in concert to affect conflicts. For example, a German American man and a Chinese American woman who work together in a small software company may have a disagreement over how to invest their limited research and development budget. As they discuss their different approaches to the budget, cultural and gendered messages about how to conduct conflict influence this particular conflict between them. For instance, some gendered prescriptions suggest that women should be harmonizers and conflict avoidant, and some cultural messages suggest that Asians should do the same. In order to define conflict, it's important to remember that all conflicts take place between people who are gendered and who come from a specific cultural background.

GENDER AND SEX

When we talk about gender, as we have mentioned in previous chapters, we are referring to gender socialization. Men and women are not inherently different in their orientations to conflict or in their conflict behaviors; rather, they have been taught a set of responsibilities and norms that affect their conflict interactions. Furthermore, not all men or all women are socialized to the same degree (DeFrancisco & Palczewski, 2014). Thus, we may see great variety in how women and men enact gendered social norms.

Because in the United States women are taught to be keepers of relational life and men are socialized to pay attention to public life (Sullivan & Turner, 1996), women often want to talk about relationship issues, and men do not. This imbalance itself may cause conflict within relationships. For example, when Moira tells Jack that she wants to talk about their relationship, Jack may perceive her statement as an indication that their relationship is in trouble and, as a result, try to avoid the conversation. Moira may not have intended

© CREATISTA/Shutterstock.com

to imply that she wanted to discuss specific problems; she just wanted to connect with Jack about the topic of their life together.

Some research suggests that women are more collaborative and men are more competitive in conflict interactions (for a summary, see Keener, Strough, & DiDonato, 2012). However, other studies call this generalization into question. One study examining college students found that women were more likely than men to report that they used both cooperative and competitive conflict strategies (Rudawsky, Lundgren, & Grasha, 1999). Another study (Messman & Mikesell, 2000) found that women and men in romantic relationships did not differ in their use of competition as a conflict strategy. Keener and her colleagues found that women were more collaborative in conflicts with women friends, but not with romantic partners, thus suggesting that context interacts with gender in terms of how conflict is conducted. Hurley and Reese-Weber (2012) concur, finding that men's and women's conflict behavior is contingent on other variables—the duration of the relationship, for instance—in interaction with sex, rather than simply their sex alone.

Some evidence does point to more enduring differences between women and men in conflict. For instance, Levenson and Gottman (1985) showed that men and women react differently to the stress of relational conflict. Whereas women seemed to be able to tolerate high levels of the physiological arousal found in conflict with a partner, men were more bothered by this arousal and sought to avoid it. In a study conducted in Belgium (Buysse et al., 2000) to test that conclusion, the researchers found that men desired to avoid marital conflict more than women did.

CULTURE

As we have discussed many times throughout this text, we live in a world of increasing diversity. Differing cultural practices and norms may put us in conflict with one another (Croucher et al., 2012). In the 21st century,

> direct contact with culturally different people in our neighborhoods, schools, and workplaces is an inescapable part of life. With immigrants and minority group members representing nearly 30% of the present workforce in the United States, an understanding of competent conflict management is especially critical in today's society. (Ting-Toomey & Oetzel, 2001, pp. 1–2)

All humans wish to be respected and shown approval, but the ways in which respect and approval are expressed often differ from culture to culture. Even the meaning of the word *conflict* may differ across cultures. For instance, for the French the term means warlike opposition. The negative connotations of conflict are extremely strong for the French. For the Chinese, the meaning of the word *conflict* involves intense struggle and fighting. Not surprisingly, Chinese people report that they do not like conflict, which they consider disruptive to the harmoniousness of interpersonal relationships. Although the value of harmony predominates in Chinese culture, conflict style differences do exist within the culture. One study (Zhang, 2007) found that modern-day Chinese families seem to endorse conversation in conflict rather than simple conformity to preserve harmony. It may be the case that the Chinese are being influenced by Western values and losing some of their traditional approaches to conflict.

People from the United States may not enjoy conflict, either, but they define the word more broadly than the French or the Chinese do, allowing for more posible responses to the interaction itself. Some other cultures may have even more positive responses to conflict than the United States does. For example, the Spanish word for conflict doesn't have very many negative connotations, and many Latino/a cultures consider conflict an interesting exercise, allowing for dramatic flair that is enjoyable (Ting-Toomey & Oetzel, 2001).

© Blend Images/Shutterstock.com

Culture affects our conduct of interpersonal conflict in myriad ways. A person whose primary orientation is toward individualism might come into conflict with a person whose primary orientation is toward collectivism because of their different values. An individualistic orientation leads to a concern with one's own image (self-face), whereas a collectivistic orientation leads to a concern for the other person's image (other-face). The individualist wishes to resolve a conflict so that the solution is equitable or fair. The collectivist wishes to resolve a conflict so that the solution benefits the community. The two people will have opposing communication behaviors (e.g., competition vs. avoidance) during conflict, probably leading to an escalation of conflict and misunderstanding.

Croucher and his colleagues (2012) examined the impact of high- and low-context cultures on conflict styles. In Chapter 2, we stated that people in high-context cultures reveal most of what they mean through contextual cues in the environment and embodied nonverbally by a person, thus relying less on direct verbal expression. In low-context cultures, the opposite approach exists, and people depend on verbal clarity to make meaning known. The United States is an example of a low-context culture, and Thailand is an example of a high-context culture. Croucher and his colleagues found, as expected, that people in high-context cultures did choose avoiding and obliging conflict styles more than those in low-context cultures; people in low-context cultures preferred the dominating conflict style more than those in high-context cultures did.

Some research examines conflict in interracial couples beginning with the premise that their racial differences will be the catalyst for more conflict than same-race couples experience. Two studies (Troy, Lewis-Smith, & Laurenceau, 2006) found that this was not the case. In fact, partners in interracial relationships reported higher relational satisfaction than same-race couples. There was no difference in the conflict patterns they reported.

9-2 COMMUNICATION PATTERNS IN CONFLICT

Long-term relational partners often notice that their communication behaviors form repeating patterns (Turk & Monahan, 1999). Although these patterns are sometimes negative and the participants wish to break out of them, they generally find it difficult to do so. Other times, the patterns are more productive. In this section, we review four conflict patterns—three negative and one positive.

9-2a Symmetrical Escalation

Symmetrical escalation exists when each partner chooses to increase the intensity of the conflict. When Mike yells at Sally and she yells back at him, they begin the symmetrical escalation pattern. If Mike then advances on Sally with a menacing look, she might slap his face. Each partner matches the other's escalating fight behaviors. Sometimes this pattern is called "fight-fight" (Knapp, Vangelisti, & Caughlin, 2014).

This pattern cannot go on indefinitely. Because the amount of escalation that is possible is limited, and because the intensity in the conflict is negative, this pattern is a futile one for communicators.

9-2b Symmetrical Withdrawal

Symmetrical withdrawal means that when conflict occurs, neither partner is willing to confront the other. Thus, one person's move away is reciprocated by the other's move away. For example, if Jolene stops speaking to Marianne because she feels she did all the work for their joint presentation in Organizational Communication, and Marianne responds in kind, they both withdraw from their relationship. This pattern, like symmetrical escalation, spells the end of the

relationship if it's carried to its logical conclusion. If both partners move away from each other when conflict happens, they will soon be so far apart that they may have difficulty reuniting.

9-2c Pursuit-Withdrawal/ Withdrawal-Pursuit

The previous two patterns are symmetrical, meaning that the partners mirror each other (or each behaves in the same way as the other). So, if Mike yells, Sally does too. When Jolene stops talking to Marianne, Marianne stops talking to Jolene. The **pursuit-withdrawal** and **withdrawal-pursuit** patterns are asymmetrical. This means that the behavior of one partner is the opposite of the other's behavior. In the pursuit-withdrawal pattern, when one partner presses for a discussion about a source of conflict, the other partner withdraws. For example, Pam tells her son, Nicky, that they have to talk about his staying out so late on school nights, and Nicky disappears into his room and shuts the door. Withdrawal-pursuit is just the opposite. In this pattern, a partner's withdrawal prompts the other's pursuit. When Anthony retreats to the attic to work on a project and Missy runs up to the attic several times to try to get him to continue arguing about buying a new car, they are exhibiting withdrawal-pursuit.

These patterns are extremely unsatisfying to the participants; they have the quality of a dog chasing its tail. Gregory Bateson (1972) referred to these types of conflicts as *schismogenesis*: both partners do what they wish the other would do for them, and both are rebuffed. Missy wants Anthony to come talk to her about their conflict, so she pursues him. Anthony wants to avoid talking about it, so he withdraws. Anthony's withdrawal spurs Missy to advance more, which in turn causes Anthony to withdraw further. Caughlin and Vangelisti (2000) noted that even though these patterns are so unsatisfying and are related to discord within relationships, they are extremely common in conflict behavior. The researchers suggest that personality characteristics such as extroversion and introversion might be related to the use of this pattern; in general, the extroverts pursue and the introverts withdraw.

9-2d Symmetrical Negotiation

Symmetrical negotiation is the one positive pattern we discuss. In this pattern, each partner mirrors the other's negotiating behaviors. They listen to each other and reflect back what they have heard. They offer

symmetrical escalation In a conflict, when each partner chooses to increase the intensity of the conflict.

symmetrical withdrawal In a conflict, neither partner being willing to confront the other.

pursuit-withdrawal In a conflict, a pattern consisting of one party pressing for a discussion about a conflictual topic while the other party withdraws.

withdrawal-pursuit In a conflict, a pattern in which one party withdraws, which prompts the other party to pursue.

symmetrical negotiation In a conflict, each party mirroring the other's negotiating behaviors.

Masterfile

suggestions for dealing with the conflict and are willing to talk as much or as little as necessary to come to a mutually satisfying resolution.

People in relationships don't use only one of these patterns exclusively to communicate. Even satisfied couples may use a negative pattern, but they are likely to break out of it and get back to discussing the problem in a more positive manner fairly quickly, using techniques we discuss at the end of the chapter. Now that we've reviewed negative and positive patterns of communicating during conflict, we'll turn our attention to negative and positive outcomes of conflict: the destructive and constructive sides to interpersonal conflict.

9-3 THE DESTRUCTIVE AND CONSTRUCTIVE SIDES OF INTERPERSONAL CONFLICT

As we stated at the beginning of the chapter, conflicts between people are inevitable and inescapable. Therefore, we engage in conflict frequently. Sometimes we feel better about ourselves and others after a conflict, while other times we may feel more upset and frustrated than we did before the conflict began. We may emerge from a conflict with a friend with a

stronger sense of our friendship; we may leave a conflict with our boss feeling diminished and impotent. Often, the key to the outcome is found in the way the conflict is managed. We'll now discuss ways that conflict communication can be negative and destructive for people individually and for their relationships with others. Later, we'll talk about the more constructive aspects of conflict communication.

9-3a Destructive Aspects of Interpersonal Conflict

There is a strong association between children who are exposed to a lot of family conflict and a host of negative psychological consequences in adulthood such as depression, anger, anxiety, and so forth (Aloia & Solomon, 2013). Furthermore, when children experience a lot of conflict in their family they are likely to become desensitized to verbal aggression, which may result in them becoming verbally aggressive themselves as adults (Aloia & Solomon). When conflict is constant and not well managed, negative consequences ensue. Here we discuss two: bullying and violence.

BULLYING
Bullying is described as a particular form of conflict in which the abuse is persistent, and the person receiving the abuse finds it very difficult to defend himself or herself against it (Hoel & Cooper, 2000). As a result, bullying often takes place in situations in which there is a distinct power difference between partners. Such unequal power relationships occur often, but not exclusively, in schools (Smith-Sanders & Harter, 2007) or at work (Tracy, Alberts, & Rivera, 2007). By some estimates, 15 percent of any given population in a school or workplace has been involved in bullying, as either the bully or the victim (Bullying Awareness Week, 2014).) Others cite higher numbers, especially with reference to cyber-bullying (or bullying behavior online). According to some statistics, over half of all adolescents in the United States have been bullied online, and about the same number have engaged in bullying behaviors online (Bullying Statistics, 2014). The National Education Association reports that 6 out of 10 American teens witness bullying daily in schools (*Daily Herald*, 2013).

> **bullying** A particular form of conflict in which the abuse is persistent and the person being bullied finds it very difficult to defend himself or herself.

Communication behaviors characteristic of bullying include isolating or ignoring, nit-picking or excessively criticizing, humiliating, and even physically abusing someone (Tracy, Lutgen-Sandvik, & Alberts, 2006). Some research indicates that a big problem for those who are bullied at work involves convincing others to believe them. This research offers suggestions for getting others to listen to and believe accounts of bullying including: speak rationally but express appropriate emotion; tell a plausible story with consistent, relevant, specific details; emphasize your own competence; and show consideration for others' perspectives (Tracy et al., 2007).

VIOLENCE AND AGGRESSION

Violence within interpersonal relationships is relatively common in the United States; FBI statistics show that 35 percent of the women killed in the United States in 2012, whose murderers were known, died at the hands of a husband or a boyfriend. Furthermore, in 2012, for those murders where the circumstances of the crime were known, over 40 percent occurred during conflicts (Federal Bureau of Investigation, 2013). Acts of violence are common between couples. Used when conflicts get out of hand, these behaviors—which include minor acts of violence such as pushing and shoving—might affect as many as 50 percent of couples in the United States (Olson, 2002, 2008).

Violence and aggression may be seen as conflict going to extremes, occurring when one person imposes his or her will on someone else through verbal and nonverbal acts geared to hurt or cause suffering. Violence and aggression can be psychological (as when parents belittle their children) or physical (as when someone is hit or battered). These two types may often be seen together. Someone who's verbally aggressive may also be physically abusive (Roberto, Carlyle, & McClure, 2006). Because these two are related, teaching more constructive forms of conflict management to reduce verbal aggression could also reduce physical abuse (Wilson, Hayes, Bylund, Rack, & Herman, 2006).

In the communication discipline, most of the research on violence has focused on the family. Family violence ranges from child abuse to spousal abuse to sibling abuse to elder abuse to incest. Some recent research examines how families can reconcile after violence (Cahn & Abigail, 2007). In this line of research, reconciliation doesn't mean excusing the violence or forgetting it happened but instead means focusing on forgiveness and moving forward.

While violence and aggression are significant social problems, the topic is beyond the scope of this text, and we won't discuss them more extensively here. Interpersonal conflict can be managed without resorting to violence and aggression, and it may even have positive outcomes. We now turn to those and discuss conflict's constructive side.

9-3b Constructive Aspects of Interpersonal Conflict

As we have previously discussed, relationships cannot exist without conflict. Furthermore, there are many positives to engaging in conflict with a relational partner. Managing conflict with sensitivity leads to positive evaluations of communication competence (Lakey & Canary, 2002). In addition, dealing productively with conflict in romantic relationships promotes positive feelings, and contributes to each partner feeling understood (Hubbard, Hendrickson, Fehrenbach, & Sur, 2013). The following benefits can come from conflict that's handled constructively: getting feelings out in the open and increasing knowledge of one another, promoting feelings of confidence in relationships that survive conflicts, promoting genuine human contact, increasing the depth of a relationship, maximizing the chances of making a good decision, and shaking a relationship out of a rut. Although all conflict doesn't automatically produce positive outcomes for relationships, the possibility almost always exists.

Additionally, it may be the case that it's not the presence of conflict *per se* that's an issue in marriage. For instance, if Ella and Larry fight an average of five times a week while Grace and Steven argue 10 times a week, it is still possible that Grace and Steven have a happy marriage. In fact, they could be happier than Ella and Larry. If during Grace and Steven's arguments they have a **positive interaction ratio** (i.e., they say more nice things to each other than negative things), they could be more satisfied in their relationship than Ella and Larry who fight less but have a **negative interaction ratio** (i.e., they're more negative than positive in their encounters).

This line of thinking began with psychologist John Gottman's work examining positive-to-negative ratios in marriage (i.e., Gottman & DeClaire, 2001). Gottman claims that five positives to one negative is the *magic ratio,* supporting this claim with substantial research data from couples in his Seattle lab. He and his colleagues predicted with 94 percent accuracy whether 700 newlywed couples would stay together or divorce based on whether or not they exhibited the magic ratio during conflict encounters.

9-4 EXPLAINING CONFLICT

In this section, we review two theoretical models that help us sort us out the complex phenomenon of conflict by diagramming its component parts. The four-part model (Satir, 1972) and the explanatory process model (Cupach & Canary, 2000) are useful in helping us think about the nature and the process of interpersonal conflict. This should help us be better communicators in conflict.

9-4a The Four-Part Model

The **four-part model** depicts conflict as a circle divided into four sections that represent the critical parts of any conflict (see Figure 9.2): you, me, the context, and the subject. *You* refers to one of the participants in the conflict and *me* refers to the other. *Context* comprises the emotional background surrounding the conflict—for

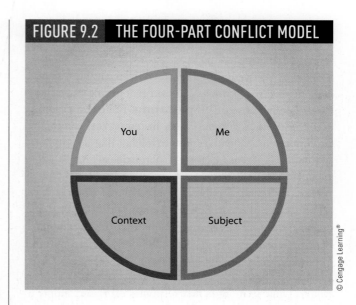

FIGURE 9.2 THE FOUR-PART CONFLICT MODEL

© Cengage Learning®

example, whether it's the first conflict on this topic, whether the two participants are highly and equally invested in the conflict, whether the topic is extremely important to the relationship between the two parties, and so forth. *Subject* means what the parties are arguing about—for example, whether to move, whether the report is ready to be turned in to the boss, whether to go to the basketball game or to the movies, whether universal health care is needed in the United States, whether the household chores are distributed fairly, and so forth.

Satir (1972) uses the model to show that effective conflict management requires that each part be considered completely. All four parts are equally important, and if each part is not attended to, the conflict won't be managed successfully. The model assumes that the nature of conflict consists of the interdependence of all these parts; if one segment is ignored, the overall conflict cannot be completely resolved. As we've noted, people generally fear or dislike conflict interaction. Perhaps because of this, they try to resolve conflicts as quickly as possible. However, if in our haste to conclude an argument we ignore one or more of the four integral segments, ineffective conflict management results. Let's

positive interaction ratio An interpersonal encounter in which the participants say more positive things to each other than negative things.

negative interaction ratio An interpersonal encounter in which the participants say more negative things to each other than positive things.

four-part model A way to explain conflict interactions that describes conflict as consisting of four parts—you, me, subject, and context—all of which must be considered in effective conflict management.

take a look at the consequences of ignoring or disqualifying any portion of the conflict.

When people disqualify the *me* in a conflict, they are being passive or ignoring their own needs in the situation. This passive response, which cancels out one's own position in a conflict, is called **placating**. For example, when George wants to compete with his coworker, Dina, for a promotion but instead decides to tell her that he'll defer in her favor, George is placating. George doesn't have to fight Dina for the promotion; it is possible to opt out of competition with another for various reasons. For example, George might think that Dina is more qualified or might acknowledge that she has more seniority with the company than he does. Or it's possible that George is having problems at home, and he realizes that now isn't the right time to assume a more demanding position. However, if deferring to Dina is George's first response, exercised simply to avoid a conflict, the model tells us that is a mistake.

When people disqualify the *you* in a conflict, they respond in an aggressive manner without acknowledging the needs of the other person in the conflict. This is **pouncing**. If George yells at Dina, telling her that she's a jerk for applying for a promotion that she knows he wants, he is pouncing. Anything that George might do to ignore Dina's side of the conflict and advance his own is considered pouncing, another ineffective strategy for conflict resolution. The *context* is the part of the model containing the emotional aspects of conflict. If someone disqualifies the context, then he or she is ignoring the conflict's emotional aspects and focusing only on the rational aspects, and Satir (1972) calls this response **computing**. As we discussed in Chapter 7, emotions are intimately related to rationality, and perhaps that is nowhere more true than in the case of conflict communication. Conflicts touch emotions deeply and won't be effectively managed unless these emotions

are addressed. For example, let's say that Dina is upset when she learns that George is also interested in the promotion. She raises her voice, pointing out that in a previous instance when she and George both competed for something at work, she'd stepped aside, so she feels that in fairness, George needs to step aside now. If George responds by telling Dina not to yell, not to feel upset, and to talk about this rationally he'd be shutting down an important aspect of their conflict. George and Dina have to confront the emotions involved in their conflict to resolve it.

If Dina comes into George's office to discuss her interest in the promotion, and George interrupts her to talk about a different topic, George would be disqualifying the subject of the conflict. This response is called **distracting** because it draws the participants' attention away from the subject of a conflict. People who laugh, cry, change the topic, or run out of the room when presented with a conflict engage in distracting responses.

In placating, pouncing, computing, and distracting, one portion of the conflict is ignored or disqualified. In so doing, the conflict interaction is rushed or skipped altogether. This accomplishes the immediate goal of minimizing the time that two people spend in conflict. However, in the long run, none of these responses will provide a long-term solution to a conflict. All four segments of the conflict circle are equally important, and if one is ignored, the conflict is not managed properly. When people give adequate attention to all the parts of a conflict, Satir (1972) labels their response **integrating**, and observes that this is their best hope for productively managing conflict.

9-4b The Explanatory Process Model

The four-part model that we've just described pictures each of the elements of a conflict as occurring simultaneously within a conflict interaction. In contrast, in the **explanatory process model**, Cupach and Canary (2000) visualize conflict as a process that occurs in the following episodes: distal context, proximal context, conflict interaction, proximal outcomes, and distal outcomes. In this section, we discuss each of these episodes in turn. Figure 9.3 illustrates how the episodes fit together to make up the conflict process.

Conflict begins with a **distal context**, or the background that frames the specific conflict. The distal context sets the stage for conflict and contains the history between the two parties and the areas of disagreement they have discussed in the past. For example, when Ryan and Geoff became roommates, they had a history going back to the second grade. Geoff knows that Ryan is messier than he is and that Ryan doesn't care about his physical surroundings nearly as much as he does. In addition, Geoff knows

---

placating Being passive or ignoring our own needs in a conflict.

pouncing Responding in an aggressive manner without acknowledging the needs of another person in a conflict.

computing Disqualifying the emotional aspects of a conflict (the context) and focusing on the rational aspects.

distracting Disqualifying the subject of a conflict by distracting both people in the conflict with behaviors such as laughing, crying, or changing the subject.

integrating Responding to conflict by giving full attention to all its parts.

explanatory process model A model that illustrates how conflict between people follows a certain sequence and every prior conflict affects how a future conflict will be handled.

distal context The background that frames a specific conflict.

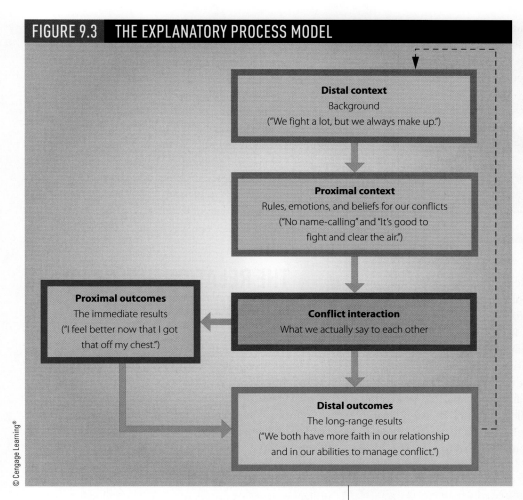

FIGURE 9.3 THE EXPLANATORY PROCESS MODEL

Distal context
Background
("We fight a lot, but we always make up.")

Proximal context
Rules, emotions, and beliefs for our conflicts
("No name-calling" and "It's good to
fight and clear the air.")

Proximal outcomes
The immediate results
("I feel better now that I got
that off my chest.")

Conflict interaction
What we actually say to each other

Distal outcomes
The long-range results
("We both have more faith in our relationship
and in our abilities to manage conflict.")

© Cengage Learning®

This episode includes what messages the two exchange and the patterns of their communication as they talk about the problem in their apartment.

The next episode is **proximal outcomes**, or the immediate results after the conflict interaction. For instance, Ryan and Geoff might decide that they don't want to be roommates any longer because they can't come up with a plan to clean the apartment that satisfies them both. Or they might get sick of arguing about it and ignore the problem for a while until Geoff can't stand the mess anymore, then the conflict begins again. Or they might decide that Ryan will pay for a cleaning person to come in once a month.

Finally, this model shows that conflicts are never completely over. The proximal outcomes affect the **distal outcomes**, which include the residue of having engaged in the conflict and the feelings that both the participants have about their interaction. For instance, if they've decided that Ryan will hire a cleaning person, Geoff and Ryan might feel proud that they came up with a great idea that pleases them both—Geoff is glad that he gets to live in a clean apartment, and Ryan is relieved that he doesn't have to change lifelong habits. Alternatively, Ryan could feel a little resentful about the solution. Even though he agreed to do it, he might feel that it's unfair that he has to pay a monthly fee beyond the rent just to keep Geoff happy.

that Ryan is quiet, and less inclined to enjoy conflict than he does. They had talked about how they would deal with these differences before moving in together. All of this background information forms the distal context.

The second episode in this model is the **proximal context**, which refers to the rules, emotions, and beliefs of the individuals involved in the conflict. If Ryan and Geoff set some rules about how to conduct conflict when it arises (e.g., no yelling, or no complaining behind the other's back), those rules will become part of the proximal context. Geoff's goal to keep the apartment clean and nice and Ryan's goal not to have to fuss about his living space also comprise the proximal context. The proximal context combines with the distal context, creating a background for any overt conflict Geoff and Ryan may have.

The next episode is **conflict interaction**. This occurs when the differences between the partners become a problem and one or both people begin to address the issue. For instance, Geoff tells Ryan he has to start picking up the stuff he leaves lying out in the common spaces of the apartment, and Ryan responds by saying that he knows it's bothering Geoff, and he feels badly about that, but he's tired of trying to live in a "magazine-ready" apartment.

proximal context The rules, emotions, and beliefs of the individuals involved in a conflict.

conflict interaction The point in the conflict process at which the differences between two individuals become a problem and one or both people begin to address the issue.

proximal outcomes The immediate results after a conflict interaction.

distal outcomes The residue of having engaged in a conflict and the feelings that both the participants have about their interaction.

© pryzmat/Shutterstock.com

In addition to the parties' responses to the solution, they both have feelings about the ways they interacted during the conflict. Geoff, for example, might congratulate himself for not losing his temper and confronting Ryan before building up too much resentment. Geoff might also feel grateful to Ryan for listening to his point of view and empathizing even though Ryan can't see the point of thoroughly cleaning the apartment. For his part, Ryan might think he did a great job of listening and might feel happy that Geoff explained his position in such a way that it began to make sense to him. It is also possible that both men could feel a bit resentful about the way the conflict interaction unfolded. One or both of them might feel that he got pushed around by the other.

As we saw in Figure 9.3, the distal outcomes feed into the distal context for the next conflict. For instance, if Geoff feels grateful to Ryan for his behavior during the conflict about cleaning the apartment, that will set the stage for how a later conflict—perhaps whether they should pitch in together to buy a flat-screen TV—unfolds. Geoff may be inclined to listen more carefully to Ryan's point of view in this conflict because he feels that Ryan was so cooperative in their previous conflict. Thus, we see in this model how conflicts affect relationships and shape relational life.

9-5 THE RELATIONSHIP OF CONFLICT TO POWER

Power can be defined as the ability to control the behavior of another. In conflict situations, power often influences the outcome as well as the process of the interaction. As we discussed in Chapter 1, power has relevance in all communication encounters; even simple conversations used to exchange demographic or superficial information may reflect power issues between the partners. Whether or not you agree that *all* communication rests on power differentials, it is true that conflict communication utilizes power in a variety of ways. The following sections discuss how people use power, sex differences in power, and the concept of empowerment.

9-5a Using Power

Researchers (Folger, Poole, & Stutman, 2013) discuss four ways that people use power in conflict interactions: direct application, direct and virtual use, indirect application, and hidden use. See Table 9.2 for a brief summary of these ways of using power.

THEORY SPOTLIGHT:

Explanatory Process Model

Think of a conflict that you have had with a roommate or any friend at school. Briefly describe the conflict, and then map the conflict onto the parts of this model: distal context, proximal context, conflict interaction, proximal outcomes, and distal outcomes. Explain what formed the distal context for the conflict, the proximal context, and so forth. In what ways does this model help you understand the conflict?

TABLE 9.2	USING POWER
Method	**Definition**
Direct application	Using any means to get your way
Direct and virtual use	Using threats and promises
Indirect application	Using an implicit approach
Hidden use of power	Having the other follow your wishes without having to say anything

© Cengage Learning®

power The ability to control the behavior of another.

Direct application of power in a conflict situation involves using any resources at your disposal to compel the other to comply, regardless of their desires. When Marla spanks her 2-year-old son, Jerry, and sends him to his room, she is using direct application of power. Related to this use, a second way that people use power, **direct and virtual use of power**, involves communicating the *potential* use of direct application. The use of threats and promises are good illustrations of this way of using power. For example, when Dr. Moore says that he will fail Lorna in his Introduction to Communication class unless she rewrites a paper to his satisfaction, he is exercising a threat. When Dr. Seltzer promises the students in his Communication Theory class that they will all receive As if they complete all the written work on time, he is offering a promise. Threats and promises are two sides of the same coin.

The **indirect application of power** concerns employing power without making its employment explicit. For instance, if Gerard has heard his boss, Colleen, mention that she likes to be copied on all office memos, and he does that even though it's not an official office policy, Colleen has used indirect application of power. One example of the indirect application of power is the relational message. When people send **relational messages**, they define the relationship (and implicitly state that they have the power to do this). For instance, when Tim tells Sue how much he gave up so they could move to Ohio to be near her parents, he sends a message that in their relationship, Sue is indebted to him. Of course, partners may accept or contest the implicit message. If Sue agrees that Tim has done her an enormous favor at some cost to himself, she accepts his relationship definition and his power. If she argues with him that he really wanted to move, too, or that he didn't give up that much, they will conflict over the relationship definition.

Most of the time we think of power as the ability to talk someone else into complying with what we want, but in the case of **hidden power** (also called *unobtrusive power*), we don't have to say a word. For example, if Sam doesn't bring up a topic for discussion because he knows his friend, Dale, won't agree with him, Dale is exercising hidden power. And when Liz complies with her mother's wishes for a big, lavish wedding, although she and her fiancé really want a small, more conservative ceremony, Liz succumbs to her mother's hidden power. Liz doesn't even broach the subject, and she and her mother do not argue about it; Liz just lets her mother be in charge without argument even though she doesn't agree with her plans.

Throughout this discussion, we adopt a relational perspective on power. In other words, we see power, like conflict, as a process that is co-constructed by relational partners. Thus, although one partner may try to utilize direct application of power or any of the other power modes we have discussed, the power loop is not closed until the other partner responds. For instance, when Marla spanks her son, Jerry, and sends him to his room, she checks in on him later to find that Jerry has thrown all his toys on the floor and ripped all the pages out of his books. Thus, Marla's direct application of power is not met with compliance; rather, it encounters resistance in the form of an exercise of direct power on Jerry's part.

© Sunny studio/Shutterstock.com

direct application of power In a conflict situation, the use of any resource at our disposal to compel another to comply, regardless of that person's desires.

direct and virtual use of power Communicating the potential use of a direct application of power.

indirect application of power Employing power without making its employment explicit.

relational message A message that defines a relationship and implicitly states that the sender has the power to do so.

hidden power A type of power in which one person in a relationship suppresses or avoids decisions in the interest of one of the parties. Also called *unobtrusive power*.

9-5b Sex Differences

Sex role stereotypes in the United States suggest that husbands have more power in decision making than their wives. But one study (Vogel, Murphy, Werner-Wilson, Cutrona, & Seeman, 2007) suggests that sex differences do not operate in stereotypical ways in marital decision making. In fact, wives exhibited more power in a decision-making exercise than their husbands did. Power was measured both by the verbal and nonverbal behaviors of the spouses and also by the results (i.e., who "gave in" to whom). The researchers found that wives talked more than their husbands, and husbands accepted their wives' opinions and followed their lead in the study. In discussing the study, the lead author commented, "There's been research that suggests that's a marker of a healthy marriage—that men accept influence from their wives" (Iowa State University News Service, 2007).

Another study (Dunbar & Burgoon, 2005) examined the verbal and nonverbal indicators of power in married couples. This study found that men and women tended to mirror one another's communication of power. In other words, men and women were not significantly different in how they expressed power verbally and nonverbally; what one did—such as interrupt—the other did as well.

9-5c Empowerment

Another consideration concerning the relationship between power and conflict revolves around **empowerment**, or helping to actualize people's power. Stephen Littlejohn and Kathy Domenici (2001) note that some mediators refer to empowerment as "power balancing," or the efforts of a third party to equalize the power distribution so that the participants in the conflict can both listen and be heard. However, Littlejohn and Domenici find the term *power balancing* problematic:

> The problem is that the mediator, who is really an outsider, cannot know what sources of power parties might have available to them. It might look as though a man is out-powering a woman by dominating the conversation, but the woman may have a great

empowerment Helping to actualize our own or another person's power.

deal of power in her silence. It may look as though a well-to-do businessperson has more power than a blue-collar customer, but the customer may have connections and buying power that give him or her a great deal of power. It may look as though a parent has more power than a teen, but anyone who has raised teenagers might disagree. . . . Rather than judge who has the power, we want to empower both parties to do and say what needs to be done and said, to identify the problem in their own terms, to establish what a successful outcome would mean for them, and to create ideas for achieving that outcome. (pp. 78–79)

Whether you call the intricate power dynamics within our relationships power balancing or empowerment, managing conflict necessitates that each party is listened to and really heard.

9-6 SKILL SET FOR EFFECTIVE CONFLICT MANAGEMENT

Researchers have examined many ways that people seek to cope with conflict as it occurs. Some researchers (e.g., Behrendt & Ben-Ari, 2012; Rahim, 1983) have followed the lead of Blake and Mouton (1964) and have examined styles of approaching conflict. Blake and Mouton said that people adopt one of five styles for conflict based on their concern for the other and their concern for themselves in a conflict situation. These five styles include (1) competing (high concern for self, low concern for other); (2) obliging (high concern for other and low concern for self); (3) integrating (high concern for both self and other); (4) compromising (moderate concern for self and other); and (5) avoiding (low concern for self and other). Ting-Toomey and Oetzel (2001) added three more styles to the list based on emotional aspects and strategy: (6) emotional (a style that relies on emotional responses to cope with conflict); (7) neglect (a coping response that's passive-aggressive); and (8) the third-party style (asking for help from someone outside the conflict).

In examining styles for dealing with conflict, researchers are looking at the big picture. Another approach is to focus on specific skills or techniques that work well in managing conflict. These techniques may fit in one or more of the styles we've just discussed. Consider the following techniques for conflict management in your interactions with others.

Law Enforcement Officers and Conflict Management Skills

Law enforcement professionals have demanding jobs that require many varied skills. According to the Career Profiles (2014) website, "the qualities of top law enforcement professional go far beyond the obvious to include less obvious qualities including refined interpersonal communication skills." It is important that those in the law enforcement professions cultivate some of the same skills we've discussed in this chapter. Although they deal with criminals, they also deal with the general public, and so can benefit by expressing and expecting goodwill. In doing this, they demonstrate their commitment to helping others. The Career Profiles website suggests that law enforcement professionals want to resolve issues without having to resort to physical confrontations. As such, effective interpersonal communication skills in conflict management are

© Glynnis Jones/Shutterstock.com

essential to law enforcement professionals. "Effective verbal communication is probably the number one asset and quality of any law enforcement professional." Additionally, law enforcement professionals need to develop cultural sensitivity in order to manage conflicts with those of a variety of cultures, different from their own.

9-6a Lighten Up and Reframe

Lightening up refers to your ability to stay cool-headed when others get "hot." Techniques that can help you do this include staying in the present and acknowledging that you have heard what your relational partner just said. Maintain eye contact and nod to show that you heard your partner's contribution. You can say, "I understand you have a concern"; or you can reframe, a skill we've mentioned in previous chapters, by changing something that has a negative connotation to something with a more positive connotation. Rather than becoming annoyed because a friend has a different political view than yours, you can reframe your differences to see them as interesting opportunities for discussion. Finally, lightening up might involve your asking permission to state your views: "May I tell you my perspective?" Keep your nonverbal communication genuine—avoid sarcasm.

9-6b Presume Goodwill and Express Goodwill

Go into each conflict interaction believing that you and your partner both want to come to a constructive resolution. Build rapport by focusing on the areas where you do agree. Reach out to your partner and expect that your

partner will do the same for you. While you are engaging in conflict, tell your partner the things about him or her that you respect. Keep it real, but mix in praise with your complaints.

9-6c Ask Questions

Focus on the other. After you both have had a chance to speak, ask your partner if he or she has anything further to add. Reflect back what you have heard and ask if you understood it correctly. Ask, "What would

© Andrey_Popov/Shutterstock.com

make this situation better?" "What would you like to see happen now?" "How can I understand your position better?" "What can you tell me that I seem to be misunderstanding?"

9-6d Listen

We detailed the role of listening in Chapter 6 and again highlight its importance here. It's difficult to manage conflict unless we spend time listening to the other person. Remember to practice all of the behaviors associated with effective listening, including looking at the other person, focusing on the words, and allowing the full story to unfold. In conflict situations, listening to another person is more than just hearing the words spoken; it's a way to show him or her that the conflict is important to resolve and that the relationship between the two of you is valuable in your life.

9-6e Practice Cultural Sensitivity

Be mindful, and tune into your own culture's norms and assumptions first before evaluating others (Sandri, 2013). Slow down your judgments of others; suspend your evaluations until you have had a chance to engage in an internal dialogue. Ask yourself questions such as these:

"Am I respectful of the different cultural background of the other person?" "Am I using my own cultural lens to understand what is being said?" "What types of strategies am I using to make sure that I don't inadvertently evaluate the person rather than the message?" These are just a few of the questions to consider as you remember the cultural backgrounds of others.

STUDY TOOLS

DON'T FORGET TO CHECK OUT COURSEMATE AT WWW.CENGAGEBRAIN.COM!

CHAPTER 9 FEATURES THE FOLLOWING RESOURCES:

☐ Ethics & Choice: Daryl

☐ Communication Assessment Test: Argumentativeness Scale

☐ Interactive Activities

USE THE TOOLS.

- Rip out the Review Cards in the back of your book to study.
Or Visit CourseMate to:
- Read, search, highlight, and take notes in the Interactive eBook
- Review Flashcards (Print or Online) to master key terms
- Test yourself with Auto-Graded Quizzes
- Bring concepts to life with Games, Videos, and Animations!

Go to CourseMate for (PKG IPC 2e and Student Website Access Code) to begin using these tools.
Access at www.cengagebrain.com

Complete the Speak Up survey in CourseMate at www.cengagebrain.com

f Follow us at www.facebook.com/4ltrpress

10 | Communicating in Close Relationships

LEARNING OUTCOMES

10-1 Develop a definition of close relationships

10-2 Detail the ways that we talk and think about close relationships

10-3 Explain the influences impacting close relationships

10-4 Discuss stage model approaches to relationship development

10-5 Understand explanations for communication in close relationships

10-6 Demonstrate a variety of skills and techniques to enhance and maintain your communication in close relationships

After you finish this chapter, go to **PAGE 217** for **STUDY TOOLS.**

THEORY/MODEL PREVIEW

Social Information Processing; Systems Theory; Dialectics Theory; Social Exchange Theory; Knapp's Stage Model of Relationship Development

© Monkey Business Images/Shutterstock.com

Our close relationships mean a great deal to us. For one thing, they help satisfy our need for connection (Waytz, 2013).

Abraham Maslow's (1968) famous hierarchy of needs (see Figure 10.1), which ranks people's needs in order of importance, places social needs (such as love, inclusion, and connection) in the third ranking, immediately after physical and safety needs. Satisfying social needs constitutes an enduring human occupation. In 1998, a Gallup survey showed that 83 percent of people between the ages of 18 and 34 rated a close-knit family as their highest priority, and 64 percent of all those surveyed said that "relationships with loved ones are always on their minds" (cited in Harvey & Weber, 2002, p. 4). Fifteen years later, a 2013 survey of 4,000 people in various age groups showed that the 1998 results still held true. This survey revealed that the most important factor for quality of life for those aged 60 and older was strong

relationships with friends and family. In addition, for both seniors as well as adults aged 18 to 59, family and friends were critically important and made up the way respondents defined community (National Council on Aging, 2013).

And, we know that communication is central to relationships. One researcher (Dindia, 2003) observes, "To maintain a relationship, partners must communicate with one another. Conversely, as long as people communicate, they have a relationship" (p. 1). We think of communication as both an indicator of our closeness with another person ("You're the only one I'd tell this to") and a means for developing a sense of closeness ("I feel so much closer to you now that we've talked about this"). Ironically, intimate partners and family members

FIGURE 10.1 MASLOW'S HIERARCHY OF NEEDS

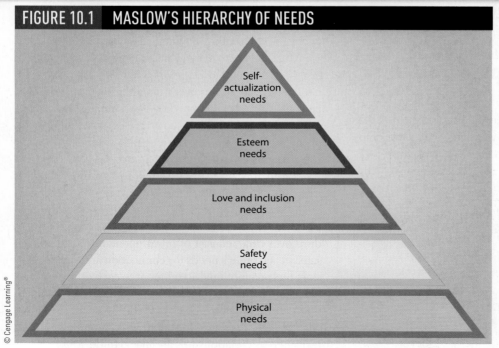

- Self-actualization needs
- Esteem needs
- Love and inclusion needs
- Safety needs
- Physical needs

© Cengage Learning®

tend to talk to each other with less consideration than they accord friends and less intimate partners (Emmers-Sommer, 2003; Lannutti, 2013). Researchers suggest this is because in developed, intimate relationships people feel confident that the connection will endure even if they communicate less than optimally to one another. They aren't that confident with less intimate relationships so they have to be more polite.

As we've introduced the topic of this chapter, we've been speaking as though everyone has the same

Personal Trainers and Clients' Relationships

One career that offers the possibility of changing a role relationship into a close one is personal training. Even if the trainer and the client do not become close friends, it is necessary for the trainer to establish him- or herself as someone who is compatible with the client as well as experienced in training skills. As a result, it's important for trainers to be skilled in many of the same things that people find beneficial in their friendships. The Aerobics and Fitness Association of America (AFAA, 2013) discusses personality traits and communication skills on their website before addressing the certifications needed to become a personal trainer. The AFAA

© Kzenon/Shutterstock.com

website suggests that being a good listener and having a nurturing approach to others are critical skills for succeeding in the profession.

understanding of a *close relationship*. Although we do have intuitive definitions for close relationships because they are such an important and ubiquitous part of our lives, we still need to establish a common definition to frame our approach in this chapter. Here we'll map out the foundations of close relationships, and detail theoretical thinking about how people communicate in close relationships generally. In Chapter 11, we'll specifically apply this information to friendships, family relationships, and relationships with romantic partners.

10-1 UNDERSTANDING CLOSE RELATIONSHIPS

One reason why it's difficult to define **close relationships** is that we experience many kinds of relationships in our lives. Some relationships are **role relationships** (Guerrero, Andersen, & Afifi, 2007), meaning that the partners are interdependent while accomplishing a

close relationship A relationship that endures over time and consists of interdependent partners who satisfy each other's needs for connection and social inclusion, feel an emotional attachment to each other, are irreplaceable to each other, and enact unique communication patterns.

role relationship A relationship in which the partners are interdependent while accomplishing a specific task, such as a server and a customer at a restaurant.

specific task. The server and customer at a restaurant, for instance, have a role relationship. One key characteristic of role relationships is that the people in them are relatively interchangeable. That is, while you might like one server better than another, you can still eat in a restaurant as long as someone is the server—anyone could fill the role, and the relationship still exists. Role relationships may be fleeting and your interdependence on each other doesn't endure. When Jane wanted to buy a condo, she hired a realtor, Laura, who specialized in condo sales. Over the two months it took Jane to find the perfect place, she and Laura talked frequently. After Jane settled in her new place, they no longer saw one another.

Role and close relationships can overlap, however. For instance, as an employee, John has a role relationship with his boss, Malcolm. But over time, they begin to talk about personal subjects, discover they have similar senses of humor, and come to feel that the other person could not simply be replaced with a new boss or a new employee. Their role relationship has evolved into a close relationship.

From this brief discussion distinguishing between role and close relationships, some important elements of the definition emerge. To be clear, our definition of a close relationship is as follows: close relationships endure over time, consist of interdependent partners who satisfy each other's needs for connection and social inclusion, feel an emotional attachment to each other, are irreplaceable to one another, and enact unique communication patterns (Guerrero et al., 2007). Now, let's examine what research suggests the unique communication patterns in close relationships are like (Hinde, 1995):

- **The content of the interactions contains variety and depth**: What do people talk about and do together? Robert and Nelson have a close relationship if they hang out together, engage in conversations beyond the superficial, and discuss a variety of topics in some depth.

- **There's a diversity of interactions**: How many different experiences do people share? Melanie and Lorraine are close if they go to the movies together, play together on the basketball team, study together, and spend time talking with one another about their futures and their jobs.

- **The interactions contain affection and conflict**: How do the partners talk to one another? Most people agree that affectionate communication is extremely important in close relationships (Horan & Booth-Butterfield, 2013). Affection can be expressed in a variety of ways—directly ("You're my best friend," "I love you") or indirectly (through giving support, compliments, or planning future activities together). As we discussed in Chapter 9, conflict is also an inevitable part of relationships. People who speak affectionately to one another but also sometimes get into heated arguments probably have a close relationship.

- **The interactions are intimate**: How much do the partners self-disclose? Is their conversation characterized by a private language that identifies them as part of a unique, closed circle? What nonverbal behaviors do they exhibit? For example, Carla and Kevin share their problems with one another. They also call one another private nicknames based on elementary school experiences. Carla is "Tootsie" because Tootsie Rolls were her favorite candy, and Kevin is "Slurps" because he was famous for slurping his milk in the cafeteria. They always hug one another hello and take walks together arm in arm. Their willingness to self-disclose, create a private language, share activities, and nonverbal behaviors all create intimacy, and mark their relationship as close, compared to their more casual acquaintances.

- **The partners perceive the interactions to be intimate**: How do the partners see each other and talk about their relationship? Kelly and Ray are in a close relationship because they perceive each other in a similar fashion and feel understood by each other. They share a perception that their relationship is a close one, and their communication reflects this, as they both describe their friendship in similar terms and talk about each other using the same relationship label: BFFs.

- **The interactions reflect commitment**: Does each partner feel the other is committed to the relationship? Diana and Cal have a close relationship because they speak openly about how devoted they are to one another. They participated in a marriage ceremony where they publicly declared their commitment to each other.

- **The interactions express satisfaction**: How closely do the partners' interactions fit their ideal? Camille and Pat have a close relationship because they frequently say that they

© Phaendin/Shutterstock.com

couldn't want a better sister than each other. They each praise the other and talk about how fulfilling their relationship is.

10-2 THINKING AND TALKING ABOUT CLOSE RELATIONSHIPS

We can understand more about close relationships when we explore how people think and talk about them. Close relationships are represented in several ways that shed light on what they mean to people. In an effort to illustrate how that process works, we'll explore close relationships as cultural performances, as cognitive constructs, and as linguistic constructions.

10-2a Relationships as Cultural Performances

Close relationships are seen as cultural performances (Baxter & Braithwaite, 2002) when they are defined by ongoing public and private exchanges. These exchanges include myriad communication practices such as private conversations and public rituals such as weddings and commitment ceremonies as well as public discourse by politicians and others indicating what marriages, families, and other relationships should be like and what values should define them. Thus, relationships are both defined by and enacted in the culture that surrounds them.

From this perspective, we would say that Brea and Tal have a close relationship because they do things that people in close relationships do. They had a wedding and publicly vowed that they were in a close relationship, labeled marriage. They go to parties together, own a home together, make budgets, take out loans, and have a joint checking account. In other words, they are performing a close relationship according to U.S. cultural and social rules.

10-2b Relationships as Cognitive Constructs

Some research examines the notion of **relationship scripts**, which are cognitive structures containing a pattern for the key events we expect in a relationship (Holmberg & MacKenzie, 2002; Patterson, Ward, & Brown, 2013). In the United States, we have both *narrow* scripts (what should happen on a first date) and *broad* scripts (how a friendship should progress). Relationship scripts serve several functions for people: They conserve brain energy, allowing us to process information about the relationship efficiently and rapidly; they help guide behavior, making it easier for us to know what to do in certain relational situations; and they enhance satisfaction when there's a match between the script and a person's actual experience of a close relationship.

We also frame close relationships as cognitive constructs when we define them as partners sharing mental images of the relationship (Wilmot, 1995). Mental images of relationships occur on two levels. At a basic level, people are simply aware of each other and the fact that they're in a relationship with one another. The second level is more complex. On this level, several things happen in a specific order:

1. The communication between the partners becomes patterned, as we talked about previously, and they can imagine with some predictive accuracy what the other will say or do in different situations.

2. The partners perceive a past, present, and future together. They're able to bring the past forward into the present and future by holding a mental image of what the partner has done in the past and generalizing it to the present or the future ("When we went skiing last winter, she liked it, so she'll probably want to go again this year"). This can be called "carrying the relationship with you," and it happens whenever people imagine what a relational partner's reaction to something might be.

3. People label their relationship ("This is my best friend," "This is my daughter," or "This is my girlfriend"). In the following section, we address the question of language and close relationships in more detail.

10-2c Relationships as Linguistic Constructions

Language influences our sense of close relationships. Giving a relationship a label (friendship, love, etc.) helps us feel "in relationship" to another. Yet, as we discussed in Chapter 4 when addressing lexical gaps, some relationships don't

Relationship scripts, such as what should happen in a dating relationship, are useful because they allow us to process information about a relationship quickly and efficiently, help us know how to behave in certain relational situations, and make us feel good when our scripts and our lived relationships match. What are some of your relationship scripts? Where do you think they came from? Do some of your scripts differ from those of the mainstream U.S. culture?

have convenient labels. What do you call your father's second wife, her children by her first marriage, your brother's former wife, or a person you're dating when both of you are in your 50s? What do children of gay parents call their two mothers or fathers? Language has not always kept pace with the relationships we live in now (Nelson, 2014).

Another way that relationships exist in language is through figurative language, also discussed in Chapter 4. Figurative language—specifically, metaphors and similes—helps us understand relationships by comparing them to other phenomena (Lakoff, 2013; Lakoff & Johnson, 1980). In such linguistic comparisons, the qualities of the phenomenon to which a relationship is linked shed light on the qualities of the relationship itself (Burrell, Buzzanell, & McMillan, 1992; Butler, 2013; Turner & Shuter, 2004). Dana understands her relationship with her mother better when she is able to come up with a comparison for it, like a Mama Bear defending her cub.

In addition to offering a vocabulary for understanding our relationships, figurative language also *shapes* our understanding of them. Using a metaphor highlights some elements of the relationship while downplaying other elements. For example, the metaphor of relationship-as-dance emphasizes the coordination and enjoyment elements of a relationship while it downplays the conflicts and struggles. Table 10.1 lists common relational metaphors.

Researchers (e.g., Owen, 1989; Thibodeau & Boroditsky, 2013) argue that metaphors influence our thinking and communication. For instance, if Ben and

relationship scripts Cognitive structures containing a pattern for the key events we expect in a relationship.

TABLE 10.1 COMMON METAPHORS USED TO DESCRIBE CLOSE RELATIONSHIPS

Nature	Thunderstorm
	Volcano
	Sunny day
	Meadow with flowers
	Tree with deep roots
Machines	Well-oiled machine
	Leaky boat
	Merry-go-round
	Roller coaster
	Broken record
Food	Stew
	Gooey cake with ice cream
	TV dinner
	Milkshake
	Tossed salad
Clothing	Ripped sweater
	Comfortable old shoes
	Tie that's choking me
	Pair of pants with an elastic waist
	Party outfit

© Cengage Learning®

Leslie picture their marriage as a "well-oiled machine," they may adopt communication behaviors that focus on efficiency ("keeping the wheels turning") and functioning ("we don't want a breakdown in communication") at the expense of emotional communication. If Melody and Kim picture their relationship as volcanic, their communication behaviors will probably highlight conflict and emotion ("If we don't talk about this, I'll just explode").

10-3 INFLUENCES ON CLOSE RELATIONSHIPS

Like all the topics in this book, close relationships are affected by many influences. In this section we'll detail four factors that exert influence on interpersonal communication in close relationships. These include attraction, culture, gender or sex, and electronic media. Attraction influences both the inception and the continuance of close relationships, as well as how partners express themselves to one another. Cultural practices and beliefs influence how people think they should talk and act in a close relationship.

© Rehan Qureshi/Shutterstock.com

The stereotype that women are relational experts and men are relational idiots is common in the United States—check out most TV commercials. Yet research shows that although women and men do differ in what they learn about relationships, ultimately what they want from relationships is quite similar.

Gender and sex have an impact on how people enact roles in close relationships. Finally, social media sites offer new ways for close relationships to form and endure, and for the partners to communicate with one another.

10-3a Attraction

Attraction, especially what is known as short-term attraction, initiates relationships. **Short-term attraction**, a judgment of relationship potential, propels us into beginning a relationship with someone. **Long-term attraction**, which makes us want to continue a relationship over time, sustains and maintains relationships. Sometimes the things that attract you to someone in the short term may be the same things that turn you off in the long term. For example, Maggie may have initially struck up a friendship with Anita because she saw Anita as outgoing and friendly. However, later in their relationship, Maggie may come to see Anita's outgoing ways as egocentric and childish. She may wonder why Anita never seems to reflect on anything and always has to be with a lot of people. Anita's outgoing personality may begin to seem negative to Maggie as the relationship grows.

Both types of attraction are based on several elements, such as physical attractiveness, charisma, physical closeness (or proximity), similarity, complementary needs, positive outcomes, and reciprocation. Furthermore, people are attracted to others who fit their

short-term attraction A judgment of relationship potential that propels us into beginning a relationship with someone.

long-term attraction The things about another that make you want to continue, sustain, and maintain a relationship with them.

cultural ideal of attractiveness, but they are more likely to initiate relationships with others who tend to match their own level of attractiveness, which is known as the **matching hypothesis** (Carter & Gibbs, 2013; Cash & Derlega, 1978; Hinsz, 1989). In other words, we feel more comfortable talking with people who are about as physically attractive as we see ourselves to be. We also like people who are confident and exude charisma. In addition, it's more likely that we'll be attracted to those who are in physical proximity to us than to those who are more distant, because, at least before the advent of social media, it's more difficult to enter the initiating stage with someone who is far away.

We are also motivated to initiate conversations with those who share some of our own attributes, values, and opinions. A study investigating why people are attracted to one another found that a "likes-attract" rule was much stronger than an "opposites-attract" rule for heterosexual couples in Western cultures (Buston & Emlen, 2003). Yet, too much similarity can be boring, so we may seek a partner with some attributes that complement ours as well. For example, if Chris is quiet and Glenn is talkative, they may want to initiate a conversation because Chris' listening behavior is a good complement for Glenn's tendency to hold forth at length. Finally, we are attracted to others who seem attracted to us, or who reciprocate our interest. For instance, when Renny smiles at Natalie at a party and she doesn't smile back, Renny probably won't go any further with the relationship (Montoya & Horton, 2013).

10-3b Culture

As we have discussed in Chapter 2, and throughout this book, cultural norms, values, and expectations shape us in important ways. Thus, it should come as no surprise that culture plays a role in how we define close relationships and how we communicate within them. For example, traditional Hawaiian culture is fundamentally collectivistic, which affects how Hawaiians define family (or *'ohana*). For traditional Hawaiians, *'ohana* is extended and expanded; it consists of the immediate family (people with blood and marital ties), those who have been adopted into the family (a common practice), and spiritual ancestors (Miura, 2000). Hawaiian culture reflects values similar to the Latino/a concept of *familism*, which focuses on an extended family that includes aunts, uncles, cousins,

matching hypothesis We feel most comfortable in relationships with people who are about as attractive as we perceive ourselves to be.

relational culture The notion that relational partners collaborate and experience shared understandings, roles, and rituals that are unique to their relationship.

and dear friends. The African value of *collectivism* is also similar but emphasizes the entire race or community, as reflected in the proverb "It takes a village to raise a child."

Even within cultures, attitudes about close relationships may vary over time. One researcher (Allendorf, 2013) studied people's scripts for arranged marriages and love marriages in a small village in India. Arranged marriages were the dominant type of marriage in the past, but now love marriages are more common. Allendorf found that respondents thought the ideal marriage was a hybrid of the two types. She concludes that respondents' scripts for the ideal marriage reflect "multiple layers of local beliefs and culture" (p. 453).

Some researchers speak of **relational culture** (Turner & West, 2013), observing that what defines a close relationship and influences what's appropriate to say and do within one has to do with the partners' shared understandings, roles, and rituals that are unique to their relationship. Elaine and Sophia define their friendship by doing things together such as shopping, walking their dogs, and sitting and talking at the coffee shop. Jorge and Raul define their friendship by the fact that they grew up together. Each of these pairs of friends has created their own relational culture.

10-3c Gender and Sex

As we've discussed throughout this book, differences between men and women permeate our understanding of interpersonal communication. Close relationships provide another context in which gender differences (or perceived differences) have an impact. We take the perspective that differences between the sexes are learned—in other words, that cultural instructions guide girls to behave in ways that society has deemed feminine and teach boys to engage in what are considered masculine behaviors (McGeorge, 2001). Furthermore, our notions of sex and gender are somewhat fluid and can change over time.

This perspective does not deny that biological sex as well as learned gendered behaviors and values make a difference in our definitions of close relationships. In fact, one study (Marano, 2004) indicates that biological differences between men and women, like responses to stress and propensity to depression, may affect how people think about close relationships. Some research (Reissman, 1990) investigating reasons that people divorced found that men became dissatisfied with their marriages when their wives stopped doing certain things for them, such as fixing dinner and greeting them at the door. Women's dissatisfaction came from a different source—they felt their marriages were headed

IPC Around Us

Olga Khazan (theatlantic.com, 2013) writes about differences in how men and women approach close relationships, and what that might mean for online dating sites. Khazan talks about what a psychology professor, Edward Royzman, thinks about men's and women's approaches to close relationships. Khazan attributes the following to Royzman: "Men and women make mating decisions very differently. Men tend to act like single-issue voters: If a prospect is not attractive enough, he or she usually doesn't qualify for a first date, period. For women, however, 'It's a more complex choice,' he said. 'What tends to matter for females is that the overall package is good,' meaning that women might accept a less-attractive mate if he was outstanding in some other way." Khazan also comments on other research showing that although women and men said they wanted different things from mates (men ranked good looks as their top priority, while women ranked money first) there was no difference in the type of mates women and men actually chose in a speed-dating exercise. Overall, Khazan concludes that even though apps like Tinder can help both men and women increase their pool of possible mates, they cannot really determine who will be compatible mates. That's still up to individuals.

©Chris Howey/Shutterstock.com

for divorce when they and their husbands stopped talking to each other. Yet, both women and men attributed their dissatisfaction to the same overarching reason— they no longer felt cherished in the relationship. Thus, both sexes desired the feeling of being cherished, but men tended to feel that way when their wives did concrete favors for them, whereas women felt most cherished when they experienced good communication with their husbands.

Although women and men differ in what they have learned about, what they expect from, and what they experience within close relationships, popular writers like John Gray (who wrote *Men Are from Mars, Women Are from Venus* in 1992, as well as 12 subsequent books on the topic) and Deborah Tannen (who wrote *Talking from 9 to 5* in 1994, as well as multiple other books on the topic) have taken our cultural interest in sex differences to an extreme. They construct some differences where

none really exist, overestimate the differences that do appear, and fail to talk about the cultural context framing these differences (DeFrancisco & Palczewski, 2014).

10-3d Electronic Media

Communication between and among individuals is forever changed because of technology. Electronic media, like social networking sites, have provided important channels for conducting interpersonal relationships as well as communicating about them (Fox, Warber, & Manstaller, 2014; Turkle, 2011). Unquestionably, social network sites such as Facebook have had an impact on how users approach close relationships. Yet, research suggests that the impact is a complex one. Some researchers suggest that online dating is a good idea. Judith Silverstein and Michael Lasky (2004), for instance, observe that "traditional dating

© dolphfyn/Shutterstock.com

is fundamentally random" (p. 10). What they mean is that during the dating stage, people tend to "stumble" onto others at a social gathering. You might find yourself in the right place at the right time and meet the right person. Or, you might not. Regardless, this way of meeting people involves a lot of luck.

However, developing an online relationship is not as random; online dating "reverses the standard rules of dating" (Shin, 2003, p. D2). Silverstein and Lasky (2004) note a number of advantages to meeting someone online:

▶ Many people online are available and seeking companionship.

▶ Before you exchange personal information, you have the power to secure a profile of the other person.

▶ You know something about how the other person thinks and writes.

▶ You know how to contact him or her.

▶ You have the chance to exchange email and talk on the phone without ever revealing your identity.

▶ You can do all of this for less than what it might cost for a typical first date, such as dinner at a moderately priced restaurant.

Other research (Fox et al., 2014) finds that there are both upsides and downsides to relationships online. Fox and his colleagues found that Facebook has dramatically changed the way people acquire information about potential romantic partners (because they can learn so much about the person without ever interacting with them) and Facebook has introduced a new category for romantic relationships: FBO (Facebook Official). But this study also found that people felt Facebook could be detrimental to romantic relationships and respondents in the study stated that they preferred to meet potential romantic partners offline.

hyperpersonal Communication online that is overly intense and personal because, online, communicators are able to make their self-presentations very positive.

Another study (Yang, Brown, & Braun, 2013) found that college students reported a sequence for new media use in developing relationships. Respondents said that they used Facebook in the early stages of relational development. Later they moved to instant messaging and then to cell phones as the relationship matured. Respondents noted that they used the medium that most matched their goals for the relationship at the time. The authors found some sex differences in that women were more explicit about this sequence than were men, except when men were talking about relationships with women.

One theory detailing the ways that people communicate online is social information processing theory (SIP) (Walther, 1996, 2011). SIP alleges that online relationships may be just as close and important to partners as offline ones. Joseph Walther, the theorist who created SIP, talks about the notion that online communication may be **hyperpersonal**, or overly intense and intimate, because participants have the ability to strategically present themselves, highlighting their positive qualities. Furthermore, as people receive information online about others, they "fill in the blanks" to make attributions about the other. This often results in overattributing similarities and a positivity bias. Additionally, online communication is often asynchronous, meaning that the communicators are not required to be online at the same time. This asynchronous nature allows for editing, retracting, and polishing messages so they are of high quality, and again, provide a positive impression. Finally, the feedback online often contributes to the positive, intimate, or hyperpersonal nature of online communication and relationships. As Walther (2011) states: "when a receiver gets a selectively self-presented message and idealizes its source, that individual may respond in a way that reciprocates and reinforces the partially modified personae, reproducing, enhancing, and potentially exaggerating them" (p. 463). In this manner, SIP predicts that relationships conducted online may become intimate rather quickly, and may intensify much faster than offline relationships. When, or if, partners meet offline, however, there may be disappointment.

 10-4 # DEVELOPING INTERPERSONAL RELATIONSHIPS THROUGH STAGES

Stage models of relational development are concerned with how relationships develop (primarily offline) and how communication changes as we deepen or weaken

TABLE 10.2 KNAPP'S MODEL OF RELATIONSHIP DEVELOPMENT

Coming Together Stage	Sample Communication
Initiating	"Hi, how are you?"
Experimenting	"Do you like water polo?"
Intensifying	"Let's take a vacation together this summer. We can play water polo!"
Integrating	"You are the best friend I could ever have!"
Bonding	"Let's wear our team shirts to the party. I want everyone to know we're on the same team!"

Coming Apart Stage	Sample Communication
Differentiating	"I am surprised that you supported a Republican. I am a longtime Democrat."
Circumscribing	"Maybe we'd be better off if we didn't talk about politics."
Stagnating	"Wow, I could have predicted you'd say that!"
Avoiding	"I have too much homework to meet you for coffee."
Terminating	"I think we shouldn't hang out together anymore. It's just not fun now."

© Cengage Learning®

our relational ties with another. Perhaps the best known of the many stage models that describe relational life was originated by Mark Knapp (1978). The model answers the following questions: "Are there regular and systematic patterns of communication that suggest stages on the road to a more intimate relationship? Are there similar patterns and stages that characterize the deterioration of relationships?" (Knapp & Vangelisti, 2000, p. 36). The model provides five stages of coming together and five stages of coming apart. See Table 10.2 for a summary of the model.

Knapp and his colleagues argue that the model is useful for all kinds of relationships because it provides for relationships that end after only a couple of stages as well as relationships that do not move beyond an early stage. The model also provides for relationships that move back and forth between stages or skip stages. In addition, the model explains the movement of friendships as well as love relationships (Knapp, Vangelisti, & Caughlin, 2014).

Some people have criticized all stage models for presenting a linear picture of relationship development. These critics note that a linear picture doesn't provide an accurate representation of relationships that "cycle" or go back and forth between episodes of breaking up and renewal (Vennum, Lindstrom, Monk, & Adams, 2013). Furthermore, critics note that relational development doesn't happen neatly in stages and that the model doesn't clarify what happens when one partner moves to a new stage and the other doesn't. For example, stage models can't show us what happens when one partner wants to terminate the relationship while the other resists.

Stage models simplify a complicated process. Each stage may contain some behavior from other, earlier stages, and people sometimes slide back and forth between stages as they interact in their relationship. Thus, stage models give us a snapshot of the process of relationship development, but they don't tell the entire story. In the following sections, we briefly discuss each of the stages in the Knapp model. As you read about these stages, keep in mind the criticisms of stage models.

10-4a Initiating

This stage is where a relationship begins. In the **initiating stage**, two people notice one another and indicate to each other that they are interested in making contact: "I notice you, and I think you're noticing me, too. Let's talk and see where it goes." Initiation depends on attraction, which as we've previously mentioned, can be either short-term or long-term.

Some of our relationships stay in the initiating stage. You may see the same person often in a place that you frequent, such as a supermarket, bookstore, or coffee shop. Each time you see this person, you might exchange smiles and pleasantries. You may have short, ritualized conversations about the weather or other topics but never move on to any of the other stages in the model. Thus, you could have a long-term relationship that never moves out of the initiating stage.

10-4b Experimenting

In the second stage, the **experimenting stage**, people become acquainted by gathering information about one another. They engage in **small talk**—interactions that are relaxed, pleasant, uncritical, and casual. Through

initiating stage The first step in Knapp's stage model when two people notice one another and indicate to each other that they are interested in making contact.

experimenting stage The second stage in Knapp's model when people become acquainted by gathering superficial information about one another.

small talk Interactions that are relaxed, pleasant, uncritical, and casual.

small talk, people learn about one another, reduce their uncertainties, find topics that they might wish to spend more time discussing, "test the waters" to see if they want to develop the relationship further, and maintain a sense of community.

Many of our relationships stay in the experimenting stage. We may have many friends whom we know through small talk but not at a deeper level. If you see a friend in the coffee shop and go beyond "Hi, can you believe that how cold it is today?" to small talk (including gossip about mutual friends, comments about sports teams, low-level observations about your job, etc.), then you have deepened the relationship some, but you still have kept it at a low level of commitment. Furthermore, even people in close relationships spend time in this stage, perhaps in an effort to understand their partner more, to pass the time, or to avoid uncomfortable feelings stirred up by a more intense conversation.

10-4c Intensifying

The **intensifying stage** begins to move the relationship to a closeness not seen in the previous stages. Intensifying refers to deepening intimacy in the relationship. During this stage, partners self-disclose, forms of address become more informal, and people may use nicknames or terms of endearment to address one another ("I miss you, Boomer"; "Hi, honey"). Relational partners begin to speak of a "we" or "us," as in "We like to go to basketball

intensifying stage The third stage in Knapp's stage model refers to deepening intimacy in the relationship. During this stage, partners self-disclose, forms of address become more informal, and people may use nicknames or terms of endearment to address one another.

integrating stage The fourth stage in Knapp's model represents the two people forming a clear identity as a couple.

bonding stage The fifth stage in Knapp's model (and the final stage in the Coming Together part) refers to a public commitment of the relationship.

games" or "It'll be nice for us to get a break from studying and go for a walk."

In this stage, people begin to develop their own language based on private symbols for past experiences or knowledge of each other's habits, desires, and beliefs. For instance, Missy and her mother still say "hmmm" to each other, because that's what Missy said when she was little to mean "I want more." And Neil says, "It's just like walking on a rocky path" when he wants Trudy to do something because when they first became friends, he made her take a walk along a path scattered with rocks when Trudy wanted to go the movies instead.

In addition, this stage is marked by more direct statements of commitment—"I have never had a better friend than you" or "I am so happy being with you." Often these statements are met with reciprocal comments—"Me neither," or "Same here." In intensifying, the partners become more sophisticated nonverbally. They are able to read each other's nonverbal cues accurately, may replace some verbalizations with a touch, and may mirror one another's nonverbal cues— how they stand, gesture, dress, and so forth may become more similar. One way Candi intensified her friendship with Tricia was to stop dressing like her old friends did, and to start wearing clothes and makeup that made her look more like Tricia.

10-4d Integrating

In the fourth stage, the **integrating stage**, the partners seem to coalesce. Integrating has also been called "coupling" (Davis, 1973) because it represents the two people forming a clear identity as a couple. Coupling is often acknowledged by the pair's social circles; they cultivate friends together and are treated as a unit by their friends. They are invited to places together, and information shared with one is assumed to be shared with the other.

Sometimes the partners designate common property. They may pick a song to be "our song," open a joint bank account, buy a dog together, or move into an apartment together. In our case as authors of this book, coauthoring a series of books together has created a couple identity for us. We are often referred to together, and if people ask one of us to do something (such as make a presentation at a convention), they usually assume that the other will come along as well.

10-4e Bonding

The final stage in the coming together part of the model is the **bonding stage**, which refers to a public commitment of the relationship. Bonding is easier in some types of relationships than in others. For heterosexual couples, and now, in many states for gay couples as well, the marriage ceremony is a traditional bonding ritual. Having a bonding ritual provides a certain social sanction for the relationship, which may explain in part why gay and lesbian couples continue fighting to gain the legal right to marry. There are bonding ceremonies for other relationships as well. Examples include commitment ceremonies, naming ceremonies for new babies to welcome them to the family, and initiation ceremonies to welcome new "sisters" or "brothers" to sororities and fraternities.

10-4f Differentiating

The first stage in the coming apart section of the model is the **differentiating stage**. This refers to highlighting the individuality of the partners. This is unlike the coming together stages, which featured the partners' similarities. The most dramatic episodes of differentiating involve conflict, as we discussed in Chapter 9. However, people can differentiate without engaging in conflict. For example, the following seemingly inconsequential comment exemplifies differentiation: "Oh, you like that sweater? I never would have thought you'd wear sweaters with Christmas trees on them. I guess our taste in clothes is more different than I thought."

People switch from "we" to "I" in this stage and talk more about themselves as individuals than as part of a couple. According to the model, this stage is the beginning of the relationship's unraveling process. However, we know that relationships oscillate between differentiation and some of the coming together stages, such as intensifying. No two people can remain in a coming together stage such as intensifying, integrating, or bonding without experiencing some differentiating.

10-4g Circumscribing

The next stage, the **circumscribing stage**, refers to restraining communication behaviors so that fewer topics are raised (for fear of conflict) and more issues are out of bounds. The couple interacts less. This stage is characterized by silences and comments such as "I don't want to talk about that anymore," "Let's not go there," and "It's none of your business." Again, all relationships may experience some taboo topics or behaviors that are typical of circumscribing. But when relationships enter the circumscribing stage (in other words, if the biggest proportion of their communication is of this type), that's a sign of a decaying relationship. If measures aren't taken to repair the situation—sitting down and talking about why there's a problem, going to counseling, taking a vacation, or some other remedy—the model shows that people enter the next stage.

10-4h Stagnating

The third stage of coming apart, the **stagnating stage**, consists of extending circumscribing so extensively that the partners no longer talk much. They express the feeling that there is no use to talk because they already know what the other will say. "There's no point in bringing this up—I know she won't like the idea" is a common theme during this stage. People feel "stuck," and their communication is draining, awkward, stylized, and unsatisfying.

Each partner may engage in **imagined conversations** (Bodie, Honeycutt, & Vickery, 2013; Honeycutt, 2003), where one partner plays the parts of both partners in a mental rehearsal of the negative communication that characterizes this stage. Me: "I want to go visit my parents." Me in Role of Partner: "Well, I'm too busy to go with you." Me: "You never want to do stuff with my family." Me in Role of Partner: "That may be true, but you certainly can't stand my family!" After this rehearsal, people usually decide that it's not worth the effort to engage in the conversation for real.

10-4i Avoiding

If a relationship stagnates for too long, the partners may decide that the relationship is unpleasant. As a result, they move to the **avoiding stage**, a stage where partners try to stay out of the same physical environment. Partners make excuses for why they can't see one another ("Sorry, I have too much work to go out tonight," "I'll be busy all week," or "I've got to go home for the weekend"). They may vary their habits so that they do not run into their partner as they used to. For example, if people used to meet at a particular restaurant or a certain spot on campus, they change their routines and no longer stop by these places.

differentiating stage The first stage in the coming apart phase of Knapp's stage model refers to highlighting the individuality of the partners.

circumscribing stage The second stage of coming apart in Knapp's model refers to restraining communication behaviors so that fewer topics are raised (for fear of conflict) and more issues are out of bounds for the partners.

stagnating stage The third state of coming apart in Knapp's model consists of extending circumscribing so far that the partners no longer talk much.

imagined conversations Where one partner plays the parts of both partners in a mental rehearsal of possible communication that might take place between them.

avoiding stage The fourth stage of coming apart, where partners try to stay out of the same physical environment.

Sometimes it isn't possible to physically avoid a partner. If a couple is married and unable to afford two residences, or if siblings still live in their parents' home, it's difficult for the partners to be completely separate. In such cases, partners in the avoiding stage simply ignore one another or make a tacit agreement to segregate their living quarters as much as possible. For example, the married couple may sleep in separate rooms, and the siblings may come into the den at different times of day. When partners in the avoiding stage accidentally run into one another, they turn away without speaking.

© Aleksandar Mijatovic/Shutterstock.com

10-4j Terminating

The **terminating stage** comes after the relational partners have decided, either jointly or individually, to part permanently. Terminating refers to the process of ending a relationship. Some relationships enter terminating almost immediately: you meet someone at a party, go through initiating and experimenting, and then decide you don't want to see them anymore, so you move to terminating. Other relationships go through all or most of the stages before terminating. Some relationships endure in one stage or another and never go through terminating. And other relationships go through terminating and then begin again (people remarry and estranged friends and family members reunite). Furthermore, some relationships terminate in one form and then begin again in a redefined way. When Sam and Virginia got divorced, they ended their relationship as married partners. However, because they have two children, they redefined their relationship and became friends.

Terminating a relationship can be simple ("We have to end this") or complicated (involving lots of discussion and even the intervention of third parties such as counselors, mediators, and attorneys). It may happen suddenly or drag out over a long time. It can be accomplished with a lot of talk that reflects on the life of the relationship and the reasons for terminating it, or it can be accomplished with relatively little or no discussion between the partners.

---

terminating stage The final stage of coming apart comes after the relational partners have decided, either jointly or individually, to part permanently. Terminating refers to the process of ending a relationship.

systems theory von Bertalanffy's theory comparing relationships to living systems with six important properties: wholeness, interdependence, hierarchy, boundaries or openness, calibration or feedback, and equifinality.

wholeness A principle of systems theory stating that we can't fully understand a system by simply picking it apart and understanding each of its parts in isolation from one another.

10-5 EXPLAINING COMMUNICATION IN CLOSE RELATIONSHIPS

A stage model gives us a description of what might happen in the life of a relationship, but it doesn't really explain why these things occur. Given the importance of communication in close relationships, it's understandable that researchers have provided many theories to explain it. In fact, trying to explain communication in our relationships is something everyone spends a lot of time doing. Most people frequently wonder why relationships develop the way they do, and why some communication behaviors help relationships, while others make things worse. In this section, we review the basic tenets of three major theories—systems theory, dialectics, and social exchange theory—advanced by researchers in an effort to help us understand close relationships.

10-5a Systems Theory

Systems theory (von Bertalanffy, 1968) compares relationships to living systems (such as cells or the body), which have six important properties:

1. **Wholeness**
2. **Interdependence**
3. **Hierarchy**
4. **Boundaries or openness**
5. **Calibration or feedback**
6. **Equifinality**

Systems researchers find that understanding how each of these six properties operates allows them to understand how communication in relationships works. We'll now consider each of the properties in turn.

WHOLENESS

Wholeness means that you can't understand a system by taking it apart and understanding each of its parts in isolation from one another. Wholeness indicates that knowing Bert and Ernie separately is not the same as knowing about the relationship between Bert and Ernie. The relationship between people is like a third entity that extends beyond each of the people individually. If you think of a specific relationship that you are in, the concept of wholeness becomes quite clear. The way you act and communicate in that relationship is probably different from the way you act and communicate in other relationships. The other person's reactions, contributions, and perceptions of you make a difference in how you behave, and vice versa. Furthermore, the way you perceive the relationship between the two of you matters. If you are longtime friends with someone, you don't have to explain things to that person the same way you might to someone who is a newer friend of yours. Wholeness tells us that just because Karen knows Cara and Susie individually doesn't mean she knows them *in relationship* to each other.

INTERDEPENDENCE

Interdependence builds on the notion of wholeness by asserting that members of systems depend on each other and are affected by one another. If Derek's sister, Dina, is injured in a car accident, of course that changes Dina's life. But, interdependence says that Derek's life is also affected because of his relationship with Dina. When you talk to the people in your close relationships, you monitor their behavior and respond to it—you are affected by their shifts in mood and tone, and your communication shifts accordingly.

HIERARCHY

Hierarchy states that these shifts and accommodations we're making don't exist in a vacuum. Derek's relationship with his sister, Dina, is embedded in the larger system of his family, which consists of his mother and four siblings (all of the members of which are interdependent), and his family is embedded in the larger system of his extended family, his neighborhood, his culture, and so forth. Lower-level systems are called **subsystems**, and higher-levels systems

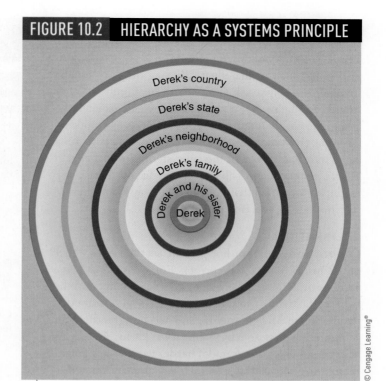

FIGURE 10.2 HIERARCHY AS A SYSTEMS PRINCIPLE

Derek's country
Derek's state
Derek's neighborhood
Derek's family
Derek and his sister
Derek

© Cengage Learning®

are called **suprasystems**. Derek and his sister form a subsystem of his immediate family. Derek's neighborhood is a suprasystem around his family (see Figure 10.2).

BOUNDARIES/OPENNESS

Boundaries or openness refers to the fact that hierarchy forms because we create boundaries around each separate system, making them distinct from one another (i.e., Derek and Dina, the family as a whole, etc.). However, human systems are inherently open, and information passes through these boundaries. (Therefore, some researchers call this element "openness," and some call it "boundaries.") For example, Marsha and Hal are best friends who have a very close relationship, and they tell

interdependence A principle that builds on the notion of wholeness by asserting that members of systems depend on each other and are affected by one another.

hierarchy A principle of systems theory stating that all relationships are embedded within larger systems.

subsystems Lower-level systems of relationship, such as a sibling relationship within a family.

suprasystems Higher-level systems of relationship, such as a neighborhood consisting of several families.

boundaries or openness A systems theory principle referring to the fact that hierarchy is formed by creating boundaries around each separate system. Human systems are inherently open, which means that information passes through these boundaries. Therefore, some researchers call this principle "openness," and some call it "boundaries."

© iStock.com/Skip ODonnell

each other things that they don't tell other people. This closeness forms the boundary around their relationship. Yet, if Marsha confides something to Hal that he finds disturbing, such as that she is abusing drugs or feeling suicidal, Hal might ask members of his family or other friends for help. In so doing, Hal would expand the boundaries of their subsystem. Boundaries exist to keep information in the subsystem, but they also act to keep some information out of the subsystem. For instance, if Terry's mother doesn't like Terry's boyfriend, Ron, Terry might work to keep that information away from the subsystem that she and Ron create.

CALIBRATION

Calibration centers on how systems set their rules, check on themselves, and self-correct. For example, Maggie and her grandmother have a close relationship, and the two of them form a subsystem of Maggie's extended family. When Maggie was 10, she and her grandmother calibrated their system by setting a weekly lunch date. As Maggie got older, she found it harder to meet her grandmother every Saturday for lunch because she wanted to do more activities with her friends. She expressed this to her grandmother, and they **recalibrated** (or reset the rules of their system) by changing their lunch date to once a month. When systems experience such a change, it's a result of **positive feedback** (or feedback that produces change). If they stay the same, the feedback is judged as **negative feedback** (or feedback that maintains the status quo).

EQUIFINALITY

Equifinality means the ability to achieve the same goals (or ends) by a variety of means. For instance, you may have some friends with whom you spend a lot of time and other friends with whom you spend less time. Some of your friends may be people you play tennis with, and others may be those you like to go to movies

calibration The process of systems setting their parameters, checking on themselves, and self-correcting.

recalibrate To adjust a relationship to accommodate changing needs of the parties.

positive feedback Feedback that causes a system to recalibrate and change.

negative feedback Feedback that causes a system to reject recalibration and stay the same.

equifinality A principle of systems theory asserting the ability to achieve the same goals (or ends) by a variety of means.

dialectics theory A theory that explains how we want to have conflicting, seemingly incompatible, things at the same time and how we try to deal with the tensions raised by this conflict.

TABLE 10.3   SYSTEM PROPERTIES AND COMMUNICATION

Property	Communication Outcome
Wholeness	The Thompson family is considered outgoing and funny. Ella Thompson is quiet and shy.
Interdependence	"I can't talk to you when you act like that!"
Hierarchy	Jake talks to his son, Marcus, about how his problems at work are making it hard for him to spend time with Marcus.
Boundaries or openness	Frieda tells a secret to her sister, Laya, and trusts her not to tell the rest of the family.
Calibration or feedback	Hap tells Miles that they can't play basketball every Wednesday because he needs to spend more time with his son.
Equifinality	Laura and Roy are happily married, and they tell each other everything. Nadine and Bob are happily married, and they keep many things private and don't confide in each other as much.

© Cengage Learning®

with. Each of these friendships may be close, but you become close (and maintain your closeness) in different ways. Equifinality is often used to explain how a variety of families with very different ways of interacting may all be happy (i.e. there is no one way to be a happy family).

Table 10.3 illustrates how each of the six properties of systems theory relates to communication behaviors. Systems theory doesn't explain all communication with our relational partners; it isn't specific enough to give us answers to questions such as why some couples argue more than others or why some communication in friendships is more satisfying than others. However, it does give us an overall impression of how relationships work and how communication behaviors function within relationships.

10-5b Dialectics Theory

A different explanation for communication in close relationships comes from dialectics theory (Baxter, 2011). This theory explains relational life as consisting of tensions resulting from people's desire to have two things at the same time that are polar opposites of each other. **Dialectics theory** explains how we want to have conflicting, seemingly incompatible, things at the same time and how we try to deal with the tensions raised by this conflict. For instance, dialectics theory assumes that we all want to have *both* privacy *and* the comfort that comes from being known by others, even though these two things seem like polar opposites. According to dialectics theory, the core of relational life consists of partners engaging in a search for seemingly incompatible goals; a search partners engage in to have *both/and* rather than *either/or* in their relationships.

Research (Baxter, 2011) suggests that the most common tensions in close relationships are those between autonomy and connection, openness and protection, and novelty and predictability. The contradiction in an **autonomy and connection dialectic** centers on our desire to be independent or autonomous while simultaneously wanting to feel a connection with our partner. This tension is apparent when Donna wants her friendship with Jessie to be really close, but at the same time she wants to be an independent individual, and it bugs her when their other friends talk about the two of them like they were one person. When we have an **openness and protection dialectic**, we want to self-disclose our innermost secrets to a friend, but we also want to keep quiet so we protect ourselves from the chance that our friend will use the information against us somehow. This tension surfaces when Mika agonizes about telling Claire that he feels inadequate at work. Mika wants Claire's empathy, but he's a little afraid she might think less of him if she knew how he feels. The tension in a **novelty and predictability dialectic** manifests in our simultaneous desires for excitement and stability. Malcolm feels bored with the everyday routines he's established in his relationship with Brandon, but he also feels comforted and reassured by them. It's scary to leave familiar routines, even when you might find them tedious. These three basic contradictions or dialectics are all seen as dynamic. This means that the interplay between the two opposites permeates the life of a relationship and is never fully resolved.

In addition to these, some other dialectics are found specifically in friendships (Rawlins, 1992), including the following:

▶ Judgment and acceptance

▶ Affection and instrumentality

▶ Public and private

▶ Ideal and real

The tension caused by the **judgment and acceptance dialectic** involves criticizing a friend as opposed to accepting them. People are often torn between offering (unwanted) advice and accepting a friend's behavior. If Maria has a friend, Josh, who is dating someone Maria thinks is wrong for him, should she offer her opinion or simply accept Josh's choice? Most people want both things simultaneously; they want to be able to make and hear judgments, but they also want unconditional acceptance. The **affection and instrumentality dialectic** poses a tension between framing your friendship with someone as an end in itself (affection) or seeing it as a means to another end (instrumentality). This dialectic suggests that in close friendships, people want to both just enjoy their friends and get some help from them. For example, if Tony often gets a ride to work from his close friend, Michael, then that friendship serves an instrumental function. But Tony values the friendship for affectionate reasons as well, such as the fun he and Michael have talking to each other on the way to work.

The two previous tensions are considered **internal dialectics** because they focus on how the partners communicate with one another. The next two are **external dialectics** because they have to do with how friends negotiate the more public aspects of their

© Antonio Guillem/Shutterstock.com

autonomy and connection dialectic The tension between our desire to be independent or autonomous while simultaneously wanting to feel a connection with our partner.

openness and protection dialectic The tension resulting when we want to self-disclose our innermost secrets to a friend, but we also want to keep quiet so we protect ourselves from the chance that our friend will use the information against us somehow.

novelty and predictability dialectic Our simultaneous, opposing desires for excitement and stability in our relationships.

judgment and acceptance dialectic Our desire to criticize a friend as opposed to accepting a friend for who he or she is.

affection and instrumentality dialectic The tension between framing a friendship with someone as an end in itself (affection) or seeing it as a means to another end (instrumentality).

internal dialectics Tensions resulting from oppositions inherent in relational partners' communication with each other.

external dialectics Tensions between oppositions that have to do with how relational partners negotiate the public aspects of their relationship.

friendship. The **public and private dialectic** specifically centers on how much of the friendship is demonstrated in public and what parts are kept private. Some emblems of friendship are fine for public consumption (such as the fact that Kelly and Amy both like horror movies and they have a few rituals around how they watch them—they have to have popcorn and Pepsi, and the room has to be completely dark), while other things (such as the silly nicknames they have for one another) might be kept between them. Some friendships, especially in adolescence, are kept more private. Ted, the football team captain at Metropolitan High School, doesn't always share publicly that he's friends with Paul, a computer geek. In private, Ted and Paul get along well, but neither especially wants to publicize their friendship.

Finally, the **ideal and real dialectic** reveals the tension between an idealized vision of friendship and the real friends that one has. We may carry images in our heads of how self-sacrificing, other-oriented, and altruistic friends should be. We get these mental images in large part from popular culture: TV shows, buddy movies, books, and magazines that show examples of friendships. Although Georgia recognizes that these idealized images of friendship are fantasies, she can't help feeling some tension when her best friend, Ada, goes on a ski trip, even though Georgia can't make it. Georgia had hoped that Ada would refuse to go without her. (Table 10.4 presents a summary of the dialectics.)

Dialectics theory says that to reduce the tension arising from our competing desires, we use several coping strategies including: cyclic alternation, segmentation, selection, and integration (Baxter, 1988, 2011).

▶ **Cyclic alternation** helps communicators handle tension by featuring the oppositions at alternating times.

---

public and private dialectic The tension between how much of a friendship is demonstrated in public and what parts are kept private.

ideal and real dialectic The tension between an idealized vision of friendship and the real friends one has.

cyclic alternation A way to help communicators cope with dialectic tensions by featuring the oppositions at alternating times.

segmentation A way to help communicators cope with dialectic tensions by allowing people to isolate separate arenas for using privacy and openness.

selection A strategy for dealing with dialectic tensions that allows us to choose one of the opposite poles of a dialectic and ignore our need for the other.

neutralizing A type of integrating that helps communicators cope with dialectic tensions through compromising.

disqualifying A type of integrating that helps communicators cope with dialectic tensions by exempting some behaviors from the general pattern.

TABLE 10.4 SUMMARY OF DIALECTICS

Most Common Relational Dialectics
1. Autonomy and connection
2. Openness and protection
3. Novelty and predictability

Additional Dialectics Found in Friendships
1. Judgment and acceptance
2. Affection and instrumentality
3. Public and private
4. Ideal and real

© Cengage Learning®

If Eileen discloses a great deal with her mother when she is in high school and then keeps much more information private from her mother when she goes to college, she is engaging in cyclic alternation. By sometimes being open and other times keeping silent, cyclic alternation allows Eileen to satisfy both goals in her relationship with her mom.

▶ **Segmentation** allows people to isolate separate arenas for using privacy and openness. For example, if Mac works in a business with his father, Nathan, they may not disclose to one another at work but do so when they are together in a family setting.

▶ **Selection** means that you choose one of the opposites and ignore your need for the other. Rosie might decide that disclosing to her friend, Wendy, isn't working. Wendy often fails to be empathic and has occasionally told something that Rosie told her in confidence to another friend. Rosie can use selection and simply stop disclosing to Wendy altogether, making their relationship less open but also less stressful.

Integration can take one of the following three forms:

▶ **Neutralizing** involves compromising between the two oppositions. If Traci and her sister Reva have been arguing because Reva feels that Traci is leaving her out of her life and not telling her anything, then Traci might decide to use neutralizing with Reva. Traci would then disclose a moderate amount to her—maybe telling Reva a little less than Reva wants to hear but a little more than she would normally tell her. The strategy of neutralizing copes with the tension by creating a happy medium.

▶ **Disqualifying** allows people to cope with tensions by exempting certain issues from the general pattern. Emily might make some topics, such as her love life, off limits for disclosure with her mom but otherwise engage in a lot of self-disclosure with her. This coping strategy

Dialectics Theory

How do you define reframing as a method for dealing with the dialectic tensions that exist in your close relationships? Give some examples from your own experiences in interpersonal communication encounters when you reframed.

creates **taboo topics**, or issues that are out of bounds for discussion. Most relationships contain topics that are not talked about by unspoken mutual consent. Many families avoid discussing sex and money. Even when couples engage in the most intimate of sexual behaviors, they may not talk about sex to each other. Another example of a taboo topic might be a family member's alcoholism. Disqualifying provides for a lot of disclosure on topics other than those considered taboo.

▶ **Reframing** refers to rethinking the opposition. In doing so, people redefine the tension. For instance, couples may say that they actually feel closer to each other if they don't tell each other everything. Reframing is illustrated in a couple's belief that if they keep some secrets, that makes what they do tell each other more significant. You'll notice that this is a specialized definition of reframing and it differs from how we've used the term in other chapters.

Like systems theory, dialectics theory is rather general. Although it provides a framework for understanding how people struggle with oppositions in relationships and helps us understand some communication behavior as strategies for dealing with these tensions, it doesn't clearly predict which strategies people will use, nor does it tell us why some relationships are more stressed than others by these tensions. However, dialectics theory is a good starting place for revealing some of the undercurrents that guide communication in close relationships.

10-5c Social Exchange Theory

Social exchange theory (Roloff, 1981) comes from a different line of thinking than systems and dialectics theories. Rather than providing a large framework for understanding communication in close relationships, **social exchange theory** is more specific and points us more directly toward testable predictions about it. First,

social exchange theory makes three basic assumptions about human nature: people are motivated by rewards and wish to avoid costs, people are rational, and people evaluate costs and rewards differently. For example, according to the first assumption, social exchange theorists believe that Jennifer and Laurie each want to do things that they find rewarding (such as going to the movies together) and that neither want to do things that seem like punishment (e.g., Jennifer wouldn't want to do Laurie's laundry). The next assumption clarifies the first by asserting that people are thinking rationally most of the time, enabling them to calculate accurately what are the costs and rewards of any given relationship. People keep mental balance sheets about relational activities (e.g., "I had to spend 2 hours helping Dan with his economics homework, and he repaid me by buying my lunch yesterday").

Finally, according to the third assumption of social exchange theory, what is costly for one person might seem rewarding for another. For example, Matt finds babysitting for his cousin a drag. But Meg majored in early childhood education and doesn't have a chance to spend time with children, so she welcomes the opportunity to babysit for her cousin. Furthermore, both people in a relationship may see their costs and rewards differently. Hillary thinks that the fact that her parents don't like Patrick is a huge cost to their relationship, but Patrick isn't concerned about parental approval, so he ranks the cost much lower.

As you can see by these assumptions, the heart of social exchange thinking lies in two concepts: costs and rewards. **Costs** are those things in relational life that people judge as negative. Examples include having to do favors for friends, listening to Uncle Al's boring stories at family gatherings, or babysitting for a bratty younger cousin. **Rewards** are those parts of being in a relationship that are pleasurable to people. Examples include having your partner listen to your problems and offer empathy, sharing favorite activities with a friend, and laughing about private jokes with your brother. Social exchange

taboo topics Issues that are out of bounds for discussion between the partners.

reframing A type of integrating that helps communicators cope with dialectic tensions by rethinking the opposition so that it no longer seems to be an opposition.

social exchange theory A theory that makes three basic assumptions about human nature: people are motivated by rewards and wish to avoid costs, people are rational, and people evaluate costs and rewards differently.

costs Those things in relational life that we judge as negative.

rewards Those parts of being in a relationship that we find pleasurable.

© iStock.com/julos

theory asserts that people are motivated to maximize their rewards while minimizing their costs (Lusch, Brown, & O'Brien, 2011; Molm, 2001) and predicts that when costs exceed rewards, people will leave the relationship.

Yet, we can all think of some examples of people who stay in relationships that seem, at least to outsiders, to be very costly. Abusive relationships (either physically or verbally), relationships where one person seems to have to do all the work, relationships where one person is wealthy and always pays for her poorer friend when they do expensive activities all provide examples of situations where it looks like the costs outweigh the rewards for at least one member of the relationship. Social exchange theory (Thibaut & Kelley, 1959) explains these relationships with two other concepts: comparison level and comparison level for alternatives.

Comparison level consists of a person's expectations for a given relationship. People learn from a variety of sources—such as the media, their families, and their past experiences—what to expect from relationships. Your comparison level might tell you that friendship is a relationship in which you should expect to give and take in equal proportions, whereas love relationships require more giving than taking. Social exchange theory predicts that people will be satisfied in relationships where the actual relationship matches or exceeds their comparison level.

Comparison level for alternatives refers to comparing the costs and rewards of a current relationship to the possibility of doing better in a different relationship. For example, Melanie calculates that she has more costs than rewards in her relationship with her husband, Erik. However, she still might stay with Erik if she also calculates that her chances of doing better without him, either by finding a better relationship or being alone, are poor. Some researchers (e.g., Kreager, Felson, Warner, & Wenger, 2013; Walker, 1984) have used this theory to explain why women stay in abusive relationships.

10-6 SKILL SET FOR COMMUNICATING IN CLOSE RELATIONSHIPS

This section presents several ways to improve communication in close relationships. As we have emphasized in this chapter, communicating with people in close relationships is our source of greatest pleasure and greatest grief, so people are usually quite motivated to improve their communication with important relational partners. Because many factors affect relationship development, we are necessarily broad in offering these suggestions.

10-6a Communication Skills for Beginning Relationships

Beginning a relationship requires a fair amount of skill, although you may not think about developing these skills. Most people meet new people fairly frequently, and they don't consciously think about how they go about striking up conversations and cultivating new friends. One study (Douglas, 1987) examined the following skills needed to initiate relationships:

▶ **Networking**: finding out information about the person from a third party. Easing into a relationship with the help of a third person means that you're behaving efficiently and in a socially acceptable fashion.

▶ **Offering**: putting yourself in a good position for another to approach you. If you sit near a person you'd like to get to know better, or walk along the same route as he or she does, you're putting physical proximity to work for you.

---

comparison level A person's standard level for what types of costs and rewards should exist in a given relationship.

comparison level for alternatives A comparison of the costs and rewards of a current relationship to the possibility of doing better in a different relationship.

networking In relational development, finding out information about a person from a third party.

offering Putting ourselves in a good position for another to approach us in a social situation.

- ▶ **Approaching**: actually going up to a person or smiling in that person's direction to give a signal that you would like to initiate contact. Approaching allows the relationship to begin, with both parties involved in some interaction.

- ▶ **Sustaining**: behaving in a way that keeps the initial conversation going. Asking appropriate questions is a way to employ sustaining.

- ▶ **Affinity seeking**: emphasizing the commonalities you think you share with the other person. Sometimes affinity seeking goes hand in hand with asking appropriate questions; you first ask questions to determine areas of common interest or experience and then you comment on them. "Do you like reality shows?" "No kidding? I'm a big fan, too." According to research, people use a variety of affinity-seeking strategies to get others to like them (Bell & Daly, 1984; see Table 10.5 for a summary of their strategies).

10-6b Communication Skills for Maintaining Relationships

Some people focus all their attention on beginning a relationship, thinking that after they have a friend, a boyfriend, or a girlfriend, they have achieved their goal. They fail to realize that close relationships need attention, and some amount of work, to keep them functioning. Some people have recognized how much nurturing a close relationship requires, however, and many popular books offer advice on enhancing relational quality (Egbert & Polk, 2006). Of course, close relationships aren't all work, or we wouldn't enjoy them so much. But if you ignore your closest relationships, they'll begin to falter and perhaps deteriorate. **Preventative maintenance** involves both partners paying attention to the relationship even when it's not experiencing trouble. According to Canary and Stafford (1992) and Stafford, Dainton, and Haas (2000), some relational maintenance behaviors include:

- ▶ Offering assurances ("I am committed to our relationship")

- ▶ Expressing openness ("Here's how I feel about our relationship")

- ▶ Reflecting positivity ("You did such a great job on that!")

- ▶ Sharing tasks ("If you'll clean the bathroom, I'll do the kitchen")

- ▶ Social networking ("Why don't you ask your sister to come to the movies with us?")

We review two additional skills for preventative maintenance in a bit more detail: expressing support and humor. A supportive communication climate, which encourages relational growth and maintenance, is conducive to maintaining relationships. However, supportive

© bikeriderlondon/Shutterstock.com

climates do not happen by chance; skillful communication is necessary to build this type of climate. The overall guidelines for developing supportive climates for communication (Gibb, 1961, 1964, 1970) are as follows:

- ▶ Make *descriptive* rather than evaluative comments. ("You have interrupted me twice" rather than "You are the rudest person!")

- ▶ Speak in *provisional* ways rather than in an absolute manner. ("I'm not sure, but I think that's the case" rather than "That's the only possible way it can be.")

- ▶ Be more *spontaneous* than strategic. ("Let's go on a picnic today—it's so beautiful out!" rather than "Let's plan a picnic for next week.")

- ▶ Strive for a *problem orientation* rather than a control orientation. ("How can we solve this so we're both happy?" rather than "You need to do it this way in order for things to work well between us.")

- ▶ Provide *empathy* instead of neutrality to your partner. ("I can tell that you're upset. Do you want to talk to me about it?" rather than simply waiting for your partner to come to you with a problem.)

- ▶ Establish *equality* between partners rather than superiority of one over the other. ("What do you think? I really want to know your opinion" rather than "Here's what I think and we're done talking about this!")

Humor also serves a preventative maintenance function. Joking and kidding are both indicators of enjoyment. Research supports the notion that humor

approaching Providing nonverbal signals that indicate we'd like to initiate contact with another person, such as going up to a person or smiling in that person's direction.

sustaining Behaving in a way that keeps an initial conversation going, such as asking questions.

affinity seeking Emphasizing the commonalities we think we share with another person.

preventative maintenance Paying attention to our relationships even when they are not experiencing troubles.

TABLE 10.5 AFFINITY-SEEKING STRATEGIES

1.	**Altruism**	Help the other person and offer to do things for him or her.
2.	**Assume control**	Take a leadership position.
3.	**Assume equality**	Don't show off. Treat the other as an equal.
4.	**Comfort**	Act at ease.
5.	**Concede control**	Allow the other to be in charge.
6.	**Conversational rules**	Follow the cultural norms for a conversation.
7.	**Dynamism**	Project excitement and enthusiasm.
8.	**Elicit disclosure**	Ask questions and encourage the other to talk.
9.	**Inclusion**	Include the other in activities and conversations.
10.	**Facilitate enjoyment**	Make time together enjoyable.
11.	**Closeness**	Indicate that the two of you have a close relationship.
12.	**Listening**	Lean in, listen intently, and respond appropriately.
13.	**Nonverbal immediacy**	Display good eye contact, appropriate touching, and so forth.
14.	**Openness**	Disclose appropriate personal information.
15.	**Optimism**	Display cheerfulness and positivity.
16.	**Personal autonomy**	Project independence.
17.	**Physical attraction**	Try to look good.
18.	**Present self as interesting**	Highlight past accomplishments and things of interest about yourself.
19.	**Reward association**	Offer favors and remind the other about past favors.
20.	**Confirmation**	Flatter the other.
21.	**Inclusion**	Spend time with the other.
22.	**Sensitivity**	Display empathy appropriately.
23.	**Similarities**	Point out things you have in common.
24.	**Support**	Be encouraging of the other and avoid criticism.
25.	**Trustworthiness**	Be dependable and sincere.

© Cengage Learning®

promotes bonding and cohesion as well as stress management (Hall, 2013). You can probably think of a time when you shared a joke with a friend or broke the tension with a humorous statement. Humor is a way of bringing people together (Young & Bippus, 2001). Bonding over something that's seen as amusing by both partners helps maintain relationships (Ledbetter, 2013).

relational transgressions Negative behaviors in close relationships, such as betrayals, deceptions, and hurtful comments.

10-6c Communication Skills for Repairing Relationships

As we've discussed throughout this chapter, having close relationships is critically important to people. However, some communication in close relationships can be unhealthy or toxic. In close relationships, people can betray, deceive, and say hurtful things to each other. Researchers call these negative behaviors **relational transgressions** (Bachman & Guerrero, 2006; Guerrero et al., 2007). When people in close relationships

experience a relational transgression, they have to decide whether to repair or terminate the relationship. If they decide not to terminate the relationship, they must engage in the difficult task of **corrective maintenance or repair** (Dindia, 1994). Repair skills are more difficult to implement than maintenance skills because repair involves correcting a problem, whereas maintenance is simply aimed at keeping things moving. We briefly discuss two repair skills: meta-communication and apology.

Meta-communication means communicating about communication. If communication is the problem in the relationship, the partners need to address how to improve their communication. For example, if Mary tells her friend, Mike, that she doesn't like it when he raises his voice to her, she is engaging in meta-communication. Mike might respond that he raises his voice when he gets excited. Mary can then tell him that she interprets it as anger. After the two define the problem through meta-communication, they can work on figuring out how to repair the problem.

Apologies (Goffman, 1967) have several parts: an expression of remorse; a promise not to repeat the transgression; an acknowledgment of fault; a promise to make it up to the victim; and a request for forgiveness. Sometimes apologies are accompanied by **accounts**, or explanations for the transgression (Carr & Wang, 2012). Accounts may include justifications ("It's really not as bad as you think—look at it from my perspective") and

excuses ("I couldn't help being late—my boss gave me a huge project just as I was leaving"). As an example of how apologies can help repair relationships, consider Keisha and May. The two had been really close friends all through high school. They had kept in touch after graduation, even though they had moved to opposite ends of the country. For several years, they exchanged Christmas cards, and they even saw each other from time to time. Each time they met, it was as if they had just been together, and they talked and talked, catching up with each other's lives. However, one year, Keisha sent May her usual Christmas card, and May didn't respond. After a couple of years, Keisha stopped sending the cards, and the two ceased contact.

Then out of the blue, May called and apologized, providing an account of her behavior. She told Keisha that problems she had been having with her family had demanded all her concentration. She said she just hadn't had the energy for keeping up with any of her long-distance friendships. Keisha felt a lot better when she heard May's explanation, and the two were able to resume their friendship. Apologies are not always successful, but they are one way that relational partners strive to repair their relationship after a transgression, and they often help (Morse & Metts, 2011).

corrective maintenance or repair Efforts to restore a relationship after it runs into trouble.

meta-communication Communication about communication.

apology A way to repair relationships after relational transgressions. Apologies consist of: an expression of remorse; a promise not to repeat the transgression; an acknowledgment of fault; a promise to make it up to the victim; and a request for forgiveness.

account An explanation for a transgression that may accompany an apology.

STUDY TOOLS

DON'T FORGET TO CHECK OUT COURSEMATE AT WWW.CENGAGEBRAIN.COM!

CHAPTER 10 FEATURES THE FOLLOWING RESOURCES:

☐ Ethics & Choice: Connie and Paul

☐ Communication Assessment Test: Relational Communication Scale

☐ Interactive Activities

11 | Communicating in Context: Families, Friends, and Romantic Partners

LEARNING OUTCOMES

11-1 Identify and describe the types of family configurations in the United States

11-2 Explain the various stages of childhood and adult friendships

11-3 Articulate the dimensionality of romantic relationships

11-4 Use skills that help improve communication in families, close friendships, and romantic relationships

After you finish this chapter go to **PAGE 237** for **STUDY TOOLS.**

THEORY/MODEL PREVIEW

Triangular Theory of Love; Selman's Stages of Childhood Friendships; Rawlins's Stages of Friendship Development

©djem/Shutterstock.com

The enduring nature of our close relationships cannot be disputed. Throughout this book, we have underscored the value of having long-term, satisfying close relationships with others.

In Chapter 10, you learned the various theoretical foundations that frame these relationships. By now, we're sure you know that our interpersonal communication with others provides us ample opportunities to make our relationships more or less compelling and valuable to us.

Relationships are sometimes messy. People are unpredictable and we can't always confidently project what will happen to us or the influences of others upon us. Challenges exist, including those related to finances, housing, child raising, fidelity, time management, jealousy, among others, making relational life very tough for many. And yet, we persevere because relationships are important and we find ourselves among people who care for us and who help us grow. These types of connections are the focus of this chapter.

Of all the interpersonal relationships in which we engage, three types figure prominently in the lives of most people: family, friends, and romantic partners. Although we understand that each of these relational types are discrete and unique in many ways, it's also true that each overlap in some significant ways. For example, some married couples refer to each other as a "best friend." In addition, close friends can, at times, turn into romantic partners, with various levels of relationship satisfaction. Or, consider the fact that some family members view other family members as close friends.

Despite this overlapping, each of the three close relationship types we're about to explore has distinct

characteristics and expectations. And, to be sure, it's also true that while each may resemble the other, it is the interpersonal communication that exists within each relationship that creates the uniqueness we're about to discuss.

Among the many relational types we find ourselves in, and as we noted above, we wish to focus on family, friends, and romantic relationships. The media have been influential in communicating images of these three. Historically, for instance, television shows have been instrumental in communicating various examples of (1) family life (e.g., *All in the Family* in 1971 and *Here Comes Honey Boo Boo* in 2014), (2) friends (e.g., *Friends* in 1994 and *The Game* in 2014), and (3) romantic relationships (e.g., *I Love Lucy* in 1951 and *Sister Wives* in 2014). Using this television vantage point, you can quickly see that these three relationship types can vary tremendously. And, outside of a Hollywood set, this variation continues. Let's begin our discussion with the sort of relationship that remains as one of the most provocative of all groups in a person's life: family.

11-1 FAMILY RELATIONSHIPS

Families are unique close relationships for many reasons. First, family ties can be voluntary or involuntary. Some families consist of people who come together of their own free will, such as married partners, communes, or **intentional families** who band together by choice rather than by blood relationships. But many family members have relationships with others they did not choose, such as parents, grandparents, cousins, siblings, and so forth, which form different relationships within this family type (e.g., sibling/grandparent, husband/mother-in-law, etc.).

Families are also distinctive because for many members, the close relationship is lifelong. Some research (Serewicz, Dickson, Morrison, & Poole, 2007) indicates that even though Western families expect children to leave

intentional families Family members who band together by choice rather than by blood relationships.

© Derek Latta/Shutterstock.com

the nest as they reach adulthood, continuity of relationships with family members is just as important as increasing autonomy. In fact, if you have a sibling, it's likely that your sibling experience will be the longest-lasting relationship you have in your life (Kreppner & Lerner, 2013). Finally, unlike friendship or dating relationships, family is a close relationship that receives social, cultural, and legal sanctions through, for example, marriage, adoption, and inheritance. Let's address "family" a bit further so you can see its relevancy, function, and possibilities in your interpersonal relationships. We begin by defining the family, discussing some interpersonal communication practices in the family, and identifying various family types.

Elsewhere, we have discussed the difficulties with defining family (Turner & West, 2015). We noted that interpreting the term family could be problematic because of all of the different incarnations existing. Further, we posited that "defining family often is a problem that bedevils policy makers, laypeople, and scholars alike" (p. 10). That is, we have multiple family types (e.g., single parent) that we know through research and we also know that there are various options and choices (e.g., reproductive technologies) that influence the interpretation of family. Furthermore, family types exist that are not universally known and, of course, there are family types yet to be realized, given the influence of culture, technology, gender, sexual identity, among others.

There is some controversy in the family communication research concerning how to define a family. Some researchers (Floyd, Mikkelson, & Judd, 2006) advocate the definition of family as a "socially, legally, and genetically oriented relationship" (p. 37). Others

(Galvin, 2006) argue for allowing functions such as communication to define the family. In other words, if a group of people function like a family by sharing affection and resources, and refer to themselves as a family, then they are a family. Still others (Turner & West, 2015) advance an expansive definition of family that includes the notion of choice; if you choose a person to be considered a family member, then that person is recognized as such. We refer to this as **voluntary kin**, or individuals who feel like family but who are not related either by blood or law. So, for example, when he was a teenager, after telling his father that he was gay, 17-year-old Tony was kicked out of his house. In the 2 years subsequent to his father's directive, Tony became close to one of his "street friends," Amber. In fact, Amber allowed him to stay with her in her apartment and the two became quite close. Today, if we were to ask Tony who he would identify as a family member, according to an expansive view of family, he would probably mention Amber. In all likelihood, he would not mention his father, despite the DNA connecting the two. What do you think about including people such as Amber in Tony's definition of family?

We believe in a more inclusive, communication-based definition. And, we contend that it's valuable for us, as we try to understand what a family is, to be vigilant in addressing the diversity that characterizes much family life.

Families are created through interpersonal communication. To illustrate why we take this position, we provide you two examples of how communication influences family life. One interpersonal communication practice that has been examined as unique to families is storytelling. **Family stories** are those bits of narrative about family members and activities that are told and retold and that have been seen as a way for members to construct a sense of family identity and meaning (Kellas & Kranstuber-Horstman, 2015). Some researchers argue that families don't just tell stories, but that storytelling is a way of creating a family (Langellier & Peterson, 2006). When Marie brings her new friend, Danielle, home to

voluntary kin Individuals who feel like family but who we're not related to by blood or law.

family stories Pieces of narrative about family members and activities that are told and retold.

© iStock.com/leezsnow

meet her parents, for instance, the stories that are told to Danielle are a way to bring the family alive for her and to integrate Danielle into the family fold.

Family stories can be pleasurable and entertaining as well as difficult to listen to. The stories can sometimes serve as cautionary tales about family members who went astray in some way. Blake recalls hearing the story about his great-uncle Thomas, who lost the family fortune by gambling. Blake always got the impression that the story was told repeatedly to warn his generation to keep working hard and avoid developing bad habits. Or, consider the family stories that may not be as clear or coherent as other stories. For example, stories handed down by African Americans regarding slavery are often incomplete. Because slavery tore families apart, it's sometimes difficult to find connected, linked stories regarding family life. In fact, "every African American family has a history, but not every African American family knows much about their history" because the family lineage is difficult to trace (Thomas, 2013, p. 1).

A second important family interpersonal communication practice is the **ritual**, or a repeated patterned communication event in a family's life (Bryant, 2006). Rituals can take three forms: everyday interactions (e.g., the Gilbert family members always say a prayer together before going to bed), traditions (e.g., Rollie and Elizabeth mark their anniversary each year by eating dinner at McDonald's because that's where they met each other), and celebrations (e.g., Ben and Rachel eat Thanksgiving dinner with their children). Celebrations differ from traditions because they involve holidays that are shared throughout a culture as opposed to traditions, which are practices that evolve in a specific family. Still, both celebrations and holidays involve the back and forth nature of conversations and each provides for enhanced intimacy as well as enhanced conflict. We will talk a bit further about these interpersonal possibilities a bit later in the chapter.

Now that you have a general understanding of what family is and a few interpersonal communication practices, let's move deeper into understanding current family life. First, we are all born into a **family-of-origin**. This is the family in which we have been raised and this family is usually important in establishing our values and our worldviews. The family-of-origin is also instrumental to our interpersonal communication style. That is, the family in which we were raised can be—and often is—responsible, directly or indirectly, for how we

TABLE 11.1 PRIMARY FAMILY TYPES IN THE UNITED STATES

Type	Definition
I. Nuclear	Married couple living with their biological children
A. Traditional	Father/husband is financial provider
	Mother/wife is responsible for domestic duties
B. Contemporary	Stay-at-home father with mother working outside the home
	Dual-career couple working outside the home, both providing care for their children
II. Gay and Lesbian	Same-sex intimate couple caring for at least one child
III. Multigenerational	A number of generations living together, including parents, children, grandparents, aunts, uncles, etc.
IV. Single Parent	One adult serving as the primary parent to at least one child

© Cengage Learning®

communicate with others today. Certainly, as we grow older, we develop and nurture effective interpersonal communication patterns and skills—otherwise, why would you be in this course? Still, we also need to acknowledge that our parents, siblings, grandparents, and other family members likely have (had) an extraordinary influence upon our interpersonal skills today.

Understanding our family-of-origin helps us realize about one family foundation. Yet, recognizing family types widens our understanding of different families. We now touch a bit on different family types that are found around us. As we examine each, keep in mind that even if we had 100 pages to write on this subject, we could never capture every family type! In fact, we present you with a group of family types that are representative and not meant to be exhaustive. So, let's discuss the definition, roles, rules, and/or patterns of interpersonal communication in four very different family types: nuclear family, gay and lesbian family, multigenerational family, and single-parent family (see Table 11.1).

Nuclear families were named this way, in part, because the "nucleus," or center, was the core where others would gravitate. In this case, it was the father and mother who served as the family's "center." In a sense, a **nuclear family** was the original foundation of family life and all the remaining family types coalesced or diverted from this configuration. Nuclear

ritual A repeated patterned communication event.

family-of-origin The family into which we are all born.

nuclear family The original foundation of family life in the United States.

families can be categorized in two ways. First, the **traditional nuclear family** is composed of a married couple living with their biological children, with a husband/father providing financial support (e.g., breadwinner) to the family and the wife/mother providing domestic support, cleaning, cooking, and so forth. The **contemporary nuclear family** is a modernized version of the nuclear family and can include two situations: a stay-at-home dad with a mom working outside of the home and a dual-career couple that includes both father and mother working outside the home and both providing primary care to their children. The U.S. Census Bureau (2011) reports that 21.6 percent of households are defined as nuclear (their definition of "nuclear" includes a more traditional view of this family type). Furthermore, the upswing of stay-at-home dads (SAHDs) cannot be ignored. There are 213,000 SAHDs compared with 5.2 million stay-at-home moms (Current Population Survey, 2013). Clearly, SAHDs are growing in number, but they still comprise a relatively small group compared to stay-at-home moms.

© iStock.com/Juanmonino

Interpersonal communication within nuclear families can be both comfortable and defensive. For instance, in a traditional family arrangement, because both the husband and wife understand and embrace traditional gender roles (Fitzpatrick, 1988; Ivy, 2012), interpersonal communication conflict is generally limited. Yet, some internal conflict may exist as this family arrangement bumps up against some external forces, namely the macro-culture. That is, consider the challenge that Maria Venegas experiences as she helps out at the annual Christmas pageant at school. Because she is a stay-at-home mom, Maria did not have to have permission to leave work or take a vacation day. This situation caused other mothers who work outside the

home to feel rather envious, causing Maria to avoid talking about her family arrangement.

Interpersonal communication challenges occur with the contemporary traditional family. Why? Stay-at-home dads may experience some intrapersonal conflict between their domestic style and the Westernized cultural expectations of men serving as the primary financial provider; in fact, most cultures around the globe have a pretty limited view of men's roles in the home. The U.S. recession during 2008–2012, however, stimulated more of this family arrangement as men were either laid off or terminated during company downsizing. In addition, despite the growing numbers of SAHDs, role conflict may occur as men perceive themselves as less effective than stay-at-home moms. Finally, some individuals still believe that upending traditional gender norms in this way is nothing but an "embarrassment"—for wives, in particular (see, e.g., Chen, 2013).

When two people of the same sex maintain an intimate relationship and care for at least one child, they are part of a **gay- and lesbian-headed family**. Although this family type has existed for decades, in 2004, the year that the Massachusetts Supreme Judicial Court declared it unconstitutional to deny gay men and lesbians the right to marry, the cultural tides of support turned. Although this family configuration enjoys much more support than it did even a decade ago, the United States is far from universal in its embrace. Many states have "approved" same-sex marriage—either through court decision, legislative action, or citizen vote. Yet, the march toward economic and legal parity with heterosexual couples continues. **Homophobia**, or an irrational fear and/or anxiety of gay men or lesbians (or bisexual and transgender people), as well as **heterosexism**, which is the assumption that heterosexuality is universal, will always thwart efforts toward full cultural support of gay and lesbian-headed households.

traditional nuclear family A married couple living with their biological children, with the husband/father as the financial provider and the wife/mother as the domestic provider.

contemporary nuclear family A modernized version of the nuclear family with two variations: (1) stay-at-home dad with the mom working outside the home and (2) a dual-career couple that includes both parents working outside the home, and both providing primary child care.

gay- and lesbian-headed family Two people of the same sex who maintain an intimate relationship and who serve as parents to at least one child.

homophobia An irrational fear and/or anxiety of gay men or lesbians.

heterosexism The assumption that heterosexuality is universal.

Research notes that 3.4 percent of adults are gay, lesbian, bisexual, or transgender (Jayson, 2012). Furthermore, the last U.S. Census (2011a) showed that there were over 900,000 same-sex couple households in the United States, although it is not always clear whether individuals are willing or accurate in reporting the presence of children. Regardless, an 84 percent growth in same-sex households from 2000 to 2010 (IMPACT Program, 2013) cannot be ignored and has supplied communication researchers with some information.

What do we know about the interpersonal communication within families with gay fathers and lesbian mothers? The "coming out" process of gay fathers is often different than mothers (West & Turner, 1995) (look at Chapter 8 for more information on self-disclosure). Perhaps because both gay fathers and lesbian mothers feel that they are targets of homophobia (Suter, 2015), this family type experiences unique challenges unlike other family types. Furthermore, "legitimacy challenges" are experienced, including direct attacks, discriminating silence, and legal discrimination. All of these life events likely undermine the interpersonal communication taking place in any family. Yet, Suter and others (Biblarz & Savci, 2010) note that there is much resilience in this family type, resulting in interpersonal communication and parenting skills that are typically supportive, nonjudgmental, and functional.

Many people belong to families where several generations live under the same roof. **Multigenerational families** are considered to be extended families, meaning that they "extend" from the nuclear arrangement we talked about earlier. Mutigenerational families include multiple generations living together, including parents and children, as well as other relatives such as aunts, uncles, and grandparents. This family type has become more commonplace for a few reasons. First, economic reasons have forced unexpected family dynamics, including college students who may not have a job after graduating (called "boomerang kids"). Couple economic factors with demographic factors; people are living longer and therefore, many families have found themselves with aging relatives living with them. Third, because of the influx of immigrants over the past several decades, multigenerational households have soared. Children, in particular, have altered the multigenerational immigrant home, accounting for about 75 percent of the growth of the child population (Landale, Thomas, & Van Hook, 2011).

The Pew Research Center (2010) reports that nearly 49 million people, or about 16 percent of the population, live in a multigenerational household. The U.S. Census Bureau (2011b) reports that by 2050,

about 100 million U.S. citizens will be over the age of 65, resulting in an obvious uptick in the numbers of this family type. Furthermore, as alluded to earlier, with 61 percent of 25- to 34-year-olds reporting that they have friends or family members who have moved back in with their parents (Parker, 2012), prompting new forms of family communication, the growth of this household type will continue.

Multigenerational families, as we have noted, who experience the addition of older family members, will be especially affected by this newly formed family configuration. Grandparents, in particular, will influence the interpersonal communication within the family. Jake Harwood (2004), for example, claims that the grandparent-grandchild relationship "can be a place in which confidences are shared and family histories are learned, in an environment perceived as more 'free' than in conversations with parents" (p. 301). Communication between family members with grandparents may be problematic, however, if a grandparent is around every day—all day—causing expectations to be placed on him or her (e.g., laundry, dishes, etc.). In fact, in what some may view as an interesting twist with respect to babysitting, Lynn Turner (2012) notes that "as grandparents age, their adult children begin to take over some responsibilities for them. Yet, these same children also turn to their parents to take care of their children in times of crisis" (p. 237). The **sandwich generation**, or the generation of people who simultaneously cares for its (aging) parents and their own children, will become even more prominent in multigenerational households, creating a bit of role confusion (Beren, 2014).

Thus far, we've addressed nuclear families, gay- and lesbian-headed families, and multigenerational families. One additional family type is the **single-parent family**. Images of single parents have evolved over the years. Presentations of single parents were usually relegated to single mothers, most of whom were created as a result of divorce and allegations that for whatever reason, the mother "did something wrong." Today, we have a myriad of images related to single-parent families, which comprise one adult serving as the primary parent to at least one child. Although it's true that many still hold an antiquated image of this family type, and some even believe

multigenerational families Extended family members (children, parents, grandparents, etc.) living under the same roof.

sandwich generation a generation of people who simultaneously take care of their (aging) parents and their own children.

single-parent family Families that consist of one adult serving as a parent and at least one child.

Family Life and Child Protective Specialists

Nearly all families have a child or children. In fact, in many family configurations, children are instrumental to a family's dynamic. The communication in a single-parent family, nuclear family, multigenerational family, among others, is impacted by the presence of children and children can be sources of pride, stress, conflict, and joy in many families. A child welfare specialist works to ensure that children live in safe, supportive, and violence-free home environments (Inside Jobs, 2013). These child-centered professionals are busy people. They are responsible for a multitude of tasks that ensure that children are given the best protection and support structures. In addition to managing caseloads that relate to children in various family situations, the child welfare specialist also is often required to understand a number of different difficult issues, including poverty, unemployment, substance abuse, illness, and other factors that impact the child's

© TOMO/Shutterstock.com

well-being. Each of these topics requires skills in interpersonal communication and also a sensitivity to multiple populations. This career is not for those who wish to "conquer the world" as it requires endless sleepless nights and much worry. Consequently, a specialist should be prepared for many bouts of relational repair. In the end, however, child protective specialists point out the authentic joy they feel as they work toward assisting the most vulnerable in society.

that the number of single parents is "alarming" (Mathur, Fu, & Hansen, 2013), we have come a long way. Portraits of single parents include both men and women who are capable of quality parenting.

Demographically, according to the *Statistical Abstract of the United States* (U.S. Bureau of Labor Statistics, 2012), over 10 million single-parent households exist in the United States, comprising nearly 30 percent of all households in the country. Yes, this is a large percentage of all family types, and single parents have more than tripled as a share of all U.S. households since 1960. Breaking down the numbers a bit further, there are 2.7 million single fathers and nearly 10.3 million single mothers (InfoPlease, 2013).

Day-to-day interpersonal communication in single-parent households is somewhat unique. Consider the reasons that a single-parent household may exist: death, divorce, choice, among others. Think about Victoria, for example, who as a single mom, must not only deal with the untimely death of her husband, but also the economic and communicative challenges of parenting three children under the age of 11. Or, imagine the

interpersonal communication in a family with Robby, who was awarded joint custody of his 14-year-old, Isabella. And, think about the different discourses taking place in a family with Julien, who, at the age of 35, successfully adopted twin 8-year-old sisters from Russia. Each of these affords opportunities for various interpersonal struggles and triumphs.

In addition, the parent-child relationship in single parents is complicated by the dynamics contained within each family. For instance, suppose a single parent decided to date. What sort of communication might exist between the dating partner and the parent? Or, how is co-parenting done in divorced families? Some research shows that a "good divorce" is possible and that cooperative co-parenting can result in close relationships (Ahrons, 2011). Also, if a single parent adopted a child, how might that parent address a child's request to meet her biological parents? Each of these scenarios, and so many others, requires a template of interpersonal communication skills. We will address a skill set later in the chapter that we believe would assist this, and other family types.

11-2 CLOSE FRIENDSHIPS

In a first of its kind, the 2013 *State of Friendship in America* report (Styles, 2013) presented a national snapshot of friendships in the United States. The report identifies several conclusions related to close friends. Five are of particular relevance:

▶ Most people are not fully satisfied with the state of their friendships. Seniors (age 70 and over) and Millennials/Generation Yers (ages 16–34) are more likely to say they're extremely satisfied than are Generation Xers (ages 35–49).

▶ People who say they have close friends report more happiness and more fulfillment in life than those without close friends.

▶ Women report more close friends, but they are no happier than men in their close friendships.

▶ Social media is fairly insignificant in long-term close friendships. In fact, there is no relationship between the number of Facebook friends and a person's satisfaction with his or her friends.

▶ Individuals who observe weekly religious services, who are ideologically conservative, and who reside in an urban center report the highest levels of satisfaction in their friendships.

The report concludes by noting that **friendship** runs deep and requires us to toss out our stereotypes and predispositions to friendship formation. And, unlike most family relationships, friendship is voluntary.

For our purposes, we adopt the following view of friendship: Friendship is a significant close relationship of choice that exists over a period of time between individuals who provide social support and who share various commonalities (e.g., time together, etc.). Still, despite this expansive view, friendship continues to be a slippery concept because the term has been tossed around in popular culture with a multitude of meanings. You will recall in Chapter 4 that language can be problematic. When you hear the word *friend*, a number of difficulties can arise because of the various uses of the term. People use the word in ways that don't foster emotional closeness or social support. For instance, politicians refer to their political enemies as "friends" (e.g., "I will not yield the floor to my good friend because he has already wasted our time"). And, of course, today we have "Facebook friends," and these are often people we've never met but whom we're comfortable labeling a "friend." We take friendships for granted, yet we rarely understand their importance in our lives. Victoria DeFrancisco and Catherine Palczewski (2014) summed up this "take-for-granted" rationale by stating, "Friendships receive no ceremonial celebration; no legal, political, religious, or other institutional support" (p. 145).

In this chapter, we are focused on **authentic friends**—those individuals whom we identify as close friends, with whom we share our personal feelings, and whom we hold in high esteem. Because there are no formal ceremonies to sanction friendships or any legal bonds to make dissolving them difficult, friendships are often amorphous, making it a somewhat fragile close relationship. Friends may be sacrificed for family in the belief that family relationships are more primary. For instance, Maggie had to exclude her best friend, Leah, from her son's wedding rehearsal because only family members were invited. Friends may also come and go based on situational factors. Randi, for example, found it hard to stay friends with Marlene after she got married and moved to California while Randi remained single in Chicago. She wanted to stay friends with Marlene, but the long distance and their different circumstances doomed the friendship.

Although we have a wide variety of differences in perceptions and experiences with friends, the truth is that we believe that our close friends need to possess certain qualities. So, let's now discuss the expectations we hold of a friend. We close our conversation about friendships by taking a lifespan approach to understanding friendships.

friendship A significant close relationship of choice that exists over a period of time between individuals who provide social support and who share various commonalities.

authentic friends Those individuals whom we identify as close friends and whom we hold in high esteem.

Friendships at work are inevitable. So says Dorie Clark (forbes.com, 2013), who writes that today, more and more businesses have co-workers who also define themselves as friends. The "work-life division is eroding," bringing with it new friendships that even a few years ago were unimaginable. Today's workplace requires people to work in teams and spend long hours together. Clark states that we need to "debunk the myth" that friendships should not happen at work and in fact, celebrate "friend-friendly workplaces" as part of the future. She believes that friendships at work have business advantages, including increased productivity and employee retention. Further, workers indicate that they have higher job satisfaction if they are able to cultivate friendships with their co-workers. In the end, Clark concludes, there must be a cultural framework in place that accommodates

© StockLite/Shutterstock.com

the development and maintenance of friendships. It's a "win-win" scenario for both employee and company.

A close friend provides us both tangible and intangible support. Whether we are asking her to borrow a truck so we can move to another apartment or hugging him after we receive devastating news about the death of a family member, we have come to rely on this close relationship in many ways. Embedded in this reliance are expectations; we wish for our close friends to possess certain attributes and behave in ways that we expect. Jeffrey Hall (2011) argues that expectations play a major role in establishing, maintaining, and terminating friendships. He also presents four expectations or highly valued qualities we have of friendships that we wish to explore: symmetrical reciprocity, communion, solidarity, and agency (Figure 11.1).

Hall (2011) states that **symmetrical reciprocity** includes a number of factors, including trust, loyalty, and genuineness. When symmetrical reciprocity exists, both members of the friendship strategically choose to enact behaviors that sustain friendship. Hall claims that

---

symmetrical reciprocity An expectation in friendship that occurs when both members of the friendship strategically choose to enact behaviors that sustain friendship.

communion An expectation in friendship whereby two friends are trying to unite in a compatible way.

solidarity An expectation in friendship that includes a sharing of mutual activities and the companionship of friends.

agency An expectation in friendship that arises when close friends perceive each other as possible resources and benefits.

---

symmetrical reciprocity is highly valued by both women and men and that without qualities such as these bonding behaviors, "a close friendship would not exist" (p. 725).

A second friendship expectation is called **communion**. Hall (2011) believes that communion is a "traditional dimension" (p. 726) of close friendships and includes self-disclosure, empathy, loyalty, and emotional availability. Communion is connection, meaning that two friends are trying to unite in some way. Two elements are at the core of a communion expectation: trust and intimacy. Hall notes that both qualities are especially important for women in their same-sex friendships. He adds that communion has often been undertaken in stressful times. In particular, because females have highly valued intimacy more than males, Hall concludes that from an evolutionary perspective, females have habitually formed "protective female coalitions" (p. 726).

Solidarity, a third expectation of friendship, refers to "sharing mutual activities and the companionship of friends" (Hall, 2011, p. 726). To understand solidarity, think of the times that you and a close friend go out for coffee, meet at a social event, or just chill together. These are all elements of a solidarity dimension. Hall indicates that time spent together is what promotes and sustains friendship solidarity. Research indicates that both males and females perceive solidarity to be an essential ingredient in a close friendship.

Hall (2011) also includes **agency** as a fourth expectation in close friendships. Agency expectations,

FIGURE 11.1　FRIENDSHIP EXPECTATIONS

Agency

⇓

Symmetrical Reciprocity ⇒ **FRIENDSHIP EXPECTATIONS** ⇐ **Solidarity**

⇑

Communion

© Cengage Learning®

according to Hall, arise when close friends are perceived as vehicles from whom benefits can be derived. Think of agency this way: In what ways can I benefit from the resources and talents of my close friend? Agency includes such factors as wealth, attractiveness, intellect, popularity/status, and physical abilities. An agency expectation is not suggesting that we exploit our close friends. Rather, we (and they) find various qualities that can come in handy should we be in need of them. Agency is more profound than, say, simply borrowing $10 from a close friend. This is the expectation that a friend would be available and able to lend the money to you. Hall found that males hold higher agency expectations than females.

The four expectations outlined by Hall (2011)—symmetrical reciprocity, communion, solidarity, and agency—are essential attributes that others would like their close friends to possess. Yet, many others exist, including expectations of compatibility, ego-reinforcement, a sense of humor, and a good personality. What others can you identify that have facilitated a close bond with your friends?

We continue our conversation about friendship by asking you to consider the following: As a 5-year-old, Anthony loved to play house. His mom set up a tent in the basement and he and his neighbor, Meghan, also a 5-year-old, would play "mom and dad." Anthony loved to "cook the meals" while Meghan loved to "plant flowers around the house."

Flash-forward a decade. While Anthony and Meghan still live next door to each other, they have taken drastically different friendship routes. Anthony is a soccer player at school and at times mixes with some other boys who, on occasion, smoke cigarettes. He's a "gamer" and loves to hang out with his three close friends, Evan, Jessie, and Terry. Meghan, however, goes to the mall with her best friend, Alicia, and the two often sit in the food court, texting other friends and although less than two feet from each other, text each other.

Now, as both Anthony and Meghan turn 21, they find themselves in different colleges and both have

"abandoned" their friends from a few years ago. Anthony still talks to his mother every week, but Meghan has a rather tense relationship with her parents and doesn't talk to them often. Both have started new friendships, and both were also a bit overwhelmed by all the demands that college required.

As they both approach 35, Anthony and Meghan are fully employed in jobs that they both really like. Anthony's closest friend is his work colleague and the two men are married and both have children. Meghan's college roommate, Angelique, remains her closest friend and although Meghan is not married, she and her friend reside in the same city and socialize quite a bit. The two also are tennis partners and they belong to a team that meets every other week.

Turning 50 saw the two childhood friends reflecting on their close friends. While Meghan remains single, she is still close friends with Angelique. Anthony's friends have expanded beyond his work colleagues and he is busy with his children and spends much more time with his wife than his close friends. Yet, he makes time for Eric, a neighbor whom he has lived next to for 11 years. They two hang out in the garage a lot, talking about sports, food, and their favorite TV reality show. And, during this time, Anthony and Meghan reconnected at their high school reunion. They were quite excited to meet up after so many years and exchanged email addresses.

Friendship is a lifespan experience. We are not inoculated from the ebbs and flows that go along with being a close friend to someone and others experience the same relational ups and downs with us. And, this friendship journey can be an exciting one! As the following two approaches explain, friendships between people typically fall along particular life markers. We start friendships a few years after we're born and like Anthony and Meghan, these friendships undergo quite a bit and continue in unforeseen ways. In this section of the chapter, we provide you two templates to understand friendship across the lifespan. We begin with a model representing our childhood.

11-2a Model of Childhood Friendship

Our friends we establish and maintain (and lose) as children may appear to be unimportant, but they are instrumental as a foundation for our future friends. Robert Selman (1981, 1997) has examined children's friendship development and considered children to be "friendship philosophers" (p. 242) insofar as they have the capacity to determine the ethical, moral, emotional, and cognitive dimensions of being a friend.

The following are considered Selman's Stages of Friendship in Childhood (see Table 11.2) and should be understood as age-related and hierarchical in complexity (Curtis-Tweed, 2011). A bit later, we explore friendship in adulthood.

Between the ages of 3 and 7, we engage in **momentary playmateship**, which we can identify as Stage 0. A friend occurs because this person lives in close proximity. The friendship is clearly on a physical level since it relies upon the children to play together and children who are conveniently located near each other.

momentary playmateship A stage in childhood friendship (ages 3–7) in which children play together because they are conveniently located near each other.

one-way assistance A stage in childhood friendship (ages 4–9) in which children show arrogance and egocentrism because they are incapable of being other-centered.

TABLE 11.2	STAGES OF CHILDHOOD FRIENDSHIP

Stage 0: Momentary Playmateship (Ages 3–7)

Description: Proximity defines the friendship and friends are valued because of their possessions

Perspective: "I want that!"

Stage 1: One-Way Assistance (Ages 4–9)

Description: Arrogance and egocentrism exists because children are incapable of being other-centered

Perspective: "What's in it for me?"

Stage 2: Two-Way, Fair-Weather Cooperation (Ages 6–12)

Description: Children begin to have self-reflection and conversational turn-taking

Perspective: "What do you think?"

Stage 3: Caring and Sharing (Ages 8–15)

Description: Mutuality begins to set in and children take an objective view of the friendship

Perspective: "Let me see if I can help you"

Stage 4: Mature Friendship (Ages 15 and up)

Description: More complex friendships are established because of interdependency and autonomy

Perspective: "We're trusting friends"

Interestingly, however, at this level, young children are viewed as philosophers who have instincts about how friendships develop and conflicts are resolved (Selman, 1981). Eileen Kennedy-Moore (2012) asserts that this level is similar to the claim "I want it my way" because children usually fight over such things as toys or space.

The level of **one-way assistance** occurs between the ages of 4 and 9. Stage 1 includes children who show arrogance and egocentrism because they are incapable of adopting an other-centeredness in their friendship ("I like her because she lets me play with her toys"). Friends at this stage are "close" because they are perceived as performing tasks that the "self" wants accomplished. The name of this stage says it all: it's all about getting and

receiving. This stage asks the question "What's in it for me?" (Kennedy-Moore, 2012).

When children are between the ages of roughly 6 to 12, they start to become newly aware of what an interpersonal relationship is. They begin being concerned with fairness and reciprocity and embrace turn taking in conversations. This second stage, called **two-way, fair-weather cooperation**, includes children understanding that friendship includes two people sharing (e.g., "two-way"), but if the exchange does not include something pleasant for them, they will exit the friendship (e.g., "fair-weather"). Kennedy-Moore (2012) contends that at this level, children "invent secret clubs" which involve a lot of rules and procedures. Yet, like the fleeting friendships at this level, the clubs don't last long.

Stage 3 begins the process of self-disclosure (see Chapter 8) between children and usually occurs between the ages of 8 and 15. This level includes early developments of "best friends" since there are many confidences shared between the two friends. This "**caring and sharing**" level (Kennedy-Moore, 2012) also finds children reflecting on the value of intimacy and the notion of "mutuality." Children begin to find a transactional friendship as having lasting importance and particularly in the early teen years, children are able to adopt an objective perspective of the friendship. Still, some jealousy and possessiveness may enter this stage and cause some unexpected conflict. This conflict, however, does not mean the end of the relationship, but merely an opportunity to adjust to the relational intimacy.

Stage 4 is the **mature friendship** and occurs from ages 12 and up. These friendships are rather stable, given the age group, and a sense of interdependence and autonomy begins to foster between the friends. Close friends at the mature friendship level accept the fact that they each have external relationships with others, and yet each will still rely on the other for social support. Close friends at this stage grow as they begin to understand the complexity of emotions and feelings related to being a friend.

Each of these stages, while unique, is not always discrete when we're talking about children. That is, some kids may be influenced by, say, family size in their friendship development. Others may have a certain family structure that will affect how their friends are formed. And, still others may be less comfortable or competent in their communication skills in establishing a friendship. Finally, regardless whether children develop close friendships in stages, researchers state that they will gain quite a bit through their friendships, including heightened self-esteem, an increased ability to cope with challenges, improved skills in decision making and problem solving, and healthier levels of empathy (Kennedy-Moore, 2013).

11-2b Adult Friendships

Like children, adults' friendships follow a path that is rather predictable. However, we don't want you to think that adult friendship models are finite and stage restricted. As we all know, friendships are often filled with surprises, especially in adulthood as we try to balance and negotiate a number of issues, including children, marriage, aging, death, birth, college, among many others. Furthermore, we are quick to point out that cultural background influences friendship formation and these cultural variations need to be acknowledged as you review the following. So, let's look at a practical approach to close friendship development that focuses on adults as conceptualized by Bill Rawlins (1992, 2008). As you consider this model, keep in mind how you might map

© iStock.com/Images_Bazaar

© Stokkete/Shutterstock.com

two-way, fair-weather cooperation A stage in childhood friendship (ages 6–12) in which children understand friendship as reciprocal, but if the friendship is unpleasant, they will exit the relationship.

caring and sharing A stage in childhood friendship (ages 8–15) in which children reflect on the value of intimacy and the notion of mutuality.

mature friendship A stage in childhood friendship (ages 12 and up) in which a sense of interdependence and autonomy begin to foster between friends.

out the stages in a close friendship of yours. The following reflects the stages of adult friendship development (see Table 11.3).

When we rely on polite conversations, engage in a fixed view of gender and cultural roles, and employ cliché forms of discourse, we are part of the first stage of adult friendships: **role-limited interaction**. When meeting someone, we stick with our social expectations and guidelines because the relationship is new to us. Our preliminary conversations are marked by what we call basic demographic information (e.g., "Where are you from?"; "What's your major?"; "You come here often?" etc.). Those who meet on Facebook or on a similar website, too, may start with standard, less vulnerable communication before meeting. Although this cliché level of dialogue may seem unimportant, it allows for both interactants to assess the similarities and differences between them. Here, a "friendship foundation" is laid for future meetings and interpersonal communication.

Rawlins (2008) notes that the second stage, **friendly relations**, is characterized by friends checking each other out and becoming less guarded about what they say. The small talk that depicted role-limited interaction has now shifted in terms of its content and risk level. We are more inclined to discuss something to figure out if we have something in common with the other person. At the friendly relations stage, we try to determine whether or not this early relationship has enough substance to become more long-term. In other words, we're trying to figure out the possibilities of this relationship.

Moving toward friendship, the third stage, is concerned with even more personal disclosures to the other. Rawlins admits that

TABLE 11.3 STAGES OF ADULT FRIENDSHIP DEVELOPMENT

Stage 1: Role-Limited Interaction ("Let's check this person out")

Perceptions and Behaviors: We stick with cultural rules and civility practices for talking to another person; we rely on the exchange of basic demographic information; we are cautious about opening ourselves up to another

Stage 2: Friendly Relations ("Do we have shared interests?")

Perceptions and Behaviors: We begin to engage in small talk and are less guarded about what we say to another; we assess the possibility of a long-term relationship; we place more focus on commonalities with the other person

Stage 3: Moving Toward Friendship ("I think this may be the one")

Perceptions and Behaviors: Increased self-disclosure occurs; we begin to move toward identifying the other as a close friend; we invite the other person to locations; if an Internet friendship, we agree to meet face-to-face

Stage 4: Nascent Friendship ("Let's work on making this a great friendship")

Perceptions and Behaviors: Communication patterns and routines set in; friends develop rules for conversations and the time they spend together

Stage 5: Stabilized Friendship ("What time should we get to their birthday party?")

Perceptions and Behaviors: We begin to trust the other person more than ever; there is a common belief that this is an enduring friendship; close friends and social circles merge; there are few "my" or "his" or "her" and more "our" and we

(Stage X) Waning Friendship ("Wow, what happened to us?")

Perceptions and Behaviors: Friendship intimacy bonds begin to decay; friends spend less and less time together, and the marker "best friend" is no longer used; friendship can be "repaired and saved" and trust can be rebuilt, prompting the relationship to move to a previous stage of development

© Cengage Learning®

this stage can be an experimental stage of sorts. That is, both friends begin to cautiously move toward identifying the other as a close friend, unsure of whether the vulnerability of disclosure will turn out poorly. It's likely that we may invite the other to locations so that both of you have the opportunity to spend time together. For instance, you may ask a classmate to study together for a midterm or ask a coworker to lunch. If you met over the Internet, you may decide to meet up in person to put a face to the words the two of you have shared.

Rawlins (2008) identifies the fourth stage as a **nascent friendship**, meaning that friendships start to blossom and build. During this stage, both friends agree to spend time together that would widen their activities

role-limited interaction A stage of adult friendship development whereby we adhere to social expectations and cultural guidelines for conversation.

friendly relations The second stage in adult friendship development characterized by friends checking each other out and becoming less guarded about what they say.

moving toward friendship The third stage in adult friendship development whereby friends begin to move cautiously toward more personal disclosures and more time spent together.

nascent friendship The fourth stage in adult friendship development whereby friends begin to widen their activities together; communication patterns and routines begin to emerge.

© Monkey Business Images/Shutterstock.com

and communication together. Patterns begin to emerge. Also, routine sets in. For example, we may go to Starbucks every Sunday evening or watch a college game every Saturday during football season. We will also likely hang out more in less strategic and more spontaneous ways, suggesting that high levels of security and belongingness needs are being met (see Chapter 10 for more on the hierarchy of relational needs). During this stage, friends begin to develop rules for their conversations and time together. The rules are co-constructed and are usually a result of much discussion. This stage sees the inevitable emergence of a very close friend.

A great deal of trust typifies those close friends who enter a **stabilized friendship**. Learning how to trust and how to be trustworthy is an essential component of a stabilized friendship. During this stage, friendship partners admit that they are close and their emotional bond suggests this is an enduring friendship. Those in the stabilized stage recognize that the friendship is primary and that if conflict ensues, they will have some relational rules that provide them ways to manage/resolve the conflict. Stabilized friendships witness close friends merging social circles; there are few "my" or "his" or "her" friends, but rather "our" friends. This integration necessitates an appreciation for the other's friendship values.

Interestingly, despite Rawlins's focus on friendship formation and development, he also contends that friends may also drift apart and for various reasons, decouple. He calls this the **waning friendship**. Intimacy bonds become broken, time spent together is reduced, and identifying the other as a "best friend" now seems so removed. Why does this happen? Well, for various reasons, whether it's related to a job, family, health, school, boredom, or new interests/activities, people may not sustain their close friendships. Both face-to-face and virtual relationships decay and breakups (via texting or social media) exist. Sometimes, it's beyond the control of the two people: graduation happens, one person needs to move to take care of a sick relative, as well as other events that are usually outside the control of friends. Other

times, however, a violation of trust may have occurred or another person may now occupy your time. These are clearly choices that are (or were) in the control of the close friend. So, waning may take place slowly or it may be abrupt, depending on the reasons for deterioration.

Waning may also prompt attitudinal and behavioral change. If both friends recognize that the relationship is important and wish to rebuild trust and compatibility, the waning stage may not last long. Depending on the severity of the waning period, the friendship may be able to stabilize.

Rawlins's proposed stages are not intended to capture all of our adult friendships, but rather present an evolutionary approach to how close friends develop their relationships. We have friendships that fall under each stage and in many cases, we may remain at a stage for years. Still, Rawlins identifies a process by which friends grow, and he marks the kinds of communication that indicate each stage.

As we've learned so far, friendships, then, are close relationships in which interpersonal communication plays a vital role—either in friendship escalation or in its deescalation. Friends communicate social support, solidarity, and positive affect as well as engage in other daily interactions that can intensify feelings of connection. But not all communication in friendship is positive; some communication behaviors may have toxic results and thus, what was once a close friendship can become a relationship to dissolve.

What happens when a friendship becomes much more intimate than we expected? In Western cultures, these may turn into romantic relationships. It is this close relationship that we now wish to examine to provide you further understanding of the diversity of close relationships in our lives.

11-3 ROMANTIC RELATIONSHIPS

Romance is often viewed as necessary and essential in lifelong relationships with others. As we begin our discussion about romantic relationships, think about your, well, romantic notions of the word *romantic*. We've all seen and listened to the nostalgic messages about being romantic, often depicted by a candlelight dinner, roses,

stabilized friendship The fifth stage in adult friendship development whereby close friends merge social circles, establish emotional bonds, and begin to appreciate the others' values on friendship.

waning friendship The stage in an adult friendship development that includes friends drifting apart for various reasons (e.g., job, health, school, boredom, etc.).

chocolates, tender touches and kisses, walking on a summer night on a beach, and so forth. Now think about the reality in most romantic relationships: paying bills, being exhausted, handling physical challenges, working long hours, shuttling children, and so forth. These two images of "romantic" are not incompatible; rather, they are reflective of the complexity and vastness of what takes place in our romantic relationships.

Early conceptions of romantic relationships focused on mating and creating a family. These days, however, most of us will agree that this option is rather limited. People establish and maintain romantic relationships for various purposes and numerous qualities of romantic relationships exist. And, given the diversity in the population, it's nearly impossible to develop one universal model of what constitutes romance. Therefore, we wish to elaborate on one of the primary and crucial foundations of romance: love (Lehmiller, 2014). We will close this section by providing representative research on romantic relationships.

The word *love* is one of those terms that people think they understand but have a tough time defining. We frequently use the term in ways that do not always reflect its value and importance ("I love this picture of a goat!"). Loving romantic relationships, however, reflect unique communication patterns, patterns that differentiate these relationships from, say, your friends or family.

The dimensionality of love has been discussed by Robert Sternberg (1998, 2006) through his **triangular theory of love**. He contends that love can be understood by examining three components, or dimensions, that, together, form the vertices of a triangle (see Figure 11.2): intimacy, passion, and commitment.

When a romantic relationship has closeness, connectedness, and bonding, it has **intimacy**. These qualities each play an essential role in love over and above other qualities. While we don't wish to reiterate this component of the triangle in too much detail (we detailed intimacy in Chapter 10), a few points merit attention as they relate to the triangle articulated by Sternberg. He observes that 10 elements are included in this vertex on the triangle:

► Desire to promote the welfare of the loved one

► Experiencing happiness with the loved one

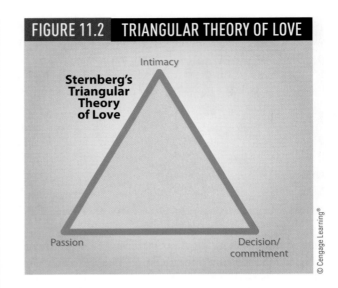

FIGURE 11.2   TRIANGULAR THEORY OF LOVE

Sternberg's Triangular Theory of Love

Intimacy

Passion

Decision/commitment

© Cengage Learning®

► Holding the loved one in high regard

► Being able to count on the loved one in times of need

► Having mutual understanding with the loved one

► Sharing oneself and one's possessions with the loved one

► Receiving emotional support from the loved one

► Giving emotional support to the loved one

► Communicating intimately with the loved one

► Valuing the loved one

It's not necessary, Sternberg believes, to experience all of these in order to experience intimacy. Rather, there is a "feeling" by one or both romantic partners that love is present; the couple may experience a small number of these to feel love. Or, maybe many are practiced at the right time. For instance, when Erika's dog died, Zack stayed with her for three days, holding her and letting her cry. Which of the preceding 10 qualities are represented in this example?

The component of **passion**, as Sternberg (1998) notes, refers to those drives that lead to desires, such as self-esteem, nurturance, affiliation, and sexual fulfillment. When people think of the word *passion*, they often think about it in sexual ways. Yet, while that is part of this dimension, other arousals also exist that demonstrate passion in a relationship. Think about the times where you strongly, but sensitively, expressed your opinion on an issue, such as whether you believe in cohabitating before marriage or waiting until marriage before living together. As long as the passion is undertaken with civility and other-centeredness (two components we identified in Chapter 1), this passion may demonstrate to another person that you have a relational spark and that you are willing to defend your perceptions.

A symbiotic relationship exists between passion and intimacy, according to Sternberg (1998). He contends that

triangular theory of love A theoretical perspective of love that includes three components: intimacy, passion, and commitment.

intimacy A component of the triangular theory of love that encompasses giving and receiving emotional support, holding a loved one in high regard, and so forth.

passion A component of the triangular theory of love that refers to those drives leading to desires such as nurturance, affiliation, and sexual fulfillment.

"intimacy in a relationship may be largely a function of the extent to which the relationship meets a person's need for passion. Conversely, passion may arouse intimacy" (p. 10). So, a romantic relationship may be passionate at first and this passion fuels the intimacy that eventually characterizes all close romantic relationships.

A third element in the triangular theory of love is **commitment** (or, decision/commitment), which is the likelihood to which a person will stick with another person. This vertex includes two aspects: **short-term commitment**, which is the decision to love a certain person, and **long-term commitment**, which is the decision to maintain that love. Sternberg cautions that there can sometimes be a commitment to a relationship in which a person didn't make the decision, such as those in arranged marriages. Most often, though, decisions precede commitment. Further, he states that conflict may ensue because of different perceptions of commitment. That is, two people may interpret their commitments differently and may not always be able to work out these disagreements. Imagine, for instance, the challenge that Ezra feels after 8 years of marriage to Henry. Although he professed commitment during the marriage ceremony, he now feels differently about the relationship. Ezra is committed and loves his husband, but he has had a change of heart with respect to the long-term nature of the marriage. Such a perceptual change occurs quite frequently in marriages across the country (Abela, Walker, & Pryor, 2013).

THEORY SPOTLIGHT:

Triangular Theory of Love

The three primary elements of the triangular theory of love are intimacy, passion, and commitment. Each is ever-present in most romantic relationships. Yet, can you, or have you ever, experienced a relationship whereby one or two of these are not present? Or, one or two (or all three) evolved slowly in the relationship. What did this evolution look like? Are you still in this relationship? If so, how do you maintain each of the components? If not, how were they affected in the relationship decay?

So, what does this theory have to say about the sorts of romantic relationships we find ourselves in? First, let's reiterate that these are not always distinct qualities; they are related. This means that you can simultaneously experience two or three qualities or you can experience one without the other. Second, think of these triangular elements as foundations of love. They each (along with other qualities we talk about throughout this book) provide an important relational "structure" that is needed to form a loving, lasting relationship with another. Third, sometimes, intimacy starts and stops in our romantic partnerships. As Sternberg (1998) explained: "The swinging back and forth of the intimacy pendulum provides some of the excitement that keeps many relationships alive" (p. 9).

Thus far, we've given you a sense of a valuable theoretical model related to the development and maintenance of romantic relationships. The triangular theory of love elaborates on one of the most significant components in romance: love. Let's now briefly talk about some research related to romantic relationships to illustrate the complexity and diversity in this area of study.

11-3a Saying "I Love You"

One area that has received some research attention relates to expressions of romantic affection. A pioneering study (Ackerman, Griskevicious, & Li, 2011) looked at the phrase "I love you" and questioned who—men or women—was more likely to confess this first to the other. Researchers asked the following question of heterosexual couples who had been together for an average of 84 months: Who is most likely to express romantic commitment first in a relationship? Ackerman and his team found that contrary to popular conception, men expressed love first in a romantic relationship (70 percent of couples agreed to this). In fact, men first thought about expressing their love an average six weeks before their female partners. What has been your experience with this phrase in your romantic relationships?

Additional research on romantic relationships has been both diverse and expansive. Much of this research is framed around relational scripts, a topic we addressed in Chapter 10. For our purposes here, think of *relational scripts* as mental stories we have about how people are to behave and the various roles they play in our various

---

commitment A component of the triangular theory of love that relates to the likelihood of an individual sticking with another individual.

short-term commitment The decision to love a certain person.

long-term commitment The decision to maintain love with another person.

relationships (Honeycutt & Bryan, 2011). For instance, although we know that couples break up and divorce, relational scripts suggest that romantic partners, in particular, will experience a relationship termination in a way that is usually different from, say, a close friend.

© Jason Winter/Shutterstock.com

As we already know, regardless of whether we're studying a same-sex or mixed-sex relationship, relational scripts function prominently. And, some research (e.g., Hall, Carter, Cody, & Albright, 2010; Knobloch, Miller, Bond, & Mannone, 2007; Levine, Aune, & Park, 2006) suggests that individual scripts for communicating in romantic relationships, in particular, can vary widely. For example, one group of researchers found that an individual's love style—passionate, stable, playful, other-centered, logical, or obsessive—made a difference in three communication practices during three stages of a relationship: opening lines for picking up someone as a potential partner, intensification strategies for moving a relationship along to greater intimacy, and secret tests for checking on the state of a developing relationship. For example, if Manny believes that love is playful, he'll use cute, flippant (and trite) pick-up lines like "God must be a thief. He stole the stars from the skies and put them in your eyes" (Levine et al., p. 478) to initiate a relationship, sexual intimacy to intensify it, and indirect secret tests like joking and hinting to check the state of a romance.

Other researchers (Guerrero & Bachman, 2006) found that how secure a person is affects how he or she communicates to maintain romantic relationships. People who are more secure tend to use more positive or prosocial behaviors. For example, if Amina is a secure person who's not anxious about relationships, she'll be likely to try to maintain her relationship with Jerome by saying "I love you," touching Jerome affectionately, complimenting him, and being open in her conversations with him. A different group of researchers (Knobloch et al., 2007) made a similar finding that married people who are uncertain about their marriages tend to interpret conversations pessimistically, whereas those who are more confident in their marriages draw more favorable conclusions.

One type of romantic relationship that has received recent research attention is the long-distance relationship (LDR), which is, as we know, a couple who continues to maintain a romantic relationship while separated geographically. While it would seem that being apart would strain LDRs, some research has found that LDRs persevere in profound ways. For example, in a study on romantic relationships following wartime deployment (Karakurt, Christiansen, Wadsworth, & Weiss, 2014), couples indicated that it was challenging to relearn how to be interdependent (again) and that there was an ongoing renegotiation of roles. Furthermore, the researchers found that during deployment, the couples relied on others for social support; once reunited, they gradually shifted back to relying on romantic partners for their social support. In a similar way, Lee Ann Knobloch and Jennifer Theiss (2014) identify relational turbulence following a tour of duty and that the reunion was emotionally volatile with heightened expectations. The research team discovered that couples found it tough returning to "normalcy," given the nuances of being separated for long periods of time.

In addition to military couples, some interpersonal communication research focuses on gay and lesbian couples (Suter, 2013) and multiracial couples (Thompson & Collier, 2006). Although many communication issues are the same across all romantic relationships, these relationships must also contend with issues of discrimination and identity. In both gay and multiracial relationships, the partners are aware of social disapproval. In some instances, they are alienated from friends and families. They are required to consider social and historical forces concerning race and sexual identity in ways that other couples are not and communication behaviors reflect this. So, for example, Danica (an African American woman) may tell her partner, Brad (a white man) that they need to be alert when they're visiting his hometown because many of the people there are racist. Brad may respond with some strategies they can use to manage any racist comments they might hear on the visit.

If you are in a romantic relationship now, chances are you're trying to make it work. Yet, we understand that like the relationships with our family members and friends, no matter how hard we try, unforeseen events will occur. As we know, we cannot control the future. To help you in this area, we close our chapter with some suggestions

TABLE 11.4 PEOPLE'S NOTIONS OF LOVE

Addiction	Strong anxious attachment; clinging behavior; anxiety at thought of losing partner
Art	Love of partner for physical attractiveness; importance to person of partner's always looking good
Business	Relationships as business propositions; money is power
Cookbook	Doing things a certain way (recipe) results in relationship being more likely to work out
Fantasy	To be saved by a knight in shining armor, or marry a princess and live happily ever after
Game	Love as a game or sport
Horror	Relationships become interesting when you terrorize or are terrorized by your partner
Mystery	Love is a mystery and you shouldn't let too much of yourself be known
Police	You've got to keep close tabs on your partner to make sure he/she "toes the line"
Science	Love can be understood, analyzed, and dissected, just like any other natural phenomenon
Sewing	Love is whatever you make it
Theatre	Love is scripted, with predictable acts, scenes, and lines
War	Love is a series of battles in a devastating but continuing war

Source: Sternberg (2013, p. 99).

© Cengage Learning®

of how to sustain quality interpersonal relationship with a family member, close friend, and/or romantic partner.

11-4 SKILL SET: STRATEGIES TO IMPROVE YOUR INTERPERSONAL COMMUNICATION WITH FAMILY MEMBERS, CLOSE FRIENDS, AND ROMANTIC PARTNERS

In Chapter 10, we identified numerous skills that are relevant to close relationships overall. As you may recall, we incorporated a myriad of strategies to consider as you initiate, maintain, and repair your relationships. In this chapter, although many of the skills we identified in Chapter 10 are clearly relevant to consider in this chapter, we

believe that taken together, there are three primary qualities to put in motion as you communicate with your family, close friends, and romantic partners. Of course, as you reflect on many of the skills we've already identified throughout this book (e.g., listening, nonverbal effectiveness, cultural awareness), you will soon see that much of what we've presented already can be applied to a number of your interpersonal relationships. Nonetheless, let's outline three different skills and along the way, we will include examples from the three relational types we discussed in this chapter.

11-4a Take Time to C.A.R.E.

To suggest that we should care about another person may seem a bit far removed as you have arguments or heated discussions with say, a spouse who won't clean up after himself. Still, as we think about this suggestion and its roots in Carol Gilligan's ethical system (discussed in Chapter 1), we need to be diligent in this connection.

We think that C.A.R.E. (Constantly Assessing Relationship Excellence) can take many forms. We demonstrate care/C.A.R.E. by practicing some of the skills of empathy and other-centeredness, behaviors we addressed in Chapter 6. Caring also includes the willingness to be mindful of the relationship's value to you. Consider a family relationship. It's easy to lose sight of a family member's value if we are mad at her because of her words or insensitive remarks. Think about, for instance, 45-year-old Shannon's experience with Mary, her 50-year-old sister. As the two discussed what to do with their aging mother, a lot of very tense back-and-forth ensued. One dialogue especially stood out:

Mary: "You have no idea what it's like because you chose not to have kids! It's killing her to know that she has to leave this house! If you weren't so wrapped up in your little life and worrying about your Caribbean vacations, you'd know that this is tough for her."

Shannon: "I'm going to listen to someone who has secretly written checks from mom's account to pay for your teeth whitening? I don't think so!"

Clearly, the two are in a difficult conflict and although they have been quite close over the years, the stress related to their mother's fragility has obviously wreaked havoc on this family relationship. We would suggest that the two take time to extend caring qualities to each other. Families, in particular, are prone to lapses in care because there is a "take-for-granted" quality; in most cases, we believe we know what makes our family members tick. Yet, especially in challenging times, retaining an ethic of care should remain paramount.

11-4b Recognize Your History Together

Caring is best accompanied by an understanding of the relation's past. Staying aware of relational history is a valued skill to practice in our relationships with family members, close friends, and romantic partners. The time and co-created experiences help to establish a foundation as the relationship evolves and this foundation will be instrumental to draw upon for future reference. For example, think about your closest friend. Now, think about what the two of you have gone through. There may have been late night conversations about boyfriends, endless dialogues over coffee about careers, frequent bouts of shared anxieties about finances, among many other situations that have bonded the two of you. This relational history should not be discarded as the friendship moves to higher levels of intimacy. As we know from Chapter 8, self-disclosure is essential in relationship-building. We also know that reciprocal self-disclosure is essential to relational growth.

Our times with a close friend serve to facilitate a long-term cooperative relationship. Recall that friendship generally goes through various stages in our lifespan. Furthermore, consider, too, that throughout our lives, we will cultivate friendships with people from all cultural backgrounds. Particularly as adults, we need to be cognizant of our relationship development and all the various factors that contributed to its importance.

relationship ruts Patterns of relationship behavior that become dull and unproductive.

11-4c Find Ways to Keep the Relationship "Alive"

The fundamental assumption sustained throughout this chapter is that our family, close friendships, and romantic relationships are central in our lives. Still, it's likely that you find yourself in **relationship ruts**, or patterns of relational behavior that become dull and unproductive. Romantic relationships sometimes become lackluster and fall prey to rituals that undercut the vibrancy of the relationship. We already know that connection is closer to intimacy than disconnection. So, when there is "routinized intimacy," habitual arguments about petty issues (e.g., "Why do you keep leaving the freezer door open?!"), an absence of affection, or a job that takes priority over your relational partner, a rut is setting in.

What helps us to avoid relationship ruts? First, practice random acts of romance (Gray, 2011). This includes doing things that have been missing for years, such as having a "date night," a weekend getaway, or providing "love notes" in unexpected places (e.g., next to your partner's toothbrush, etc.). Even everyday actions can be repackaged to avoid ruts. Stale and boring do not have to replace new and exciting. Think about greeting your partner at the door with a prolonged hug or kiss, rather than a "hello." Or, consider getting a romantic card and placing it between the screen and keyboard of your partner's laptop. You might even leave a sexy note on the bathroom mirror as a reminder of the passion that was once present.

Although we have focused on romantic relationships, all interpersonal relationships can use some spice! We should confront any relational rut head on and talk openly with the other person. Together, two people will be able to resolve an unwelcomed stale relationship productively.

11-4d Ensure Equity When Possible

In its basic form, equity is fairness. And, equity comes in many forms, including emotional, financial, physical, as well as other dimensions of a relationship (Kelley, 2012). Today, more than ever, couples and families are demanding that they live in equitable relationships. Spouses share domestic duties. Children collaborate with their parents. Close friends return phone calls and contribute equally to a costly night out.

Despite these overtures of relational justice, we still find ourselves in relationships that are very imbalanced. Although husbands may be doing more around the house, for instance, a gendered division of household labor continues with women experiencing a "second shift" (Hochschild & Machung, 2003), which describes a woman working outside the home and returning home to take care of the children. Imbalances occur, too, with dating couples.

One who discloses more personal information without the other reciprocating can be distressing and cause a partner to feel guilty or angry (Hatfield & Rapson, 2011).

Family members, close friends, and romantic partners need to keep in mind that caring about the other requires communication that is equitable and just. No matter how good a relationship is, in order for it to survive the various challenges, individuals need to be equal. When interpersonal desires and needs conflict, both people in the relationship need to be "communally oriented" (Hatfield & Rapson, 2011, p. 207) and work toward ensuring an equitable outcome.

In the end, every relationship experiences various levels of intimacy. It's the responsibility of both partners to construct an action plan that will ensure the relationship's vitality for years to come.

STUDY TOOLS

DON'T FORGET TO CHECK OUT COURSEMATE AT WWW.CENGAGEBRAIN.COM!

CHAPTER 11 FEATURES THE FOLLOWING RESOURCES:

☐ Communication Assessment Test: The Listening Inventory

☐ Interactive Activities

REFERENCES

A

Abela, A., Walker, J., & Pryor, J. (2013). *Marriage and divorce in the Western world*. Oxford: Wiley-Blackwell.

Ackerman, J. M., Griskevicius, V., & Li, N. (2011). Let's get serious: Communicating commitment in romantic relationships. *Journal of Personality and Social Psychology, 100,* 1079–1094.

Aerobics and Fitness Association of America (AFAA). (2013). Become a personal trainer. Retrieved from http://www.afaa.com/Personal-Trainer.html

Afifi, T. D., McManus, T., Hutchinson, S., & Baker, B. (2007). Inappropriate parental divorce disclosures, the factors that prompt them, and their impact on parents' and adolescents' well-being. *Communication Monographs, 74,* 78–102.

Afifi, W. A., & Guerrero, L. K. (2000). Motivations underlying topic avoidance in close relationships. In S. Petronio (Ed.), *Balancing the secrets of private disclosures* (pp. 165–179). Mahwah, NJ: Erlbaum.

Ahrons, C. R. (2011). Divorce: An unscheduled family transition. In M. McGoldrick, B. Carter, & N. Garcia Preto (Eds.), *The expanded family life cycle: Individual, family, and social perspectives* (pp. 292–306). Boston: Allyn & Bacon.

Alim, H. S. (2012). Interview with Geneva Smitherman. *Journal of English Linguistics, 40,* 357–377.

Allendorf, K. (2013). Schemas of marital change: From arranged marriages to eloping for love. *Journal of Marriage and Family, 75,* 453–469.

Aloia, L. S., & Solomon, D. H. (2013). Perceptions of verbal aggression in romantic relationships: The role of family history and motivational systems. *Western Journal of Communication, 77,* 411–423.

Altman, I., & Taylor, D. (1973). *Social penetration: The development of interpersonal relationships.* New York: Holt, Rinehart & Winston.

Andersen, J. (1996). *Communication theory: Epistemological foundations.* New York: Guilford.

Andersen, P. (2008). *Nonverbal communication: Forms and functions.* Long Grove, IL: Waveland.

Anderson, R., & Ross, V. (2002). *Questions of communication: A practical introduction to theory.* New York: St. Martin's.

Aoki, S., & Uchida, O. (2011). An automatic method to generate the emotional vectors of emoticons using blog articles. *International Journal of Computers, 5,* 346–353.

Asante, M. K. (1998). *The Afrocentric idea.* Philadelphia: Temple University Press.

Asante, M. K., Miike, Y., & Yin, J. (Eds.). (2013). *The global intercultural communication reader.* New York: Routledge.

Aschwanden, C. (2013, December 24). The joy of pain and what we get out of it. *New York Times.* Retrieved from http://www.nytimes.com

Aune, K. S., & Aune, R. K. (1996). Cultural differences in the self-reported experience and expression of emotions in relationships. *Journal of Cross-Cultural Psychology, 27,* 67–81.

B

Bachman, G. F., & Guerrero, L. K. (2006). Relational quality and communicative responses following hurtful events in dating relationships: An expectancy violations analysis. *Journal of Social and Personal Relationships, 23,* 943–963.

Baddeley, A. (2012). Working memory: Theories, models, and controversy. *Annual Reviews of Psychology, 63,* 1–29.

Ballard, D. I., & Seibold, D. R. (2000). Time orientation and temporal variation across work groups: Implications for group and organizational communication. *Western Journal of Communication, 64,* 218–242.

Barner, D., Inagaki, S., & Li, P. (2009). Language, thought, and real nouns. *Cognition, 111,* 329–344.

Barnes, S. B. (2003). *Computer-mediated communication: Human-to-human communication across the Internet.* Boston: Allyn & Bacon.

Barnlund, D. C. (1970). A transactional model of communication. In K. K. Sereno & C. D. Mortensen (Eds.), *Foundations of communication theory* (pp. 83–102). New York: Harper & Row.

Barr, D., & Selman, R. L. (1997) Pair therapy and pairing for prevention: Two developmental approaches for a spectrum of needs. In N. E. Alessi, T. J. Coyle, S. Harrison, & S. Eth (Eds.), *Handbook of child and adolescent psychiatry: Vol. 6. Basic psychiatric science and treatment* (pp. 423–431). New York: Wiley.

Batanova, M. D., & Loukas, A. (2013). Maternal psychological control and peer victimization in early adolescence: An application of the family relational schema model. *Journal of Early Adolescence, 32,* 206–228.

Bateson, G. (1972). *Steps to an ecology of mind.* New York: Ballantine Books.

Bauerlein, M. (2009). *The dumbest generation: How the digital age stupefies young Americans and jeopardizes our future (or, don't trust anyone under 30).* London: Penguin Books.

Bavelas, J. B. (1994). Gestures as part of speech: Methodological implications. *Research on Language and Social Interaction, 27,* 201–222.

Baxter, L. A. (1988). A dialectical perspective on communication strategies in relationship development. In S. Duck (Ed.), *A handbook of personal relationships* (pp. 257–273). New York: Wiley.

Baxter, L. A. (2011). *Voicing relationships: A dialogic perspective.* Thousand Oaks, CA: Sage.

Baxter, L. A., & Braithwaite, D. O. (2002). Performing marriage: Marriage renewal rituals as cultural performance. *Southern Communication Journal, 67,* 94–109.

Bazarova, N. N., Taft, J. G., Choi, Y. H., & Cosley, D. (2013). Managing impressions and relationships on Facebook: Self-presentational and relational concerns revealed through the analysis of language style. *Journal of Language and Social Psychology, 32,* 121–141.

BBC News. (1999, June 1). New technology makes work harder. Retrieved from http://news.bbc.co.uk

Bechar-Israeli, H. (1996). From <Bonehead> to <cLoNehEAd>: Nicknames, play and identity on the Internet Relay Chat. Retrieved from http://www.ascusc.org

Bedrosian, T. A., Vaughn, C. A., Galan, A., Daye, G., Weil, Z. M., & Nelson, R. J. (2013). Nocturnal light exposure impairs affective responses in a wavelength-dependent manner. *Journal of Neuroscience, 33,* 13081–13087.

Behrendt, H., & Ben-Ari, R. (2012). The positive side of negative emotion: The role of guilt and shame in coping with interpersonal conflict. *Journal of Conflict Resolution, 56,* 1116–1138.

Belin, P., Campanella, S., Ethofer, T. (2013). (Eds.). *Integrating face and voice in person perception.* New York: Springer.

Bell, R. A., & Daly, J. A. (1984). The affinity-seeking function of communication. *Communication Monographs, 51,* 91–115.

Bem, S. (1993). *The lenses of gender: Transforming the debate on sexual inequality.* New Haven, CT: Yale University Press.

Benjamin, B., & Werner, R. (2004). Touch in the Western world. *Massage Therapy Journal, 43,* 28–32.

Bentley, S. C. (2000). Listening in the 21st century. *International Journal of Listening, 14,* 129–142.

Beren, S. A. (2014). *The sandwich generation's guide.* Seattle: Amazon Digital.

Berg, J. H., & Archer, R. L. (1980). Disclosure or concern: A second look at liking for the norm-breaker. *Journal of Personality, 48,* 245–257.

Bevan, J. L., Tidgewell, K. D., Bagley, K. C., Cusanelli, L., Hartstern, M., Holbeck, D., & Hale, J. L. (2007). Serial argumentation goals and their relationships to perceived resolvability and choice of conflict tactics. *Communication Quarterly, 55,* 61–77.

Biblarz, T. J., & Savci, E. (2010). Lesbian, gay, bisexual, and transgender families. *Journal of Marriage and Family, 72,* 480–497.

Bippus, A., & Young, S. (2012). *Using appraisal theory to predict emotional and coping responses to hurtful messages.* Retrieved from http://interpersona.psychopen.eu/article/view/99/111.

Bizumic, B. (2014). Who coined the concept of ethnocentrism? A brief report. *Journal of Social and Political Psychology, 2.* doi:10.5964/jspp.v2i1.264

Blake, R. R., & Mouton, J. S. (1964). *The managerial grid: Key orientations for achieving production through people.* Houston: Gulf.

Blumer, H. (1969). *Symbolic interactionism: Perspective and method.* Englewood Cliffs, NJ: Prentice Hall.

Bochner, A. P. (1982). On the efficacy of openness in close relationships. In M. Burgoon (Ed.), *Communication yearbook 5* (pp. 109–124). New Brunswick, NJ: Transaction Books.

Bodie, G. D., Honeycutt, J. M., & Vickery, A. J. (2013). An analysis of the correspondence between imagined interaction attributes and functions. *Human Communication Research, 39,* 157–183.

Bodie, G. D., Worthington, D. W., & Fitch-Hauser, M. (2011). A comparison of four measurement models for the Watson-Barker listening test (WBLT)—Form C. *Communication Research Reports, 28,* 32–42.

Bohannon, L. S., Herbert, A. M., Pelz, J. B., & Rantanen, E. M. (2013). Eye contact and video-mediated communication: A review. *Displays, 34,* 177–185.

Bond, C. D. (2012). An overview of best practices to teach listening skills. *International Journal of Listening, 26,* 61–63.

Booth-Butterfield, M., & Booth-Butterfield, S. (1998). *Emotionality and affective orientation.* In J. C. McCroskey, J. A. Daly, M. M. Martin, & M. J. Beatty (Eds.), *Communication and personality: Trait perspectives* (pp. 171–190). Cresskill, NJ: Hampton.

Boston Herald. (2010, March 1). Rally aims to make 'retard' new dirty word.

Bostrom, R. N. (1990). *Listening behavior: Measurement and application.* New York: Guilford.

Bostrom, R. N., & Waldhart, E. S. (1988). Memory models in the measurement of listening. *Communication Education, 37,* 1–12.

Boyle, L. (2013, July 3). Big Brother *contestants' racist and homophobic rants caught on live feed but are edited out of episodes by CBS.* Retrieved from http://www.dailymail.co.uk/news/article-2354948 /Big-Brother-contestants-racist-homophobic-rants -caught-live-feed-edited-CBS-network.html.

Bradford, L. (1993). *A cross-cultural study of strategic embarrassment in adolescent socialization.* Unpublished doctoral dissertation, Arizona State University. *Dissertation Abstracts International. A: The humanities and social sciences, 29,* 2003.

Bradford, L., & Petronio, S. (1998). Strategic embarrassment: The culprit of emotion. In P. A. Andersen & L. K. Guerrero (Eds.), *The handbook of communication and emotion* (pp. 99–121). San Diego, CA: Academic Press.

Brody, J. E. (2002, May 28). Why angry people can't control the short fuse. *New York Times,* D7.

Brownell, J. (2012). *Listening: Attitudes, principles, and skills.* Boston: Pearson.

Bryant, L. E. (2006). Ritual (in)activity in postbereaved stepfamilies. In L. H. Turner & R. West (Eds.), *Sourcebook of family communication* (pp. 281–296). Thousand Oaks, CA: Sage.

Bryner, J. (2007, April 11). Hip e-mail addresses bad for résumés. Retrieved from http://www.msnbc .msn.com

Buber, M. (1970). *I and thou* (W. Kaufmann, Trans.). New York: Scribner.

Bullying Awareness Week. (2014). http:// www .bullyingawarenessweek.org

Bullying Statistics. (2014). Cyber bullying statistics. Retrieved from http://www.bullyingstatistics. org/content/cyber-bullying-statistics.html

Burgoon, J. K. (1978). A communication model of personal space violation: Explication and an initial test. *Human Communication Research, 4,* 129–142.

Burgoon, J. K. (2009). Expectancy violations theory. In S. W. Littlejohn & K. Foss (Eds.), *Encyclopedia of communication theory* (pp. 367–369). Thousand Oaks, CA: Sage.

Burgoon, J. K., Buller, D. B., & Woodall, W. G. (1996). *Nonverbal communication: The unspoken dialogue.* New York: McGraw-Hill.

Burgoon, J. K., & Hoobler, G. D. (2002). Nonverbal signals. In M. L. Knapp & J. A. Daly (Eds.), *Handbook of interpersonal communication* (pp. 240–299). Thousand Oaks, CA: Sage.

Burgoon, J. K., Stern, L. A., & Dillman, L. (1995). *Interpersonal adaptation: Dyadic interaction patterns.* New York: Cambridge University Press.

Burleson, B. R. (2003). Emotional support skills. In J. O. Greene & B. R. Burleson (Eds.), *Handbook of communication and social interaction skills* (pp. 551–594). Mahwah, NJ: Erlbaum.

Burleson, B. R., Holmstrom, A. J., & Gilstrap, C. M. (2005). "Guys can't say *that* to guys": Four experiments assessing the normative motivation account for deficiencies in the emotional support provided by men. *Communication Monographs, 72,* 468–501.

Burrell, N. A., Buzzanell, P. M., & McMillan, J. J. (1992). Feminine tensions in conflict situations as revealed by metaphoric analyses. *Management Communication Quarterly, 6,* 115–149.

Buston, P. M., & Emlen, S. T. (2003). Cognitive processes underlying human mate .choice: The relationship between self-perception and mate preference in Western society. *Proceedings of the National Academy of Sciences, 100,* 8805–8810.

Butler, J. (2013). Metaphorically examining organizational communication: A student's perspective. *Communication Teacher, 27,* 161–164.

Buysse, A., De Clercq, A., Verhofstadt, L., Heene, E., Roeyers, H., & Van Oost, P. (2000). Dealing with relational conflict: A picture in milliseconds. *Journal of Social and Personal Relationships, 17,* 574–597.

Buzzanell, P. M. (1999). Tensions and burdens in interviewing processes: Perspectives of non-dominant group applicants. *Journal of Business Communication, 36,* 134–162.

Buzzanell, P. M., & Turner, L. H. (2003). Emotion work revealed by job loss discourse: Backgrounding-foregrounding of feelings, construction of normalcy, and (re)instituting of traditional masculinities. *Journal of Applied Communication Research, 31,* 27–57.

Buzzanell, P. M., & Turner, L. H. (2012). Effective family communication and job loss: Crafting the narrative for family crisis. In F. C. Dickson & L. M. Webb (Eds.), *Communication for families in crisis: Theories, research, strategies* (pp. 281–306). New York: Lang.

Byers, D. (2013, April 3). 'An African American', or 'a black'? On Media, *Politico.*

C

Cahn, D., & Abigail, R. (2007). *Conflict management through communication.* Boston: Allyn & Bacon.

Callaghan, D. E., Graff, M. G., & Davies, J. (2013). Revealing all: Misleading self-disclosure rates in laboratory-based online research. *Cyberpsychology, Behavior, and Social Networking, 16,* 690–694.

Campbell, A., Carrick, L., & Elliott, R. (2013). A hierarchy of personal agency for people with life-limiting illness. *American Journal of Hospice and Palliative Medicine, 30,* 2–9.

Campbell, D. (2013, September 5). *Abundant photography: The misleading metaphor of the image flood.* Retrieved from http://www.david -campbell.org/2013/09/05/abundant-photography -misleading-metaphor-image-flood/

Canary, D. J., Cupach, W. R., & Serpe, R. T. (2001). A competence-based approach to examining interpersonal conflict: Test of a longitudinal model. *Communication Research, 28,* 79–104.

Canary, D. J., & Hause, K. S. (1993). Is there any reason to research sex differences in communication? *Communication Quarterly, 41,* 129–144.

Canary, D. J., & Stafford, L. (1992). Relational maintenance strategies and equity in marriage. *Communication Monographs, 59,* 243–267.

Capps, R., Bachmeier, J. D., Fix, M., & Van Hook, J. (2013). *A demographic, socioeconomic, and health coverage profile of the unauthorized immigrants in the United States.* Issue Brief No. 5, May. Washington, DC: Migration Policy Institute. Retrieved from http://migrationpolicy.org/research /demographic-socioeconomic-and-health-coverage -profile-unauthorized-immigrants-united-states

Carbaugh, D. (1999). "Just listen": "Listening" and landscape among the Blackfeet. *Western Journal of Communication, 63,* 250–270.

Career Profiles. (2014). *Qualities of top law enforcement professionals.* Retrieved from http://www .careerprofiles.info/law-enforcement-professional-qualities.html

Carmel, S. (2012). Lack of self-disclosure and verbal communication about emotions as a precipitant of affairs. *Couple and Family Psychoanalysis, 2,* 181–197.

Carmon, A .F. (2014). Is it necessary to be clear? An examination of strategic ambiguity in family business mission statements. *Qualitative Research Reports in Communication, 14,* 87–96.

Carnevale, A. P., & Smith, N. (2013). Workplace basics: The skills employees need and employers want. *Human Resource Development, 16,* 491–501. doi: 10.1080/13678868.2013.821267

Carr, K., & Wang, T. R. (2012). "Forgiveness isn't a simple process: It's a vast undertaking": Negotiating and communicating forgiveness in nonvoluntary family relationships. *Journal of Family Communication, 12,* 40–56.

Carr, K., Schrodt, P., & Ledbetter, A. M. (2012). Rumination, conflict intensity, and perceived resolvability as predictors of motivation and likelihood of continuing serial arguments. *Western Journal of Communication, 76,* 480–502.

Carrasquillo, H. (1997). Puerto Rican families in America. In M. K. DeGenova (Ed.), *Families in cultural context: Strengths and challenges in diversity* (pp. 155–172). Mountain View, CA: Mayfield.

Carter, B. (2013, November 15). *MSNBC suspends Alec Baldwin and his talk show.* Retrieved from http://www.nytimes.com

Carter, P. J., & Gibbs, R. J. (2013). *Using horrific body and avatar creation as an extension of the Proteus effect.* Retrieved from http://eprints.hud .ac.uk

Cash, T. F., & Derlega, V. J. (1978). The matching hypothesis: Physical attractiveness among same-sexed friends. *Personality and Social Psychology Bulletin, 4,* 240–243.

Cass, C. (2013, December 1). *Survey finds Americans losing trust in each other.* Retrieved from http://www.bostonglobe.com/news/nation /2013/12/01/god-trust-maybe-but-not-each-other /TXYOuxPsqEDPF4WcGNO7lL/story.html?s _campaign=8315

Castro, D. R., Cohen, A., Tohar, G., & Klugar, A. N. (2013). The role of active listening in teacher-parent relations and the moderating role of attachment style. *International Journal of Listening, 27.* 136–145.

Caughlin, J. P., & Vangelisti, A. L. (2000). An individual difference explanation of why married couples engage in the demand/withdraw pattern of conflict. *Journal of Social and Personal Relationships, 17,* 523–551.

Chen, G. M. (2013). Losing *face* on social media: Threats to *positive face* lead to an indirect effect on retaliatory aggression through negative affect. *Communication Research, 12.* doi: 10.1177/0093650213510937

Chen, G. M., & Starosta, W. J. (2006). Intercultural awareness. In L. A. Samovar, R. E. Porter, & E. McDaniel (Eds.), *Intercultural communication: A reader* (pp. 357–365). Belmont, CA: Wadsworth.

Chen, V. (2013, December 9). When stay-at-home husbands are embarrassing to their wives. *Time.* Retrieved from http://ideas.time.com/2013/12/09/the-househusbands-of-wall-street/

Cherwin, K. A. (2011, August). Using emotional intelligence to teach. Retrieved from http://www.higheredjobs.com/Articles/articleDisplay.cfm?ID=285

Chopra, R. (2001). Retrieving the father: Gender studies, "father love" and the discourse of mothering. *Women's Studies International Forum, 24,* 445–455.

Chui, J., Manyika, J., Bughin, J., Dobbs, R., Roxburgh, C., Sarrazin, H., Sands, G., & Westergren, M. (2012, July). *The social economy: Unlocking value and productivity through social technologies.* Washington, DC: McKinsey Global Institute. Retrieved from http://www.mckinsey.com/insights/high_tech_telecoms_internet/the_social_economy

Clark, D. (2013). Debunking the "no friends at work" rule: Why friend-friendly workplaces are the future. Retrieved from http://dorieclark.com/debunking-the-no-friends-at-work-rule-why-friend-friendly-workplaces-are-the-future/

Coates, J., & Cameron, D. (Eds.). (1989). *Women and their speech communities.* New York: Longman.

Cole, S. W., Kemeny, M. E., Taylor, S. E., Visscher, B. R., & Fahey, J. L. (1996). Accelerated course of human immunodeficiency virus infection in gay men who conceal their homosexual identity. *Psychosomatic Medicine, 58,* 219–231.

Colyn, L. A., & Gordon, A. K. (2013). Schadenfreude as a mate-value-tracking mechanism. *Personal Relationships, 20,* 524–545.

Cooks, L. (2000). Family secrets and the lie of identity. In S. Petronio (Ed.), *Balancing the secrets of private disclosures* (pp. 197–211). Mahwah, NJ: Erlbaum.

Corballis, M. C. (2011). *The recursive mind.* Princeton, NJ: Princeton University Press.

Côté, S., DeCelles, K. A., McCarthy, J. M.,Van Kleef, G. A., & Hideg, I. (2011). The Jekyll and Hyde of emotional intelligence: Emotion-regulation knowledge facilitates both prosocial and interpersonally deviant behavior. *Psychological Science, 22,* 1073–1080.

Coupland, N., & Nussbaum, J. F. (Eds.). (1993). *Discourse and lifespan identity.* Newbury Park, CA: Sage.

Craig, H. K., & Grogger, J. T. (2012). Influences of social and style variables on adult usage of African American English features. *Journal of Speech, Language, and Hearing Research, 55,* 1274–1288.

Craig, R. T. (2003). *Discursive origins of a communication discipline.* Paper presented at the annual meeting of the National Communication Association, Miami, FL.

Craig, R. T. (2007). Pragmatism in the field of communication theory. *Communication Theory, 17,* 125–145.

Craig, R. T. (2013). Communication theory and social change. *Communication & Social Change, 1,* 5–18 doi: 10.4471/csc.2013.01

Crane, D. R., Dollahite, D. C., Griffin, W., & Taylor, V. L. (1987). Diagnosing relationships with spatial distance: An empirical test of a clinical principle. *Journal of Marital and Family Therapy, 13*(3), 307–310.

Croucher, S. M., Bruno, A., McGrath, P., Adams, C., McGahan, C., Suits, A., & Huckins, A. (2012). Conflict styles and high-low context cultures: A cross-cultural extension. *Communication Research Reports, 29,* 64–73.

Cupach, W. R., & Canary, D. G. (2000). *Competence in interpersonal conflict.* Prospect Heights, IL: Waveland Press.

Cupach, W. R., & Imahori, T. T. (1993). Identity management theory communication competence in intercultural episodes and relationships. In R. L. Wiseman, & J. Koester (Eds.), *Intercultural communication competence* (pp. 112–131). Newbury Park, CA: Sage.

Cupach, W. R., & Metts, S. M. (1994). *Facework.* Thousand Oaks, CA: Sage.

Cupach, W. R., & Spitzberg, B. H. (2014). *The dark side of relationship pursuit: From attraction to obsession and stalking.* New York: Routledge.

Current Population Survey. (2013). Retrieved from http://timewellness.files.wordpress.com/2013/11/stay-at-home-parents.png

Curtis-Tweed, P. (2011). Selman's stages of friendship development. In S. Goldstein & J. Neglieri (Eds.), *Encyclopedia of child behavior and development* (pp. 1327–1328). New York: Springer.

D

Daily Herald (Provo, UT). (2013, May 19). Scared in school: Bullying statistics. Retrieved from http://www.heraldextra.com/news/local/education/precollegiate/scared-in-school-bullying-statistics/article_74844177-1669-5ef5-9609-2c7234e92987.html

Davis, E., Greenberger, E., Charles, S., & Chen, C., Zhao, L., & Dong, Q. (2012). Emotion experience and regulation in China and the United States: How do culture and gender shape emotion responding? *International Journal of Psychology, 47,* 230–239.

Davis, K. (2012). Friendship 2.0: Adolescents' experiences of belonging and self-disclosure online. *Journal of Adolescence, 35,* 1527–1536.

Davis, M. S. (1973). *Intimate relations.* New York: Free Press.

Deakin, M. B. (2013, Winter). A crazy gift of tragedy. *UUWorld, 27,* 8–11.

DeFrancisco, V. P, & Palczewski, C. (2014). *Gender in communication: A critical introduction.* Thousand Oaks, CA: Sage.

Dell'Antonia, K. (2013, November 21). A stillbirth's living silver linings. Motherlode blog, *New York Times* online.

Demby, G. (2013, April 8). How code-switching explains the world. *Code Switch: Frontiers of Race, Culture, and Ethnicity,* NPR. Retrieved from http://www.npr.org/blogs/codeswitch/2013/04/08/176064688/how-code-switching-explains-the-world

Denn, R. (2012, January 18). No sympathy for deep-fried queen Paula Deen's diabetes. Retrieved from http://seattletimes.com/html/allyoucaneat/2017267798_sympathy_for_paula_deens_diabe.html

Derlega, V. J., Metts, S., Petronio, S., & Margulis, S. T. (1993). *Self-disclosure.* Newbury Park, CA: Sage.

Dickson, F. C., & Walker, K. L. (2001). The expression of emotion in later-life married men. *Qualitative Research Reports in Communication, 2,* 66–71.

Diggs, R. C., & Clark, K. D. (2002). It's a struggle but worth it: Identifying and managing identities in an interracial friendship. *Communication Quarterly, 50,* 368–390.

Dillard, C., Browning, L. D., Sitkin, S. B., & Sutcliffe, K. M. (2000). Impression management and the use of procedures at the Ritz-Carlton: Moral standards and dramaturgical discipline. *Communication Studies, 51*(4), 404–414.

Dindia, K. (1998). "Going into and coming out of the closet": The dialectics of stigma disclosure. In B. M. Montgomery & L. A. Baxter (Eds.), *Dialectical approaches to studying personal relationships* (pp. 83–108). Mahwah, NJ: Erlbaum.

Dindia, K. (2003). Definitions and perspectives on relational maintenance communication. In D. J. Canary & M. Dainton (Eds.), *Maintaining relationships through communication: Relational, contextual, and cultural variations* (pp. 1–28). Mahwah, NJ: Erlbaum.

Dindia, K., & Allen, M. (1992). Sex-differences in self-disclosure: A meta-analysis. *Psychological Bulletin, 112,* 106–124.

Donaghue, E. (2007, July 25). Communication now part of the cure. *USA Today,* D1.

Douglas, W. (1987). Affinity-testing in initial interaction. *Journal of Social and Personal Relationships, 4,* 3–16.

Du, J., Fan, X., & Feng, T. (2011). Multiple emotional contagions in service encounters. *Journal of the Academy of Marketing Science, 39,* 449–466.

DuBrin, A. J. (2014). *Human relations: Interpersonal job-oriented skills.* New York: Prentice Hall.

Duck, S. (2007). *Human relationships.* Thousand Oaks, CA: Sage.

Duck, S. W., & McMahan, D. T. (2014). *Communication in everyday life: A survey of communication.* Thousand Oaks, CA: Sage.

Duck, S. W., & Wood, J. T. (1995). For better, for worse, for richer, for poorer: The rough and smooth of relationships. In S. Duck & J. T. Wood (Eds.), *Confronting relationship challenges* (pp. 1–21). Thousand Oaks, CA: Sage.

Dunbar, R. (1998). *Grooming, gossip, and the evolution of language.* Cambridge, MA: Harvard University Press.

Dunbar, N. E., & Burgoon, J. K. (2005). Perceptions of power and interactional dominance in interpersonal relationships. *Journal of Social and Personal Relationships, 22,* 207–233.

E

Earp, B. D. (2012). The extinction of masculine generics. *Journal for Communication and Culture, 2,* 4–19.

Egbert, N., & Polk, D. (2006). Speaking the language of relational maintenance: A validity test of Chapman's (1992) five love languages. *Communication Research Reports, 23,* 19–26.

Eisenberg, E. M. (1984). Ambiguity as strategy in organizational communication. *Communication Monographs, 51,* 227–242.

Ekman, P. (1972). Universals and cultural differences in facial expressions of emotion. In J. Cole (Ed.), *Nebraska Symposium on Motivation, 1971* (pp. 207–283). Lincoln: University of Nebraska Press.

Ekman, P. (1973). Cross-cultural studies of facial expressions. In P. Ekman (Ed.), *Darwin and facial expressions* (pp. 169–229). New York: Academic Press.

Ekman, P., & Friesen, W. V. (1971). Constants across cultures in the face and emotion. *Journal of Personality and Social Psychology, 17,* 124–129.

Elphinston, R. A., Feeney, J. A., Noller, P., Connor, J. P., & Fitzgerald, J. (2013). Romantic jealousy and relationship satisfaction: The costs of rumination. *Western Journal of Communication, 77,* 293–304.

Emmers-Sommer, T. M. (2003). When partners falter: Repair after a transgression. In D. J. Canary & M. Dainton (Eds.), *Maintaining relationships through communication: Relational, contextual, and cultural variations* (pp. 185–205). Mahwah, NJ: Erlbaum.

Emmrich, S. (2014, January 2). "In other news": TV personalities' low-key coming out: How gay news anchors broke their own coming out stories. *New York Times,* E6.

Englehardt, E. E. (2001). *Ethical issues in interpersonal communication.* Fort Worth, TX: Harcourt.

Evans, R. (2013, October 16). Culture clashes provide benefits in the long run. *Construction News.* Retrieved from http://www.cnplus.co.uk/opinion/editors-comment/culture-clashes-provide-benefits-in-the-long-run/8654365.article#.U2EBD4lOU5s

F

Federal Bureau of Investigation (FBI). (2013). *Uniform Crime Report: Crime in the United States, 2012: Expanded homicide data.* Retrieved from http://www.fbi.gov

Fehr, B., & Russell, J. A. (1984). Concept of emotion viewed from a prototype perspective. *Journal of Experimental Psychology, 113,* 464–486.

Fernandez, R. M., & Greenberg, J. (2013). Race, identity, hiring, and statistical discrimination. In S. McDonald (Ed.), *Networks, work, and inequality* (pp. 81–102). Bradford, UK: Emerald Group.

Ferrari, B. (2012). *Power listening.* New York: Penguin Books.

Field, T. (1999). American adolescents touch each other less and are more aggressive toward their peers as compared with French adolescents. *Adolescence, 34,* 753–759.

Fischer, A. H. (2000). Introduction. In A. H. Fischer (Ed.), *Gender and emotion: Social psychological perspectives* (pp. 97–117). Cambridge: Cambridge University Press.

Fitzpatrick, M. A. (1988). *Between husbands and wives: Communication in marriage.* Thousand Oaks, CA: Sage.

Floyd, K., Mikkelson, A. C., & Judd, J. (2006). Defining the family through relationships. In L. H. Turner & R. West (Eds.), *The family communication sourcebook* (pp. 21–39). Thousand Oaks, CA: Sage.

Folger, J. P., Poole, M. S., & Stutman, R. K. (2013). *Working through conflict: Strategies for relationships, groups, and organizations.* Boston: Pearson.

Fong, J. H., & Longnecker, N. (2010, Spring). Doctor-patient communication: A review. *Ochsner Journal, 10,* 38–43.

Forbes. (2012, April 3). What your clothes say about you. http://www.forbes.com

Forgas, J. P. (2002). How to make the right impression. In J. A. DeVito (Ed.), *The interpersonal communication reader* (pp. 28–33). Boston: Allyn & Bacon.

Fox, J., Warber, K. M., & Makstaller, D. C. (2013). The role of Facebook in romantic relationship development: An exploration of Knapp's relational stage model. *Journal of Social and Personal Relationships, 30,* 771–794.

Franzoi, S. L., & Klaiber, J. R. (2007). Body use and reference group impact. *Sex Roles, 55,* 205–214.

Friedrich, G. W., & Boileau, D. M. (1999). The communication discipline. In A. L. Vangelisti, J. A. Daly, & G. W. Friedrich (Eds.), *Teaching communication: Theory, research and methods* (2nd ed., pp. 3–13). Mahwah, NJ: Erlbaum.

Frymier, A. B., & Nadler, M. K. (2013). *Persuasion: Integrating theory, research, and practice* (3rd ed.). Dubuque, IA: Kendall-Hunt.

Fulghum, R. (1989). *All I really need to know I learned in kindergarten.* New York: Ivy.

G

Galvin, K. M. (2006). Diversity's impact on defining the family: Discourse-dependence and identity. In L. H. Turner & R. West (Eds.), *The family communication sourcebook* (pp. 3–19). Thousand Oaks, CA: Sage.

Gangestad, S. W., & Snyder, M. (2000). Self-monitoring: Appraisal and reappraisal. *Psychological Bulletin, 126,* 530–555.

Gardner, H., & Davis, K. (2013). *The App generation: How today's youth navigate identity, intimacy, and imagination in a digital world.* New Haven, CT: Yale University Press.

Gastil, J. (1990). Generic pronouns and sexist language: The oxymoronic character of masculine generics. *Sex Roles, 23,* 629–641.

Gay & Lesbian Alliance Against Defamation (GLAAD). (2013). GLAAD media reference guide—Transgender glossary of terms. Retrieved from http://www.glaad.org/reference/transgender

Geary, J. (2011). *I is an other: The secret life of metaphor and how it shapes the way we see the world.* New York: HarperCollins.

Gensler, H. J. (2013). *Ethics and the golden rule.* New York: Routledge.

Germino, B. B., Mishel, M. H., Crandell, J., Porter, L., Blyler, D., Jenerette, C., & Gil, K. (2012). Outcomes of an uncertainty management intervention in younger African American and Caucasian breast cancer survivors, *Oncology Nursing Forum,* 1–11.

Gerth, H., & Mills, C. W. (1964). *Character and social structure: The psychology of social institutions.* New York: Harcourt, Brace & World.

Gibb, J. (1961). Defensive communication. *Journal of Communication, 11,* 141–148.

Gibb, J. (1964). Climate for trust formation. In L. Bradford, J. Gibb, & K. Benne (Eds.), *T-group theory and laboratory method* (pp. 279–309). New York: Wiley.

Gibb, J. (1970). Sensitivity training as a medium for personal growth and improved interpersonal relationships. *Interpersonal Development, 1,* 6–31.

Gibbs, J. L, & Ellison, N. B., & Heino, R. D. (2006). Self-presentation in online personals: The role of anticipated future interaction, self-disclosure, and perceived success in Internet dating, *Communication Research, 33,* 152–177.

Giles, H., & Le Poire, B. A. (2006). The ubiquity and social meaningfulness of nonverbal communication: An introduction. In V. Manusov & M. Patterson (Eds.), *Handbook of nonverbal behavior* (pp. xv–xxvii). Thousand Oaks, CA: Sage.

Gilligan, C. (1982). *In a different voice: Psychological theory and women's development.* Cambridge, MA: Harvard University Press.

Glass, L. (2013). *The body language of liars: From little white lies to pathological deceptions.* Pompton Plains, NJ: Career Press.

Goffman, E. (1959). *The presentation of self in everyday life.* New York: Anchor Books.

Goffman, E. (1967). *Interaction ritual.* Garden City, NY: Doubleday Anchor Books.

Goldsmith, D. J., & Fulfs, P. A. (1999). "You just don't have the evidence": An analysis of claims and evidence in Deborah Tannen's *You Just Don't Understand.* In M. E. Roloff (Ed.), *Communication yearbook 22* (pp. 1–49). Thousand Oaks, CA: Sage.

Goleman, D. (2006). *Social intelligence: The new science of human relationships.* New York: Bantam.

Gosselin, P., Kirouac, G., & Dore, F. Y. (1995). Components and recognition of facial expression in the communication of emotion by actors. *Journal of Personality and Social Psychology, 68,* 83–96.

Gottman, J. M., & DeClaire, J. (2001). *The relationship cure.* New York: Three Rivers Press.

Gottman, J. M., Katz, L. F., & Hooven, C. (1997). *Metaemotion: How families communicate emotionally.* Mahwah, NJ: Erlbaum.

Goudreau, J. (2012). The 20 best-paying jobs for people persons. ForbesWoman blog, *Forbes.com.*

Graham, E. E. (1997). Turning points and commitments in postdivorce relations. *Communication Monographs, 64,* 350–368.

Graham, E. E. (2003). Dialectic contradictions in postmarital relationships. *Journal of Family Communication, 4,* 193–214.

Grant, A. (2014, January 2). The dark side of emotional intelligence. *The Atlantic.* Retrieved from http://www.theatlantic.com/health/archive/2014/01/the-dark-side-of-emotional-intelligence/282720/

Gray, J. (2011). Random romance acts can help a relationship rut. Retrieved from http://www.creators.com/advice/men-mars-women-venus/random-romance-acts-can-help-a-relationship-rut.html

Green, M. (2012). *The human side of a mediated life: How mediated communication is affecting relationships and nonverbal literacy.* Unpublished manuscript, California Polytechnic State University, San Luis Obispo.

Grice, H. P. (1975). Logic and conversation. In P. Cole & J. L. Morgan (Eds.), *Syntax and semantics: Vol. 3. Speech acts* (pp. 41–58). New York: Seminar.

Griffin, C. L. (2014). *Invitation to public speaking.* Boston: Wadsworth/Cengage.

Grognet, A., & Van Duzer, C. (2002). *Listening skills in the workplace.* Denver: Spring Institute for International Studies.

Grossman, T. (2013). The early development of processing emotions in face and voice. In P. Belin, S. Campanella, & T. Ethofer (Eds.), *Integrating face and voice in person perception* (pp. 95–116). New York: Springer.

Gueguen, N., & De Gail, M. (2003). The effect of smiling on helping behavior: Smiling and Good Samaritan behavior. *Communication Reports, 16,* 133–140.

Guerrero, J. (2012). *Investigating the relationship between acculturation and metabolic syndrome among a bi-national sample of Mexicans and Mexican-Americans.* Unpublished doctoral dissertation, Texas A&M University, College Station, TX.

Guerrero, L. K., & Afifi, W. A. (1995). What parents don't know: Topic avoidance in parent-child relationships. In T. J. Socha & G. H. Stamp (Eds.), *Parents, children, and communication: Frontiers of theory and research* (pp. 219–245). Mahwah, NJ: Erlbaum.

Guerrero, L. K., Andersen, P. A., & Afifi, W. A. (2007). *Close encounters: Communication in relationships.* Los Angeles: Sage.

Guerrero, L. K., & Bachman, G. F. (2006). Associations among relational maintenance behaviors, attachment-style categories, and attachment dimensions. *Communication Studies, 57,* 341–361.

Guy, D. (2012, May 22). *Why Isn't the Sky Blue?* www.radiolab.org

H

Hall, A. (2013, May 17). Listening to customers yields success. Entrepreneurs blog, *Forbes.com.* Retrieved from http://www.forbes.com/sites/alanhall/2013/05/17/listening-to-customers-yields-success

Hall, B. J. (2005). *Among cultures: The challenge of communication.* Fort Worth, TX: Harcourt.

Hall, E. T. (1959). *The silent language.* New York: Doubleday.

Hall, E. T., & Hall, M. R. (1990). *Understanding cultural differences.* Yarmouth, ME: Intercultural Press.

Hall, J. A. (2011). Sex differences in friendship expectations: A meta-analysis. *Journal of Social and Personal Relationships, 28,* 723–747. doi: 10.1177/0265407510386192

Hall, J. A. (2013). Humor in long-term romantic relationships: The association of general humor styles and relationship-specific functions with relationship satisfaction. *Western Journal of Communication, 77,* 272–292.

Hall, J. A., Carter, J. D., & Horgan, T. G. (2000). Gender differences in nonverbal communication of emotion. In A. H. Fischer (Ed.), *Gender and emotion: Social psychological perspectives* (pp. 97–117). Cambridge: Cambridge University Press.

Hall, J. A., Carter, S., Cody, M. J., Albright, J. (2010). Individual differences in the communication of romantic interest: Development of the flirting styles inventory. *Communication Quarterly, 58,* 365–392.

Hamid, P. N. (2000). Self-disclosure and occupational stress in Chinese professionals. *Psychological Reports, 87,* 1075–1082.

Hamilton, W. L. (2004, July 5). For Bantu refugees, hard-won American dreams. *New York Times,* A1, A14.

Hanna, A., & Walther, J. B. (2013). What perceptions do people form after viewing Facebook profiles? In K. Schultz & A. K. Goodboy (Eds.), *Introduction to communication studies: Translating scholarship into meaningful practice* (pp. 11–17). Dubuque, IA: Kendall/Hunt.

Hareli, S., & Hess, U. (2012). The social signal value of emotions. *Cognition and Emotion, 26,* 385–389.

Harvey, J. H., & Weber, A. L. (2002). *Odyssey of the heart: Close relationships in the 21st century.* Mahwah, NJ: Erlbaum.

Harwood, J. (2004). Relational, role, and social identity as expressed in grandparents' personal web sites. *Communication Studies, 55,* 300–318.

Hashem, M. (2004). The power of Wastah in Lebanese speech. In A. Gonzalez, M. Houston, & V. Chen (Eds.), *Our voices: Essays in culture, ethnicity, and communication* (pp. 169–173). Los Angeles: Roxbury.

Hastie, B., & Cosh, S. (2013). "What's wrong with that?" Legitimating and contesting gender inequality. *Journal of Language and Social Psychology, 32,* 369–389.

Hastings, S. O. (2000). "Egocasting" in the avoidance of disclosure: An intercultural perspective. In S. Petronio (Ed.), *Balancing the secrets of private disclosures* (pp. 235–248). Mahwah, NJ: Erlbaum.

Hatfield, E., & Rapson, R. (2013). Equity theory in close relationships. In P. Van Lange, A. W. Kruglanski, & E. T. Higgins (Eds.), *The handbook of theories of social psychology* (pp. 200–217). London: Sage.

Hathaway, G. (2013, May 3). Diversity then and now. *Inside Higher Ed.* Retrieved from http://www.insidehighered.com/advice/2013/05/03/essay-evolving-role-diversity-director

Haug, J. (2013). *The diversity movement: Defeating itself, destroying society.* Retrieved from http://www.americanthinker.com/2013/01/the_diversity_movement_defeating_itself_destroying_society.html

Heider, F. (1958). *The psychology of interpersonal relations.* New York: Wiley.

Heisterkamp, B., & Alberts, J. K. (2000). Control and desire: An analysis of teasing and joking interactions among gay couples. *Communication Studies, 51,* 388–404.

Hendrick, B. (2010, September 27). Mindfulness meditation vs. multiple sclerosis: Mindfulness meditation helps multiple sclerosis patients, researchers say. Retrieved from http://www.webmd.com/multiple-sclerosis/news/20100927/mindfulness-meditation-vs-multiple-sclerosis

Hesse, C., & Rauscher, E. A. (2013). Privacy tendencies and revealing/concealing: The moderating role of emotional competence. *Communication Quarterly, 61,* 91–112. doi: 10.1080/01463373.2012.720344

Hinde, R. A. (1995). A suggested structure for a science of relationships. *Personal Relationships, 2,* 1–15.

Hinsz, V. B. (1989). Facial resemblance in engaged and married couples. *Journal of Social and Personal Relationships, 6,* 223–229.

Hochschild, A. R., & Machung, A. (2003). *The second shift: Working families and the revolution at home.* New York: Viking.

Hochschild, A. R. (1983). *The managed heart: Commercialization of human feeling.* Berkeley: University of California Press.

Hoel, H., & Cooper, C. L. (2000). *Destructive conflict and bullying at work.* Manchester School of Management, University of Manchester Institute of Science and Technology.

Hofstede, G. (1980). *Culture's consequences.* Beverly Hills, CA: Sage.

Hofstede, G. (1984). The cultural relativity of the quality of life concept. *Academy of Management Review, 9,* 389–398.

Hofstede, G. (1991). *Cultures and organizations: Software of the mind.* New York: McGraw-Hill.

Hofstede, G. (2001). *Culture's consequences: Comparing values, behaviors, institutions, and organizations across nations.* Thousand Oaks, CA: Sage.

Hofstede, G. (2003). Geert Hofstede cultural dimensions. Retrieved from http://www.geert-hofstede.com/

Hoijer, H. (1994). The Sapir-Whorf hypothesis. In L. A. Samovar & R. E. Porter (Eds.), *Intercultural communication: A reader.* Belmont, CA: Wadsworth.

Holland, K. (2013, July 23). Importance of body language in nursing communication. *NurseTogether.com.* Retrieved from http://www.nursetogether.com/value-body-language-nursing-communication

Hollenbaugh, E. E., & Everett, M. K. (2013). The effects of anonymity on self-disclosure in blogs: An application of the online disinhibition effect. *Journal of Computer-Mediated Communication 18,* 283–302.

Holmberg, D., & MacKenzie, S. (2002). So far, so good: Scripts for romantic relationship development as predictors of relational well-being. *Journal of Social and Personal Relationships, 19,* 777–796.

Honeycutt, J. M. (2003). *Imagined interactions.* Cresskill, NJ: Hampton Press.

Honeycutt, J. M., & Bryan, S. P. (2011). *Scripts and communication for relationships.* New York: Lang.

Honeycutt, J. M., Pence, M. E., & Gearhart, C. C. (2013). Using imagined interactions to predict covert narcissism. *Communication Reports, 26,* 26–38.

Horan, S. M., & Booth Butterfield, M. (2013). Understanding the routine expression of deceptive affection in romantic relationships. *Communication Quarterly, 61,* 195–216.

Houston, M. (2004). When black women talk with white women: Why dialogues are difficult. In A. Gonzalez, M. Houston, & V. Chen (Eds.), *Our voices: Essays in culture, ethnicity, and communication* (4th ed., pp. 133–139). Los Angeles: Roxbury.

Hubbard, A. S. (2009). Perspective taking, adaptation, and coordination. In W. F. Eadie (Ed.), *21st century communication* (pp. 119–127). Thousand Oaks, CA: Sage.

Hubbard, A. S., Hendrickson, B., Fehrenbach, K. S., & Sur, J. (2013). Effects of timing and sincerity of an apology on satisfaction and changes in negative feeling during conflicts. *Western Journal of Communication, 77,* 323–339.

Hui, S. (2013, November 19). *Year of the "selfie": Oxford Dictionary crowns its word of the year.* Retrieved from http://news.nationalpost.com/2013/11/19/its-official-2013-is-the-year-of-the-selfie-oxford-dictionaries-crowns-its-word-of-the-year/

Hurley, L., & Reese-Weber, M. (2012). Conflict strategies and intimacy: Variations by romantic relationship development and gender. *Interpersona, 6,* 200–210.

Hurtado-de-Mendoza, A., Molina, C., & Fernández-Dols, J.-M. (2013). The archeology of emotion concepts: A lexicographic analysis of the concepts *shame* and *vergüenza. Journal of Language and Social Psychology, 32,* 272–290.

I

Ijams, K., & Miller, L. D. (2000). Perceptions of dream-disclosure: An exploratory study. *Communication Studies, 51,* 135–148.

Imahori, T. T. (2006). On becoming "American." In M. W. Lusting & J. Koester (Eds.), *AmongUS: Essays on identity, belonging, and intercultural competence* (pp. 258–269). Boston: Pearson.

IMPACT Program. (2013). How many LGBT families are there? Retrieved from http://www.impactprogram.org/youth/how-many-lgbt-familes-are-there/

IndexMundi. (2012). Country comparison: Exports. Retrieved from http://www.indexmundi.com/g/r.aspx?t=t10&v=85

InfoPlease. (2007). Mothers by the numbers: Info about mothers from the Census Bureau. Retrieved from http://www.infoplease.com/spot/momcensus1.html

Inside Jobs. (2013). Child welfare specialist. Retrieved from http://www.insidejobs.com/careers/child-welfare-specialist

Iowa State University News Service. (2007, June 29). ISU study finds wives have greater power in marriage problem-solving behavior. Retrieved from http://www.iastate.edu/~nscentral/news/2007/jun/wifepower.shtml

Ivy, D. K. (2012). *GenderSpeak: Personal effectiveness in gender communication* (5th ed.). Boston: Pearson.

Ivy, D. K., Bullis-Moore, L., Norvell, K., Backlund, P., & Javidi, M. (1995). The lawyer, the babysitter, and the student: Inclusive language usage and instruction. *Women and Language, 18,* 13–21.

J

Jack, R. E., Caldara, R., & Schyns, P. G. (2012). Internal representations reveal cultural diversity in expectations of facial expressions of emotion. *Journal of Experimental Psychology, 141,* 19–25.

Jäger, C., & Bartsch, A. (2006). Meta-emotions. *Grazer Philosophische Studien, 73,* 179–204.

Jandt, F. E. (2013). *An introduction to intercultural communication.* Thousand Oaks, CA: Sage.

Jayson, S. (2012, October 18). New survey: 3.4% of U.S. adults are LGBT. *USA Today.* Retrieved from http://williamsinstitute.law.ucla.edu/press/new-survey-3–4–of-u-s-adults-are-lgbt/

Jensen, J. V. (1997). *Ethical issues in the communication process.* Mahwah, NJ: Erlbaum.

Johannesen, R. L., Valde, K. S., & Whedbee, K. E. (2007). *Ethics in human communication* (6th ed.). Lake Zurich, IL: Waveland Press.

Johnson, E. N., Kuhn, J. R., Apostolou, B. A., & Hassell, J. M. *(2013)* Auditor perceptions of client narcissism as a fraud attitude risk factor. *AUDITING: A Journal of Practice & Theory, 32,* 203–219.

Johnson, F. L. (2000). *Speaking culturally: Language diversity in the United States.* Thousand Oaks, CA: Sage.

Johnston, M. K., Weaver, J. B., Watson, K. W., & Barker, L. B. (2000). Listening styles: Biological or psychological differences? *International Journal of Listening, 14,* 32–46.

Jonas, M. (2007, August 5). The downside of diversity. *Boston Globe,* D2, D4.

Jones, D. (2004, January 9). Women trump the men in first episode. *USA Today,* 3B.

Jones, S. E., & Yarbrough, A. E. (1985). A naturalistic study of the meanings of touch. *Communication Monographs, 52,* 19–56.

Jones, S. M., & Wirtz, J. G. (2007). "Sad monkey see, monkey do:" Nonverbal matching in emotional support encounters. *Communication Studies, 58,* 71–86.

Jourard, S. M. (1971). *The transparent self.* New York: Van Nostrand–Reinhold.

K

Kádár, D. Z., & Haugh, M. (2013). *Understanding politeness.* New York: Cambridge University Press.

Kant, I. (1785). *The groundwork for the metaphysics of morals.* Peterborough, Ontario: Broadview Press.

Karakurt, G., Christiansen, A. T., Wadsworth, M. M., & Weiss, H. M. (2013). Romantic relationships following wartime deployment. *Journal of Family Issues, 34,* 1427–1441.

Kayyal, M. H., & Russell, J. A. (2013). Language and emotion: Certain English–Arabic translations are not equivalent. *Journal of Language and Social Psychology, 32,* 261–271.

Keeley, M. P. (2007). 'Turning toward death together': The functions of messages during final conversations in close relationships. *Journal of Social and Personal Relationships, 24,* 225–253.

Keener, E., Strough, J., & DiDonato, L. (2012). Gender differences and similarities in strategies for managing conflict with friends and romantic partners. *Sex Roles, 67,* 83–97.

Kellas, J. K., & Kranstuber-Horstman, H. (2015). Communicated narrative sense-making: Understanding family narratives, storytelling, and the construction of meaning through a communicative lens. In L. H. Turner & R. West (Eds.), *The SAGE handbook of family communication* (pp. 76–90). Thousand Oaks, CA: Sage.

Keller, B. (2013, December 5). *Nelson Mandela, South Africa's liberator as prisoner and president, dies at 95.* Retrieved from http://www.nytimes.com/2013/12/06/world/africa/nelson-mandela_obit.html?hp

Kelley, H. H. (2013). *Personal relationships: Their structures and processes.* New York: Psychology Press.

Kennedy-Lightsey, C. D., & Dillow, M. R. (2011). Initiating and avoiding communication with mothers: Young adult children's perceptions of hurtfulness and affirming styles. *Southern Communication Journal, 76,* 1–20.

Kennedy-Lightsey, C. D., Martin, M. M., Thompson, M., Himes, K. L., & Clingerman, B. Z. (2012). Communication privacy management theory: Exploring coordination and ownership between friends. *Communication Quarterly, 60,* 665–680.

Kennedy-Moore, E. (2012). Children's growing friendships. Retrieved from http://www.psychologytoday.com/blog/growing-friendships/201202/childrens-growing-friendships.

Khazan, O. (2013a, December 11). A psychologist's guide to online dating: Can we predict romantic prospects just from looking at a face? *The Atlantic.* Retrieved from http://www.theatlantic.com/health/archive/2013/12/a-psychologists-guide-to-online-dating/282225/

Khazan, O. (2013b, December 23). Why families fight during holidays: A time for good food, comfort, joy, and . . . "you could be so pretty if you only lost a little weight." *The Atlantic.* Retrieved from http://www.theatlantic.com/health/archive/2013/12/why-families-fight-during-holidays/282584/

King, G., Baxter, D., Rosenbaum, P., Zwaigenbaum, & Bates, A. (2009). Belief systems of families of children with autism spectrum disorders or Down syndrome. *Focus on Autism and other Developmental Disabilities, 24,* 50–64.

Kirtley, M. D., & Honeycutt, J. (1996). Listening styles and their correspondence with second-guessing. *Communication Research Reports, 13,* 1–9.

Kirtley, M. D., & Weaver, J. B. III (1999). Exploring the impact of gender role self-perception on communication style. *Women's Studies in Communication, 22,* 190–204.

Kitzinger, C. (2000). How to resist an idiom. *Research on Language and Social Interaction, 33,* 121–154.

Knapp, M. L. (1978). *Social intercourse: From greeting to goodbye.* Boston: Allyn & Bacon.

Knapp, M. L., Hall, J.A., & Horgan, T. (2014). *Nonverbal communication in human interaction.* Boston: Cengage/Wadsworth.

Knapp, M. L., & Vangelisti, A. L. (2000). *Interpersonal communication and human relationships.* Boston: Allyn & Bacon.

Knapp, M. L., & Vangelisti, A. L. (2005). *Interpersonal communication and human relationships* (5th ed.). Boston: Allyn & Bacon.

Knapp, M. L., Vangelisti, A. L., & Caughlin, J. P. (2014). *Interpersonal communication and human relationships.* Boston: Pearson.

Knobloch, L. K., Miller, L. E., Bond, B. J., & Mannone, S. E. (2007). Relational uncertainty and message processing in marriage. *Communication Monographs, 74,* 154–180.

Knobloch, L. K., & Theiss, J. A. (2014). Relational turbulence with military couples during reintegration following deployment. In S. M. Wadsworth & D. Riggs (Eds.), *Military deployment and its consequences for families* (pp. 37–60). New York: Springer.

Korzybski, A. (1958). *Science and sanity: An introduction to non-Aristotelian systems and general semantics.* Lakeville, CT: International Non-Aristotelian Library Publishing Company.

Kosky, C., & Schlisselberg, G. (2013, June). Oral communication skills in senior citizens: A community service model. *Perspectives: American Speech-Language-Hearing Association, 16*(1), 28–38.

Kovecses, Z. (2000). *Metaphor and emotion: Language, culture, and body in human feeling.* Cambridge: Cambridge University Press.

Kowalski, R. M. (2001). The aversive side of social interaction revisited. In R. M. Kowalski (Ed.), *Behaving badly: Aversive behaviors in interpersonal relationships* (pp. 297–309). Washington, DC: American Psychological Association.

Kramarae, C. (1981). *Women and men speaking.* Rowley, MA: Newbury House.

Kreager, D. A., Felson, R. B., Warner, C., & Wenger, M. R. (2013). Women's education, marital violence, and divorce: A social exchange perspective. *Journal of Marriage and Family, 75,* 565–581.

Kreppner, K., & Lerner, R.M. (2013). *Family systems and lifespan development.* Hillsdale, NJ: Erlbaum.

Kristof, N. (2013, November 27). *Where is the love?* Retrieved from http://www.nytimes.com/2013/11/28/opinion/kristof-where-is-the-love.html

Kroeber, A. L., & Kluckhohn, C. (1993). *Culture: A critical review of concepts and definitions.* New York: Vintage.

Kumar, A. (2013). The plight of Dalit women: Why it's time to end the caste system both in India and in the UK. Retrieved from http://blogs.independent.co.uk/2013/07/04/the-plight-of-dalits-women-why-its-time-to-end-the-caste-system-both-in-india-and-the-uk/

L

Labov, W. (1972). *Sociolinguistic patterns.* Philadelphia: University of Pennsylvania Press.

Lakey, S. G., & Canary, D. J. (2002). Actor goal achievement and sensitivity to partner as critical factors in understanding interpersonal communication competence and conflict strategies. *Communication Monographs, 69,* 217–235.

Lakoff, G. (2013). Neural social science. In D. D. Franks & J. H. Turner (Eds.), *Handbook of neurosociology* (pp. 9–25). Amsterdam: Springer.

Lakoff, G., & Johnson, M. (1980). *Metaphors we live by.* Chicago: University of Chicago Press.

Lakoff, R. (1975). *Language and women's place.* New York: Harper & Row.

Landale, N. S., Thomas, K. J., & Van Hook, J. (2011). The living arrangement of children in immigrant families. *The Future of Children, 21,* 43–70.

Langellier, K. M., & Peterson, E. E. (2006). Narrative performance theory: Telling stories, doing family. In D. O. Braithwaite & L. A. Baxter (Eds.), *Engaging theories in family communication* (pp. 99–114). Thousand Oaks, CA: Sage.

Langer, E. (1989). *Mindfulness.* Reading, MA: Addison-Wesley.

Lannutti, P. J. (2013) Same-sex marriage and privacy management: Examining couples' communication with family members. *Journal of Family Communication, 13,* 60–75.

Latour, F. (2014). How blind people see race. *Boston Globe,* K2.

Lazarus, R. S. (1991). *Emotion and adaptation.* New York: Oxford University Press.

Lecheler, S., & De Vreese, C. H. (2012). A mediation analysis of framing effects on political attitudes. *Journalism & Mass Communication Quarterly, 89,* 185–204.

Ledbetter, A. M. (2013). Relational maintenance and inclusion of the other in the self: Measure development and dyadic test of a self-expansion theory approach. *Southern Communication Journal, 78,* 289–310.

Leggitt, J. S., & Gibbs, R. W. (2000). Emotional reactions to verbal irony. *Discourse Processes, 29,* 1–24.

Lehmiller, J. (2014). *The psychology of human sexuality.* Hoboken, NJ: Wiley.

Levenson, R. W., & Gottman, J. M. (1985). Physiological and affective predictors of change in relationship satisfaction. *Journal of Personality and Social Psychology, 45,* 587–597.

Levine, T. R., Aune, K. S., & Park, H. S. (2006). Love styles and communication in relationships: Partner preferences, initiation, and intensification. *Communication Quarterly, 54,* 465–486.

Lewis, R. D. (1999). *When cultures collide: Managing successfully across cultures.* London: Brealey.

Linguistic Society of America. (1997, January). *LSA resolution on the Oakland "Ebonics" issue.* Retrieved from http://www.linguistlist.org/topics /ebonics/lsa-ebonics.html

Lippert, T., & Prager, K. J. (2001). Daily experiences of intimacy: A study of couples. *Personal Relationships, 8,* 283–298.

Lippman, W. (1922). *Public opinion.* New York: Macmillan.

Littlejohn, S. W., & Domenici, K. (2001). *Engaging communication in conflict.* Thousand Oaks, CA: Sage.

Liu, L. (2008, September 1). *Intercultural communication apprehension.* Saarbrücken, Germany: VDM.

Lo, S.-K. (2008). The nonverbal communication functions of emoticons in computer-mediated communication. *CyberPsychology and Behavior, 11,* 595–597.

Locock, L., Mazanderani, F., & Powell, J. (2012). Metaphoric language and the articulation of emotions by people affected by motor neurone disease. *Chronic Illness, 8,* 201–213.

Lohrey, J. (2014). Verbal communication guidelines for the restaurant business. Retrieved from http://smallbusiness.chron.com/verbal-communication-guidelines-restaurant-business-73650.html

Luft, J. (1970). *Group process: An introduction to group dynamics.* Palo Alto, CA: Mayfield.

Lumley, M., & Wilkinson, J. (2014). *Developing employability for business.* Oxford: Oxford University Press.

Lusch, R. F., Brown, J. R., & O'Brien, M. (2011). Protecting relational assets: A pre and post field study of a horizontal business combination. *Journal of the Academy of Marketing Science, 39,* 175–197.

Lustig, M. W., & Koester, J. (1999a). *AmongUS: Essays on identity, belonging, and intercultural competence.* New York: Longman.

Lustig, M. W., & Koester, J. (1999b). *Intercultural competence: Interpersonal communication across cultures.* New York: Longman.

Lytle, R. (2011, June 13). *How slang affects students in the classroom.* Retrieved from http://www.usnews .com/education/high-schools/articles/2011/06/13 /how-slang-affects-students-in-the-classroom

M

Mackay, H. (2011, June 23). Listen if you want to learn. Retrieved from http://harveymackay.com /column/listen-if-you-want-to-learn/

Malis, R. S., & Roloff, M. E. (2006). Features of serial arguing and coping strategies: Links with stress and well-being. In B. A. Le Poire & R. M. Dailey (Eds.), *Applied interpersonal communication matters: Family, health, and community relations* (pp. 39–66). New York: Lang.

Maltz, D. J., & Borker, R. A. (1982). A cultural approach to male-female miscommunication. In J. J. Gumpertz (Ed.), *Language and social identity* (pp. 196–216). Cambridge: Cambridge University Press.

Marano, H. E. (2003). The new sex scorecard. *Psychology Today, 36*(4), 38.

Martin, J., & Nakayama, T. (2013). *Intercultural communication in contexts.* New York: McGraw-Hill.

Martin, J., & Nakayama, T. (2014). *Experiencing intercultural communication: An introduction.* New York: McGraw-Hill.

Martinez, R. (2000, July 16). The next chapter: America's next great revolution in race relations is already underway. *New York Times Magazine,* 11–12.

Martyna, W. (1978). What does 'he' mean? Use of the generic masculine. *Journal of Communication, 28,* 131–138.

Mashru, R. (2012). *It's a girl! The three deadliest words in the world.* Retrieved from http://blogs .independent.co.uk/2012/01/16/it%E2%80%99s-a -girl-the-three-deadliest-words-in-the-world/

Maslow, A. H. (1970). *Motivation and personality.* New York: Harper & Row. (Originally published 1954.)

Maslow, A. H. (1968). *Toward a psychology of being.* New York: Van Nostrand Reinhold.

Matchan, L. (2009, June 2). They love being grandparents, but call them something else. Retrieved from http://www.boston.com/community /moms/articles/2009/06/02/baby_boomers_say_call _me_just_dont_call_me_grandma/

Mather, D. (2013, August 28). Restoring the lost art of listening. *The Epoch Times,* B4.

Mathews, A., Derlega, V. J., & Morrow, J. (2006). What is highly personal information and how is it related to self-disclosure decision-making? The perspective of college students. *Communication Research Reports, 23,* 85–92.

Mathur, A., Fu, H., & Hansen, P. (2013). *The mysterious and alarming rise of single parenthood in America.* Retrieved from http://www.theatlantic .com/business/archive/2013/09/the-mysterious -and-alarming-rise-of-single-parenthood-in -america/279203/

Matsumoto, D., Frank, M. G., & Hwang, H. (2013). *Nonverbal communication: Science and applications.* Thousand Oaks, CA: Sage.

Maurer, S. (2013). How to become a mental health counselor. Retrieved from http://www.innerbody .com/careers-in-health/how-to-become-mental -health-counselor.html

McCroskey, J. C., & Richmond, V. P. (1995). Correlates of compulsive communication: Quantitative and qualitative characteristics. *Communication Quarterly, 43,* 39–52.

McGeorge, C. (2001). Mars and Venus: Unequal planets. *Journal of Marital and Family Therapy, 27,* 55–68.

McFedries, P. (2004). *Word spy: The word lover's guide to modern culture.* New York: Broadway Books.

McGlone, M. S., Beck, G., & Pfiester, A. (2006). Contamination and camouflage in euphemisms. *Communication Monographs, 73,* 261–282.

McLuhan, M. (1964). *Understanding media: The extensions of man.* New York: McGraw-Hill.

Mead, G. H. (1934). *Mind, self and society: From the standpoint of a social behaviorist.* Chicago: University of Chicago Press.

Meghani, A. (2009). Color your world. *School Planning and Management, 2,* 3.

Mehrabian, A., & Ferris, S. R. (1967). Inference of attitudes from nonverbal communication in two channels. *Journal of Consulting Psychology, 21,* 248–252.

Meldrum, H. (2011). The listening practices of exemplary physicians. *International Journal of Listening, 25,* 145–160.

Merriam-Webster Online Dictionary. (2013). Retrieved from http://www.merriam-webster.com/

Merrill, A. F., & Afifi, T. D. (2012). Examining the bidirectional nature of topic avoidance and relationship dissatisfaction: The moderating role of communication skills. *Communication Monographs, 79,* 499–521.

Messman, S. J., & Mikesell, R. L. (2000). Competition and interpersonal conflict in dating relationships. *Communication Reports, 13,* 21–34.

Mickelson, W. T., & Welch, S. A. (2013). Improving the performance of the listening competency scale: Revision and validation. *International Journal of Listening, 27,* 75–78.

Mill, J. S. (1863). *Utilitarianism.* London: Parker, Son, & Bourn.

Miller, G. R., & Steinberg, M. (1975). *Between people: A new analysis of interpersonal communication.* Chicago: Science Research Associates.

Miller, J. B., Plant, E. A., & Hanke, E. (1993). Girls' and boys' views of body type. In C. Berryman-Fink, D. Ballard-Reisch & L. H. Newman (Eds.), *Communication and sex-role socialization* (pp. 49–58). New York: Garland.

Miller, K. I. (2007). Compassionate communication in the workplace: Exploring processes of noticing, connecting, and responding. *Journal of Applied Communication Research, 35,* 223–245.

Miura, S. Y. (2000). The mediation of conflict in the traditional Hawaiian family: A collectivistic approach. *Qualitative Research Reports in Communication, 1,* 19–25.

Modern Language Association. (2010). *New MLA survey report finds that the study of languages other than English is growing and diversifying at U.S. colleges and universities.* New York: Author.

Molloy, J. T. (1978). *Dress for success.* New York: Warner.

Molm, L. D. (2001). Theories of social exchange and exchange networks. In G. Ritzer & B. Smart (Eds.), *Handbook of social theory* (pp. 260–272). London: Sage.

Montoya, R. M., & Horton, R. S. (2014). A two-dimensional model for the study of interpersonal attraction. *Personality and Social Psychology Review, 18,* 59–86.

Moore, N., Hickson, M., & Stacks, D. (2009). *Nonverbal communication: Studies and application.* New York: Oxford University Press.

Moors, R., & Webber, R. (2013). The dance of disclosure: Online self-disclosure of sexual assault. *Qualitative Social Work, 12,* 799–815.

Morris, D. (2002): *Peoplewatching: The Desmond Morris guide to body language.* New York: Vintage Books.

Morse, C. R., & Metts, S. (2011). Situational and communicative predictors of forgiveness following a relational transgression. *Western Journal of Communication, 75,* 239–258.

Mulac, A., Bradac, J. J., & Gibbons, P. (2001). Empirical support for the gender-as-culture hypothesis: An intercultural analysis of male/female language differences. *Human Communication Research, 27,* 121–152.

Murphy, D. E. (2002, May 26). Letting go: Beyond justice: The eternal struggle to forgive. *New York Times,* C1–C3.

Myers, S. A., Byrnes, K. A., Frisby, B. N., & Mansson, D. H. (2011). Adult siblings' use of affectionate communication as a strategic and routine relational maintenance behavior. *Communication Research Reports, 28,* 151–158.

Myers, S. A., & Claus, C. J. (2012). The relationship between students' motives to communicate with their instructors and classroom environment. *Communication Quarterly, 60,* 386–402.

N

National Council on Aging. (2013, July). *The United States of Aging Survey 2013.* Retrieved from http://www.ncoa.org/assets/files/pdf/united-states -of-aging/2013-survey/USA13-Full-Report.pdf

National Governors Association. (2008, May 4). *Promoting STEM education: A communications toolkit.* Washington, DC. Retrieved from http:// www.nga.org/cms/home/nga-center-for-best -practices/center-publications/page-edu -publications/col2-content/main-content-list /promoting-stem-education-a-commu.html

Nelson, M. K. (2014). Whither fictive kin? Or, what's in a name? *Journal of Family Issues, 35,* 201–222.

Nettle, D., & Romaine, S. (2000). *Vanishing voices: The extinction of the world's languages.* Oxford: Oxford University Press.

Neuliep, J. W. (2012). *Intercultural communication: A contextual approach.* Thousand Oaks, CA: Sage.

Newman, K. (2013). *The accordion family: Boomerang kids, anxious families, and the private toll of global competition.* Boston: Beacon.

Nguyen, M., Bin, Y. S., & Campbell, A. (2012). Comparing online and offline self-disclosure: A systematic review. *Cyberpsychology, Behavior, and Social Networking, 15,* 103–111.

Nilsen, T. (1966). *Ethics of speech communication.* Indianapolis, IN: Bobbs-Merrill.

Novack, J. (2013, September 30). Federal government begins first shutdown in 17 years. *Forbes.* Retrieved from http://www.forbes.com/sites /janetnovack/2013/09/30/clock-ticks-to-first-federal -shutdown-in-17-years/

Nunberg, G. (2003, May 29). *Fresh Air* interview [radio show].

O

O'Callaghan, A. (2013). Emotional congruence in learning and health encounters in medicine: Addressing an aspect of the hidden curriculum. *Advances in Health Sciences Education, 18,* 305–317.

Ogden, C. K., & Richards, I. A. (1923). *The meaning of meaning.* London: Kegan, Paul, Trench, Trubner.

Olson, L. N. (2002). Compliance gaining strategies of individuals experiencing "common couple violence." *Qualitative Research Reports in Communication, 3,* 7–14.

Olson, L. N. (2008). Relational control-motivated aggression: A theoretical framework for identifying various types of violent couples. In D. D. Cahn (Ed.), *Family violence: Communication processes* (pp. 27–47). Thousand Oaks, CA: Sage.

Omarzu, J. (2000). A disclosure decision model: Determining how and when individuals will self-disclose. *Personality and Social Psychology Review, 4,* 174–185.

Orbe, M. P. (1998). *Constructing co-cultural theory: An explication of culture, power, and communication.* Thousand Oaks, CA: Sage.

Orbe, M. P., & Roberts, T. L. (2012). Co-cultural theorizing: Foundations, applications, and extensions. *Howard Journal of Communications, 23,* 293–311.

Ortony, A., Clore, G. L., & Foss, M. (1987). The referential structure of the affective lexicon. *Cognitive Science, 11,* 361–384.

Osborn, P., Berg, C. A., Hughes, A. E., Pham, P., & Wiebe, D. J. (2013). What Mom and Dad don't know CAN hurt you: Adolescent disclosure to and secrecy from parents about type 1 diabetes. *Journal of Pediatric Psychology, 38,* 141–150.

Owen, W. F. (1989). Image metaphors of women and men in personal relationships. *Women's Studies in Communication, 12,* 37–57.

Oxford English dictionary. (2013). Recent updates to the OED. http://public.oed.com/the -oed-today/recent-updates-to-the-oed/

P

Palmer, K. S. (2002, October 10). Cultures clash in workplaces. *USA Today,* 13A.

Pan, Y. (2000). *Politeness in Chinese face-to-face interaction.* Stamford, CT: Ablex.

Parker, K. (2012, March 15). The boomerang generation: Feeling OK about living with Mom and Dad. Retrieved from http://www.pewsocialtrends .org/2012/03/15/the-boomerang-generation

Parks, M. R. (1982). Ideology in interpersonal communication: Off the couch and into the world. In M. Burgoon (Ed.), *Communication yearbook 6* (pp. 79–107). Newbury Park, CA: Sage.

Patterson, G. E., Ward, D. B., & Brown, T. B. (2013). Relationship scripts: How young women develop and maintain same-sex romantic relationships. *Journal of GLBT Family Studies, 9,* 179–201.

Pearson, J. C., West, R., & Turner, L. H. (1995). *Gender and communication.* Madison, WI: Brown & Benchmark.

Pellegrini, A. D. (2010). The role of physical activity in the development and function of human juveniles' sex segregation. *Behaviour, 147,* 1633–1656.

Pennebaker, J. W., Barger, S. D., & Tiebout, J. (1989). Trauma and health among Holocaust survivors. *Psychosomatic Medicine, 51,* 577–589.

Peterson, B. (2013, October 19). Baseball, shaper of language: Why linguists love America's favorite pastime. *Boston Globe.*

Petronio, S. (2000). Preface. In S. Petronio (Ed.), *Balancing the secrets of private disclosures* (pp. xiii–xvi). Mahwah, NJ: Erlbaum.

Petronio, S. (2002). *Boundaries of privacy: Dialectics of disclosure.* Albany, NY: SUNY Press.

Petronio, S. (2010). Communication privacy management theory: What do we know about family privacy regulation? *Journal of Family Theory & Review, 2,* 175–196.

Petronio, S. (2013). Brief status report on communication privacy management theory. *Journal of Family Communication, 13,* 6–14.

Petrow, S. (2013, October 22). Why can Neil Patrick Harris say that's "too gay" and straights can't? *New York Times.*

Pew Research Center. (2010, March 18). *The return of the multi-generational family household.* Washington, DC. Retrieved from http://www .pewsocialtrends.org/2010/03/18/the-return-of-the -multi-generational-family-household/

Pfeiffer, R. S., & Forsberg, R. L. (2005). *Ethics on the job: Cases and strategies.* Belmont, CA: Wadsworth.

Piff, P. K., Stancato, D. M., Martinez, A. G., Kraus, M. W., & Keltner, D. (2012). Class, chaos, and the construction of community. *Journal of Personality and Social Psychology, 103,* 949–962. doi: 10.1037/a0029673

Planalp, S. (1999). *Communicating emotion: Social, moral, and cultural processes.* Cambridge: Cambridge University Press.

Planalp, S., & Fitness, J. (1999). Thinking/feeling about social and personal relationships. *Journal of Social and Personal Relationships, 16,* 731–750.

Plutchik, R. (1984). Emotions: A general psycho-evolutionary theory. In K. R. Scherer & P. Ekman (Eds.), *Approaches to emotion* (pp. 197–219). Hillsdale, NJ: Erlbaum.

Poole, M., & Walther, J. (Eds.) (2002). *Communication: Ubiquitous, complex, consequential.* Washington, DC: National Communication Association.

Porter, K. (2013, April 22). 12 skills you need to keep your job in sales. Salesforce.com. Retrieved from http://blogs.salesforce.com/company/2013/04 /12-skills-you-need-to-keep-your-job-in-sales.html

Powers, R. (2013). Preface. In R. Powers (Ed.), *Bartlett's familiar Black quotations: 5,000 years of literature, lyrics, poems, passages, phrases, and proverbs from voices around the world* (pp. xv–xx). New York: Little, Brown.

Pressman, S. D., Gallagher, M. D., & Lopez, S. (2013). Is the emotion-health connection a "first-world problem"? *Psychological Science, 24,* 544–549.

Pryor, J. (2013) Marriage and divorce in the Western world. In A. Abela & J. Walker (Eds.), *Contemporary issues in family studies: Global perspectives on partnerships, parenting and support in a changing world.* Oxford: Wiley. doi: 10.1002/9781118320990.ch4

Pullum, G. K. (1991). *The great Eskimo vocabulary hoax and other irreverent essays on the study of language.* Chicago: University of Chicago Press.

Purdy, M. (2004). *Listen up, move up.* Retrieved from http://www.featuredreports.monster.com

Q

Quek, K. M.-T., & Fitzpatrick, J. (2013). Cultural values, self-disclosure, and conflict tactics as predictors of marital satisfaction among Singaporean husbands and wives. *Family Journal, 21,* 208–216.

R

Rahim, M. A. (1983). A measure of styles of handling interpersonal conflict. *Academy of Management Journal, 26,* 368–376.

Ravitch, D. (2003). *The language police: How pressure groups restrict what students learn.* New York: Knopf.

Rawlins, W. K. (1992, 2008). *Friendship matters: Communication, dialectics, and the life course.* New York: Aldine de Gruyter.

Reissman, C. (1990). *Divorce talk: Women and men make sense of personal relationships.* New Brunswick, NJ: Rutgers University Press.

Reyes, R. (2013, December 15). Obama was right to shake Castro's hand. RGJ.com. http://www.rgj .com/article/20131215/OPED04/312150006 /Raul-Reyes-Obama-right-shake-Castro-s-hand

Ribeau, S. A., Baldwin, J. R., & Hecht, M. L. (2000). An African American communication perspective. In L. A. Samovar & R. E. Porter (Eds.), *Intercultural communication: A reader* (pp. 128–135). Belmont, CA: Wadsworth.

Richards, R.D . (2013). Compulsory process in cyberspace: Rethinking privacy in the social networking age. *Harvard Journal of Law and Public Policy, 36,* 519–548.

Richmond, V. P., Wrench, J., & McCroskey, J. C. (2012). *Communication apprehension avoidance and effectiveness.* Boston: Pearson.

Roberto, A. J., Carlyle, K. E., & McClure, L. (2006). Communication and corporal punishment: The relationship between parents' use of verbal and physical aggression. *Communication Research Reports, 23,* 27–33.

Roethlisberger, F. L., & Dickson, W. (1939). *Management and the worker.* New York: Wiley.

Roloff, M. E. (1981). *Interpersonal communication: The social exchange approach.* Beverly Hills, CA: Sage.

Roloff, M. E. (1987). Communication and conflict. In C. R. Berger & S. H. Chaffee (Eds.), *Handbook of communication science* (pp. 484–534). Newbury Park, CA: Sage.

Roloff, M. E., & Ifert, D. E. (2000). Conflict management through avoidance: Withholding complaints, suppressing arguments, and declaring topics taboo. In S. Petronio (Ed.), *Balancing the secrets of private disclosures* (pp. 151–163). Mahwah, NJ: Erlbaum.

Rosenfeld, L. B. (2000). Overview of the ways privacy, secrecy, and disclosure are balanced in today's society. In S. Petronio (Ed.), *Balancing the secrets of private disclosures* (pp. 3–17). Mahwah, NJ: Erlbaum.

Ross, E. D., Shayya, L, Champlain, A., Monnot, M., & Prodan, C. I. (2013). Decoding facial blends of emotion: Visual field, attentional and hemispheric biases. *Brain Cognition, 83,* 252–261.

Rough guide. (2007, August). *Harper's,* 22–23. Retrieved from http://harpers.org/archive/2007/08 /rough-guide/

Rourke, L., Anderson, T., Garrison, D. R., & Archer, W. (2001). Assessing social presence in asynchronous text-based computer conferencing. *Journal of Distance Education, 14,* 50–71.

Rudawsky, D. J., Lundgren, D. C., & Grasha, A. F. (1999). Competitive and collaborative responses to negative feedback. *International Journal of Conflict Management, 10,* 172–190.

Russell, J. A. (1978). Evidence of convergent validity of the dimensions of affect. *Journal of Personality and Social Psychology, 36,* 1152–1168.

Russell, J. A. (1980). A circumplex model of affect. *Journal of Personality and Social Psychology, 39,* 1161–1178.

Russell, J. A. (1983). Pancultural aspects of the human conceptual organization of emotions. *Journal of Personality and Social Psychology, 45,* 1281–1288.

S

Sadka, D. (2004). *The Dewey color system.* New York: Three Rivers

Samovar, L. E., Porter, R. E., & McDaniel, E. R. (2013). (Eds.). *Intercultural communication: A reader.* Boston: Cengage/Wadsworth.

Samovar, L.E., Porter, R. E., McDaniel, E. R, & Roy, C. (2013). *Communicating between cultures.* Boston: Cengage/Wadsworth.

Sandri, G. (2013, September/October). Choosing conflict resolution by culture. *Industrial Management,* 10–15.

Sargent, S. L., Weaver, J. B., III, & Kiewitz, C. (1997). Correlates between communication apprehension and listening style preferences. *Communication Research Reports, 14,* 74–78.

Satir, V. (1972). *Peoplemaking.* Palo Alto, CA: Science & Behavior Books.

Schramm, W. L. (1954). *The process and effects of mass communication.* Urbana: University of Illinois Press.

Schrodt, P., Ledbetter, A. M., & Ohrt, J. K. (2007). Parental confirmation and affection as mediators of family communication patterns and children's mental well-being. *Journal of Family Communication, 7,* 23–46.

Schwartz, A. L., Galliher, R. V., & Rodríguez, M. M. D. (2011). Self-disclosure in Latinos' intercultural and intracultural friendships and acquaintanceships: Links with collectivism, ethnic identity, and acculturation. *Cultural Diversity and Ethnic Minority Psychology, 17,* 116–121.

Scollo, M., & Carbaugh, D. (2013). Interpersonal communication: Qualities and culture. *Russian Journal of Communication, 5,* 95–103. doi: 10.1080 /19409419.2013.805664

Seay, E. (2004, February 11). Lost city, lost languages. *Princeton Alumni Weekly, 17,* 43.

Seiter, J. S., & Bruschke, J. (2007). Deception and emotion: The effects of motivation, relationship type, and sex on expected feelings of guilt and shame following acts of deception in United States and Chinese samples. *Communication Studies, 58,* 1–16.

Selman, R. (1981). The child as friendship philosopher. In S. Asher & J. M. Gottman (Eds.), *The development of children's friendships* (pp. 242–272). New York: Cambridge University Press.

Selman, R. L. (2009). The evolution of pair therapy. In R. L. Selman, C. L. Watts, & L. H. Schultz (Eds.), *Pair therapy for treatment and prevention* (pp. 3–18). Brunswick, NJ: Transaction Books.

Serewicz, M. C. M., Dickson, F. C., Morrison, J. H. T. A., & Poole, L. L. (2007). Family privacy orientation, relational maintenance, and family satisfaction in young adults' family relationships. *Journal of Family Communication, 7,* 123–142.

Shannon, C. E., & Weaver, W. (1949). *The mathematical theory of communication.* Urbana: University of Illinois Press.

Shannon, C. E., & Weaver, W. (1999). *The mathematical theory of communication* (50th ed.). Urbana: University of Illinois Press.

Sharma, S., & Chakravarthy, B. K. (2013). How people view abstract art: An eye movement study to assess information processing and viewing strategy. In A. Chakrabarti & R. V. Prakash (Eds.), *IcoRD'13 Global Product Development: Lecture notes in mechanical engineering* (pp. 477–487). New York: Springer.

Sheldon, P. (2013). Examining gender differences in self-disclosure on Facebook versus face-to-face. *Journal of Social Media in Society, 2,* 88–104.

Shellenbarger, S. (2013, October 15). Teens are still developing empathy skills: Vital social skill ebbs and flows in adolescent boys; how to cultivate sensitivity. Work & Family, *Wall Street Journal.* Retrieved from http://online.wsj.com/news/articles/SB 10001424052702304561004579137514122387446

Shields, S. A. (2000). Thinking about gender, thinking about theory: Gender and emotional experience. In A. H. Fischer (Ed.), *Gender and emotion: Social psychological perspectives* (pp. 3–23). Cambridge: Cambridge University Press.

Shields, S. A., & Crowley, J. C. (1996). Appropriating questionnaires and rating scales for a feminist psychology: A multimethod approach to gender and emotion. In S. Wilkinson (Ed.), *Feminist social psychologies* (pp. 218–232). Philadelphia: Open University Press.

Shimanoff, S. B. (1980). *Communication rules: Theory and research.* Beverly Hills, CA: Sage.

Shimanoff, S. B. (1985). Expressing emotions in words: Verbal patterns of interactions. *Journal of Communication, 35,* 16–31.

Shimanoff, S. B. (1987). Types of emotional disclosures and request compliance between spouses. *Communication Monographs, 54,* 85–100.

Shin, L. (2003, May 9). Ah, sweet mystery of e-mail. *New York Times,* D2.

Shuter, R., & Turner, L. H. (1997). African American and European American women in the workplace: Perceptions of conflict communication. *Management Communication Quarterly, 11,* 74–96.

Sillars, A. L., Roberts, L., Leonard, K. E., & Dun, T. (2000). Cognition during marital conflict: The relationship of thought and talk. *Journal of Social and Personal Relationships, 17,* 479–502.

Silva-Corvalán, C. (1994). *Language contact and change: Spanish in Los Angeles.* New York: Oxford University Press.

Silverstein, J., & Lasky, M. (2004). *Online dating for dummies.* Indianapolis, IN: Wiley.

Simonson, P., Peck, J., Craig, R. T., & Jackson, J. P. (2013). The history of communication history. In P. Simonson, J. Peck, R. T. Craig, & J. P. Jackson (Eds.), *The handbook of communication history* (pp. 13–57). New York: Routledge.

Simpson, L. (2003). Get around resistance and win over the other side. *Harvard Management Communication Letter,* 3–5

Siner, E. (2013, October 24). What's a "glitch" anyway? A brief linguistic history. Retrieved from http:// www.npr.org/blogs/alltechconsidered/2013/10/24 /239788307/whats-a-glitch-anyway-a-brief-linguistic -history-meaning-definition

Smitherman, G. (2000). *Black talk: Words and phrases from the hood to the amen corner.* Boston: Houghton Mifflin.

Smith-Sanders, A. K., & Harter, L. M. (2007). Democracy, dialogue, and education: An exploration of conflict resolution at Jefferson Junior High School. *Southern Communication Journal, 72,* 109–126.

Smyth, J. M., Pennebaker, J. W., & Arigo, D. (2012). What are the health effects of disclosure? In A. Baum, T. A. Revenson, & J. Singer (Eds.), *Handbook of health psychology* (pp. 175–192). New York: Psychology Press.

Snorton, R. (2004). New poll shows at least 5% of America's high school students identify as gay or lesbian. Retrieved from http://www.glsen.org/cgi-bin/iowa/all/library/record/1724.html

Snyder, M. (1979). Self-monitoring processes. In L. Berkowitz (Ed.), *Advances in experimental social psychology* (pp. 86–131). New York: Academic Press.

Sonnentag, S., Unger, D., & Nägel, I. J. (2013). Workplace conflict and employee well-being: The moderating role of detachment from work during off-job time. *International Journal of Conflict Management, 24,* 166–183.

Sopory, P. (2006). Metaphor and attitude accessibility. *Southern Communication Journal, 71,* 251–272.

Spiegel, D., & Kimerling, R. (2001). Group psychotherapy for women with breast cancer: Relationships among social support, emotional expression, and survival. In C. D. Ryff & B. H. Singer (Eds.), *Emotion, social relationships, and health* (pp. 97–123). Oxford: Oxford University Press.

Spinello, R. (2014). *Global capitalism, culture, and ethics.* New York: Routledge.

Spitzberg, B. H., & Cupach, W. R. (1984). *Interpersonal communication competence.* Beverly Hills, CA: Sage.

Spitzberg, B. H., & Cupach, W. R. (1989). *Handbook of interpersonal communication research.* New York: Springer.

Sprecher, S., Treger, S., & Wondra, J. D. (2013). Effects of self-disclosure role on liking, closeness, and other impressions in get-acquainted interactions. *Journal of Social and Personal Relationships, 30,* 497–514.

Sprecher, S., Treger, S., Wondra, J. D., Hilaire, N., & Wallpe, K. (2013). Taking turns: Reciprocal self-disclosure promotes liking in initial interactions. *Journal of Experimental Social Psychology, 49,* 860–866.

Stafford, L., Dainton, M., & Haas, S. (2000). Measuring routine and strategic relational maintenance: Scale revision, sex versus gender roles, and the prediction of relational characteristics. *Communication Monographs, 67,* 306–323.

Stearns, P. N. (1994). *American cool: Constructing a twentieth-century emotional style.* New York: New York University Press.

Stern, K. (2013, March 20). Why the rich don't give to charity. *The Atlantic.* Retrieved from http://www.theatlantic.com/magazine/archive/2013/04/why-the-rich-dont-give/309254/

Sternberg, R. (2013, February). Searching for love. *The Psychologist, 26*(2), 98–101. Retrieved from http://www.thepsychologist.org.uk/archive/archive_home.cfm?volumeID_26-editionID_222-ArticleID_2217_getfile_getPDF/thepsychologist/0213ster.pdf

Sternberg, R. J. (1998). *Cupid's arrow.* New York: Cambridge University Press.

Sternberg, R. J. (2006). *Cognitive psychology.* Belmont, CA: Thomson/Wadsworth.

Sternberg, R. J., & Whitney, C. (2002). How to think clearly about relationships. In J. A. DeVito (Ed.), *The interpersonal communication reader* (pp. 152–161). Boston: Allyn & Bacon.

Stevenson, S. (2012). There's magic in your smile: How smiling affects your brain. *Psychology Today.* Retrieved from http://www.psychologytoday.com/blog/cutting-edge-leadership/201206/there-s-magic-in-your-smile

Stoller, G. (2013, December 29). Expert etiquette tips for doing business in China. *USA Today.* Retrieved from http://www.usatoday.com/story/travel/destinations/2013/12/29/cultural-studies-pay-in-china/4240917/

Strelan, P., McKee, I., Calic, D., Cook, L., Shaw, L. (2013). For whom do we forgive? A functional analysis of forgiveness. *Personal Relationships, 20,* 124–139.

Stringer, J. L., & Hopper, R. (1998). Generic *he* in conversation? *Quarterly Journal of Speech, 84,* 209–221.

Stuart, E. J. (2010). *Listening skills for the 21st century.* n.p.: Lulu.

Styles, R. (2013, September 29). Looking for love? Try the office! *Daily Mail* (UK). Retrieved from http://www.dailymail.co.uk/femail/article-2437181/Relationships-begin-workplace-likely-result-marriage-new-study-reveals.html

Su, H. (2013). *Economic justice and liberty: The social philosophy in John Stuart Mill's Utilitarianism.* New York: Routledge.

Such, J. M., Espinosa, A., García-Fornes, A., & Sierra, C. (2012). Self-disclosure decision making based on intimacy and privacy. *Information Sciences, 211,* 93–111.

Suter, E. A. (2015). Communication in gay and lesbian families. In L. H. Turner & R. West (Eds.), *The SAGE handbook of family communication* (pp. 235–247). Thousand Oaks, CA: Sage.

Sweeney, N. (2004, March 7). Cyber cool: Teens' witty screen names don't always seem so at college time. *Milwaukee Journal Sentinel,* B1–B2.

T

Taheri, M. A. (2013). *Human worldview.* Glenside, PA: Interuniversal Press.

Tannen, D. (2001). *Talking from 9 to 5: Women and men at work.* New York: HarperCollins.

Tardy, C. H. (2000). Self-disclosure and health: Revisiting Sidney Jourard's hypothesis. In S. Petronio (Ed.), *Balancing the secrets of private disclosures* (pp. 111–122). Mahwah, NJ: Erlbaum.

Tavernise, S. (2012, September 20). Life spans shrink for least-educated whites in the U.S. *New York Times,* A1.

Tavris, C. (2001). Anger defused. In K. Scott & M. Warren (Eds.), *Perspectives on marriage: A reader* (pp. 243–253). New York: Oxford University Press.

TenHouten, W. D. (2012). *Emotion and reason: Mind, brain, and the social domains of work and love.* London: Routledge.

Theiss, J. A., & Solomon, D. H. (2007). Communication and the emotional, cognitive, and relational consequences of first sexual encounters between partners. *Communication Quarterly, 55,* 179–206.

Thibaut, J., & Kelley, H. (1959). *The social psychology of groups.* New York: Wiley.

Thibodeau P. H., & Boroditsky L. (2013). Natural language metaphors covertly influence reasoning. *PLoS ONE* 8: e52961. doi: 10.1371/journal.-pone.0052961

Thomas, P. M. (2013., October). *Researching African American family history.* Harrisonburg, VA: Coming to the Table, Eastern Mennonite University. Retrieved from http://comingtothetable.org/wp-content/uploads/2013/10/07-Researching_African_American_Family_History.pdf

Thompson, J., & Collier, M. J. (2006). Toward contingent understandings of intersecting identifications among selected U.S. interracial couples: Integrating interpretive and critical views. *Communication Quarterly, 54,* 487–507.

Thompson, M. L. (2013). *Imagination in Kant's critical philosophy.* New York: Walter de Gruyter.

Thoth, C. A., Tucker, C., Leahy, M., & Stewart, S. M. (2013). Self-disclosure of serostatus by youth who are HIV-positive: A review. *Journal of Behavioral Medicine.* doi: 10.1007/s10865-012-9485-2

Tine, M. (2013). Working memory differences between children living in rural and urban poverty. *Journal of Cognition and Development, 24.* doi: 10.1080/15248372.2013.797906

Ting-Toomey, S., & Chung, L. C. (2005). *Understanding intercultural communication.* Los Angeles: Roxbury.

Toma, C. L., & Hancock, J. T. (2010). Looks and lies: The role of physical attractiveness in online dating self-presentation and deception. *Communication Research, 37,* 335–351.

Tracy, S. J. (2005). Locking up emotion: Moving beyond dissonance for understanding emotion labor discomfort. *Communication Monographs, 72,* 261–283.

Tracy, S. J., Alberts, J. K., & Rivera, K. D. (2007, January 31). How to bust the office bully. Report # 0701, The Project for Wellness and Work-Life, The Hugh Downs School of Human Communication.

Tracy, S. J., Lutgen-Sandvik, P., & Alberts, J. K. (2006). Nightmares, demons and slaves: Exploring the painful metaphors of workplace bullying. *Management Communication Quarterly, 20,* 148–185.

Treichler, P. A., & Kramarae, C. (1983). Women's talk in the ivory tower. *Communication Quarterly, 31,* 118–132.

Trenholm, S. (1986). *Human communication theory.* Englewood Cliffs, NJ: Prentice Hall.

Troy, A. B., Lewis-Smith, J., & Laurenceau, J.-P. (2006). Interracial and intraracial romantic relationships: The search for differences in satisfaction, conflict, and attachment style. *Journal of Social and Personal Relationship, 23,* 65–80.

Turk, D. R., & Monahan, J. L. (1999). "Here I go again": An examination of repetitive behaviors during interpersonal conflicts. *Southern Communication Journal, 64,* 232–244.

Turkle, S. (2011). *Alone together: Why we expect more from technology and less from each other.* New York: Basic Books.

Turner, L. H., Dindia, K., & Pearson, J. C. (1995). An investigation of female/male verbal behaviors in same-sex and mixed-sex conversations. *Communication Reports, 8,* 86–96.

Turner, L. H., & Shuter, R. (2004). African American and European American women's visions of workplace conflict: A metaphorical analysis. *Howard Journal of Communications, 15,* 169–183.

Turner, L. H., & West, R. (2013). *Perspectives of family communication.* New York: McGraw-Hill.

Turner, L. H., & West, R. (2015). The challenge of defining "family." In L. H. Turner & R. West (Eds.), *The SAGE handbook of family communication* (pp. 10–25). Thousand Oaks, CA: Sage.

U

Ullrich, P. M., & Lutgendorf, S. K. (2002). Journaling about stressful events: Effects of cognitive processing and emotional expression. *Annals of Behavioral Medicine, 24,* 244–250.

Ury, W. (2010, November). The walk from "no" to "yes." Retrieved from http://www.ted.com/talks/william_ury.html

U.S. Bureau of Labor Statistics, Census Bureau. (2012). Single-parent households, 1980 to 2009. Table 1337. Retrieved from http://www.census.gov/compendia/statab/2012/tables/12s1337.pdf

U.S. Census Bureau. (2011a). *Older Americans month.* Retrieved from http://www.census.gov/newsroom/releases/archives/facts_for_features_special_editions/cb08–ff14.html

U.S. Census Bureau. (2011b). *Resident population of the United States.* Retrieved from http://www.census.gov/hhes/families

U.S. Census Bureau. (2012). *2010 Census shows multiple-race population grew faster than single-race population.* CB12-82, September 27. Washington, DC: Author. Retrieved from http://www.census.gov/newsroom/releases/archives/race/cb12–182.html

Vallejo, J. A. (2012). Socially mobile Mexican Americans and the minority culture of mobility. *American Behavioral Scientist, 56,* 666–681.

Vanden Bosch, J. (2012). "We're not twenty-two anymore": Intimacy in long-lived marriages. *The Gerontologist, 52,* 866–868.

Vangelisti, A. L., Caughlin, J. P., & Timmerman, L. (2001). Criteria for revealing family secrets. *Communication Monographs, 68,* 1–27.

Vangelisti, A. L., Knapp, M., & Daly, J. (1990). Conversational narcissism. *Communication Monographs, 57,* 251–274.

Vennum, A., Lindstrom, R., Monk, J. K., & Adams, R. (2013). "It's complicated": The continuity and correlates of cycling in cohabiting and marital relationships. *Journal of Social and Personal Relationships.* doi: 10.1177/0265407513501987

Victor, D. A. (1992). *International business communication.* New York: HarperCollins.

Vittengl, J. R., & Holt, C. S. (2000). Getting acquainted: The relationship of self-disclosure and social attraction to positive affect. *Journal of Social and Personal Relationships, 17,* 53–66.

Vogel, D. L., Murphy, M. J., Werner-Wilson, R. J., Cutrona, C. E., & Seeman, J. (2007). Sex differences in the use of demand and withdraw behavior in marriage: Examining the social structure hypothesis. *Journal of Counseling Psychology, 54,* 165–177.

von Bertalanffy, L. (1968). *General system theory.* New York: Braziller.

Waldman, K. (2013, December 9). *Society tells men that friendship is girly. Men respond by not having any friends.* Retrieved from http://www.slate.com/blogs/xx_factor/2013/12/09/white_heterosexual_men_can_t_have_friends_gender_norms_are_to_blame.html?wpisrc=hpsponsoredd2

Waldron, V. R., & Kelley, D. L. (2008). *Communicating forgiveness.* Thousand Oaks, CA: Sage.

Walker, L. (1984). *The battered woman syndrome.* New York: Springer.

Walther, J. B. (1992). Interpersonal effects in computer-mediated interactions. *Communication Research, 19,* 52–90.

Walther, J. B. (1996). Computer-mediated communication: Impersonal, interpersonal, and hyperpersonal interaction. *Communication Research, 23,* 3–43.

Walther, J. B. (2011). Theories of computer-mediated communication and interpersonal relations. In M. L. Knapp & J. A. Daly (Eds.), *The handbook of interpersonal communication* (pp. 443–479). Thousand Oaks, CA: Sage.

Walther, J. B. (2012). Interaction through technological lenses: Computer-mediated communication and language. *Journal of Language and Social Psychology, 31,* 397–414.

Walther, J. B., & Jang, J.-W. (2012). Communication processes in participatory web sites. *Journal of Computer-Mediated Communication, 18,* 2–15. doi: 10.1111/j.1083-6101.2012.01592.x

Walther, J. B., Van Der Heide, B., Ramirez, A., Jr., Burgoon, J. K., & Pena, J. (2014). Interpersonal and hyperpersonal aspects of computer-mediated communication. In S. S. Sundar (Ed.), *The handbook of psychology and communication technology.* West Sussex, England: Wiley-Blackwell.

Wang, Q., Fink, E. L., & Cai, D. A. (2012). The effect of conflict goals on avoidance strategies: What does not communicating communicate? *Human Communication Research, 38,* 222–252.

Watson, K. W., & Barker, L. L. (1995). *Winning by listening around.* Tega Cay, SC: SPECTRA.

Watzlawick, P., Beavin, J., & Jackson, D. D. (1967). *Pragmatics of human communication.* New York: Norton.

Waytz, N. (2013). Social connection and seeing human. In C. N. DeWall (Ed.), *The Oxford handbook of social exclusion* (pp. 251–256). Oxford: Oxford University Press.

Weber, K., Goodboy, A. K., & Cayanus, J. L. (2010). Flirting competence: An experimental study on appropriate and effective opening lines. *Communication Research Reports, 27,* 184–191.

West, R., & Turner, L. H. (2014). *Introducing communication theory: Analysis and application* (5th ed.). New York: McGraw-Hill.

Whorf, B. (1956). *Language, thought, and reality.* Cambridge, MA: MIT Press.

Wile, J., & Weisenthal, R. (2013, May 28). 13 things that Americans do that the rest of the world just finds bizarre. *Business Insider.* Retrieved from http://www.businessinsider.com

Williams, A. (2007, July 29). (-: Just between you and me ;-). *New York Times,* D1, D9.

Williams, R. B. (2011, August 6). Why we pay more attention to beautiful people. Wired for Success blog, *Psychology Today.* Retrieved from http://www.psychologytoday.com

Wilmot, W. W. (1995). *Relational communication.* New York: McGraw-Hill.

Wilson, S. R., Hayes, J., Bylund, C., Rack, J. J., & Herman, A. P. (2006). Mothers' trait verbal aggressiveness and child abuse potential. *Journal of Family Communication, 6,* 279–296.

Wolvin, A. D. (2010). Introduction: Perspectives on listening in the 21st century. In A. D. Wolvin (Ed.), *Listening and human communication in the 21st century* (pp. 1–4). Oxford: Wiley-Blackwell. doi: 10.1002/9781444314908.fmatter

Wolvin, A. D., & Coakley, C. G. (1996). *Listening.* Madison, WI: Brown & Benchmark.

Wood, J. T. (1998). *But I thought you meant … misunderstandings in human communication.* Mountain View, CA: Mayfield.

Wood, J. T. (2013). *Gendered lives.* New York: Wadsworth.

Worthington, D.L, & Fitch-Hauser, M. (2012). *Listening: Processes, functions, and competency.* Boston: Allyn & Bacon.

Wright, K. B., Rosenberg, J., Egbert, N., Ploeger, N. A., Bernard, D. R., & King, S. (2013). Communication competence, social support, and depression among college students: A model of Facebook and face-to-face support network influence. *Journal of Health Communication, 18,* 41–57.

Yadegaran, J. (2013, December 11). Are selfies good or bad for our self-esteem? *San Jose Mercury News.* Retrieved from http://www.mercurynews.com/ci_24696982/are-selfies-good-or-bad-our-self-esteem

Yang, C., Brown, B. B., & Braun, M. T. (2014). From Facebook to cell calls: Layers of electronic intimacy in college students' interpersonal relationships. *New Media & Society, 16,* 5–23.

Yang, S. (2013, November 15). China easing one-child policy amid elderly boom. *USA Today.* Retrieved from http://www.usatoday.com/story/news/world/2013/11/15/china-one-child-policy/3570593/

Young, S. L., & Bippus, A. M. (2001). Does it make a difference if they hurt you in a funny way? Humorously and nonhumorously phrased hurtful messages in personal relationships. *Communication Quarterly, 49,* 35–52.

Zak, D. (2013, November 19). "Selfie"-reliance: The word of the year is the story of our individualism. *Washington Post.* Retrieved from http://www.washingtonpost.com

Zhang, Q. (2007). Family communication patterns and conflict styles in Chinese parent-child relationships. *Communication Quarterly, 55,* 113–128.

Zohoori, A. (2013). A cross-cultural comparison of the HURIER listening profile among Iranian and U.S. students. *International Journal of Listening, 27,* 50–60.

INDEX

A

Ability, perception and, 54
Abstract, defined, 73
Abstraction
    ladder of, 73, 86–87
    words varying in level of, 73–75
Abuse, conflict and, 186
Accounts, relational transgression and, 217
Acculturation, 30
Acronyms, 114
Action-centered listening style, 122
Active listening, 115, 127–129, 150–151
Activity (emotion), 132
Activity, time and, 102–103
Actual self, 64
Adult friendships, 229–231
Aeschylus, 28
Affection and instrumentality dialectic, 211
Affinity seeking strategies, 215, 216
African Americans
    family stories among, 221
    muted language and, 83
    racist language and, 84–85
African American Vernacular English (AAVE), 76
Age
    email addresses and, 80
    multileveled nature of co-culture and, 31–32
    perception and, 54
    verbal symbols and, 80
Agency, 226–227
Aggression, in interpersonal relationships, 186
All I Really Need to Know I Learned in Kindergarten
    (Fulghum), 128
Ambiguity
    in nonverbal communication, 91
    strategic, 74–75
    in touch behavior, 98
Ambushing, 119, 121
American Cancer Society, 14
American Cool (Stearns), 142
American Sign Language (ASL), 116
Ancient Greece and Rome, 4
Androgynous, 52–53, 159
Anxiety
    immigration causing, 32–33
    intercultural communication and, 40–41
Apologies, 217
Apprehension, communication, 2–3
Approaching, 215
Arabic language, 78, 140
Aristotle, 4, 23
Arranged marriages, 202
As Good As It Gets (film), 15
ASL (American Sign Language), 116
Assumption of similarity, 41–42
Attending and selecting stage of perception, 48–49
Attraction, in close relationships, 201–202
Attractiveness, physical, 95
Attributes of verbal symbols, 70–75
Attribution theory, 62, 63

Autonomy and connection dialectic, 211
Avoiding stage in relationship, 207–208

B

Baby Boomers, 80
    grandparent names for, 80
Barnes, Sue, 54
Bechar-Israeli, Haya, 61
Beginning relationships, communication skills for, 213–214
Behavior. *See* Nonverbal behavior; Verbal behaviors
Belonging, perceptions of, 40–41
Bem, Sandra, 53
Biases
    knowing your, 42–43
    speaker, 115
    Western, 159
Biases, intercultural communication and, 42–43
Bilingualism, 77
Biological theory of emotion, 134–135, 136
Black English, 76, 83
Blackfeet Indians, 123
Blind people, eye behavior and, 104
Blind self, 166
Body artifacts, 94–95
Body movement (kinesics), 93–94, 103, 105
Body orientation, 94
Body posture, 93–94
Bonding stage in relationship, 206–207
Boomerang kids, 59
Boundaries or openness, 209–210
Breadth of self-disclosure, 165
Bullying, 185–186
Bus rider phenomenon, 162

C

Calibration, 210
C.A.R.E. (Constantly Assessing Relationship Excellence), 235
Careers
    child protective specialists, family life and, 224
    human resource management, cultural awareness and, 29
    journalism, self-disclosure in, 172
    law enforcement officers, conflict management and, 193
    mental health counselors, 127
    nursing, body language and, 108
    "people-centered" professions, 15
    personal trainers, client's relationship with, 198
    restaurant business, verbal clarity and, 87
    sales professionals, 64
    teaching, I-messages and, 150
Caring and sharing level of friendships, 229
Castro, Raúl, 99
Categorical imperative, 21–22, 24
Catharsis, 167
Channel, 8
Chicano English, 76–77
Child protective specialists, 224
China
    concept of love in, 140
    conflict and, 183

China (*continued*)
    customs and culture, 28
    emotions and, 140
    shame in, 140
    silence in, 39–40
Choice, self-disclosure and, 153–154
Chronemic cues, 106
Chronemics, 102
Chunking, 114–115
Circumscribing stage in relationship, 207
Citing gestures, 93
Civil communication, 25
"Clicking," 158
Close friendships, 225–231
Close relationships, 196–217
    attraction and, 201–202
    C.A.R.E. (Constantly Assessing Relationship Excellence)
        in, 235–236
    as cognitive constructs, 200
    communication in, 196–197
    communication patterns in, 198–199
    communication skills for beginning, 213–214
    communication skills for maintaining, 215–216
    communication skills for repairing, 216–217
    as cultural performances, 199
    culture influencing, 202
    defined, 198
    dialectics theory on, 210–213
    electronic media and, 203–204
    equitable, 236–237
    explaining communication in, 208–214
    family, 219–224
    importance of, 196
    influences on, 201–204
    Knapp's model of development in, 205–208
    as linguistic construction, 200–201
    metaphors describing, 200–201
    overlapping of types of, 218
    recognizing history together, 236
    role relationships and, 198
    skill set for communicating in, 214–217, 235–237
    social exchange theory on, 213–214
    stage models of, 204–205
    stages in development of, 204–208
    stages of, 205–208
    systems theory on, 208–210
Clothing, nonverbal communication and, 94–95
Co-cultures, 30–31
    personal space in, 98
    speech communities and, 77
Codability, 78
Codes, nonverbal communication. *See* Nonverbal
    communication codes
Code switching, 69–70
Cognitive constructs, close relationships as, 200
Collectivism/collectivistic cultures, 38
    conflict in, 183
    emotional communication and, 140–141
    family and, 202
    listening and, 123
Color, nonverbal communication and, 101
Commitment, 233
Communicating emotionally, 136
Communication. *See also* Interpersonal communication; Nonverbal
    communication; Verbal communication
    civil, 25
    phatic, 76
    types of, 4–5

Communication apprehension, 2–3
    defined, 2
    intercultural, 2–3
Communication competency, 25
Communication models
    defined, 7
    evolving, 12
    interactional, 9–10
    linear, 7–9
    transactional, 10–12
Communication privacy management theory (CPM), 163–164
Communication studies
    history of, 4
    origins, 4
    value of, 14
Communion, 226
Community
    culture creating, 30–31
    defined, 30
Comparison level for alternatives, 214
Compassion, communicating, 138
Complexity, message, 118
Computing, 188
Concrete words, 73
Confirmation, 85
Conflict(s), 174–194. *See also* Interpersonal conflict
    in close relationships, 199
    communication patterns in, 184–185
    content, 179, 180
    cultural influences on, 183
    defining, 175–176
    explaining, 187–190
    explanatory process model of, 188–190
    four-part model of, 187–188
    gender and sex influencing, 182–183
    during holidays, 176
    image, 178–179, 180
    incompatible goals and, 176, 178
    interaction and, 176–177
    meta, 180
    myths about communication and, 181–182
    power and, 190–192
    relational, 179
    serial, 180–181
    techniques for managing, 192–194
    as unavoidable, 174
    value, 179, 180
Conflict interaction, 189
Conflict management techniques
    asking questions, 193–194
    cultural sensitivity, 194
    law enforcement officers and, 193
    lightening up, 193
    listening, 194
    presuming and expressing goodwill, 193
    styles for, 192
Connotative meaning, 73
Consistency, between verbal and nonverbal communication, 171
Contact codes, 97–101
Contemporary nuclear family, 222
Content-centered listening style, 122
Content conflicts, 179, 180
Content level, 18
Context
    cultural, 8
    defined, 8
    distal, 188–189
    emotional communication and, 142–143

in explanatory process model of conflict, 188–189
in four-part model of conflict, 187, 188
historical, 9
intercultural communication and, 38–39
in linear model of communication, 8–9
nonverbal communication placed in, 108
physical, 8
proximal, 189
self-disclosure and, 171
social-emotional, 8–9
touch behavior and, 98
verbal symbols and, 80–81
Context orientation theory, 38–39
Continuum of interpersonal communication, 12–14
Conversation
imagined, 207
Conversational narcissism, 119
Corporate social responsibility, communication ethics and, 22
Corrective maintenance or repair, 217
Costs, in social exchange theory, 213–214
Cues, for emotional communication, 138–139
Cultural awareness, human resource management and, 29
Cultural context, 8
Cultural empathy, 44
Cultural imperialism, 44
Cultural performances, close relationships as, 199
Cultural respect, 44
Cultural sensitivity, 194
Cultural variability theory, 38
Culture(s). See also High-context cultures; Intercultural
      communication; Low-context cultures
   close relationships and, 202
   components of, 29
   defining, 28–32
   dimensions of, 36–39
   educating yourself about, 44–45
   feminine, 37
   Hofstede's cultural dimensions and, 38–39
   identity and, 28
   influence on communication types, 5
   influence on emotional communication, 139–141
   influence on perception, 52
   interpersonal communication differences and, 20
   interpersonal conflict and, 183
   as learned, 29–30
   listening process and, 123–124
   masculine, 37
   meaning and, 6–7
   as multileveled, 31–32
   nonverbal communication and, 89
   self-disclosure and, 158–159
   verbal symbols and, 75–79
Culture clash, 31
Cyclic alteration, 212

D

Darwin, Charles, 134, 135
Dating
   cultural differences in, 30
   online, 5, 203–204
Decoding, 70
Defensive listening, 119, 121
Delivery gestures, 93
Demby, Gene, 69
Demographic imperative, 34, 36
Denotative meaning, 72–73

Depth of self-disclosure, 165
Descartes, René, 133
Dialectics
   affection and instrumentality, 211
   autonomy and connection, 211
   external, 211–212
   ideal and real, 212
   internal, 211
   judgment and acceptance, 211
   novelty and predictability, 211
   openness and protection, 211
   public and private, 212
Dialectics theory, 210–213
Dialogue enhancers, 128
Differentiating stage in relationship, 207
Direct and virtual use of power, 191
Direct application of power, 191
Disclosure. See Self-disclosure
Disconfirmation, 85
Disqualifying, 212–213
Distal context, 188–189
Distal outcomes, 189
Distance
   intimate, 98–99, 100
   personal, 99, 100
   power, 36–37
   public, 99, 100
   social, 99, 100
Distance, nonverbal communication and, 98–101
Distracting, 188
Distractions, nonverbal, 108
Distribution of power, 36–37
Diversity, 32–33
Doctor-patient communication, 14
Dualism, 133–134
Duration, 102–103
Dyadic effect, 162

E

Eastern emoticons, 143
Ebonics, 76
Economic imperative, 34–35, 36
Education of self, 44–45
Electronic communication. See Online communication
Email addresses, 80
Embarrassment, strategic, 132
Emoticons, 106, 143–144
Emotion(s), 130–151. See also Emotional communication
   biological theory of, 134–135, 136
   classifying, 132–133
   conflict and, 188
   defining, 131–132
   dualism and, 133–134
   emotions about (meta-emotion), 139
   identifying reasons for your, 148
   interpersonal communication and, 136–139
   metaphors for, 137–138
   negative, 144
   owning your, 149
   physiological component to, 134
   real vs. manufactured feelings, 131
   reason and, 133–134
   recognizing your, 147–148
   sharing with others, 148–149
   social interaction theory of, 135–136
   stating your, 148
Emotional afterglow, 136

Emotional communication
    constructive aspects of, 145–147
    context and, 142–143
    cues for, 138–139
    cultural influences on, 139–141
    defined, 137
    destructive aspects of, 144–145
    electronic media and, 143–144
    gender and sex differences in, 141–142
    increasing competence in, 147–151
    influences on, 139–144
    meta-emotion and, 139
    nonverbal cues for, 138, 139
    verbal cues for, 138–139
Emotional contagion, 136
Emotional effects, 136–137
Emotional experience, 136
Emotional intelligence, 147
Emotional labor, 131
Emotion cone, 133
Empathy, 125–126
    active listening and, 150–151
    cultural, 44
    defined, 125–126
    listening and, 125–126
    by low-income *vs.* high-income, 150
    in responses, 125–126
    supportive climate in communication through, 215
    of teens, 125
Employment. *See also* Careers
    listening and, 116
    outsourcing and, 35
    work friendships, 226
Empowerment, 192
Encoding, 70
Enculturation, 30
English language
    African American vernacular, 76
    baseball and, 83
    Chicano, 76–77
    "English only" movement, 32
    idioms in, 75–76
    Inuit words for "snow" and, 78
    power of words in, 72
    translation of words for emotions, 140
English Language Empowerment Act (1996), 32
Environment, nonverbal communication and, 101–102
Equifinality, 210
Equitable relationships, 236–237
Equivocation, 75
Ethical imperative, 35, 36
Ethic of care, 23, 24
Ethics
    categorical imperative in, 21–22, 24
    corporate social responsibility and, 22
    defined, 18
    ethic of care in, 23, 24
    golden mean and, 23, 24
    in interpersonal communication, 18–19, 20–24
    significant choice in, 23–24
    utilitarian, 22–23, 24
    values and, 24
Ethnicity, verbal symbols and, 75–79
Ethnocentrism, 39–40, 42
Euphemisms, 75
Evans, Rebecca, 30
Evolution of interpersonal communication, 4–6
Evolution of words, 71–72
Expectancy violations theory, 100
Experimenting stage in relationship, 205–206

Explanatory process model of conflict, 188–190
External dialectics, 211–212
External feedback, 9
Eye behavior/contact, 95–96, 103–104, 108

F

Face, 59–60
    defined, 59
    "losing," 60
    negative, 60
    positive, 59–60
Facebook, 63, 204, 225
Face-to-face communication, 47, 59
Face-to-face relationships, online relationships vs., 106
Facework, identity management and, 59–60
Facial communication
    cultural variations in, 103–104
    emotional communication and, 138
    nonverbal communication and, 95–96
Facts
    defined, 65
    inferences *vs.*, 65, 115
    as verifiable, 115
Families
    child protective specialists and, 224
    conflict in, 176, 185
    gay and lesbian, 222–223
    multigenerational, 223
    nuclear, 221–222
    single-parent, 223–224
    types of, 221–224
    violence and aggression in, 186
Familism, Latino concept of, 202
Family-of-origin, 221
Family relationships, 219–224
    defining, 220
    intentional, 219
    interpersonal communication practices, 220–221
    as lifelong, 219–220
    types of, 221
Family stories, 220–221
FBO (Facebook Official), 204
Feedback
    defined, 9
    external, 9
    in interactional model of communication, 9
    internal, 9
    negative, 210
    nonjudgmental, 126–127
    positive, 210
    in responding, 114
    in systems theory, 210
Feeling rules, 142–143
Feelings. *See also* Emotion(s)
    knowing your, 147–148
    owning your, 149
    real *vs.* manufactured, 131
Feminine cultures, 37
Feminist movement, 6, 84
Field of experience, 11
"Fight-fight" pattern, 184
Figurative language, 137, 200
Forgiveness, 146–147
Formal time, 102
Four-part model on conflict, 187–188
Four "Rs" of listening, 113–115
Framing theory, 74
Friendly relations, 230

Friendships, 225–231
    adult, 229–231
    authentic, 225
    childhood, 228–229
    defined, 225
    expectations of, 225–227
    over a lifespan, 227–231
    State of Friendship in America report on, 225
    at work, 226

G

Gap fillers, 120–121
Gap filling, 119
Gay- and lesbian-headed families, 221, 222–223
Gay men, use of "girl" by, 68–69
Gays and lesbians, 234
    homophobic language and, 85
    self-disclosure in journalism, 172
    statistics, 223
    terminology about, 71
Gender
    close relationships and, 202–203
    defined, 52
    emotional communication and, 141–142
    influence on perception, 52–54
    influence on verbal symbols, 78–79
    interpersonal communication differences and, 20
    interpersonal conflict and, 182–183
    power and, 192
    self-disclosure and, 159
    smiling and, 142
    vocabulary and, 79
Gender roles, in communication, 53
Gender role socialization, 53
Gender schema, 53
Gender stereotypes, emotion and, 141
Gender tagging, 84
Generations, verbal language and, 80
Generic *he*, 83
Gen Y, 80
Gestures, 93, 103
    citing, 93
    delivery, 93
    seeking, 93
    turn, 93
Gilligan, Carol, 23, 235
Global village, 34
Goals
    incompatible, 176, 178
    setting personal, 66
Goffman, Erving, 59
Golden mean, 23, 24
Goodwill, presuming and expressing, 193
Grammar, 70
Gray, John, 203
Greatest Generation, 80
Gut reactions, 133

H

Hall, Edward T., 33, 98, 102
Halo effect, 62
Handshakes, 99
Haptics (touch), 97–98
Hawaiian culture, 202
Hearing
    defined, 111
    listening *vs.*, 111–112

Heterosexism, 222
Hidden power, 191
Hidden self in Johari Window, 166
Hierarchy, 209
    of needs (Maslow), 196, 197
High-context cultures
    conflict in, 183
    defined, 39
    self-disclosure in, 159
Himba, the, 77–78
Historical context, 9
History
    of close relationships, 236
    of communication studies, 4
    defined, 156
    relational, 13
    self-disclosure and, 156
Hofstede, Geert, 36, 37, 38
Holidays, conflict during, 176
Home pages, personal, 61–64
Homophobia, 222
Homophobic language, 85
Honesty in self-disclosure, 171
Human resource management, cultural awareness and, 29
Humor, preventative maintenance through, 215–216
Hunches, 133
Hurt, avoiding, 169–170
Hybrid touch, 98
Hyperpersonal, 204

I

"I" communication orientation, 37, 123. *See also* Individualism/
        individualistic cultures
Ideal and real dialectic, 212
Ideal self, 64
Identity, culture and, 28. *See also Self*, the
Identity management
    explained, 58–59
    facework and, 59–61
    online, 61–64
    risk and, 59
    self-monitoring and, 60–61
Identity management theory, 58–59
Identity marker, 61
Idioms, 75–76
Image conflicts, 178–179, 180
Imagined conversations, 207
I-messages, 149
    owning and using, 86
    with self-disclosure, 171
    teaching profession and, 150
Immediate reciprocity, 162
Immigration, anxiety related to, 32–33
Imperative
    categorical, 21–22, 24
    demographic, 34, 36
    economic, 34–35, 36
    ethical, 35, 36
    peace, 35, 36
    self-awareness, 35, 36
    technological, 33–34, 36
Imperialism, cultural, 44
Impersonal communication, 12–14
Implicit personality theory, 62
Impression, asking others for their, 107–108
Incompatible goals, conflict and, 176, 178
Indexing, 87
India, power distance in, 37

Indirect application of power, 191
Individualism/individualistic cultures
    conflict in, 183
    emotional communication and, 141
    intercultural communication and, 37–38
    listening and, 123
Individual *vs.* the culture, relating to, 45
Inferences, facts vs., 65, 115
Informal time, 102–103
Information, public *vs.* private, 154–155
Ingham, Harry, 165
In-groups, 40–41
Initiating stage in relationships, 205
Integrating stage in relationships, 206
Integration, 188
Intensifying stage in relationships, 206
Intensity (emotion), 132–133
Intentional families, 219
Intentionality, self-disclosure and, 153–154
Interaction, conflict and, 176–177
Interaction adaptation theory, 90
Interactional model of communication, 9–10, 12
Intercultural communication, 26–45. *See also* Culture(s)
    anxiety and uncertainty in, 40–41
    apprehension in, 2
    assumption of similarity and difference in, 41–42
    being prepared for consequences in, 45
    biases in, 42–43
    challenges of, 39–42
    comfort in, 40–41
    context and, 38–39
    cultural respect for, 44–45
    defined, 27
    demographic imperative in, 34
    distribution of power in, 36–37
    diversity in, 32–33
    economic imperative in, 34–35
    ethical imperative in, 35
    ethnocentrism in, 39–40
    improving your, 42–45
    individualism-collectivism in, 37–39
    masculinity-femininity in, 37
    misinterpretation of nonverbal and verbal behaviors in, 41
    nonverbal and verbal differences in, 41
    peace imperative in, 35
    power distance in, 36–37
    reasons for studying, 33–35, 36
    relating to the individual *vs.* the culture in, 45
    requirements for, 28
    self-awareness imperative, 35
    stereotyping and, 40, 42–43
    technological imperative in, 33–34
    tolerance for, 43–44
    uncertainty avoidance in, 36
Intercultural relationships, 5
Intercultural Sensitivity Scale, 43
Interdependence, 177–178
    defined, 177
    interpersonal conflict and, 177–178
    in systems theory, 209, 210
Internal dialectics, 211
Internal feedback, 9
Internet. *See also* Online communication; Social media
    dating on, 5, 203–204
    email addresses and, 80
    identity management on, 61–64
    perceptions and, 54
    personal home pages, 61–64
    three selves on, 64

Interpersonal communication, 2–25
    as common sense, 20
    content levels of message in, 18
    continuum of, 12–14
    "dark side" of, 19
    defined, 5, 6
    defining, 6–7
    emotion and, 136–139
    ethical choices in, 18–19
    ethics of, 20–24
    evolution of, 4–6
    as face-to-face, 20
    in families, 220–224
    family stories, 220–221
    field of experience in, 11
    interpersonal relationships and, 20
    as irreversible, 16
    as learned, 17–18
    meaning in, 6–7
    message exchange in, 6
    myths about, 19–20
    nonverbal communication and, 90–91
    principles of, 15–19
    as a process, 6
    relationship level of message in, 18
    relationship problems and, 19
    rules governing, 17
    self, perception, and, 62–63
    as unavoidable, 16
    value of, 14–15
Interpersonal conflict, 176. *See also* Conflict(s)
    constructive aspects of, 186–187
    destructive aspects of, 185–186
    factors influencing, 182–183
    incompatible goals and, 178
    interaction and, 176–177
    interdependence and, 177–178
    perception and, 178
    types of, 178–181
Interpersonal relationships. *See also* Online relationships
    interpersonal communication as synonymous with, 20
    self-disclosure for escalating, 169
    self-disclosure for initiating new, 168
    self-disclosure for maintaining existing, 168–169
    self-disclosure patterns during life of, 157–158
    verbal language and, 68
    violence and aggression in, 186
Interpreting stage of perception, 48, 50–51
Interracial relationships, 183
Intimacy
    in close relationships, 199
    defined, 232
    in romantic relationships, 232–233
Intimate distance, 98–99, 100
Intrapersonal communication, 5
Inuit, the, 78
Irreversibility of interpersonal communication, 16
Issues
    private, 179
    public, 179

J

Japan
    body movement in, 103, 105
    conflict between couples and families in, 140
    eye contact in, 52
    self-disclosure in, 158–159
    silence in, 39

Johari Window, 165–167
Jourard, Sidney, 163
Judgment and acceptance dialectic, 211

K

Kant, Immanuel, 21–22, 133
Kinesics (body movement), 93–94, 103, 105
King, Martin Luther Jr., 10
Knapp, Mark, 205
Knapp's model of relationship development, 205–208

L

Ladder of abstraction, 86–87
Langer, Ellen, 48
Language. *See also* Verbal symbols
    Arabic, 78
    Black English, 76, 83
    close relationships existing in, 200–201
    codability and, 78
    defined, 70
    determining or influencing perceptions and thoughts, 77–78
    evolution of, 71–72
    figurative, 137, 200
    as flexible, 83
    generational differences in, 80
    homophobic, 85
    of inclusion, 85–86
    metaphors for emotions, 137–138
    of Mexican Americans, 76–77
    racist, 84–85
    sexist, 83–84
    sign, 116
    technology influencing, 80
Latino/a(s)
    Chicano English and, 76–77
    close relationships among, 202
    conflict and, 183
    countries making up, 76
    Hispanic vs., 71
    language of, 76–77
    self-disclosure among, 159
Laughing, 97
Law enforcement professionals, 193
Leadership style, 49
Lebanese Americans, cultural influence on perception
        and, 52
Lexical gaps, 82
Lightening up, conflict management and, 193
Lighting, nonverbal communication and, 101
Linear model of communication, 7, 12
Linguistic constructions, close relationships as, 200–201
Linguistic determination, 77–78
Linguistic relativity, 78
Linguistic Society of America, 76
Listening, 110–129
    action-centered style of, 122
    active, 115, 127–129, 150–151
    barriers to, 115–119
    conflict management and, 194
    content-centered style of, 122
    culture and, 123–124
    defensive, 121
    defined, 113
    with empathy, 125–126
    evaluating your skills in, 124
    four "Rs" of, 113–115

habits associated with poor, 119–121
    mindful, 113
    with nonjudgmental feedback, 126–127
    people-centered style of, 122
    personal styles of, 121–123
    preparation for, 124–125
    rating in, 115
    recalling in, 114–115
    receiving in, 113–114
    responding in, 114
    selective, 119–120
    silent, 128–129
    skills for improving, 124–129
    time-centered style of, 122–123
    training for, 118–119
    value and importance of, 115–116
Listening gap, 119
Liu, Ling, 2
Lohrey, Jackie, 87
Long-distance relationships (LDRs), 234
Long-term attraction, 201
Long-term commitment, 233
Low-context cultures
    conflict in, 183
    defined, 39
    self-disclosure in, 159
Luft, Joseph, 165

M

Magic ratio, 187
Mandela, Nelson, 99, 146
Man-linked words, 84
Manufactured feelings, real feelings vs., 143
Marriage
    commitment in, 233
    culture and, 202
    gender differences in dissatisfaction with, 202–203
Masculine cultures, 37
Masculinity-femininity, 37
Maslow, Abraham, 14–15, 196, 197
Maslow's hierarchy of needs, 196, 197
Mass communication, 5
Matching hypothesis, 202
Mature friendships, 229
Mead, George Herbert, 56
Meaning
    connotative, 73
    context orientation and, 38–39
    culture and, 6–7
    defined, 6
    denotative, 72–73
    shared, 10–12, 89
    triangle of, 70–71
Mechanistic thinking, 7–9
Memory (recall), 114–115
Men. *See also* Gender
    coming out by gay fathers, 223
    communication differences between women and, 79
    derogatory names for, 84
    report talk preferred by, 79
    stay-at-home dads, 222
    as unemotional, 141
Message
    complexity of, as barrier to listening, 118
    defined, 7
    in linear model of communication, 7
    mixed, 92
    nonverbal, 6, 9–10

Message (*continued*)
    rating a, 115
    recalling a, 114–115
    receiving, 113
    responding to, 114
Message exchange, 6
Message overload, as barrier to listening, 118
Meta-communication, 217
Meta-conflicts, 180
Meta-emotion, 139
Metaphors, 73–74
    describing close relationships, 200–201
    for emotion, 137–138
Mexican Americans, language of, 76–77
Middle ground, probing, 87
Migration Policy Institute, 32
Mill, John Stuart, 22–23
Millennials, 32, 80
Mindful listening, 113
Mindfulness, 48
Miscommunication, 181
Misinterpretation of verbal and nonverbal behaviors, 41
Mixed messages, 92
Mnemonic devices, 114
Moaning, 97
Momentary playmateship, 228
Moving toward friendship stage, 230
Multigenerational families, 221, 223
Multiracial romantic relationships, 234
Muslims, 7, 31
Muted group theory, 82–83
Muting, verbal symbols and, 82–83
Myths, conflict and communication, 181–182

N

Names, screen, 61
Narcissism, conversational, 119
Nascent friendship, 230–231
National Association of Academic Teachers of Public Speaking, 4
National Association of Colleges and Employers, 14
National Communication Association, 4
National Council of Teachers of English, 4
National Institutes of Health, 14
Native Americans, listening and, 123–124
Negative emotions, 144
Negative face, 59–60
Negative feedback, 210
Negative halo, 62
Negative interaction ratio, 187
Negotiation, symmetrical, 184–185
Networking, 214
Neutralizing, 212
Newman, Katherine, 59
New Zealand, dating in, 30
Nilsen, Thomas, 23
Noise
    as barrier to listening, 117–118
    defined, 8
    in linear model of communication, 8
    physiological, 118
    psychological, 118
    semantic, 117–118
Nonjudgmental feedback, 126–127
Nonverbal behavior
    misinterpretation of, 41
    monitoring your, 107
    in nursing profession, 108
    tentativeness in interpreting, 107

Nonverbal communication, 88–109. *See also* Nonverbal communication codes
    adapting our behavior to others and, 90
    ambiguity in, 91
    believability of, 92
    codes in, 92–103
    conflicting with verbal communication, 92
    consistency between verbal communication and, 171
    culture and, 89, 103–105
    defined, 89
    electronic communication and, 89
    increasing effectiveness in, 106–109
    influence of, 90
    intercultural communication and, 41
    intertwined with verbal message systems, 69–70
    percent of message meaning conveyed by, 88, 89
    principles of, 90–92
    relationship with verbal communication, 106–107
    speech regulated by, 91–92
    technology and, 105–106
    verbal communication *vs.*, 90
Nonverbal communication codes, 93–104
    body movement, 93–94
    contact, 97–101
    facial communication, 95–96, 103–104
    paralanguage (voice), 96–97
    personal space, 98–101, 104
    physical appearance, 94–95
    physical environment, 101–102
    place and time, 101–103
    silence, 97
    space and distance, 98–101
    touch, 97–98, 104–105
Nonverbal cues in emotional communication, 138
Nonverbal distractions, avoiding, 108
Nonverbal messages, 6
    in interactional model of communication, 9–10
Novelty and predictability dialectic, 211
Nuclear family, 221–222
Nursing profession, 108

O

Obama, Barack, 99
Offering, 214
One-way assistance, 228–229
Online communication. *See also* Social media
    asynchronous nature of, 204
    close relationships influenced by, 203–204
    emotional communication and, 143–144
    as hyperpersonal, 204
    nonverbal communication and, 89
    positive face on, 60
    selfies, 55, 57
Online dating, 5, 203–204
Online identity management, 61–64
Online relationships
    listening and, 111
    self-disclosure and, 160
    social information processing theory (SIP) on, 204
    upsides and downsides to romantic, 204
Openness and protection dialectic, 211
Open self, in Johari Window, 165–166
Organizational communication, 5
Organizing stage of perception, 48, 49–50
Ought self, 64
Out-groups, 40–41
Outsourcing, 35
Owning (feelings), 149
Oxford English Dictionary (OED), 72

P

Paralanguage (voice), 96–97
Paraphrasing, 127–128
Passion, 232–233
Patient-physician communication, 14
Peace imperative, 35, 36
People-centered listening style, 122
"People-centered" professions, 15
Perception, 46, 47–48. *See also* Self, the
   age and, 54
   attending and selecting stage of, 48–49
   of belonging, 40–41
   of color, 101
   defined, 48
   incompleteness of, 65
   influences on, 52–55
   interpersonal conflict and, 178
   interpreting stage in, 50–51
   link between self, interpersonal communication and, 62–63
   online relationship development and, 63–64
   organizing stage in, 49–50
   physical factors in, 54
   process of, 47–48
   reason, body, and emotion, 133–134
   retrieving stage in, 51–52
   selective, 48–49
   sense of self in, 54–55
   sex and gender in, 52–54
   stereotypes and, 49–50
   technology influencing, 54
Perception checking, improving, 64–67
Personal distance, 99, 100
Personal expectations, perception and, 50
Personal goals, setting, 66
Personal home pages, 61–64
Personal information, sharing of. *See* Self-disclosure
Personal issues, 179
Personal space, 97, 98, 99, 100, 104
Personal worldview, self-awareness of, 35
Perspective taking, 86
Phatic communication, 76
Physical abuse, 186
Physical appearance, nonverbal communication and, 94–95
Physical context, 8
Physical health
   perception and, 54
   self-disclosure and, 163, 167–168
Physical makeup, perception and, 54
Physical noise, 8, 117
Physician-patient communication, 14
Physiological component to emotion, 134
Physiological noise, 8, 118
Placating, 188
Place and time codes, 101–103
Playful function of touch, 98
Polarization, 82
Positive face, 59–60
Positive feedback, 210
Positive halo, 62
Positive interaction ratio, 187
Posture, body, 93–94
Pouncing, 188
Power
   defined, 190
   empowerment and, 192
   gender differences and, 192
   hidden, 191
   ways of using, 190–191
Power balancing, 192

Power distance, 36–37
Prejudices, being aware of your, 42–43
Preoccupation, as barrier to listening, 117, 119
Preventative maintenance, 215
Prison vocabulary, 77
Private information, 154–155
Private issues, 179
Probing the middle ground, 87
Process, defined, 6
Process of abstraction, 74
Proxemics, 98
Proximal context, 189
Proximal outcomes, 189
Pseudolistening, as barrier to communication, 119, 120
Psychological health, self-disclosure and, 163, 167
Psychological noise
   as barrier to listening, 118
   defined, 8, 118
Public and private dialectic, 212
Public communication, 5
Public distance, 99, 100
Public information, 154, 155
Public issues, 179
Puerto Rican culture, 38
Punctuality, 102–103
Pursuit-withdrawal, 184

Q

Questions
   conflict management and, 193–194
   listening and, 128

R

Racist language, 84–85
Rapport talk, 79
Rating (listening process), 115
Real feelings, manufactured feelings vs., 131
Reason, emotion and, 133–134
Recalibrate, 210
Recalling (listening process), 114–115
Receiver
   defined, 7
   in linear model of communication, 7
Receiving (listening process), 113–114
Reciprocity, self-disclosure and, 162–163
Reddit survey (2013), 427
Referent, 73
Reframing, 149, 193, 213
Reification, verbal symbols and, 82
Rejection, avoiding, 169–170
Relational conflicts, 179, 180
Relational culture, 202
Relational history, 13
Relational messages, 191
Relational rules, 13
Relational schema, 49
Relational transgressions, 216–217
Relational uniqueness, 13
Relational uppers, 65–66
Relationship level of message, 18
Relationship ruts, 236
Relationships. *See* Close relationships; Interpersonal relationships;
   Online relationships
Relationship scripts, 200, 233–234
Relevancy, self-disclosure and, 171–172
Report talk, 79
Respect, practicing cultural, 44

Responding
  empathic, 125–126
  in listening process, 114
Retention, selective, 51
Retrieving stage of perception, 48, 51–52
Rewards, in social exchange theory, 213–214
Rhetoric (Aristotle), 4
Ritualistic touch, 98
Rituals, 21
Role-limited interaction, 230
Role relationships, 198
Romantic love, cultural differences on, 140
Romantic relationships, 231–235
  online, 204
  relationship ruts in, 236
Room design, nonverbal communication and, 101–102
Rules
  defined, 17
  feeling, 142–143
  interpersonal communication, 17
  relational, 13

S

Sales professionals, 64
Sandwich generation, 223
Sapir, Edward, 77
Sapir-Whorf hypothesis, 77, 78
Schadenfreude, 144
Schema
  gender, 53
  relational, 49
Schismogenesis, 184
Screen names, 61
Second-guessing, 122
Seeking gestures, 93
Segmentation, 212
Selecting and attending stage of perception, 48–49
Selection, 212
Selective listening, as barrier to listening, 119–120
Selective perception, 48–49
Selective retention, 51
Self, the, 46, 47–48. *See also* Perception
  presentation of, online, 63–64
Self-actualization, 14–15
Self-awareness
  defined, 56
  self-disclosure and, 168
Self-awareness imperative, 35, 36
Self-concept
  changing, 65–66
  components of, 56
  defined, 54, 55–56
  identity management and, 58–64
  improving, 65–66
  online identity management and, 61–64
  perception and, 54–55
  self-awareness and, 56
  self-esteem and, 56–57
  self-fulfilling prophecy and, 57–58
Self-disclosure, 152–173
  amount of, in the course of a day, 160–162
  choice and, 153–154
  defined, 153
  factors affecting, 157–160
  importance of, 152
  individual differences in, 157
  intentionality and, 153–154

Johari Window and, 165–167
  nature of relationship and, 162
  occurring over time, 163
  online, 160
  patterns of, over the life of relationships, 157–158
  principles of, 160–163
  of private *vs.* public information, 154–155
  reasons against, 169–171
  reasons for, 167–169
  reciprocity in, 162–163
  as a subjective process, 156–157
  techniques for building skills in, 171–173
  theories explaining, 163–165
  trust and, 155–156
Self-esteem, 55, 56–57
Self-fulfilling prophecy, 57–58
Selfies, 55, 57
Self-imposed prophecies, 58
Self-monitoring, 60–61
Self-worth, 56–57
Semantic derogation, 84
Semantic noise
  as barrier to listening, 117–118
  defined, 8, 117
Semantic triangle, 70–71
Semiotics theory, 16–17
Sender, 7
Serial conflicts, 180–181
Sex
  close relationships and, 202–203
  defined, 52
  emotional communication and, 141–142
  influence on verbal symbols, 78–79
  interpersonal conflict and, 182–183
  perception and, 52–54
  self-disclosure and, 158–159
  verbal symbols and, 79–80
Sexist language, 83–84
Sexual assault, disclosing, 160
Sexual self-disclosures, 155
Shared meaning, 6, 10–12, 89
Short-term attraction, 201
Short-term commitment, 233
Significant choice, 23–24
Silence
  listening and, 128–129
  nonverbal communication and, 97
Similarity, assumption of, 41–42
Similes, 73–74
Single parent families, 223–224
Single parent family, 221
Slang, 71, 80
Small group communication, 5
Smiling, 96, 138, 142
Social distance, 99, 100
Social-emotional context, 8–9
Social exchange theory, 213–214
Social identity
  co-cultures and, 30–31
  defined, 30
Social information processing (SIP) theory, 106
Social interaction theory of emotion, 135–136
Social media, 5
  close relationships and, 203–204
  generational differences in language and, 80
  self-disclosure and, 155
  self-presentation in, 63–64
  used by salespeople, 64
Social penetration theory, 164–165

Solidarity, 226
Somalia, time perception in, 52
Space, nonverbal communication and, 98–101
Spatial distances, 104
Speaker bias, 115
Speech communities, 77
Spot listening, 119–120
Stabilized friendship, 231
Stagnating stage in relationship, 207
State of Friendship in America report, 225
Static evaluation, 81–82, 87
Stay-at-home dads (SAHDs), 222
Stereotyping
    defined, 40, 49
    emotion and gender, 141
    intercultural communication and, 40, 42–43
    perception and, 49–50
Sternberg, Robert, 232–233
Stimuli, 48–54
    emotion and, 134
    hearing *vs.* listening and, 112
Stories, 156
    family, 220–221
Strangers, self-disclosure to, 162
"Strangers on a train," 162
Strategic ambiguity, 74–75
Strategic embarrassment, 132
Stress, self-disclosure and, 170–171
Subjective process, self-disclosure as a, 156–157
Subsystems, 209
Suprasystems, 209
Sustaining, 215
Symbolic, interpersonal communication as, 16–17
Symbolic interactionism theory, 56, 77
Symbols, 16. *See also* Verbal symbols
Symmetrical escalation, 184
Symmetrical negotiation, 184–185
Symmetrical reciprocity, 226
Symmetrical withdrawal, 184
Systems theory, 208–210

T

Taboo topics, 212–213
Talkaholism, as barrier to listening, 119, 120
Tannen, Deborah, 203
Task function of touch, 98
Technical time, 102
Technological imperative, 33–34, 36
Technology. *See also* Online communication; Online relationships
    influence on communication, 5–6, 12
    influence on language, 80
    intercultural communication and, 33–34
    listening and, 116, 119
    nonverbal communication and, 105–106
    perception and, 54
Terminating stage, 208
Territoriality, 100
Territorial markers, 100–101
Theories
    attribution, 63
    identity management, 58–64
    implicit personality, 62
Thinking
    dialectic, 213
    mechanistic, 7–9
Time (chronemics), 102–103
Time, perception of, 52
Time-centered listening style, 122–123

Tolerance, intercultural communication and, 43–44
Topical intimacy, 156–157
Touch
    cultural differences in, 104–105
    functions of, 98
Touch behavior, 97–98
Traditional nuclear family, 222
Transactional model of communication, 10–12
Transgender community, terminology about, 71
Triangle of meaning, 70–71
Triangular theory of love, 232–233
Trust, self-disclosure and, 155–156
Turn gestures, 93
Turn taking, 91–92
Two-culture theory, 79
Two-way, fair-weather cooperation, 229

U

Uncertainty, intercultural communication and, 40–41
Uncertainty avoidance, 36
Undifferentiated traits, 53
Uniqueness, relational, 13
Unknown, tolerating the, 43–44
Unknown self, in Johari Window, 166
Unobtrusive power, 191
U.S. Department of Labor, Occupational Information Network
    (O°NET), 15
Utilitarianism, 22–23, 24

V

Valence, 132
Value(s)
    ethics and, 24
    of interpersonal communication, 14–15
    of listening, 115–116
Value conflicts, 179, 180
Verbal aggression, 185, 186
Verbal behaviors
    of African Americans, 76
    of Mexican Americans, 76–77
    misinterpretation of, 41
    relationship with nonverbal behavior, 106–107
Verbal clarity, 87
Verbal communication
    believability of, 92
    conflicting with nonverbal communication, 92
    consistency between nonverbal communication and, 171
    I-messages and, 86
    improving, 86–87
    indexing and, 87
    intercultural communication and, 41
    ladder of abstraction and, 86–87
    nonverbal communication *vs.*, 90
    percent of message meaning conveyed by, 89
    perspective taking, 86
    probing the middle ground for, 87
Verbal cues, for emotional communication, 138–139
Verbal messages, 6
Verbal symbols, 68–87
    attributes of, 70–75
    connection and differentiation with others through, 68–70
    connotative meaning of, 73
    constructive side of, 85–86
    context and, 80–81
    culture and ethnicity influencing, 75–79
    defined, 70

Verbal symbols (*continued*)
  denotative meaning of, 72–73
  destructive side of, 81–85
  factors affecting, 75–81
  generational differences and, 80
  intertwined with nonverbal message systems, 69–70
  muting and, 82–83
  polarization and, 82
  reification and, 82
  sex and gender influencing, 79–80
  static evaluation and, 81–82
  understanding, 70–75
Violence, 186
Visual-auditory contact codes, 93–97
Vocabulary. *See also* Verbal symbols; Words
  gender differences in, 79
  prison, 77
Vocal characterizers, 96, 97
Vocal distractors, 96
Vocal qualities, 96
Voice
  emotional communication and, 138
  nonverbal communication and, 96–97
Voluntary kin, 220

W

Walther, Joseph, 204
Waning friendships, 231
"We" communication orientation, 38, 123. *See also* Collectivism/collectivistic cultures
Western bias, 159
Western emoticons, 143
Western thought, dualisms in, 133
Whining, 97
Wholeness, 209, 210

Whorf, Benjamin, 77, 78
Withdrawal-pursuit, 184
Women. *See also* Gender
  changing roles of, 6
  communication differences between men and, 79
  derogatory terms for, 84
  as emotional, 141
  rapport talk preferred by, 79
  taking husband's surname, 84
Words
  concrete, 73
  evolving over time, 71–72
  man-linked, 84
  power of, 72
  as symbolic, 70–71
  varying in level of abstraction, 73–75
Working memory theory, 112
Workplace. *See* Careers; Employment
Worldview
  defined, 35, 65
  intercultural communication and, 35
  perception checking and, 65

Y

You-messages, 86
Youth
  boomerang kids, 59
  bullying and, 185–186
  childhood friendships, 228–229
  teaching empathy to, 125

Z

Zak, Dan, 55

KEY CONCEPTS

To help you succeed, we have designed a review card for each chapter.

We often take our ability to communicate for granted, and the majority of people living in the United States believe that they communicate well. However, many people have a tough time communicating with others and need some help in their relationships with others. Regardless of the information available to us, each of us can certainly improve our interpersonal communication skills in some way.

1.1

The evolution of interpersonal communication. Interpersonal communication is a com~~_____~~ forms of communication, such ~~_____~~ mass, and public. The definition of inte~~_____~~ *This section presents a summary of* ~~____~~ e years as several models of communi~~____~~ *the Learning Objectives, which give an overview of important chapter concepts.*

1.2

Defining interpersonal communication. Another way to understand the nature of interpersonal communication is to look at the interpersonal communication continuum. Interactions come in all degrees of closeness, not just the extremes of impersonal and interpersonal, which are at either end of the continuum. Where an interaction falls on the continuum depends on the relational history, relational rules, and relational uniqueness of the people involved.

1.3

Models of communication. The three prevailing models are the linear model, the interactional model, and the transactional model.

1.4

The value of interpersonal communication. After you understand the definition, evolution, and nature of interpersonal communication, you can appreciate its value. Effective communication skills can reap countless professional and personal benefits. Most of us desire long-term, satisfying relationships, and effective communication can help us establish such relationships. Learning the intricacies of interpersonal communication can improve our lives physically, emotionally, and psychologically, and can aid in self-actualization.

1.5

Principles of interp~~____~~

interpersonal communi~~____~~
shape it. Interpersonal c~~____~~
Further, what we say is i~~____~~
understood by everyon~~____~~
choose whether or not ~~____~~
both on the content an~~____~~

How to use this card:
1. **Look over the card to preview the concepts you'll be introduced to in the chapter.**
2. **Read your chapter in detail to understand the material.**
3. **Go to class (and pay attention!).**
4. **Review the card to make sure you've registered the key concepts.**
5. **Don't forget, this card is only one of many IPC learning tools available to help you succeed in your communications course.**

1.6

Myths about interpe~~____~~
people operate under several misconceptions about interpersonal communication. These myths impede our understanding and enactment of effective communication. Despite the stereotype, interpersonal communication does not solve all problems. It is usually a good thing, but it can also be used to manipulate and abuse. Interpersonal communication is not necessarily synonymous with interpersonal relationships, nor does it always occur face to face.

1.7

Interpersonal communication ethics. Finally, you have to understand the ethics involved in interpersonal communication. Five systems—categorical imperative,

KEY TERMS

Here, you'll find key terms and definitions in the order that they appear in the chapter.

communication apprehension (p. 2) A fear or anxiety pertaining to the communication process.

intercultural communication apprehension (p. 2) A~~____~~ comm~~____~~ cultura~~____~~

interpers~~_____~~ The process of message transaction between two people to create and sustain shared meaning.

process (p. 6) When used to describe interpersonal communication, an ongoing, unending, vibrant activity that always changes.

message exchange (p. 6) The transaction of verbal and nonverbal messages being sent simultaneously between two people.

meaning (p. 6) What communicators create together through the use of verbal and nonverbal messages.

communication models (p. 7) Visual, simplified representations of complex relationships in the communication process.

linear model of communication (p. 7) A characterization of communication as a one-way process that transmits a message from a sender to a receiver.

sender (p. 7) The source of a message.

message (p. 7) Spoken, written, or unspoken information sent from a sender to a receiver.

receiver (p. 7) The intended target of a message.

channel (p. 8) A pathway through which a message is sent.

noise (p. 8) Anything that interferes with accurate transmission or reception of a message. See also physical noise, physiological noise, psychological noise, and semantic noise.

physical noise (p. 8) Any stimuli outside of a sender or a receiver that interfere with the transmission or reception of a message. Also called *external noise*.

physiological noise (p. 8) Biological influences on a sender or a receiver that interfere with the transmission or reception of a message.

psychological noise (p. 8) Biases, prejudices, and feelings that interfere with the accurate transmission or reception of a message. Also called *internal noise*.

semantic noise (p. 8) Occurs when senders and receivers apply different meanings to the same message; may take the form of jargon, technical language, and other words and phrases that are familiar to the sender but that are not understood by the receiver.

context (p. 8) The environment in which a message is sent.

physical context (p. 8) The tangible environment in which communication occurs.

cultural context (p. 8) The cultural environment in which communication occurs; refers to the rules, roles, norms, and patterns of communication that are unique to a particular culture.

social-emotional context (p. 8) The relational and emotional environment in which communication occurs.

historical context (p. 9) A type of context in which messages are understood in relationship to previously sent messages.

interactional model of communication (p. 9) A characterization of communication as a two-way process in which a message is sent from sender to receiver and from receiver to sender.

feedback (p. 9) A verbal or nonverbal response to a message. *See also* internal feedback and external feedback.

internal feedback (p. 9) The feedback we give ourselves when we assess our own communication.

external feedback (p. 9) The feedback we receive from other people.

transactional model of communication (p. 10) A characterization of communication as the reciprocal sending and receiving of messages. In a transactional encounter, the sender and receiver do not simply send meaning from one to the other and then back again; rather, they build shared meaning through simultaneous sending and receiving.

field of experience (p. 11) The influence of a person's culture, past experiences, personal history, and heredity on the communication process.

relational history (p. 13) The prior relationship experiences that two people share.

relational rules (p. 13) Negotiable rules that indicate what two relational partners expect and allow when they talk to each other.

relational uniqueness (p. 13) The ways in which the particular relationship of two relational partners stands apart from other relationships they experience.

utilitarianism, ethic of care, golden mean, and significant choice—can guide you, but ultimately you need to understand your own values as well as the consequences of your actions.

1.8
The communication core: competency and civility. Effectiveness in communication with others requires two critical ingredients: competency and civility. **Communication competency**, or the ability to communicate with knowledge, skills, and thoughtfulness, should be foremost when trying to meet a communication challenge. When we are competent, our communication is both appropriate and effective. Civil communication requires sensitivity to the experiences of the other communicator. Learning about interpersonal communications makes us part of civilization.

ONLINE RESOU...

Every chapter has online resources and activities that will help you master the concepts in the chapter.

Use Enhanced CourseMa... study resources that accompany this text:

• **Ethics & Choice:** Lenora's got a problem, and you can help her solve it.

INTERACTIVE ACTIVITIES

1.1 Interactive Models of Communication—Check out interactive versions of the models of communication.

1.2 Communication Skills Test—Assess your current communication skills.

self-actualization (p. 15) The process of gaining information about ourselves in an effort to tap our full potential, our spontaneity, and our talents, and to cultivate our strengths and eliminate our shortcomings.

irreversibility (p. 16) The fact that our communication with others cannot be "unsaid" or reversed.

semiotics theory (p. 16) The study of signs and symbols in relation to their form and content.

symbols (p. 16) Arbitrary labels or representations (such as words) for feelings, concepts, objects, or events.

rule (p. 17) A prescribed guide that indicates what behavior is obligated, preferred, or prohibited in certain contexts.

content level (p. 18) The verbal and nonverbal information contained in a message that indicates the topic of the message.

relationship level (p. 18) The information contained in a message that indicates how the sender wants the receiver to interpret the message.

ethics (p. 18) The perceived rightness or wrongness of an action or behavior.

categorical imperative (p. 22) An ethical system, based on the work of philosopher Immanuel Kant, advancing the notion that

individuals follow moral absolutes. The underlying tenet in this ethical system suggests that we should act as an example to others.

utilitarianism (p. 22) An ethical system, developed by John Stuart Mill, suggesting that what is ethical will bring the greatest good for the greatest number of people.

golden mean (p. 23) An ethical system, articulated by Aristotle, proposing that a person's moral virtue stands between two vices, with the middle, or the mean, being the foundation for a rational society.

ethic of care (p. 23) An ethical system, based on the concepts of Carol Gilligan, that is concerned with the connections among people and the moral consequences of decisions.

significant choice (p. 23) An ethical system, conceptualized by Thomas Nilsen, underscoring the belief that communication is ethical to the extent that it maximizes our ability to exercise free choice. In this system, information should be given to others in a noncoercive way so that people can make free and informed decisions.

communication competency (p. 25) The ability to communicate with knowledge, skills, and thoughtfulness.

civil communication (p. 25) The acceptance of another person as an equal partner in achieving meaning during communication.

KEY CONCEPTS

We often take our ability to communicate for granted, and the majority of people living in the United States believe that they communicate well. However, many people have a tough time communicating with others and need some help in their relationships with others. Regardless of the information available to us, each of us can certainly improve our interpersonal communication skills in some way.

1.1

The evolution of interpersonal communication. Interpersonal communication is a complex process that is unique from other forms of communication, such as intrapersonal, small group, organizational, mass, and public. The definition of interpersonal communication has evolved over the years as several models of communication have been advanced.

1.2

Defining interpersonal communication. Another way to understand the nature of interpersonal communication is to look at the interpersonal communication continuum. Interactions come in all degrees of closeness, not just the extremes of impersonal and interpersonal, which are at either end of the continuum. Where an interaction falls on the continuum depends on the relational history, relational rules, and relational uniqueness of the people involved.

1.3

Models of communication. The three prevailing models are the linear model, the interactional model, and the transactional model.

1.4

The value of interpersonal communication. After you understand the definition, evolution, and nature of interpersonal communication, you can appreciate its value. Effective communication skills can reap countless professional and personal benefits. Most of us desire long-term, satisfying relationships, and effective communication can help us establish such relationships. Learning the intricacies of interpersonal communication can improve our lives physically, emotionally, and psychologically, and can aid in self-actualization.

1.5

Principles of interpersonal communication. To better understand interpersonal communication, one has to explore some of the major principles that shape it. Interpersonal communication is unavoidable—you cannot *not* communicate. Further, what we say is irreversible. Words are symbolic, and verbal symbols are not understood by everyone. Interpersonal communication is rule-governed, but we can choose whether or not we wish to follow any given rule. Messages contain information both on the content and relationship level.

1.6

Myths about interpersonal communication. For one reason or another, people operate under several misconceptions about interpersonal communication. These myths impede our understanding and enactment of effective communication. Despite the stereotype, interpersonal communication does not solve all problems. It is usually a good thing, but it can also be used to manipulate and abuse. Interpersonal communication is not necessarily synonymous with interpersonal relationships, nor does it always occur face to face.

1.7

Interpersonal communication ethics. Finally, you have to understand the ethics involved in interpersonal communication. Five systems—categorical imperative,

KEY TERMS

communication apprehension (p. 2) A fear or anxiety pertaining to the communication process.

intercultural communication apprehension (p. 2) A fear or anxiety pertaining to communication with people from different cultural backgrounds.

interpersonal communication (p. 6) The process of message transaction between two people to create and sustain shared meaning.

process (p. 6) When used to describe interpersonal communication, an ongoing, unending, vibrant activity that always changes.

message exchange (p. 6) The transaction of verbal and nonverbal messages being sent simultaneously between two people.

meaning (p. 6) What communicators create together through the use of verbal and nonverbal messages.

communication models (p. 7) Visual, simplified representations of complex relationships in the communication process.

linear model of communication (p. 7) A characterization of communication as a one-way process that transmits a message from a sender to a receiver.

sender (p. 7) The source of a message.

message (p. 7) Spoken, written, or unspoken information sent from a sender to a receiver.

receiver (p. 7) The intended target of a message.

channel (p. 8) A pathway through which a message is sent.

noise (p. 8) Anything that interferes with accurate transmission or reception of a message. See also physical noise, physiological noise, psychological noise, and semantic noise.

physical noise (p. 8) Any stimuli outside of a sender or a receiver that interfere with the transmission or reception of a message. Also called *external noise*.

physiological noise (p. 8) Biological influences on a sender or a receiver that interfere with the transmission or reception of a message.

psychological noise (p. 8) Biases, prejudices, and feelings that interfere with the accurate transmission or reception of a message. Also called *internal noise*.

CHAPTER REVIEW 1

semantic noise (p. 8) Occurs when senders and receivers apply different meanings to the same message; may take the form of jargon, technical language, and other words and phrases that are familiar to the sender but that are not understood by the receiver.

context (p. 8) The environment in which a message is sent.

physical context (p. 8) The tangible environment in which communication occurs.

cultural context (p. 8) The cultural environment in which communication occurs; refers to the rules, roles, norms, and patterns of communication that are unique to a particular culture.

social-emotional context (p. 8) The relational and emotional environment in which communication occurs.

historical context (p. 9) A type of context in which messages are understood in relationship to previously sent messages.

interactional model of communication (p. 9) A characterization of communication as a two-way process in which a message is sent from sender to receiver and from receiver to sender.

feedback (p. 9) A verbal or nonverbal response to a message. *See also* internal feedback and external feedback.

internal feedback (p. 9) The feedback we give ourselves when we assess our own communication.

external feedback (p. 9) The feedback we receive from other people.

transactional model of communication (p. 10) A characterization of communication as the reciprocal sending and receiving of messages. In a transactional encounter, the sender and receiver do not simply send meaning from one to the other and then back again; rather, they build shared meaning through simultaneous sending and receiving.

field of experience (p. 11) The influence of a person's culture, past experiences, personal history, and heredity on the communication process.

relational history (p. 13) The prior relationship experiences that two people share.

relational rules (p. 13) Negotiable rules that indicate what two relational partners expect and allow when they talk to each other.

relational uniqueness (p. 13) The ways in which the particular relationship of two relational partners stands apart from other relationships they experience.

utilitarianism, ethic of care, golden mean, and significant choice—can guide you, but ultimately you need to understand your own values as well as the consequences of your actions.

1.8
The communication core: competency and civility. Effectiveness in communication with others requires two critical ingredients: competency and civility. **Communication competency**, or the ability to communicate with knowledge, skills, and thoughtfulness, should be foremost when trying to meet a communication challenge. When we are competent, our communication is both appropriate and effective. Civil communication requires sensitivity to the experiences of the other communicator. Learning about interpersonal communications makes us part of civilization.

ONLINE RESOURCES

Use Enhanced CourseMate for quick access to the electronic study resources that accompany this text:

- **Ethics & Choice:** Lenora's got a problem, and you can help her solve it.

INTERACTIVE ACTIVITIES

1.1 Interactive Models of Communication—Check out interactive versions of the models of communication.

1.2 Communication Skills Test—Assess your current communication skills.

self-actualization (p. 15) The process of gaining information about ourselves in an effort to tap our full potential, our spontaneity, and our talents, and to cultivate our strengths and eliminate our shortcomings.

irreversibility (p. 16) The fact that our communication with others cannot be "unsaid" or reversed.

semiotics theory (p. 16) The study of signs and symbols in relation to their form and content.

symbols (p. 16) Arbitrary labels or representations (such as words) for feelings, concepts, objects, or events.

rule (p. 17) A prescribed guide that indicates what behavior is obligated, preferred, or prohibited in certain contexts.

content level (p. 18) The verbal and nonverbal information contained in a message that indicates the topic of the message.

relationship level (p. 18) The information contained in a message that indicates how the sender wants the receiver to interpret the message.

ethics (p. 18) The perceived rightness or wrongness of an action or behavior.

categorical imperative (p. 22) An ethical system, based on the work of philosopher Immanuel Kant, advancing the notion that

individuals follow moral absolutes. The underlying tenet in this ethical system suggests that we should act as an example to others.

utilitarianism (p. 22) An ethical system, developed by John Stuart Mill, suggesting that what is ethical will bring the greatest good for the greatest number of people.

golden mean (p. 23) An ethical system, articulated by Aristotle, proposing that a person's moral virtue stands between two vices, with the middle, or the mean, being the foundation for a rational society.

ethic of care (p. 23) An ethical system, based on the concepts of Carol Gilligan, that is concerned with the connections among people and the moral consequences of decisions.

significant choice (p. 23) An ethical system, conceptualized by Thomas Nilsen, underscoring the belief that communication is ethical to the extent that it maximizes our ability to exercise free choice. In this system, information should be given to others in a noncoercive way so that people can make free and informed decisions.

communication competency (p. 25) The ability to communicate with knowledge, skills, and thoughtfulness.

civil communication (p. 25) The acceptance of another person as an equal partner in achieving meaning during communication.

KEY CONCEPTS

Our cultural background shapes our identity, our communication practices, and our responses to others. Intercultural communication refers to communication between and among individuals and groups whose cultural backgrounds differ. As the populations of countries become more diverse, communicators today need to have knowledge of others' cultural values and practices to inform their communication.

2.1

Defining culture. The United States is a heterogeneous mix of various cultures, with 2.4 percent of the population identifying with more than one race. We can experience intercultural communication at the national level or at the small scale of a neighborhood. The United States generally supports cultural newcomers, including Latinos, the fastest-growing cultural group.

Family, friends, and the media teach us culture. The national culture is made up of numerous co-cultures, or cultures within cultures, membership in which is determined by factors such as sexual identity, gender, and race. Cultures and co-cultures create a sense of community for members.

2.2

Diversity in the United States: a nation of newcomers. Intercultural contact is pervasive in the United States. This diversity affects family structures, corporations, religious institutions, schools, and the media. The increase in diversity in recent years raises new challenges: anxiety, misunderstandings, and relational challenges. Learning how to communicate effectively with members of different cultures is a hallmark of a thoughtful and effective communicator.

2.3

Why study intercultural communication? In today's world, there are six reasons, or imperatives, to study intercultural communication. The technology imperative shows that technology makes communication with those in other countries easier than ever before. The demographic imperative recognizes that the United States is a symphony of cultures that should accommodate and appreciate each other. The economic imperative states that all societies—and their businesses—are interconnected in a global village. The peace imperative says that looking at world affairs from other countries' perspectives is a step in the right direction, especially if you have taken advantage of the self-awareness imperative, which encourages us to have a clear understanding of our own worldview. Finally, according to the ethical imperative, we have an obligation to ensure that cultural behaviors are depicted in the context of cultural values.

2.4

Dimensions of culture. Culture has four dimensions. Cultures vary in the degree that they desire predictability (the uncertainty avoidance dimension) and how much they show respect for status (the distribution of power dimension). They also differ on what they value, such as competitiveness or quality of life (the masculinity-femininity dimension) and individual or group accomplishments (the individualism-collectivism dimension). Another important ingredient in culture is context; members of high-context cultures draw the meaning of the message from the surroundings, whereas people in low-context cultures derive the meaning from the message itself.

2.5

Challenges of intercultural communication. The chapter discusses five obstacles to intercultural communication. Ethnocentrism makes us judge other cultures using the standards of our own culture. As we learned in Chapter 2, stereotyping is an

KEY TERMS

intercultural communication (p. 27) Communication between and among individuals and groups from different cultural backgrounds.

culture (p. 28) The shared, personal, and learned life experiences of a group of individuals who have a common set of values, norms, and traditions.

enculturation (p. 30) The process that occurs when a person—either consciously or unconsciously—learns to identify with a particular culture and a culture's thinking, way of relating, and worldview.

acculturation (p. 30) The process that occurs when a person learns, adapts to, and adopts the appropriate behaviors and rules of a host culture.

community (p. 30) The common understandings among people who are committed to coexisting.

co-culture (p. 30) A culture within a culture.

social identity (p. 30) The part of one's self that is based on membership in a particular group.

culture clash (p. 31) A conflict over cultural expectations and experiences.

global village (p. 34) The concept that all societies, regardless of size, are connected in some way. The term also can be used to describe how communication technology ties the world into one political, economic, social, and cultural system.

outsourcing (p. 35) A practice in which a nation sends work and workers to a different country because doing so is cost-efficient.

worldview (p. 35) A unique way of seeing the world through one's own lens of understanding, directly derived from our cultural identity.

cultural variability theory (p. 36) A theory that describes the four value dimensions (uncertainty avoidance, distribution of power, masculinity-femininity, individualism-collectivism) that offer information regarding the value differences in a particular culture.

uncertainty avoidance (p. 36) A cultural mind-set that indicates how tolerant (or intolerant) a culture is of uncertainty and change.

power distance (p. 36) How a culture perceives and distributes power.

masculine culture (p. 37) A culture that emphasizes characteristics stereotypically associated with masculine people, such as

CHAPTER REVIEW 2

achievement, competitiveness, strength, and material success.

feminine culture (p. 37) A culture that emphasizes characteristics stereotypically associated with feminine people, such as sexual equality, nurturance, quality of life, supportiveness, affection, and a compassion for the less fortunate.

individualism (p. 37) A cultural mind-set that emphasizes self-concept and personal achievement and that prefers competition over cooperation, the individual over the group, and the private over the public.

collectivism (p. 38) A cultural mind-set that emphasizes the group and its norms, values, and beliefs over the self.

context orientation theory (p. 38) The theory that meaning is derived from either the setting of the message or the words of a message and that cultures can vary in the extent to which message meaning is made explicit or implicit.

high-context culture (p. 39) A culture in which there is a high degree of similarity among members and in which the meaning of a message is drawn primarily from its context, such as one's surroundings, rather than from words.

low-context culture (p. 39) A culture in which there is a high degree of difference among members and in which the meaning of a message must be explicitly related, usually in words.

ethnocentrism (p. 39) The process of judging another culture using the standards of one's own culture.

stereotypes (p. 40) Fixed mental images of a particular group and communicating with an individual as if he or she is a member of that group.

in-group (p. 40) A group to which a person feels he or she belongs.

out-group (p. 40) A group to which a person feels he or she does not belong.

cultural imperialism (p. 44) The process whereby individuals, companies, and/or the media impose their way of thinking and behaving upon another culture.

cultural empathy (p. 44) The learned ability to understand the experiences of people from diverse cultures and to convey that understanding responsively.

often misguided process that associates certain traits with individuals just because they are part of a group. Anxiety influences our communication; feeling like a member of an in-group or out-group can affect our relationships. Nonverbal behaviors differ across cultures. Finally, if we assume that we are similar to those in other cultures, we don't appreciate the differences between us, and the reverse is also true.

2.6

Skill set for intercultural understanding. You can make positive choices to improve your intercultural understanding, including knowing and eliminating your biases, tolerating the unknown, practicing cultural respect, educating yourself, being prepared for consequences, and relating to the individual instead of the culture. Intercultural communication requires patience, knowledge, sensitivity, and respect. We hope that you work toward establishing and maintaining intercultural relationships with the information we outline in this chapter.

ONLINE RESOURCES

Use Enhanced CourseMate for quick access to the electronic study resources that accompany this text:

• **Ethics & Choice:** Roommates clash over each other's culture.
• **Communication Assessment Test:** Revised Ethnocentrism Scale

INTERACTIVE ACTIVITIES

2.1 Effects of Globalization—Explore the effects of globalization on cultural diversity, women, and more.

2.2 Hofstede's Dimensions of Culture—View a summary of Hofstede's four dimensions of culture and an extensive list of representative countries.

KEY CONCEPTS

A significant part of our interpersonal communication effectiveness is based upon our perceptions and on our self-concepts. Our perceptions are influenced by our self-identity, and our self-identity is influenced by our perceptions. The two are inseparable in our communication with others.

3.1

Understanding perception: a "see/saw" experience. In most of our interpersonal encounters, we form an impression of the other person. These impressions, or perceptions, are critical to achieving meaning. Perception is an active and challenging process that involves all five senses: touch, sight, taste, smell, and hearing. Through perception, we gain important information about the interpersonal communication skills of others and of ourselves. The perception process generally occurs in four stages: attending and selecting, organizing, interpreting, and retrieving.

3.2

Influences on perception. Perception is the process of using our physical senses to respond to the world around us. The perception process occurs in four stages: attending and selecting, organizing, interpreting, and retrieving. In the attending and selecting stage, we use our senses to respond to our interpersonal environment and then decide which stimuli we will attend to. In the organizing stage, we order the information we have selected so that it is understandable and accessible. In the interpreting stage, we assign meaning to what we perceive based on our relational history, personal expectations, and knowledge of ourselves and others. In the retrieving stage, we recall information we have stored in our memories, which affects how we communicate with others. Perception is influenced by many factors, including culture, sex and gender, physical factors, technology, and self-concept.

3.3

Understanding the self: the "I's" have it. A person's self-concept is the relatively stable set of perceptions a person holds of himself or herself. Our self-concept is shaped by self-awareness, self-esteem, and self-fulfilling prophecy. Self-awareness is an understanding of who we are. Though we begin our lives as blank slates, self-awareness is instigated by our earliest relationships. Self-esteem is an evaluation of who we perceive ourselves to be. We develop self-esteem as a result of overcoming setbacks, achieving our goals, and helping others in their pursuits. Self-fulfilling prophecies are predictions about our future that are likely to come true because we believe them.

3.4

Identity management. An important component of the self is identity management, or the ways we handle various interpersonal situations to influence how others perceive us. When we present our identity to others, we are presenting a particular sense of self. The image of the self we present to others is called *face*, and we typically present two types of face in our interactions with others: positive face and negative face. Positive face is our desire to be liked, understood, and respected by others. Negative face is our desire for others to respect our individuality and to refrain from imposing their will on us.

3.5

Online identity management. After ridding yourself of your predisposed biases, you can employ several skills to improve your perceptual abilities. First, understand your personal worldview. Second, be aware of why you choose to select and attend to particular stimuli over others, and check your perceptions as needed. Third, check in with others to make sure that you are accurately perceiving a person,

KEY TERMS

perception (p. 48) The process of using our senses to understand and respond to stimuli. The perception process occurs in four stages: attending and selecting, organizing, interpreting, and retrieving.

attending and selecting stage (p. 48) The first stage of the perception process, requiring us to use our visual, auditory, tactile, and olfactory senses to respond to stimuli in our interpersonal environment.

mindful (p. 48) Having the ability to engage our senses so that we are observant and aware of our surroundings.

selective perception (p. 48) Directing our attention to certain stimuli while ignoring other stimuli.

organizing stage (p. 49) The second stage of the perception process in which we place what are often a number of confusing pieces of information into an understandable, accessible, and orderly arrangement.

relational schema (p. 49) A mental framework or memory structure that we rely on to understand experience and to guide our future behavior in relationships.

stereotyping (p. 49) Categorizing individuals according to a fixed impression, based upon the group to which they belong.

interpreting stage (p. 50) The third stage of the perception process in which we assign meaning to what we perceive.

retrieving stage (p. 51) The fourth and final stage of the perception process in which we recall information stored in our memories.

selective retention (p. 51) Recalling information that agrees with our perceptions and selectively forgetting information that does not.

sex (p. 52) The biological makeup of an individual (male or female).

gender (p. 52) The learned behaviors a culture associates with being a male or female, known as masculinity or femininity.

gender role socialization (p. 53) The process by which women and men learn the gender roles appropriate to their sex. This process affects the way the sexes perceive the world.

gender schema (p. 53) A mental framework we use to process and categorize beliefs, ideas, and events as either masculine or feminine in order to understand and organize our world.

self-concept (p. 54) A relatively stable set of perceptions we hold of ourselves.

symbolic interactionism theory (p. 56) The theory that our understanding of ourselves and of the world is shaped by our interactions with those around us.

self-awareness (p. 56) Our understanding of who we are.

self-esteem (p. 56) An evaluation of who we perceive ourselves to be.

self-worth (p. 56) How we feel about our talents, abilities, knowledge, expertise, and appearance.

self-fulfilling prophecy (p. 58) A prediction or expectation about our future behavior that is likely to come true because we believe it and thus act in ways that make it come true.

identity management theory (p. 58) The theory that explains the manner in which you handle your "self" in various circumstances; includes competency, identity, and face.

face (p. 59) The image of the self we choose to present to others in our interpersonal encounters.

facework (p. 59) The set of coordinated behaviors that help us either reinforce or threaten our competence.

positive face (p. 59) Our desire to be liked by significant people in our lives and have them confirm our beliefs, respect our abilities, and value what we value.

negative face (p. 60) Our desire that others refrain from imposing their will on us, respect our individuality and our uniqueness, and avoid interfering with our actions or beliefs.

self-monitoring (p. 60) Actively thinking about and controlling our public behaviors and actions.

identity marker (p. 61) An electronic extension of who someone is (e.g., screen name).

implicit personality theory (p. 62) The theory that we rely on a set of a few characteristics to draw inferences about others and use these inferences as the basis of our communication with them.

halo effect (p. 62) The result of matching like qualities with each other to create an overall perception of someone or something.

positive halo (p. 62) The result of placing positive qualities (e.g., warm, sensitive, and intelligent) together.

negative halo (p. 62) The result of grouping negative qualities (e.g., unintelligent, rude, and temperamental) together.

situation, or event. Fourth, distinguish facts from inferences. And fifth, practice being patient and tolerant.

In addition, you can implement five strategies to improve your self-concept. First, have the desire and will to work at changing your self-concept. Second, make the decision to change and be specific about what you will change. Third, set reasonable personal goals. Fourth, review and revise your self-concept as needed, retaining the changes that are beneficial. And fifth, surround yourself with "relational uppers"— people who support and trust you.

ONLINE RESOURCES

Use Enhanced CourseMate for quick access to the electronic study resources that accompany this text:

- **Ethics & Choice:** Karena and Nick's conflict underscores how important perceptions of the self are in interpersonal relationships.
- **Communication Assessment Test**: Self-Monitoring Scale

INTERACTIVE ACTIVITIES

3.1 Optical Illusions and Perception—Dramatic (and fun) examples of how our visual capabilities affect our perceptions.

3.2 Pygmalion in the Classroom—Read about a famous and interesting study that tested the power of self-fulfilling prophecies in an elementary school class.

attribution theory (p. 62) A theory that explains how we create explanations or attach meaning to another person's behavior or our own.

impression management (p. 63) A component of Walther's social information processing theory; the unconscious or strategic effort to influence another's perceptions.

actual self (p. 64) Attributes of an individual.

ideal self (p. 64) Attributes an individual ideally possesses.

ought self (p. 64) Attributes an individual should possess.

worldview (p. 65) A unique personal frame for viewing life and life's events.

fact (p. 65) A piece of information that is verifiable by direct observation.

inference (p. 65) A conclusion derived from a fact, but it does not reflect direct observation or experience.

relational uppers (p. 67) People who support and trust us as we improve our self-concept.

KEY CONCEPTS

We use words, or verbal symbols, to achieve our ultimate goal: sharing meaning with others. Verbal symbols are only symbolic representations, but they still can be quite powerful and flexible. As we use language, we are both expressing our thoughts and creating our thoughts, and even deciding what is worth thinking about.

4.1

Understanding verbal symbols. The lexicon is ever-changing; new words are coined as new technology emerges. Other words are discarded because the things they refer to are obsolete or because the words of one generation are ignored by the next, replaced by language that characterizes a generational in-group. In addition, the meanings of existing words evolve. For example, although a word's denotative meaning (its dictionary definition) might stay the same, its connotative meaning (the ideas or feelings people associate with a term) might change.

4.2

Factors affecting verbal symbols. Words are affected by factors such as culture and ethnicity. Idioms (words or phrases that have an understood meaning in a culture) such as phatic communication (words not meant to be literally translated) complicate communication between people of different cultures. Some people who navigate two cultures engage in code switching, or shifting between languages in the same conversation. Other variables, such as gender, generation, and context, also influence our use of verbal symbols.

Our use of verbal symbols or language can be explained in many ways. Symbolic interactionism holds that the meanings of words are determined by cultural agreement, not by anything inherent in the words themselves. Linguistic determinism states that words determine our ability to perceive and think, and linguistic relativity proposes that language influences, but doesn't determine, our thinking.

4.3

The destructive and constructive sides of verbal symbols. Words can be inflammatory. Language can be perceived as sexist, such as use of the generic *he* (using the pronoun *he* for all people, male and female) and the prevalence of man-linked words (such as *salesman*). Other words, (such as *blackmail*), can be considered racist. We can also use phrases, such as "that's so gay," which communicate homophobia. Language can be problematic when it encourages speakers to ignore change (static evaluation), to characterize another person as either good or bad (polarization), and to respond to the symbol rather than the thing itself (reification).

4.4

Skill set for improving verbal communication. Language can be restorative. We can use it to express confirmation and to develop inclusion. When we practice perspective taking, we acknowledge the viewpoints of those with whom we interact. We can also use I-messages to own our behaviors and feelings. We can choose to communicate using concrete or abstract terms, depending on the circumstances. In addition, we can index the time frame of our judgments to avoid static evaluation. Lastly, we can probe the middle ground to avoid polarization.

KEY TERMS

code switching (p. 69) Shifting back and forth between languages, sometimes in the same conversation or in different situations.

language (p. 70) A system comprised of vocabulary and rules of grammar that allows us to engage in verbal communication.

verbal symbols (p. 70) Words or vocabulary that make up a language.

grammar (p. 70) The rules that dictate the structure of language.

encoding (p. 70) The process of putting thoughts and feelings into verbal symbols, nonverbal messages, or both.

decoding (p. 70) The process of developing thought based on hearing verbal symbols, observing nonverbal messages, or both.

denotative meaning (p. 72) The literal, conventional meaning that most people in a culture have agreed upon.

connotative meaning (p. 73) The meaning of a verbal symbol that is derived from our personal and subjective experience with that symbol.

concrete (p. 73) Able to be seen, smelled, tasted, touched, or heard.

referent (p. 73) The thing a verbal symbol represents.

abstract (p. 73) Not able to be seen, smelled, or tasted.

framing theory (p. 74) A theory arguing that when we compare two unlike things in a figure of speech, we are unconsciously influenced by the comparison—it acts like a frame to filter our thinking.

process of abstraction (p. 74) The ability to move up and down the ladder of abstraction from specific to general and vice versa.

strategic ambiguity (p. 74) Leaving out cues in a message on purpose to encourage multiple interpretations by others.

equivocation (p. 75) A type of ambiguity that involves choosing our words carefully to give a listener a false impression without actually lying.

euphemism (p. 75) A milder or less direct word substituted for another word that is more blunt or negative.

idiom (p. 75) A word or a phrase that has an understood meaning within a culture but whose meaning is not derived by exact translation.

CHAPTER REVIEW 4

phatic communication (p. 76) Communication consisting of words and phrases that are used for interpersonal contact only and are not meant to be translated verbatim.

speech community (p. 77) A group of people who share norms about how to speak; what words to use; and when, where, and why to speak.

symbolic interaction theory (p. 77) The theory that our understanding of ourselves and of the world is shaped by our interactions with those around us.

Sapir-Whorf hypothesis (p. 77) A theory that points to connections among culture, language, and thought. In its strong form, this theory is known as linguistic determinism, and in its weak form, it is known as linguistic relativity.

linguistic determinism (p. 77) A theory arguing that our language determines our ability to perceive and think about things. If we don't have a word for something in our language, this theory predicts that we won't think about it or notice it.

linguistic relativity (p. 78) A theory stating that language influences our thinking but doesn't determine it. Thus, if we don't have a word for something in our language, this theory predicts that it will be difficult, but not impossible, to think about it or notice it.

codability (p. 78) The ease with which a language can express a thought.

two-culture theory (p. 79) A theory asserting that sex operates in the same way as culture in establishing different rules, norms, and language patterns for men and women.

static evaluation (p. 81) The tendency to speak and respond to someone today the same way we did in the past, not recognizing that people and relationships change over time.

polarization (p. 82) The tendency to use "either/or" language and speak of the world in extremes.

reification (p. 82) The tendency to respond to words, or labels for things, as though they were the things themselves.

lexical gaps (p. 82) Experiences that are not named.

muted group theory (p. 82) Theory that explains what happens to people whose experiences are not well represented in verbal symbols and who have trouble articulating their thoughts and feelings

verbally because their language doesn't give them an adequate vocabulary.

sexist language (p. 83) Language that is demeaning to one sex.

generic _he_ (p. 83) The use of the masculine pronoun _he_ to function generically when the subject of the sentence is of unknown gender or includes both men and women.

man-linked words (p. 84) Words that include the word _man_ but are supposed to operate generically to include women as well, such as _mankind_.

confirmation (p. 85) A response that acknowledges and supports another.

disconfirmation (p. 85) A response that fails to acknowledge and support another, leaving the person feeling ignored and disregarded.

perspective taking (p. 86) Acknowledging the viewpoints of those with whom we interact.

indexing (p. 87) Avoiding generalizations by acknowledging the time frame in which we judge others and ourselves.

ONLINE RESOURCES

Use Enhanced CourseMate for quick access to the electronic study resources that accompany this text:

• **Ethics & Choice:** When a sports team trivializes Native American culture, it has ethical implications.

• **Communication Assessment Test:** Vocabulary Test

INTERACTIVE ACTIVITIES

4.1 Politically Correct Language—Explore language reform and political correctness.

4.2 Gender-Free Language—Test your skills at replacing man-linked words with gender-neutral ones by taking the Gender-Free Language Quiz.

KEY CONCEPTS

5.1

Principles of nonverbal communication. Nonverbal communication plays a significant role in our interpersonal relationships. It is often ambiguous, meaning different things to people of different cultures and co-cultures. People use nonverbal cues to regulate conversation, such as using body language to facilitate turn taking. Nonverbal communication is more credible than verbal communication because it is harder to mask. Sometimes, nonverbal and verbal communication are at odds, resulting in mixed messages.

5.2

Nonverbal communication codes. Nonverbal communication manifests itself in many forms. Kinesics includes gestures and body posture/orientation. Physical appearance encompasses the physical characteristics of an individual (including attractiveness) and body artifacts such as clothing, jewelry, and tattoos. Facial expressions, especially the eyes and smiling, are the nonverbal cues that give the most insight into how someone is feeling.

Paralanguage, or vocalics, involves vocal qualities such as vocal distractors (the "ums" and "ers" of conversation); the use of silence; and pitch, rate, volume, inflection, tempo, and pronunciation. Paralanguage also encompasses vocal characterizers such as crying, laughing, whining, and so on. Touch communication, or haptics, the most primitive form of communication, represents the ultimate in privileged access to people and can perform diverse functions.

Proxemics, the study of distance, involves people's personal space (which can vary by circumstance and culture) as well as their territoriality, or their need to "own" certain spaces. Aspects of the physical environment, such as color, lighting, and room design, can affect our nonverbal communication. And chronemics, or the study of a person's use of time, explains how people perceive and structure time, including how the management of time is associated with status and power.

5.3

Cultural variations in nonverbal communication. Culture affects nonverbal behavior and interpretation of nonverbal behavior. People of different cultures vary in their mode of greeting and gesturing, how much they engage in eye contact, the personal space they require, and their acceptance of touching. Unless you are sensitive to this variation, you may have a tough time communicating with someone with a different cultural background from your own.

5.4

Technology and nonverbal communication. The interplay between the digital environment and nonverbal communication is an important area. The evolution of technology has been occurring for centuries, and yet, each generation must deal with the technological challenges that accompany these changes. We discuss social information processing theory, which contends that online relationships have the same potential for intimacy as do our face-to-face relationships.

5.5

Skill set for increasing nonverbal communication effectiveness. To improve our nonverbal communication, we must remember that verbal and nonverbal communication work together. We also need to avoid jumping to conclusions about what certain nonverbal cues mean. Furthermore, we need to monitor our nonverbal behavior

KEY TERMS

nonverbal communication (p. 89) All behaviors other than spoken words that communicate messages and create shared meaning between people.

interaction adaptation theory (p. 90) A theory that suggests individuals simultaneously adapt their communication behavior to the communication behavior of others.

turn taking (p. 91) In a conversation, nonverbal regulators that indicate who talks when and to whom.

mixed message (p. 92) The incompatibility that occurs when our nonverbal messages are not congruent with our verbal messages.

kinesics (p. 93) The study of a person's body movement and its effect on the communication process.

delivery gestures (p. 93) Gestures that signal shared understanding between communicators in a conversation.

citing gestures (p. 93) Gestures that acknowledge another's feedback in a conversation.

seeking gestures (p. 93) Gestures that request agreement or clarification from a sender during a conversation.

turn gestures (p. 93) Gestures that indicate another person can speak or that are used to request to speak in a conversation.

body orientation (p. 94) The extent to which we turn our legs, shoulders, and head toward or away from a communicator.

physical characteristics (p. 94) Aspects of physical appearance, such as body size, skin color, hair color and style, facial hair, and facial features.

body artifacts (p. 94) Items we wear that are part of our physical appearance and that have the potential to communicate, such as clothing, religious symbols, military medals, body piercings, and tattoos.

paralanguage (p. 96) The study of a person's voice. Also called *vocalics*. Nonverbal behaviors that include pitch, rate, volume, inflection, tempo, and pronunciation as well as the use of vocal distractors and silence.

vocal qualities (p. 96) Nonverbal behaviors such as pitch, rate, volume, inflection, tempo, and pronunciation.

CHAPTER REVIEW 5

vocal distractors (p. 96) The "ums" and "ers" used in conversation.

vocal characterizers (p. 96) Nonverbal behaviors such as crying, laughing, groaning, muttering, whispering, and whining.

haptics (p. 97) The study of how we communicate through touch.

proxemics (p. 98) The study of how people use, manipulate, and identify their personal space.

personal space (p. 98) The distance we put between ourselves and others.

intimate distance (p. 98) The distance that extends about 18 inches around each of us that is normally reserved for people with whom we are close, such as close friends, romantic partners, and family members.

personal distance (p. 100) Ranging from 18 inches to 4 feet, the space most people use during conversations.

social distance (p. 100) Ranging from 4 to 12 feet, the spatial zone usually reserved for professional or formal interpersonal encounters.

public distance (p. 100) The spacial distance of 12 or more feet used in communication to allow listeners to see a person while he or she is speaking.

expectancy violations theory (p. 100) A theory stating that we expect other people to maintain a certain distance from us in their conversations with us.

territoriality (p. 100) Our sense of ownership of space that remains fixed.

territorial markers (p. 100) Items or objects that humans use to mark their territories, such as a newspaper set on a table in a coffee shop.

physical environment (p. 101) The setting in which our behavior takes place.

chronemics (p. 102) The study of a person's use of time.

social information processing (SIP) theory (p. 106) a theory that contends that people have the ability to establish online relationships and that these relationships are equal to or greater than the intimacy achieved in face-to-face relationships.

and ask others for their impressions of our nonverbal cues. Finally, we must not only avoid nonverbal distractions during our conversations but also must ensure that we interpret nonverbal communication within its context.

ONLINE RESOURCES

Use Enhanced CourseMate for quick access to the electronic study resources that accompany this text:

- **Ethics & Choice:** Kyle wants a job so badly that he is considering lying.
- **Communication Assessment Test:** Touch Avoidance Inventory

INTERACTIVE ACTIVITIES

5.1 Mixed Messages in Negotiations—Read about mixed messages within the context of business negotiations.

5.2 Test Your Paralanguage Skills—Test your accuracy in interpreting another's paralanguage.

5.3 Nonverbal Behavior in Japan—Compare your nonverbal behaviors with those used by people in another country.

KEY CONCEPTS

Listening is called a 21st century skill because it is essential in all arenas, including home, school, and work. Indeed, employers rank listening as the most important skill on the job, and listening is important in our friendships and other personal relationships. When we listen effectively, we are communicating to senders that their messages are important to us.

6.1

Lend me your ear: differences between hearing and listening.
Listening and hearing are not the same thing. Hearing occurs when a soundwave hits an eardrum and stimuli are sent to the brain. It's a physical process. Listening is much more than letting in audible stimuli. It's a communication activity that requires us to be thoughtful.

6.2

The components of the listening process. We define listening as the dynamic, transactional process of the four "Rs": receiving, responding to, recalling, and rating stimuli and/or messages from another communicator. When we receive messages, we are being mindful and acknowledging the speaker verbally and nonverbally. When we respond, we provide nonverbal and verbal feedback to the speaker. When we recall the message, we understand it and store it for later retrieval using the following strategies: repetition, use of mnemonic devices, and chunking. When we rate messages, we have to be sure that we don't confuse facts with inferences and opinions.

6.3

The value and importance of listening. Listening is an ongoing interpersonal activity that requires lifelong training. Relationships, education, and employment all require that we hone the skill of listening. New technology and changes in business practices have changed our listening styles and skills and raised new roadblocks.

6.4

The barriers: why we don't listen. There are many barriers to listening. Physical distractions such as semantic, psychological, or physiological noise interfere. Modern phenomena such as multitasking, telecommuting, and being bombarded by many messages from numerous media can lead to message overload. Messages that are too complex—such as those filled with unfamiliar jargon or challenging arguments—can be difficult to listen to and understand. Businesses and schools seldom offer listening training or courses. Preoccupation with personal issues, including extreme self-focusing (conversational narcissism), can inhibit the processing of messages. Lastly, the time difference between the mental ability to interpret words and the speed at which they arrive at the brain (the listening gap) can cause the mind to wander.

Our poor listening habits also interfere with listening. When we selectively listen, we tend to lose focus on those messages that are uninteresting to us. Talkaholics hog the conversational stage, resulting in one-sided conversations. We may or may not fool others when we pseudolisten, or pretend to listen, to a message. Gap fillers interrupt because they believe that they know the rest of the message. When we defensively listen, we perceive innocent comments as hostile in intent. Ambushers retrieve information so that they can later use it to discredit or manipulate another person.

KEY TERMS

hearing (p. 111) The physical process of letting in audible stimuli without focusing on the stimuli.

working memory theory (p. 112) A theory stating that we can pay attention to several stimuli and simultaneously store stimuli for future reference.

listening (p. 113) The dynamic, transactional process of receiving, recalling, rating, and responding to stimuli, messages, or both.

four "Rs" of listening (p. 113) The four components of the listening process: receiving, responding, recalling, and rating.

receiving (p. 113) The verbal and nonverbal acknowledgment of a message.

mindful listening (p. 113) Listening that requires us to be engaged with another person—the words, the behaviors, and the environment.

responding (p. 114) Providing observable feedback to a sender's message.

recalling (p. 114) Understanding a message, storing it for future encounters, and remembering it later.

chunking (p. 114) Placing pieces of information into manageable and retrievable sets.

rating (p. 115) Evaluating or assessing a message.

opinion (p. 115) A view, judgment, or appraisal based on our beliefs or values.

American Sign Language (ASL) (p. 116) A visual rather than auditory form of communication that is composed of precise hand shapes and movements.

physical noise (p. 117) External disturbances that interrupt the meaning between a sender and receiver.

semantic noise (p. 117) Disruption that results from a sender using language that is not readily understood by a receiver.

physiological noise (p. 118) Interference in message reception because of physical, biological, or chemical functions of the body.

psychological noise (p. 118) The biases or prejudices of a sender or receiver that interrupts the meaning of a message.

message overload (p. 118) The result when senders receive more messages than they can process.

conversational narcissism (p. 119) Engaging in an extreme amount of self-focusing during a conversation to the exclusion of another person.

CHAPTER REVIEW 6

listening gap (p. 119) The time difference between our mental ability to interpret words and the speed at which they arrive at our brain.

selective listening (p. 119) Responding to some parts of a message and rejecting others.

talkaholic (p. 120) A compulsive talker who hogs the conversational stage and monopolizes encounters.

pseudolisten (p. 120) To pretend to listen by nodding our heads, looking at the speaker, smiling at the appropriate times, or practicing other kinds of attention feigning.

gap fillers (p. 120) Listeners who think that they can correctly guess the rest of the story a speaker is telling and don't need the speaker to continue.

defensive listening (p. 121) Viewing innocent comments as personal attacks or hostile criticisms.

ambushing (p. 121) Listening carefully to a message and then using the information later to attack the sender.

listening style (p. 121) A predominant and preferred approach to listening to the messages we hear.

people-centered listening style (p. 122) A listening style associated with concern for other people's feelings or emotions.

action-centered listening style (p. 122) A listening style associated with listeners who want messages to be highly organized, concise, and error free.

second-guess (p. 122) To question the assumptions underlying a message.

content-centered listening style (p. 122) A listening style associated with listeners who focus on the facts and details of a message.

time-centered listening style (p. 122) A listening style associated with listeners who want messages to be presented succinctly.

empathy (p. 125) The process of identifying with, or attempting to experience, the thoughts, beliefs, and actions of another.

nonjudgmental feedback (p. 126) Feedback that describes another's behavior and then explains how that behavior made us feel.

paraphrasing (p. 127) Restating the essence of a sender's message in our own words.

dialogue enhancers (p. 128) Supporting statements, such as "I see" or "I'm listening," that indicate we are involved in a message.

silent listening (p. 128) Listening that requires individuals to listen attentively and nonverbally to another person.

6.5
Poor listening habits. Poor listening is something that occurs over a lifetime. We pick up behaviors, some of which occur more frequently than others, that affect the reception and meaning of a message: selective listening, talkaholism, pseudolistening, gap filling, defensive listening, and ambushing.

6.6
Personal styles of listening. Researchers have identified four listening styles. Your listening style may vary depending on the situation and the purpose of the personal encounter. People-centered listeners are concerned with other people's feelings or emotions. Action-centered listeners are listeners who want messages to be highly organized and who sometimes second-guess, or question, the assumptions underlying the message. Content-centered listeners focus on the facts and details of a message and are likely to play devil's advocate. Time-centered listeners discourage wordy explanations from speakers and set time guidelines for conversations.

6.7
Culture and the listening process. In addition to noting a communicator's listening style, keep in mind that people from different cultures provide different types of feedback (direct or indirect), which may affect message meaning. Individualistic cultures value direct communication, or speaking one's mind. Some collectivistic cultures, such as Japan, respect others' words, desire harmony, and believe in conversational politeness. Cultures vary in their value systems, yet listening remains a critical part of the various cultural communities. Staying culturally aware of these variations as you consider the message of another person is important.

6.8
Skill set for effective listening. To improve your listening skills, you need to evaluate your current skills, prepare to listen, provide empathic responses, use nonjudgmental feedback, and practice active listening. When we actively listen, we communicate reinforcing messages to the speaker through paraphrasing (restatements), dialogue enhancers (supporting expressions), questioning, and the use of silence. When you work on your listening skills, you are striving to become a more engaged and competent communicator.

ONLINE RESOURCES

Use Enhanced CourseMate for quick access to the electronic study resources that accompany this text:
- **Ethics & Choice:** Gabe has to decide whether to excuse himself from a gaggle of gossiping frat brothers.
- **Communication Assessment Test:** The Listening Inventory

INTERACTIVE ACTIVITIES

6.1 The Importance of Listening—Read an article that reinforces the importance of listening and offers steps to effective listening.

6.2 Identify Your Listening Problems—Identify the areas in which you can improve your listening skills.

6.3 Overcome Bad Listening Habits—Read about strategies you can use to become a better listener.

6.4 Keys to Better Listening—Check out seven strategies to better listening.

KEY CONCEPTS

7.1

Defining emotion: more than just a feeling. Emotional language and emotional communication are inevitable in our daily interactions. Emotional experiences shape our lives and our relationships and are often what we remember most about interpersonal encounters. The term *emotion* encompasses both the internal feelings of one person (e.g., when Joe feels anxious before he meets Ana's parents) as well as feelings that can be experienced only in a relationship (e.g., when Joyce feels competitiveness when she hears how well Barb did on the chemistry exam). Emotion relates to the affective, or feeling tone, of our experiences.

7.2

Explaining emotion: biology and social interaction. The biological theory of emotion, based mainly on Darwin's ideas, states that emotions are related to instinct and are universal. This view places emphasis on observable emotional expressions, or "gestures" of emotion. On the other hand, the social theory of emotion, attributed to Hans Gerth and C. Wright Mills, states that the social situation, as well as biology, affects the experience of emotion. This view studies how the reactions of others to our gestures help us define our feelings. The social interaction theory acknowledges that biology affects emotion and emotional communication. Proponents of this theory, however, are also interested in how people interact with social situations before, during, and after the experience of emotion. The theory adds social factors, like interactions with others, to the biological basis for explaining emotion.

7.3

Emotion and communication. People often use metaphors to talk about emotion, many of which make it seem as if emotional forces are beyond our control. Tools for emotional communication include facial expressions, vocal cues, gestures, and verbal cues. Although it is not as well researched as the face, the voice is probably equally important in conveying emotion. How loudly people talk, how high-pitched their tone, how fast they talk, how many pauses they take, and so forth give clues to emotion. Culture, gender, and context are three of the many factors that also influence emotional communication.

7.4

Influences on emotional communication. Emotional communication is not a fixed behavior in our conversations with others. Emotional communication is influenced by several factors, including meta-emotion, culture, gender and sex, and context.

7.5

Recognize destructive and constructive aspects of with emotional communication. Communication that offers comfort, social support, warmth, affection, forgiveness, or desire falls on the constructive end of the emotional spectrum. Embarrassment, guilt, hurt, jealousy, anger, depression, and loneliness fall on the destructive side. Some destructive emotions are the polar opposites of constructive emotions. For example, empathy, a constructive emotion, is the opposite of the destructive emotion *schadenfreude*. Emotions are often experienced in blends, and constructive and destructive, love and hate, are entangled with one another. There

KEY TERMS

emotion (p. 131) The critical internal structure that orients us to, and engages us with, what matters in our lives: our feelings about ourselves and others. Emotion encompasses both the internal feelings of one person (e.g., anxiety or happiness) as well as feelings that can be experienced only in a relationship (e.g., jealousy or competitiveness).

valence (p. 132) An attribute of emotion that refers to whether the emotion reflects a positive or negative feeling.

activity (p. 132) An attribute of emotion that refers to whether the emotion implies action or passivity.

intensity (p. 132) An attribute of emotion that refers to how strongly an emotion is felt.

dualism (p. 133) A way of thinking that constructs polar opposite categories to encompass the totality of a thing. Dualism prompts us to think about things in an either/or fashion.

emotional contagion (p. 136) The process of transferring emotions from one person to another.

emotional experience (p. 136) The feeling of emotion.

communicating emotionally (p. 136) Communicating such that the emotion is not the content of the message but rather a property of it.

emotional effects (p. 136) The ways in which an emotional experience impacts communication behavior.

emotional communication (p. 137) Talking about an emotional experience.

meta-emotion (p. 139) Emotion felt about experiencing another emotion.

feeling rules (p. 142) The cultural norms used to create and react to emotional expressions.

emoticon (p. 143) An icon that can be typed on a keyboard to express emotions; used to compensate for the lack of nonverbal cues in computer-mediated communication.

owning (p. 149) Verbally taking responsibility for our own thoughts and feelings.

I-message (p. 149) A message phrased to show we understand that our feelings belong to us and aren't caused by someone else.

reframe (p. 149) To change something that has a negative connotation to something with a more positive connotation (e.g., a problem can become a concern, or a challenge can become an opportunity).

active listening (p. 150) Suspending our own responses while listening so we can concentrate on what another person is saying.

are no simple guidelines specifying when positive emotions are healthier than negative ones, because the context, the receiver, the sender, and the social goal all make a difference.

7.6

Skill set for emotional communication. Becoming competent in emotional communication requires practicing the following techniques: knowing your feelings, analyzing the situation, owning your feelings, reframing when needed, and empathizing. Emotional communication is a complex activity that involves sensitivity, awareness, insight, and empathy. Just like any proficiency, emotional communication requires patience and persistence, but the rewards are worth the effort.

ONLINE RESOURCES

Use Enhanced CourseMate for quick access to the electronic study resources that accompany this text:

- **Ethics & Choice:** Marco decides what to do about work that conflicts with his moral beliefs.

- **Communication Assessment Test:** Emotional Intelligence (E-IQ)

INTERACTIVE ACTIVITIES

7.1 Feeling Emotion—Read an interesting article about how the brain and body change when recalling emotional experiences.

7.2 Emotions, the Body, and the Mind—More about the links among emotion, the body, and the mind.

7.3 Theories of Emotion—Check out several additional theories of emotion.

KEY CONCEPTS

8.1

Definition of self-disclosure: opening up. Self-disclosure is a complex, well-researched communication process. We define it as verbal communication that intentionally reveals personal information about ourselves that our listener would be unlikely to discover without being told. This means that self-disclosing is a choice we make; we always have the option of not telling.

8.2

Factors affecting disclosure. We generally choose to disclose in the context of a close, trusting relationship because self-disclosure is scary and implies risk. Not everyone self-discloses in the same way or at the same rate. Our disclosures are affected by individual differences, relational factors, cultural values, and gender and sex, as well as the channel through which the disclosure is made. We wish to emphasize that our knowledge of and attitude toward self-disclosure is heavily influenced by cultural norms; for example, in the United States, the culture favors openness over secrecy.

8.3

Principles of self-disclosure. One norm of self-disclosure is that we disclose a great deal in a few interactions; only about 2 percent of our communication time is involved in this activity. Another principle is that self-disclosures occur between two people in a close relationship; however, exceptions to this rule include self-disclosing in public forums (such as on a TV talk show) or to a stranger while traveling ("the bus rider phenomenon"). Another guideline self-disclosures follow is that they are reciprocal; the dyadic effect describes the tendency for us to return another's self-disclosure with one that matches it in level of intimacy. Lastly, self-disclosures occur in the context of time—that is, self-disclosures get more intimate as a relationship progresses, and time affects the meaning of disclosure.

8.4

Explaining self-disclosure. One way we can understand the process of self-disclosing is through the theory of communication privacy management. This theory explains how people believe they own private information about themselves and think about how to (and whether to) share it with others. We can also get a handle on self-disclosure from social penetration theory. This theory pictures relational development as a gradual, incremental process facilitated by self-disclosures (like peeling back layers of an onion). Finally, the Johari Window provides information about self-disclosure by showing how the four panes of the window (the open self, the hidden self, the blind self, and the unknown self) shrink or expand as we disclose and get feedback.

8.5

Reasons for revealing and concealing personal information.
People have both individual and relational reasons for disclosing to others. Reasons that provide primarily individual benefits include catharsis, psychological health, physical health, and self-awareness. Reasons involving relational life encompass developing a new relationship, maintaining a relationship, fulfilling the expectations for what should happen within a relationship, and escalating the intensity of a relationship.

Reasons for not engaging in self-disclosure include avoiding hurt and rejection, avoiding conflict and protecting a relationship, keeping our image intact and maintaining our individuality, and reducing stress.

KEY TERMS

self-disclosure (p. 153) Evaluative and descriptive information about the self, shared intentionally, that another would have trouble finding out without being told.

public information (p. 154) Personal facts, usually socially approved characteristics, that we make part of our public image.

private information (p. 154) Assessments, both good and bad, that we make about ourselves, including our personal values and our interests, fears, and concerns.

history (p. 156) Information that may sound personal to another person but is relatively easy for us to tell.

story (p. 156) Information we feel we are taking a risk telling another.

topical intimacy (p. 156) The level of intimacy inherent in a topic.

androgynous (p. 159) Having both masculine and feminine traits.

dyadic effect (p. 162) The tendency for us to return another's self-disclosure with one that matches it in level of intimacy.

reciprocity (p. 162) The tendency to respond in kind to another's self-disclosure.

communication privacy management theory (CPM) (p. 163) A theory focusing on how people manage information that they consider to be private.

social penetration theory (p. 164) A theory of self-disclosure and relational development that illustrates how sharing increasingly more personal information intensifies a relationship's intimacy level.

breadth (p. 165) A dimension of self-disclosure indicating the number of topics discussed within a relationship.

depth (p. 165) A dimension of self-disclosure indicating how much detail we provide about a specific topic.

Johari Window (p. 165) A model used to understand the process of self-disclosure consisting of a square with four panels that provides a pictorial representation of how "known" we are to ourselves and others.

open self (p. 165) In the Johari Window, the pane that includes all the information about us that we know and have shared with others through disclosures.

CHAPTER REVIEW 8

hidden self (p. 166) In the Johari Window, the pane that includes the information about ourselves that we are aware of but have chosen not to disclose.

blind self (p. 166) In the Johari Window, the pane that includes information others know about us that we are unaware of.

unknown self (p. 166) In the Johari Window, the pane that includes the information about ourselves that neither we nor others are aware of.

catharsis (p. 167) A therapeutic release of tensions and negative emotion as a result of self-disclosing.

8.6

Skill set for effective disclosing. Understanding self-disclosure contributes to an understanding of interpersonal communication. To engage in skillful self-disclosure, you need to learn how to use I-statements, and you must be honest and consistent with your verbal and nonverbal communication. Remember to focus your nonverbal communication, and be sure that your content and topic are relevant. Practice estimating the risks and benefits of self-disclosure and predicting how your partner will respond. Be sure that the amount and type of disclosure are appropriate, and try to estimate the effect of the disclosure on your relationship.

ONLINE RESOURCES

Use Enhanced CourseMate for quick access to the electronic study resources that accompany this text:

• **Ethics & Choice:** Theo wonders if he should reveal anything about his disability, multiple sclerosis (MS), to his prospective employers.

• **Communication Assessment Test:** Exploring Your Approach to Self-Disclosure

INTERACTIVE ACTIVITIES

8.1 Disclosing Health Information—Access guidelines detailing how to disclose private information about your health.

8.2 Self-Disclosure Assessment—Assess your own willingness to self-disclose in various situations.

8.3 Fear of Self-Disclosure—Read an article about how the fear of self-disclosure prevents some people from seeking psychological help.

8.4 The Johari Window in a Professional Setting—Explore some uses of the Johari Window in a professional context.

KEY CONCEPTS

9.1

Defining conflict. Even though most people think that conflict is unpleasant and even nasty, interpersonal conflict is a pervasive fact of relational life. Conflicts are interactions about important differences between interdependent people. When people first meet, they usually focus on their similarities, thus reducing opportunities for conflict. However, later in the relationship, they usually notice and discuss differences. These interactions can focus on image, content, values, and/or relational questions. Meta-conflicts can happen at any time, but they are especially likely in long-term relationships. Serial conflicts occur when partners engage in repeated conflicts about the same thing over time.

9.2

Communication patterns in conflict. During conflicts, communication partners often repeat patterns of behavior, including symmetrical escalation, symmetrical withdrawal, withdrawal-pursuit or pursuit-withdrawal, and symmetrical negotiation. The only one of these patterns that is positive is symmetrical negotiation, in which each partner mirrors the other's negotiating behaviors.

9.3

The destructive and constructive sides of interpersonal conflict. Conflicts between people are inevitable and inescapable, and we engage in conflict frequently. The key to the outcome is often in the way the conflict is managed. Destructive styles, such as bullying and violence and aggression, provide poor outcomes as opposed to constructive styles such as getting feelings out in the open and increasing knowledge of one another, and promoting confidence and human contact.

9.4

Explaining conflict. We can conceptualize conflict by using the four-part model, which shows that conflict has four interdependent parts: you, me, context, and subject. Ignoring even one of these components results in ineffective conflict management. Another approach that is helpful in thinking about conflict is the explanatory process model, which explains conflict as a process with five episodes (distal context, proximal context, conflict interaction, proximal outcomes, and distal outcomes).

9.5

The relationship of conflict to power. Power often influences the outcome as well as the process of conflict. Power may be used through direct application, direct and virtual use, indirect application, and hidden use. Sex difference research indicates that either women have more power than men in marriage or power is equal. Empowerment is a way to manage power positively, thus encouraging good conflict outcomes.

9.6

Skill set for effective conflict management. To manage your conflicts, use the following strategies: lighten up and reframe, presume and express goodwill, ask questions, listen, and practice cultural sensitivity. Although no one can avoid conflict, these techniques should improve your satisfaction in conflict encounters. Effectively managed conflict will help you acquire necessary tools for satisfaction in your interpersonal interactions.

KEY TERMS

interpersonal conflict (p. 176) The interaction of interdependent people who perceive incompatible goals and interference from each other in achieving those goals.

interaction (p. 176) A condition necessary for conflict, given that conflicts are created and sustained through verbal and nonverbal communication.

interdependence (p. 177) A condition necessary for conflict, given that people involved in conflict rely on each other, need each other, and are in a relationship with each other.

image conflict (p. 178) A conflict with another about one's sense of self.

content conflict (p. 179) A conflict that revolves around an issue. Also called substantive conflict.

public issue (p. 179) An issue outside a relationship that can cause a content conflict.

private issue (p. 179) An issue related to a relationship that can cause a content conflict.

value conflict (p. 179) A conflict in which the content is specifically about a question of right and wrong.

relational conflict (p. 179) A conflict that focuses on issues concerning the relationship between two people.

meta-conflict (p. 180) A conflict about the way a conflict is conducted.

serial conflicts (p. 180) Conflicts that recur over time in people's everyday lives, without a resolution.

symmetrical escalation (p. 184) In a conflict, when each partner chooses to increase the intensity of the conflict.

symmetrical withdrawal (p. 184) In a conflict, neither partner being willing to confront the other.

pursuit-withdrawal (p. 184) In a conflict, a pattern consisting of one party pressing for a discussion about a conflictual topic while the other party withdraws.

withdrawal-pursuit (p. 184) In a conflict, a pattern in which one party withdraws, which prompts the other party to pursue.

symmetrical negotiation (p. 184) In a conflict, each party mirroring the other's negotiating behaviors.

bullying (p. 185) A particular form of conflict in which the abuse is persistent and the person being bullied finds it very difficult to defend himself or herself.

positive interaction ratio (p. 187) An interpersonal encounter in which the participants say more positive things to each other than negative things.

negative interaction ratio (p. 187) An interpersonal encounter in which the participants say more negative things to each other than positive things.

four-part model (p. 187) A way to explain conflict interactions that describes conflict as consisting of four parts—you, me, subject, and context—all of which must be considered in effective conflict management.

placating (p. 188) Being passive or ignoring our own needs in a conflict.

pouncing (p. 188) Responding in an aggressive manner without acknowledging the needs of another person in a conflict.

computing (p. 188) Disqualifying the emotional aspects of a conflict (the context) and focusing on the rational aspects.

distracting (p. 188) Disqualifying the subject of a conflict by distracting both people in the conflict with behaviors such as laughing, crying, or changing the subject.

integrating (p. 188) Responding to conflict by giving full attention to all its parts.

explanatory process model (p. 188) A model that illustrates how conflict between people follows a certain sequence and every prior conflict affects how a future conflict will be handled.

distal context (p. 188) The background that frames a specific conflict.

proximal context (p. 189) The rules, emotions, and beliefs of the individuals involved in a conflict.

conflict interaction (p. 189) The point in the conflict process at which the differences between two individuals become a problem and one or both people begin to address the issue.

proximal outcomes (p. 189) The immediate results after a conflict interaction.

distal outcomes (p. 189) The residue of having engaged in a conflict and the feelings that both the participants have about their interaction.

Power (p. 190) The ability to control the behavior of another.

direct application of power (p. 191) In a conflict situation, the use of any resource at our disposal to compel another to comply, regardless of that person's desires.

direct and virtual use of power (p. 191) Communicating the potential use of a direct application of power.

indirect application of power (p. 191) Employing power without making its employment explicit.

ONLINE RESOURCES

Use Enhanced CourseMate for quick access to the electronic study resources that accompany this text:

• **Ethics & Choice:** Daryl decides if she should change her appearance to fit in or toughen up.

• **Communication Assessment Test:** Argumentativeness Scale

INTERACTIVE ACTIVITIES

9.1 Conflict Styles—Read an interesting article about the different styles people use in communicating about conflict.

9.2 Techniques for Resolving Conflict—Practice techniques that can help you deal with conflict effectively.

relational message (p. 191) A message that defines a relationship and implicitly states that the sender has the power to do so.

hidden power (p. 191) A type of power in which one person in a relationship suppresses or avoids decisions in the interest of one of the parties. Also called *unobtrusive power*.

empowerment (p. 192) Helping to actualize our own or another person's power.

CHAPTER REVIEW 10
Communicating in Close Relationships

CONCEPTS IN REVIEW

In this chapter, we tackled a huge topic: communication in close relationships. According to Maslow's hierarchy of needs, establishing relationships is the third most important human need, behind only physical and safety needs.

10.1

Understanding close relationships. To organize the information, we distinguished between close relationships and role relationships, concluding that close relationships endure over time, consist of interdependent partners who satisfy each other's needs, feel an emotional attachment to each other, are irreplaceable to one another, and enact unique communication patterns.

10.2

Thinking and talking about close relationships. We examined close relationships from a cultural performance perspective as well as a cognitive and linguistic perspective. We observed that the cultural performance perspective attends to the rituals and rules in a specific culture that define close relationships and the communication practices that should take place within them. Cognitive approaches to close relationships focus on how people think about what should happen within these relationships, and develop scripts and mental images for them. Linguistic perspectives attend to how we label our close relationships, and the metaphors we develop to describe them.

10.3

Influences on close relationships. We consider the ways in which attraction, culture, gender and sex, and electronic communication influence our communication in close relationships. We distinguish between short-term and long-term attraction, and note that different cultures may view and define close relationships differently. We examine research on gendered behaviors and expectations around close relationships. Finally, we present some findings about how electronic media are changing communication in close relationships.

10.4

Developing close relationships through stages. We examine how relationships have been pictured through stages of coming together and coming apart. We illustrate how the model approach allows for different types of communication in each stage. We present some arguments for and against using this approach to understand communication in close relationships.

10.5

Explanations for communication in close relationships. Three frameworks offer some explanation for how we communicate in close relationships. We discussed systems thinking, which allows us to see close relationships as highly interdependent, open, self-adjusting systems. We illustrated seven common relational dialectics, and we explored the central premise of social exchange.

10.6

Skill set for communicating in close relationships. Different communication guidelines help us begin, maintain, and repair close relationships. For instance, apologies and accounts may be useful strategies for repairing relationships, while networking and offering may help initiate relationships. Given the variety of close relationships and the factors that influence them, no one can provide a single list of skills that will always be successful. Yet, the more we understand about communicating in close relationships, the more successful and life enhancing our relationships will be.

KEY TERMS

close relationship (p. 198) A relationship that endures over time and consists of interdependent partners who satisfy each other's needs for connection and social inclusion, feel an emotional attachment to each other, are irreplaceable to each other, and enact unique communication patterns.

role relationship (p. 198) A relationship in which the partners are interdependent while accomplishing a specific task, such as a server and a customer at a restaurant.

relationship scripts (p. 200) Cognitive structures containing a pattern for the key events we expect in a relationship.

short-term attraction (p. 201) A judgment of relationship potential that propels us into beginning a relationship with someone.

long-term attraction (p. 201) The things about another which make you want to continue, sustain, and maintain a relationship with them.

matching hypothesis (p. 202) We feel most comfortable in relationships with people who are about as attractive as we perceive ourselves to be.

relational culture (p. 202) The notion that relational partners collaborate and experience shared understandings, roles, and rituals that are unique to their relationship.

hyperpersonal (p. 204) Communication online that is overly intense and personal because, online, communicators are able to make their self-presentations very positive.

initiating stage (p. 205) The first step in Knapp's stage model when two people notice one another and indicate to each other that they are interested in making contact.

experimenting stage (p. 205) The second stage in Knapp's model when people become acquainted by gathering superficial information about one another.

small talk (p. 205) Interactions that are relaxed, pleasant, uncritical, and casual.

intensifying stage (p. 206) The third stage in Knapp's stage model refers to deepening intimacy in the relationship.

integrating stage (p. 206) The fourth stage in Knapp's model represents the two people forming a clear identity as a couple.

bonding stage (p. 206) The fifth stage in Knapp's model (and the final stage in the Coming Together part) refers to a public commitment of the relationship.

differentiating stage (p. 207) The first stage in the coming apart phase of Knapp's stage model refers to highlighting the individuality of the partners.

circumscribing stage (p. 207) The second stage of coming apart in Knapp's model, refers to restraining communication behaviors so that fewer topics are raised (for fear of conflict) and more issues are out of bounds for the partners.

stagnating stage (p. 207) The third state of coming apart in Knapp's model consists of extending circumscribing so far that the partners no longer talk much.

imagined conversations (p. 207) Where one partner plays the parts of both partners in a mental rehearsal of possible communication that might take place between them.

avoiding stage (p. 207) The fourth stage of coming apart, where partners try to stay out of the same physical environment.

terminating stage (p. 208) The final stage of coming apart comes after the relational partners have decided, either jointly or individually, to part permanently. Terminating refers to the process of ending a relationship.

systems theory (p. 208) von Bertalanffy's theory comparing relationships to living systems with six important properties: wholeness, interdependence, hierarchy, boundaries or openness, calibration or feedback, and equifinality.

wholeness (p. 209) A principle of systems theory stating that we can't fully understand a system by simply picking it apart and understanding each of its parts in isolation from one another.

interdependence (p. 209) A principle that builds on the notion of wholeness by asserting that members of systems depend on each other and are affected by one another.

hierarchy (p. 209) A principle of systems theory stating that all relationships are embedded within larger systems.

subsystems (p. 209) Lower-level systems of relationship, such as a sibling relationship within a family.

suprasystems (p. 209) Higher-level systems of relationship, such as a neighborhood consisting of several families.

boundaries or openness (p. 209) A systems theory principle referring to the fact that hierarchy is formed by creating boundaries around each separate system.

calibration (p. 210) The process of systems setting their parameters, checking on themselves, and self-correcting.

recalibrate (p. 210) To adjust a relationship to accommodate changing needs of the parties.

positive feedback (p. 210) Feedback that causes a system to recalibrate and change.

negative feedback (p. 210) Feedback that causes a system to reject recalibration and stay the same.

equifinality (p. 210) A principle of systems theory asserting the ability to achieve the same goals (or ends) by a variety of means.

dialectics theory (p. 210) A theory that explains how we want to have conflicting, seemingly incompatible, things at the same time and how we try to deal with the tensions raised by this conflict.

autonomy and connection dialectic (p. 211) The tension between our desire to be independent or autonomous while simultaneously wanting to feel a connection with our partner.

openness and protection dialectic (p. 211) The tension resulting when we want to self-disclose our innermost secrets to a friend, but we also want to keep quiet so we protect ourselves from the chance that our friend will use the information against us somehow.

novelty and predictability dialectic (p. 211) Our simultaneous, opposing desires for excitement and stability in our relationships.

judgment and acceptance dialectic (p. 211) Our desire to criticize a friend as opposed to accepting a friend for who he or she is.

affection and instrumentality dialectic (p. 211) The tension between framing a friendship with someone as an end in itself (affection) or seeing it as a means to another end (instrumentality).

internal dialectics (p. 211) Tensions resulting from oppositions inherent in relational partners' communication with each other.

external dialectics (p. 211) Tensions between oppositions that have to do with how relational partners negotiate the public aspects of their relationship.

public and private dialectic (p. 212) The tension between how much of a friendship is demonstrated in public and what parts are kept private.

ideal and real dialectic (p. 212) The tension between an idealized vision of friendship and the real friends one has.

cyclic alternation (p. 212) A way to help communicators cope with dialectic tensions by featuring the oppositions at alternating times.

segmentation (p. 212) A way to help communicators cope with dialectic tensions by allowing people to isolate separate arenas for using privacy and openness.

selection (p. 212) A strategy for dealing with dialectic tensions that allows us to choose one of the opposite poles of a dialectic and ignore our need for the other.

neutralizing (p. 212) A type of integrating that helps communicators cope with dialectic tensions through compromising.

disqualifying (p. 212) A type of integrating that helps communicators cope with dialectic tensions by exempting some behaviors from the general pattern.

taboo topics (p. 213) Issues that are out of bounds for discussion between the partners.

reframing (p. 213) A type of integrating that helps communicators cope with dialectic tensions by rethinking the opposition so that it no longer seems to be an opposition.

social exchange theory (p. 213) A theory that makes three basic assumptions about human nature: people are motivated by rewards and wish to avoid costs, people are rational, and people evaluate costs and rewards differently.

costs (p. 213) Those things in relational life that we judge as negative.

rewards (p. 213) Those parts of being in a relationship that we find pleasurable.

comparison level (p. 214) A person's standard level for what types of costs and rewards should exist in a given relationship.

comparison level for alternatives (p. 214) A comparison of the costs and rewards of a current relationship to the possibility of doing better in a different relationship.

networking (p. 214) In relational development, finding out information about a person from a third party.

offering (p. 214) Putting ourselves in a good position for another to approach us in a social situation.

approaching (p. 215) Providing nonverbal signals that indicate we'd like to initiate contact with another person, such as going up to a person or smiling in that person's direction.

sustaining (p. 215) Behaving in a way that keeps an initial conversation going, such as asking questions.

affinity seeking (p. 215) Emphasizing the commonalities we think we share with another person.

preventative maintenance (p. 215) Paying attention to our relationships even when they are not experiencing troubles.

relational transgressions (p. 216) Negative behaviors in close relationships, such as betrayals, deceptions, and hurtful comments.

corrective maintenance or repair (p. 217) Efforts to restore a relationship after it runs into trouble.

meta-communication (p. 217) Communication about communication.

apology (p. 217) A way to repair relationships after relational transgressions.

account (p. 217) An explanation for a transgression that may accompany an apology.

KEY CONCEPTS

11.1

Family Relationships. Families are unique relationships for many reasons. Family ties can be voluntary or involuntary. Some families consist of people who come together of their own free will, such as married partners, communes, or intentional families who band together by choice rather than by blood relationships. But many family members have relationships with others they did not choose, such as parents, grandparents, cousins, siblings, and so forth, which form different relationships within this family type. Families may be nuclear (traditional or contemporary), families of origin, gay- and lesbian-headed, multigenerational, single-parent or even voluntary.

11.2

Close Friendships. Friendship is a significant close relationship of choice that exists over a period of time between individuals who provide social support and who share various commonalities. It runs deep and requires us to toss out our stereotypes and predispositions. And, unlike most family relationships, friendship is voluntary.

In childhood we experience such stages of friendship as momentary playmateship, one-way assistance, two-way fair-weather cooperation, caring and sharing, and mature friendship. As adults, we can experience role-limited interaction, friendly relations, moving toward friendship, nascent friendship, stabilized friendship, and waning friendship.

11.3

Romantic Relationships. Romance is often viewed as necessary and essential in lifelong relationships with others. Early conceptions of romantic relationships focused on mating and creating a family. Today, this option is rather limited. People establish and maintain romantic relationships for various purposes and numerous qualities of romantic relationships exist.

One of the primary and crucial foundations of romance is love. Robert Sternberg's triangular theory of love contends that love can be understood by examining three components, or dimensions, which, together, form the vertices of a triangle: intimacy, passion, and commitment.

11.4

Skill Set: Strategies to Improve Your Interpersonal Communication with Family Members, Close Friends, and Romantic Partners. There are several skills to put in motion when communicating with family, close friends, and romantic partners. C.A.R.E. (Constantly Assessing Relationship Excellence); recognizing a shared history; finding ways to keep a relationship "alive"; and insuring equity in the relationship when possible are primary among these.

ONLINE RESOURCES

Use Enhanced CourseMate for quick access to the electronic study resources that accompany this text:

- **Ethics & Choice:** Bernadette decides if she should fess up to her online romantic interest.

- **Communication Assessment Test:** A Chat Self Test

KEY TERMS

intentional families (p. 219) Family members who band together by choice rather than by blood relationships.

voluntary kin (p. 220) Individuals who feel like family but who we are not related to by blood or law.

family stories (p. 220) Pieces of narrative about family members and activities that are told and retold.

ritual (p. 221) A repeated patterned communication event.

family-of-origin (p. 221) The family into which we are all born.

nuclear family (p. 221) The original foundation of family life in the United States.

traditional nuclear family (p. 222) A married couple living with their biological children, with the husband/father as the financial provider and the wife/mother as the domestic provider.

contemporary nuclear family (p. 222) A modernized version of the nuclear family with two variations: (1) stay-at-home dad with the mom working outside the home; and (2) a dual-career couple that includes both parents working outside the home, and both providing primary child care.

gay- and lesbian-headed family (p. 222) Two people of the same sex who maintain an intimate relationship and who serve as parents to at least one child.

homophobia (p. 222) An irrational fear and/or anxiety of gay men or lesbians.

heterosexism (p. 222) The assumption that heterosexuality is universal.

multigenerational families (p. 223) Extended family members (children, parents, grandparents, etc.) living under the same roof.

sandwich generation (p. 223) A generation of people who simultaneously take care of their (aging) parents and their own children.

single-parent family (p. 223) Families that consist of one adult serving as a parent and at least one child.

friendship (p. 225) A significant close relationship of choice that exists over a period of time between individuals who provide social support and who share various commonalities.

CHAPTER REVIEW 11

authentic friends (p. 225) Those individuals whom we identify as close friends and who we hold in high esteem.

symmetrical reciprocity (p. 226) An expectation in friendship that occurs when both members of the friendship strategically choose to enact behaviors that sustain friendship.

communion (p. 226) An expectation in friendship whereby two friends are trying to unite in a compatible way.

solidarity (p. 226) An expectation in friendship that includes a sharing of mutual activities and the companionship of friends.

agency (p. 226) An expectation in friendship that arises when close friends perceive each other as possible resources and benefits.

momentary playmateship (p. 228) A stage in childhood friendship (ages 3–7) in which children play together because they are conveniently located near each other.

one-way assistance (p. 228) A stage in childhood friendship (ages 4–9) in which children show arrogance and egocentrism because they are incapable of being other-centered.

two-way, fair-weather cooperation (p. 229) A stage in childhood friendship (ages 6–12) in which children understand friendship as reciprocal, but if the friendship is unpleasant, they will exit the relationship.

caring and sharing (p. 229) A stage in childhood friendship (ages 8–15) in which children reflect on the value of intimacy and the notion of mutuality.

mature friendship (p. 229) A stage in childhood friendship (ages 12 and up) in which a sense of interdependence and autonomy begin to foster between friends.

role-limited interaction (p. 230) A stage of adult friendship development whereby we adhere to social expectations and cultural guidelines for conversation.

friendly relations (p. 230) The second stage in adult friendship development characterized by friends checking each other out and becoming less guarded about what they say.

moving toward friendship (p. 230) The third stage in adult friendship development whereby friends begin to move cautiously toward more personal disclosures and more time spent together.

nascent friendship (p. 230) The fourth stage in adult friendship development whereby friends begin to widen their activities together; communication patterns and routines begin to emerge.

stabilized friendship (p. 231) The fifth stage in adult friendship development whereby close friends merge social circles, establish emotional bonds, and begin to appreciate the others' values on friendship.

waning friendship (p. 231) The stage in an adult friendship development that includes friends drifting apart for various reasons (e.g., job, health, school, boredom, etc.).

triangular theory of love (p. 232) A theoretical perspective of love that includes three components: intimacy, passion, and commitment.

intimacy (p. 232) A component of the triangular theory of love that encompasses giving and receiving emotional support, holding a loved one in high regard, and so forth.

passion (p. 232) A component of the triangular theory of love that refers to those drives leading to desires such as nurturance, affiliation, and sexual fulfillment.

commitment (p. 233) A component of the triangular theory of love that relates to the likelihood of an individual sticking with another individual.

short-term commitment (p. 233) The decision to love a certain person.

long-term commitment (p. 233) The decision to maintain love with another person.

relationship ruts (p. 236) patterns of relationship behavior that become dull and unproductive.